PREPARING FOR THE
NEW

EVIDENCE-BASED
READING AND WRITING

AMSCO

AMSCO SCHOOL PUBLICATIONS, INC.,

a division of Perfection Learning®

Editorial Director:	Sue Thies
Editor:	Andrea Stark
Proofreading Coordinator:	Sheri Cooper
Art Director:	Randy Messer
Designer:	Ronan Design

Reviewers:

Gary Lemco
English Teacher
San Jose, California

Patrick J. Mangan
Reading and English Teacher
Frederick Douglass Academy #1
New York City Department of Education
New York, New York

Amanda B. Morey
English Teacher
Rancocas Valley Regional High School
Mount Holly, New Jersey

Beth Olson
SAT Tutor
Boulder, Colorado

Susie Weber
Writer and Tutor
Boulder, Colorado

When ordering this book, please specify:
Softcover ISBN: 978-1-63419-813-4 or **2679101**
eBook ISBN: 978-1-68240-452-2 or **26791D**

4 5 6 7 EBM 21 20 19 18 17 16

Printed in the United States of America

Table of Contents

Writing and Language Domain

Essay Section

Introduction

You are reading this book because you are preparing to take the SAT. Luckily, you have been preparing for the SAT your whole life, whether you knew it or not. Your life experiences, the classes you've taken, the books you've read, and the essays you've written are all a part of what you will bring with you on test day. Nonetheless, the SAT is still a test, and you need to prepare for it in order to get the best score you can. This book will help you identify your weak areas by providing you with lessons on important skills and by giving you a chance to answer practice problems and take full-length practice tests. Using this book will help you be confident and prepared on test day.

The New SAT

The new SAT (Spring 2016) is meant to more closely align with your classroom learning, creating a bridge between your high school work and the academics you will encounter in college.

The SAT has four components: a Reading Test, a Writing and Language Test, a Math Test, and an optional Essay Test. The test is scored on a scale of 400 to 1600, instead of a scale of 600 to 2400. The sections include:

- Evidence-Based Reading Test and Writing and Language Test: 200 to 800 possible points

- Mathematics Test: 200 to 800 possible points

- Optional Essay: 2 to 8 possible points on each of three traits (reading, analysis, and writing). Two scorers will grade your essay on each trait on a 1 to 4 scale, then the two scores will be combined for a maximum total score of 8. Your essay score will not affect your Writing and Language test score.

This book will help prepare you to take the Reading Test, the Writing and Language Test, and the Essay task on the new SAT. (To prepare to take the Math section of the test, see our companion book, *Preparing for the SAT Mathematics*, which can be purchased at perfectionlearning.com.)

The Reading Test allows 65 minutes to answer 52 questions.

You will be required to

- analyze sources: The Reading Test will always contain 5 reading passages that include

    – One passage from a classic or contemporary work of U.S. or world literature (10 questions)

    – One passage or a pair of passages from either a U.S. founding document or a text in the great global conversation they inspired. The U.S. Constitution or a speech by Nelson Mandela, for example. (10 to 11 questions)

    – A selection about economics, psychology, sociology, or some other social science. (10 to 11 questions)

    – Two science passages (or one passage and one passage pair) that examine foundational concepts and developments in Earth science, biology, chemistry, or physics. (10 to 11 questions on each passage or paired passage)

    The passages will range from easier (9–10 grade reading level) to difficult (12 + or college level) in no particular order. They will not be arranged from easy to difficult.

- use evidence: You will be asked to identify parts of the passages that support your answers to some of the questions.

- interpret data in informational graphics: Some passages will include charts or graphs that you will have to interpret or relate to the ideas presented in the passage.

- determine the meanings of words in context: Passages will contain unfamiliar words. You will be asked to use the context to figure out their meanings. However, these word are unlikely to be archaic or specialized words that you will never use again.

- make inferences and conclusions based on what you have read, identify the main idea, discover the author's purpose and tone, and find supporting details.

The Language and Writing Test allows 35 minutes to answer 44 questions.

You will be required to

- edit passages so that they follow standard written English conventions, including grammar, usage, and punctuation.
- revise passages by keeping, adding, deleting, or changing words and phrases to improve order, create transitions, or maintain tone.
- determine which sentence would best support the central claim of a passage, provide a logical transition between paragraphs, or bring the passage to a satisfying conclusion.
- relate information in charts and graphs to information in the text.

In the optional Essay section of the test, you will have 50 minutes to complete the essay.

You will be required to

- read a text from a previously published source. These texts will explore issues or trends in the arts, sciences, or in cultural life.
- write a clear analysis that explains how the author of the text built an effective argument to persuade his or her audience.
- identify and analyze the techniques the author employed to successfully build his or her argument.
- use clear organization and essay structure, as well as follow standard English conventions.

Scoring

On the SAT you will earn points for questions you answer correctly, but you will not lose points for questions that you answer incorrectly. This means that you should definitely guess, even if you have no idea what the right answer is. If you are running out of time on a section, you should fill in answers even if you don't have time to read the questions. (On the old version of the SAT there was a "guessing penalty," which meant students lost a quarter of a point for wrong answers. This meant that only making careful, educated guesses was advisable.)

For more information about the format and scoring of the test, see the College Board's SAT Web site at sat.collegeboard.org/home.

Preparing to Take the SAT

Long-term Preparation

The best way to prepare for the SAT is to learn all you can from your classes in school. Whether for a class or on your own, it is important to

- read broadly: Choose both challenging and entertaining texts.
- read deeply and critically: Think about an author's message, purpose, and tone.
- expand your vocabulary: As you read, use context to figure out what unknown words mean, look up unfamiliar words you see online or hear in conversations, and learn new words whenever you can.
- improve your writing: Get feedback from teachers, friends, or parents. Notice the effective techniques that other writers use. Write frequently.

Short-term Preparation

If you will be taking the SAT in the next few months, start practicing. Follow the How to Use this Book section at the end of this Introduction.

- Learn the format of the test and the directions for each section so that there are no surprises on test day.

- Work through the lessons in this book, particularly in your weaker areas.

- Get help from someone who can explain areas in which you are struggling.

Before the Test

- Set up a study schedule: Devote time each day or week to work through this book.

- Don't cram: The SAT assesses your ability to read, think, problem-solve, and write. It does not test knowledge that you can cram before the test. This test requires thorough preparation, which comes from extensive practice.

- Take care of yourself: A rested brain and a healthy body will serve you well on test day. Therefore, it is important to get sleep, eat well, exercise, stay hydrated, and engage in other activities that contribute to your overall health and well-being.

- Manage anxiety: If test taking makes you nervous, practice ways of calming your brain. If you find yourself feeling stressed as you work through this book, take a few deep breaths, take a break, go on a walk, or practice some other way of managing your emotions. Finding stress-management skills that work for you will help you on test day.

On Test Day

- Allow for plenty of time to get to the testing center.

- Bring the necessary documents and identification.

- Wear a watch so that you can keep track of time during the test. You will *not* be permitted to use your phone.

- Bring an approved calculator with fresh batteries for the Math section. (Consult the College Board website to see calculator specifications.)

- Bring water and a snack in case you need them during the breaks.

Test-Taking Strategies

Here are some strategies to help you on each section of the test. They are assembled in one list and are also repeated in the Reading and Writing and Language sections of the book in the Quick Tips sidebars.

On the Reading Test

- You must read the passages in order to answer the questions. Do not read all the questions first and then search in the passage. This method is time-consuming and ineffective.

- As you read the passage, underline the main idea. There will always be questions about the main idea of the text.

- Underline key phrases in each paragraph of the text so that you can easily find important information later.

- When you read the questions, put them in your own words so you understand what information you are trying to find.

- Find the part of the passage that relates to the question and re-read it.

- If you can, generate an answer in your mind before you look at the choices. If you need to, use the answer choices to get on the right track.

- Cross out obviously wrong choices.

- Keep in mind that sometimes you will find an answer choice that is true according to the passage, but is not the correct answer to the question. Don't be fooled!

- The directions may say pick the "best" possible answer. However, you may not find the answer you're looking for among the choices. In this case, you will have to find a choice that is true according to the passage and is a good enough fit for the question.

- Find proof for the answer you choose.

- When in doubt, pick an answer that represents the main idea of the passage.

On the Writing and Language Test

- Answer the questions in this section as you go, rather than reading the entire text and then tackling the questions. Questions will point you to a numbered and underlined section of the passage. The questions will relate to possible errors in the sentences.

- You will almost always need to read the entire sentence, and sometimes the sentence before and after the underlined part in order to correctly identify the mistake and how to fix it.

- Often one of the answer choices will be "NO CHANGE." Pick this choice if you are sure the sentence is written correctly.

- In many cases, the clearest and shortest answer choice is correct because it represents concise language.

Timing and Pacing

- Work through the questions at a steady pace. Don't get stuck too long on any one question—after all, they are all worth the same amount. It is better to get two easier questions correct than to use up time struggling with one difficult question.

- Mark difficult questions and return to these if you have extra time. You probably won't have time to check all your answers. However, if you have marked difficult questions, go back and try these again.

- Check your answer sheet frequently to make sure you are in the right place. If you skip a question, be sure to skip a space on your answer sheet.

- Keep track of time. If you are running out of time, answer the easier questions first, and then make an educated guess on the more difficult ones.

Process of Elimination

- Remember, this is a multiple-choice test, so you should use the answer choices to help you. It also means that you don't have to completely understand a passage or a question or a word in order to find the right answer. Right off the bat, you have a 25% chance of getting the question correct!

- After you read the question and think of an answer, consult the choices. Immediately see if you can eliminate one or two choices that are obviously incorrect. Look for choices that are off topic or are the opposite of the answer you want and cross these off.

- There are often two answers that are very similar. One of these is probably correct.

- Beware of choices that are partially correct or true, but also contain an incorrect part. The correct answer choice has to be *completely* correct. Don't fall for the first correct-sounding answer right away.

Stress Management

- Focus on what you know, not what you don't. When you read a question, ask yourself, "What do I know?"

- Think of the test as a treasure hunt for questions you can get right. You can get many questions incorrect and still do well.

- Try to stay positive. You have prepared well so be confident in your ability.

- Don't forget to breathe. Oxygen is your friend. Your brain needs it to think clearly and effectively.

How to Use This Book

This book was developed to prepare you to do well on the SAT. It accomplishes this, first, by helping you review the skills tested on the SAT. The College Board (developer of the SAT) has published a list of all the reading and language skills you could possibly be tested over on the Reading and Writing and Language section of the SAT. The lessons in this book explain all of these skills in clear, concise language using many examples. The lessons help you master the skill by giving you isolated practice over a specific objective.

This book also provides practice with the format and types of questions found on the SAT. You will become familiar with the way questions are worded so that you can easily identify how to answer the question. Test-taking tips will help you avoid silly mistakes and increase your ability to focus on the best answers quickly.

The reading passages in the lessons (and the practice tests) provide practice with reading literature, historical texts, and informational passages on science and social studies topics. Some will be easier and others will be more difficult, just like the reading passages on the SAT.

Here are some steps for using this book:

1. Take the Diagnostic Test (pp. 11–56). Score your test and then consult the chart that correlates each question with a lesson in the book (pp. 51–55). Identify which skills will need the most practice. Plan to spend more time working through these lessons.

2. Work through the lessons for the Reading (pp. 57–216) and the Writing and Language (pp. 243–362) sections in the book. The lesson format is as follows:

   Explain: Summary of skills taught in the lesson.

   Think It Through: Explanation of skill using examples.

   Practice: Provides practice questions to answer or text to edit. Exercises are not necessarily in multiple-choice format.

   Model SAT Questions: Multiple-choice questions in SAT format. Answers are explained.

   Practice SAT Questions: More multiple-choice SAT questions without explanations.

   Section Practice Tests: These tests reflect SAT format and cover all skills taught in the lessons.

3. Take the Full-length Model SAT Tests (pp. 379–494). These practice exams closely mirror the SAT. Taking these tests under the timed conditions (outlined at the beginning of the test) will help you learn to manage your time and will build your confidence. You can grade your test and translate your raw score into what you would likely receive on the Reading and Writing sections of the SAT. (See pages 55–56.)

4. If you plan to take the Essay Test, work through the Diagnostic Essay section (pp. 495–506). Then work through Lesson 14 (pp. 507–519). Finally, practice by writing one or more of the essay prompts provided (pp. 520–554). You will give your essay a preliminary grade and then compare it with graded student samples.

Diagnostic Test Instructions

The following Diagnostic Test will assess your current knowledge of the skills tested on the SAT Reading and Writing and Language tests. The questions and passages on this Diagnostic Test match those you will encounter on the SAT. Your results will help you focus your review and provide you with a benchmark against which you can measure your progress as you move through the lessons in this book.

Student Instructions

When you take this Diagnostic Test, you should

- be in a quiet place where you will not be disturbed.

- time yourself. You will have 65 minutes for the Reading section and 35 minutes for the Writing and Language section.

- take a 3-minute break after taking the Reading section and before taking the Writing and Language section.

After you complete the Diagnostic Test,

- use the Answer Key on p. 41 to check your answers.

- study the answer explanations to any questions you missed.

- use the correlation charts to spot error trends and identify your areas of strengths and weaknesses for focused review. Follow these steps:

  1) Circle or highlight any questions you missed.

  2) Use the chart on page 51 (Reading) or page 54 (Writing and Language) to identify which lessons in the book will help you improve your knowledge of the skills you missed.

  3) Focus on these lessons as you work through this book. For example, if you answered question 1 incorrectly, pay close attention to the information in Lesson 1: Identifying Characterization.

- determine your estimated SAT score by using the Score Conversion Chart on pp. 55–56.

Answer Sheet

SAT Reading and Writing and Language Diagnostic Test

Use a No. 2 pencil. Fill in the circle completely. If you change your answer, erase completely. Incomplete erasures may be read as answers.

Reading Section

1 Ⓐ Ⓑ Ⓒ Ⓓ	11 Ⓐ Ⓑ Ⓒ Ⓓ	21 Ⓐ Ⓑ Ⓒ Ⓓ	31 Ⓐ Ⓑ Ⓒ Ⓓ	41 Ⓐ Ⓑ Ⓒ Ⓓ	51 Ⓐ Ⓑ Ⓒ Ⓓ
2 Ⓐ Ⓑ Ⓒ Ⓓ	12 Ⓐ Ⓑ Ⓒ Ⓓ	22 Ⓐ Ⓑ Ⓒ Ⓓ	32 Ⓐ Ⓑ Ⓒ Ⓓ	42 Ⓐ Ⓑ Ⓒ Ⓓ	52 Ⓐ Ⓑ Ⓒ Ⓓ
3 Ⓐ Ⓑ Ⓒ Ⓓ	13 Ⓐ Ⓑ Ⓒ Ⓓ	23 Ⓐ Ⓑ Ⓒ Ⓓ	33 Ⓐ Ⓑ Ⓒ Ⓓ	43 Ⓐ Ⓑ Ⓒ Ⓓ	
4 Ⓐ Ⓑ Ⓒ Ⓓ	14 Ⓐ Ⓑ Ⓒ Ⓓ	24 Ⓐ Ⓑ Ⓒ Ⓓ	34 Ⓐ Ⓑ Ⓒ Ⓓ	44 Ⓐ Ⓑ Ⓒ Ⓓ	
5 Ⓐ Ⓑ Ⓒ Ⓓ	15 Ⓐ Ⓑ Ⓒ Ⓓ	25 Ⓐ Ⓑ Ⓒ Ⓓ	35 Ⓐ Ⓑ Ⓒ Ⓓ	45 Ⓐ Ⓑ Ⓒ Ⓓ	
6 Ⓐ Ⓑ Ⓒ Ⓓ	16 Ⓐ Ⓑ Ⓒ Ⓓ	26 Ⓐ Ⓑ Ⓒ Ⓓ	36 Ⓐ Ⓑ Ⓒ Ⓓ	46 Ⓐ Ⓑ Ⓒ Ⓓ	
7 Ⓐ Ⓑ Ⓒ Ⓓ	17 Ⓐ Ⓑ Ⓒ Ⓓ	27 Ⓐ Ⓑ Ⓒ Ⓓ	37 Ⓐ Ⓑ Ⓒ Ⓓ	47 Ⓐ Ⓑ Ⓒ Ⓓ	
8 Ⓐ Ⓑ Ⓒ Ⓓ	18 Ⓐ Ⓑ Ⓒ Ⓓ	28 Ⓐ Ⓑ Ⓒ Ⓓ	38 Ⓐ Ⓑ Ⓒ Ⓓ	48 Ⓐ Ⓑ Ⓒ Ⓓ	
9 Ⓐ Ⓑ Ⓒ Ⓓ	19 Ⓐ Ⓑ Ⓒ Ⓓ	29 Ⓐ Ⓑ Ⓒ Ⓓ	39 Ⓐ Ⓑ Ⓒ Ⓓ	49 Ⓐ Ⓑ Ⓒ Ⓓ	
10 Ⓐ Ⓑ Ⓒ Ⓓ	20 Ⓐ Ⓑ Ⓒ Ⓓ	30 Ⓐ Ⓑ Ⓒ Ⓓ	40 Ⓐ Ⓑ Ⓒ Ⓓ	50 Ⓐ Ⓑ Ⓒ Ⓓ	

Writing and Language Section

1 Ⓐ Ⓑ Ⓒ Ⓓ	11 Ⓐ Ⓑ Ⓒ Ⓓ	21 Ⓐ Ⓑ Ⓒ Ⓓ	31 Ⓐ Ⓑ Ⓒ Ⓓ	41 Ⓐ Ⓑ Ⓒ Ⓓ
2 Ⓐ Ⓑ Ⓒ Ⓓ	12 Ⓐ Ⓑ Ⓒ Ⓓ	22 Ⓐ Ⓑ Ⓒ Ⓓ	32 Ⓐ Ⓑ Ⓒ Ⓓ	42 Ⓐ Ⓑ Ⓒ Ⓓ
3 Ⓐ Ⓑ Ⓒ Ⓓ	13 Ⓐ Ⓑ Ⓒ Ⓓ	23 Ⓐ Ⓑ Ⓒ Ⓓ	33 Ⓐ Ⓑ Ⓒ Ⓓ	43 Ⓐ Ⓑ Ⓒ Ⓓ
4 Ⓐ Ⓑ Ⓒ Ⓓ	14 Ⓐ Ⓑ Ⓒ Ⓓ	24 Ⓐ Ⓑ Ⓒ Ⓓ	34 Ⓐ Ⓑ Ⓒ Ⓓ	44 Ⓐ Ⓑ Ⓒ Ⓓ
5 Ⓐ Ⓑ Ⓒ Ⓓ	15 Ⓐ Ⓑ Ⓒ Ⓓ	25 Ⓐ Ⓑ Ⓒ Ⓓ	35 Ⓐ Ⓑ Ⓒ Ⓓ	
6 Ⓐ Ⓑ Ⓒ Ⓓ	16 Ⓐ Ⓑ Ⓒ Ⓓ	26 Ⓐ Ⓑ Ⓒ Ⓓ	36 Ⓐ Ⓑ Ⓒ Ⓓ	
7 Ⓐ Ⓑ Ⓒ Ⓓ	17 Ⓐ Ⓑ Ⓒ Ⓓ	27 Ⓐ Ⓑ Ⓒ Ⓓ	37 Ⓐ Ⓑ Ⓒ Ⓓ	
8 Ⓐ Ⓑ Ⓒ Ⓓ	18 Ⓐ Ⓑ Ⓒ Ⓓ	28 Ⓐ Ⓑ Ⓒ Ⓓ	38 Ⓐ Ⓑ Ⓒ Ⓓ	
9 Ⓐ Ⓑ Ⓒ Ⓓ	19 Ⓐ Ⓑ Ⓒ Ⓓ	29 Ⓐ Ⓑ Ⓒ Ⓓ	39 Ⓐ Ⓑ Ⓒ Ⓓ	
10 Ⓐ Ⓑ Ⓒ Ⓓ	20 Ⓐ Ⓑ Ⓒ Ⓓ	30 Ⓐ Ⓑ Ⓒ Ⓓ	40 Ⓐ Ⓑ Ⓒ Ⓓ	

Diagnostic Test

65 MINUTES, 52 QUESTIONS

Turn to the Reading section of your answer sheet to answer the questions in this section.

Directions

The following is a diagnostic test that covers every skill that could possibly be tested by the Reading and the Writing and Language sections of the SAT. Take this test BEFORE working through any of the lessons in the book. After you take the test, check your answers with those on pages 41 and following. On pages 51 and 54, you will find a table that matches each numbered question with the associated skill. The table explains which pages give in-depth teaching and practice on this skill.

Each passage or pair of passages below is followed by a number of questions. After reading each passage or pair, choose the best answer to each question based on what is stated or implied in the passage or passages and in any accompanying graphics (such as a table or graph).

Questions 1–11 are based upon the following passage.

This passage is adapted from Harold Brodkey's short story "Sentimental Education," originally published in 1954 by Peter Farb. In it, a Harvard student dreams of falling in love.

It was eight o'clock on a warm September evening, and all the bells of Harvard were striking the hour. Elgin Smith, tired of studying, was standing on the steps of Widener Library—those
5 wide, Roman, inconvenient steps—blinking his eyes and staring into the distance, because that was supposed to refresh the corneas and the retina. He was thinking, but not of his schoolwork. He was thinking of what it would be like to fall in
10 love, to worship a girl and to put his life at her feet. He despised himself, because he feared he was incapable of passion and he believed that only passionate people were worthwhile and all other kinds were shallow. He was taking courses in
15 English Literature, in German Literature, in Italian Literature, in History, ancient and medieval, and every one of them was full of incidents that he thought mocked him, since they seemed to say that the meaning of life, the peak of existence, the core
20 of events was one certain emotion, to which he was a stranger, and for which he was very likely too rational. Therefore, he stood on the steps of Widener, so cracked by longing that it seemed only gravity held him together.

25 He was very tall, six feet three, and gangling. He had a small head, curiously shaped (his roommate, Dimitri, sometimes accused him of looking like a wedge of cheese), and a hooked nose. He wanted to

CONTINUE →

be a professor in the field of comparative philology, and he believed in Beauty. He studied all the time, and there were moments when he was appalled by how hard he worked. He was known for his crying in movies. He was not unathletic. Somehow, he had become convinced that he was odd and that only odd girls liked him, pitiable girls who couldn't do any better, and this singed his pride.

It was his fate that this particular night he should see a girl walking up the steps of Widener Library. She was of medium height and had black hair cut short; she was wearing a light-colored coat that floated behind her because she was walking so fast, nearly running, but not quite; and the curve of her forehead and the way her eyes were set took Elgin's breath away. She was so pretty and carried herself so well and had a look of such healthy and arrogant self-satisfaction that Elgin sighed and thought here was the sort of not odd girl who could bestow indescribable benefits on any young man she liked— and on his confidence. She was that very kind of girl, that far from unhappy, that world-contented kind, he believed would never fall for him. . . .

"Surely this year," he thought, looking up at the sky. "Now that I'm almost nineteen." He stretched out his arms, and the leaves on the trees, already growing dry at the approach of autumn, rustled in the breezes.

He thought about that girl once or twice in the days that followed, but the longing for her didn't really take root until he saw her again, two weeks later, at a Radcliffe Jolly-Up in Cabot Hall. It was in one of the dimly lit common rooms, where couples were indefatigably dancing in almost total darkness. Elgin was swaying in place (he was not a good dancer) with a girl who helped him on his German, when he caught sight of his Widener Library vision. When the next dance began, he wound through the couples looking for her, to cut in on her, but when he drew near her, he turned and walked over to the wall, where he caught his breath and realized he was frightened.

This was the stroke that fatally wounded him. Knowing he was frightened of that girl, he longed for her, the way men who think they are cowards long for war so they can prove they're not. Or perhaps it was some other reason. The girl had a striking appearance; there was her youth and her proud, clean look to recommend her.

But whatever the reason, he did begin to think about her in earnest. She rose up in clouds of brilliant light in his head whenever he came across certain words in his reading. ("Mistress" was one, "beautiful" another; you can guess the rest.) He did a paper on "The Unpossessable Loved One in Troubadour Poetry." When he walked through the Yard on his way to classes, his eyes revolved nervously and never rested, searching all the faces on all the walks in the hope of seeing her. In fact, on his walks to classes he looked so disordered that a number of his friends asked him if he was feeling ill, and it pleased Elgin, after the first two times this happened, to reply that he was. He was ill with longing. . . .

When he slept, he dreamed of carnage, horses, and speeding automobiles. He went to French movies and ground his knees against the seat in front

CONTINUE

95 of him. He laughed at himself, and decided to break this absurd habit he had gotten into of thinking all the time about this girl he had never met, but he didn't quite succeed. At last, he admitted to himself that he was in love with her; and one night, sleeping

100 in his lower bunk while Dimitri breathed heavily over his head, he had tears in his eyes because he was so foolish and did desire that girl whom he had seen the two times mentioned and only twice more besides.

1

Elgin can best be described as

A) self-critical.

B) overbearing.

C) condescending.

D) apathetic.

2

Which of the following details best supports your answer to question 1?

A) lines 11–13 ("He despised himself . . . kinds were shallow")

B) lines 27–30 ("He wanted to be . . . believed in Beauty")

C) lines 44–49 ("She was so pretty . . . and on his confidence")

D) lines 71–73 ("Knowing he was frightened . . . prove they're not")

3

Which choice best summarizes the passage?

A) A Harvard student seeks security in the esteem of a young woman whom he admires.

B) A Harvard boy yearns to fall madly in love and finds an object for his desire.

C) Boy meets girl on the steps of the Widener Library, and against all odds the two fall madly in love.

D) An insecure Harvard student summons the courage to approach an attractive, confident Radcliffe girl.

4

Why does the author compare Elgin's head to "a wedge of cheese" in lines 27–28?

A) to suggest Elgin has an odd appearance

B) to indicate Elgin is downright ugly

C) to imply that Elgin is overweight

D) to point out Elgin has a truly unique beauty

5

The word "Beauty" is capitalized in line 30 to express the idea that Elgin

A) associates beauty with the girl on the library steps.

B) believes in the transcendent idea of beauty.

C) seeks out the artistic in the disciplines he's studying.

D) may give up philology for the study of aesthetics.

6

Which choice best characterizes the girl Elgin longs for?

A) proud, unkind

B) striking, talkative

C) young, self-confident

D) athletic, restless

CONTINUE →

7

Which lines provide the best support for the answer to question 6?

A) lines 39–44 ("She was of medium . . . took Elgin's breath away")

B) lines 44–49 ("She was so pretty . . . on his confidence")

C) lines 65–69 ("When the next dance . . . realized he was frightened")

D) lines 74–80 ("The girl had a . . . words in his reading")

8

The use of words and phrases such as "cracked by longing" (line 2) and "ill with longing" (line 90–91) give the story a tone that can best be described as

A) dreamy.

B) mysterious.

C) fanciful.

D) romantic.

9

The imagery in lines 78–80 ("She rose . . . reading") conveys which of the following ideas?

A) Elgin is passionate about romantic literature.

B) Elgin needs someone in his life to think about.

C) Elgin has an idealized love for the girl.

D) The girl has no idea of the feelings Elgin has for her.

10

Which choice best describes the narrator's point of view?

A) It reflects the thoughts and feelings of both Elgin and the girl.

B) It reveals the narrator's feelings about Elgin and the girl.

C) It provides other characters' perceptions of Elgin.

D) It captures Elgin's thoughts and feelings, but not the girl's.

11

The voice of the narrator is most accurately described as

A) critical.

B) empathetic.

C) cynical.

D) accusatory.

Questions 12–19 are based upon the following passage.

The following passage is adapted from "The Ecology of Language" from Word Play: What Happens When People Talk *by Peter Farb. It discusses the influence of language upon the lives of peoples past and present.*

Toward the end of the [19th] century people began to speak of languages as being "born," producing "daughter" languages, and eventually "dying"—undoubtedly because the metaphor of a living

5 organism came naturally to a generation that had recently learned about Darwinian evolution. Some languages were also thought to "give birth" to weak mutations, in which case euthanasia could always be practiced upon them by the eternally vigilant guardians

10 of correct usage. The metaphor of language as a living organism persists to this day, but it is inherently false. A language does not live or die. And unless it is to be considered merely a code to be broken (like Egyptian or Mayan hieroglyphics) or an intellectual pastime

15 (like speaking Latin), a language has no life apart from the lives of the people who speak it.

Today a more fitting metaphor might be the "ecology" of language—the web formed by strands uniting the kind of language spoken, its history, the

20 social conventions of the community in which it is spoken, the influence of neighboring languages, and

CONTINUE

even the physical environment in which the language is spoken. This metaphor emphasizes that the function of language is to relate its speakers to one another and

25 to the world they live in. Eskimo, for example, is a language whose grammar makes it difficult to express certain ideas but very easy to say other things. It is spoken in the particular physical environment of the Arctic Circle, which makes it understandable that this

30 language should have a large vocabulary for describing different kinds of snow and seals. Its vocabulary has also been influenced by the presence of neighboring Indian tribes and of Europeans. And the strategies for using the language are unconscious conventions of

35 the social environment into which native speakers are born—a speech community with its own ideas about the "rightness" or "wrongness" of whatever is said.

An Eskimo's language affords him a tremendous, possibly infinite, number of ways he can

40 communicate whatever he wishes to say—whether it be to impart information, to convince someone of the rightness of his cause, or just to be sociable. But in actuality his choice of exactly what he will say at any particular moment is much more limited because

45 his environment severely restricts the strategies he can use. He will express the same thought differently in the igloo than he will on a hunt. And he will unconsciously be influenced by his relationship to his listener, the role he intends to play in his society,

50 whether or not an audience is present, and so on— with the result that out of the many possible things he might say, only a few choices are acceptable at the moment. Everything I have stated about the Eskimo holds true for speakers of other languages any place

55 on earth.

12

Which of the following statements best expresses the main idea of the passage?
- A) An Eskimo's language affords him a tremendous, possibly infinite, number of ways he can communicate.
- B) Languages do not live and die like organisms.
- C) The Eskimo's vocabulary has been influenced by the presence of neighboring Indian tribes and of Europeans.
- D) A language is part of the ecology and culture of the people who speak it.

13

Which of the following details best support your answer to question 12?
- A) lines 15–16 ("a language has no life. . . who speak it")
- B) lines 23–25 ("This metaphor emphasizes . . . to the world they live in")
- C) lines 27–31 ("It is spoken in the . . . of snow and seals")
- D) lines 38–42 ("An Eskimo's language . . . just to be sociable")

14

As used in line 8, "euthanasia" most nearly means
- A) eradicating the new forms of language.
- B) correcting the mutations.
- C) developing a strategy for using language.
- D) preserving new languages.

15

Although an Eskimo has a tremendous number of ways he can communicate, he is nevertheless restricted by his
- A) education.
- B) environment.
- C) financial circumstances.
- D) status in his group.

CONTINUE

16

The passage indicates that the author

A) supports the metaphor of language as a living organism.

B) believes studying and speaking Latin is a waste of time.

C) doesn't believe in the superiority or inferiority of any language.

D) rejects the idea that environment influences language.

17

Which of the following ideas is closest to the concept expressed in lines 17–23: "the 'ecology' of language . . . is spoken"?

A) Language is a form of human reason, which has its internal logic of which man knows nothing.

B) Our language is the reflection of ourselves. A language is an exact reflection of the character and growth of its speakers.

C) The limits of my language means the limits of my world.

D) Language is the house of the truth of being.

18

The author makes the statement in lines 27–31 ("It is spoken . . . of snow and seals") in order to

A) describe why so many things are hard to explain in Eskimo.

B) illustrate how directly a natural setting influences language.

C) question the standard metaphor of language as a living organism

D) demonstrate that Eskimo is far more complex than most languages.

19

What function do lines 45–55 serve in the passage as a whole?

A) They describe in detail the frustrations that occur when speaking a limited language.

B) They offer a final argument for replacing the "language as organism" metaphor.

C) They provide examples of the "unconscious conventions" mentioned in lines 34–35.

D) They support the idea in lines 27–31 that physical environment influences language.

Questions 20–30 are based upon the following passage.

The following passage describes the influence of polling on America's political process.

The intrusive polls of recent years have poisoned the political climate and subverted the aims of democracy. The entire political process is tainted by the daily rating changes, as though a presidential
5 election is a day on Wall Street or an afternoon at the racetrack. For those who bet on horses, minute-to-minute changes indicate, by the odds posted, which horse is favored and which might as well take the day off. Presidential races now seem similar,
10 with constant changes in the expected percentages favoring a particular candidate.

Harmless? No. A major danger is that fewer voters may go to the polls because they feel that the election has already been settled. If their candidate is
15 winning in the polls, why waste a pleasant Tuesday afternoon voting to assure what is already assured? If their candidate is behind, why waste that same afternoon in a hopeless cause? In an article in *American Heritage*, Bernard A. Weisberger reports,

CONTINUE ➡

20 "Some countries even forbid the publication of poll results immediately before the election or projections until the last voting booth is closed."

There are two separate elements in Weisberger's statement: the polls before the election and the

25 projections of winners on the night of the election. The former might limit First Amendment freedoms. The second might encounter geographical problems.

On the latter point: withholding projections in a country as large as the United States would

30 require that voters wait until the wee hours of the next morning for results. But why not? Voters in the 2000 presidential election had to wait weeks to find out who had won. Projections are an inexact science at best. In that 2000 election, Al Gore was

35 at first projected to win the crucial electoral votes of Florida. Then the projection was reversed, and George W. Bush was the projected winner. On the basis of this projection, Al Gore conceded the election. Then some discrepancies in the vote count

40 were discovered, and Gore withdrew his concession. From then on, legal battles delayed the naming of the president for many weeks. So much for projections.

Pre-election polls, however, are another matter.

45 This daily polling procedure could be eliminated by general consensus. However, such a consensus is probably doubtful. Nevertheless, an examination of the place of polls in American life can still be helpful.

50 What would be the advantage of giving up polls? For one thing, as noted already, it might minimize some of the notorious American voter apathy generated by knowing who will win anyway. There

is another serious problem. Some commentators

55 believe that constant poll-taking tempts candidates to modify their strategies, and ultimately their goals, in trying to follow the polls instead of leading. Still another disadvantage is the reluctance of financial backers to provide funds for an able candidate who

60 is lower in the polls. Why support a candidate who is projected a loser?

Polling may have a legitimate place in consumer surveys, but choosing a president is another matter. If we must have polls, educate the public to

65 recognize their pitfalls and misleading messages.

20

As used in line 2, the word "subverted" most nearly means
A) undermined. C) perverted.
B) lessened. D) altered.

21

Which choice best describes the tone created by the use of words such as "intrusive," "poisoned," "subverted," and "tainted" in lines 1–3?
A) contemplative C) morose
B) cynical D) sarcastic

22

The central claim of the passage is that
A) polls contaminate the political process, threatening our democracy.
B) polls should be removed from the political process.
C) polls inform voters and tell them their opinions count.
D) polls have a range of pitfalls, such as giving misleading messages.

CONTINUE ➡

23

The author uses all of the following reasons to support the main argument, EXCEPT

A) candidates change their goals because of polls.

B) fewer people vote because of polls.

C) polls prevent financial backers from supporting a candidate.

D) polls may produce erroneous data.

24

As used in line 39, the word "conceded" most nearly means

A) relinquished

B) acknowledged

C) confessed to

D) admitted to

25

The author's attitude toward polls can best be described as

A) ambiguous because he suggests that polls could be given up or kept.

B) unbiased because he gives equal attention to the positive and negative aspects of polls.

C) critical because he reveals the problems with polls.

D) humorous because he pokes fun at polls.

26

Which choice provides the best support for the answer to question 25?

A) lines 3–4 ("The entire political process. . . daily ratings changes")

B) lines 20–22 ("Some countries even . . . booth is closed")

C) lines 29–32 ("On the latter point: . . . But why not?")

D) lines 45–50 ("Pre-election polls, however, . . . can still be helpful")

27

What solution does the author propose if polls are to be kept?

A) only administer them following an election

B) teach the public about their dangers

C) design more effective and less error-ridden polls

D) give them to a larger sample of the population

28

Which choice provides the best support for the answer to question 27?

A) lines 12–14 ("A major danger is. . . already been settled")

B) lines 29–32 ("On the latter point. . . But why not")

C) lines 51–54 ("What would be the advantage . . . knowing who will win anyway")

D) lines 65–66 ("If we must have polls. . . misleading messages")

29

Which of the following is a reason the author might be opposed to government regulation of pre-election poll reporting as a way to improve voter turnout in the United States?

A) Regulation would likely conflict with freedom of speech and the press.

B) People often decide whether or not to vote on the basis of published polls.

C) Not enough countries have tried poll-reporting regulations to know if it works.

D) Poll reporting is only one of many issues connected with poor voter turnout.

CONTINUE ▶

30

Which conclusion can be drawn from the information in the passage about the 2000 presidential election (line 32–44)?

A) Misleading polls can change the outcome of an election.

B) Polls can influence the actions of candidates as well as voters.

C) More people would vote if they could trust the accuracy of polls.

D) Polls affect the popular vote far more than they effect the electoral vote.

Questions 31–41 are based upon the following passage and supplementary material.

The following is adapted from the article "The Flap Over Fluoride: Should It Be in Our Water?"

For more than 60 years, the element fluoride has been added to the drinking water supplies of many cities in the United States. In fact, nearly three quarters of the U.S. population drinks fluoridated

5   water. Fluoride compounds, which are mostly a waste product from fertilizer plants, are even added to some toothpastes and mouthwashes. The reason for this is that fluoride is thought to function as a tooth-decay preventive. In particular, fluoride is

10 targeted to prevent tooth decay in children, although it can also protect the teeth of adults.

While children's teeth have improved since the 1940s, it is debatable whether this is due to better diet and health care or to fluoride in the public water

15 system. People who are in favor of fluoridation claim that the addition of fluoride has improved dental health. Those who are opposed maintain that fluoride is a toxic substance that can actually harm the teeth and bones of children and adults. In fact,

20 they want to see fluoride removed from the public's water supplies.

The first studies that claimed fluoride's success in combating cavities were performed in the 1940s in several U.S. and Canadian cities. Since then,

25 there has been conflicting proof of its success. Early studies showed a 60 percent reduction in tooth decay among youth in fluoridated areas. Yet some recent studies have shown no significant differences in cavity rates between children in fluoridated and

30 non-fluoridated cities. In fact, one study has even shown results to the contrary, that children in non-fluoridated cities had less tooth decay than those in fluoridated cities.

Most countries do not add fluoride to their

35 public water supplies. There are several reasons why so many people are cautious about its use. One reason is that fluoridation has been shown, on rare occasions, to cause permanent discoloration in children's teeth, a condition known as dental

40 fluorosis. But this condition may not be the worst problem.

There are those who believe that (based on animal studies) fluoridation can lead to a variety of ill effects in people, such as lower IQ in children.

45 Other possible ill effects that have been attributed to fluoridation include bone cancer; changes in bone structure (leading to more hip fractures); osteoarthritis; birth defects and infant deaths; increased lead and arsenic exposure; an increase in

50 dental cavities; impaired immune system (causing chronic disorders); adverse reactions such as joint pains, headaches, and fatigue; inhibition of many key enzymes; suppression of thyroid function; acute poisoning; and "severe skeletal fluorosis" when

CONTINUE ➡

55 exposure levels are high. Yet none of these effects have been scientifically proved to occur.

There is another major objection to fluoridation of public water supplies: Some people consider it unethical to "mass medicate" the public without
60 their consent, especially when the health benefits have not been proved and there could even be adverse effects. Most recently, a county in Florida voted to stop adding fluoride to its public water supply; this was done for health reasons and as a
65 cost-cutting measure. About 200 other cities in the United States have chosen to stop fluoridation in the past five years, partly due to doubts about its benefits. Although scientists, doctors, and dentists have been among those making these decisions,
70 there are still many who favor the fluoridation of water. The U.S. Public Health Service and the Centers for Disease Control and Prevention continue to support the practice, claiming that the benefits outweigh the risks. In particular, they claim that
75 fluoridation benefits the many people who cannot afford dental care; at least this way they get some dental protection through their water supply.

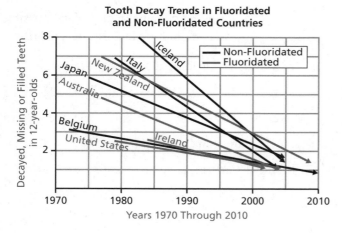

Tooth Decay Trends in Fluoridated and Non-Fluoridated Countries

Source: fluoridealert.org

Which choice best supports the idea that fluoride has lowered the rate of tooth decay?
A) lines 1–5 ("For more than 60 years, . . . fluoridated water")
B) lines 5–11 ("Fluoride compounds, which . . . the teeth of adults")
C) lines 25–27 ("Early studies showed . . . in fluoridated areas")
D) lines 27–33 ("Yet some recent studies . . . in fluoridated cities")

Both the text and graph indicate that fluoride in public water systems
A) has resulted in increased cavity rates in both children and adults.
B) may not be responsible for lower rates of dental decay in recent years.
C) caused twelve-year-olds to have fewer cavities.
D) has lowered the rate of dental decay between 1970 and 2010.

It can be inferred from the text and graph that the rate of dental decay decreased in recent years
A) because people have greater access to dental care.
B) because people are using fluoride toothpaste.
C) for reasons other than adding fluoride to the water supply.
D) because more fluoride was added to the water supply.

All of the following are potential dangers of adding fluoride to the public water supply, EXCEPT
A) lower IQ in children.
B) changes in bone structure.
C) acute poisoning.
D) pancreatic cancer.

CONTINUE

35

The author mentions both the pros and cons of adding fluoride to drinking water supplies in order to

A) convince readers that the cons outweigh the pros.

B) persuade readers to lobby to have fluoride removed from drinking water supplies.

C) assure readers they can safely drink water from the tap.

D) give readers a full picture of the benefits and drawbacks of fluoridation.

36

The central claim of the fifth paragraph (lines 42–56) is that

A) fluoridation may lead to ill effects in people, but these haven't been proven.

B) fluoridation has been shown to cause a variety of health problems in animals.

C) there are several possible negative health effects of fluoride on bones.

D) the pros of fluoridation do not outweigh the cons.

37

The phrases such as "Early studies showed" (line 26) and "scientifically proved" (line 56) give this passage which of the following tones?

A) informal and subjective

B) formal and objective

C) critical and conventional

D) earnest and forthright

38

What function do lines 35–41 serve in the passage as a whole?

A) They present data that help support the author's overall argument.

B) They develop an argument introduced in lines 22–33.

C) They provide another supporting reason for the idea expressed in lines 17–19.

D) They provide an opposing viewpoint to the central argument.

39

The author's perspective on adding fluoride to drinking water supplies can best be described as

A) clearly neutral.

B) vehemently opposed.

C) strongly in favor.

D) essentially indifferent.

40

Which of the following may have influenced the results of early studies of the benefits of adding fluoride to public water supply?

A) The studies may have included people using fluoride toothpaste.

B) The Centers for Disease Control and Prevention supported the practice.

C) The diet of many people in the country improved around the same time.

D) The studies focused mainly on people who could not afford dental care.

41

Which conclusion can be drawn based on information in the passage?

A) It is wrong to "mass medicate" a population even for public health reasons.

B) Saving money is the main reason many cities have stopped fluoridating water.

C) The majority of scientists, doctors, and dentists now question the use of fluoride.

D) Both the potential benefits and possible risks of fluoride lack strong scientific proof.

CONTINUE ➡

Questions 42–52 are based upon the following passages.

In the 1896 case, Plessy v. Ferguson, *the Supreme Court upheld the constitutionality of the "separate but equal" doctrine. Passage 1 is an excerpt from a recent article on pbs.org about the case, written by Alex McBride. Passage 2 is an excerpt from a primary document: the lone dissenting argument against the ruling by Justice John Marshall Harlan.*

Passage 1

Plessy v. Ferguson (1896)

In *Plessy v. Ferguson* the Supreme Court considered the constitutionality of a Louisiana law passed in 1890 "providing for separate railway carriages for the white and colored races." The law,
5 which required that all passenger railways provide separate cars for blacks and whites, stipulated that the cars be equal in facilities, banned whites from sitting in black cars and blacks in white cars, and penalized passengers or railway employees for
10 violating its terms.

Homer Plessy, the plaintiff in the case, was seven-eighths white and one-eighth black, and had the appearance of a white man. On June 7, 1892, he purchased a first-class ticket for a trip and took
15 possession of a vacant seat in a white-only car. Duly arrested and imprisoned, Plessy was brought to trial in a New Orleans court and convicted of violating the 1890 law. He then filed a petition against the judge in that trial, arguing that the segregation
20 law violated the Equal Protection Clause of the Fourteenth Amendment, which forbids states from denying "to any person within their jurisdiction the equal protection of the laws," as well as the Thirteenth Amendment, which banned slavery.

25 The Court ruled that, while the object of the Fourteenth Amendment was to create "absolute equality of the two races before the law," such equality extended only so far as political and civil rights, not "social rights." As Justice Henry Brown's
30 opinion put it, "if one race be inferior to the other socially, the Constitution of the United States cannot put them upon the same plane." Furthermore, the Court held that the Thirteenth Amendment applied only to the imposition of slavery itself.

35 The Court expressly rejected Plessy's arguments that the law stigmatized blacks "with a badge of inferiority," pointing out that both blacks and whites were given equal facilities under the law and were equally punished for violating the law. "We consider
40 the underlying fallacy of [Plessy's] argument" contended the Court, "to consist in the assumption that the enforced separation of the two races stamps the colored race with a badge of inferiority. If this be so, it is not by reason of anything found in the act,
45 but solely because the colored race chooses to put that construction upon it."

Until the mid-twentieth century, *Plessy v. Ferguson* gave a "constitutional nod" to racial segregation in public places, foreclosing legal
50 challenges against increasingly segregated institutions throughout the South.

Passage 2

Judge Harlan's Dissent

In respect of civil rights, common to all citizens, the Constitution of the United States does not, I think, permit any public authority to know the race

CONTINUE

of those entitled to be protected in the enjoyment of such rights. But I deny that any legislative body or judicial tribunal may have regard to the race of citizens which the civil rights of those citizens are involved. Indeed, such legislation as that here in question is inconsistent not only with that equality of rights which pertains to citizenship, national and state but with the personal liberty enjoyed by everyone within the United States. . . . The white race deems itself to be the dominant race in this country. But in the view of the Constitution, in the eye of the law, there is in this country no superior, dominant, ruling class of citizens. Our Constitution is color-blind and neither knows nor tolerates classes among citizens. In respect of civil rights, all citizens are equal before the law.

The arbitrary separation of citizens, on the basis of race, while they are on a public highway, is a badge of servitude wholly inconsistent with the civil freedom and the equality before the law established by the Constitution. It cannot be justified upon any legal grounds.

If evils will result from the commingling of the two races upon public highways established for the benefit of all, they will be infinitely less than those that will surely come from state legislation regulating the enjoyment of civil rights upon the basis of race. We boast of the freedom enjoyed by our people above all other peoples. But it is difficult to reconcile that boast with the state of the law which, practically, puts the brand of servitude and degradation upon a large class of our fellow citizens, our equals before the law. The thin disguise of "equal" accommodations for passengers in railroad coaches will not mislead anyone, nor atone for the wrong this day done. . . .

For the reasons stated, I am constrained to withhold my assent from the opinion and judgment of the majority.

42

The author of Passage 1 quotes Justice Henry Brown's opinion in lines 30–32 in order to
A) explain the meaning of "social rights."
B) apply the Thirteenth Amendment to the issue at hand.
C) point out the popular rationale about racial equality at that time.
D) illustrate the justification for how one race is inferior to another.

43

As used in line 46, "construction" most nearly means
A) building.
B) creation.
C) constraint.
D) liberty.

44

In Passage 1 the author refers to a "constitutional nod" in line 48 in order to
A) suggest that the *Plessy v. Ferguson* case contributed to racial harmony.
B) invoke the Constitution's rejection of institutions throughout the South.
C) prove that *Plessy v. Ferguson* foreclosed institutions in the South.
D) explain how the Supreme Court gave tacit approval to segregation.

CONTINUE ➤

45

Which of the following best describes the relationship *Plessy v. Ferguson* had to increasing incidences of racial segregation in the South through the mid-twentieth century?

A) It defended the practice of racial segregation by deeming it constitutional.

B) It claimed the Fourteenth Amendment applied only to political and civil rights.

C) It introduced the concept of "separate but equal" to public transportation.

D) It encouraged racial segregation by introducing the concept of "social rights."

46

The author of Passage 2 makes the statement in lines 52–55 ("In respect of civil rights . . . protected in the enjoyment of such rights") in order to

A) prove to the audience that the Constitution permits authorities to know the race of those entitled to protection.

B) convince the audience that the Constitution restricts using knowledge of race when protecting rights.

C) cast doubt on the Constitution's role in racial issues.

D) deny that knowing the race of an individual would influence public authority.

47

Which choice provides the best evidence for the answer to question 46?

A) lines 56–59 ("But I deny that any legislative body . . . those citizens are involved")

B) lines 63–65 ("The white race . . . in this country")

C) lines 77–82 ("If evils will result . . . upon the basis of race")

D) lines 83–87 ("But it is difficult to reconcile . . . our equals before the law")

48

As used in line 84 "reconcile" most nearly means

A) make one consistent with another.

B) restore friendly relations between.

C) find a disagreement between.

D) cause to coexist in harmony.

49

The author of Passage 2 refers to a "badge of servitude" (line 73) and a "brand of servitude" (line 85) in order to

A) argue that segregation should have been outlawed by the Thirteenth Amendment.

B) suggest that the evils of "separate but equal" facilities are easily seen by everyone.

C) make the point that upholding the law can be viewed as a privilege or burden.

D) show how strongly he feels that segregation denies freedom just as slavery once had.

50

How would the author of Passage 2 respond to lines 25–29 in Passage 1 ("The Court ruled that . . . 'social rights'")?

A) Human rights cannot be divided into categories in order to deny certain types of rights to certain individuals.

B) The Constitution does not allow policy-makers to know the race of individuals when determining their rights.

C) Citizens of the United States have more liberty than citizens of other countries.

D) The white race believes it is the dominant race and therefore should be granted more social rights.

CONTINUE ➡

Which statement best describes the relationship between Passage 1 and Passage 2?

A) Passage 2 refutes the court decision explained in Passage 1.

B) Passage 2 illustrates the reasons behind the court decision discussed in Passage 1.

C) Passage 2 argues against the amendments mentioned in Passage 1.

D) Passage 2 criticizes the author of Passage 1.

It can be inferred that the author of Passage 2

A) treats all human beings equally, regardless of race.

B) interprets parts of the Constitution to mean that no race is superior to another.

C) believes that the Constitution does not regulate the enjoyment of civil rights.

D) believes that personal liberty is more important than civil rights.

STOP

**If you finish before time is called, you may check your work on this section only.
Do not turn to any other section.**

Diagnostic Test

35 MINUTES, 44 QUESTIONS

Turn to the Writing and Language section of your answer sheet to answer the questions in this section.

Directions

Each passage below is accompanied by a number of questions. For some questions, you will consider how the passage might be revised to improve the expression of ideas. For other questions, you will consider how the passage might be edited to correct errors in sentence structure, usage, or punctuation. A passage or a question may be accompanied by one or more graphics (such as a table or a graph) that you will consider as you make revising and editing decisions.

Some questions will direct you to an underlined portion of a passage. Other questions will direct you to a location in a passage or ask you to think about the passage as a whole.

After reading each passage, choose the answer to each question that most effectively improves the quality of writing in the passage or that makes the passage conform to the conventions of standard written English. Many questions include a "NO CHANGE" option. Choose that option if you think the best choice is to leave the relevant portion of the passage as it is.

Questions 1–8 are based upon the following passage.

The number of farmers markets operating in communities across the nation has increased rapidly in recent years, owing in large part to growing concerns of consumers about where and how their food is grown. The trend has been a positive one **1** for farmers, and ranchers, as well as consumers, by offering new outlets for their products. The reasons for this growth are concisely summarized in the opening of the mission statement of *Know Your Farmer, Know Your Food*, an initiative of the United States Department of Agriculture (USDA), which states: "A surge in consumer demand for locally produced food is creating jobs and opportunity throughout rural America."

1
A) NO CHANGE
B) for farmers, and ranchers;
C) for: farmers, ranchers,
D) for farmers and ranchers,

CONTINUE

Local and regional food is already a multibillion-dollar market and growing rapidly. The number of farmers markets has grown by more than 70 percent since 2008. A recent survey conducted by the USDA reports that there are now more than 8,400 farmers markets listed **2** in the USDAs National Farmers Market Directory. The survey reported that in addition to the growth in numbers, there was a sense among market managers that **3** they continued to grow in their role as popular community gathering places.

The survey also identified trends in the following areas: increasing customer demand; a need for more vendors; greater customer access to nutritional assistance programs; the addition of nutritional education programs; and the growing presence of organic produce vendors.

4 The trend to provide access to nutritional assistance at farmers markets is seen as a potential benefit for both low-income customers and vendors. Almost three-quarters of farmers markets have at least one vendor accepting federal nutrition assistance as payment. Programs like Supplemental Nutrition Assistance Program (SNAP), the Women, Infants and Children Farmers Market Nutrition Program (WIC FMNP) and Senior Farmers Market Nutrition program (SFMNP) expand the customer base for farmers, **5** will give recipients access to healthy foods, and encourage the sale of locally sourced produce. **6** At the same time, farmers markets have also stepped up nutritional education efforts. Most farmers markets feature healthier eating programs, such as distributing healthy-recipe cards to customers and sponsoring health-themed cooking demonstrations.

2
A) NO CHANGE
B) in the USDAs National Farmer's
C) in the USDA's National Farmers
D) in the USDAs' National Farmers

3
A) NO CHANGE
B) it
C) vendors
D) farmers markets

4
The writer is considering deleting the underlined sentence. Should the writer do this?
A) Yes, because it does not directly support the main topic of the passage.
B) Yes, because it does not provide a good transition from the previous paragraph.
C) No, because it briefly introduces important elements described in the paragraph.
D) No, because it just repeats and rephrases information from an earlier paragraph.

5
A) NO CHANGE
B) give
C) gave
D) has given

6
A) NO CHANGE
B) However,
C) Consequently,
D) As a result,

CONTINUE

But the biggest draw for most customers at farmers markets is the opportunity to purchase farm-fresh **7** fruits; vegetables; eggs; and meats. Fresh produce continues to be the **8** dominant feature of markets, and most markets these days offer organic options. Virtually all market managers surveyed sold locally grown fresh fruits or vegetables at their markets. Nearly two-thirds of market managers had at least one USDA-certified organic vendor.

7

A) NO CHANGE
B) fruits, vegetables, eggs, and meats
C) fruits, vegetables; eggs, meats
D) fruits and vegetables; eggs and meats

8

A) NO CHANGE
B) significant factor
C) primary element
D) notable offering

CONTINUE

Questions 9–17 are based upon the following passage.

White-nose syndrome (WNS) is an emergent disease of hibernating bats that has spread from the northeastern to the central United States at an alarming rate. Since the winter of 2007–2008, millions of insect-eating bats in 25 states and five Canadian provinces have died **9** from this super nasty sickness. The disease is named for the white fungus, *Pseudogymnoascus destructans*, that **10** infects skin of the muzzle, ears, and wings of hibernating bats.

The U.S. Geological Survey's National Wildlife Health Center (NWHC), along with the U.S. Fish and Wildlife Service and other partners, continue to play a primary role in WNS research.

9
A) NO CHANGE
B) from this rather nasty sickness
C) from this unbelievably bad illness
D) from this devastating disease

10
A) NO CHANGE
B) infected
C) had infected
D) will infect

CONTINUE →

To [11] figure out if bats are affected by white-nose syndrome, scientists look for a characteristic microscopic pattern of skin erosion caused by *P. destructans*. Field signs of WNS can include visible white fungal growth on the bat's muzzle and/or wing tissue, but this is [12] not a very reliable and dependable indicator. Infected bats also often display abnormal behaviors in [13] its hibernation sites (hibernacula), such as movement toward the mouth of caves and daytime flights during winter. These abnormal behaviors [14] have got to be what's behind the untimely consumption of stored fat reserves causing emaciation, a characteristic documented in a portion of the bats that die from WNS.

11

A) NO CHANGE
B) tell
C) estimate
D) determine

12

A) NO CHANGE
B) not a very reliable indicator
C) not a very reliable, dependable indicator
D) not a very reliable or very dependable indicator

13

A) NO CHANGE
B) it's
C) his or her
D) their

14

A) NO CHANGE
B) probably could explain
C) may contribute to
D) are maybe what is behind

CONTINUE →

15 [1] Current estimates of bat population declines in the northeastern U.S. since the emergence of WNS are approximately 80%. [2] It is unlikely that species of bats affected by WNS will recover quickly because most are long-lived and have only a single pup per year. [3] Consequently, even in the absence of disease, bat populations do not fluctuate widely in numbers over time. [4] This sudden and widespread mortality associated with WNS is unprecedented in hibernating bats, among which disease outbreaks have not been previously documented.

The true ecological consequences of large-scale population reductions currently underway among hibernating bats **16** are not yet known however, farmers might feel the impact. In temperate regions, **17** they are primary consumers of insects, and a recent economic analysis indicated that insect suppression services (ecosystem services) provided by bats to U.S. agriculture is valued between 4 to 50 billion dollars per year.

To make the fourth paragraph most logical, sentence 4 should be placed

A) Where it is now

B) Before sentence 1

C) After sentence 1

D) Before sentence 3

A) NO CHANGE

B) are not yet known, however. Farmers

C) are not yet known. However, farmers

D) are however not yet known and farmers

A) NO CHANGE

B) bats

C) populations

D) these

Questions 18–25 are based upon the following passage.

Do cell phones pose a health hazard?

Many people are concerned that cell phone radiation will cause cancer or other serious health hazards.

Cell phones emit low levels of radiofrequency energy (RF). Over the past 15 years, scientists have conducted hundreds of studies looking at the biological effects of the radiofrequency energy emitted by cell phones. While some researchers have reported biological changes associated with RF energy, these studies **18** are failing to be replicated. The majority of studies published have failed to show an association between exposure to radiofrequency from a cell phone and health problems.

The low levels of RF cell phones emit while in use are in the microwave frequency range. They also emit RF at substantially reduced time intervals when in the stand-by mode. **19** Whereas high levels of RF can produce health **20** affects (by heating tissue), exposure to low-level RF that does not produce heating effects causes no known adverse health effects.

18
A) NO CHANGE
B) failed
C) will fail
D) have failed

19
A) NO CHANGE
B) Consequently,
C) However,
D) Furthermore,

20
A) NO CHANGE
B) affect
C) effects
D) effectiveness

CONTINUE →

The biological effects of radiofrequency energy should not be confused with the effects from other types of electromagnetic energy.

Very high levels of electromagnetic **21** energy, such as is found in X-rays and gamma rays can ionize biological tissues. Ionization is a process where electrons are stripped away from **22** its normal locations in atoms and molecules. **23** It can permanently damage biological tissues including DNA, the genetic material.

The energy levels associated with radiofrequency energy, including both radio waves and microwaves, are not great enough to cause the ionization of atoms and molecules. Therefore, RF energy is a type of non-ionizing radiation. Other types of non-ionizing radiation include visible light, infrared radiation (heat), and other forms of electromagnetic radiation with **24** kind of low frequencies.

While RF energy doesn't ionize particles, large amounts can increase body temperatures and cause tissue damage. The eyes are particularly vulnerable to RF **25** heating. There is relatively little blood flow in them to carry away excess heat.

21
A) NO CHANGE
B) energy; such as is found in X-rays and gamma rays can
C) energy such as is found in X-rays, and gamma rays, can
D) energy, such as is found in X-rays and gamma rays, can

22
A) NO CHANGE
B) their
C) it's
D) your

23
The writer is considering deleting the underlined sentence. Should the writer do this?
A) Yes, because it does not provide a good transition into the next paragraph.
B) Yes, because it fails to support the rest of the information in the paragraph.
C) No, because it clarifies the reason why ionization of tissue is such a hazard.
D) No, because it develops the argument that cell phones are not a health concern.

24
A) NO CHANGE
B) relatively
C) continually
D) different kinds of

25
Which choice most effectively combines the two sentences at the underlined portion?
A) heating and there
B) heating, and so there
C) heating because there
D) heating, and this is because there

CONTINUE

Questions 26–31 are based upon the following passage.

It was long believed that life could exist only within certain narrow limits of temperature and 26 air quality, and there are living organisms that challenge common sense and astound scientists every year with new discoveries. The 27 bacteria are so numerous and abundant that a single gram of fertile soil may contain as many as 100 million bacteria. 28 As separate individuals, other organisms are outnumbered by bacteria. 29 They exist everywhere; in the bodies of all living creatures, inside Antarctic rocks, in all parts of the ocean, even in the stratosphere. Sulfur-loving bacteria provide a life-enhancing function in the ecosystem huddled around volcanic vents in the ocean, where sunlight never reaches and temperatures exceed the boiling point of water.

30 [1] Bacteria are paradoxical: they keep us alive … and sometimes try to kill us. [2] The words *bacterial infection* reminds us that there are harmful bacteria that can seriously impact the quality of life. [3] Antibiotics, vaccinations, and tetanus shots have been effectively used to fight bacteria for many years, but in the course of natural selection, mutations arise that prove immune to the weapons. [4] The human body is fortunately equipped to counteract bacterial infections with antibodies, but the immune system cannot handle all infections by itself.

The very word *bacteria* 31 frightens people, the vast majority of bacteria are either harmless or even beneficial to mankind. Bacteria assist in decomposition of organic matter, in soil enrichment, pickling, fermentation, cheese making, and other specialized processes. On balance, bacteria are life-enhancing.

26
A) NO CHANGE
B) air quality, also there are living organisms that challenge common sense
C) air quality, but there are living organisms that challenge common sense
D) air quality, however there are living organisms that challenge common sense

27
A) NO CHANGE
B) bacteria are numerous and abundant
C) bacteria are so numerous
D) bacteria are so numerous and so abundant

28
A) As separate individuals, the number of bacteria surpasses that for other organisms.
B) Other organisms, as separate individuals are outnumbered by bacteria.
C) As separate individuals, bacteria outnumber any other type of organism.
D) As separate individuals, there are more bacteria than any other type of organism.

29
A) NO CHANGE
B) They exist everywhere: in the bodies
C) They exist everywhere, in the bodies
D) They exist everywhere in the bodies

30
To make the second paragraph most logical, sentence 3 should be placed
A) Where it is now
B) Before sentence 1
C) After sentence 1
D) After sentence 4

31
A) NO CHANGE
B) frightens people: the vast majority
C) frightens people the vast majority
D) frightens people; however, the vast majority

Questions 32–41 are based upon the following passage.

Prying Open the Black Box of the Brain

The human brain is the most complex biological structure on Earth. It has about 100 billion **32** neurons—each of which has thousands of connections to other neurons, or nerve cells.

33 For example, as we age, our brains lose nerve cells. In addition, **34** the wiring of our brains is continually altered as we learn, socialize, undergo stress, and encounter varied environmental conditions. Our brains are anatomically and physiologically changed by normal intellectual and physical experiences.

35 [1] So each of us—continually subjected to new and different brain-changing experiences—has a unique brain. [2] What's more, brain injuries may trigger various types of changes in the anatomy and physiology of the brain to compensate for lost function and/or maximize remaining functions. [3] Largely because the brain is so complex and dynamic, it is still akin to a locked black box— 3 pounds of mystery lodged between our ears. [4] **36** For instance, our understanding of the brain remains downright rudimentary compared to our understanding of other organs.

32
A) NO CHANGE
B) neurons each
C) neurons, each
D) neurons; each

33
Which choice provides the most appropriate opening sentence to the second paragraph?
A) To make things more complicated, these neurons are continually in flux.
B) Brains are the most interesting area of study in modern times.
C) Aging affects the brain as well as all parts of the body.
D) Indeed, neurons number in the billions.

34
A) NO CHANGE
B) the wiring of our brains is continual,
C) the wiring of our brains are continually
D) our brains and the wiring is continually

35
The writer is considering adding the following sentence to the third paragraph.

In fact, even the brains of identical twins differ from one another.

The writer should
A) add it before sentence 1 because it establishes the main idea of the paragraph.
B) add it after sentence 1 because it provides a supporting example.
C) add it after sentence 4 because it includes a minor detail.
D) not add the sentence to the paragraph.

36
A) NO CHANGE
B) Indeed,
C) In contrast,
D) Needless to say,

CONTINUE

Desperately Seeking a Theory

37 [5] Despite major technological advances in brain research during recent decades, scientists have yet to describe all of the various types of cells that comprise the brain and determine their functions. [6] Complicating matters further, the brain is more than the sum of its parts. [7] That is, the various components of the brain do not operate in isolation from one another; they must communicate with one another and work together to process information and produce memories, thoughts, and behaviors. [8] In other words, scientists are studying brain injuries to understand how the brain works.

But scientists still don't understand how information is processed in any organism, whether it be a lowly worm whose nervous system comprises only a few hundred neurons or **38** a brain that is complex. We simply do not know what happens in the brain when an organism thinks, maneuvers through the world, takes in sensory information, or sleeps.

In other words, scientists lack a basic, overarching theory about healthy brain function that would explain how memories, thoughts, and behaviors emerge from dynamic activities in the brain—any brain.

This theoretical vacuum has persisted even though molecular, cellular and neuronal activities in the brains of many species have been well studied, as has behavior in many species, including humans. Nevertheless, the relationships between these two types of phenomena and the sequence of events that translates one to the other remain **39** strange.

37

The writer is considering deleting a sentence from this paragraph. Which is the best choice?

A) Keep all sentences
B) Delete sentence 6
C) Delete sentence 7
D) Delete sentence 8

38

A) NO CHANGE
B) or a human with a complex nervous system.
C) or a complex vertebrate.
D) or a few million neurons.

39

A) NO CHANGE
B) furtive
C) clandestine
D) mysterious

CONTINUE ➡

By providing a framework for predicting how micro events in the brain produce behaviors, and vice versa, a theory of healthy brain function would contribute as much to neuroscience as the theory of evolution contributes to the tree of life, the theory of plate tectonics contributes to geology, and the theory of relativity contributes to cosmology. But still unable to explain how a normal brain functions, scientists cannot yet explain how traumatic injuries and brain diseases, such as Alzheimer's, schizophrenia, autism, and epilepsy, impair function. [9] Neither can they **40** get a handle on how brain injuries and diseases should be treated. **41**

40
A) NO CHANGE
B) wrap their brains around
C) determine
D) do anything about

41

The writer is considering adding the following sentence immediately after sentence 9.

By comparison, imagine a mechanic trying to fix a car's engine without a parts list and an understanding how it runs!

Should the writer add the information here?
A) Yes, because it illustrates the idea that scientists have much to learn about the brain.
B) Yes, because it shows how different experiences produce different results.
C) No, because it indicates how scientists study the brain versus how mechanics fix cars.
D) No, because it contradicts the main idea of sentence 9.

CONTINUE

Questions 42–44 are based upon the following passage and graph.

The number of children receiving food stamps in 2014 is significantly higher than before the start of the Great Recession in 2007, according to the U.S. Census Bureau.

The rate of children living with married parents who receive food stamps 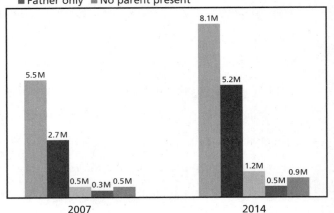**42** has nearly doubled since 2007. In 2014, an estimated 16 million children, or about one in five, received food stamp assistance compared with the roughly 9 million children, or one in eight, that received this form of assistance **43** prior to the recession.

These statistics come from the 2014 Current Population Survey's Annual Social and Economic Supplement, which has collected statistics on **44** families, and living arrangements for more than 60 years. Today's table package delves into the characteristics of households, including the marital status of the householders and their relationship to the children residing in the household.

Nutrition Assistance
Number of Children Receiving Food Stamps
by Living Arrangement

In millions
■ Mother only ■ Married parents ■ Two unmarried parents
■ Father only ■ No parent present

2007: 5.5M, 2.7M, 0.5M, 0.3M, 0.5M
2014: 8.1M, 5.2M, 1.2M, 0.5M, 0.9M

Source: United States Census Bureau, census.gov.

42

A) NO CHANGE
B) was significantly higher than it was
C) has tripled
D) was slightly higher than it was

43

A) NO CHANGE
B) prior from
C) prior in
D) prior for

44

A) NO CHANGE
B) families: and living
C) families—and living
D) families and living

STOP

If you finish before time is called, you may check your work on this section only.
Do not turn to any other section.

Answers and Explanations

Reading Test

Item	Answer	Explanation
1	A	Evidence for choice A: "He was appalled at how hard he worked," "he had become convinced that he was odd," "he was so foolish." Choice B: There is no evidence that he is overbearing; in fact, he is the opposite, because he never approaches or talks to the girl. Choice C: The passage does not show Elgin's interactions with anyone, so there is no evidence that he is condescending. Choice D: Elgin doesn't act on his desires, but this doesn't make him apathetic. He does care and wishes that he could meet the girl.
2	A	Evidence for choice A: The phrases "despised himself," "incapable of passion," "shallow" show self-criticism. Choice B: This shows Elgin's career desires. Choice C: This shows the aspects of the girl whom he admires. Choice D: This provides evidence that Elgin longs for the girl and feels cowardly, but it doesn't show him being critical of this.
3	B	Evidence for choice B: The passage repeatedly shows Elgin's admiration of and desire for the girl. She becomes the object of his desire. Choice A: Although Elgin yearns for the girl, he doesn't ever get to "seek security" in her esteem because he never makes contact with her. Choice C: They never meet and never fall in love. Choice D: Elgin never summons the courage to approach the girl.
4	A	Evidence for choice A: This choice supports the information that "He had a small head, curiously shaped." Choice B: This choice is too extreme and there isn't evidence that Elgin is "downright ugly." Choice C: There is no evidence that he is overweight. Choice D: This choice is too positive and is the opposite of Elgin's head being "curiously shaped."
5	B	Evidence for choice B: Capitalizing an abstract noun such as "Beauty" suggests a broader meaning of the word. Choice A: No link is made here about the girl and Beauty. Choice C: There is no evidence about Elgin seeking out the artistic. Choice D: The passage says that he wanted to be a professor in philology.
6	C	Evidence for choice C: "She was so pretty and carried herself so well and had a look of such healthy and arrogant self-satisfaction…" Choice A: There is no evidence that she is unkind. She is never described interacting with anyone. Choice B: Although "striking" may work in terms of the descriptions of her beauty, she is not described as being talkative. Choice D: Although she may be athletic, given that she was "walking so fast, nearly running," there isn't solid evidence for this. There is no evidence that she is restless.
7	B	See explanations for item 6.

Item	Answer	Explanation
8	D	Evidence for choice D: These words and phrases all refer to romantic feelings felt by a man toward a woman. Choice A: "Dreamy" is a less accurate form of "romantic" because it connotes a dreamlike feeling, whereas "romantic" has to do with love. Choice B: The words do not lend a mysterious tone. Choice C: "Fanciful" means existing in the imagination, but Elgin is truly feeling these emotions.
9	C	Evidence for choice C: The words show that Elgin is idealizing her (making her into more than she may actually be in real life). Choice A: Elgin may be passionate about romantic literature, but the line in question does not show this. Choice B: Again, he may need someone to think about, but this line shows *how* he thinks about her. Choice D: This choice is true but not an answer to the question.
10	D	Evidence for choice D: Throughout the passage, the narrator provides insight into what Elgin is thinking and how he is feeling, but does not provide any information about the girl's thoughts or feelings. Choice A: This contradicts the above explanation about choice D. Choice B: The narrator's feelings are rarely included in the passage. Choice C: There is one reference to Dimitri's perception of Elgin's looks, but this is not the overall effect of the narrator's point of view.
11	B	Evidence for choice B: The narrator shows empathy toward Elgin with phrases such as, "cracked by longing," "it was his fate," "the stroke that fatally wounded him." Choice A: "Critical" is the opposite of empathetic. Elgin is critical of himself, but the narrator is not critical of him. Choice C: "Cynical" means showing distrust or contempt, which is far more negative than the narrator's voice actually is. Choice D: "Accusatory" is also too negative.
12	D	Evidence for choice D: The last sentence of the first paragraph and the first sentence of the second paragraph capture this idea, and the rest of the passage goes on to illustrate it. Choice A: This is a detail and is contradicted by the passage: "Eskimo, for example, is a language whose grammar makes it difficult to express certain ideas but very easy to say other things." Choice B: The passage does state this idea, but it is not the *main* idea of the whole passage. Choice C: This is a true statement, but it is not the main idea of the passage. It is a detail.
13	A	Evidence for choice A: This line supports the main idea of the passage: Language is connected to the people who speak it and therefore to their history, community, and environment. Choice B: This line has to do with the function of language, not with the main idea (see above). Choice C: This line provides a supporting detail to the main idea but does not capture the entire passage's main idea. Choice D: Again, these are supporting details related to the Eskimo language, not the main idea.

Item	Answer	Explanation
14	A	Evidence for choice A: The passage says that "vigilant guardians of correct usage" could practice "euthanasia" on the "weak mutations," suggesting that they would be eradicated, or gotten rid of. Choice B: More than simply correcting mutant languages, the "vigilant guardians" would want to get rid of them. Choice C: There is no context to support the idea of developing a strategy for using the language. Choice D: There is no context to support the idea of preserving new languages.
15	B	Evidence for choice B: The passage states, "what he will say. . . is much more limited because his *environment* severely restricts the strategies he can use." Choice A: There is no discussion of education in the passage. Choice C: There is no discussion of financial circumstances. Choice D: There is discussion of relationships but not of social status.
16	C	Evidence for choice C: Although the author doesn't explicitly state this, it can be assumed that he believes this because of his focus on how language develops based on environment, history, and community. Choice A: The author states that this idea is "inherently false." Choice B: The author calls speaking Latin "an intellectual pastime," but this doesn't necessarily mean he thinks it is a waste of time. Choice D: He doesn't reject this idea; it is his main argument.
17	C	Evidence for choice C: The author states that language is influenced by the environment. Choice C extends this concept to suggest that because language is affected by environment language is therefore limited by the limits of one's world. Choice A: The lines do not mention the idea that man has no idea of the internal logic of language. Choice B: The lines discuss language being influenced by the world around the speaker, not as an "exact reflection" of the speaker. Choice D: The lines do not allude to aspects of truth and language.
18	B	Evidence for choice B: The author makes a clear connection in those lines between "the physical environment of the Arctic Circle" and "a large vocabulary for describing different kinds of snow and seals." Choice A: The author does mention that Eskimo "is a language whose grammar makes it hard to express certain ideas" (lines 26–27), but that is not the idea developed in lines 27–31. Choice C: This choice expresses a central theme of the passage, but it does not directly relate to the lines in question. Choice D: The author does say that the Eskimo language affords "a tremendous, possibly infinite, numbers of ways" to say things (lines 38–40), but that is not what he intends to convey in lines 27–31.

Item	Answer	Explanation
19	C	Evidence for choice C: In lines 47 to 50, the author writes that an Eskimo speaker in a given situation "will unconsciously be influenced by his relationship to his listener, the role he intends to play in his society, whether or not an audience is present, and so on." In other words, the speaker observes certain social conventions of communicating, even if he or she is not consciously aware of doing so. Choice A: While the lines describe how different situations might limit what an Eskimo speaker can appropriately say, no mention is made of these limitations resulting in "frustrations." Choice B: The lines do not directly argue against the "language as organism" metaphor; rather, they provide further support for the "language as ecosystem" idea. Choice D: Lines 44–45 have more to do with a speaker's social environment than his physical environment.
20	A	Evidence for choice A: The sentence says that polls have "poisoned the political climate" and "subverted the aims of democracy." Therefore "subverted" has a negative connotation that means "damaged" or "weakened," which is the definition of "undermined." Choice B: It doesn't make sense to say polls have "lessened" the aims of democracy. Choice C: In this context, "perverted" means corrupted, which also doesn't make sense to use with "the aims of democracy." Choice D: Although "altered" could make sense here, the context suggests a more negative word than one that simply means "changed."
21	B	Evidence for choice B: "Cynical" means showing contempt for accepted standards. By using the words identified in this question, the author reveals his cynicism, or negative, view of the effect of polls on the political process. Choice A: "Contemplative" means "thoughtful." The words the author uses are too negative for this choice to be correct. Choice C: "Morose" means "sullen" or "ill-tempered." The words the author uses do not suggest this tone. Choice D: Although the author could be interpreted as sarcastic because of his negative tone, he is not being ironic; he means what he says.
22	A	Evidence for choice A: This claim is clearly expressed in the first two sentences of the passage and the author goes on to support it with details throughout the passage. Choice B: The author states that removing polls would be one solution, but he also provides other options. This is not his central claim. Choice C: This statement is not supported in the text. Choice D: This answer choice is true, but it is not the author's central claim.
23	D	Evidence for choice D: The passage does not state this. This question asks you to identify the one item that is NOT stated in the passage. Choice A: The passage states this in lines 55–58. Choice B: The passage states this in lines 12–13. Choice C: The passage states this in lines 58–61.

Item	Answer	Explanation
24	A	Evidence for choice A: In the context of the passage, Al Gore "conceded" the election because it was projected that George W. Bush would win. Al Gore "relinquished," or gave up, the election. Choice B: It does not make sense to say that Gore "acknowledged" the election. Choice C: It does not make sense to say that Gore "confessed to" the election. Choice D: It does not make sense to say that Gore "admitted to" the election.
25	C	Evidence for choice C: The author makes clear criticisms of polls, backing up each one with evidence. Choice A: Although the author suggests that polls could be kept or relinquished, his opinion is not ambiguous; he clearly feels negatively toward polls. Choice B: The author is not unbiased, because he makes his criticism of polls very clear. He also does not give equal weight to the positives and negatives; his focus is on the negative aspects of polls. Choice D: The author criticizes polls but is not making fun of them.
26	A	Evidence for choice A: This statement sums up the author's central claim, which contains his opinion about the topic: he believes there are many problems with polls. Choice B: This statement refers to what other countries do, but it doesn't indicate the author's opinion about it. Choice C: This statement identifies the consequences of withholding projections, but again, this doesn't reveal the author's opinion. Choice D: This statement acknowledges how difficult it would be to get consensus on pre-election polls, but this is not the strongest evidence for identifying the author's opinion.
27	B	Evidence for choice B: In the last paragraph the author says, "if we must have polls, educate the public to recognize their pitfalls and misleading messages." Choice A: Although the author mentions getting rid of pre-election polls, he does not propose keeping post-election polls as one of the solutions to the problem. Choice C: The author does not explicitly state that polls should be redesigned. Choice D: The author does not explicitly state that polls should be given to more people.
28	D	Evidence for choice D: In this sentence, the author provides the solution: if polls are to be kept, the public must be educated about them. Choice A: This sentence identifies a problem not a solution. Choice B: These lines talk about the idea of withholding projection, but the author does not offer it as a solution. Choice C: These lines discuss an advantage of giving up polls, but the author is not offering this as a solution.

Item	Answer	Explanation
29	A	Evidence for choice A: In lines 26–27, the writer states that restricting pre-election poll reporting "might limit First Amendment freedoms." This is a way of saying that the practice would likely be at odds with the Constitution's guarantee of freedom of the press.
		Choice B: The author would probably agree with this statement, and he sees it as a fundamental problem with polls. In other words, this is the type of reason that would make him favor some kind of regulation.
		Choice C: There is no evidence to support this statement. On the contrary, the suggestion is that at least some countries feel poll-reporting regulations are important enough to successful elections that they impose restrictions on the press.
		Choice D: While this statement is likely true, based on information in the passage, there is nothing to suggest the writer would see this as a reason to oppose regulation.
30	B	Evidence for choice B: In lines 39–41, the author notes that poll projections led presidential candidate Al Gore to concede the election, then later withdraw his concession "when discrepancies in the vote count were discovered."
		Choice A: This statement may be true in some cases, but it is not a conclusion that can be drawn from the information about the 2000 presidential election.
		Choice C: There is no evidence in the passage to support this.
		Choice D: Electoral votes are mentioned in the passage, but there's no discussion to support this statement as a conclusion.
31	C	Evidence for choice C: This sentence provides facts about how fluoride reduced tooth decay.
		Choice A: This sentence merely states that fluoride has been added to water; it does not tell the effects of this.
		Choice B: This sentence tells where fluoride comes from but does not tell its effects.
		Choice D: This sentence contradicts the argument that fluoride has had positive effects.
32	B	Evidence for choice B: This is stated in lines 12–15 and lines 27–30. The graph indicates that tooth decay has declined in all countries regardless of whether they have fluoridated water. This indicates that some other factors common to all countries is causing the rate of tooth decay to decrease.
		Choice A: The graph and text indicate that tooth decay has decreased not increased.
		Choice C: The graph shows some countries have had more cavities even though the water was fluoridated. (For example, New Zealand has had more than Japan.)
		Choice D: Although the graph shows this, the text states that fluoride was added to U.S. water supplies in the 1940s, therefore, this cannot explain the reduction in decay from 1970 to 2010. Given that the rate of decay has gone down in all countries during this period of time, whether fluoridated or not, fluoride cannot completely explain this reduction.
33	C	Evidence for choice C: The graph shows that dental decay has decreased in all countries, whether fluoridated or not. The passage states that there is not clear evidence that fluoride is the reason for the reduction and mentions the possibility of better diet and health care as contributing factors.
		Choice A: Although this may be true, the graph does not show this, and the passage only alludes to better health care but does not prove that better dental care is the reason for decreased decay.
		Choice B: The text mentions fluoride in toothpaste but does not analyze its results. The graph does not indicate data about users of fluoride toothpaste.
		Choice D: The author does not discuss more fluoride being added to the water supply.

Item	Answer	Explanation
34	D	Evidence for choice D: This is not stated in the passage. This question asks you to identify the one item that is NOT stated in the passage. Choice A: This is stated in line 44. Choice B: This is stated in lines 46–47. Choice C: This is stated in lines 53–54.
35	D	Evidence for choice D: Throughout the passage, the author presents the pros and cons of fluoride. He gives equal weight to both sides. Choice A: The author presents both sides, giving equal weight to each. He is not trying to convince readers to believe that fluoride is bad. Choice B: There is no mention of lobbying to remove fluoride, and the tone is not persuasive. Choice C: Because the author presents both sides, he is not necessarily assuring readers that fluoride is safe. He is simply showing the positives and the negatives.
36	A	Evidence for choice A: This paragraph lists several possible negative results of fluoride, but ends by stating that none of these effects have been proven. Choice B: The paragraph does mention animal studies, but this is not the central claim (main idea) of the whole paragraph. Choice C: This is mentioned but is not the central claim. Choice D: This paragraph does not discuss pros and cons.
37	B	Evidence for choice B: These phrases show that the author is referencing scientific data, which gives the passage objectivity and a formal tone. Choice A: This is the opposite of choice B. "Informal" would mean the passage had a more talkative tone, and "subjective" would mean that the author's bias could be seen. Choice C: Because the author presents both sides, he is not simply being critical. "Conventional" is a somewhat irrelevant word in the context of this passage. Choice D: Although the author is being forthright in that he is presenting the facts on the issue, "earnest" suggests an intense conviction, which would suggest more of a bias than the author reveals.
38	C	Evidence for choice C: Lines 17–19 state "Those who are opposed maintain that fluoride is a toxic substance that can actually harm the teeth and bones of children and adults." The lines referred to in this question provide additional reasons people object to fluoride. Choice A: The author does not present an argument for or against fluoride; he simply presents both sides of the debate. Choice B: These lines do not support the idea that "The first studies that claimed fluoride's success in combating cavities were performed in the 1940s in several U.S. and Canadian cities." They support the opposite viewpoint. Choice D: The author is not making an argument for or against fluoride, so these lines are not in opposition to the central argument.

Item	Answer	Explanation
39	A	Evidence for choice A: Because of the author's equal presentation of the pros and cons of fluoride, his perspective is clearly neutral; he does not favor one side over the other. Choice B: This choice is too extreme and too negative. The author does discuss some of the benefits of fluoride. Choice C: This choice is too positive. The author does discuss the drawbacks of fluoride. Choice D: This choice sounds similar to choice A, but "indifferent" suggests that the author has no interest in the subject, which is not accurate.
40	C	Evidence for choice C: Lines 12–14 note that improvements in children's teeth since the 1940s might in part be "due to better diet and health care," rather than just fluoride. Choice A: While fluoride toothpaste is mentioned in the passage, there is no mention of it in conjunction with those first studies. Choice B: The article only mentions that the Centers for Disease Control and Prevention currently supports fluoridating water supplies. Choice D: This statement is not supported by evidence in the passage.
41	D	Evidence for choice D: Of the potential benefits of fluoride, the writer states (in lines 28–30) that "recent studies have shown no significant differences in cavity rates between children in fluoridated and non-fluoridated cities." Of the possible risks of fluoride, the writer lists a number of "possible ill effects" of fluoride (lines 55–56) and then closes the paragraph by saying, "Yet none of these effects have been scientifically proven to occur." Choice A: This states a belief of some opponents of fluoride (lines 58–60), but there are others, including entire federal health agencies, that disagree. Choice B: The author states that hundreds of cities have stopped fluoridating water and goes on to explain that while "cost-cutting" is often a factor, the decision is also "due to doubts about its (fluoride's) benefits" (lines 65–68). Choice C: There is no evidence to support the conclusion that "the majority" of scientists, doctors, and dentists now question the use of fluoride. However, the passage does make it clear there is a divided opinion on the issue.
42	C	Evidence for choice C: In this quotation, Justice Brown states that the Constitution can't help if one race is "socially" inferior to another. This implies that blacks were not as intelligent or educated and reveals the attitudes that contributed to racial inequality at that time in history. Choice A: Social rights is mentioned earlier, but Justice Brown is not explaining its meaning here. Choice B: The Thirteenth Amendment abolished slavery, which isn't directly related to what Justice Brown says. Choice D: Justice Brown isn't justifying one race's inferiority to another. He is explaining his interpretation of category of rights that the Constitution upholds.
43	C	Evidence for choice C: A constraint is a limitation. In this context, Justice Brown believes that if one race feels inferior to another, it is because they are choosing to limit themselves in that way. Choice A: "Building" is another definition of "construction" but not a correct interpretation in this context. Choice B: "Creation" is another definition of "construction" but does not work in this context. Choice D: "Liberty" means freedom, which is the opposite of the meaning of "construction" in this context.

Item	Answer	Explanation
44	D	Evidence for choice D: A "nod" in this context means a gesture of acknowledgment or concession. The ruling in the court case essentially gave permission for continued racial segregation without issuing a ruling approving of it.
		Choice A: Racial harmony is the opposite of what the case resulted in.
		Choice B: This choice uses some of the language in the passage but the part in question does not suggest "rejecting" institutions in the South.
		Choice C: The passage states that the case foreclosed legal challenges not institutions.
45	A	Evidence for choice A: The author of passage 1 states in lines 47–48 that the Supreme Court's decision in *Plessy v. Ferguson* "gave a 'constitutional nod' to racial segregation in public places." By claiming to base its decision on constitutional grounds, the Supreme Court greatly influenced the continuation of racial segregation well into the mid-twentieth century.
		Choice B: This statement is true in itself, and it did play a part in the Supreme Court's decision. But it was only a part of the court's argument that racial segregation was constitutional.
		Choice C: The concept of "separate but equal" facilities existed prior to *Plessy v. Ferguson* and was the central issue debated in the case.
		Choice D: This statement may be true. However, it is not supported in the passage, and, as with Choice B, it was an element of the court's overall argument that segregation in public places was constitutional.
46	B	Evidence for choice B: Justice Harlan states that he thinks the Constitution "does not . . . permit any public authority to know the race" of those whose rights are in question.
		Choice A: This is the opposite of what Justice Harlan says.
		Choice C: He is not doubting the Constitution's role; he is identifying it.
		Choice D: This choice is also the opposite of the concern at hand. The concern is that if authorities know the race of a person, it will affect their ability to offer fair protection of rights.
47	A	Evidence for choice A: This sentence restates the previous sentence in which Justice Harlan states that authorities should not know the race of those whose rights they are to protect.
		Choice B: This statement does not directly support the previous question.
		Choice C: This statement relates to the idea of desegregation of railway cars.
		Choice D: This statement has to do with the fact that our country prides itself on its citizens' freedom yet it restricts the liberty of some.
48	C	Evidence for choice C: Justice Harlan states that it is difficult to "reconcile" the fact that the U.S. boasts of freedom for its citizens, yet a class of its citizens is discriminated against. In this context reconcile means to make consistent with one another.
		Choice A: This definition of the word would make sense in the context of friendship.
		Choice B: This definition of the word "reconcile" would make sense in the context of a friendship, but not in this case.
		Choice D: This is the opposite of the correct definition.

Item	Answer	Explanation
49	D	Evidence for choice D: The author of passage 2 writes that the Court's ruling is "inconsistent" with "personal liberty" and "a degradation" to fellow citizens who should be "our equals before the law." He also states that "the white race deems itself to be the dominant race in this country" (lines 64–65), which meant blacks continued in a type of servitude, despite the end of slavery. Choice A: While this choice is related to the author's opinions, it is not the best description of why he chose to use the word "servitude." Choice B: The fact that the Supreme Court ruled as it did shows that not everyone saw the evils of racial segregation as clearly as Justice Harlan did. Choice C: The author of passage 2 makes it clear that he is strongly opposed to "separate but equal" laws and would rather end them than be forced to "uphold" them.
50	A	Evidence for choice A: In Passage 1, lines 25–29 explain that the Court determined that the Constitution guarantees equal political and civil rights but not social rights. In Passage 2, Justice Harlan makes the argument that all citizens are entitled to the same rights. Choice B: This is a statement that Justice Harlan makes, but it is not directly related to the part of Passage 1 in question. Choice C: Justice Harlan makes this statement, but it is the opposite of the idea that only certain rights of certain people are protected. Choice D: Justice Harlan would not agree with this statement because it is in opposition to the points he makes in his argument.
51	A	Evidence for choice A: Passage 1 explains the ruling in *Plessy v. Ferguson*, which made it legal to segregate railway cars. In Passage 2, Justice Harlan disagrees with the decision on the case. "Refutes" means argues against. Choice B: Passage 2 does not explain the reasons behind the ruling in the case; it argues against it. Choice C: The Thirteenth and Fourteenth Amendments are discussed in Passage 1. The author of Passage 2 is in support of these amendments. Choice D: The author of Passage 2 criticizes the ruling discussed in Passage 1, but does not disagree with the author. The author of Passage 1 is simply reporting on the case, not arguing for it.
52	B	Evidence for choice B: In the first sentences of Passage 2, Justice Harlan discusses his interpretation of the Constitution to mean that race should not be involved when determining citizens' rights. Choice A: Although one could assume that Justice Harlan treats all humans equally, based on his interpretation of the Constitution, there is not proof in the passage to support this. Choice C: This is the opposite of Justice Harlan's interpretation. Choice D: This concept is not addressed.

If you missed these questions on the Reading Test . . .	study this lesson. (Please note that some questions test multiple skills; thus some question numbers appear twice in this chart.)
	Closely Reading Literature
6	Lesson 1: Understanding explicit and implicit ideas (p. 57)
3	Lesson 1: Understanding main ideas and purpose (p. 65)
4, 5, 8, 9	Lesson 1: Analyzing word choice and imagery for tone (p. 74)
1, 6	Lesson 1: Identifying characterization (p. 85)
10, 11	Lesson 1: Identifying narrator's point of view (p. 92)
2, 7	Lesson 1: Citing textual evidence (p. 99)
	Closely Reading Literature and Informational Texts
14, 20, 24, 43, 48	Lesson 2: Understanding meanings of words and phrases (p. 107)
	Closely Reading Informational Texts
15, 17, 27	Lesson 3: Understanding explicit meanings (p. 115)
12, 15, 22, 36	Lesson 3: Determining central ideas and summarizing (p. 121)
23, 31, 34	Lesson 3: Identifying supporting details (p. 127)
30, 33, 40, 41, 52	Lesson 4: Making inferences (p. 137)
29, 50	Lesson 4: Using analogical reasoning (p. 146)
13, 26, 28, 31, 47	Lesson 4: Citing textual evidence (p. 152)
16, 18, 19, 25, 35, 39, 42, 49	Lesson 5: Analyzing author's point of view and purpose (p. 159)
22, 23, 35, 45	Lesson 5: Analyzing the use of arguments (claims, counterclaims, reasoning, and evidence) (p. 168)
21, 37, 38, 44, 49	Lesson 6: Analyzing use of word choice to shape meaning and tone (p. 177)
19, 38	Lesson 6: Analyzing text structures (p. 184)
50, 51	Lesson 7: Synthesizing information from multiple texts (p. 193)
32, 33	Lesson 7: Analyzing and synthesizing information from graphic organizers and texts (p. 204)

Writing and Language Test

Item	Answer	Explanation
1	D	A comma is not needed between two words connected by the word "and."
2	C	The USDA is a singular noun, since it is a single institution. As such, the apostrophe indicating possession comes before the "s."
3	D	The pronoun "they" is confusing here because its antecedent, "farmers markets," does not appear in the sentence; the pronoun appears at first to be referring to "market managers." Corrected: that **farmers markets** continued to grow . . .
4	C	The sentence previews the topic of the paragraph, which is how nutritional assistance programs benefit both customers and vendors.
5	B	In this sentence, the verbs "expand," "give," and "encourage" should all be in the same tense — the present tense in this case.
6	A	The information that follows the transitional phrase "In addition" adds complementary information to the discussion of nutrition, rather than contrasting with what's been said ("However") or being causally related to it ("Consequently," "As a result").
7	B	Since all of the items in the series are one word and hence easily distinguished from each other, semicolons are unnecessary; commas are the correct choice.
8	A	In the context of the passage, the most accurate description of the presence of fresh produce at farmers markets is "dominant feature."
9	D	The choice "devastating disease" is consistent with the tone of the rest of the passage and also an accurate description of the situation.
10	A	The sentence describes an event in the present, so "infects" is correct.
11	D	While "figure out" and "tell" convey the nature of the action, "determine" is the most precise and stylistically best way to describe it. "Estimate" is inaccurate.
12	B	The words "reliable" and "dependable" are synonyms. Using both words is redundant.
13	D	The antecedent for the pronoun is "bats," so the plural possessive form "their" is correct. Corrected: Infected bats also often display abnormal behaviors in **their** hibernation sites . . .
14	C	The phrase "may contribute to" best matches the formal style and tone of the passage.
15	C	The sentence expands on information given in sentence 1, so it's best to place it after that opening sentence.
16	C	A period after "known" provides the clearest presentation of information, as well as being the best way to correct the run-on sentence.
17	B	In the original sentence, the pronoun "they" is a long way from its antecedent, "bats." Replacing the pronoun with the noun makes for clearer reading. Corrected: In temperate regions, **bats** are primary consumers
18	D	The present perfect tense, "have failed," is the correct tense because it describes something that happened in the past and also continues into the present—in this situation, experiments. Corrected: While some researchers have reported biological changes associated with RF energy, these studies **have failed** to be replicated.

19	A	The word "whereas" provides the best transition and also prepares the reader for contrasting elements in the sentence it begins.
20	C	The word refers to conditions caused by radio frequency energy, so "effects" is the correct word.
21	D	The clause "such as is found in X-rays and gamma rays" is a nonrestrictive clause, meaning it is not essential to the meaning of the sentence and should be set off by commas.
22	B	The pronoun refers back to the antecedent "electrons" and should therefore be plural in form — in this case, "their." Corrected: where electrons are stripped away from **their** normal locations
23	C	If it were not for that final sentence, readers would not have a clear understanding of how dangerous ionization of tissue can be, and that information is vital to understanding the overall discussion.
24	B	The use of "kinds of" is vague, and it's also incorrect wording. The word "relatively" is correct, clear, and appropriate.
25	C	The second clause explains a condition described in the first (that the eyes are vulnerable to RF heating), so "because" is the appropriate conjunction. Choice D uses "because," but it also contains unnecessary words ("and this is").
26	C	This sentence is made up of two independent clauses (complete sentences) that are connected by a comma and a conjunction (and). The second clause contradicts the first, so it should begin with "but." "However" is also a contradiction, but it would need a semicolon before it and a comma after it in this sentence construction.
27	C	"Numerous" and "abundant" have close definitions. Using both words is redundant.
28	C	The phrase "as separate individuals" modifies "bacteria." The correct placement of it is next to the word it is modifying.
29	B	Use a colon to introduce a list.
30	D	Sentence 3 is a response to sentence 4. Sentence 4 contains the fact that the immune system cannot handle all infections by itself. Sentence 3 follows this up with examples of medical interventions that can help the immune system.
31	D	This sentence contains two independent clauses (complete sentences) that are connected by a comma. This error is called a comma splice. Choice D fixes this by correctly using a semicolon.
32	A	This is the correct use of a dash.
33	A	The second paragraph explains how the brain changes. Choice A summarizes this idea.
34	A	The subject "wiring" is singular and takes the singular verb "is." None of the other choices improve the sentence.
35	B	This sentence starts with "in fact," which means that it is providing an example of something mentioned earlier. Sentence 1 presents the information that each of us has a unique brain. By inserting the new sentence after sentence 1, there is an illustration of the point that was just made.
36	B	"For instance" means that an example will be provided, but instead the sentence supports the statement in the previous sentence. "Indeed" indicates this relationship.
37	D	Sentence 8 introduces a new topic (brain injuries), which is not related to the topic of the paragraph.

38	B	Compare and contrast like to like. Here a worm is contrasted to a brain. Instead, a worm should be compared to another creature. Choice C is too vague ("vertebrate").
39	D	"Mysterious" is a more accurate word when referring to aspects of the brain that have not yet been figured out.
40	C	To keep a consistent tone with the rest of the passage, "determine" is a more formal form of "get a handle on."
41	A	The sentence provides an analogy between scientists trying to figure out the brain and mechanics trying to fix a car without a parts list. This supports the main idea of the passage: that there is much not known about the brain.
42	A	The graph indicates that the rate of children living with married parents who receive food stamps has jumped from 2.7 to 5.2. The means the rate has almost doubled. The sentence is correct.
43	A	The phrase "prior to" is correct.
44	D	A comma is not needed between two items connected by the word "and."

If you missed these questions on the Writing and Language Test . . .	study this lesson from the Writing and Language Domain. (Please note that some questions test multiple skills; thus some question numbers appear twice in this chart.)
4, 15, 23, 33, 35, 37, 41	Lesson 8: Revising texts for clarity, focus, and purpose (p. 243)
42	Lesson 8: Relating information presented in graphs, charts, and tables to information presented in texts (p. 252)
30	Lesson 9: Revising for cohesion and logical order (p. 261)
6, 19, 36	Lesson 9: Revising beginnings or endings of a text or paragraphs to ensure transitional words, phrases, and sentences are used effectively (p. 267)
11, 8, 39	Lesson 10: Revising texts to improve word choice for exactness and content (p. 275)
12, 27, 34	Lesson 10: Revising to eliminate wordiness (p. 279)
9, 14, 40	Lesson 10: Revising text for consistency of style and tone or to match style and tone to purpose (p. 288)
16, 31	Lesson 11: Editing to correct sentence fragments and run-ons (p. 295)
25	Lesson 11: Combining sentences for clarity (p. 304)
28, 26	Lesson 11: Editing to correct problems with subordination/coordination, parallel structure, and modifier placement (p. 306)
5, 10, 18	Lesson 11: Editing to correct shifts in verbs (tense, voice, and mood) and pronouns (person and number) (p. 313)
3, 17	Lesson 12: Using pronouns correctly (p. 323) Lesson 12: Correcting unclear or ambiguous pronouns or antecedents (p. 325)
13, 22, 34	Lesson 12: Correcting problems with pronoun/antecedent, subject/verb, and noun agreement (p. 329)

20	Lesson 12: Correcting misuse of confusing words (p. 337)
38	Lesson 12: Correcting cases in which unalike terms are compared (p. 337)
24, 43	Lesson 12: Correcting nonstandard written English (p. 338)
1, 7, 16, 21	Lesson 13: Using end punctuation and commas (p. 343)
29, 31	Lesson 13: Using semicolons and colons (p. 349)
32	Lesson 13: Using parentheses, dashes, and quotation marks (p. 354)
2, 44	Lesson 13: Using possessives and correcting use of unnecessary punctuation (pp. 358–359)

Score Conversions

You are probably wondering how your score on this Diagnostic Test converts to the SAT point scale of 200–800 for the Reading and Writing and Language section. On the next page is a chart that you can use to convert your raw scores into scaled scores and finally into an estimated total section score. This chart can also be used to compute your scores on the three Model SAT Exams.

Keep in mind: the conversions in the chart are estimates only. Visit https://collegereadiness.collegeboard.org/about/scores for more information and the latest scoring conversions.

Use these steps:

1) Add up the number of questions you answered correctly for the Reading section and the Writing and Language section. Do not subtract points for questions you answered incorrectly or failed to answer.

2) Use the score conversion chart on page 56 to find your scaled scores.

3) Add your scaled scores for the Evidence-based Reading and the Writing and Language sections together. (See the chart on the bottom of page 56.)

4) Multiply your total from Step 3 times 10. This is your estimated score for the section.

The SAT reports your score on the Math section (200–800) and the Evidence-based Reading and Writing sections (200–800) separately and also as a total SAT score of 400–1600.

Score Conversion Charts

1) Total your correct answers on the Reading Test and the Writing and Language Test. This is your raw score. Use the chart to find the scaled score for each section of the test.

Raw Score (Number of Correct Answers)	Reading Test Scaled Score	Writing and Language Test Scaled Score	Raw Score (Number of Correct Answers)	Reading Test Score	Writing and Language Test Score
0	10	10	30	27	30
1	10	10	31	28	30
2	10	10	32	29	31
3	11	11	33	29	32
4	12	12	34	30	32
5	13	13	35	30	33
6	14	14	36	31	33
7	15	14	37	31	34
8	15	15	38	32	35
9	16	16	39	32	36
10	17	17	40	33	36
11	18	17	41	33	37
12	18	18	42	34	38
13	19	19	43	34	39
14	19	19	44	35	40
15	20	20	45	36	
16	21	21	46	36	
17	21	22	47	37	
18	22	22	48	38	
19	22	23	49	38	
20	23	24	50	39	
21	23	24	51	40	
22	23	25	52	40	
23	24	26			
24	24	26			
25	25	27			
26	25	27			
27	26	28			
28	26	28			
29	27	29			

2) Fill in the boxes below with your scaled scores from the chart above. Add them together and then multiply by 10 to find your estimated section score.

Reading Scaled Score (10–40 from table)		Writing and Language Score (10–40 from table)		Reading and Writing Test Score (20–80)		Evidence-Based Reading and Writing Section Score (200–800)
	+		=		x 10	

LESSON 1:
Closely Reading Literature

- Determining explicit and implicit meanings

- Understanding main ideas and purpose

- Analyzing word choice and imagery for tone

- Identifying characterization

- Identifying narrator's point of view

- Citing textual evidence

Explain Determining Explicit and Implicit Meanings

The SAT Reading test will include one passage of literature with approximately 10 questions. The literature may be from a classic or contemporary novel or short story. The sections in this lesson will review how to review and interpret a work of fiction, based upon the types of questions asked on the SAT.

SAT questions fall into two categories: those that test over explicit meanings and those that test over implicit meanings. **Explicit** meanings are those that are clearly stated in the text. Explicit questions ask you about specific things the narrator says or the characters do. Answers for explicit questions can be easily found in the text.

Examples of explicit questions include:

- The passage indicates that a character's behavior was caused by . . .

- As presented in the passage, the reason an event occurs is because . . .

- In the passage, character 1 . . .

Implicit meanings are implied or suggested, but not clearly stated. To make an inference, you must go a step beyond the text and draw a conclusion. An inference is always based upon the text but requires you to add some of your prior knowledge in order to interpret the character's or narrator's words and actions. Many of the skills you will study in this lesson will require you to make inferences. For example, the writer almost never comes out and states the theme of a work of literature. You must infer it from many details found in the text. Some examples of questions that require you to make inference include the following:

- The passage most clearly implies that . . .

- The narrator implies that . . .

- The question the narrator asks in lines xx-xx most nearly implies that . . .

- Lines xx–xx suggests that . . .

Read the following passage from the opening of the story "The Revolt of 'Mother'" by Mary Wilkins Freeman. Notice how the reader underlined explicit details in the passage. Note the inferences made in the margin.

"Father!"

The old man slapped the saddle upon the mare's back.

"Look here, Father, I want to know what them men are diggin' over in the field for, an' I'm goin' to know."

5   "I wish you'd go into the house, Mother, an' 'tend to your own affairs," the old man said then. He ran his words together, and his speech was almost as inarticulate as a growl.

Father avoids answering Mother's questions. Perhaps he is not used to questions from his wife.

But the woman understood; it was her most native tongue. "I ain't goin' into the house till you tell me what them men are doin' over there in the field," 10 said she.

Then she stood waiting. She was a small woman, short and straight-waisted like a child in her brown cotton gown. Her forehead was mild and benevolent between the smooth curves of gray hair; there were meek downward lines about her nose and mouth; but her eyes, fixed upon the old 15 man, looked as if the meekness had been the result of her own will, never of the will of another.

Description of Mother: meek by choice, mild, childlike

They were in the barn, standing before the wide open doors. The spring air, full of the smell of growing grass and unseen blossoms, came in their faces. The deep yard in front was littered with farm wagons and piles of 20 wood; on the edges, close to the fence and the house, the grass was a vivid green, and there were some dandelions.

Setting: peaceful description of the farm, spring air, and growing grass is in contrast with the confrontation between Mother and Father

Read these explicit and implicit ideas based upon the passage. Do all the inferences seem appropriate, based upon the passage?

Explicit Ideas:

- An older man and woman are talking in a barn.
- The woman questions the man about why men are digging in a field. Although she asks him several times, he doesn't answer, instead telling her to attend to her own affairs.
- The setting is a barn. There is a yard with wagons and wood. There are surrounding fields.

Implicit Ideas (Inferences):

- The man is probably a farmer and the setting is a farm.

- Although the woman calls the man "Father," they must be husband and wife. They appear similar in age and interact as if they are married. This emphasizes their roles in the family rather than their individual personalities.

- Mother is described as "meek" but seems stubborn because she keeps asking Father why the men are digging. She seems unhappy that he hasn't told her.

- Father is dismissive of Mother, telling her to "'tend to your own affairs." He doesn't like to communicate; his speech is "inarticulate as a growl."

- Mother and Father appear to have clearly defined roles. He is in charge of the farm; she takes care of the house. Mother seems to be breaking out of these roles by asking about the digging in the field.

Notice that the inferences require you to draw conclusions not specifically stated in the passage. Inferences are supported by direct quotations and also by paraphrases of details from the passage.

The SAT will test your ability to identify lines of text that support an inference. See pages 99–106 on citing evidence.

Practice

Directions: As you read the following text, mark the text, underlining important ideas and writing inferences in the margin. Then answer the questions that follow.

In the following excerpt from The Interlopers *by Saki, Ulrich von Gradwitz and Georg Znaeym fight over a strip of forest that lies between their lands. Although a court ruled that the von Gradwitzs own the land, the Znaeym family has never accepted this judgment. One night the two enemies confront each other on the disputed land.*

The two enemies stood glaring at one another for a long silent moment.
Each had a rifle in his hand, each had hate in his heart and murder uppermost
in his mind. The chance had come to give full play to the passions of a
lifetime. But a man who has been brought up under the code of a restraining
5 civilization cannot easily nerve himself to shoot down his neighbor in cold
blood and without word spoken, except for an offence against his hearth and
honor. And before the moment of hesitation had given way to action a deed of
Nature's own violence overwhelmed them both. A fierce shriek of the storm
had been answered by a splitting crash over their heads, and ere they could
10 leap aside a mass of falling beech tree had thundered down on them. Ulrich
von Gradwitz found himself stretched on the ground, one arm numb beneath
him and the other held almost as helplessly in a tight tangle of forked branches,
while both legs were pinned beneath the fallen mass. His heavy shooting-boots
had saved his feet from being crushed to pieces, but if his fractures were not as
15 serious as they might have been, at least it was evident that he could not move
from his present position till someone came to release him. . . . At his side,

so near that under ordinary circumstances he could almost have touched him, lay Georg Znaeym, alive and struggling, but obviously as helplessly pinioned down as himself. All round them lay a thick-strewn wreckage of splintered
20 branches and broken twigs.

Relief at being alive and exasperation at his captive plight brought a strange medley of pious thank-offerings and sharp curses to Ulrich's lips. Georg, who was early blinded with the blood which trickled across his eyes, stopped his struggling for a moment to listen, and then gave a short, snarling
25 laugh.

"So you're not killed, as you ought to be, but you're caught, anyway," he cried; "caught fast. Ho, what a jest, Ulrich von Gradwitz snared in his stolen forest. There's real justice for you!"

And he laughed again, mockingly and savagely.

30 "I'm caught in my own forest-land," retorted Ulrich. "When my men come to release us you will wish, perhaps, that you were in a better plight than caught poaching on a neighbour's land, shame on you."

Georg was silent for a moment; then he answered quietly:

"Are you sure that your men will find much to release? I have men, too, in
35 the forest tonight, close behind me, and THEY will be here first and do the releasing. When they drag me out from under these branches it won't need much clumsiness on their part to roll this mass of trunk right over on the top of you. Your men will find you dead under a fallen beech tree. For form's sake I shall send my condolences to your family."

40 "It is a useful hint," said Ulrich fiercely. "My men had orders to follow in ten minutes time, seven of which must have gone by already, and when they get me out—I will remember the hint. Only as you will have met your death poaching on my lands I don't think I can decently send any message of condolence to your family."

45 "Good," snarled Georg, "good. We fight this quarrel out to the death, you and I and our foresters, with no cursed interlopers to come between us."

Explicit meanings

1. What reason does the passage give for the two men not immediately shooting each other?

   4-6 describes

   _____

   _____

   _____

2. Describe what happens to the men in the first paragraph.

   _____

   _____

   _____

Implicit meanings

3. What does Georg imply when he says, "When they drag me out from under these branches it won't need much clumsiness on their part to roll this mass of trunk right over on the top of you"?

   _____

   _____

   _____

   _____

4. What does Georg mean by saying, "There's real justice for you!"? Why does he laugh at their situation?

   _____

   _____

   _____

   _____

For answers, see page 555.

Directions: These Model SAT Questions show how the skills in this lesson might be tested on the SAT. The answers and explanations immediately follow the questions. Try the questions and then review the answers and the explanations.

This passage is from The House of Mirth, *a novel published by Edith Wharton in 1905. Lily Bart, a young woman who has been raised to marry a rich man, decides to pursue a romance with a man named Selden, a relationship based on love instead of money or social standing.*

Miss Bart was a keen reader of her own heart, and she saw that her sudden preoccupation with Selden was due to the fact that his presence shed a new light on her surroundings. Not that he was notably brilliant or exceptional; in his own profession he was surpassed by more than one man who had bored Lily

5 through many a weary dinner. It was rather that he had preserved a certain social detachment, a happy air of viewing the show objectively, of having points of contact outside the great gilt cage in which they were all huddled for the mob to gape at. How alluring the world outside the cage appeared to Lily, as she heard its door clang on her! In reality, as she knew, the door never clanged: it stood

10 always open; but most of the captives were like flies in a bottle, and having once flown in, could never regain their freedom. It was Selden's distinction that he had never forgotten the way out. . . .

Lily smiled at her classification of her friends. How different they had seemed to her a few hours ago! Then they had symbolized what she was

15 gaining, now they stood for what she was giving up. That very afternoon they had seemed full of brilliant qualities; now she saw that they were merely dull in a loud way. Under the glitter of their opportunities she saw the poverty of their achievement. It was not that she wanted them to be more disinterested; but she would have liked them to be more picturesque. And she had a shamed

20 recollection of the way in which, a few hours since, she had felt the centripetal force of their standards. She closed her eyes an instant, and the vacuous routines of the life she had chosen stretched before her like a long white road without dip or turning: it was true she was to roll over it in a carriage instead of trudging it on foot, but sometimes the pedestrian enjoys the diversion of a short

25 cut which is denied to those on wheels.

1. The passage indicates that in the past Lily has been very influenced by
   A) her own observations about the world.
   B) large groups of people she calls "the mob."
   C) the opinions of her friends.
   D) Selden and his family.

Strategy: The important phrase in the question is "in the past." Choice A is not correct, because clearly Lily is still guided by her own mind, as a "clear reader of her own heart." Choice D is also incorrect because she is currently being influenced by Selden. Choice B references the idea that Lily feels trapped in a cage for "the mob to gape at." Although clearly Lily feels like everyone is watching and perhaps judging her, she does not say that she is influenced by them. The best choice is C. This is supported by the phrase "a few hours since, she had felt the centripetal force of their standards."

2. The narrator's description of Lily Bart's way of life as "the great gilt cage in which they were all huddled for the mob to gape at" most nearly implies that Lily believes that she and her friends
   A) help protect each other from the outside world.
   B) seem to be confined by society's standards.
   C) care too much about what other people think of them.
   D) can't ever escape from society's harsh standards.

Strategy: The image of huddling in a cage does not imply protection so choice A is incorrect. Choice C suggests that people are scrutinizing Lily and her friends, but no mention is made of how they feel about this attention. The idea that they can't ever escape is contradicted by the statement that the door "stood always open." However, the idea that Lily and her friends are confined and trapped by the rules of their social circles is implied. The best answer is choice B.

SAT-Type Questions

Directions: Questions 1–5 are based on the following passage.

This passage is from "The Flowers," a short story by Alice Walker. In it a girl named Myop, whose family lives on a sharecropper's farm, makes a startling discovery.

It seemed to Myop as she skipped lightly from hen house to pigpen to smokehouse that the days had never been as beautiful as these. The air held a keenness that made her nose twitch. The harvesting of the corn and cotton, peanuts and squash, made each day a golden surprise that caused excited
5 little tremors to run up her jaws. . . .

She had explored the woods behind the house many times. Often, in late autumn, her mother took her to gather nuts among the fallen leaves. Today she made her own path, bouncing this way and that way, vaguely keeping an eye out for snakes. She found, in addition to various common but

10 pretty ferns and leaves, an armful of strange blue flowers with velvety ridges
and a sweet suds bush full of the brown, fragrant buds.

By twelve o'clock, her arms laden with sprigs of her findings, she was a mile
or more from home. She had often been as far before, but the strangeness of the
land made it not as pleasant as her usual haunts. It seemed gloomy in the little
15 cove in which she found herself. The air was damp, the silence close and deep.

Myop began to circle back to the house, back to the peacefulness of the
morning. It was then she stepped smack into his eyes. Her heel became
lodged in the broken ridge between brow and nose, and she reached down
quickly, unafraid, to free herself. It was only when she saw his naked grin
20 that she gave a little yelp of surprise.

He had been a tall man. From feet to neck covered a long space. His head
lay beside him. When she pushed back the leaves and layers of earth and debris
Myop saw that he'd had large white teeth, all of them cracked or broken, long
fingers, and very big bones. All his clothes had rotted away except some threads
25 of blue denim from his overalls. The buckles of the overall had turned green.

Myop gazed around the spot with interest. Very near where she'd stepped
into the head was a wild pink rose. As she picked it to add to her bundle
she noticed a raised mound, a ring, around the rose's root. It was the rotted
remains of a noose, a bit of shredding plowline, now blending benignly into
30 the soil. Around an overhanging limb of a great spreading oak clung another
piece. Frayed, rotted, bleached, and frazzled-—barely there—but spinning
restlessly in the breeze. Myop laid down her flowers.

And the summer was over.

1. At the beginning of the passage, Myop is
   A) working on her family's farm.
   B) gathering nuts for her mother.
   C) going into the woods to pick flowers.
   D) exploring a new path in the forest.

2. The use of the words "strangeness" (line 13) and "close and deep"
   (line 15) imply that the cove is
   A) an exciting place to play.
   B) mysterious and foreboding.
   C) a good place to have a picnic.
   D) shady and welcoming.

3. According to the passage, Myop steps on a
   A) skull.
   B) sleeping man's head.
   C) piece of rope.
   D) a plundered grave.

4. It is implied that the tall man
   A) was the victim of a lynching.
   B) lost his way in the forest.
   C) was shot for trespassing.
   D) fell out of the tree and died.

5. The final line "And the summer was over" implies that Myop
   A) must return to school soon.
   B) must get home before the people who killed the man find her.
   C) has discovered that the world can be an evil place.
   D) will never tell her family about finding the man's remains.

For answers, see page 555.

Explain Understanding Main Ideas and Purpose

One of the most commonly asked questions about literature is about the **main idea** of the text. You will be asked to identify the central theme of the text—the central idea the author is communicating. Some questions will ask you to identify the best **summary** of a passage. A good summary must include the key events or ideas in the story. Examples of questions about main idea and summary include:

- Which choice describes what happens in this passage?
- This passage is mainly about . . .
- Which choice best summarizes the passage?

Other questions ask about **purpose**. Purpose has to do with what a story seeks to communicate. Some questions focus on the purpose of a specific line or paragraph as it relates to the entire passage. Examples of questions about purpose include:

- The main purpose of (sentence, paragraph) is to . . .
- The sentence in lines xx-xx mainly serves to . . .

Think It Through

As you read the passage, underline important details. Remember that literature communicates meaning through description of events, character, and setting. As you read the passage, jot notes in the margin. Identify lines of text that

- reveal a character's personality or motives
- create the emotional tone or mood
- use figurative language, such as metaphor or simile
- reveal the narrator's point of view

QUICK TIP

Main idea is what the passage is about (meaning) whereas summary is what happens (plot).

The following passages are excerpted from The Great Gatsby *by F. Scott Fitzgerald, published in 1925. Notice how the reader underlined the text, identifying the main ideas of the passage.*

There must have been moments even that afternoon when Daisy <u>tumbled</u> <u>short of his dreams</u>—not through her own fault, but because of the <u>colossal</u> <u>vitality of his illusion</u>. It had gone <u>beyond her</u>, beyond everything. He had thrown himself into it with a creative passion, adding to it all the time,

5 decking it out with every bright feather that drifted his way. <u>No amount of</u> <u>fire or freshness</u> can <u>challenge</u> what a man will <u>store up</u> in his <u>ghostly heart</u>.

Gatsby's view of Daisy isn't grounded in reality.

Main Idea: Gatsby had created a false vision of Daisy that wasn't based in reality.

Purpose: In this paragraph the writer reveals Gatsby's state of mind toward Daisy and hints at future events. Gatsby has placed Daisy on a pedestal from which she is likely to fall.

He [Gatsby] smiled understandingly—much more than understandingly. It was one of those rare smiles with a quality of <u>eternal reassurance</u> in it, that you may come across four or five times in life. It faced—or seemed to face—the whole eternal world for an instant, and then concentrated on you

5 with an <u>irresistible prejudice in your favor</u>. It understood you just as far as you wanted to be understood, believed in you as you would like to believe in yourself, and assured you that it had precisely the <u>impression of you</u> that, <u>at your best</u>, you hoped to convey.

Summary: Gatsby's smile makes people feel understood and accepted.

Which of the following is the best summary of the paragraph?

- Gatsby commands attention from the narrator.
- The narrator describes the effect Gatsby has on people.
- Gatsby never judges anyone.
- The narrator explains how Gatsby's radiant smile attracts people.

A good summary focuses on the big ideas of the passage. It shouldn't focus on minor details; it must not contain erroneous facts.

- Gatsby commands attention from the narrator. (True, but not the main idea.)
- The narrator describes the effect Gatsby has on people. (Main idea)
- Gatsby never judges anyone. (Not what the passage says.)
- The narrator explains how Gatsby's radiant smile attracts people. (This can be inferred from the paragraph, but is not the central focus of the passage.)

Questions about purpose may ask you to think about what role a sentence or paragraph plays within an entire passage. Ask yourself, "Why did the writer include this detail? How does it help me understand the main ideas?"

In the paragraph describing Gatsby above, what is the main purpose of describing

QUICK TIP

Summary/main idea questions answer "What?" Purpose questions answer "Why?"

Gatsby's uncommonly reassuring smile "that you may come across four or five times in life"?

- to compare Gatsby with other men like him
- to detail how unusual it was to meet a man like Gatsby
- to describe how often Gatsby smiled at his friends

By returning to the passage, you notice that the narrator describes Gatsby's smile as "rare." This supports the idea that Gatsby is uncommon. The purpose is to explain how unusual men like Gatsby are.

Practice

Directions: As you read the following text, mark up the text, underlining explicit main ideas. Then answer the questions that follow.

This passage is from The Red Badge of Courage *by Stephen Crane, published in 1895. The following passage describes how Henry decides to become a soldier in the American Civil War.*

He had burned several times to enlist. Tales of great movements shook the land. They might not be distinctly Homeric, but there seemed to be much glory in them. He had read of marches, sieges, conflicts, and he had longed to see it all. His busy mind had drawn for him large pictures extravagant in

5 color, lurid with breathless deeds.

But his mother had discouraged him. She had affected to look with some contempt upon the quality of his war ardor and patriotism. She could calmly seat herself and with no apparent difficulty give him many hundreds of reasons why he was of vastly more importance on the farm than on the

10 field of battle. She had had certain ways of expression that told him that her statements on the subject came from a deep conviction. Moreover, on her side, was his belief that her ethical motive in the argument was impregnable.

At last, however, he had made firm rebellion against this yellow light thrown upon the color of his ambitions. The newspapers, the gossip of the

15 village, his own picturings, had aroused him to an uncheckable degree. They were in truth fighting finely down there. Almost every day the newspaper printed accounts of a decisive victory.

One night, as he lay in bed, the winds had carried to him the clangoring of the church bell as some enthusiast jerked the rope frantically to tell the twisted

20 news of a great battle. This voice of the people rejoicing in the night had made him shiver in a prolonged ecstasy of excitement. Later, he had gone down to

his mother's room and had spoken thus: "Ma, I'm going to enlist."

"Henry, don't you be a fool," his mother had replied. She had then covered her face with the quilt. There was an end to the matter for that night.

25 Nevertheless, the next morning he had gone to a town that was near his mother's farm and had enlisted in a company that was forming there. When he had returned home his mother was milking the brindle cow. Four others stood waiting. "Ma, I've enlisted," he had said to her diffidently. There was a short silence. "The Lord's will be done, Henry," she had finally replied, and
30 had then continued to milk the brindle cow.

When he had stood in the doorway with his soldier's clothes on his back, and with the light of excitement and expectancy in his eyes almost defeating the glow of regret for the home bonds, he had seen two tears leaving their trails on his mother's scarred cheeks.

35 Still, she had disappointed him by saying nothing whatever about returning with his shield or on it. He had privately primed himself for a beautiful scene. He had prepared certain sentences which he thought could be used with touching effect. But her words destroyed his plans. She had doggedly peeled potatoes and addressed him as follows: "You watch out, Henry, an' take good
40 care of yerself in this here fighting business—you watch, an' take good care of yerself. Don't go a-thinkin' you can lick the hull rebel army at the start, because yeh can't. Yer jest one little feller amongst a hull lot of others, and yeh've got to keep quiet an' do what they tell yeh. I know how you are, Henry."

1. What is this passage is mainly about?

_____

_____

_____

2. From what sources does Henry get his information about the war?

_____

_____

_____

3. What is the main purpose of paragraph 4 (lines 18–22)?

_____

_____

_____

4. What can be inferred about Henry's mother's attitude about Henry going to war? Identify lines of text that support your answer.

_____

_____

_____

5. What can be inferred about Henry's views of what going to war is like based upon the passage? Identify lines of text that support your answer.

_____

_____

_____

6. Summarize paragraphs 7 and 8 (lines 31–43).

_____

_____

_____

_____

_____

For answers, see page 555.

Directions: These Model SAT Questions show how the skills in this lesson might be tested on the SAT. The answers and explanations immediately follow the questions. Try the questions and then review the answers and the explanations.

This passage is from The House of Mirth, *a novel published by Edith Wharton in 1905. Lily Bart, a young woman who has been raised to marry a rich man, decides to pursue a relationship with a man named Selden, a relationship based on love instead of money or social standing.*

Miss Bart was a keen reader of her own heart, and she saw that her sudden preoccupation with Selden was due to the fact that his presence shed a new light on her surroundings. Not that he was notably brilliant or exceptional; in his own profession he was surpassed by more than one man who had bored

5 Lily through many a weary dinner. It was rather that he had preserved a certain social detachment, a happy air of viewing the show objectively, of having points of contact outside the great gilt cage in which they were all huddled for the mob to gape at. How alluring the world outside the cage appeared to Lily, as she heard its door clang on her! In reality, as she knew, the door never

10 clanged: it stood always open; but most of the captives were like flies in a bottle, and having once flown in, could never regain their freedom. It was Selden's distinction that he had never forgotten the way out. . . .

Lily smiled at her classification of her friends. How different they had seemed to her a few hours ago! Then they had symbolized what she was

15 gaining, now they stood for what she was giving up. That very afternoon they had seemed full of brilliant qualities; now she saw that they were merely dull in a loud way. Under the glitter of their opportunities she saw the poverty of their achievement. It was not that she wanted them to be more disinterested; but she would have liked them to be more picturesque. And she

20 had a shamed recollection of the way in which, a few hours since, she had felt the centripetal force of their standards. She closed her eyes an instant, and the vacuous routines of the life she had chosen stretched before her like a long white road without dip or turning: it was true she was to roll over it in a carriage instead of trudging it on foot, but sometimes the pedestrian enjoys

25 the diversion of a short cut which is denied to those on wheels.

1. Which choice best summarizes the second paragraph?
   A) A woman's viewpoint of her friends drastically changes.
   B) A woman decides to take a different path from the rest of society.
   C) The main character rejects her rich upbringing and embraces poverty.
   D) Because a woman's friends are ignoring her, she decides to make new ones.

Strategy: Nothing is mentioned about embracing poverty or her friends ignoring her, so choices C and D can be eliminated. Choice B is implied by lines 15–16, but it is a detail and not the central idea. The passage is mainly about how Lily's view of her friends has changed. The correct answer is choice A.

2. The sentences in lines 15–19 mainly serve to
   A) demonstrate the influence Lily's friends had over her.
   B) explain the narrator's point of view of Lily's choices.
   C) indicate how Lily's attitude toward her friends is evolving.
   D) explain an incident when Lily's friends shamed her.

Strategy: The sentence indicates that when Lily remembers her friends, she is ashamed of how they had influenced her. Choices B and D can be eliminated. Choices A and C are both mentioned in the sentence. However, the main purpose is not to explain the extent of her friends' influence. It is an example of how her attitude is changing. She is now ashamed of her friends. Choice C is the best answer.

• • • SAT-Type Questions •

Directions: Question 1 is based on the following passage.

This passage comes from The Snow Leopard *by Peter Matthiessen. He is quoting philosopher Carl Jung.*

The fact that many a man who goes his own way ends in ruin means nothing. . . . He must obey his own law, as if it were a daemon whispering to him of new and wonderful paths. . . . There are not a few who are called awake by the summons of a voice, whereupon they are at once set apart from
5 the others, feeling themselves confronted with a problem about which the others know nothing. In most cases it is impossible to explain to the others what has happened, for any understanding is walled off by impenetrable prejudices. "You are no different from anybody else," they will chorus, or, "there's no such thing," . . . . He is at once set apart and isolated, as he
10 has resolved to obey the law that commands him from within. "His *own* law!" everybody will cry. But he knows better: it is *the* law. . . . The only meaningful life is a life that strives for the individual realization—absolute

and unconditional—of its own particular law. . . . To the extent that a man is untrue to the law of his being . . . he has failed to realize his life's meaning.

1. Which of the following best summarizes the passage?
   A) People have no tolerance for those who obey their own laws.
   B) People who stand out from the crowd have more meaningful lives.
   C) People must obey their own laws in order to have a meaningful life.
   D) Some people purposefully refuse to follow the crowd.

Often answer choices with extremely positive or negative wording (always, never) are incorrect.

Directions: Questions 2–6 are based on the following passage.

The following passage is from James Baldwin's short story "Sonny's Blues," which was originally published in 1957. In this scene, the narrator comes to learn who his troubled brother Sonny really is.

All I know about music is that not many people ever really hear it. And even then, on the rare occasions when something opens within, and the music enters, what we mainly hear, or hear corroborated, are personal, private, vanishing evocations. But the man who creates the music is hearing

5 something else, is dealing with the roar rising from the void and imposing order on it as it hits the air. What is evoked in him, then, is of another order, more terrible because it has no words, and triumphant, too, for that same reason. And his triumph, when he triumphs, is ours. I just watched Sonny's face. His face was troubled, he was working hard, but he wasn't with it. And I

10 had the feeling that, in a way, everyone on the bandstand was waiting for him, both waiting for him and pushing him along. But as I began to watch Creole, I realized that it was Creole who held them all back. He had them on a short rein. Up there, keeping the beat with his whole body, wailing on the fiddle, with his eyes half closed, he was listening to everything, but he was listening

15 to Sonny. He was having a dialogue with Sonny. He wanted Sonny to leave the shoreline and strike out for the deep water. He was Sonny's witness that deep water and drowning were not the same thing—he had been there, and he knew. And he wanted Sonny to know. He was waiting for Sonny to do the things on the keys which would let Creole know that Sonny was in the water.

20   And, while Creole listened, Sonny moved, deep within, exactly like someone in torment. I had never before thought of how awful the relationship must be between the musician and his instrument. He has to fill it, this instrument, with the breath of life, his own. He has to make it do what he wants it to do. And a piano is just a piano. It's made out of so much wood and wires and little

25 hammers and big ones, and ivory. While there's only so much you can do with

it, the only way to find this out is to try; to try and make it do everything.

And Sonny hadn't been near a piano for over a year. And he wasn't on

much better terms with his life, not the life that stretched before him now.

He and the piano stammered, started one way, got scared, stopped; started

30 another way, panicked, marked time, started again; then seemed to have

found a direction, panicked again, got stuck. And the face I saw on Sonny

I'd never seen before. Everything had been burned out of it, and, at the same

time, things usually hidden were being burned in, by the fire and fury of the

battle which was occurring in him up there.

35 Yet, watching Creole's face as they neared the end of the first set, I had

the feeling that something had happened, something I hadn't heard. Then

they finished, there was scattered applause, and then, without an instant's

warning, Creole started into something else, it was almost sardonic, it was

Am I Blue. And, as though he commanded, Sonny began to play. Something

40 began to happen. And Creole let out the reins. The dry, low, black man said

something awful on the drums, Creole answered, and the drums talked

back. Then the horn insisted, sweet and high, slightly detached perhaps, and

Creole listened, commenting now and then, dry, and driving, beautiful, calm

and old. Then they all came together again, and Sonny was part of the family

45 again. I could tell this from his face. He seemed to have found, right there,

beneath his fingers, a damn brand-new piano. It seemed that he couldn't get

over it. Then, for a while, just being happy with Sonny, they seemed to be

agreeing with him that brand-new pianos certainly were a gas.

Then Creole stepped forward to remind them that what they were playing

50 was the blues. He hit something in all of them, he hit something in me,

myself, and the music tightened and deepened, apprehension began to beat the

air. Creole began to tell us what the blues were all about. They were not about

anything very new. He and his boys up there were keeping it new, at the risk

of ruin, destruction, madness and death, in order to find new ways to make

55 us listen. For, while the tale of how we suffer, and how we are delighted, and

how we may triumph is never new, it must always be heard. There isn't any

other tale to tell, it's the only light we've got in all this darkness.

2. According to the lines 27–31, Sonny is
    A) starting to play piano again after a long break from performing.
    B) a beginner who is performing with Creole's group for the first time.
    C) regaining his confidence after an attack of stage fright.
    D) switching from the drums to the piano.

3. Lines 15–19 imply that Creole wants Sonny to change his playing by
    A) finding the rhythm of the music.
    B) putting in more sustained effort.
    C) playing from the heart.
    D) accurately hitting each note.

4. The narrator's description in paragraph 3 (lines 27–34) serves mainly to
    A) describe how the parts of a piano work to create music.
    B) describe what is happening on stage.
    C) explain the musical interchange between Creole and Sonny.
    D) describe the interaction between a musician and his instrument.

5. This passage implies all of the following about the relationship of music to life EXCEPT
    A) music connects us to others.
    B) music speaks to the soul.
    C) music reveals the essence of a person.
    D) music creates a dark atmosphere.

6. Which choice best summarizes the passage?
    A) A pianist turns to music to heal the pain of his past.
    B) A character describes how the blues speaks about suffering and hope.
    C) Two characters discover how playing in a blues band brings meaning to life.
    D) A character observes the powerful effects of music on his brother's soul.

For answers, see page 556.

Explain Analyzing Word Choice and Imagery for Tone and Mood

Writers carefully choose each word in order to create meaning and establish a particular tone and mood. On the SAT you will be required to analyze how specific words or phrases in a text imply a specific meaning, create the mood, or reflect the author's tone, or attitude.

In order to figure out how a word shapes tone, you'll first need to figure out its meaning. Look at the words surrounding the word in question. Sometimes context will hint at the definition of the word. Other times examples will help reveal the word's meaning or a synonym or antonym in the sentence will. Also think about the word's **denotation**, or dictionary definition, and its **connotations**, that is, the emotional associations it carries. For example, the words "fancy" and "flamboyant" both mean "excessively showy," but "flamboyant" implies an excessive lack of taste. "Fancy" has a more positive connotation, implying that something is expensive and posh.

Once you know a word's meaning, think about how the word contributes to the mood and tone of a passage. **Tone** is an author's attitude toward a subject. It encourages readers to read a text as positive, negative, serious, humorous, sardonic, mournful, and so forth. **Mood** is the emotion the words create in the reader. Consider this example from *The Great Gatsby:* "So we beat on, boats against the current, borne back ceaselessly into the past." The use of the preposition "against" and the adverb "ceaselessly" set a mournful mood, since they suggest that any attempts to escape the past and move forward are ultimately futile. The author's tone is reflective and perhaps melancholic.

Questions about tone or mood may be worded like this:

- The references to x and x mainly have which effect?

- The author's use of the words "x" and "x" are intended to . . .

Imagery is the use of descriptive words and phrases that appeal to all of our physical senses. Writers use imagery not only to beautify a literary text but to help create a visual picture in the reader's mind. Take this example from Kate Chopin's story "A Pair of Silk Stockings:" "But she went on feeling the soft, sheeny luxurious things—with both hands now, holding them up to see them glisten, and to feel them glide serpent-like through her fingers."

The descriptive language not only helps you "feel" the silk stockings, it suggests that the stockings have a seductive, slightly menacing quality ("serpent-like").

When you come across a few sentences or a paragraph that includes good descriptive details, ask yourself: What am I seeing, hearing, smelling, tasting, and feeling? Then think about how the imagery helps you understand what's happening in the text.

Imagery is often found in combination with other **figures of speech** including similes, metaphors, and personification. Questions on the SAT will ask you to identify the purpose of a specific simile or metaphor.

Simile—compares two unlike things using the words "like" or "as"

> **Example:** I would have given anything for the power to soothe her frail soul, tormenting itself in its invincible ignorance like a small bird beating about the cruel wires of a cage.
>
> **Purpose:** The comparison helps the reader realize that the speaker has compassion for the woman being described.

Metaphor—compares two dissimilar things that have a few common characteristics

> **Example:** Let us be grateful to people who make us happy; they are the charming gardeners who make our souls blossom.
>
> **Purpose:** The comparison helps the reader understand that positive people help us grow into healthy human beings.

Personification—gives human qualities to inanimate objects

> **Example:** The woods are getting ready to sleep—they are not yet asleep but they are disrobing and are having all sorts of little bed-time conferences and whisperings and good-nights.
>
> **Purpose:** The comparison creates a calming, peaceful feeling.

Questions about imagery might look like this:

- The author uses imagery in lines xx–xx in order to . . .

- The imagery in lines xx–xx primarily serves to . . .

- It can be inferred from the imagery in line xx that . . .

- The comparisons of . . . in line xx serve mainly to . . .

- The description of . . . in line xx reinforce the idea . . .

In the following passages, words that shape tone, mood, and meaning are underlined and notes about the effect of these words are in the margin. Add your own notes by filling in the blank in the third note.

This passage comes from The Pillow Book *by Sei Shonagon, a lady-in-waiting to Japan's Princess Sadako at the beginning of the 11th century.*

In spring it is the dawn that is most beautiful. As the light creeps over the hills, their outlines are dyed a faint red and wisps of purplish cloud trail over them.

In summer the nights. Not only when the moon shines, but on dark nights
5 too, as the fireflies flit to and fro, and even when it rains, how beautiful it is!

In autumn, the evenings, when the glittering sun sinks close to the edge of the hills and the crows fly back to their nests in threes and fours and twos; more charming still is a file of wild geese, like specks in the distant sky. When the sun has set, one's heart is moved by the sound of the wind and the
10 hum of the insects.

In winter the early mornings. It is beautiful indeed when snow has fallen during the night, but splendid too when the ground is white with frost; or even when there is no snow or frost, but it is simply very cold and the attendants hurry from room to room stirring up the fires and bringing charcoal, how well
15 this fits the season's mood! But as noon approaches and the cold wears off, no one bothers to keep the braziers alight, and soon nothing remains but piles of white ashes.

Conclusions about tone and mood: Overall, the tone and mood are reflective and peaceful. The use of the color "white" conjures images of pure snow but also ashes from a fire, which evokes images of death and turn the mood mournful.

In the following passage, examples of imagery and figures of speech are underlined. Notes about how they add meaning to the text are in the margin.

This excerpt is from Alice Munro's "Deep-Holes." The following paragraphs describe the woods where an accident happens.

The entrance to the woods looked quite ordinary and unthreatening. Sally understood, of course, that these woods were on top of a high bluff, and she expected a daunting lookout somewhere. She did not expect the danger that had to be skirted almost immediately in front of them.

QUICK TIP

Questions about imagery may also test your ability to identify purpose or to make inferences.

Words create a calm, dreamy mood.

Words set a romantic mood.

In the final line, the mood becomes _____

QUICK TIP

Tone is the author's attitude. Mood is the reader's attitude. Sometimes they are similar; sometimes they are different.

5   Deep chambers, really, some the size of a coffin, some much bigger than that, like rooms cut out of the rocks. Corridors zigzagging between them, and ferns and mosses growing out of the walls. Not enough greenery, however, to make any sort of cushion over the rubble below. The path went meandering between them, over hard earth and shelves of not quite level rock.

The visual imagery suggests a menacing landscape.

In the following excerpt, the narrator and her husband find their injured son.

Alex had reached him. He bent and lifted him. Kent gave a beseeching scream of pain. Alex draped him around his shoulders, Kent's head hanging down on one side and useless legs—one so unnaturally protruding—on the other. He rose, stumbled a couple of steps, and while still hanging on to Kent

5   dropped back down to his knees. He had decided to crawl and was making his way—Sally understood this now—to the rubble that partly filled the far end of the crevasse. He shouted some order to her without raising his head, and though she could not make out any word she knew what he wanted. She got up off her knees—why was she on her knees?—and pushed through some

10 saplings to that edge of the rim, where the rubble came to within perhaps three feet of the surface. Alex was still crawling along with Kent dangling from him like a shot deer.

Personification: meandering path implies that the path is wandering without purpose. The path is indifferent to their purpose.

Auditory imagery: scream of pain

Visual imagery: protruding leg

Simile compares the boy to a dead deer

Conclusions about imagery: In the first paragraph, the detail "deep chambers . . . the size of a coffin" gives the reader a picture of the size of the chambers, as well as suggests that danger is lurking over this family outing.

The image of Alex "crawling along with Kent dangling from him like a shot deer" gives the reader a visual picture of how badly Kent is injured. The image is foreboding and frightening because the boy is compared to a dead or dying animal. It implies that the narrator's state of mind is uneasy.

Practice

Directions: Read the following passages. In the text, mark the following:

- words that suggest the tone
- imagery that evokes emotion
- figures of speech that reveal tone or characterization

Then answer the questions that follow each passage.

In this excerpt from Edgar Allan Poe's "The Fall of the House of Usher," published in 1839, the narrator describes the house of the title.

Shaking off from my spirit what *must* have been a dream, I scanned more narrowly the real aspect of the building. Its principal feature seemed to be that

QUICK TIP

To identify mood, ask yourself how a particular passage makes you feel. Often thinking about your own emotional reaction to a text can help you recognize its mood.

of an excessive antiquity. The discoloration of ages had been great. Minute
fungi overspread the whole exterior, hanging in a fine tangled web-work

5 from the eaves. Yet all this was apart from any extraordinary dilapidation.
No portion of the masonry had fallen; and there appeared to be a wild
inconsistency between its still perfect adaptation of parts, and the crumbling
condition of the individual stones. In this there was much that reminded me
of the specious totality of old wood-work which has rotted for long years in

10 some neglected vault, with no disturbance from the breath of the external
air. Beyond this indication of extensive decay, however, the fabric gave little
token of instability. Perhaps the eye of a scrutinizing observer might have
discovered a barely perceptible fissure, which, extending from the roof of the
building in front, made its way down the wall in a zigzag direction, until it

15 became lost in the sullen waters of the tarn.

1. Describe the mood of the passage. What specific words help create this mood?

_____

_____

_____

2. When the writer includes this line: "In this there was much that reminded me
   of the specious totality of old wood-work which has rotted for long years in
   some neglected vault, with no disturbance from the breath of the external air,"
   what comparison is he making?

_____

_____

_____

_____

3. What effect on the meaning of the passage as a whole does this comparison
   have?

_____

_____

_____

This passage is from Amy Tan's novel The Joy Luck Club. *The speaker is an American-born daughter of Chinese parents who is a chess champion.*

I knew it was a mistake to say anything more, but I heard my voice speaking, "Why do you have to use me to show off? If you want to show off, then why don't you learn to play chess?"

My mother's eyes turned into dangerous black slits. She had no words for
5 me, just sharp silence.

I felt the wind rushing around my hot ears. I jerked my hand out of my mother's tight grasp and spun around, knocking into an old woman. Her bag of groceries spilled to the ground.

"Aii-ya! Stupid girl!" my mother and the woman cried. Oranges and tin
10 cans careened down the sidewalk. As my mother stooped to help the old woman pick up the escaping food, I took off.

I raced down the street, dashing between people, not looking back as my mother screamed shrilly, "Meimei! Meimei!" I fled down an alley, past dark, curtained shops and merchants washing the grime off their windows. I sped
15 into the sunlight, into a large street crowded with tourists examining trinkets and souvenirs. I ducked into another dark alley, down another street, up another alley. I ran until it hurt and I realized I had nowhere to go, that I was not running from anything. The alleys contained no escape routes.

My breath came out like angry smoke. It was cold. I sat down on an
20 upturned plastic pail next to a stack of empty boxes, cupping my chin with my hands, thinking hard. I imagined my mother, first walking briskly down one street or another looking for me, then giving up and returning home to await my arrival. After two hours, I stood up on creaking legs and slowly walked home. The alley was quiet and I could see the yellow lights shining
25 from our flat like two tiger's eyes in the night. I climbed the sixteen steps to the door, advancing quietly up each so as not to make any warning sounds. I turned the knob; the door was locked. I heard a chair moving, quick steps, the locks turning—click! click! click!—and then the door opened.

"About time you got home," said Vincent. "Boy, are you in trouble."

30 He slid back to the dinner table. On a platter were the remains of a large fish, its fleshy head still connected to bones swimming upstream in vain

escape. Standing there waiting for my punishment, I heard my mother speak in a dry voice.

"We not concerning this girl. This girl not have concerning for us."

35 Nobody looked at me. Bone chopsticks clinked against the inside of bowls being emptied into hungry mouths.

I walked into my room, closed the door, and lay down on my bed. The room was dark, the ceiling filled with shadows from the dinnertime lights of neighboring flats.

40 In my head, I saw a chessboard with sixty-four black and white squares. Opposite me was my opponent, two angry black slits. She wore a triumphant smile. "Strongest wind cannot be seen," she said.

Her black men advanced across the plane, slowly marching to each successive level as a single unit. My white pieces screamed as they scurried 45 and fell off the board one by one. As her men drew closer to my edge, I felt myself growing light. I rose up into the air and flew out the window. Higher and higher, above the alley, over the tops of tiled roofs, where I was gathered up by the wind and pushed up toward the night sky until everything below me disappeared and I was alone.

50 I closed my eyes and pondered my next move.

4. What does the comparison "shining from our flat like two tiger's eyes" (lines 24–25) suggest?

_____

_____

_____

5. Describe the mood established by the image of the fish in lines 30–32.

_____

_____

_____

6. How does the image of the chessboard in lines 40–50 reveal the character of the narrator?

_____

_____

_____

7. What tone is created by the description of "growing light" and being "pushed up toward the night sky until everything below me disappeared and I was alone"? Support your answer with lines from the text.

_____

_____

_____

_____

_____

For answers, see page 556.

For answers, see page 556.

Model SAT Questions

Directions: These Model SAT Questions show how tone, imagery, and figurative language might be tested on the SAT. The answers and explanations immediately follow the questions. Try the questions and then review the answers and the explanations.

> *This passage is from Laura Esquivel's novel* Like Water for Chocolate.
>
> Each of us is born with a box of matches inside us but we can't strike them all by ourselves; we need oxygen and a candle to help. In this case, the oxygen for example, would come from the breath of the person you love; the candle would be any kind of food, music, caress, word, or sound that engenders the explosion
> 5 that lights one of the matches. For a moment we are dazzled by an intense emotion. A pleasant warmth grows within us, fading slowly as time goes by, until a new explosion comes along to revive it. Each person has to discover what will set off those explosions in order to live, since the combustion that occurs when one of them is ignited is what nourishes the soul. That fire, in short, is its
> 10 food. If one doesn't find out in time what will set off these explosions, the box of matches dampens, and not a single match will ever be lighted.

1. The imagery in lines 5–7 primarily suggests that "explosions"
   A) overwhelm a person so that he or she can't think.
   B) feel both thrilling and frightening at the same time.
   C) emotionally crush a person with their intensity.
   D) feel all-consuming at first and less so over time.

Strategy: The details in the description "dazzled by an intense emotion" and "a pleasant warmth grows . . . fading slowly" over time suggest that an explosion is a positive experience. Therefore, choice C can be eliminated. Nowhere does the author include imagery that suggests explosions prevent people from thinking. Therefore, A is also incorrect. The positive connotations of the word "dazzled" mean that "frightening" (B) is not the right word to describe the sensations produced by an explosion. Choice D is the best answer.

2. The author's use of "nourishes the soul" and "food" when describing the explosions of light imply that
   A) connections with loved ones are essential for one's happiness.
   B) fire is needed to properly prepare food.
   C) it is impossible to live without human companionship.
   D) good food and music is better when shared with someone you love.

Strategy: The explosions discussed in the passage are a combination of being with a loved one and a catalyst that creates a positive emotion. The passage describes these catalysts as food, music, touches, or words. The use of the words "nourish" and "food" imply that the explosions are necessary to one's inner life—their spirit or soul. What is being spoken of is not literal food, so choice B is incorrect. The idea that "good food and music is better" when shared with loved ones, choice D, isn't appropriate with the connotation of the words "nourish" and "food." Choice C can't be supported by the passage. The passage does suggest that these moments of emotional connection are essential for happiness. Choice A is the best answer.

QUICK TIP

Don't be fooled by answer choices that are partially correct. (See question 1, choice B.) If any part of the answer is wrong, it is incorrect.

SAT-Type Questions

Directions: Read the following passages, marking words that create images or tone. Answer the questions that follow.

In the following excerpt from Willa Cather's short story "A Wagner Matinee," a young man takes his elderly aunt to a concert in Boston. Once a teacher at the Boston conservatory, Aunt Georgiana has lived for the past thirty years in rural Nebraska.

From the time we entered the concert-hall, however, she was a trifle less passive and inert, and seemed to begin to perceive her surroundings. I had felt some trepidation lest she might become aware of the absurdities of her attire, or might experience some painful embarrassment at stepping suddenly

5 into the world to which she had been dead for a quarter of a century. But again I found how superficially I had judged her. She sat looking about her with eyes as impersonal, almost as stony, as those with which the granite Rameses in a museum watches the froth and fret that ebbs and flows about

his pedestal, separated from it by the lonely stretch of centuries. I have seen
10 this same aloofness in old miners who drift into the Brown Hotel at Denver,
their pockets full of bullion, their linen soiled, their haggard faces unshorn,
and who stand in the thronged corridors as solitary as though they were still
in a frozen camp on the Yukon, or in the yellow blaze of the Arizona desert,
conscious that certain experiences have isolated them from their fellows by
15 a gulf no haberdasher could conceal.

The audience was made up chiefly of women. One lost the contour of
faces and figures, indeed any effect of line whatever, and there was only the
color contrast of bodices past counting, the shimmer and shading of fabrics
soft and firm, silky and sheer, resisting and yielding: red, mauve, pink, blue,
20 lilac, purple, écru, rose, yellow, cream, and white, all the colors that an
impressionist finds in a sunlit landscape, with here and there the dead black
shadow of a frock-coat. My Aunt Georgiana regarded them as though they
had been so many daubs of tube paint on a palette.

When the musicians came out and took their places, she gave a little stir
25 of anticipation, and looked with quickening interest down over the rail at that
invariable grouping; perhaps the first wholly familiar thing that had greeted
her eye since she had left old Maggie and her weakling calf. I could feel how
all those details sank into her soul, for I had not forgotten how they had sunk
into mine when I came fresh from ploughing forever and forever between
30 green aisles of corn, where, as in a treadmill, one might walk from daybreak to
dusk without perceiving a shadow of change in one's environment. I reminded
myself of the impression made on me by the clean profiles of the musicians,
the gloss of their linen, the dull black of their coats, the beloved shapes of the
instruments, the patches of yellow light thrown by the green-shaded stand-
35 lamps on the smooth, varnished bellies of the 'cellos and the bass viols in the
rear, the restless, wind-tossed forest of fiddle necks and bows; I recalled how, in
the first orchestra I had ever heard, those long bow strokes seemed to draw the
soul out of me, as a conjurer's stick reels out paper ribbon from a hat.

The first number was the Tannhäuser overture. When the violins drew out the
40 first strain of the Pilgrim's chorus, my Aunt Georgiana clutched my coat-sleeve.
Then it was that I first realized that for her this singing of basses and stinging
frenzy of lighter strings broke a silence of thirty years, the inconceivable silence

of the plains. . . . I saw again the tall, naked house on the prairie, black and grim as a wooden fortress; the black pond where I had learned to swim, the

45 rain-gullied clay about the naked house; the four dwarf ash-seedlings on which the dishcloths were always hung to dry before the kitchen door. The world there is the flat world of the ancients; to the east, a cornfield that stretched to daybreak; to the west, a corral that stretched to sunset; between, the sordid conquests of peace, more merciless than those of war.

1. The comparisons in lines 6–15 serve mainly to
   A) provide a contrast between the narrator and his aunt.
   B) indicate Aunt Georgiana's disapproval of the concert.
   C) show Aunt Georgiana's disregard for her inappropriate dress.
   D) describe the narrator's anxiety about his aunt's visit.

2. The clothing imagery in the second paragraph primarily serves to suggest that
   A) the women who attend concerts of this kind are wealthy.
   B) Aunt Georgiana longs for her former, artistic life in Boston.
   C) Aunt Georgiana merely appreciates their bright colors and not their style.
   D) Aunt Georgiana yearns to be like the women who wear such finery.

3. The phrases "forever and forever between green aisles of corn" and "as in a treadmill" in lines 29–30 have which effect?
   A) They evoke the narrator's gratification of growing up on a farm.
   B) They reflect the monotony of the narrator's childhood home.
   C) They emphasize the continuous stress of farming.
   D) They reveal the narrator's longing to go back home.

4. The description of the musicians and their instruments and the farmland where the narrator grew up mainly serves to
   A) show that the narrator has been swept away by the wonders of music.
   B) contrast the concert hall with the starkness of the prairie.
   C) provide a flashback to a life-changing childhood event.
   D) give background information about the narrator's relationship with his aunt.

5. What key idea does the imagery in the final sentence convey?
   A) The prairie resembles the landscape of ancient Greece and Rome.
   B) The prairie in Nebraska stretches as far as the eye can see.
   C) Farm life in Nebraska is fraught with constant struggle and hard work.
   D) Georgiana wants to remain in Boston instead of returning to Nebraska.

For answers, see page 557.

Characterization is the process by which a writer develops the personality of a character. Since understanding characters is key to understanding the main themes of literature, you can expect to see questions on characterization on the SAT. To infer what a character's personality is like, watch for the following:

- physical description (e.g., how the character looks and dresses)
- observations about the character made by the narrator or by other characters
- the character's thoughts, actions, words, and feelings
- how the character interacts with other characters

Notice as much as you can about a character as you read a passage. Look for specific words used to describe or refer to the character. Also keep an eye out for dialogue and actions that reveal personality traits.

Questions about characterization might look like this:

- In lines xx–xx, the narrator suggests that [the character] is . . .
- The passage indicates [character's] behavior was mostly caused by . . .
- The passage most clearly implies that other people regarded [character] as . . .
- The description of [character] (lines xx–xx) mainly serves to . . .
- As presented in the passage, [character] is best described as . . .

Think It Through

As you examine the following passage, consider how the reader marked details that reveal characterization. Add your own notes to the ones in the margin.

The following passage from Look Homeward, Angel *by Thomas Wolfe suggests the essence of a colorful character.*

Seated before a roast or a fowl, Gant began a heavy clangor on his steel and carving knife, distributing thereafter Gargantuan portions to each plate. Eugene feasted from a high chair by his father's side, filled his distending belly until it was drumtight, and was permitted to stop eating by his watchful sire only

5 when his stomach was impregnable to the heavy prod of Gant's big finger.

"There's a soft place there," he would roar, and he would cover the scoured plate of his infant son with another heavy slab of beef. That their machinery withstood this hammerhanded treatment was a tribute to their vitality and Eliza's cookery. Gant ate ravenously and without caution.

10 He was immoderately fond of fish, and he invariably choked upon a bone while eating it. This happened hundreds of times, but each time he would look up suddenly with a howl of agony and terror, groaning and crying out strongly while a half-dozen hands pounded violently on his back.

Gant has a voracious appetite.

Gant's eating puts him in danger of choking, but he won't change.

"Merciful God!" he would gasp finally, "I thought I was done for that time."

15 "I'll vow, Mr. Gant," Eliza was vexed. "Why on earth don't you watch what you're doing? If you didn't eat so fast you wouldn't always get choked."

The children, staring, but relieved, settled slowly back in their places.

Eliza finds Gant's behavior irritating.

Conclusions about characterization:

• Gant has an insatiable appetite and believes his son should enjoy food as he does. His behavior suggests he loves his son and wants him to be satisfied.

• Words and phrases such as "roar," "hammerhanded," "ravenously," and "howl of agony and terror," together function to present Gant as a coarse man.

• Eliza's observation about Gant in line 16 implies that he doesn't learn from his past mistakes.

Practice

Directions: As you read the passage, underline details about Miss Emily.

This passage from "A Rose for Emily" by William Faulkner describes a confrontation between Miss Emily, an elderly Southern woman, and local government officials when she refuses to pay her taxes.

A deputation waited upon her, knocked at the door through which no visitor had passed since she ceased giving china-painting lessons eight or ten years earlier. They were admitted by the old Negro into a dim hall from which a stairway mounted into still more shadow. It smelled of dust

5 and disuse—a close, dank smell. The Negro led them into the parlor. It was furnished in heavy, leather-covered furniture. When the Negro opened the blinds of one window, they could see that the leather was cracked; and when they sat down, a faint dust rose sluggishly about their thighs, spinning with slow motes in the single sun-ray. On a tarnished gilt easel before the

10 fireplace stood a crayon portrait of Miss Emily's father.

They rose when she entered—a small, fat woman in black, with a thin gold chain descending to her waist and vanishing into her belt, leaning on an ebony cane with a tarnished gold head. Her skeleton was small and spare; perhaps that was why what would have been merely plumpness in another

15 was obesity in her. She looked bloated, like a body long submerged in motionless water, and of that pallid hue. Her eyes, lost in the fatty ridges of her face, looked like two small pieces of coal pressed into a lump of dough as they moved from one face to another while the visitors stated their errand.

She did not ask them to sit. She just stood in the door and listened quietly
20 until the spokesman came to a stumbling halt. Then they could hear the
invisible watch ticking at the end of the gold chain.

Her voice was dry and cold. "I have no taxes in Jefferson. Colonel Sartoris
explained it to me. Perhaps one of you can gain access to the city records and
satisfy yourselves."

25 "But we have. We are the city authorities, Miss Emily. Didn't you get a
notice from the sheriff, signed by him?"

"I received a paper, yes," Miss Emily said. "Perhaps he considers himself
the sheriff . . . I have no taxes in Jefferson."

"But there is nothing on the books to show that, you see. We must go by
30 the—"

"See Colonel Sartoris. I have no taxes in Jefferson."

"But, Miss Emily."

"See Colonel Sartoris." (Colonel Sartoris had been dead almost ten years.)

"I have no taxes in Jefferson. Tobe!" The Negro appeared. "Show these
35 gentlemen out."

1. Describe Miss Emily's appearance. What can you infer about her based upon
   her appearance? Support your answer with lines from the passage.

   _____

   _____

   _____

   _____

   _____

2. What do you learn about Miss Emily from her interaction with her visitors?
   Support your answer with lines from the passage.

   _____

   _____

   _____

   _____

   _____

3. What can you infer about Miss Emily from the description of her house?
   Support your answer with lines from the passage.

_____

_____

_____

_____

_____

For answers, see page 557.

Model SAT Question

Directions: This Model SAT Question shows how characterization might be tested on the SAT. The answer and explanation immediately follow the question. Answer the question and then review the answer and the explanation.

> *The following excerpt is from the novel* Beloved *(1987) by Toni Morrison. The the main character, Sethe, has a reunion with Paul D.*
>
> "Eighteen years," she said softly.
>
> "Eighteen," he repeated. "And I swear I been walking every one of them. Mind if I join you?" He nodded toward her feet and began unlacing his shoes.
>
> "You want to soak them? Let me get you a basin of water." She moved closer
> 5 to him to enter the house.
>
> "No, uh uh. Can't baby feet. A whole lot more tramping they got to do yet."
>
> "You can't leave right away, Paul D., you got to stay awhile."
>
> "Well, long enough to see Baby Suggs, anyway. Where is she?"
>
> "Dead."
>
> 10 "Aw no. When?"
>
> "Eight years now. Almost nine."
>
> "Was it hard. I hope she didn't die hard."
>
> Sethe shook her head. "Soft as cream. Being alive was the hard part. Sorry you missed her though. Is that what you came by for?"

15 "That's some of what I came for. The rest is you. But if all the truth be known, I go anywhere these days. Anywhere they let me sit down."

"You looking good."

"Devil's confusion. He lets me look good as long as I feel bad." He looked at her and the word bad took on another meaning.

20 Sethe smiled. This is the way they were—had been. All of the Sweet Home men, before and after Halle, treated her to a mild brotherly flirtation, so subtle you had to scratch for it.

Except for a heap more hair and some waiting in his eyes, he looked the way he had in Kentucky. Peachstone skin; straight-backed. For a man with an 25 immobile face it was amazing how ready it was to smile, or blaze or be sorry with you. As though all you had to do was get his attention and right away he produced the feeling you were feeling. With less than a blink, his face seemed to change—underneath it lay activity.

1. As presented in the passage, Paul D. is best described as
   A) kindly, anxious, and eager to please.
   B) sensitive, flirtatious, and restless.
   C) coy, lighthearted, and ill at ease.
   D) unruly, apprehensive, and bashful.

Strategy: The dialogue indicates that Paul D. has never stayed in one place for long. Sethe's observations reveal that Paul D. enjoys flirting, and the narrator's physical description of him suggests that he feels compassion toward others. Given this information, it is reasonable to infer that he is restless, flirtatious, and empathetic. Choice A captures one component of his personality—kindliness—but not the others. Choice B, which fits with the information above, is a possibility. Choices C and D don't capture the three aspects of his personality revealed in this passage. Therefore, B must be the correct answer.

SAT-Type Questions

Directions: Read the passage and answer the questions that follow.

In the following excerpt from the short story "A Cup of Tea" by Katherine Mansfield, an upper-class woman, Rosemary, picks up a street person and brings her home to tea.

"Rosemary, may I come in?" It was Philip.

"Of course."

He came in. "Oh, I'm so sorry," he said, and stopped and stared.

"It's quite all right," said Rosemary smiling. "This is my friend, Miss—"

5 "Smith, madam," said the languid figure, who was strangely still and unafraid.

"Smith," said Rosemary. "We are going to have a little talk."

"Oh, yes," said Philip. "Quite," and his eye caught sight of the coat and hat on the floor. He came over to the fire and turned his back to it. "It's a 10 beastly afternoon," he said curiously, still looking at that listless figure, looking at its hands and boots, and then at Rosemary again.

"Yes, isn't it?" said Rosemary enthusiastically. "Vile."

Philip smiled his charming smile. "As a matter of fact," said he, "I wanted you to come into the library for a moment. Would you? Will Miss Smith 15 excuse us?"

The big eyes were raised to him, but Rosemary answered for her. "Of course she will." And they went out of the room together.

"I say," said Philip, when they were alone. "Explain. Who is she? What does it all mean?"

20 Rosemary, laughing, leaned against the door and said: "I picked her up in Curzon Street. Really. She's a real pick-up. She asked me for the price of a cup of tea, and I brought her home with me."

"But what on earth are you going to do with her?" cried Philip.

"Be nice to her," said Rosemary quickly. "Be frightfully nice to her. Look 25 after her. I don't know how. We haven't talked yet. But show her—treat her—make her feel—"

"My darling girl," said Philip, "you're quite mad, you know. It simply can't be done."

"I knew you'd say that," retorted Rosemary. "Why not? I want to. Isn't that 30 a reason? And besides, one's always reading about these things. I decided—"

"But," said Philip slowly, and he cut the end of a cigar, "she's so astonishingly pretty."

"Pretty?" Rosemary was so surprised that she blushed. "Do you think so? I—I hadn't thought about it."

35 "Good Lord!" Philip struck a match. "She's absolutely lovely. Look again, my child. I was bowled over when I came into your room just now. However . . . I think you're making a ghastly mistake. Sorry, darling, if I'm crude and all that. But let me know if Miss Smith is going to dine with us in time for me to look up *The Milliner's Gazette.*"

40 "You absurd creature!" said Rosemary, and she went out of the library, but not back to her bedroom. She went to her writing-room and sat down at her desk. Pretty! Absolutely lovely! Bowled over! Her heart beat like a heavy bell. Pretty! Lovely! She drew her cheque-book towards her. But no, cheques would be no use, of course. She opened a drawer and took out five pound
45 notes, looked at them, put two back, and holding the three squeezed in her hand, she went back to her bedroom.

Half an hour later Philip was still in the library, when Rosemary came in.

"I only wanted to tell you," said she, and she leaned against the door again and looked at him with her dazzled exotic gaze, "Miss Smith won't dine with
50 us tonight."

1. Lines 20–22 indicate that Rosemary's immediate purpose in bringing the stranger home is to
   A) make a friend of Miss Smith.
   B) provide entertainment for Philip.
   C) indulge a sudden impulse.
   D) highlight her own generosity.

2. Rosemary's answering for Miss Smith (lines 16–17) suggests that Rosemary
   A) has real interest in Miss Smith's welfare.
   B) wants to make her guest feel comfortable.
   C) feels superior to Miss Smith.
   D) is insensitive to Philip's feelings.

3. Rosemary's response to Philip's question (lines 20–22) reveals that she is motivated by
   A) the novelty of bringing home a beggar.
   B) the need to help Miss Smith.
   C) loneliness.
   D) the desire to shock her husband.

4. The line "one's always reading about these things" (line 30) suggests which of the following about Rosemary's character?
   A) She understands human motivation.
   B) She lives in a world of fantasy.
   C) She wants adoration from people of a lower class.
   D) She feels superior to Miss Smith.

5. It is implied that the change in Rosemary's attitude toward Miss Smith is mostly motivated by

    A) her husband's lack of enthusiasm.

    B) a fear of what people might think.

    C) jealousy over Miss Smith's beauty.

    D) a realization that she is inadequate to help Miss Smith.

For answers, see page 558.

Explain Identifying Narrator's Point of View

The **narrative voice** refers to the person who is telling the story or describing events. Understanding the narrator is important to understanding the themes of the story. On the SAT you are most likely to read literature written in first-person **point of view** or third-person point of view.

First-person point of view: For this point of view, a character—either a main or a secondary character—relates events that occurred. This may include the main character telling his or her own story using the pronoun *I*.

Third-person point of view: The narrator is a voice outside the story who refers to the characters as *he, she*, and *they*. This narrator may reveal the thoughts, observations, and feelings of just one character or of all of the characters.

Examples of questions about narrator's point of view include:

- During paragraph x, the narrator's focus shifts from . . .
- Over the course of the passage, the narrator's attitude shifts from . . .
- Which choice best describes the narrator's view of _____ ?
- The passage indicates that the narrator views _____ as . . .
- The narrator implies/indicates that . . .

Think It Through

As you read the literature, identify who is telling the story. Use these questions to help you understand how the point of view is influencing the meaning of the passage:

If the story is in first-person point of view, ask

- Is this the voice of the main character or a minor character?
- Is the narrator's ability to relate events limited by age, time, or ability? (Is the narrator a child? Is he/she remembering events that happened long ago?)
- Where does the narrator reveal his/her feelings and motivations?
- Can the narrator's perspective be trusted or is there something he/she is not saying?
- Does the narrator's point of view of the events shift or change over the course of the passage? Why?

If the story is in third-person point of view, ask

- Is the narrator impartial or does the narrator make judgments about the characters?

- Does the narrator share the feelings of one character or all the characters?

Notice how these questions can help you evaluate the following passages. Words that reveal narrative voice are underlined, and notes about point of view and narrative voice in the right margin.

The following is from Edgar Allan Poe's "The Tell-Tale Heart," published in 1843.

TRUE!—nervous—very, very dreadfully nervous I had been and am; but why will you say that I am mad? The disease had sharpened my senses—not destroyed—not dulled them. Above all was the sense of hearing acute. I heard all things in the heaven and in the earth. I heard many things in hell.

5 How, then, am I mad? Hearken! and observe how healthily—how calmly I can tell you the whole story.

It is impossible to say how first the idea entered my brain; but once conceived, it haunted me day and night. Object there was none. Passion there was none. I loved the old man. He had never wronged me. He had never given

10 me insult. For his gold I had no desire. I think it was his eye! yes, it was this! He had the eye of a vulture—a pale blue eye, with a film over it. Whenever it fell upon me, my blood ran cold; and so by degrees—very gradually—I made up my mind to take the life of the old man, and thus rid myself of the eye forever.

First person narrator

The narrator insists that he is not crazy, which makes him appear defensive—and possibly crazy.

The narrator claims he is not mad, but then he says he decided to kill the man because of his eye.

Conclusions: The first-person narrator can't be trusted. He repeatedly claims he is not crazy, but his own statements contradict this. He says he can hear sounds from heaven and hell. He says he killed an old man because his vulture-like eye was tormenting him.

In this excerpt from Jane Austen's book Persuasion, *the narrator describes the character of Sir Walter Elliot.*

Vanity was the beginning and the end of Sir Walter Elliot's character; vanity of person and of situation. He had been remarkably handsome in his youth; and, at fifty-four, was still a very fine man. Few women could think more of their personal appearance than he did, nor could the valet of any new

5 made lord be more delighted with the place he held in society. He considered the blessing of beauty as inferior only to the blessing of a baronetcy; and the Sir Walter Elliot, who united these gifts, was the constant object of his warmest respect and devotion.

Third-person point of view. Narrator doesn't appear to like Sir Walter Elliot because he/she says he is vain.

Conclusions: The narrator gently mocks Sir Walter Elliot for being obsessed with his own appearance and standing in society.

Directions: As you read the following passage, underline important details that help you understand the narrator's perspective. Jot notes in the margin. Use the questions to guide your notes.

This excerpt is from Mary Shelley's novel, Frankenstein, *which tells the story of Victor Frankenstein, a scientist who brings a creature to life.*

It was on a dreary night of November that I beheld the accomplishment of my toils. With an anxiety that almost amounted to agony, I collected the instruments of life around me, that I might infuse a spark of being into the lifeless thing that lay at my feet. It was already one in the morning; the rain

5   pattered dismally against the panes, and my candle was nearly burnt out, when, by the glimmer of the half-extinguished light, I saw the dull yellow eye of the creature open; it breathed hard, and a convulsive motion agitated its limbs.

How can I describe my emotions at this catastrophe, or how delineate the

10 wretch whom with such infinite pains and care I had endeavoured to form? His limbs were in proportion, and I had selected his features as beautiful. Beautiful! Great God! His yellow skin scarcely covered the work of muscles and arteries beneath; his hair was of a lustrous black, and flowing; his teeth of a pearly whiteness; but these luxuriances only formed a more horrid

15 contrast with his watery eyes, that seemed almost of the same colour as the dun-white sockets in which they were set, his shrivelled complexion and straight black lips.

The different accidents of life are not so changeable as the feelings of human nature. I had worked hard for nearly two years, for the sole purpose

20 of infusing life into an inanimate body. For this I had deprived myself of rest and health. I had desired it with an ardour that far exceeded moderation; but now that I had finished, the beauty of the dream vanished, and breathless horror and disgust filled my heart. Unable to endure the aspect of the being I had created, I rushed out of the room and continued a long time traversing

25 my bed-chamber, unable to compose my mind to sleep. At length lassitude succeeded to the tumult I had before endured, and I threw myself on the bed in my clothes, endeavouring to seek a few moments of forgetfulness. But it was in vain; I slept, indeed, but I was disturbed by the wildest dreams. I thought I saw Elizabeth, in the bloom of health, walking in the streets of

30 Ingolstadt. Delighted and surprised, I embraced her, but as I imprinted the

first kiss on her lips, they became livid with the hue of death; her features

appeared to change, and I thought that I held the corpse of my dead mother

in my arms; a shroud enveloped her form, and I saw the grave-worms

crawling in the folds of the flannel. I started from my sleep with horror; a

35 cold dew covered my forehead, my teeth chattered, and every limb became

convulsed; when, by the dim and yellow light of the moon, as it forced

its way through the window shutters, I beheld the wretch—the miserable

monster whom I had created.

1. Who is telling the story? What is the point of view?

Victor Frankenstein

"I" = 1st Person

_____

2. How would you describe the narrator's attitude toward his creation? What details support your description?

he is "disgusted" & "horrified" — line 23

calli

_____

_____

_____

3. What does the narrator's description of his dreams imply? What details support this implication?

_____

_____

_____

_____

Students Do in class

The narrator's attitude greatly influences the tone of a passage.

4. What can you conclude about the narrator based upon the following line: "With an anxiety that almost amounted to agony, I collected the instruments of life around me, that I might infuse a spark of being into the lifeless thing that lay at my feet"?

_____

_____

_____

_____

5. Overall, how would you describe the narrator's attitude toward life and human nature?

_____

_____

_____

_____

For answers, see page 558.

Model SAT Question

Directions: This Model SAT Question shows how point of view might be tested on the SAT. The answer and explanation immediately follow the question. Try the question and then review the answer and the explanation.

In the following excerpt from Zora Neale Hurston's novel Their Eyes Were Watching God, *Janie explains to Pheoby why she has returned to the town alone.*

They sat there in the fresh young darkness close together. Pheoby eager to feel and do through Janie, but hating to show her zest for fear it might be thought mere curiosity. Jane was full of that oldest human longing—self-revelation. Pheoby held her tongue for a long time, but she couldn't help
5 moving her feet. So Janie spoke.

"They don't need to worry about me and my overhalls long as Ah still got nine hundred dollars in de bank. Tea Cake got me into wearing 'em—following behind him. Tea Cake ain't wasted up no money of mine, and he ain't left me for no young gal, neither. He give me every consolation in de world. He'd tell
10 'em so too, if he was here. If he wasn't gone."

Pheoby dilated all over with eagerness, "Tea Cake gone?"

"Yeah, Pheoby, Tea Cake is gone. And dat's de only reason you see me back here—cause Ah ain't got nothing to make me happy no more where Ah was at. Down in the Everglades there, down on the muck."

1. The narrator's description of Janie and Pheoby's conversation implies that Pheoby
   A) longs to listen to Janie's stories.
   B) wants to leave town with Janie.
   C) doesn't approve of Janie's clothing.
   D) is happy that Tea Cake and Janie's relationship is over.

Strategy: The narrator gives the reader some insight into Pheoby and Janie. Pheoby desires to "feel and do through Janie." She longs to hear what has happened to Janie. This supports choice A. Pheoby's eagerness to hear Janie's tales doesn't support choice B. While Janie's statement that "They don't need to worry about me and my overhalls" indicates that some people don't like her clothing, there is no mention that Pheoby shares that opinion (choice C). As for choice D, Pheoby is eager to hear about Tea Cake, but that doesn't necessarily imply that she is happy about it. The best answer is choice A.

SAT-Type Questions

Directions: Read each passage and answer the questions that follow.

The following is an excerpt from "The Story of an Hour" by Kate Chopin. At the beginning of the story, Louise Mallard, a frail young woman, receives the news that her husband has been killed in a train accident. Her protective family gently breaks the news to her, and then she retreats to her room to think.

There would be no one to live for during those coming years; she would live for herself. There would be no powerful will bending hers in that blind persistence with which men and women believe they have a right to impose a private will upon a fellow-creature. A kind intention or a cruel intention

5 made the act seem no less a crime as she looked upon it in that brief moment of illumination.

And yet she had loved him—sometimes. Often she had not. What did it matter! What could love, the unsolved mystery, count for in the face of this possession of self-assertion which she suddenly recognized as the strongest

10 impulse of her being!

"Free! Body and soul free!" she kept whispering.

Josephine was kneeling before the closed door with her lips to the keyhole, imploring for admission. "Louise, open the door! I beg; open the door—you will make yourself ill. What are you doing, Louise? For heaven's

15   sake open the door."

"Go away. I am not making myself ill." No; she was drinking in a very elixir of life through that open window.

Her fancy was running riot along those days ahead of her. Spring days, and summer days, and all sorts of days that would be her own. She breathed

20   a quick prayer that life might be long. It was only yesterday she had thought with a shudder that life might be long.

She arose at length and opened the door to her sister's importunities. There was a feverish triumph in her eyes, and she carried herself unwittingly like a goddess of Victory. She clasped her sister's waist, and together they

25   descended the stairs. Richards stood waiting for them at the bottom.

Someone was opening the front door with a latchkey. It was Brently Mallard who entered, a little travel-stained, composedly carrying his grip-sack and umbrella. He had been far from the scene of the accident, and did not even know there had been one. He stood amazed at Josephine's

30   piercing cry; at Richards' quick motion to screen him from the view of his wife.

When the doctors came they said she had died of heart disease—of the joy that kills.

1. The passage indicates that the narrator views Louise as
   A) weak-minded and totally dependent on her husband.
   B) a timid soul who longs for independence.
   C) physically abused.
   D) a woman who is emotionally strong.

2. The point of view of the story causes the reader to sympathize with
   A) Louise's family.
   B) Brently Mallard.
   C) Louise.
   D) the doctors.

3. In the final line of the story, the narrator's focus shifts from Louise's thoughts to the doctors' diagnosis. This serves mainly to emphasize
   A) how little people understood her.
   B) the dangers of surprising someone with a health problem.
   C) how greatly Louise's inner life affected her physical life.
   D) that life is unpredictable.

For answers, see page 559.

Explain Citing Textual Evidence

The SAT will test your ability to identify lines that support conclusions about the text. You will need to find evidence for what the text states clearly, as well as for what it implies. For every passage or pair of passages, at least one question will ask you to decide which part of the text best supports the answer to a previous question.

One question format you'll encounter is two related questions. The first will test your understanding of theme, plot, character, or point of view, while the second will ask you to determine which part of the passage provides the best support for the answer to the first question. Or you may be asked to choose which of four answer choices is best supported by a specific line from the passage.

Here is an example of what textual evidence questions will look like:

1. Which choice best characterizes the girl Elgin longs for?
   A) proud, unkind
   B) striking, talkative
   C) young, self-confident
   D) athletic, restless

2. Which lines provide the best support for the answer to question 1?
   A) lines 38–43 ("She was of medium . . . took Elgin's breath away")
   B) lines 43–48 ("She was so pretty . . . on his confidence")
   C) lines 68–72 ("When the next dance . . . realized he was frightened")
   D) lines 77–83 ("The girl had a . . . words in his reading")

Think It Through

Study the following passage, noticing how the reader underlined key details about the character's thoughts and motivations.

The following excerpt is from the James Joyce story "The Dead." It follows a scene in which Gretta has told her husband, Gabriel, the story of her first love, Michael Furey, who died after waiting outside her window in the cold.

The air of the room chilled his shoulders. He stretched himself cautiously along under the sheets and lay down beside his wife. One by one, they were all becoming shades. Better pass boldly into that other world, in the full glory of some passion, than fade and wither dismally with age. He thought of how
5 she who lay beside him had locked in her heart for so many years that image of her lover's eyes when he had told her that he did not wish to live.

Better to live a short, passionate life than a long life without passion.

Generous tears filled Gabriel's eyes. He had never felt like that himself towards any woman, but he knew that such a feeling must be love. The tears gathered more thickly in his eyes and in the partial darkness he imagined he

10 saw the form of a young man standing under a dripping tree. Other forms were near. His soul had approached that region where dwell the vast hosts of the dead. He was conscious of, but could not apprehend, their wayward and flickering existence. His own identity was fading out into a grey impalpable world: the solid world itself, which these dead had one time reared and lived

15 in, was dissolving and dwindling.

Gabriel is sad he never experienced the passionate love for a woman the way Michael Furey had.

Gabriel will eventually die.

Question: Which of the following is the best definition of the word "shade" (line 3)?

- a cover for a window that keeps out the sun

- an area protected from the sun's light and heat

- a shadow or ghost

Answer: Gabriel is thinking about how everyone is becoming shades. This implies that everyone is slowing dying. He believes it would be better to burn out with passion than "fade and wither dismally with age." The evidence supports the idea that a shade is a shadow or a ghost, a being that has faded to almost nothing.

Question: Which line from the text supports the conclusion that Gabriel is becoming more aware of his feelings?

Answer: When Gabriel understood that he had never loved a woman, "generous tears filled [his] eyes" (line 7). This supports the idea that Gabriel is realizing the importance of love.

Practice

Directions: Read the following story, marking important details as you read.

In the following excerpt from the short story "Dead Men's Path" by Chinua Achebe, modern ideas and traditions collide at an African school.

Michael Obi's hopes were fulfilled much earlier than he expected. He was appointed headmaster of Ndume Central School in January 1949.

It had always been an unprogressive school, so the Mission authorities decided to send a young and energetic man to run it. Obi accepted this

5 responsibility with enthusiasm. He had many wonderful ideas and this was an opportunity to put them into practice. He had had sound secondary school education which designated him a "pivotal teacher" in the official records and set him apart from the other headmasters in the mission field. He was outspoken in his condemnation of the narrow views of these older and often

10 less educated ones.

"We shall make a good job of it, shan't we?" he asked his young wife when they first heard the joyful news of his promotion.

"We shall do our best," she replied. "We shall have such beautiful gardens and everything will be just modern and delightful . . ." In their two years of
15 married life she had become completely infected by his passion for "modern methods" and his denigration of "these old and superannuated people in the teaching field who would be better employed as traders in the Onitsha market." She began to see herself already as the admired wife of the young headmaster, the queen of the school.

20 The wives of the other teachers would envy her position. She would set the fashion in everything . . . Then, suddenly, it occurred to her that there might not be other wives. Wavering between hope and fear, she asked her husband, looking anxiously at him.

"All our colleagues are young and unmarried," he said with enthusiasm
25 which for once she did not share. "Which is a good thing," he continued.

"Why?"

"Why? They will give all their time and energy to the school."

Nancy was downcast. For a few minutes she became skeptical about the new school; but it was only for a few minutes. Her little personal misfortune
30 could not blind her to her husband's happy prospects. She looked at him as he sat folded up in a chair. He was stoop-shouldered and looked frail. But he sometimes surprised people with sudden bursts of physical energy. In his present posture, however, all his bodily strength seemed to have retired behind his deep-set eyes, giving them an extraordinary power of penetration.
35 He was only twenty-six, but looked thirty or more. On the whole, he was not unhandsome.

1. Which inference regarding Mr. Obi and his wife is best supported by the text?
   A) Mr. Obi and his wife are somewhat humbled by the task ahead of them.
   B) Mr. Obi and his wife are young, energetic, and somewhat overconfident.

2. Which choice provides the best evidence for the answer to question 1?
   A) lines 14–18 ("In their two years . . . the Onitsha market")
   B) lines 20–21 ("The wives of the other . . . fashion in everything")

3. Which detail from the text best supports the idea that Mrs. Obi enjoys feeling superior to others?
   A) lines 28–29 ("Nancy was downcast . . . only for a few minutes")
   B) lines 20–21 ("The wives of . . . set the fashion in everything")

For answers, see page 559.

Model SAT Questions

Directions: These Model SAT Questions show using textual evidence might be tested on the SAT. The answers and explanations immediately follow the questions. Try the questions and then review the answers and the explanations.

In the following excerpt from David Guterson's novel Snow Falling on Cedars, *Hatsue, the daughter of Japanese immigrants to the northwestern United States, is being taught how to be a proper Japanese lady.*

Shigemura, on Wednesday afternoons, taught Hatsue the intricacies of the tea ceremony as well as calligraphy and scene painting. She showed her how to arrange flowers in a vase and how, for special occasions, to dust her face with rice powder. She insisted that Hatsue must never giggle and must never look at
5 a man directly. In order to keep her complexion immaculate—Hatsue, said Mrs. Shigemura, had skin as smooth as vanilla ice cream—she must take care to stay out of the sun. Mrs. Shigemura taught Hatsue how to sing with composure and how to sit, walk, and stand gracefully. It was this latter that remained of Mrs. Shigemura: Hatsue still moved with a wholeness of being that began in
10 the balls of her feet and reached right through to the top of her head. She was unified and graceful.

Mrs. Shigemura taught Hatsue to sit without moving and claimed that she would not mature properly unless she learned to do so for extended periods. Living in America, she said, would make this difficult, because here there
15 was tension and unhappiness. At first Hatsue, who was only thirteen, could not sit still for even thirty seconds. Then later, when she had stilled her body, she found it was her mind that would not be quiet. But gradually her rebellion against tranquility subsided. Mrs. Shigemura was pleased and claimed that the turbulence of her ego was in the process of being overcome. She told Hatsue

20 that her stillness would serve her well. She would experience harmony of being in the midst of the changes and unrest that life inevitably brings.

But Hatsue feared, walking home over forest trails from Mrs. Shigemura's, that despite her training she was not to be calmed. She dallied and sometimes sat under trees, searched for lady's slippers or white trilliums to pick, and

25 contemplated her attraction to the world of illusions—her craving for existence and entertainment, for clothes, makeup, dances, movies. It seemed to her that in her external bearing she had succeeded only in deceiving Mrs. Shigemura; inwardly she knew her aspiration for worldly happiness was frighteningly irresistible. Yet the demand that she conceal this inner life was great, and by

30 the time she entered high school she was expert at implying bodily a tranquility that did not in fact inhabit her. In this way she developed a secret life that disturbed her and that she sought to cast off.

1. The narrator indicates that Hatsue feels
   A) torn between the Japanese and American cultures.
   B) at peace with her dual nationalities.
   C) that she is inferior to Mrs. Shigemura.
   D) that her lessons with Mrs. Shigemura have made her a better person.

Strategy: Read through the answer choices and eliminate any that you know are not correct. No evidence is given for choice B; in fact the opposite is true. The text does not indicate that she feels inferior to Mrs. Shigemura, but she does feel that she has deceived her. Choice C is incorrect. Mrs. Shigemura is the one who says the Hatsue would "experience harmony of being in the midst of the changes and unrest" of life, making her a better person, but Hatsue feels worse for having pretended that she is calm. The best choice is A.

2. Which of the following could best be used as evidence to support the idea that Hatsue is torn between two cultures—Japanese and American?
   A) lines 9–11 ("Hatsue still moved . . . to the top of her head")
   B) lines 12–15 ("Mrs. Shigemura taught Hatsue to sit . . . tension and unhappiness")
   C) lines 22–26 ("But Hatsue feared . . . dances, movies")
   D) lines 31–32 ("In this way she developed . . . she sought to cast off")

Strategy: The question asks you to identify details in the passage that support the idea Hatsue is torn between two cultures. The details in choice A suggest that Hatsue has learned to move like a proper Japanese woman. Therefore, it can be eliminated. Choice B explains Mrs. Shigemura's views and not Hatsue's, removing it from the running. Choice C is possible, since the details in these lines suggest that Hatsue can't calm down and is attracted to an American lifestyle. Choice D is only tangentially related to the idea of being torn between two cultures. Choice C provides the most direct evidence.

Directions: Read the passage and answer the questions that follow.

The following excerpt continues the short story "Dead Men's Path" by Chinua Achebe, in which modern ideas and traditions collide at an African school.

One evening as Obi was admiring his work he was scandalized to see an old woman from the village hobble right across the compound, through a marigold flower-bed and the hedges. On going up there he found faint signs of an almost disused path from the village across the school compound to the
5 bush on the other side.

"It amazes me," said Obi to one of his teachers who had been three years in the school, "that you people allowed the villagers to make use of this footpath. It is simply incredible." He shook his head.

"The path," said the teacher apologetically, "appears to be very important
10 to them. Although it is hardly used, it connects the village shrine with their place of burial."

"And what has that got to do with the school?" asked the headmaster.

"Well, I don't know," replied the other with a shrug of the shoulders. "But I remember there was a big row some time ago when we attempted to close it."

15 "That was some time ago. But it will not be used now," said Obi as he walked away. "What will the Government Education Officer think of this when he comes to inspect the school next week? The villagers might, for all I know, decide to use the schoolroom for a pagan ritual during the inspection."

Heavy sticks were planted closely across the path at the two places where
20 it entered and left the school premises. These were further strengthened with barbed wire.

Three days later the village priest of Ani called on the headmaster. He was an old man and walked with a slight stoop. He carried a stout walking-stick which he usually tapped on the floor, by way of emphasis, each time he
25 made a new point in his argument.

"I have heard," he said after the usual exchange of cordialities, "that our ancestral footpath has recently been closed . . ."

"Yes," replied Mr. Obi. "We cannot allow people to make a highway of our school compound."

30 "Look here, my son," said the priest bringing down his walking-stick, "this path was here before you were born and before your father was born. The whole life of this village depends on it. Our dead relatives depart by it and our ancestors visit us by it. But most important, it is the path of children coming in to be born . . ."

35 Mr. Obi listened with a satisfied smile on his face.

"The whole purpose of our school," he said finally, "is to eradicate just such beliefs as that. Dead men do not require footpaths. The whole idea is just fantastic. Our duty is to teach your children to laugh at such ideas."

"What you say may be true," replied the priest, "but we follow the
40 practices of our fathers. If you re-open the path we shall have nothing to quarrel about. What I always say is: let the hawk perch and let the eagle perch." He rose to go.

"I am sorry," said the young headmaster. "But the school compound cannot be a thoroughfare. It is against our regulations. I would suggest your
45 constructing another path, skirting our premises. We can even get our boys to help in building it. I don't suppose the ancestors will find the little detour too burdensome."

"I have no more words to say," said the old priest, already outside.

Two days later a young woman in the village died in childbed. A diviner
50 was immediately consulted and he prescribed heavy sacrifices to propitiate ancestors insulted by the fence.

Obi woke up the next morning among the ruins of his work. The beautiful hedges were torn up not just near the path but right round the school, the flowers trampled to death and one of the school buildings pulled down . . .
55 That day, the white Supervisor came to inspect the school and wrote a nasty report on the state of the premises but more seriously about the "tribal-war situation developing between the school and the village, arising in part from the misguided zeal of the new headmaster."

1. Based upon the passage the central conflict is
   A) Mr. Obi and the local priest disagree about an ancient path.
   B) Mr. Obi is concerned about being evaluated by his Supervisor.
   C) Mr. Obi loves his flowers more than the school children.
   D) Mr. Obi's modern thinking disregards the ancient ways of the local villagers.

2. What evidence provides the best support for the answer to question 1?
   A) lines 13–14 ("Well, I don't. . . attempted to close it")
   B) lines 16–17 ("What will the Government. . . school next week")
   C) lines 36–38 ("The whole purpose of our school. . . laugh at such ideas")
   D) lines 52–54 ("Obi woke up. . . pulled down")

3. As used in line 38, the word "fantastic" most nearly means
   A) extremely good.
   B) very strange or unusual.
   C) not based in reality.
   D) humorous.

4. Which of the following details best supports the answer to question 3?
   A) lines 28–29 ("We cannot allow . . . school compound")
   B) lines 36–37 ("The whole purpose . . . require footpaths")
   C) lines 39–40 ("What you say . . . practices of our fathers")
   D) lines 40–41 ("If you re-open . . . to quarrel about")

5. One can infer that the white Supervisor
   A) had more sympathy for the ancient ways than the headmaster.
   B) was prejudiced against Mr. Obi.
   C) didn't really understand the African culture.
   D) thought the pagan ways should be discouraged at all costs.

6. Which of the following details best supports the answer to question 5?
   A) lines 16–17 ("What will the Government Education . . . next week")
   B) lines 41–42 ("What I always say . . . eagle perch")
   C) lines 52–54 ("The beautiful . . . buildings pulled down")
   D) lines 55–58 ("That day, the white Supervisor. . . new headmaster")

For answers, see page 559.

LESSON 2:
Defining Words and Phrases in Context

• • • **Explain** **Understanding Meanings of Words and Phrases**

Vocabulary-in-context questions play an important role in the SAT. These questions require you to determine a word's meaning by using **context,** or the words and sentences surrounding the word. Remember, vocabulary-in-context questions aren't asking you to choose the most common dictionary definition of a word, but rather the definition of the word according to how it is used in the passage. Often the answer choices will include definitions that are correct according to the dictionary, but which are not how the word is being used in the passage.

The types of words you can expect to be tested over are not obscure or out-of-date. They are words you will see in passages on different subjects and which you will use in college or in the workplace. Some questions will ask you to choose the best definition of a phrase from a passage.

Questions over word meaning may look like this:

- As used in lines xx–xx, "x" most nearly means . . .

- Which choice most closely captures the meaning of the phrase x used in lines xx–xx?

• • • **Think It Through** •

There are several different ways to use context to figure out a word's meaning.

- **Check surrounding words and sentences for suggested meanings.**
  Notice how the underlined words provide a clue to the meaning of the word "deleterious."

  Example:
  Climate change has several **deleterious** consequences, including the damaging onslaught of severe weather events. (The underlined words imply that *deleterious* means "damaging.")

- **Look for examples that suggest the word's meaning**. Words that signal the presence of examples include: *for instance, such as, for example,* and *like*.

  Example:
  Ty is an **assiduous** note taker. Throughout the class, I can hear him typing the teacher's words into his laptop. (The example given indicates that Ty is constantly taking notes. This implies that *assiduous* means "persistent" or "diligent.")

- **Look for nearby synonyms.** Writers regularly use synonyms to explain new or complex terms. Phrases that signal a synonym is nearby include *called, known as, in other words,* and *that is.*

  Example:
  Our neighbors celebrate **Diwali**, also known as the Indian festival of lights.

QUICK
TIP

The SAT includes ten questions on defining words in context: two in each of the reading passages, including the literature passage and the four nonfiction passages on science and social studies.

- **Look for nearby antonyms.**

  > **Example:**
  > Janet is so humble and friendly that John was shocked when someone referred to her as **condescending**. (John's shock when someone calls Janet "condescending" suggests it means the opposite of *humble*. Therefore, it must mean "superior.")

- **Consider common prefixes, roots, and suffixes.** English draws upon a large number of Greek and Latin words. A basic understanding of common prefixes, root words, and suffixes can help you discern the meaning of an unfamiliar word. A few are listed below. Many more can be found online.

Prefix/Root/Suffix	Meaning	Example
a-	not; without	apathy; atheist
dis-	not; opposite	distrust; disable
auto-	self	autobiography; autonomous
micro-	small	microscope; microcosm
mono-	one	monotonous; monologue
-able, -ible	is; can be	affordable; sensible
-ous, -eous, -ious	having qualities of	riotous; courageous; gracious

  > **Example:**
  > One of the only primate examples of monogamy, Lar gibbons have long been documented living in close-knit families. The coupled male and female will spend time grooming each other and (literally) hanging out together in the trees. (The root *mono* means "one." This fact along with the context clues "close-knit families" and "coupled" implies that *monogamy* means "having a relationship with one mate.")

- **Generate your own synonym.** Think of your own simple synonym for the word in question. Choose an answer choice that is closest to your synonym.

  > **Example:**
  > Scientists now realize that the brain is very plastic; the neurons adapt and change as circumstances change. (From the context, a synonym for *plastic* is "adaptable." If the answer choices include *creative, artificial, malleable,* and *sculptural,* you know that the closest in meaning is *malleable.*)

The following passages show unfamiliar words underlined. As you read the following passages, underline context clues that will help you determine the meanings.

Researchers at the Robert Wood Johnson Clinical Scholars Program at Yale University found that the more closely knit people reported their neighborhood to be, the less exposure to violence they had. By collecting data from roughly 150 New Haven residents through community-based surveys
5 conducted in 2014, the study authors concluded that strong social ties may help reduce gun violence and produce more resilient neighborhoods.

1. In context, "resilient" suggests the neighborhoods are
   A) strong.
   B) flexible.

Answer: "Resilient" is used as an adjective to describe neighborhoods; since having strong social ties results in safer neighborhoods, the word must have a positive connotation. The best answer is choice A since the preceding sentence suggests communities with strong social ties are particularly hardy.

Although the study was specific to a single city in Connecticut with historically high crime rates, it illustrates the importance of social cohesion, or a community's willingness to cooperate in order to prosper. The concept may sound <u>mawkish</u> in theory, but it has far-reaching empirical benefits.

5 And these matter at a time when the national conversation about gun violence has seen renewed fervor.

2. In line 4, "mawkish" most nearly means
   A) overly sentimental.
   B) having a sickly flavor.

Answer: Both answers are dictionary definitions of "mawkish," and both convey a negative connotation. However, "having a sickly flavor" does not logically describe *concept*, so A is the correct answer.

In *Bowling Alone*, the sociologist Robert Putnam argued that even affluent areas have seen decreased social interaction in recent decades. . . . Putnam found that Americans had joined fewer civic organizations, socialized with friends less frequently, and signed fewer petitions. The title of the book came

5 from the fact that while Americans had bowled more in the preceding twenty years than ever before, fewer of them did so in leagues (instead they "bowled alone"). Putnam concluded that the United States was bleeding <u>social capital</u>, and therefore democratic values.

3. In context, which is the best definition of "social capital" in lines 7–8?
   A) political events with like-minded people
   B) valuable relationships with other people

Answer: Since the paragraph focuses on decreased social interaction, the meaning of "social capital" might be along the lines of "social participation." Both answers incorporate this idea, but the following detail suggests the author is referring to relationships in the passage, not events: "Americans had joined fewer civic organizations, socialized with friends less frequently . . . ." Thus choice B is correct.

QUICK TIP

Some questions will test your understanding of multiple-meaning words. The answer choices may include several definitions of the word in question, which are accurate according to the dictionary. However, make sure the meaning fits the one used in the context of the passage.

Directions: As you read the following passage, underline any context clues that explain the meaning of the underlined words. Then answer the question(s) that follow each passage.

Where does one begin with the most prolific of major modern composers? Philip Glass has written more than two dozen operas along with a considerable amount of incidental music for plays. By next season, his symphonies will number nine. There are concertos galore, film scores
5 galore, solo pieces galore, and an impossible-to-categorize repertory for his Philip Glass Ensemble . . . .

Glass' list of collaborators is also profligate. Along with film and theater directors—high and low—Glass has worked with musicians from a startling wide range of classical, pop, jazz and world music traditions and cultures.
10 He gets along, and his music gets along.

It is that companionable aspect of Glass that has no doubt been most responsible for the trajectory of his career. One of the founders of hard-core, anti-establishment Minimalism in the 1960s, the 74-year-old composer has entered the mainstream, be it big-box opera, big-budget movies or, the ultimate
15 pop-culture accolade, having your style ripped off by television commercials.

1. The word "prolific" in line 1 means

_____

_____

2. In context, "collaborators" most nearly means

_____

_____

3. In context, "companionable" suggests Glass is

_____

_____

4. In line 15, "accolade" most nearly means

_____

_____

The following is from The Master of the World *by Jules Verne, published in 1904.*

Then suddenly, toward three o'clock in the morning, another alarm! Flames leaped up above the rocky wall of the Great Eyrie. Reflected from the clouds, they illuminated the atmosphere for a great distance. A crackling, as if of many burning trees, was heard.

5   Had a fire spontaneously broken out? And to what cause was it due? Lightning could not have started the conflagration; for no thunder had been heard. True, there was plenty of material for fire; at this height the chain of the Blueridge is well wooded. But these flames were too sudden for any ordinary cause.

10   "An eruption! An eruption!"

The cry resounded from all sides. An eruption! The Great Eyrie was then indeed the crater of a volcano buried in the bowels of the mountains. And after so many years, so many ages even, had it reawakened? Added to the flames, was a rain of stones and ashes about to follow? Were the lavas going 15 to pour down torrents of molten fire, destroying everything in their passage, annihilating the towns, the villages, the farms, all this beautiful world of meadows, fields and forests, even as far as Pleasant Garden and Morganton?

5. In line 5, "spontaneously" suggests the fire began
   A) with no apparent cause.
   B) with no restraint.

6. In line 11, "cry" most nearly means
   A) wail.
   B) shout.

7. In line 15, "torrents" most nearly means
   A) a violent outburst of nature.
   B) a powerful, rushing stream of liquid.

For answers, see page 560.

Directions: This Model SAT Question shows how defining words in context might be tested on the SAT. The answers and explanations immediately follow the questions. Try the questions and then review the answers and the explanations.

This passage is from Mary Wollstonecraft's A Vindication of the Rights of Women, *written in 1792.*

Contending for the rights of women, my main argument is built on this simple principle, that if she be not prepared by education to become the companion of man, she will stop the progress of knowledge, for truth must be common to all, or it will be inefficacious with respect to its influence on

5 general practice. And how can woman be expected to co-operate, unless she know why she ought to be virtuous? Unless freedom strengthen her reason till she comprehend her duty, and see in what manner it is connected with her real good? If children are to be educated to understand the true principle of patriotism, their mother must be a patriot; and the love of mankind, from which

10 an orderly train of virtues spring, can only be produced by considering the moral and civil interest of mankind; but the education and situation of woman, at present, shuts her out from such investigations.

1. As used in line 5, "be expected to cooperate" most nearly means
   A) deliberate about moral choices.
   B) comply with certain standards.
   C) accomplish the bare minimum.
   D) confine to realistic hopes for the future.

Strategy: This question asks you to use context to figure out the meaning of the phrase "be expected to cooperate." The last part of the sentence, "unless she know why she ought to be virtuous," suggests that the phrase relates to reasons for behavior. The paragraph does not ponder morality at any point nor does it mention achieving as little as required, so eliminate choices A and C. The whole paragraph argues to expand the rights of women, so choice D does not make sense in this context. The ideas of a woman knowing why she should act a certain way and comprehending her duty in relation to her "real good" indicate that choice B is the correct answer.

2. As used in line 4, "inefficacious" most nearly means
   A) successful in producing a desired effect.
   B) lacking strength of character.
   C) unable to produce a certain effect.
   D) producing large amounts of something.

QUICK TIP

Try to identify if the word has a positive or negative connotation. Then look at the answer choices and eliminate words that suggest the opposite emotion.

SAT-Type Questions

Directions: Questions 1–4 are over the following passage.

Not so long ago, photography was dismissed by the art world as nothing more than a utilitarian medium. In the mid-1970s, a photograph by Edward Weston, an early 20th-century master of
5 optical precision, could be had for less than $200 (roughly $800 today). In 2014, Weston's "Nautilus Shell, 1927," a print small enough to hold in one hand, was auctioned for $461,000, an apt barometer of photography's migration to the realm
10 of high art. Cindy Sherman is a reigning example: a group of twenty-one of her grainy photographs sold for over $6 million in 2015. Single images by Ms. Sherman, Andreas Gursky and Jeff Wall have been sold for several million dollars each.

15 But the value of photography today stands in sharp contrast to the gauntlet of art world prejudices that made its coming-of-age so difficult.

1. In line 2, "utilitarian" is closest in meaning to
   A) profitable.
   B) functional.
   C) desirable.
   D) creative.

2. As used in line 9, "barometer" most nearly means
   A) an instrument used to forecast weather.
   B) anything that reflects continuity.
   C) anything that reflects change.
   D) a tool that registers atmospheric pressure.

3. In line 10, "reigning" is closest in meaning to
   A) predominating.   C) directing.
   B) ruling.   D) influencing.

4. As used in line 16, "gauntlet" most nearly refers to
   A) any of various protective gloves.
   B) an open challenge.
   C) a fight.
   D) an attack from two or more sides.

Directions: Questions 5–7 are over the following passage.

The following is adapted from an article on the mass extinction of ocean life.

A team of scientists, in a groundbreaking analysis of data from hundreds of sources, has concluded that humans are on the verge of causing unprecedented damage to the oceans and the
5 animals living in them.

There are clear signs already that humans are harming the oceans to a remarkable degree, the scientists found. Some ocean species are certainly overharvested, but even greater damage results
10 from large-scale habitat loss, which is likely to accelerate as technology advances the human footprint, the scientists reported.

The oceans are so vast that their ecosystems

15 may seem impervious to change. But Dr.

McClenachan warned that the fossil record shows

that global disasters have wrecked the seas before.

"Marine species are not immune to extinction on a

large scale," she said.

5. In line 4, "unprecedented" is closest in meaning to
   A) revolutionary.
   B) pioneering.
   C) unparalleled.
   D) unfamiliar.

6. In line 9, "overharvested" most nearly means
   A) gathered excessively.
   B) destroyed.
   C) consumed extravagantly.
   D) picked to perfection.

7. As used in line 14, "impervious" most nearly means
   A) controlled by.
   B) unaffected by.
   C) proof against.
   D) vulnerable to.

Directions: Questions 8–10 are over the following passage.

The following is an excerpt from the United States Bill of Rights.

No person shall be held to answer for a

capital, or otherwise infamous crime, unless on a

presentment or indictment of a Grand Jury, except

in cases arising in the land or naval forces, or in

5 the Militia, when in actual service in time of War

or public danger; nor shall any person be subject

for the same offense to be twice put in jeopardy

of life or limb; nor shall be compelled in any

criminal case to be a witness against himself, nor

10 be deprived of life, liberty, or property, without

due process of law; nor shall private property be taken

for public use without just compensation.

8. As used in line 4, "cases" most nearly means
   A) matters in question.
   B) official investigations.
   C) examples of something.
   D) outer coverings.

9. As used in line 12, "just compensation" most nearly means
   A) a small sum of money.
   B) a minimum amount.
   C) expected rewards.
   D) fair reimbursement.

10. As used in line 3, "indictment" most nearly means
    A) a charge of a misdemeanor, or small offense.
    B) a thing that illustrates that a situation is bad.
    C) any cause for blame.
    D) a formal charge of a serious crime.

For answers, see page 560.

Closely Reading Informational Texts for Explicit Meanings

- Understanding explicit meanings
- Determining central ideas and summarizing texts
- Identifying supporting details

• • • • **Explain** **Understanding Explicit Meanings** • • • • • • • • • • • • • •

As you read an informational passage, identify ideas, facts, and opinions that are explicitly stated. **Explicit meanings** refer to ideas and information that are clearly stated in the text. In contrast, **implied meanings** are ideas and information that a reader must infer from context. To find the answer to an explicit question, search the passage for specific words or phrases included in the question.

As you read each paragraph in a passage, determine the point the author is making. Underline key words, phrases, and facts. Then in the margin next to each paragraph, paraphrase or restate important points.

Questions about explicit meanings might look like this:

- In lines xx–xx, the author directly states . . .
- In lines xx–xx, the author mentions that . . .
- In lines xx–xx, the author indicates that . . .
- In line xx, "_____" refers to . . .
- According to the passage, which of the following is true . . .

• • • • **Think It Through** •

The following examples show key words, phrases, and facts underlined and the main points noted in the margin.

> Although there has been measurable progress in recent years in reading ability at the elementary school level, all progress appears to halt as children enter their teenage years. There is a general decline in reading among teenage and adult Americans. Most alarming, both reading ability and the habit of regular reading have greatly declined among college graduates. These negative trends have more than literary importance. As this report makes clear, the declines have demonstrable social, economic, cultural, and civic implications.
>
> How does one summarize this disturbing story? As Americans, especially younger Americans, read less, they read less well. Because they read less well, they have lower levels of academic achievement. (The shameful fact

Declines in reading ability affect society in many ways.

that nearly one-third of American teenagers drop out of school is deeply connected to declining literacy and reading comprehension.) With lower levels of reading and writing ability, people <u>do less well</u> in the <u>job market</u>. Poor reading skills correlate heavily with <u>lack of employment, lower wages,</u> and <u>fewer opportunities</u> for advancement. Significantly worse reading skills are found among prisoners than in the general adult population. And <u>deficient readers</u> are <u>less</u> likely to become <u>active in civic and cultural life,</u> most notably in <u>volunteerism and voting.</u>

Poor readers do less well in school and at work.

All of the data suggest how powerfully <u>reading transforms the lives</u> of individuals—<u>whatever their social circumstances.</u> Regular reading not only <u>boosts</u> the likelihood of an <u>individual's academic and economic success</u>—facts that are not especially surprising—but it also seems to <u>awaken a person's social and civic sense.</u> Reading correlates with almost every measurement of <u>positive personal and social behavior</u> surveyed. It is reassuring, though hardly amazing, that readers attend more concerts and theater than non-readers, but it is surprising that they exercise more and play more sports—no matter what their educational level. The cold statistics confirm something that most readers know but have mostly been reluctant to declare as fact—<u>books change lives for the better.</u>

Reading improves lives.

Explicit Details:

- While elementary students have improved their reading ability, teenagers and adults have actually declined.
- The decline in reading ability and regular reading habits have far-reaching implications, such as lower academic achievement, less success in the job market, and lower wages.
- Reading positively impacts people's lives regardless of their social class.
- People who read have greater success in life and engage in positive social behaviors such as attending concerts, going to the theater, and playing sports.

Practice

Directions: As you read the following passage, underline important ideas and write key points in the margin. Then answer the questions that follow.

Faltering under extreme weather and vanishing habitats, the yearly winter migration of monarch butterflies to a handful of forested Mexican mountains dwindled precipitously in December of 2013, continuing what scientists said was an increasingly alarming decline.

5   The migrating population has become so small—perhaps 35 million,

experts guess—that the prospects of its rebounding to levels seen even five

years ago are diminishing. At worst, scientists said, a migration widely called

one of the world's great natural spectacles is in danger of effectively vanishing.

1. According to the passage, what is causing the decrease in the migrating population of monarch butterflies?

_____

_____

_____

2. In the last paragraph, what does the author believe will happen if the monarch butterflies continue their decline?

_____

_____

_____

   Before 1883, local communities had their own time. Each town figured

noon when the sun was at the zenith. Clocks in New York City, for example,

were 10 minutes and 27 seconds ahead of those in Baltimore. Railroad

schedules were a nightmare. Then, an unsung hero, William F. Allen,

5   suggested that the country be divided into four time zones, eliminating those

hundreds of different local times. November 18, 1883, was called "The Day

of Two Noons," for on that day Washington, D.C., gained four minutes as

"local noon" was replaced by "standard noon." Some major cities resisted

change. Cincinnati held out for seven years, but gradually the entire country

10 went on Eastern, Central, Mountain, or Pacific Time. This idea, so obviously

good and so universally accepted today, was an idea whose time had come,

but the coming did not come easily.

3. What does the author directly state about the difficulty of implementing a new time code system?

_____

_____

_____

4. In what way did the railroad influence the U.S. to standardize time zone?

_____

_____

_____

    If people are asked to name dangerous animals, they suggest tigers, rhinos, wolves, leopards, and bears. Yet a far more dangerous creature is the seemingly insignificant mosquito, carrier of discomfort, disease, and sometimes death. Most people know about malaria-carrying mosquitoes,

5 but few realize that some mosquitoes in the United States carry the dreaded encephalitis. This disease, usually associated with the tropics, is found even in cold areas of the country, like LaCrosse, Wisconsin. It is transmitted by a nasty little fellow called the "tree-hole mosquito." This woodland dweller tends to bite in the late afternoon rather than the evening hours.

10 But whenever it bites, the results can be painful, even deadly. It's just one representative of a dangerous family. Throughout the world the lowly mosquito is a vicious enemy of human beings.

5. What does the author explicitly cite as the serious diseases carried by mosquitoes?

_____

_____

_____

_____

6. In lines 1–4 ("If people . . . death"), what does the author claim about mosquitoes and other animals?

_____

_____

_____

_____

For answers, see page 561.

Directions: This Model SAT Question shows how you might be tested on explicit ideas on the SAT. The answer and explanation immediately follow the question. Try the question and then review the answer and the explanation.

"Because it is there!" George Mallory's explanation of why he kept trying to scale Mt. Everest is not a satisfying answer to a nonclimber. But a true climber understands. In an exciting report on his mountain adventures, *Savage Arena*, Joe Tasker attempts to add his explanation to Mallory's. Tasker endured

5   terrible hardships on the Eigerwand in Switzerland, K2 in Kashmir, Dunagiri in India, and Everest in Nepal-Tibet. With fellow climbers he experienced hope and despair in a desperate ascent after an avalanche had covered their tents. In a climb on the West Face of K2 he lost Nich Estcourt, a beloved comrade. Yet he always went back—at last to his death in May 1982 not far

10 from the summit of Everest itself, the ultimate challenge. In the book written shortly before his death, he confessed, "In some ways, going to the mountains is incomprehensible to many people and inexplicable by those who go. The reasons are difficult to unearth and only with those who are similarly drawn is there no need to try to explain."

1. Joe Tasker contends that the reason he attempted to climb deadly mountains is
   A) comprehensible only to other climbers.
   B) because the mountains were there.
   C) because he was an adventure-seeker and risk-taker.
   D) because he wanted to achieve an extraordinary feat.

Strategy: This question asks you to identify information explicitly stated in the passage. In lines 11–14, Tasker explains his reasons for climbing deadly mountains: "In some ways, going to the mountains is incomprehensible to many people and inexplicable to those who go. The reasons are difficult to unearth and only with those who are similarly drawn is there no need to try to explain." Only choice A corresponds to the ideas revealed by Tasker's quote about how only other climbers need no explanation because they inherently understand.

SAT-Type Questions

Directions: Questions 1–3 are based on the following passage.

How large a part will solar energy play in the future? When will the nonreplaceable petroleum begin to run out? How large a role will coal play in the energy program of the future? Is nuclear energy a feasible alternative?

Can we depend upon minihydroelectric systems to produce electricity in

5   small but economical chunks? Questions like these are bandied back and

forth in television discussions, news reports, and newspaper articles. There

is, however, another possibility, that is little considered but strategically

important. We can create tiny habitats that conserve energy.

Experts estimate that energy-minded landscaping can cut home energy

10 needs by 30%. Early societies knew the value of creative plantings to

help people keep cool in summer and warm in winter. Much of today's

landscaping, however, overlooks creative possibilities for energy

conservation, wasting precious resources through inefficient planning.

Trees, shrubs, vines, and ground cover can be planted to protect against the

15 summer's blazing sun. These plants are living air conditioners, evaporating

water and cooling the air. Planting windbreaks can help keep out wintry

blasts. Even small windbreaks around a foundation reduce heat loss by

providing a wall of insulating air around the house. Replacing traditional

grass lawns with rock, gravel, and succulents conserves water and prevents

20 the air pollution of mowing. Winter and summer, living plants can work for

us and save us energy dollars.

1. According to the passage, which of the following is true of
   energy-minded landscaping?
   A) It reduces dependence on petroleum.
   B) It can provide natural air conditioning.
   C) It requires a substantial investment of time and money.
   D) It can increase people's self-sufficiency.

2. In the second paragraph (lines 9–21), what does the author claim to be a
   disadvantage of modern landscaping?
   A) It focuses too much on utility and not enough on aesthetics.
   B) It disregards innovative ideas based on cutting edge technology.
   C) It is mired in bureaucracy and overrun with regulations.
   D) It fails in creatively and efficiently using resources.

3. Which choice does the author explicitly cite as an advantage living plants
   can provide for energy conservation?
   A) They can bring color to the yard.
   B) They can substantially reduce home energy bills.
   C) They can protect a house from cold winds.
   D) They can increase home energy needs by 30%.

For answers, see page 561.

One of the most important skills when reading an informational passage is to identify the main idea. The main idea of a text is the overall idea the writer wants to communicate. To find the main idea, or central idea, ask yourself, "What is the central concept the author wants the reader to understand?" Words that signal main ideas include *most importantly*, *key*, *central*, *mainly*, and *above all*.

As you read each paragraph in a passage, underline a sentence or sentences that best express the main idea of that paragraph. This is called a **topic sentence**. Think about how the main idea of each paragraph supports the main idea of the entire passage. In the margin, write notes about the relationship between the paragraph and the central idea of the passage.

Questions about central ideas might look like this:

- The main idea of [the passage/paragraph x] is . . .

- Paragraph x is mainly about . . .

Some SAT questions will ask you to identify a summary of a passage. A **summary** explains the main idea and key supporting details of a text. As you read, take notes in the margin about the main idea of each paragraph. These notes will help you identify the main ideas in the text as well as help you find information quickly to answer questions. Remember, a summary will include only important ideas, not secondary or extraneous information.

Questions about summary might look like this:

- Which choice best summarizes the passage?

- Which choice best reflects the overall sequence of the passage?

The main idea of an entire passage is often found in the first or last sentence of the first paragraph.

In writing that presents an argument, the central idea is sometimes referred to as the central claim.

••• Think It Through •

As you read the following passage, notice how the reader underlined the main idea in each paragraph. Think about how the main idea of each paragraph supports an overall central idea.

Although scientists are still trying to learn exactly why people need sleep, <u>animal studies show that sleep is necessary for survival.</u> For example, while rats normally live for two to three years, those deprived of REM (rapid eye movement) sleep survive only about 5 weeks on average, and rats deprived

5 of all sleep stages live only about 3 weeks. Sleep-deprived rats also develop abnormally low body temperatures and sores on their tail and paws. The <u>sores may develop because the rats' immune systems become impaired.</u> Some studies suggest that sleep deprivation affects the immune system in detrimental ways.

10 <u>Sleep appears necessary for our nervous systems to work properly.</u> Too little sleep leaves us drowsy and unable to concentrate the next day. It also leads to impaired memory and physical performance and reduced ability to carry out math calculations. If sleep deprivation continues, hallucinations

The body needs sleep to avoid sickness.

and mood swings may develop. Some experts believe sleep gives neurons
15 used while we are awake a chance to shut down and repair themselves.
Without sleep, neurons may become so depleted in energy or so polluted
with byproducts of normal cellular activities that they begin to malfunction.
Sleep also may give the brain a chance to exercise important neuronal
connections that might otherwise deteriorate from lack of activity.

Sleep helps the nervous system recharge and repair itself.

20   Deep sleep coincides with the release of growth hormone in children
and young adults. Many of the body's cells also show increased production
and reduced breakdown of proteins during deep sleep. Since proteins are
the building blocks needed for cell growth and for repair of damage from
factors like stress and ultraviolet rays, deep sleep may truly be "beauty
25 sleep." Activity in parts of the brain that control emotions, decision-making
processes, and social interactions is drastically reduced during deep
sleep, suggesting that this type of sleep may help people maintain optimal
emotional and social functioning while they are awake. A study in rats also
showed that certain nerve-signaling patterns which the rats generated during
30 the day were repeated during deep sleep. This pattern repetition may help
encode memories and improve learning.

Deep sleep aids cell growth and repair and helps maintain emotional and social health.

Main Idea: Sleep is necessary for the body's physical and mental health.

Some questions may also ask you to summarize a multiple-paragraph passage. This will require you to put together the main ideas from each paragraph into one succinct statement.

Question: Which of the following best summarizes the passage?

•   Sleep is essential to the body, and sleep deprivation has many negative effects.

•   Animal studies indicate that a lack of sleep leads to sickness and even death.

•   Sleep allows the brain time to recharge.

Answer: The first summary is the best answer because it describe the overall emphasis of the passage. The second choice's inclusion of "animal studies" is true, but not the main focus. The passage mentions other types of studies to prove the central point, not merely animal studies. The third options focuses on one detail in one paragraph.

• • • • • **Practice** •

Directions: For each paragraph, underline the main idea and then write a paraphrase of the main idea in the margin. Answer the questions that follow.

Surveys have shown that bats in upstate New York caves were "mysteriously dying off by the thousands," and scientists were not sure why. The problem

was first noticed during the winter of 2005–2006. By 2007, biologists
discovered caves that had thousands of dead and dying bats. The only telltale
5   sign of illness appeared to be what they called "white-nose syndrome"—a
condition marked by a white fungus on the bats' faces. The wildlife experts
were not sure if the fungus caused the bats' illness and death, or was just a
symptom of their as-yet-unknown illness. By 2008, scientists had confirmed
that this was a new species of fungus and named it *Geomyces destructans*.

10   The biologists at first thought the die-off might be caused by any number
of other factors—bacteria, a virus, changes in weather, a toxin, or some
contaminant brought in by a cave explorer from another region. But by
2011, scientists from the U.S. Geological Survey had performed numerous
experiments and gathered enough information to be certain of the cause of
15   the huge bat die-off, which by then had spread 2,000 kilometers across the
eastern United States and into Canada. More than five million bats have died
across this area. The cause was indeed the *Geomyces* fungus, which attaches
to living bats in the middle of the winter when they are most vulnerable
during hibernation.

20   What had puzzled scientists at first is that the same white-nose fungus
condition is seen among European bats, but they are not killed by the
infection. Experiments have indicated that while the North American bats
are susceptible to fatal infection by the fungus, the European bats must have
built up immunity to it over many thousands of years of exposure. Scientists
25   are looking for clues to the European bats' ability to survive the fungus to
find ways that they may be able to save the American bats. They are also
investigating the genetics of the fungus to see how it kills and thus how it
might be stopped.

1. In your own words, what is the main idea of the first paragraph (lines 1–9)?

_____

_____

_____

_____

2. In your own words, what is the main idea of the third paragraph (lines 20–28)?

_____

_____

_____

3. Write a summary of the entire passage.

_____

_____

_____

_____

_____

For answers, see page 562.

Model SAT Question

Directions: This Model SAT Question shows how finding the main idea might be tested on the SAT. The answer and explanation immediately follow the question. Try the question and then review the answer and the explanation.

When we think about memory on an intuitive level, it often seems as though our memories just fade away with the passage of time. It is as though some physical or chemical trace of an experience decays or degenerates as time progresses. The decay interpretation of memory is an old one and is perhaps the most widely believed by the general public. But the idea that memories fade with the passage of time has not been supported by experimental research. Somewhat surprisingly, there is no direct evidence to support the decay interpretation. Although the idea is a simple one, it has not led to fruitful experimentation and must, at present, be taken as nothing more than an interesting possibility.

  1. The main idea of this paragraph is that
    A) memory loss occurs when memories fade away.
    B) the brain steadily decays as humans age.
    C) fruitful experiments have been conducted in the field of memory loss.
    D) the theory of memory decay is not adequate.

SAT-Type Questions

Directions: Question 1 is based on the following passage.

Dangerous drivers account for a disproportionately large number of traffic fatalities. Some drivers are multiple offenders. Keeping such drivers off the roads is a desirable goal, but in the past there were some difficulties in enforcing such a plan. Previously, it was possible for a driver with a suspended or revoked license in one state to get a license in another state. The National Driver Register has solved this problem. The register is a computerized database of information about drivers who have had their licenses revoked or suspended, or who have been convicted of serious traffic violations, such as driving while impaired by alcohol or drugs. A California study has shown that license sanctions are the most effective means of reducing accidents caused by problem drivers. This device is more effective than jail terms, fines, driver-improvement classes, or alcohol-treatment centers. Because the register has resulted in greater cooperation by the states and greater efficiency at the national level, the number of dangerous drivers on the highways has been reduced.

1. Which choice best summarizes the passage?
   A) Most dangerous drivers are multiple offenders.
   B) The National Driver Register helps states screen prospective applicants for a license.
   C) Denying or limiting the issuance of drivers' licenses is a more effective means of driver control than jail terms or fines.
   D) A loophole of past procedures is the ability of a problem driver to get a license in a state that does not know his or her record.

Directions: Questions 2–3 are based on the following passage.

The paradox of Gilbert and Sullivan continues to amaze music lovers. The two men, utterly different in temperament and personality, somehow managed to collaborate on more than a dozen operettas of enduring charm.

QUICK TIP

The right answer to a summary question usually is a paraphrase of the main idea sentence from the text.

Both men were told they were wasting their talents on inconsequential

5 operettas, but somehow they stayed together, through stormy years and

occasional unpleasant sessions, to create immortal songs like "Tell Me,

Pretty Maiden" from *Patience*—songs that were a fortuitous blend of lyric

and melody.

William Schwenck Gilbert, who wrote the lyrics and generally determined

10 the plot and direction of the operettas, was a rather stern Victorian, intolerant

of laziness, indifference, or lack of talent. His guiding hand in the actual

production guaranteed the quality of the production and the integrity of the

performances. His witty, often satirical, lyrics punctured Victorian pomposity

and inefficiency and, it is said, even ruffled the feathers of Queen Victoria.

15 Arthur Sullivan, who composed the lovely music for Gilbert's words, was

a contrast to Gilbert. Sullivan was a rather gentle person, aristocratic, fond of

the good life, and often melancholy. Awed by titles, he loved to hobnob with

the great. Seldom robustly healthy, he created some of the most beautiful

music while racked with pain.

20 On many occasions, Sullivan said, "I don't want to do another operetta,"

but after each refusal, Gilbert would tempt Sullivan with plots, snatches of

dialog, production ideas. In the background, Richard D'Oyly Carte acted

as impresario and referee, bringing the two men back together again and

again, despite the apparent refusal of Sullivan to go on. Somehow, despite

25 altercations, disagreements, and misunderstandings, the two men created

fourteen operettas, eleven of which are still frequently played.

2. The main idea of the second paragraph (lines 9–14) is that
   A) the appeal of Gilbert and Sullivan's works endures to today.
   B) Gilbert and Sullivan had a rocky relationship, but they still managed
      to produce 14 operettas.
   C) lyricist Gilbert was a perfectionist who was not afraid to make fun of
      societies' problems.
   D) Queen Victoria was not a fan of Gilbert's biting lyrics.

3. This passage is mainly about
   A) the famous operettas of Victorian England.
   B) how Gilbert and Sullivan's operettas became famous.
   C) how Gilbert charmed Sullivan into doing more operettas.
   D) the unlikely collaboration of Gilbert and Sullivan.

Directions: Question 4 is based on the following passage from Charles Darwin's *Origin of Species* (1859).

The eyes of moles and of some burrowing rodents are rudimentary in size, and in some cases are quite covered up by skin and fur. This state of the eyes is probably due to gradual reduction from disuse, but aided perhaps by natural selection. In South America, a burrowing rodent, the tuco-tuco,
5 or *Ctenomys*, is even more subterranean in its habits than the mole; and I was assured by a Spaniard, who had often caught them, that they were frequently blind; one which I kept alive was certainly in this condition, the cause, as appeared on dissection, having been inflammation of the nictitating membrane. As frequent inflammation of the eyes must be injurious to
10 any animal, and as eyes are certainly not indispensable to animals with subterranean habits, a reduction in their size with the adhesion of the eyelids and growth of fur over them, might in such case be an advantage; and if so, natural selection would constantly aid the effects of disuse.

4. Which statement best captures Darwin's central assumption in the passage?
   A) Natural selection encourages eye reduction among burrowing rodents.
   B) Dissection reveals that eyes are generally unnecessary for subterranean animals.
   C) Burrowing rodents frequently suffer from inflammation of the eyes.
   D) Burrowing rodents find protective fur around their eyes advantageous.

For answers, see page 562.

Explain Identifying Supporting Details

While some questions on the SAT focus on the **main idea** of a passage, other questions test your ability to identify **supporting details.** Supporting details are facts, examples, reasons, anecdotes, illustrations, or analogies that support the main idea. In other words, these details are the pillars that "hold up" the main idea. While the main idea is a broad overview of an entire passage or paragraph, details are more specific and offer convincing information that causes the reader to understand the truth of the main idea.

Some questions on the SAT will ask you to identify which answer choice contains the correct supporting detail from the passage. These types of questions are explicit knowledge questions. A careful reading of the passage will provide the correct answer. Look for words that signal a relationship between the main idea and supporting details, such as *first, second, also, in addition, another, finally, furthermore, moreover.*

Explicit knowledge questions about supporting details look like this:

- The authors indicate which of the following about _____?
- In lines xx–xx, the author . . .

Other questions will ask you to identify the relationship between the main idea and supporting details. These types of questions will ask you to consider *how* the supporting details support the main idea. For example, details may

- provide an illustration
- give examples
- explain reasons
- give background or history

Questions that test your ability to identify the purpose of supporting details may look like this:

- The examples given in lines xx–xx mainly serve to . . .
- How does the comparison in lines xx–xx support the author's claim that . . .
- In lines xx–xx, the author supports the idea that _____ by . . .

Some questions will ask you to identify the purpose of supporting details. For more on identifying author's purpose, see Lesson 5 on page 159.

Think It Through

The following paragraphs provide a model of how a reader underlined the main idea of each paragraph and noted the supporting details in the margin. As you read, think about how the details support the main idea.

The <u>Mayan Empire</u> once stretched from the Yucatan to western Honduras. <u>Its power and extent are constantly being restudied</u> as new discoveries rescue important Mayan sites from the jungle. Sites like Uxmal and Chichen-Itza in Yucatan, Tikal in Guatemala, and Copan in Honduras <u>reveal the awesome</u>
5 <u>achievements</u> of the civilization that flourished many centuries ago. The latter two, discovered in the 1840s, "rank in archaeological importance with the pyramids of Egypt."

Details: From Yucatan to Honduras; Sites reclaimed from jungle; Tikal and Copan discovered in the 1840s, as important as the pyramids.

<u>A more recent discovery is causing a complete reappraisal of the Mayan influence and the duration of the Mayan Empire.</u> It had previously been
10 thought that the Mayan civilization did not mature before A.D. 300. Then in 1978 Bruce Dahlin uncovered bits of pottery dating from 400 B.C. There, in the lost city called El Mirador, not far from Tikal, a civilization flourished centuries before the date usually assigned to its arrival.

Details: Discovery of pottery from 400 B.C. in 1978 discounts theory that Mayan civilization did not mature before A.D. 300.

The <u>architecture at El Mirador reveals the sophistication of its artisans:</u>
15 master builders, stonecutters, and sculptors. The various structures also suggest a high level of social organization. Here, too, are beautiful carvings with hieroglyphics as yet undeciphered. This graphic style of writing provided much of the communication upon which a civilization ultimately rests.

Details: Art, architecture, and hieroglyphics are evidence of an advanced society

The new discoveries suggest that the Mayan Empire lasted not 500 or so

20   years but 1500 years or more. <u>John Graham of Berkeley flatly states, "Mayan</u>

<u>civilization represents the longest sustained civilization in the New World."</u>

Further explorations at El Mirador suggest that we have just scratched the

surface of our knowledge about the Maya.

Details: Mayan empire lasted 1500 years not 500.

Main idea: New discoveries are challenging archeologists' conclusions about the Mayan empire.

Supporting details from paragraphs:

- Tikal in Guatemala and Copan in Honduras "rank in archaeological importance with the pyramids of Egypt."

- Bruce Dahlin uncovered bits of pottery in the lost city of El Mirador dating from 400 B.C., centuries earlier than originally thought.

- El Mirador reveals the Mayan's sophisticated artwork and system of hieroglyphics.

- Mayan Empire lasted 1500 years or more.

Question: How do the details support the main idea?

Answer: They explain how the discovery of the lost Mayan city of El Mirador has provided new information about how advanced and enduring the Mayan civilization was.

QUICK TIP

Transitional phrases will help you determine the relationship between main ideas and supporting details in a text. Examples of transitional phrases include "for example" and "for this reason."

Practice

Directions: For each paragraph, underline the main idea. In the right margin, take notes about the supporting details and their relationship to the main idea. Answer the questions that follow.

Biotechnology is defined as the industrial use of living organisms or

biological techniques developed through basic research; marine biotechnology

is an emerging discipline based on the use of marine natural resources. The

oceans encompass about 71% of the surface of our planet, but over 99% of the

5   biosphere (since organisms are found throughout the water column), and they

represent the greatest extremes of temperature, light, and pressure encountered

by life. Adaptation to these harsh environments has led to a rich marine bio-

and genetic-diversity with potential biotechnological applications related to

drug discovery, environmental remediation, increasing seafood supply and

10   safety, and developing new resources and industrial processes.

Drug discovery represents one of the most promising and highly visible

outcomes of marine biotechnology research. Biochemicals produced by

marine invertebrates, algae and bacteria, are very different than those from

related terrestrial organisms and thus offer great potential as new classes of

15 medicines. To date, examples of marine-derived drugs include an antibiotic
    from a fungi, two closely related compounds from a sponge that treat cancer
    and the herpes virus, and a neurotoxin from a snail that has painkiller
    properties making it 10,000 times more potent than morphine without the
    side effects. However, there are several more marine-derived compounds
20 currently in clinical trials and it is likely that many more will advance to
    the clinic as more scientists look to the sea for these biotechnological uses.
    In addition to new medicines, other uses for marine-derived compounds
    include: cosmetics (algae, crustacean and sea fan compounds), nutritional
    supplements (algae and fish compounds), artificial bone (corals), and
25 industrial applications (fluorescent compounds from jellyfish, novel glues
    from mussels, and heat resistant enzymes from deep-sea bacteria).

    NOAA NURP and its partner the National Institute of Undersea
    Science and Technology (NIUST) are committed to assessing the marine
    biotechnological potential of US coral reef organisms. In the last 3 years,
30 OBCR has surveyed and sampled the marine resources of Hawaii, Alaska,
    Puerto Rico, Guam, Saipan, and American Samoa. The repository currently
    contains over 2,000 extracts which have been tested in-house for antibiotic,
    anticancer, and antimalarial activity. These extracts have also been forwarded
    to academic and industrial partners across the United States for additional
35 screening. Over 10% of the repository samples have been flagged for
    follow-up research efforts (this compares favorably to the 0.5% "hit-rate"
    reported for terrestrial plants). In addition, this research increases our
    understanding of novel marine organisms and habitats using new and novel
    technologies.

1. According to the passage, what factors cause marine life to have such potential
   for biotechnology?

   _____

   _____

   _____

2. Which lines from the text support your answer to question 1?

   _____

   _____

3. In paragraph 2 (lines 11–26), how does the writer support his claim that marine biotechnology research has resulted in new medical discoveries?

_____

_____

_____

4. Why does the writer include the list of marine-derived compounds in lines 22–26 ("In addition to . . . deep-sea bacteria")?

_____

_____

_____

5. Why does the writer include the detail in lines 35–37 comparing the percentage of marine biotechnological samples flagged for further research efforts with those from terrestrial plants?

_____

_____

_____

For answers, see page 562.

Model SAT Questions

Directions: These Model SAT Questions show how this skill might be tested on the SAT. The answer and explanation immediately follow the questions. Try each question and then review the answer and the explanation.

This passage is excerpted from Franklin Delano Roosevelt's "Commonwealth Club Address" given on September 23, 1932. It was given in the midst of the Great Depression, a time when the economy had slowed significantly and many Americans were out of work.

Just as in older times the central government was first a haven of refuge, and then a threat, so now in a closer economic system the central and ambitious financial unit is no longer a servant of national desire, but a danger. I would draw the parallel one step farther. We did not think because national
5 government had become a threat in the 18th century that therefore we should abandon the principle of national government. Nor today should we abandon the principle of strong economic units called corporations, merely because their power is susceptible of easy abuse. In other times we dealt with the problem of an unduly ambitious central government by modifying it gradually

10 into a constitutional democratic government. So today we are modifying and controlling our economic units.

As I see it, the task of government in its relation to business is to assist the development of an economic declaration of rights, an economic constitutional order. This is the common task of statesman and business man. It is the 15 minimum requirement of a more permanently safe order of things.

Every man has a right to life; and this means that he has also a right to make a comfortable living. He may by sloth or crime decline to exercise that right; but it may not be denied him. We have no actual famine or death; our industrial and agricultural mechanism can produce enough and to spare. Our government 20 formal and informal, political and economic, owes to every one an avenue to possess himself of a portion of that plenty sufficient for his needs, through his own work. Every man has a right to his own property; which means a right to be assured, to the fullest extent attainable, in the safety of his savings.

By no other means can men carry the burdens of those parts of life which, 25 in the nature of things afford no chance of labor; childhood, sickness, old age. In all thought of property, this right is paramount; all other property rights must yield to it. If, in accord with this principle, we must restrict the operations of the speculator, the manipulator, even the financier, I believe we must accept the restriction as needful, not to hamper individualism but to protect it.

1. In the first paragraph (lines 1–11) the speaker supports his central claim about corporations by
   A) asserting that America should curb corporations in the same way they curbed an overly controlling central government.
   B) proposing that the government step in and take over large corporations that are going bankrupt.
   C) explaining how personal rights could be expanded by giving more freedom to businesses.
   D) returning to a strong central government.

Strategy: This question asks you how supporting details support a central claim. The first paragraph sets up a comparison between the central government in the 18th century and "financial units" and "corporations" currently. The final sentence explains how in "other times we dealt with the problem of an unduly ambitious central government by modifying it gradually . . . so today we are modifying and controlling our economic units." Choice B is not mentioned. Although personal rights are discussed in the third paragraph, it is implied that the power of businesses need to be limited in order to allow more personal freedom. Choice C is incorrect. No support is given for choice D. The best answer is choice A.

2. The explanation of personal rights listed in lines 22–29 ("Every . . . it") mainly serves to

   A) emphasize the importance of protecting these rights.
   B) reveal how complex the issue of government and individual rights is.
   C) convince the audience that strong central government is needed.
   D) highlight the urgent the need for a revised economic plan.

Strategy: This question asks you to identify the purpose behind the details listed in the final paragraph. The third paragraph outlines the right to life, the right to make a living or work, and the right to have possessions (property) or money (savings). Roosevelt emphasizes the importance of these rights in order to convince the reader that these rights must be protected. Choice B may be true, but it is not Roosevelt's main purpose; it is not mentioned in the passage. Choice D is not supported by the passage. Choice C is incorrect because it requires the reader to make the assumption that by stating that the actions of the financier must be restricted, Roosevelt is arguing for a stronger central government. That is not what he is saying. His main purpose is to emphasize the important of individual rights, choice A.

SAT-Type Questions

Directions: Questions 1–3 are based on the following passage.

The passage below is excerpted from "Hotspots: Mantle Thermal Plumes" published on the U.S. Geological Survey's Web site.

In 1963, J. Tuzo Wilson, the Canadian geophysicist who discovered transform faults, came up with an ingenious idea that became known as the "hotspot" theory. Wilson noted that in certain locations around the world, such as Hawaii, volcanism has been active for very long periods of time.

5 This could only happen, he reasoned, if relatively small, long-lasting, and exceptionally hot regions—called hotspots—existed below the plates that would provide localized sources of high heat energy (thermal plumes) to sustain volcanism. Specifically, Wilson hypothesized that the distinctive linear shape of the Hawaiian Island-Emperor Seamounts chain resulted

10 from the Pacific Plate moving over a deep, stationary hotspot in the mantle, located beneath the present-day position of the Island of Hawaii. Heat from this hotspot produced a persistent source of magma by partly melting the overriding Pacific Plate. The magma, which is lighter than the surrounding solid rock, then rises through the mantle and crust to erupt onto the seafloor,

15 forming an active seamount. Over time, countless eruptions cause the seamount to grow until it finally emerges above sea level to form an island

QUICK TIP

When answering a supporting detail question, peruse the selection for specific details the question is asking for. Often the answer can be found in a single sentence.

volcano. Wilson suggested that continuing plate movement eventually carries the island beyond the hotspot, cutting it off from the magma source, and volcanism ceases. As one island volcano becomes extinct, another develops

20 over the hotspot, and the cycle is repeated. This process of volcano growth and death, over many millions of years, has left a long trail of volcanic islands and seamounts across the Pacific Ocean floor.

According to Wilson's hotspot theory, the volcanoes of the Hawaiian chain should get progressively older and become more eroded the farther

25 they travel beyond the hotspot. The oldest volcanic rocks on Kauai, the northwesternmost inhabited Hawaiian island, are about 5.5 million years old and are deeply eroded. By comparison, on the "Big Island" of Hawaii— southeasternmost in the chain and presumably still positioned over the hotspot—the oldest exposed rocks are less than 0.7 million years old and

30 new volcanic rock is continually being formed.

The possibility that the Hawaiian Islands become younger to the southeast was suspected by the ancient Hawaiians, long before any scientific studies were done. During their voyages, sea-faring Hawaiians noticed the differences in erosion, soil formation, and vegetation and recognized that the islands to

35 the northwest (Niihau and Kauai) were older than those to the southeast (Maui and Hawaii). This idea was handed down from generation to generation in the legends of Pele, the fiery Goddess of Volcanoes. Pele originally lived on Kauai. When her older sister Namakaokahai, the Goddess of the Sea, attacked her, Pele fled to the Island of Oahu. When she was forced by Namakaokahai

40 to flee again, Pele moved southeast to Maui and finally to Hawaii, where she now lives in the Halemaumau Crater at the summit of Kilauea Volcano. The mythical flight of Pele from Kauai to Hawaii, which alludes to the eternal struggle between the growth of volcanic islands from eruptions and their later erosion by ocean waves, is consistent with geologic evidence obtained

45 centuries later that clearly shows the islands becoming younger from northwest to southeast.

1. According to the passage, Wilson identifies Hawaii as a possible hotspot location because it
   A) has a distinctive linear shape.
   B) provides numerous volcanoes to study.
   C) is located on the Pacific Plate.
   D) contains ancient volcano mythology.

2. The passage indicates that the formation of island volcanoes across the Pacific Ocean floor was facilitated by
   A) the Hawaiian goddess Pele.
   B) existence of a stationary hotspot.
   C) alternation of high and low heat.
   D) large breaks in the Earth's crust.

3. The myth explained in lines 40–41 ("Pele . . . Volcano") mainly serves to
   A) indicate how distinctively original Hawaiian myths are.
   B) add a human story to scientific data.
   C) explain the geography of the Hawaiian Islands.
   D) indicate that Hawaiian myths reflect scientific reality.

Directions: Questions 4–7 are based on the following passage.

The text below is excerpted from "A Guide to Health" by Mahatma Gandhi (1906).

We have got into the habit of calling in a doctor for the most trivial diseases. Where there is no regular doctor available, we take the advice of mere quacks. We labour under the fatal delusion that no disease can be cured without medicine. This has been responsible for more mischief to mankind than any

5 other evil. It is of course, necessary that our diseases should be cured, but they cannot be cured *by medicines*. Not only are medicines merely useless, but at times even positively harmful. For a diseased man to take drugs and medicines would be as foolish as to try to cover up the filth that has accumulated in the inside of the house. The more we cover up the filth, the more rapidly does

10 putrefaction go on. The same is the case with the human body. Illness or disease is only Nature's warning that filth has accumulated in some portion or other of the body; and it would surely be the part of wisdom to allow Nature to remove the filth, instead of covering it up by the help of medicines. Those who take medicines are really rendering the task of Nature doubly difficult. It is,

15 on the other hand, quite easy for us to help Nature in her task by remembering certain elementary principles,—by fasting, for instance, so that the filth may not accumulate all the more, and by vigorous exercise in the open air, so that some of the filth may escape in the form of perspiration. And the one thing that is supremely necessary is to keep our minds strictly under control.

20 We find from experience that, when once a bottle of medicine gets itself introduced into a home, it never thinks of going out, but only goes on drawing other bottles in its train. We come across numberless human beings who are afflicted by some disease or other all through their lives in spite of

their pathetic devotion to medicines. They are to-day under the treatment
25 of this doctor, to-morrow of that. They spend all their life in a futile search
after a doctor who will cure them for good. As the late Justice Stephen (who
was for some time in India) said, it is really astonishing that drugs of which
so little is known should be applied by doctors to bodies of which they
know still less! Some of the greatest doctors of the West themselves have
30 now come to hold this view. Sir Astley Cooper, for instance, admits that the
'science' of medicine is mostly mere guess-work; Dr. Baker and Dr. Frank
hold that more people die of medicines than of diseases; and Dr. Masongood
even goes to the extent of saying that more men have fallen victims to
medicine than to war, famine and pestilence combined!

4. The passage indicates that most people error by
   A) going to a doctor when they are sick.
   B) thinking the mind doesn't play a role in curing diseases.
   C) believing medicine is required to cure diseases.
   D) seeing only specialists to cure diseases.

5. According to the passage, Ghandi believes disease is nature's warning that
   A) a person has taken too many medications.
   B) filth has accumulated in the body.
   C) the body has too much fat.
   D) the mind is not under control.

6. The passage identifies which of the following as one of the best ways to naturally cure disease?
   A) commune with nature
   B) take medicine
   C) eat healthy food
   D) exercise rigorously

7. The range of doctors and their opinions listed in lines 30–34 ("Sir Astley . . . combined") mainly serves to emphasize how
   A) much the medical field has yet to learn about medicine and the human body.
   B) inconsistent doctors' views about medicine are throughout the world.
   C) strongly most doctors feel about treating patients with experimental treatments.
   D) dependable advice from medical personnel is to those seeking treatment.

For answers, see page 563.

QUICK
TIP

A supporting detail question may also test your knowledge of more than one detail. You'll need to select an answer choice including all of the details asked for.

LESSON 4:
Closely Reading Informational Text for Implicit Meanings

- Making inferences
- Using analogical reasoning
- Citing textual evidence

Explain Making Inferences

Many questions on the SAT will test your ability to figure out what a selection *suggests* or *implies*. These **implicit meaning** questions will require you to draw reasonable inferences from the text. You will also encounter questions that require you to identify the **textual evidence** that best supports the inferences you have drawn.

As you read a passage, pause after each paragraph and make inferences. Ask yourself, "What reasonable conclusions can I draw from this information?" Think about what the passage states and also what you know to be true based upon prior knowledge. In the margin, record your inferences. Then underline the evidence that supports these inferences. This will enable you to more easily find the correct answer to inference questions.

Questions about inferences often look like this:

- The passage implies that . . .
- Which of the following does the author suggest in line xx?
- It can most reasonably be inferred from Passage 2 that . . .
- An unstated assumption made by the authors is that . . .
- Based on information in the passage, it can reasonably be inferred that . . .

Think It Through

Read the following passages. Notice how the reader underlined explicit details in the passage and wrote inferences in the margin. Study the explicit and implicit details below each passage.

Passage 1

There is one creature perfectly adapted and temperamentally suited to some of the most inhospitable areas of the world: the camel. In the ecology of the Sahara Desert, the nomad and the camel are mutually dependent on each other. The nomad provides the camel with water and food. The camel provides the nomad with milk, wool, transportation, and meat. Above all, the camel provides work and gives meaning to the lives of the tribes that crisscross the Sahara. The camel provides the only means by which human beings can constructively utilize the desert. Camel herding, combined with nomadism to take advantage of seasonal rains and recurrent scattered vegetation, is the <u>only feasible solution to surviving</u> in the desert. The camel is at the heart of all efforts to live in harmony with the desert.

Inference: The camel is irreplaceable to the desert people.

Explicit Details:

- The camel is physically and temperamentally adapted to extreme areas, such as the Sahara.
- The nomad and the camel are dependent on one another to survive in the Sahara.
- The nomad provides water and food for the camel, while the camel provides milk, wool, transportation, and meat for the nomad.
- Nomadism and camel herding make survival in the desert possible.

Implicit Details (Inferences):

- Details that state that nomads and camels "are mutually dependent on each other" and camels give "meaning to the lives of tribes" suggest camels and people have a relationship based on mutual affection.
- The people of the Sahara love and depend upon their camels.

Passage 2

"Prairie fire!" The words struck terror into the hearts of many settlers. Dry grass burns rapidly. Out of control, a prairie fire can be an awesome sight. Yet today <u>controlled fires</u> are set to <u>help</u> the <u>grasslands survive</u>. <u>Without occasional fires, undesirable intruders</u> like red cedar begin to <u>take over the land</u>. <u>Unwelcome</u> smaller <u>plants</u>, like Kentucky bluegrass, soon <u>replace native grasses</u> and change the character of prairie islands preserved as examples of the American natural heritage. <u>Litter</u> on the prairie floor also changes the ecology of an area and <u>permits aggressive exotic plants to move in.</u> Fire removes litter and provides the opportunity for native grasslands to be preserved for generations to come. But the <u>fires must be set</u> only <u>after extensive study</u> and analysis of <u>wind, wind speed, relative humidity, temperature,</u> and the <u>physical factors</u> of the <u>vegetation</u> to be burned.

Inference: Controlled fires are used by ecologists/ land managers to preserve native grasslands.

Explicit Ideas

- Controlled fires help grasslands by destroying invading plants, such as red cedar and Kentucky bluegrass, that change the native landscape.
- Fires also eliminate litter, preserving the prairie and stopping exotic plants from inhabiting the area.
- Fires must be carefully set after studying many relevant factors.

Implicit Ideas (Inferences):

- Out-of-control fires are dangerous and can be deadly.
- Non-native plants are unwelcome on the prairie, and the prairie should be preserved in its natural state.
- Land managers set fires on purpose to cleanse the prairie of unwanted plants and litter.

Passage 3

Society in every state is a blessing, but Government, even in its best state, is but a necessary evil; in its worst state an intolerable one: for when we suffer, or are exposed to the same miseries BY A GOVERNMENT, which we might expect in a country WITHOUT GOVERNMENT, our calamity is heightened by reflecting that we furnish the means by which we suffer. Government, like dress, is the badge of lost innocence; the palaces of kings are built upon the ruins of the bowers of paradise. For were the impulses of conscience clear, uniform and irresistibly obeyed, man would need no other lawgiver; but that not being the case, he finds it necessary to surrender up a part of his property to furnish means for the protection of the rest; and this he is induced to do by the same prudence which in every other case advises him, out of two evils to choose the least. Wherefore, security being the true design and end of government, it unanswerably follows that whatever form thereof appears most likely to ensure it to us, with the least expense and greatest benefit, is preferable to all others.

Inference: People require government even though it is an inherently evil institution.

Explicit Ideas:

- Society is advantageous, but government is a necessary evil.
- When the government causes people suffering, it is further distressing because the people provide support for the government.
- Laws would be unnecessary if people's consciences were clear and always obeyed, but since this is not so, people must give up something to ensure protection.
- The real purpose of government is security, so people seek to find the form that is the least expensive and has the greatest benefit.

Implicit Ideas (Inferences):

- Government varies in its tolerability but is never a positive force.
- People's vices create the need for government.

Notice that the inferences require you to draw conclusions not specifically stated in the passage. However, inferences must be able to be supported by evidence from the passage.

Sometimes you'll need to read an informational passage more than once in order to understand it. In the first reading, focus on explicit information and key ideas. Then when you reread, try to decipher the implicit meanings the author conveys.

Directions: The following is from a speech by Ronald Reagan given at the Berlin Wall in Germany in 1987. Underline key ideas in the passage. Then write inferences in the margin.

Chancellor Kohl, Governing Mayor Diepgen, ladies and gentlemen:

Twenty-four years ago, President John F. Kennedy visited Berlin, speaking to the people of this city and the world at the City Hall. Well, since then two other presidents have come, each in his turn, to Berlin. And today I,
5   myself, make my second visit to your city.

We come to Berlin, we American presidents, because it's our duty to speak, in this place, of freedom. But I must confess, we're drawn here by other things as well: by the feeling of history in this city, more than 500 years older than our own nation; by the beauty of the Grunewald and the
10 Tiergarten; most of all, by your courage and determination. Perhaps the composer Paul Lincke understood something about American presidents. You see, like so many presidents before me, I come here today because wherever I go, whatever I do: *Ich hab noch einen Koffer in Berlin.* [I still have a suitcase in Berlin.] Our gathering today is being broadcast throughout
15 Western Europe and North America. I understand that it is being seen and heard as well in the East. To those listening throughout Eastern Europe, a special word: Although I cannot be with you, I address my remarks to you just as surely as to those standing here before me. For I join you, as I join your fellow countrymen in the West, in this firm, this unalterable belief: *Es*
20 *gibt nur ein Berlin.* [There is only one Berlin.]

Behind me stands a wall that encircles the free sectors of this city, part of a vast system of barriers that divides the entire continent of Europe. From the Baltic, south, those barriers cut across Germany in a gash of barbed wire, concrete, dog runs, and guard towers. Farther south, there may be no visible, no
25 obvious wall. But there remain armed guards and checkpoints all the same—still a restriction on the right to travel, still an instrument to impose upon ordinary men and women the will of a totalitarian state. Yet it is here in Berlin where the wall emerges most clearly; here, cutting across your city, where the news photo and the television screen have imprinted this brutal division of a continent upon
30 the mind of the world. Standing before the Brandenburg Gate, every man is a

German, separated from his fellow men. Every man is a Berliner, forced to look upon a scar. President von Weizsacker has said, "The German question is open as long as the Brandenburg Gate is closed." Today I say: As long as the gate is closed, as long as this scar of a wall is permitted to stand, it is not the German

35 question alone that remains open, but the question of freedom for all mankind. Yet I do not come here to lament. For I find in Berlin a message of hope, even in the shadow of this wall, a message of triumph.

In this season of spring in 1945, the people of Berlin emerged from their air-raid shelters to find devastation. Thousands of miles away, the people of the

40 United States reached out to help. And in 1947 Secretary of State—as you've been told—George Marshall announced the creation of what would become known as the Marshall Plan. Speaking precisely 40 years ago this month, he said: "Our policy is directed not against any country or doctrine, but against hunger, poverty, desperation, and chaos." In the Reichstag a few moments ago,

45 I saw a display commemorating this 40th anniversary of the Marshall Plan. I was struck by the sign on a burnt-out, gutted structure that was being rebuilt. I understand that Berliners of my own generation can remember seeing signs like it dotted throughout the western sectors of the city. The sign read simply: "The Marshall Plan is helping here to strengthen the free world." A strong, free

50 world in the West, that dream became real. Japan rose from ruin to become an economic giant. Italy, France, Belgium— virtually every nation in Western Europe saw political and economic rebirth; the European Community was founded. In West Germany and here in Berlin, there took place an economic miracle, the Wirtschaftswunder. Adenauer, Erhard, Reuter, and other leaders

55 understood the practical importance of liberty—that just as truth can flourish only when the journalist is given freedom of speech, so prosperity can come about only when the farmer and businessman enjoy economic freedom. The German leaders reduced tariffs, expanded free trade, lowered taxes. From 1950 to 1960 alone, the standard of living in West Germany and Berlin doubled.

60 Where four decades ago there was rubble, today in West Berlin there is the greatest industrial output of any city in Germany—busy office blocks, fine homes and apartments, proud avenues, and the spreading lawns of parkland. Where a city's culture seemed to have been destroyed, today there are two great universities, orchestras and an opera, countless theaters, and

65 museums. Where there was want, today there's abundance—food, clothing, automobiles—the wonderful goods of the *Ku'damm*. From devastation, from utter ruin, you Berliners have, in freedom, rebuilt a city that once again ranks as one of the greatest on earth. The Soviets may have had other plans. But my friends, there were a few things the Soviets didn't count on—*Berliner Herz,*

70 *Berliner Humor, ja, und Berliner Schnauze.* [Berliner heart, Berliner humor, yes, and a Berliner Schnauze.]

1. What is the meaning of lines 13–14 ("I still have a suitcase in Berlin")?

    _____

    _____

    _____

2. What does Reagan imply in lines 16–18 ("To those listening throughout Eastern Europe, a special word: Although I cannot be with you, I address my remarks to you just as surely as to those standing here before me")?

    _____

    _____

    _____

3. What can be inferred about Reagan's view of Germany when he says, "There is only one Berlin" in lines 19–20?

    _____

    _____

    _____

QUICK TIP

Inference questions often combine other skills. For example, question 3 requires you to infer Reagan's point of view. Question 3 is also testing you on the skill of determining purpose. (See Lesson 5.)

4. What can you infer about Reagan's purpose for delivering this speech, based on lines 30–33 ("Standing before . . . is closed' ")?

    _____

    _____

    _____

5. Based on the information in lines 53–59, what can reasonably be inferred about the Marshall Plan's effect on West Germany?

    _____

    _____

6. What does paragraph 5 (lines 60–71) imply about Berliners?

_____

_____

_____

For answers, see page 564.

Model SAT Questions

Directions: These Model SAT Questions show how making inferences might be tested on the SAT. The answer and explanation immediately follow the question. Try the question and then review the answer and the explanation.

The Information Explosion adds knowledge at an incredible rate. In the nineteenth century, it took about fifty years to double the world's knowledge. Today, the base of knowledge doubles in less than a year. What is behind this breathtaking growth? What spurs people on to new inventions and

5 broader applications of existing technology? Ralph Hinton, an American anthropologist, had an unusual answer: "The human capacity for being bored, rather than man's social or natural needs, lies at the root of man's cultural advance."

1. The author indicates which of the following about the Information Explosion?
   A) It may result in an overreliance on technology.
   B) It will eventually saturate the world's capacity for knowledge.
   C) Its major effect has been felt in the field of inventions.
   D) Its growth rate shows no signs of slowing down.

Strategy: This question asks you to identify information explicitly stated in the passage. The passage does not mention an overreliance on technology or knowledge saturation, so choices A and B are incorrect. The passage only briefly mentions inventions, so choice C is incorrect as well. The best answer is choice D because the first four sentences in the passage highlight how the Information Explosion has an incredible growth rate that is only increasing.

2. Based upon the quotation from Ralph Hinton (lines 6–7), it can be reasonably inferred that
   A) people in more advanced countries are more likely to be bored.
   B) need rarely causes people to invent new products.
   C) modern people are more likely to invent new technologies out of boredom.
   D) advancements in technology have decreased humans' capacity for boredom.

Once you make an inference, watch for new information that confirms or changes it. Based on this new evidence, revise your original inference or make a new inference.

SAT-Type Questions

Directions: Questions 1–2 are based on the following passage.

"This [sculpture of Cleopatra] was not a beautiful work, but it was a very original and very striking one. . . . [Cleopatra] is seated in a chair; the poison of the asp has done its work and the Queen is dead. The effects of death are represented with such skill as to be absolutely repellent—and it is a question
5 whether a statue of the ghastly characteristics of this one does not overstep the bounds of legitimate art."

So wrote artist William J. Clark Jr. in *Great American Sculptures* (1878) about one of the artworks on display at the Centennial Exposition of 1876 in Philadelphia. The person who created it, Edmonia Lewis, was the
10 first professional African-American and Native American sculptor. It is symptomatic of her difficult life and neglected career that her most important piece, *The Death of Cleopatra*, which caused such a stir in Philadelphia 120 years ago, soon dropped out of sight and was not rediscovered until the late 1970s. Miraculously rescued from oblivion, it was recently conserved and has
15 been placed on view at the Smithsonian's National Museum of American Art.

1. Which of the following does William J. Clark Jr. suggest about the sculpture of Cleopatra mentioned in lines 1–6?
   A) Its depiction is more gruesome than artistic.
   B) Its most striking feature is its beauty.
   C) Its focus on Cleopatra's death makes it unoriginal.
   D) Its realistic quality makes it a masterpiece.

2. It can be inferred that the author of this passage believes that Edmonia Lewis
   A) should have sculpted more pieces.
   B) was a moderately talented sculptor.
   C) had a critical view of her own work.
   D) was an underappreciated sculptor.

Directions: Questions 3–5 are based on the following passage.

"The left hand is the dreamer; the right hand is the doer."

Scientists often discover wisdom in folk sayings. There has been much recent speculation about the hemispheres of the brain and their various functions. The right hemisphere of the brain controls the left side of the body.
5 The left hemisphere controls the right side. But there is more to the division. In most people language and language-related abilities are located in the left hemisphere. Because language is so closely related to thinking and reasoning, the left hemisphere is concerned with conscious thought processes and problem solving. It was once considered the major hemisphere. But recent
10 investigations have shown that the right hemisphere also plays an important role in the total functioning of the personality. This hemisphere provides nonverbal skills and a different mode of thinking. Whereas the left hemisphere tends to be verbal and analytic, the right hemisphere tends to be nonverbal and global. The right hemisphere is not inferior to the left. It processes information
15 differently, often providing creative leaps and sudden insights not available to the left hemisphere. The left hand, controlled by the right hemisphere, is "the dreamer," but the label should not suggest inferiority or incapacity. Both hemispheres play an equivalent, though different, role in the functioning of the personality.

Asking yourself the following types of questions can help you make good inferences: What is the author's purpose? How does this detail fit into the overall text?

3. This passage implies that
   A) both hemispheres are important for a complete personality.
   B) scientists have discredited the theory that the brain has two hemispheres.
   C) the left brain is the major hemisphere.
   D) a left-handed person performs poorly in a right-handed world.

4. An unstated assumption made by the author about the left and right brain hemispheres is that both hemispheres
   A) contribute to the creation of genius within people.
   B) are divided but must function together within people.
   C) keep the brain from being overloaded with information.
   D) control individual segments related to language.

5. What can reasonably be inferred about the right hemisphere from the passage?
   A) It processes information in confusing ways.
   B) Its main function is to analyze data.
   C) It has better problem solving and language skills than the left hemisphere.
   D) Its skills would be useful for creating music.

For answers, see page 564.

Explain Using Analogical Reasoning

The SAT will test your ability to use analogical reasoning. **Analogical reasoning** takes an idea or situation and applies it to a new situation. An analogical reasoning question might test your ability to determine the similarities and differences between two things. Or it might test you on whether you can correctly apply information from a selection to a totally new scenario or situation.

Questions about analogical reasoning may look like this:

- Based upon the passage, with which of the following statements is the author most likely to agree/disagree?

- Which of the following is most like (or most similar or most analogous to) . . .

Think It Through

As you read a passage, pay close attention to the text's main ideas. Figuring out the most important ideas can help you answer questions in which you must apply an idea to a new scenario. Underline main ideas and write summaries in the margin. These notes will make it easy to find important information quickly when you answer an analogical reasoning question. Ask yourself: What situations are similar to the one in the passage? How would this author feel about a different situation?

The following passage is from George Washington's Farewell Address (1796). Notice how main ideas are underlined and a summary is included in the margin.

The unity of government which constitutes you one people is also now dear to you. It is justly so, for it is a main pillar in the edifice of your real independence, the support of your tranquility at home, your peace abroad; of your safety; of your prosperity; of that very liberty which you so highly prize. But as it is easy to foresee that, from different causes and from different quarters, much pains will be taken, many artifices employed to weaken in your minds the conviction of this truth; as this is the point in your political fortress against which the batteries of internal and external enemies will be most constantly and actively (though often covertly and insidiously) directed, it is of infinite moment that you should properly estimate the immense value of your national union to your collective and individual happiness; that you should cherish a cordial, habitual, and immovable attachment to it; accustoming yourselves to think and speak of it as of the palladium of your political safety and prosperity; watching for its preservation with jealous anxiety; discountenancing whatever may suggest even a suspicion that it can in any event be abandoned; and indignantly frowning upon the first dawning of every attempt to alienate any portion of our country from the rest, or to enfeeble the sacred ties which now link together the various parts.

Washington stresses the importance of unity. He warns against division according to areas of the country.

An analogy question about this passage might look like this:

Based upon this passage, of which of the following situations would Washington mostly likely disapprove?

A) a group of northern states that enter into an agreement to trade exclusively with each other

B) a strong central government that gives few rights to states

C) entering into a national treaty with the government of other neighboring nations

In the passage, Washington emphasizes the importance of unity and a strong central government. Evidence for this includes the phrase "indignantly frowning upon the first dawning of every attempt to alienate any portion of our country from the rest." Thus Washington would most likely disapprove of granting the states greater independence or autonomy. He would most likely disapprove of choice A because he would view some states' decision to trade exclusively with each other as alienating other parts of the country.

QUICK TIP

Many analogical reasoning questions require you to understand the writer's point of view and then infer how the writer would apply her point of view in a different situation.

Practice

Directions: As you read the following passage, underline key ideas. Write notes in the margin.

On the domestic front, Peter the Great instigated sweeping reforms in education, the economy, and the church. He decreed that the children of the nobility and government clerks learn mathematics and geometry or forfeit their right to marry and established schools for that purpose. He also

5 encouraged them to travel to other countries to learn about and experience other cultures and invited foreigners to come to Russia to share their know-how. To increase trade with foreign countries, he "[gave] orders, made dispositions, and founded institutions," and to encourage the development of commerce and industry, he created a College of Manufacturing. Finally,

10 as Prokopovich's document suggests, he became involved in the governance of the Russian Orthodox Church, which had been much more autonomous before his reign.

The tsar labored at the reform of fashions, or, more properly speaking, of dress. Until that time the Russians had always worn long beards, which

15 they cherished and preserved with much care, allowing them to hang down on their bosoms, without even cutting the mustache. With these long beards, they wore the hair very short, except the ecclesiastics, who, to distinguish themselves, wore it very long. The tsar, in order to reform that custom, ordered that gentlemen, merchants, and other subjects—except priests and

20 peasants—should each pay a tax of one hundred rubles a year if they wished to keep their beards; the commoners had to pay one kopek each. Officials

were stationed at the gates of the towns to collect that tax, which the Russians regarded as an enormous sin on the part of the tsar and as a thing which tended to the abolition of their religion.

25   These insinuations, which came from the priests, occasioned the publication of many pamphlets in Moscow, where for that reason alone the tsar was regarded as a tyrant and a pagan; and there were many old Russians who, after having their beards shaved off, saved them preciously, in order to have them placed in their coffins, fearing that they would not be allowed to
30   enter heaven without their beards. As for the young men, they followed the new custom with more readiness as it made them appear more agreeable to the fair sex.

1. Based on this passage, which of the following ideas would Peter the Great most likely support—establishing public schools for kids from every social class or providing government funding for travel abroad programs for the wealthy? Provide evidence to support your answer.

_____

_____

_____

2. What did Peter the Great do to motivate the Russian nobility and merchants to adopt Western grooming standards?

_____

_____

_____

3. How is the situation described in this passage analogous to the following: under John Calvin's leadership, the city council of Geneva imposed a strict moral code forbidding extravagance in dress?

_____

_____

_____

4. Peter the Great would most likely agree with which of the following:
   A) The government allowing smoking but taxing cigarettes at a higher rate
   B) The government providing financial aid to religious groups

   Support your answer with evidence from the text.

   _____

   _____

   _____

For answers, see page 565.

Model SAT Question

Directions: This Model SAT Question shows how analogical reasoning might be tested on the SAT. The answer and explanation immediately follow the question. Try the question and then review the answer and the explanation.

This passage is from the essay "Civil Disobedience," written by Henry David Thoreau in 1849.

Unjust laws exist; shall we be content to obey them, or shall we endeavor to amend them, and obey them until we have succeeded, or shall we transgress them at once? Men generally, under such a government as this, think that they ought to wait until they have persuaded the majority to alter them. They think that, if they should resist, the remedy would be worse than the evil. But it is the fault of the government itself that the remedy *is* worse than the evil. *It* makes it worse. Why is it not more apt to anticipate and provide for reform? Why does it not cherish its wise minority? Why does it cry and resist before it is hurt? Why does it not encourage its citizens to be on the alert to point out its faults, and *do* better than it would have them? . . . If the injustice is part of the necessary friction of the machine of government, let it go, let it go: perchance it will wear smooth . . . . but if it is of such a nature that it requires you to be the agent of injustice to another, then, I say, break the law. Let your life be a counter-friction to stop the machine. What I have to do is to see, at any rate, that I do not lend myself to the wrong which I condemn.

1. Based on the passage, Thoreau would most approve of which of the following behaviors?
   A) Reading up on an unjust war to gain knowledge.
   B) Praying for peace and the end of slavery.
   C) Expressing outrage against the system of slavery.
   D) Refusing to pay taxes that support an unjust war.

Strategy: This question asks you to figure out Thoreau's core idea in the passage and apply it to different scenarios. In the passage, Thoreau argues that when faced with a tyrannical or unjust government, honest people should rebel against that government by refusing, for example, to obey an unjust law. The first three choices are incorrect because they don't mention any actions that would put an end to an injustice (e.g., an unjust war or slavery). Choice D is correct, since it mentions an action that would take away practical support for an injustice.

SAT-Type Questions

Directions: Questions 1–5 are based on the following passage.

If changing the way you speak your language affects thinking, what happens when you switch languages altogether? Opinions on the subject date back centuries (Charlemagne once said, "To have a second language is to have a second soul"). In the 1930s, two American linguists, Edward Sapir

5 and Benjamin Lee Whorf, popularized the hypothesis that the languages we speak may shape the ways we think.

There are some 7,000 languages spoken in the world, and they exhibit tremendous variance. [Lera] Boroditsky and her colleagues' research has shown that language—from verb tenses to gender to metaphors—can shape

10 the most fundamental dimensions of human cognition, including space, time, causality, and our relationships with others.

"I was always interested in how humans become so smart. How do we build complex knowledge? How are we able to think about things that go far beyond our physical experience?" she says. "It became clear quite

15 early that there wasn't any way to explain how we build such complex and sophisticated knowledge unless you look at patterns in language."

English speakers usually describe events in terms of agents doing things: "John broke the vase." Speakers of Spanish or Japanese are less likely to mention the agent when describing an accident: "The vase broke."

20 These differences can affect how speakers of different languages actually

remember the same event. In one study, speakers of English, Spanish, and Japanese watched videos of two people popping balloons, breaking eggs, and intentionally or unintentionally spilling drinks. When asked later who broke what, speakers of Spanish and Japanese did not remember who was

25 responsible for the accidents as well as English speakers did. But they had no problem identifying who was responsible for intentional events, for which their language would mention the agent.

1. Based on the passage, Boroditsky would most likely disagree with which of the following statements?
   A) Learning another language can impact the way people think about cause and effect.
   B) It is nearly impossible to determine patterns in language.
   C) The language people speak affects their perception of the future.
   D) The language people speak may impact their understanding of space.

2. How would Boroditsky most likely respond to Sapir and Whorf's hypothesis in lines 5–6 ("the languages . . . think")?
   A) She would assert that the notion of languages shaping the way people think is more plausible to people in their era than in modern times.
   B) She would argue that there is no link between the way people think and the language they speak.
   C) She would question the possibility that the way we think is affected by language.
   D) She would point out that new research supports and expands on their hypothesis.

3. Japanese speakers watching a video of a woman accidentally spilling a bowl of cereal would most likely say
   A) "Don't cry over spilled cereal."
   B) "The woman spilled a bowl of cereal."
   C) "The bowl of cereal was spilled."
   D) "Some milk was spilled."

4. English speakers who saw a male driver unintentionally hit another car would most likely say
   A) "The car was hit."
   B) "The man hit the car."
   C) "The car sustained damage."
   D) "I hope he has insurance."

5. What similarity do English and Spanish speakers share?
   A) Both would say "John broke the vase" if John intentionally broke it.
   B) Both would say "John broke the vase" if John accidentally broke it.
   C) Both would say "the vase broke" if John intentionally broke it.
   D) Both would say "the vase broke" if John unintentionally broke it.

For answers, see page 565.

The SAT will ask you not only to accurately interpret ideas and information in a text but also to identify **textual evidence** that supports your conclusions. You will need to identify a specific line of text that supports what the text clearly states and what it implies. In considering whether a piece of evidence adequately supports the conclusion you have drawn, ask yourself: Which sentence from the passage could I use to prove that my conclusion is correct? If someone questioned my conclusion about a passage, what phrase or sentence could I use to convince them?

One format that regularly appears on the SAT is two related questions. The first question will ask you to define a word, make an inference, identify a supporting detail, or test you over another skill. A second question will ask you to determine which part of the passage provides the best evidence for the answer to the first question. Or you may be asked to figure out which of four answer choices is supported by evidence from the passage.

Here is an example of what textual evidence questions will look like:

The passage indicates that the assumption made by scientists in lines xx–xx may be
A) flawed.
B) correct.
C) unsubstantiated.
D) unverifiable.

Which choice provides the best evidence for the answer to the previous question?
A) lines xx–xx ("First . . . documented")
B) lines xx–xx ("Undoubtedly . . . determination")
C) lines xx–xx ("In . . . opinion")
D) lines xx–xx ("According . . . relationship")

Think It Through

As you read the passage, note the interpretations the reader made in the right margin. Evidence for these interpretations is underlined in the passage.

The following excerpt is from a speech by Theodore Roosevelt given on February 13, 1905, titled "Lincoln and the Race Problem."

Neither I nor any other man can say that any given way of approaching

that problem will present in our times <u>even an approximately perfect</u>

<u>solution</u>, but we can safely say that there can never be such solution at all

unless we approach it with the effort to do <u>fair and equal justice among all</u>

5 <u>men</u>; and to demand from them in return just and fair treatment for others.

Our effort should be to <u>secure to each man, whatever his color, equality</u>

<u>of opportunity</u>, equality of treatment before the law. As a people striving

to shape our actions in accordance with the <u>great law of righteousness</u>, we

cannot afford to take part in or be indifferent to <u>oppression or maltreatment</u>

10 <u>of any man</u> who, against crushing disadvantages, has by his own industry,

energy, self-respect, and perseverance struggled upward to a position which

No perfect solution exists, but we must try to be fair and just.

No perfect solution exists, but we must try to be fair and just. Since we are good people, we must act accordingly and treat people fairly, regardless of skin color.

would entitle him to the respect of his fellows, if only his skin were of a different hue.

Question: Which line from the text supports the idea that President Roosevelt believes African Americans deserve fair and equal treatment?

Answer: Evidence to support this idea is found in lines 6–7, "Our effort should be to secure to each man, whatever his color, equality of opportunity, equality of treatment before the law."

Question: Which lines of text support the idea that the word "industry" in line 10 means "hard work"?

Answer: From the context, Roosevelt is discussing the qualities of someone who has "struggled upward"(line 11) to a position of respect. The text also lists other similar adjectives to describe such a person: "energy, self-respect, and perseverance" (line 11). These details are evidence that support the idea that "industry" means "diligence" or "hard work."

Practice

Directions: The following passage is adapted from Franklin Delano Roosevelt's First Inaugural Address given in 1933 as the nation was gripped by the Great Depression. Underline the main idea in each paragraph. Write your own thoughts and observations in the margin.

I am certain that my fellow Americans expect that on my induction into the Presidency I will address them with a candor and a decision which the present situation of our people impels. This is preeminently the time to speak the truth, the whole truth, frankly and boldly. Nor need we shrink from
5 honestly facing conditions in our country today. This great Nation will endure as it has endured, will revive and will prosper. So, first of all, let me assert my firm belief that the only thing we have to fear is fear itself—nameless, unreasoning, unjustified terror which paralyzes needed efforts to convert retreat into advance. In every dark hour of our national life a leadership
10 of frankness and vigor has met with that understanding and support of the people themselves which is essential to victory. I am convinced that you will again give that support to leadership in these critical days.

In such a spirit on my part and on yours we face our common difficulties. They concern, thank God, only material things. Values have shrunken to
15 fantastic levels; taxes have risen; our ability to pay has fallen; government of all kinds is faced by serious curtailment of income; the means of exchange are frozen in the currents of trade; the withered leaves of industrial enterprise lie on every side; farmers find no markets for their produce; the savings of many years in thousands of families are gone.

20 More important, a host of unemployed citizens face the grim problem of

existence, and an equally great number toil with little return. Only a foolish

optimist can deny the dark realities of the moment.

Yet our distress comes from no failure of substance. We are stricken by no

plague of locusts. Compared with the perils which our forefathers conquered

25 because they believed and were not afraid, we have still much to be thankful

for. Nature still offers her bounty and human efforts have multiplied it.

Plenty is at our doorstep, but a generous use of it languishes in the very

sight of the supply. Primarily this is because the rulers of the exchange of

mankind's goods have failed, through their own stubbornness and their own

30 incompetence, have admitted their failure, and abdicated. Practices of the

unscrupulous money changers stand indicted in the court of public opinion,

rejected by the hearts and minds of men.

1. What is Roosevelt's tone as he speaks to the audience?

_____

_____

_____

2. What words create the tone? List examples below.

_____

_____

_____

3. What is Roosevelt's attitude toward material goods?

_____

_____

_____

4. Which sentence provides the best evidence for your answer to the previous
question?

_____

_____

5. What does the last paragraph indicate about Roosevelt's belief regarding the cause of the crisis?

_____

_____

_____

6. Which sentence provides the best evidence for your answer to the previous question?

_____

_____

_____

For answers, see page 566.

Model SAT Questions

Directions: These Model SAT Questions show how citing textual evidence might be tested on the SAT. The answers and explanations immediately follow the questions. Try each question and then review the answer and the explanation.

This passage is from a speech African American social reformer Frederick Douglass delivered in 1852 titled "The Meaning of July Fourth for the Negro."

At a time like this, scorching irony, not convincing argument, is needed. O! had I the ability, and could I reach the nation's ear, I would, to-day, pour out a fiery stream of biting ridicule, blasting reproach, withering sarcasm, and stern rebuke. For it is not light that is needed, but fire; it is not the gentle shower, but

5 thunder. We need the storm, the whirlwind, and the earthquake. The feeling of the nation must be quickened; the conscience of the nation must be roused; the propriety of the nation must be startled; the hypocrisy of the nation must be exposed; and its crimes against God and man must be proclaimed and denounced.

10 What, to the American slave, is your Fourth of July? I answer: a day that reveals to him, more than all other days in the year, the gross injustice and cruelty to which he is the constant victim. To him, your celebration is a sham; your boasted liberty, an unholy license; your national greatness, swelling vanity; your sounds of rejoicing are empty and heartless; your denunciation of

15 tyrants, brass-fronted impudence; your shouts of liberty and equality, hollow

mockery; your prayers and hymns, your sermons and thanksgivings, with

all your religious parade and solemnity are, to Him, mere bombast, fraud,

deception, impiety, and hypocrisy—a thin veil to cover up crimes which

would disgrace a nation of savages. There is not a nation on the earth guilty of

20 practices more shocking and bloody than are the people of these United States,

at this very hour.

1. The author indicates that slaves shouldn't celebrate the Fourth of July
   because it
   A) illustrates the duplicity of celebrating freedom while slavery exists.
   B) reveals the inability of slaves to gain their freedom.
   C) exposes the nation's lack of concern for slaves.
   D) celebrates a historical day which slaves were not part of.

Strategy: To answer this question correctly, you must look carefully at the evidence Douglass provides to support the idea slaves shouldn't celebrate the Fourth of July. In lines 10–19, Douglass condemns the country for failing to live up to its sacred ideals and hypocritically claiming it does. He implies that if the country were true to its ideals, slavery would be abolished. Since Douglass suggests that America's hypocrisy is revealed when it celebrates the Fourth of July while allowing slavery, choice A is the best answer.

Remember that with paired questions, it's very important to answer the first question correctly. If you don't, you're likely to get not one but two questions wrong.

2. Which choice provides the best evidence for the answer to the previous
   question?
   A) lines 8–9 ("its crimes against God . . . denounced")
   B) lines 10–12 ("a day that . . . victim")
   C) line 14 ("your sounds of . . . heartless")
   D) lines 15–16 ("your shouts of liberty . . . mockery")

Strategy: To answer this question correctly, you must look carefully at each answer to see if it offers evidence that supports your answer to question 1. Choice A mentions crimes against God and man, so it does not provide support for the idea that slaves should not celebrate the Fourth of July because of its inherent hypocrisy. Choices C and D reveal Douglass's feelings toward the Fourth of July, but only choice B identifies the Fourth of July as a day in particular slaves feel they are victims. Choice B is the correct answer.

SAT-Type Questions

Directions: Questions 1–2 are based on the following passage.

The long association of Joseph Duveen and Henry E. Huntington resulted

in an art collection of unquestioned excellence. Like many other wealthy men

of his time, Huntington distrusted his own judgment, relying instead upon the

impeccable taste of an art dealer who had the knack of matching millionaire

5 and painting. It was Joseph Duveen who bought for Huntington and his wife,

Arabella, the two famous paintings often paired in the eyes of the public: Gainsborough's *The Blue Boy* and Lawrence's *Pinkie.* Without prodding from Duveen, Huntington would never have bought Turner's *The Grand Canal.* Over the protest of Arabella Huntington, Duveen persuaded

10 Huntington to buy Reynolds' masterpiece, *Sarah Siddons as the Tragic Muse.* Arabella had at first objected to having a picture of an actress in her home.

Another Reynolds gem, *Georgiana, Duchess of Devonshire,* was added to the Huntington collection. One painting that Arabella Huntington bought,

15 with Duveen's help, is the priceless painting, Rogier van der Weyden's *The Virgin and Christ Child.* Visitors to the Huntington Gallery in San Marino, California, owe a debt to Henry E. Huntington, who accumulated the art now available to the public. But it was Joseph Duveen who made it all possible.

1. According to the passage, Henry E. Huntington would not have amassed his world-class art collection without
   A) the generosity of Joseph Duveen.
   B) the sharp eye of Joseph Duveen.
   C) funding from his wealthy friends.
   D) the impeccable taste of his wife, Arabella.

2. Which choice provides the best evidence for the answer to the previous question?
   A) lines 5–7 ("It . . . *Pinkie*")
   B) line 11–12 ("Arabella. . . home")
   C) lines 13–14 ("Another . . . collection")
   D) lines 16–18 ("Visitors … public")

Directions: Questions 3–5 are based on the following passage.

Air quality has improved significantly since the passage of the Clean Air Act in 1970; however, there are still many areas of the country where the public is exposed to unhealthy levels of air pollutants and sensitive ecosystems are damaged by air pollution. Poor air quality is responsible for an estimated 60,000

5 premature deaths in the United States each year. Costs from air pollution-related illnesses are estimated at $150 billion per year. The goal of the U.S. air quality program is to provide ozone, particulate matter and other pollutant forecasts the public can use to limit the harmful effects of poor air quality. Our goal is to save and improve lives and reduce the number of air quality-related asthma

10 attacks; eye, nose, and throat irritation; heart attacks; and other respiratory and cardiovascular problems.

QUICK TIP

Pay careful attention to words like "best" in a question. It suggests that more than one answer choice may be correct, but one is better than the others. Start by eliminating any answer choices you know are wrong. Then pick the best answer from among the remaining choices.

Risks Related to Ground Level Ozone

Ground-level ozone (O_3) is a product of nitrogen oxides (NO_x) and volatile organic compounds (VOCs) in the presence of heat and sunlight. Motor vehicle exhaust, industrial emissions, gasoline vapors,

15 and chemical solvents are among the major sources of NO_x and VOCs responsible for harmful buildup of ground-level ozone. Even at low concentrations, ozone can trigger a variety of health problems such as lung irritation and inflammation, asthma attacks, wheezing, coughing, and increased susceptibility to respiratory illnesses.

Risks Related to Particulate Matter

20 Particulate matter (PM), or airborne particles, includes dust, dirt, soot, and smoke. Some particles are directly emitted into the air by cars, trucks, buses, factories, construction sites and wood burning to name a few examples. Other particles are formed in the air when gases from burning fuels react with sunlight and water vapor. Such gases, from incomplete combustion in motor vehicles, at

25 power plants, and in other industrial processes, contribute indirectly to particulate pollution. This pollution can cause chronic bronchitis, asthma attacks, decreased lung function, coughing, painful breathing, cardiac problems and heart attacks, as well as a variety of serious environmental impacts such as acidification of lakes and streams and nutrient depletion in soils and water bodies.

3. Which choice best supports the author's claim that air pollution exacerbates health conditions?
   A) lines 1–2 ("Air . . . 1970")
   B) lines 12–14 ("Ground-level . . . sunlight")
   C) lines 16–19 ("Even . . . illnesses")
   D) lines 24–26 ("Such . . . pollution")

4. The authors indicate that poor air quality
   A) is unfortunate but unavoidable.
   B) results primarily from motor vehicle exhaust.
   C) requires immediate action by officials.
   D) contributes to costly health problems.

5. Which choice provides the best evidence for the answer to the previous question?
   A) lines 4–5 ("Poor. . . year")
   B) lines 5–6 ("Costs . . . year")
   C) lines 6–8 ("The . . . quality")
   D) lines 14–16 ("Motor . . . ozone")

For answers, see page 566.

The Reading section of the SAT will contain ten questions that ask you to identify textual evidence. There will be two questions in each of the five reading passages.

When a question asks you to find evidence to support the answer to a previous question, find the line of text where you found the answer to that question. Then see if that line is listed as one of the answer choices. If it isn't listed, you might have the wrong answer to the previous question.

LESSON 5:

Analyzing Ideas in Informational Text

- Analyzing author's point of view and purpose
- Analyzing the use of arguments

••• Explain Analyzing Author's Point of View and Purpose

The SAT will test your ability to recognize the author's **point of view**, or opinion, of the ideas presented in the passage and determine how his or her point of view affects the style of a passage. To identify the author's **point of view**, look carefully at the words and phrases the author uses, including any words with negative or positive connotations. A useful strategy is to determine if an author's perspective is positive, negative, or neutral. Then look at the answer choices and put them into similar categories. Key words and phrases for SAT questions about author's point of view include: *position, stance, attitude, views, would most likely agree with*.

SAT questions about point of view may look like this:

- The author indicates x because he feels that . . .
- During the course of the passage, the author's focus shifts from x to x . . .
- The author indicates which of the following about x?
- The author's attitude toward x can best be described as . . .

The SAT often asks questions about an **author's purpose,** or reason for writing a selection. Purpose answers the question "Why did the author write this?" It explains the author's goals. Authors may state their intent explicitly or they may expect you to infer their purpose from details in the text. Some broad common reasons why authors write are to entertain, inform, or persuade.

The chart below lists some examples of author's purpose, the text structures that are often used for this purpose, and textual clues that can help a reader determine author's purpose.

Author's Purpose	Possible Text Structure	Clues in the Text
Persuade, convince	Cause/effect Compare/contrast	Persuasive techniques such as use of statistics, personal experiences, call to action, emotionally charged language, appeal to emotions
Inform, educate	Chronological Cause/effect	Use of facts, explanations, straightforward and objective language, presentation of results/interpretations
Entertain, amuse	Narrative	Use of anecdotes, personal stories, imagery and figurative language
Criticize, condemn	Cause/effect Compare/contrast	Use of statistics, negative/opinionated language, predictions

Some SAT questions will ask you about the purpose of an entire text. Other questions will require you to identify the purpose of part of a text, such as how one paragraph relates to the rest of the passage. In these cases, the purpose of one sentence or paragraph may be different than the overall purpose of the passage. For instance, in a persuasive piece in which an author uses mostly statistics, he or she may shift to a personal anecdote to elicit an emotional response from his or her reader.

Key words and phrases for SAT questions about author's purpose include: *main purpose, primary purpose, intention, function, in order to, functions mainly to.*

SAT questions about author's purpose often look like this:

- The main (or primary) function of the passage is to . . .

- The function of paragraph x in the passage is to . . .

- The author's purpose in x is to . . .

- The author uses x in order to . . .

The introductory material before a passage may provide clues to the purpose of a passage.

Think It Through

In the following paragraphs, details that help reveal the author's point of view and purpose are underlined, and explanatory notes are included in the margin.

Last summer, researchers at Yale published a study proving that physicists, chemists and biologists are likely to view a young male scientist more favorably than a woman with the same qualifications. Presented with identical summaries of the accomplishments of two imaginary applicants,

5 professors at six major research institutions were significantly more willing to offer the man a job. If they did hire the woman, they set her salary, on average, nearly $4,000 lower than the man's. Surprisingly, female scientists were as biased as their male counterparts.

The new study goes a long way toward providing hard evidence of a

10 continuing bias against women in the sciences. Only one-fifth of physics Ph.D.s in this country are awarded to women, and only about half of those women are American; of all the physics professors in the United States, only 14 percent are women. The numbers of black and Hispanic scientists are even lower; in a typical year, 13 African-Americans and 20 Latinos

15 of either sex receive Ph.D.s in physics. The reasons for those shortages are hardly mysterious—many minority students attend secondary schools that leave them too far behind to catch up in science, and the effects of prejudice at every stage of their education are well documented. But what could still be keeping women out of the STEM fields ("STEM" being the

20 current shorthand for "science, technology, engineering and mathematics"),

Subject: Gender bias in science

Author points out gender disparities in employment.

Author presents facts to support her purpose: there is a bias against women in the sciences.

Author uses statistics to show bias persists against both women and minorities.

Author blames alarming statistics on bias and institutional barriers.

which offer so much in the way of job prospects, prestige, intellectual stimulation and income?

As one of the first two women to earn a bachelor of science degree in physics from Yale—I graduated in 1978—this question concerns me deeply.

25 I attended a rural public school whose few accelerated courses in physics and calculus I wasn't allowed to take because, as my principal put it, "girls never go on in science and math." Angry and bored, I began reading about space and time and teaching myself calculus from a book. When I arrived at Yale, I was woefully unprepared. The boys in my introductory physics class, who

30 had taken far more rigorous math and science classes in high school, yawned as our professor sped through the material, while I grew panicked at how little I understood. The only woman in the room, I debated whether to raise my hand and expose myself to ridicule, thereby losing track of the lecture and falling further behind.

Shifts to personal experience to show her reaction to feeling ill-prepared for college-level classes.

Uses details to explain why she didn't advance as quickly as male peers.

Question: Which of the following best explains the author's point of view about women in science careers?

- She believes that women are hired less often because they don't have the right education.
- She believes that there is prejudice against hiring women scientists.
- She believes that women are usually less confident than men.

Answer: In line 10, the author states her point of view that there is a "continuing bias against women in the sciences." The middle choice is the best one.

Question: What is the author's view of her educational experiences in the sciences?

Answer: The phrases "concerns me deeply," "wasn't allowed," "angry and bored," and "woefully unprepared" show a negative view of her science education. On a multiple-choice question, you would look for answer choices that are more negative than positive and that align with the phrases mentioned above.

Question: What purpose does the author's inclusion of her personal experience in lines 23–34 serve?

Answer: In addition to facts and statistics, the author shares her own educational experiences in order to further convince her audience of her argument by using a personal connection. Her story can give readers a more emotional connection with the topic.

Question: What function do these lines serve in the passage: "I grew panicked at how little I understood. The only woman in the room, I debated whether to raise my hand and expose myself to ridicule"?

Answer: The word "panicked" and the phrase "expose myself to ridicule" lend a feeling of urgency and vulnerability to the situation the author faced. This may evoke compassion in the reader and it provides a "real-life" look at the results of the bias against women in the sciences.

Directions: The passage from the previous pages continues below. As you read it, underline words and phrases that reveal the author's perspective and intent and write your conclusions about the point of view and purpose in the margin.

In the end, I graduated summa cum laude, Phi Beta Kappa, with honors in the major, having excelled in the department's three-term sequence in quantum mechanics and a graduate course in gravitational physics, all while teaching myself to program Yale's mainframe

5 computer. But I didn't go into physics as a career. At the end of four years, I was exhausted by all the lonely hours I spent catching up to my classmates, hiding my insecurities, struggling to do my problem sets while the boys worked in teams to finish theirs. I was tired of dressing one way to be taken seriously as a scientist while dressing another to feel

10 feminine. And while some of the men I wanted to date weren't put off by my major, many of them were.

Mostly, though, I didn't go on in physics because not a single professor—not even the adviser who supervised my senior thesis— encouraged me to go to graduate school. Certain this meant I wasn't

15 talented enough to succeed in physics, I left the rough draft of my senior thesis outside my adviser's door and slunk away in shame. Pained by the dream I had failed to achieve, I locked my textbooks, lab reports and problem sets in my father's army footlocker and turned my back on physics and math forever.

20 In many ways, of course, the climate has become more welcoming to young women who want to study science and math. Female students at the high school I attended in upstate New York no longer need to teach themselves calculus from a book, and the physics classes are taught by a charismatic young woman. When I first returned to Yale in the fall of 2010,

25 everyone kept boasting that 30 to 40 percent of the undergraduates majoring in physics and physics-related fields were women. More remarkable, those young women studied in a department whose chairwoman was the formidable astrophysicist Meg Urry, who earned her Ph.D. from Johns Hopkins, completed a postdoctorate at M.I.T.'s center for space research and

30 served on the faculty of the Hubble space telescope before Yale hired her

as a full professor in 2001. (At the time, there wasn't a single other female faculty member in the department.)

The key to reform is persuading educators, researchers and administrators that broadening the pool of female scientists and making
35   the culture more livable for them doesn't lower standards. If society needs a certain number of scientists, Urry said, and you can look for those scientists only among the males of the population, you are going to have to go much farther toward the bottom of the barrel than if you also can search among the females in the population, especially the females who are at the
40   *top* of their barrel.

As so many studies have demonstrated, success in math and the hard sciences, far from being a matter of gender, is almost entirely dependent on culture—a culture that teaches girls math isn't cool and no one will date them if they excel in physics; a culture in which professors rarely encourage
45   their female students to continue on for advanced degrees; a culture in which success in graduate school is a matter of isolation, competition and ridiculously long hours in the lab; a culture in which female scientists are hired less frequently than men, earn less money and are allotted fewer resources.

And yet, as I listened to these four young women laugh at the stereotypes
50   and fears that had discouraged so many others, I was heartened that even these few had made it this far, that theirs will be the faces the next generation grows up imagining when they think of a female scientist.

1. What is the main purpose of the first paragraph (lines 1–11)?

To explain why the author decided to not choose physics as a career

2. It can be inferred from the author's reactions in lines 14–16 that her perspective on abandoning science forever is

shameful - "slunk away in shame" she feels disappointed that she allowed others to influence her decision to leave her passion behind

Do in class

3. The primary purpose of the third paragraph (lines 20–34) is to suggest that women today

experience more support for their scientific aspirations "the climate has become more welcoming

4. The fourth paragraph (lines 33–40) is primarily concerned with

_____

_____

_____

5. What is the author's perspective on our current culture of science according to the final two paragraphs (lines 41–52)?

_____

_____

_____

For answers, see page 567.

Model SAT Questions

Directions: These Model SAT Questions show how this topic might be tested on the SAT. The answers and explanations immediately follow the questions. Try the questions and then review the answers and the explanations.

This passage is from the essay "Nature" by Ralph Waldo Emerson, which was published in 1836.

Our age is retrospective. It builds the sepulchres of the fathers. It writes biographies, histories, and criticism. The foregoing generations beheld God and nature face to face; we, through their eyes. Why should not we also enjoy an original relation to the universe? Why should not we have a poetry and
5 philosophy of insight and not of tradition, and a religion by revelation to us, and not the history of theirs? Embosomed for a season in nature, whose floods of life stream around and through us, and invite us by the powers they supply, to action proportioned to nature, why should we grope among the dry bones of the past, or put the living generation into masquerade out of its faded

10 wardrobe? The sun shines to-day also. There is more wool and flax in the

fields. There are new lands, new men, new thoughts. Let us demand our own

works and laws and worship.

1. The main purpose of this passage is to
    A) encourage readers to learn about the traditions of the past.
    B) motivate readers to experience God and nature directly.
    C) convince readers that nature is an expression of the divine.
    D) persuade readers to write their own poems about nature.

Strategy: Although the passage does call for humankind to write its own "poetry and philosophy of insight," this is not Emerson's main purpose in writing the passage. Therefore, choice D can be eliminated. Similarly, the idea that nature is an expression of the divine is suggested in only one sentence—the second. Choice C is incorrect. We can also eliminate choice A, since Emerson explicitly states that humankind should reject the knowledge and traditions of the past, and experience God and nature directly. Choice B is clearly the correct answer.

2. Emerson would most likely agree with which of the following statements?
    A) Past generations were more intelligent than today's population.
    B) It is better to take a walk than read a book.
    C) It is better to find your own religion rather than spend time in nature.
    D) It is important to demand new laws because the old ones are poorly written.

Strategy: The idea that past generations were smarter is not indicated anywhere in the passage, so choice A is incorrect. While part of choice C aligns with Emerson's ideas (finding one's own religion), he does not indicate that religion is more important than nature, so choice C is incorrect. Emerson does mention demanding "our own works and laws and worship," but he does not say that old laws are poorly written. Therefore, choice D is incorrect. Choice B is correct because it best represents Emerson's perspective on directly experiencing life.

SAT-Type Questions

Directions: Questions 1–3 are based on the following passage.

In William Shakespeare's Hamlet, *Polonius is the chief counselor to the king. He is often viewed as a character with many faults.*

In too many performances of *Hamlet*, Polonius is depicted as a doddering

old man, tottering shakily on the edge of senility. In productions like these,

Polonius is often played strictly for laughs. His advice to Laertes, though not

out of keeping for a typical courtier, is ridiculed by the player's exaggerated

5 infirmity of speech and decrepitude of action. His advice to Ophelia, though

reasonable in the context of the times, is made to seem arbitrarily absurd.

His admitted garrulity is overemphasized, and his interference in the action

is made the work of a clown.

Unfortunately for Polonius, there is some justification for laughing at
his expense now and then. Hamlet derides Polonius at every opportunity,
drawing a laugh from the courtier's eagerness to please at any cost. The King
often wishes Polonius would get to the point in breaking important news
or giving advice on matters concerning Hamlet. Even the generally kindly
Queen says at one time, "More matter with less art." Yet these points are not
decisive in any full appraisal of Polonius.

Despite the audience's occasional laughter at Polonius's expense, certain facts
remain indisputably true. Till his death Polonius remains a respected member
of the court. Throughout the play he has been assigned positions of respect. The
King seems to value Polonius's judgment and advice. Though Polonius's advice
has proved faulty, the King does not object when Polonius volunteers to spy on
Hamlet and his mother. Then in her room, the Queen takes Polonius's ill-fated
advice to "be round" with Hamlet. That proves to be the wrong tack.

Polonius meets his fate on an errand he interprets as serving his king,
and his death precipitates the final tragedy. Polonius is not a nonentity, not
a character provided for comic relief. He is not a pitiful dotard. He supplies
some of the humor, to be sure, but a sound case can be made for playing him
as a reasonably typical courtier—not a mental or spiritual giant, but at least a
respectable and generally honored member of the court at Elsinore.

1. The author's primary purpose in writing this passage is to
   A) argue that Polonius is commonly portrayed in a demeaning light.
   B) assert that Polonius should be played as a senile, garrulous man.
   C) prove that Polonius's advice to the Queen has terrible consequences.
   D) suggest that Polonius should be played as a respectable courtier.

2. The author's attitude toward Polonius is best described as one of
   A) adoration.
   B) frustration.
   C) appreciation.
   D) uncertainty.

3. What function does paragraph 2 serve in the passage?
   A) It points out Polonius is too verbose.
   B) It concedes that Polonius is worthy of our laughter.
   C) It implies that Hamlet dislikes Polonius.
   D) It suggests the Queen finds Polonius tiresome.

QUICK TIP

An SAT question about the author's viewpoint may use the word "attitude" instead of "point of view" or "viewpoint." No matter which word is used, this type of question is asking you to determine the author's opinion about someone or something.

Directions: Questions 4–6 are based on the following passage.

This speech was delivered by the South African activist and politician Nelson R. Mandela on July 2, 2005.

As long as poverty, injustice and gross inequality persist in our world, none of us can truly rest. We shall never forget how millions of people around the world joined us in solidarity to fight the injustice of our oppression while we were incarcerated. Those efforts paid off and we are able to stand here and join
5   the millions around the world in support of freedom against poverty.

Massive poverty and obscene inequality are such terrible scourges of our times—times in which the world boasts breathtaking advances in science, technology, industry and wealth accumulation.

We live in a world where knowledge and information have made
10   enormous strides, yet millions of children are not in school. We live in a world where the AIDS pandemic threatens the very fabric of our lives. Yet we spend more money on weapons than on ensuring treatment and support for the millions infected by HIV. It is a world of great promise and hope. It is also a world of despair, disease and hunger.

15   Overcoming poverty is not a gesture of charity. It is an act of justice. It is the protection of a fundamental human right, the right to dignity and a decent life. While poverty persists, there is no true freedom. The steps that are needed from the developed nations are clear.

The first is ensuring trade justice. I have said before that trade justice is a truly
20   meaningful way for the developed countries to show commitment to bringing about an end to global poverty. The second is an end to the debt crisis for the poor countries. The third is to deliver much more aid and make sure it is of the highest quality.

4. The main purpose of this passage is to
   A) persuade developed countries to fight against global poverty.
   B) inform people about the problem of global poverty.
   C) point out the improperly ordered priorities of developed nations.
   D) suggest global poverty can be easily defeated.

5. The stance Mandela takes in this passage is best described as that of
   A) an observer lamenting the pervasiveness of poverty.
   B) a scholar discussing the causes and consequences of poverty.
   C) an expert using collective action to fight injustice.
   D) an activist calling for global action against poverty.

6. Mandela refers to a previous struggle in lines 2–5 ("We shall . . . against poverty") in order to

    A) stress that black South Africans now have equal rights under the law.

    B) point out that many nations helped end oppressive conditions in South Africa.

    C) suggest that taking global action to end injustice can be effective.

    D) compare one injustice, racial inequality, to another, extreme poverty.

For answers, see page 567.

Explain Analyzing the Use of Arguments

In many informational passages, the writer's point of view is based upon an opinion about a debatable issue. To support his or her point of view, the writer makes a **claim**, or states an opinion. Throughout the text, the author supports his or her claim using reasons and evidence.

A **reason** is an explanation for a claim or counterclaim. Skillful writers include enough reasons to demonstrate that a particular claim is valid and should be accepted by the reader as true. Reasons are usually based in logic and appeal to correct thinking. The word *because* is often used to link a reason to a claim.

Evidence is used to support reasons. Types of evidence include facts, such as statistics, data, examples, and personal testimony. Strong evidence is relevant to the reason being supported. It is based upon accurate research. If personal testimony is included, the person is considered to be knowledgeable or an expert about the topic.

One technique that writers use to convince an audience is to include counterclaims to their own claim. A **counterclaim** is an opposing point of view to the one the author is making. For example:

- **Claim:** The government should invest in renewable energy.

- **Counterclaim:** Some may say that the government shouldn't invest in green energy because it lacks the expertise to pick the most effective companies and technology that will make a lasting difference.

Writers include counterclaims to acknowledge the opposition and then to prove why particular opposing viewpoints are inaccurate. More broadly, incorporating counterclaims shows that the author has a thorough understanding of all aspects of a topic. Often an author will follow a counterclaim with her own refutation. This may be signaled by a contrast word, such as: *however, but, although, on the other hand, yet, in contrast, otherwise, nevertheless, nonetheless, notwithstanding, in spite of,* and *on the contrary.*

SAT questions about an author's argument might look like this:

- The central claim of the passage is that . . .

- The central problem that the author describes in the passage is that . . .

- Which piece of information best supports the claim in lines xx?

- Which choice provides the best evidence for the claim in lines xx?

- How does the graph support the author's argument?

Think It Through

For the following paragraphs, main ideas are underlined. Claims, reasons, and evidence are noted in the margins.

    SOLITUDE is out of fashion. Our companies, our schools and our culture are in thrall to an idea I call the New Groupthink, which holds that creativity and achievement come from an oddly gregarious place. Most of us now work in teams, in offices without walls, for managers who prize people skills

5 above all. Lone geniuses are out. Collaboration is in.

But there's a problem with this view. Research strongly suggests that people are more creative when they enjoy privacy and freedom from interruption. And the most spectacularly creative people in many fields are often introverted, according to studies by the psychologists Mihaly

10 Csikszentmihalyi and Gregory Feist. They're extroverted enough to exchange and advance ideas, but see themselves as independent and individualistic. They're not joiners by nature.

The reader identified the author's central claim that society is wrong to place great importance on working in groups.

Question: How does the writer support his claim?

Answer: He states that creative people are often introverts and that the creative process requires solitude.

As you read the following passage, underline the main ideas. Identify the claim, reasons, evidence, or counterclaims in the right margin.

You have probably heard about fossil fuel-related problems such as high gasoline prices and environmentally damaging crude oil spills. Because of problems such as these, biochemists are working on alternative fuel sources to power our cars, ships, and planes. Corn-based ethanol is one such source,

5 but it takes a lot of corn to produce this fuel. The production of just one liter of ethanol from corn requires thousands of liters of water, and takes up land that could be used to grow food crops. Clearly, sciences must continue to look for sources of power.

Central Claim: More alternative fuels are needed to replace fossil fuels

Question: How does the author support the claim that a new type of alternative fuel source is necessary?

Answer: The author names specific negative consequences ("high gasoline prices and oil spills") of using fossil fuels.

Question: How does the author anticipate the counterclaim that we already have alternative fuel sources?

Answer: The author points out problems with the current alternative fuel source, corn-based ethanol: "it takes a lot of corn, which requires a lot of water and land that could be used to grow food crops."

Author's claim: Society is placing too much emphasis on working in teams.

Reasons: Creative people need privacy and are often introverts.

Evidence: Study by Csikszentmihalyi and Feist

Author's claim:

Reasons:

Evidence:

Directions: For each paragraph, underline the reasons and evidence and jot down any claims and counterclaims in the right margin.

Several bioengineering companies are now engaged in producing various types of fuel from blue-green algae—the unicellular organisms that produce much of the world's oxygen. This is truly a "green" technology!

Algae can be used to produce oil, ethanol, and diesel fuels. At the
5 Massachusetts-based biotech company Joule Unlimited, scientists genetically engineer the algae to excrete tiny drops of fuel as they carry out photosynthesis. All that is needed are sunlight, seawater, fertilizer, and carbon dioxide to support the process. And that's the good part—the plan is to try to use waste carbon dioxide from nearby power plants to produce this
10 new biofuel. Using up excess carbon dioxide is a plus, since it is considered a greenhouse gas that contributes to global warming. The fuel produced by the algae is said to burn cleaner than gasoline, so that's another benefit for the environment.

A company called Sapphire Energy is also using algae to make crude oil,
15 considering it the "most economical" substitute for petroleum. Even Exxon Mobil is getting involved in the business by investing in a genetic-engineering company that can produce the algae-based fuel. Clearly, "big oil" sees that this could be the fuel of the future for all forms of transportation and they do not want to miss out on the moment—or the potential money.

20 Another good thing about algae as a fuel producer is that unlike corn, the organisms do not need to be grown on good farmland. Vats of algae can be set out in the desert to grow and make fuel. The algae are more productive than corn, producing nearly eight times as much fuel per unit of biomass. And the oil that the algae produce is a pure, high-quality fuel.

25 It remains to be seen if the algae being grown in the open fields produce as well as those in the laboratories. Some data show that the algae may need more fertilizer per hectare than crops such as corn. Also, a commercial algae fuel plant would require thousands of cubic meters of carbon dioxide every day. So the problem of getting enough waste carbon dioxide gas from power
30 plants to the algae farms has to be solved, too. In addition, although the

algae could be grown in desert environments, the facilities would still require large areas of land to produce enough fuel to compete with current gasoline supplies. Fortunately, though, it is thought that the same pipelines that are used by the oil industry could be used for pumping the algae-based fuel.

35 Still, a complete switch to the algae-derived fuel will take some time, since it is still in the pilot phase of development.

1. What is the main purpose of this selection?

_____

_____

_____

2. What evidence does the author provide to support the central claim?

_____

_____

_____

3. Why does the author include the reference to Exxon Mobil in the third paragraph?

_____

_____

_____

4. Why does the author include counterclaims in the final paragraph?

_____

_____

_____

For answers, see page 568.

Directions: These Model SAT Questions show how this topic might be tested on the SAT. The answers and explanations immediately follow the questions. Try the questions and then review the answers and the explanations.

This passage is from The History of Woman's Suffrage, Volume I, 1848–1861 *by Elizabeth Cady Stanton, Susan B. Anthony, and Matilda Joslyn Gage.*

As civilization advances there is a continual change in the standard of human rights. In barbarous ages the right of the strongest was the only one recognized; but as mankind progressed in the arts and sciences intellect began to triumph over brute force. Change is a law of life, and the development of society a natural
5 growth. Although to this law we owe the discoveries of unknown worlds, the inventions of machinery, swifter modes of travel, and clearer ideas as to the value of human life and thought, yet each successive change has met with the most determined opposition. Fortunately, progress is not the result of pre-arranged plans of individuals, but is born of a fortuitous combination of circumstances that
10 compel certain results, overcoming the natural inertia of mankind. There is a certain enjoyment in habitual sluggishness; in rising each morning with the same ideas as the night before; in retiring each night with the thoughts of the morning. This inertia of mind and body has ever held the multitude in chains. Thousands have thus surrendered their most sacred rights of conscience. In all periods of human
15 development, thinking has been punished as a crime, which is reason sufficient to account for the general passive resignation of the masses to their conditions and environments.

1. What is the author's central claim about social change?
   A) It should be embraced as a constant reality in life.
   B) It is the law of life, but only comes after struggle.
   C) It only happens when people make it happen.
   D) It will not come if people aren't willing to suffer.

Strategy: The authors assert not only that change is a constant reality in life, but also that it is always met with opposition. Since choice A covers only part of the point about change, it can't be correct. Choice B sounds right since it summarizes the authors' ideas about social change. Choice C sounds right too, but it doesn't convey the idea that change is a constant reality in life. "Suffering" is not explicitly mentioned in the text, so choice D can't be right. Choice B is the correct answer.

2. The authors indicate which of the following about progress?
   A) It is born of the passive resignation of the masses.
   B) It happens only when individuals combine their efforts.
   C) It is based on an individual's pre-arranged plans.
   D) It comes from a lucky mixture of situations.

Strategy: The authors state that "progress is not the result of pre-arranged plans of individuals, but is born of a fortuitous combination of circumstances that compel certain results." Choice D is an accurate interpretation of these lines. Choice C is wrong because it states the opposite of what the passage claims (progress happens *not* because of an individual's pre-arranged plans.) Choice A refers not to progress, but to what has happened because "thinking has been punished as a crime." It is incorrect. Choice B sounds reasonable, but it is not as accurate an interpretation as the correct answer, choice D.

• • • SAT-Type Questions •

Directions: Questions 1–3 are based on the following passage.

This passage is from President Dwight Eisenhower's Farewell Address given on January 17, 1961.

A vital element in keeping the peace is our military establishment. Our arms must be mighty, ready for instant action, so that no potential aggressor may be tempted to risk his own destruction.

Our military organization today bears little resemblance to that known by
5 any of my predecessors in peacetime, or indeed by the fighting men of World War II or Korea.

Until the latest of our world conflicts, the United States had no armaments industry. American makers of plowshares could, with time and as required, make swords as well. But now we can no longer risk emergency
10 improvisation of national defense; we have been compelled to create a permanent armaments industry of vast proportions. Added to this, three and a half million men and women are directly engaged in the defense establishment. We annually spend on military security more than the net income of all United States corporations.

15   This conjunction of an immense military establishment and a large arms industry is new in the American experience. The total influence — economic, political, even spiritual — is felt in every city, every State house, every office of the Federal government. We recognize the imperative need for this development.

Yet we must not fail to comprehend its grave implications. Our toil, resources
20 and livelihood are all involved; so is the very structure of our society.

In the councils of government, we must guard against the acquisition
of unwarranted influence, whether sought or unsought, by the military-
industrial complex. The potential for the disastrous rise of misplaced power
exists and will persist.

25 We must never let the weight of this combination endanger our liberties
or democratic processes. We should take nothing for granted. Only an alert
and knowledgeable citizenry can compel the proper meshing of the huge
industrial and military machinery of defense with our peaceful methods and
goals, so that security and liberty may prosper together.

1. What evidence does Eisenhower use to support his claim that the
   military-industrial complex is immense?
   A) The U.S. has temporary, vast armaments industry, which is an
      important part of the new American experience.
   B) The U.S. has a vast armaments industry that employs millions of
      people, and it spends more on defense than any other country.
   C) Our military establishment is essential to ensuring that potential
      aggressors cannot harm our nation.
   D) U.S. corporations outspend our military, which influences our
      country's economic, political, and spiritual well-being.

2. According to Eisenhower, in what institution could the military-industrial
   complex exert unwarranted influence?
   A) the American corporation
   B) U.S. courts of law
   C) the Pentagon
   D) the United States Congress

3. What is Eisenhower's central claim in this passage?
   A) The military-industrial complex is necessary to deter other nations
      from becoming more aggressive, but it is too weak.
   B) The military-industrial complex bears little resemblance to the
      organization of the U.S. military prior to the Korean War.
   C) The military-industrial complex is necessary, but it poses a threat to
      democratic government and must be carefully monitored.
   D) The military-industrial complex has provided high-paying jobs to
      millions of Americans.

Directions: Questions 4–6 are based on the following passage.

The following paragraphs are from "Earth's Next Generation: the Pros and Cons of Renewable Energy Sources" by Javier Espinoza.

The use and prominence of renewable energy, which uses natural resources with no finite supply, such as wind and sunlight, has been on the rise. In China, the planet's biggest polluter, renewable energy could form 26% of the country's energy mix by 2030, according to a report by

5 the Renewable Energy and Energy Efficiency Partnership. In the U.K., renewable energy has been described as the "first pillar" of the country's future energy plan.

According to the Renewables 2010 Global Status Report, in 2008 about 19% of global final energy consumption came from renewables, with 13%

10 coming from biomass, which is mainly used for heating, and 3.2% from hydroelectricity. Some believe that a massive take-up of renewable energy will move governments away from using traditional carbon-emitting sources of energy such as coal, oil and gas. Despite the apparent benefits to the environment, however, skeptics argue that renewable energy is too costly,

15 it can be a blight on the landscape in many cases and that, ultimately, it is not a realistic or truly efficient way to guarantee energy security. After all, the wind only blows 30% of the time and the sun is a rare visitor in many parts of Northern Europe. How viable renewable energy is as an alternative source of energy will depend on each country's natural resources, says Peter

20 Rossbach, head of the private equity division at Impax Asset Management Group, a London-based fund manager with a particular focus on cleaner sources of energy like solar and wind. "Each country has a different resource mix. So there is no silver bullet," he says.

4. The author refers to "the 'first pillar'" of the U.K.'s energy plan (line 6) in order to
   A) prove that some countries are focusing on renewable energy.
   B) argue that all countries should have a plan like that of the U.K.
   C) stress the importance of organized plans for the future.
   D) praise the only leader in the renewable energy battle.

5. According to the author, some people believe that governments will take which of the following actions?
   A) They will set much higher fuel efficiency standards for automobiles.
   B) They will discontinue using traditional carbon-emitting sources.
   C) They will mandate that 25% of a country's energy come from renewables.
   D) They will help make solar power more affordable to citizens.

6. What opposing viewpoint does the author include in lines 13–16 ("Despite the . . . energy security")?
   A) Renewable energy can't generate the large quantity of energy that countries need.
   B) Renewable energy relies too much on the weather for its sources of power.
   C) Renewable energy isn't a realistic way to meet a country's energy needs.
   D) Renewable energy requires large tracts of land to produce enough energy.

For answers, see page 568.

LESSON 6:

Analyzing Style in Informational Text

- Analyzing use of word choice to shape meaning and tone

- Analyzing text structures

• • • • **Explain** Analyzing Use of Word Choice to Shape Meaning and Tone

Authors choose specific words in order to communicate a particular tone and message to the reader. **Tone** is the author's attitude toward his or her subject. To identify the tone of a selection, look carefully at the words the author has selected and how they are used within the text. For instance, when Theodore Roosevelt announced the death of President McKinley, he stated, "A terrible bereavement has befallen our people." The grave, somber tone is exemplified through the words "terrible," "bereavement," and "befallen."

Often, you can describe the tone of a selection with a single adjective such as "serious" or "passionate." However, in some texts the tone may change as the writer's purpose changes. Informational texts typically have an objective, matter-of-fact tone, but they can also be written with a more subjective, emotional tone.

The following are some common adjectives used to describe tone.

"TONE" ADJECTIVES:

aggressive	dogmatic	passionate
argumentative	inquisitive	apologetic
inspirational	honest	straightforward
instructional	humble	ironic
formal	informal	subjective
objective	scholarly	reflective

An author's choice of words also shapes the text's meaning. As you read, look for important words and phrases and think about how they reveal the text's meaning. Pay particular attention to any emotionally charged language the author includes. An author who uses words such as "crisis," "vital," and "critical" conveys an urgent tone and the text's meaning may reflect this urgency by presenting solutions to the problem identified and explained. In contrast, words such as "challenge," "fundamental," and "central" convey a less urgent and more objective tone, so the text may center around simply conveying information about a problem rather than offering a solution or urging any action to address it.

Questions about tone and word meanings may be worded:

- How do the words "x," "x," and "x" in the third paragraph (lines xx–xx) help establish the tone of the paragraph?

- The author uses the phrase "x" in lines xx–xx in order to convey . . .

In the following passages, words that reveal tone and meaning are underlined, and notes about the author's tone and message are included in the right margin.

Better than most renowned works of art, Georges Seurat's *Un dimanche après-midi à l'Ile de la Grande Jatte* [*A Sunday Afternoon on the Island of La Grande Jatte*] has weathered glib popularity with its dignity intact. This shimmering array of 19th-century Parisians enjoying their day of rest, spread

5 across a monumental canvas more than 7 feet high and 10 feet wide, has been shrunken countless times on murky postcards, been laughed at in cartoon parodies, made a guest appearance in *Ferris Bueller's Day Off* and inspired a Broadway musical.

Yet Seurat's pointillist picture is as verdant and modern today as when it

10 appeared in 1886, at the eighth and final Impressionist exhibition, after which it became, in the judgment of 20th-century art historian Robert L. Herbert, "the most famous painting of the decade." Its renown only escalated after it crossed the Atlantic Ocean and found a public home in 1924 at the Art Institute of Chicago.

15 Among its enduring virtues is the ability to encourage (or withstand) any amount of attention. The anecdotal diversity of the actions by its 52 figures (48 people, three dogs, one monkey) invites scrutiny of the picture's particulars. Only on close inspection does one notice the rusty butterfly that flutters off center, the several kinds of energy (steam, wind, muscle) powering

20 the eight boats. Or the variety of brushstrokes—not so much dots but dashes— and the many combinations and intensities of colors Seurat harmonized, not only on the canvas but around the frame.

The author's word choice is careful and exact, which mirrors the respectful, knowledgeable tone.

Variety of precise adjectives: monumental, shrunken, murky

The tone is contemplative, appreciative.

These words reflect the author's praise of Seurat's work: enduring virtues, encourage, diversity.

Question: How do the underlined words and phrases in the passage contribute to its appreciative tone?

Answer: The author uses very exact language to praise the painting's "enduring virtues." Examples includes "verdant and modern" and "anecdotal diversity." The word choice is scholarly but not overly academic. The writer's tone is appreciative; he doesn't dismiss pop culture's parodies of the work.

Question: What does the author mean by writing the painting "has weathered glib popularity with its dignity intact"?

Answer: The phrase "dignity intact" suggests the painting's image has not been tarnished, so despite all the parodies and spin-offs the painting has generated, it is worthy of respect.

The following passage is a continuation of the article above. As you read, underline key words that hint at tone and meaning. Then answer the questions that follow on your own before reading the answers provided.

Equally involving is the way the arrangement of figures cleverly mirrors the experience of artist and viewer. We are witnesses to a crowd enjoying the outdoors. But only a handful of the figures are physically active—a small dog racing across the foreground, a child playing with a hoop in the middle

5 ground, and a group of rowers in the upper left. Most of the others have entered a trancelike state—almost no one is looking at anyone else—not unlike the isolating spell that the picture can cast on us.

Question: What is the tone of the passage? What words and phrases establish this tone?

Answer: Words and phrases such as "enduring virtues," "anecdotal diversity," "invites scrutiny," "variety of brushstrokes," "intensities of colors," and "harmonized" suggest that the author has a deep appreciation for the painting. Therefore, the tone is reverent.

Question: How do the phrases "trancelike state," "isolating spell," and "picture can cast" in lines 6–7 suggest how viewers might feel when looking at Seurat's painting?

Answer: The phrases "trancelike state," "isolating spell," and "picture can cast" create a dreamy, magical sense, so these words suggest that viewers feel dreamy and almost spellbound when looking at the painting.

Practice

Directions: For each paragraph, underline words that reveal tone and meaning. In the right margin, jot down notes about the author's tone and message.

The following passages are from the essay "Here Is New York" by E. B. White published in 1949.

On any person who desires such queer prizes, New York will bestow the gift of loneliness and the gift of privacy. It is this largess that accounts for the presence within the city's walls of a considerable section of the population; for the residents of Manhattan are to a large extent strangers who have pulled

5 up stakes somewhere and come to town, seeking sanctuary or fulfillment or some greater or lesser grail. The capacity to make such dubious gifts is a mysterious quality of New York. It can destroy an individual, or it can fulfill him, depending a good deal on luck. No one should come to New York to live unless he is willing to be lucky.

10 New York is the concentrate of art and commerce and sport and religion and entertainment and finance, bringing to a single compact arena the gladiator, the evangelist, the promoter, the actor, the trader and the merchant. It carries on its lapel the unexpungeable odor of the long past, so that no matter where you sit in New York you feel the vibrations of great times and

15 tall deeds, of queer people and events and undertakings . . . New York blends

the gift of privacy with the excitement of participation and better than most

dense communities it succeeds in insulating the individual (if he wants it,

and almost everybody wants or needs it) against all enormous and violent

and wonderful events that are taking place every minute. . . .

20   I mention these merely to show that New York is peculiarly constructed to

absorb almost anything that comes along (whether a thousand-foot liner out

of the East or a twenty-thousand-man convention out of the West) without

inflicting the event on its inhabitants; so that every event is, in a sense,

optional, and the inhabitant is in the happy position of being able to choose

25 his spectacle and so conserve his soul. In most metropolises, small and large,

the choice is often not with the individual at all. He is thrown to the Lions.

The Lions are overwhelming; the event is unavoidable. A cornice falls, and it

hits every citizen on the head, every last man in town. . . .

The quality in New York that insulates its inhabitants from life may

30 simply weaken them as individuals. Perhaps it is healthier to live in a

community where, when a cornice falls, you feel the blow; where, when the

governor passes, you see at any rate his hat.

I am not defending New York in this regard. Many of its settlers are

probably here merely to escape, not face, reality. But whatever it means,

35 it is a rather rare gift, and, I believe it has a positive effect on the creative

capacities of New Yorkers—for creation is in part merely the business of

forgoing the great and small distractions.

Although New York often imparts a feeling of great forlornness or

forsakenness, it seldom seems dead or unresourceful; and you always feel

40 that either by shifting your location ten blocks or by reducing your fortune by

five dollars you can experience rejuvenation. Many people who have no real

independence of spirit depend on the city's tremendous variety and sources of

excitement for spiritual sustenance and maintenance of morale. In the country

there are a few chances of sudden rejuvenation—a shift in weather, perhaps, or

45 something arriving in the mail. But in New York the chances are endless. I think

that although many persons are here from some excess of spirit (which caused

them to break away from their small town), some, too, are here from a deficiency

of spirit, who find in New York a protection, or an easy substitution. . . .

1. Describe the tone of the passage. Support your answer with quotations from the text.

_____

_____

_____

2. By using the phrase "unexpungeable odor" in line 13, White asserts that the past
   A) permeates New York's streets.
   B) often crowds out the present in New York.
   C) lures New Yorkers out onto the streets.
   D) happens over and over again.

3. What effect does the mention of being "thrown to the Lions" and falling cornices in lines 26–27 have on the reader? Why does White use these two illustrations?

_____

_____

_____

4. In the final paragraph, White uses contrasting words to describe the effect New York has on people. What emotions do these words convey? How do they contribute to White's central idea?

_____

_____

_____

For answers, see page 569.

Model SAT Question

Directions: This Model SAT Question shows how this skill might be tested on the SAT. The answer and explanation immediately follow the question. Try the question and then review the answer and the explanation.

"Why bother saving wild and endangered species? It is the fate of species to become extinct someday anyway. Why bother with snail darters and wild grains? Let's spend more time on more important problems."

These arguments have a specious reasonableness, but they couldn't be more wrong. We have a selfish interest in wild species. We need to protect them for our own survival.

1. How does the repetition of the phrase "Why bother" in the first paragraph (lines 1–2) help establish the tone of the passage?
    A) It creates a mocking tone that implies that the author disagrees with those who don't believe wild and endangered species are worth saving.
    B) It creates an objective tone that implies that the author has no opinion regarding saving wild and endangered species.
    C) It creates a serious tone that implies that the author has doubts about the usefulness of wild and endangered species.
    D) It creates a scholarly tone that implies that the author believes that saving wild and endangered species is an impossible task.

Strategy: The repetition of the phrase "Why bother" suggests the author disagrees with those who don't believe wild and endangered species are worth saving. Moreover, it suggests that he is making fun of their opinion. Choices B and D seem out of the running, since the tone is not "objective" or "scholarly." The tone of the second paragraph is certainly serious (choice C), but the author does suggest that wild and endangered species are not useful. Choice A is the best answer.

SAT-Type Questions

Directions: Questions 1–6 are based on the following passage.

The following essay offers a critique of the popular mystery genre.

"Who Cares Who Killed Roger Ackroyd?"

The title of Edmund Wilson's 1945 essay clearly indicates the writer's bias. Wilson called detective stories "wasteful of time and degrading to the intellect." Since that time other critics have sneered, condescended, and scorned the whodunit, but its popularity has rarely faltered. The detective

5 story and related types like the spy story, the horror tale, and the Dashiell Hammett type of thriller are often lumped under the general heading Mystery and earn a special shelf in most libraries. The mystery shelf is one of the most popular in every library. Novels by old favorite writers like John Dickson Carr vie with current favorites like those by Ruth Rendell,

10 P.D. James, Elizabeth George, and Tony Hillerman. Why do mysteries, and especially detective stories, often outlast their critics?

In an era when much modern fiction is plotless and loosely structured, the detective story, with its solid plot, tells a story that appeals to the child in everyone. The detective story begins somewhere and ends somewhere.

15 In between, readers are treated to twists of plot, surprises in characterization, and challenging puzzles.

Detective stories and other mysteries, though often maligned, have influenced other current fiction. Even "literary" fiction has been affected by the mystery and its close relatives. Paul Theroux's *Family Arsenal,* Robert

20 Stone's *A Flag for Sunrise,* and Margaret Atwood's *Bodily Harm* all use the conventions of the thriller.

Some writers have gone further. Michiko Kakutani has pointed out that some prestigious writers "have used the conventions of the mystery to make philosophical points about the nature of storytelling itself." Joyce Carol

25 Oates in *Mysteries of Winterthurn,* Alain Robbe-Grillet in *The Erasers,* and Jorge Luis Borges in *Death and the Compass* have added a dimension to the possibilities inherent in the mystery form.

1. How does the reference to the essay titled "Who Cares Who Killed Roger Ackroyd?" help establish the tone of the passage?
   A) It creates a sympathetic and curious tone that makes clear the author is skeptical about the attraction of mysteries.
   B) It creates a witty tone that makes clear the author is actually defending detective stories.
   C) It creates a brutally callous tone that makes clear the author cares nothing for critics' opinions.
   D) It creates a straightforwardly informative tone that makes clear the author is objective about detective stories.

2. The author's use of the words "sneered," "condescended," and "scorned" in lines 3–4 in the first paragraph functions mainly to
   A) confirm that detective stories are reputed to be too predictable to be enjoyable.
   B) emphasize that detective stories have been poorly received by literary critics.
   C) counter the claim that detective stories have been viewed with indifference by readers.
   D) support the claim that detective stories have been treated as oracles by literary critics.

3. The author uses the question "Why do mysteries, and especially detective stories, often outlast their critics?" (lines 10–11) most likely to
   A) gently mock mystery writers.
   B) praise reviewers of mysteries.
   C) comment on "literary" fiction.
   D) take a swipe at critics of mysteries.

4. The author uses the phrase "often maligned" (line 17) mainly to emphasize what he/she sees as
   A) the growing number of disgruntled mystery fans.
   B) the ability of mysteries to garner both praise and criticism.
   C) the copious amount of attention paid to mysteries.
   D) the erroneous criticism of mysteries.

5. The author uses the phrase "treated to" (line 15) most likely to
   A) demonstrate the concept that mysteries are often difficult to solve.
   B) emphasize the amount of suspense mystery readers experience.
   C) highlight the idea that reading mysteries is pleasurable.
   D) underscore the sense of mystery inherent in the genre.

6. The phrase "prestigious writers" (line 23) most directly suggests that
   A) influential authors use the mystery form.
   B) mysteries only improve the fiction genre.
   C) many writers consider reading mysteries enjoyable entertainment.
   D) most fans prefer mysteries over other literary forms.

For answers, see page 569.

For answers, see page 569.

· · · · · **Explain** **Analyzing Text Structures** ·

Skilled writers carefully organize texts in order to best convey particular ideas and pieces of information. For example, the structure of a persuasive speech may present a problem and then explain solutions to the problem. Often multiple text structures are used in one text. A description of a scientific experiment may describe the steps of the experiment in chronological order and also the causes and effects of different variables within the experiment.

Some commonly used patterns of organization are problem and solution, chronological/sequential, cause and effect, compare and contrast, and description/spatial. Oftentimes, a text will combine one or more structures.

Problem and solution	features an issue or problem that needs to be solved	problem, solution, resolved, because, since, as a result, in order to
Chronological/ sequential	conveys information in time order or in a step-by-step sequence	first, then, next, later, and finally
Spatial or descriptive	description of how something looks	as, next to, behind, across from, below that, above that, and to the right of
Cause and effect	explains the effects of an event, describes reasons why something happened	due to, thanks to, because of, leading to, for this reason, therefore, on account of, in order to, resulting in
Compare and contrast	explains how two or more things are similar to or different from one another	(compare) both, similarly, and alike, (contrast) in comparison, by contrast, but, on the other hand, on the contrary, yet, however, despite, meanwhile, as opposed to

Most questions on the SAT will not ask you to simply identify the text structures above. You will likely be asked to identity the relationship between ideas or between lines or paragraphs in a text. Some questions may ask you to explain the overall structure of a text.

Questions on text structures may be worded these ways:

- The overall structure of the passage could be described as . . .
- Lines xx–xx provide . . .

Think It Through

The following passages show words that signal the different types of text structures underlined. Notes about the type(s) being used are in the right margin.

In an intermediate French class at Merced College a few years ago, the students were assigned a five-minute oral report, to be delivered in French. The second student to stand up in front of the class was a young Hmong man. His chosen topic was a recipe for la soupe de poissone: Fish Soup.

5 To prepare Fish Soup, he said, you must have a fish, and in order to have a fish, you have to go fishing. In order to go fishing, you need a hook, and in order to choose the right hook, you need to know whether the fish you are fishing for lives in fresh or salt water, how big it is, and what shape its mouth is. Continuing in this vein for forty-five minutes, the student filled the

10 blackboard with a complex branching tree of factors and options, a sort of piscatory flow chart, written in French with an overlay of Hmong. He also told several anecdotes about his own fishing experiences. He concluded with a description of how to clean various kinds of fish, how to cut them up, and, finally, how to cook them in broths flavored with various herbs. When the

15 class period ended, he told the other students that he hoped he had provided enough information, and he wished them good luck in preparing Fish Soup in the Hmong manner.

The text has a sequential structure.

Analysis: This passage is told in sequential order, but the young man's speech itself starts with the fish and then moves backward to the fishing expedition, using reverse sequential order.

American stadium design has been stuck in a nostalgic funk, with sports franchises recycling the same old images year after year.

Still, if you have to go with a retro look, New York City could have done worse than the new Yankee Stadium and Citi Field. Both were designed

5 by Populous (formerly known as HOK Sport Venue Event) and are major upgrades over the stadiums they replaced, which had been looking more and

The passage has a compare and contrast structure.

more dilapidated over the years. <u>Both</u> should be fine places to spend a few hours watching a game.

What's more, each stadium subtly reflects the character of the franchises
10 that built them. Yankee Stadium is the kind of stoic, self-conscious monument to history that befits the most successful franchise in American sports. The new home of the Mets, <u>meanwhile,</u> is scrappier and more lighthearted. It plays with history fast and loose, as if it were just another form of entertainment.

Analysis: The passage compares and contrasts the new Yankee Stadium with Citi Field. The stadiums are similar because they share the same designer, are improvements over the stadiums they replaced, and are good places to take in a game. The differences are that Yankee Stadium is more "stoic" and "self-conscious," whereas Citi Field "is scrappier and more lighthearted."

Practice

Directions: Underline words and phrases that reveal the main ideas and structure of the text, and jot down notes synthesizing these ideas in the text. Then answer the questions that follow.

In the natural world, scientists have documented a vast range of shifts in biological behavior related to climate change, from birds laying their eggs earlier to bears emerging earlier from hibernation in time for the first blossom of spring.

5   As it turns out, humans are not excluded from such behavioral changes. Over the last 30 years, a new study has found, peak park attendance has shifted by about four days, probably in response to climate change.

"The results may come as a surprise to some," said Abe Miller-Rushing, the science coordinator for Acadia National Park and the Schoodic Education
10 and Research Center in Bar Harbor, Maine, who was not involved in the study. "One of the main ways that people often think of climate change is affecting things that are far away," he said.

Past studies have examined climate-related human behavior in terms of single events like droughts or floods. To the researchers' knowledge, this is
15 the first study to examine behavioral response to temperature changes over a long period of time.

The study, published in the *International Journal of Biometeorology*, compared park temperatures and attendance records from 1979, when the

parks started keeping reliable attendance data, to those from 2008. Of nine
20 parks experiencing significant increases in average spring temperatures,
seven exhibited corresponding shifts in peak visitor attendance, said Lauren
Buckley, a biologist at the University of North Carolina at Chapel Hill and
lead author of the paper.

"Although the public is still debating the occurrence of global warming,
25 they're already changing their behaviors," she said in an interview.

Human behavioral shifts were comparable to those noted for other
species. Of the nine parks with temperature increases since 1979, 78 percent
recorded shifts in visitor rates, and 71 percent of the species at those parks
have undergone behavioral timing changes in relation to rising temperatures.

30 Some shifts were more pronounced than others: at Grand Canyon
National Park, July 4 was the peak attendance day in 1979, whereas June 24
was the peak in 2008. At Mesa Verde National Park, visitors peaked on July
10 in 1979 and on July 1 in 2008.

Across the parks, the average shift was four days.

35 Dr. Buckley also compared attendance at parks with notable temperature
changes to attendance at parks without much change in temperature. The
timing of attendance at the latter did not change much. (The study factored
in other variables like travel costs.)

Dr. Miller-Rushing suggested that the warming trend could eventually
40 lead parks to adjust their preparations for peak periods, including the hiring
of seasonal employees. "As visitor season shifts, when those employees are
hired or working would need to shift as well," he said.

Climate change could influence the timing of many types of vacations,
like ski trips, autumn leaf viewing and bird watching, he noted.

1. Why did the author begin the article by comparing animal and human
   responses to climate change?

_____

_____

_____

_____

2. What is the purpose of lines 30–33 as related to the rest of the passage?

_____

_____

_____

_____

3. Explain how the author structures the information in this passage. Support your answer with lines from the text.

_____

_____

_____

For answers, see page 570.

For answers, see page 570.

Model SAT Question

Directions: This Model SAT Question shows how text structures might be tested on the SAT. The answer and explanation immediately follow the question. Try the question and then review the answer and the explanation.

Stamp collectors sometimes have to make a key decision: whether to concentrate on stamps that have been postally used or to collect only clean, pure, unused stamps, often direct from the printing presses. Postally used stamps are not as pretty as mint stamps. Portions of their designs have been obliterated by
5 cancellation marks. Mint stamps, on the other hand, are sparkling and clear, with every design detail clearly visible. But used stamps have something extra: actual use in the mails. Often their cancellations provide information about date and place of use. They often demonstrate the romance of the mails. Collectors of only used stamps call stamps mere labels until they perform their function in the
10 mails. Postally used stamps may conveniently be put into an album with stamp hinges, without any concern about a loss in value. On the other hand, mint stamps that have been hinged lose part of their value in the marketplace. They must thus be encased in transparent envelopes and pockets that show the stamps without sticking hinges to them. Mounting mint stamps thus takes more time, energy,
15 and money. There is something to be said for both decisions, and some collectors collect both kinds of stamps. But usually a collector has a secret preference.

1. Which choice best reflects the overall sequence of events in the passage?
   A) The advantages of collecting unused stamps are highlighted and discussed.
   B) An argument that collectors should have both types of stamps in their collections is presented.
   C) The best way to preserve both postally used and unused stamps is detailed.
   D) The benefits and drawbacks of collecting two types of stamps are described.

Strategy: The author only briefly reflects on the advantages of collecting unused stamps, so choice A can be eliminated. Choice B is incorrect since the author describes collecting both types of stamps but does not advance an argument for either one. The author does describe how both types of stamps are preserved but does not mention whether there are multiple ways to preserve stamps and the preservation method is mentioned only in order to explain the pros and cons of collecting each type. Thus, choice C is incorrect. The author focuses on the benefits and drawbacks of collecting each type of stamp. Therefore, D is the right answer.

SAT-Type Questions

Directions: Question 1 is based on the following passage.

In June, 1981, Jay Johnson started out on an incredible journey—a self-propelled trip around the United States. At no time did Johnson rely on any motorized transportation, though he used a variety of methods. He started in northern Maine and backpacked south along the Appalachian Trail to
5   Georgia. Still on foot, he reached Montgomery, Alabama. He picked up a 15-foot dory in Montgomery and rowed down the wild Alabama River to the Gulf of Mexico. Rowing 1,200 miles along the Gulf Coast, he reached Brownsville, Texas. Then he chose a bicycle for his 3,000-mile trip through the Southwest. He gave up the bicycle in Southern California and
10 backpacked north on the Pacific Coast Trail all the way to British Columbia, arriving in late September, 1982. His trip had lasted 16 months and covered nearly 10,000 miles. To help him along his unusual journey, he estimated his needs in advance and then used the Postal Service for delivery of supplies to prearranged points. He plotted his journey like a military campaign,
15 with a thorough evaluation of his abilities and needs. This was a magical experience, but there was no magic behind its success.

1. Why does the author organize the different parts of Johnson's journey in chronological order?
   A) To give the reader a sense of the difficulties Johnson faced.
   B) To give the reader a visual sense of where Johnson traveled.
   C) To allow the reader to count all of the miles Johnson covered.
   D) To point out all of the transportation methods Johnson used.

Directions: Questions 2–5 are based on the following passage.

When a forest is ravaged by fire, cut down to make way for a parking lot, or harvested for timber, there is the aesthetic loss of something beautiful. A complete ecosystem is destroyed, and the habitats of forest creatures are laid waste. There is an even more serious long-range problem, however: the
5 effect upon the balance of oxygen and carbon dioxide in the atmosphere. On the one hand, the ever-expanding use of fossil fuels has liberated into the atmosphere tremendous quantities of carbon dioxide. On the other hand, deforestation has reduced the vegetation needed to recycle the carbon dioxide, store carbon, and release essential oxygen for the world's living
10 things. Too much release of stored carbon can also potentially raise the temperature of the atmosphere through the "greenhouse effect."

Forest vegetation stores 90% of the carbon held in terrestrial ecosystems. In eastern North America there has been some improvement in recent years through reforestation. But gains in the temperate zone have been offset by
15 losses in the tropics. Wholesale destruction of tropical forests is the greatest single threat, since most of the world's arboreal vegetation is found in the vast forest of the Amazon and other tropical areas. Global awareness of the problem is needed to provide a basis for sound management of forests, the crucial agents in the carbon cycle.

2. Which choice best describes the developmental pattern of the passage?
   A) A detailed depiction of how forest creatures are under threat.
   B) A definitive response to a call to action.
   C) A serious description of a problem with the carbon cycle and its solution.
   D) A thoughtful recounting of a series of events.

3. Why does the author choose to introduce the article with the example of a fire causing aesthetic loss?
   A) To assert this is a minor issue in comparison to a fire's impact on the balance of oxygen and carbon dioxide.
   B) To suggest this is a minor issue in comparison to a fire's impact on the destruction of an ecosystem.
   C) To point out that vacationing in tropical locales could lose its appeal if tropical forests are wiped out.
   D) To convey the idea that aesthetic loss and the loss of ecosystems are equally troubling consequences of fires.

4. Lines 6–10 ("On the one . . . living things) identify
   A) A solution for mitigating the greenhouse effect.
   B) An explanation of the greenhouse effect.
   C) Two causes of the greenhouse effect.
   D) Reasons for cutting back on greenhouse gas emissions.

5. What is the purpose of lines 15–19 as they relate to the rest of the passage?
   A) To present the unintended consequences of carbon emissions.
   B) To provide a key solution to the problem of carbon emissions.
   C) To describe the largest source of carbon emissions from human activity.
   D) To detail successes in combating the problem of carbon emissions.

Directions: Questions 6–8 are based on the following passage.

In the century since Albert Einstein proposed his theory of general relativity physicists have put it through the wringer with extensive experimental tests—and it has withstood them all. But these experiments were conducted in environments of relatively weak gravity. Scientists have thus been left

5 to wonder how well the theory describes the universe under more extreme conditions, like those found in the regions around black holes. To that end a new study suggests a means of testing the limits of the theory: Researchers have determined that if general relativity does break down near black holes, the effects may be detectable in x-rays blazing off the infalling matter. The study

10 was published in *Physical Review D*.

According to general relativity, the phenomenon we experience as gravitational force is a result of spacetime (the combination of the three spatial dimensions and fourth dimension of time) curving around mass. The denser an object, the more severely it warps the fabric of spacetime and

15 the stronger its gravitational field. Around objects like black holes—the

remnants of exploded massive stars that are so compact not even light can
escape their gravitational tug—spacetime is severely distorted. Physicists
have used relativity, along with the so-called no-hair theorem, which states
that black holes only have two defining characteristics (mass and rotation),
20 to predict how spacetime curves around black holes. They call that curvature
the Kerr solution.

Proving that the Kerr solution provides an accurate description of
spacetime near a black hole would show that general relativity holds up
even in environments of extreme gravity. But so far no one has been able to
25 prove the Kerr solution's correctness. Ideally, astrophysicists would record
the motions of an object as it traveled through the region around a black
hole to characterize the spacetime curvature. But some black holes are
mere kilometers across, which is tiny on the cosmic scale. Scientists are not
currently capable of tracking a single object moving in such a confined space
30 from light-years away.

6. Which choice best reflects the overall sequence of events in the passage?
   A) An unexpected finding results in a new study being done; the results
       are inconclusive, and the study is repeated.
   B) An anomaly is observed and documented; subsequent experiments
       indicate no anomaly; the anomaly is disregarded.
   C) A new discovery leads to reconsideration of a theory; a study is
       conducted, and the theory is debunked.
   D) An experiment for testing a theory is proposed; the theory is described,
       but the experiment is found to be beyond the capability of current
       technology.

7. The author uses a cause and effect structure in paragraph 3 in order to
   A) point out that the Kerr solution is currently impossible to prove.
   B) argue that the Kerr solution is an accurate description for the spacetime
       curvature near a black hole.
   C) stress that many scientists have attempted to prove the accuracy of the
       Kerr solution.
   D) suggest that scientists should focus on other theories and experiments
       instead of the Kerr solution.

8. During the course of the first paragraph, the focus shifts from
   A) a chronological account of past experiments to the testing of a new
       theory.
   B) a step-by-step explanation of a theory to a description of its limitations.
   C) an evaluation of a theory to a description of how to test the theory's
       soundness.
   D) a description of experiments testing a theory to a new testing method.

For answers, see page 570.

LESSON 7:

Synthesizing Multiple Texts and Graphics

- synthesizing information from multiple texts
- analyzing and synthesizing information from texts and graphics

Explain Synthesizing Information from Multiple Texts

On the SAT, you will encounter paired passages that share a theme or topic. The passages may agree, disagree, or complement each other, thereby enriching the point of view presented. Often the author of the second passage will express ideas that contrast or build upon the ideas found in the first passage.

Some questions will refer solely to the first passage, and others solely to the second. These questions will ask you to identify purpose or main ideas or make inferences—skills practiced in Lessons 2–6 of this book. This lesson will prepare you to answer questions that require you to synthesize information from both passages.

Synthesizing is combining ideas from different texts. You may be asked to compare and contrast the main points, structure, or style of the two passages or draw a conclusion about how the author of one passage would view a claim made by the writer of the other passage. Examples of synthesis questions include:

- The author of Passage 1 would most likely agree with which of the following statements in Passage 2?

- Which statement describes the overall relationship between Passage 1 and Passage 2?

- The author of Passage 2 would most likely claim that the information presented in lines xx–xx of Passage 1 . . .

Think It Through

To answer questions over paired passages, carefully read the introduction. Then read the passages. As you read, jot notes in the margin that reveal relationships in ideas between the passages.

To synthesize (and not merely summarize) information, you need to make connections. Think about how the passages are organized and what their key points are. As you read, consider questions such as the following:

- Do the ideas in the passages support or oppose each other?

- What evidence or reasons do the writers use to support their ideas?

- What important points does one author make that the other would support or oppose?

- Does one passage build upon an idea mentioned in the other passage?

In the paired passages on the next page, the underlined phrases and sentences indicate connections that can be made between the passages.

The first passage below, "What Makes a Life Significant?," is from a lecture that William James, a prominent American philosopher and psychologist, presented to students in 1899. The second passage is from Framley Parsonage *by Anthony Trollope. As you read, consider how the two passages comment on human nature.*

Passage 1

In my previous talk, "On a Certain Blindness," I tried to make you feel how soaked and shot-through life is with values and meanings which we fail to realize because of our external and insensible point of view. The meanings are there for the others, but they are not there for us. There lies more than a mere interest of curious speculation in understanding this. It has the most tremendous practical importance. I wish that I could convince you of it as I feel it myself. It is the basis of all our tolerance, social, religious, and political. The forgetting of it lies at the root of every stupid and sanguinary mistake that rulers over subject-peoples make. The first thing to learn in intercourse with others is noninterference with their own peculiar ways of being happy, provided those ways do not assume to interfere by violence with ours. No one has insight into all the ideals. No one should presume to judge them offhand. The pretension to dogmatize about them in each other is the root of most human injustices and cruelties, and the trait in human character most likely to make the angels weep.

People are oblivious to others' perspectives.

Human injustices occur when people interfere with others' ways.

Passage 2

She was, moreover, one of those few persons—for they are very few—who are contented to go on with their existence without making themselves the center of any special outward circle. To the ordinary run of minds it is impossible not to do this. A man's own dinner is to himself so important that he cannot bring himself to believe that it is a matter utterly indifferent to everyone else. A lady's collection of baby clothes, in early years, and of house linen and curtain fringes in later life, is so very interesting to her own eyes that she cannot believe but that other people will rejoice to behold it. I would not, however, be held as regarding this tendency as evil. It leads to conversation of some sort among people, and perhaps to a kind of sympathy. Mrs. Jones will look at Mrs. White's linen chest, hoping that Mrs. White may be induced to look at hers.

Humans are self-involved.

When two people share their interests, they develop sympathy for one another.

1. The authors of both Passage 1 and Passage 2 would most likely agree with which of the following statements?
   A) People place too little importance on themselves.
   B) A belief in one's own self-worth is key to achieving success.
   C) Rulers too often interfere with people's personal beliefs.
   D) People should tolerate others' flaws.

Answer: In Passage 1, the author argues that people shouldn't interfere with others' own "peculiar ways of being happy." In Passage 2, when discussing how people often view their own interests as disproportionately important, the narrator does not judge this tendency harshly, stating, "I would not, however, be held as regarding this tendency as evil." Neither passage discusses choice A, people's having too little self-importance, or choice B, achieving success. Only Passage 1 references rulers, so C is incorrect. Both passages suggest their authors would agree that people should tolerate others' flaws, choice D.

2. Both Passage 1 and Passage 2 explore
   A) personal ill will.
   B) self-centeredness.
   C) deep-seated prejudice.
   D) human injustices and cruelties.

Answer: The author of Passage 1 argues that people are insensible to others' perspectives on life and the world, and this indifference leads to human injustices. Therefore choices A and C can be eliminated. Human injustices and cruelties are not mentioned by the author of Passage 2. However, the author does explore human self-centeredness. Therefore, choice B is correct.

3. In comparison with the basic premise of Passage 1, Passage 2 is more concerned with
   A) the evils brought on by monopolizing conversations.
   B) generally unselfish behavior.
   C) the pointlessness of human communication.
   D) harmless human weaknesses.

Answer: In regard to monopolizing conversations, Passage 2 explains, "I would not, however, be held as regarding this tendency as evil," so choice A can be eliminated. Passage 2 primarily describes selfish behavior. It also does not indicate that human communication is pointless. Instead the author writes, "It leads to conversation of some sort among people, and perhaps to a kind of sympathy." Thus, choice C is not correct. In essence, Passage 2 discusses the human tendency to be self-centered, but not the consequences of this tendency, whereas Passage 1 covers both, so D is the best answer.

Practice

Directions: Underline phrases and sentences that reveal the main ideas, and jot down notes synthesizing these ideas from the text. Then answer the questions that follow.

Passage 1 is from a speech delivered in 1995 by then-First Lady Hillary Rodham Clinton to the United Nations Fourth World Conference on Women. Passage 2 is a speech given by Susan B. Anthony when she illegally cast a vote during the 1872 presidential elections. Anthony's vote was illegal because women did not have the right to vote at the time.

Passage 1

The great challenge of this conference is to give voice to women everywhere whose experiences go unnoticed, whose words go unheard.

Women comprise more than half the world's population. Women are

Carefully read any material introducing the two passages. This material can provide important information about the content of the passages. It can also prepare you for the types of questions you might encounter.

70 percent of the world's poor, and two-thirds of those who are not taught to read and write.

Women are the primary caretakers for most of the world's children and elderly. Yet much of the work we do is not valued—not by economists, not by historians, not by popular culture, not by government leaders.

At this very moment, as we sit here, women around the world are giving birth, raising children, cooking meals, washing clothes, cleaning houses, planting crops, working on assembly lines, running companies, and running countries.

Women also are dying from diseases that should have been prevented or treated; they are watching their children succumb to malnutrition caused by poverty and economic deprivation; they are being denied the right to go to school by their own fathers and brothers; they are being forced into prostitution, and they are being barred from the ballot box and the bank lending office.

Passage 2

The preamble of the Federal Constitution says:

We, the people of the United States, in order to form a more perfect union, establish justice, insure domestic tranquility, provide for the common defense, promote the general welfare, and secure the blessings of liberty to ourselves and our posterity, do ordain and establish this Constitution for the United States of America.

It was we, the people; not we, the white male citizens; nor yet we, the male citizens; but we, the whole people, who formed the Union. And we formed it, not to give the blessings of liberty, but to secure them; not to the half of ourselves and the half of our posterity, but to the whole people—women as well as men. And it is a downright mockery to talk to women of their enjoyment of the blessings of liberty while they are denied the use of the only means of securing them provided by this democratic-republican government—the ballot.

1. What claim does Clinton make in Passage 1?

_____

_____

_____

2. Why, according to the author of the second passage, should women have the right to vote? Support your answer with evidence from the text.

_____

_____

_____

_____

_____

_____

3. Both of the authors would most likely agree with which of the following statements about governments?
   A) Governments may be swayed by public opinion.
   B) Governments are too often outdated and disorganized entities.
   C) Governments should treat their subjects fairly and equally.
   D) Governments should provide access to education for all people.

4. How are the methods of argumentation in the passages similar?

_____

_____

_____

How are they different?

_____

_____

_____

5. Both of the authors would most likely agree with which of the following statements about women's rights?
   A) Women in the U.S. should have the right to vote, but it is unnecessary in other countries.
   B) People should focus on other issues such as poverty and disease.
   C) Women's rights supporters have too many factions to succeed.
   D) Both men and women must recognize women's rights.

For answers, see page 571.

Directions: These Model SAT Questions show how synthesizing information from multiple passages might be tested on the SAT. Try the questions and then review the answers and explanations.

The following passages celebrate two brilliant historical periods centuries apart.

Passage 1

There have been times in human history when the earth seems suddenly to have grown warmer or more radioactive . . . I don't put that forward as a scientific proposition, but the fact remains that three or four times in history, humans have made a leap forward that would have been unthinkable under
5 ordinary evolutionary conditions. One such time was about the year 3000 B.C., when quite suddenly civilization appeared, not only in Egypt and Mesopotamia but in the Indus Valley; another was in the late sixth century B.C., when there was not only the miracle of Ionia and Greece—philosophy, science, art, poetry, all reaching a point that wasn't reached again for 2000 years—but also in India
10 a spiritual enlightenment that has perhaps never been equaled. Another was round about the year 1100. It seems to have affected the whole world; but its strongest and most dramatic effect was in Western Europe—where it was most needed. It was like a Russian spring.
In every branch of life—action, philosophy, organization, technology—there
15 was an extraordinary outpouring of energy, an intensification of existence. Popes, emperors, kings, bishops, saints, scholars, philosophers were all larger than life, and the incidents of history—Henry II at Canossa, Pope Urban announcing the First Crusade, Heloise and Abelard, the martyrdom of St. Thomas à Becket—are great heroic dramas, or symbolic acts, that still stir our
20 hearts.

The evidence of this heroic energy, this confidence, this strength of will and intellect, is still visible to us. In spite of all our mechanical aids and the inflated scale of modern materialism, Durham Cathedral remains a formidable construction, and the east end of Canterbury still looks very large and very
25 complex. And these great orderly mountains of stone at first rose out of a small cluster of wooden houses; everyone with the least historical imagination has thought of that. But what people don't always realize is that it all happened quite suddenly—in a single lifetime. An even more astonishing change took

30 place in sculpture. Tournus is one of the very few churches of any size to have
survived from before the dreaded year 1000, and the architecture is rather
grand in a primitive way. But its sculpture is miserably crude, without even the
vitality of barbarism. Only fifty years later sculpture has the style and rhythmic
assurance of the greatest epochs of art. The skill and dramatic invention
35 that had been confined to small portable objects—goldsmith work or ivory
carving—suddenly appear on a monumental scale.

Passage 2

The men who had made Florence [Italy] the richest city in Europe, the bankers
and wool-merchants, the pious realists, lived in grim defensive houses strong
enough to withstand party feuds and popular riots. They don't foreshadow
40 in any way the extraordinary episode in the history of civilization known as
the Renaissance. There seems to be no reason why suddenly out of the dark,
narrow streets there arose these light, sunny arcades with their round arches
"running races in their mirth" under their straight cornices. By their rhythms and
proportions and their open, welcoming character they totally contradict the dark
45 Gothic style that preceded, and, to some extent, still surrounds them. What has
happened? The answer is contained in one sentence by the Greek philosopher
Protagoras, "Man is the measure of all things." The Pazzi Chapel, built by the
great Florentine Brunelleschi in about 1430, is in a style that has been called
the architecture of humanism. His friend and fellow-architect, Leon Battista
50 Alberti, addressed man in these words: "To you is given a body more graceful
than other animals, to you power of apt and various movements, to you most
sharp and delicate senses, to you wit, reason, memory like an immortal god."
Well, it is certainly incorrect to say that we are more graceful than other animals,
and we don't feel much like immortal gods at the moment. But in 1400 the
55 Florentines did. There is no better instance of how a burst of civilization depends
on confidence than the Florentine state of mind in the early fifteenth century.
For thirty years the fortunes of the republic, which in a material sense had
declined, were directed by a group of the most intelligent individuals who have
ever been elected to power by a democratic government. From Salutati onwards
60 the Florentine chancellors were scholars, believers in the *studia humanitatis,* in
which learning could be used to achieve a happy life, believers in the application
of free intelligence to public affairs, and believers, above all, in Florence.

1. Which choice provides the best evidence that the author of Passage 1 would most likely agree with the claim attributed to Leon Battista Alberti in lines 50–52, of Passage 2?
   A) Lines 12–14 ("It . . . needed")
   B) Lines 22–23 ("The evidence . . . us")
   C) Lines 26–28 ("And . . . that")
   D) Lines 33–34 ("Only . . . art")

Strategy: The quotation exalts man as a god with sharp senses, wit, and reason. Choice A references the location of the enlightenment, so it is incorrect. Choice C discusses architecture, and choice D describes sculpture and art, so they are incorrect. Choice B describes "heroic energy, this confidence, this strength of will and intellect," and so is the best evidence that the author of Passage 1 would agree with Alberti's claim about humans being blessed with "sharp and delicate senses . . . wit, reason, memory." Choice B is the best answer.

2. The author of Passage 1 would most likely claim that the information presented in Passage 2
   A) adds credibility to the idea that democratic leadership was critical to achieving a sudden burst of glory.
   B) demonstrates that during a leap forward every branch of life is impacted.
   C) proves that dramatic changes can take place in a few short years.
   D) validates the notion that a few times in history humans have made an extraordinary leap forward.

Strategy: Since the author of Passage 1 doesn't bring up democratic leadership, choice A isn't the best answer. He or she does mention that every branch of life was impacted—action, philosophy, organization, technology—but the author of Passage 2 only describes how architecture changed. Therefore choice B can be eliminated. Choice C seems correct, since the author of Passage 2 refers to changes that took place during a 30-year period. However, the phrase "a few short years" suggests a period of shorter duration. Choice D is the best answer, since the Renaissance was one of the few periods in history characterized by extraordinary development.

SAT-Type Questions

Directions: Read the paired selection and answer the questions that follow.

The following two passages discuss the future of the world and population growth.

Passage 1

Concern about the dangers of overpopulation is not new. In 1589, Giovanni Botero, an Italian scholar, warned of the dangerous maladjustment of population and resources. These two, he said, were on a collision course. Two centuries later, in 1798, Robert Thomas Malthus warned, in his "Essay

5 on Population," that the world faced a terrible problem. He wrote, "The power of population is indefinitely greater than the power in the earth to

provide subsistence for man." Population grows faster than the means to feed all the new mouths.

Every year, the earth is adding a hundred million people. At current rates, by the year 2100, the earth will have to support 9 to 12 billion people. They will not only have to be fed. They'll have to be provided living space, jobs, cars, recreation, material goods and services. How can the global economy provide all the necessary elements? The traffic of life will be in perpetual gridlock.

Overpopulation is felt in many related ways. To feed growing populations, fishing fleets exhaust fisheries. Tropical rain forests are destroyed to provide farmlands, then often abandoned because of infertile soil. The ozone layer becomes more and more punctured, opening the world's populations to new dangers. Some authorities believe the greenhouse effect, the result of the combustion of fossil fuels, may cause a rise in the world's temperatures, with some significant negative results all too possible.

Rich countries can ameliorate many of the growing problems. Americans have forced petroleum companies to phase out leaded gas. Twenty-three industrialized countries have drastically reduced the rate of release of the most dangerous compounds that destroy the ozone. But poorer countries, caught in the vicious cycle of ever-increasing population, cannot do the same. All human beings want a piece of the pie, but the future may find the pie divided into shreds. Somehow the world's governments must devise ways to check the disastrous growth of population. At this writing, the future looks bleak.

Passage 2

The "authorities" have been predicting catastrophes for 400 years. So far, none have arrived. The world has had its share of troubles, of course, but the horrible apocalypse so often predicted has not materialized. No one denies the dangers of unchecked population growth. Nature's incredible fertility has led many wild creatures to starvation, as resources dwindle. But nature also institutes a system of balances. When the arctic hare diminishes in numbers, the arctic fox has fewer offspring.

There is, of course, a major difference between human beings and animals. People have shown an amazing resiliency and flexibility in

dealing with seemingly insuperable problems. Malthus was right. Given the
40 productivity of the world's farmlands at his time, we'd already be starving
now. But even though population has grown, food is still plentiful. Tons of
food were shipped to Somalia to pull the inhabitants back from the brink
of starvation. These tons of food represent food surpluses elsewhere in the
world. The ability to increase food production has been phenomenal. Ansley
45 Coale of Princeton says, "If you had asked someone in 1890 about today's
population, he'd say, 'There's no way the United States can support two
hundred and fifty million people. Where are they going to pasture all their
horses?'"

In 1949, Paul Ehrlich wrote *The Population Bomb,* a depressing scenario
50 for the future. As Mann writes, "Twenty-five years ago 3.4 billion people
lived on earth. Now the United Nations estimates that 5.3 billion do—the
biggest, fastest increase in history. But food production increased faster
still. The per capita food production rose more than 10 percent from 1968
to 1990. The number of chronically malnourished people fell by more
55 than 16 percent." Though some authorities declare that the good days are
ending, others insist that by using modern agricultural methods, Third World
countries could keep that favorable trend going.

Pessimists overlook the fact that trends can be reversed. Many former
forests were cut down for farms only to return to forests when the farms were
60 abandoned. In 1875, six counties in the lower Hudson Valley contained
573,003 acres of forest. By 1980, the forests covered an area three times as
large. American forests as a whole are bigger and healthier now than they were
at the turn of the century. Salmon are returning to American rivers. White-tailed
deer, once hunted to the point of near-extinction, are now more numerous than
65 ever. Wild turkeys are reaching levels near those of their precolonial days. All
these happy events occurred while the population was growing.

1. The author of Passage 1 refers to Botero and Malthus (lines 1–8) in order
   to
   A) contrast their respective positions on population growth.
   B) quote their statistics on modern population growth.
   C) show that concerns over population growth aren't new.
   D) make use of their studies of explosive growth in populations.

2. As used in line 7, "subsistence" is closest in meaning to
   A) fortitude.
   B) survival.
   C) luxuries.
   D) fulfillment.

3. Lines 22–29 (final paragraph of Passage 1) indicate that the author believes that
   A) poor countries must work to ameliorate the problems arising from overpopulation.
   B) environmental catastrophe will happen if governments fail to intervene.
   C) wealthy countries are responsible for depleting the planet's resources.
   D) human ingenuity will prevent an apocalypse from happening.

4. Which choice best describes the developmental pattern of Passage 1?
   A) an elaborate account of a problem and solution
   B) a careful sifting of fact from fiction
   C) a definitive response to public outcry
   D) a detailed description of cause and effect

5. How do the words "concern," "danger," and "warned" in the first paragraph of Passage 1 (lines 1–2) help establish the tone?
   A) They create an urgent tone that makes clear the author considers the subject serious.
   B) They create a dubious tone that makes clear the author does not have confidence in the information provided.
   C) They create a critical tone that makes clear the author is skeptical of claims that overpopulation is a major issue.
   D) They create an alarmed tone that makes clear the author believes nothing can be done to change the outcome of overpopulation.

6. The author of Passage 2 places the hope for human survival on
   A) zero population growth.
   B) the astonishing rise in food production.
   C) significantly increasing renewable energy.
   D) human ingenuity and flexibility.

7. As used in line 32, "apocalypse" is closest in meaning to
   A) prophecy.
   B) destruction.
   C) revelation.
   D) war.

8. Which choice best states the relationship between the two passages?
   A) Passage 2 refutes the central claim advanced in Passage 1.
   B) Passage 2 advocates an alternative approach to a problem discussed in Passage 1.
   C) Passage 2 provides further evidence to support an idea introduced in Passage 1.
   D) Passage 2 exemplifies an attitude promoted in Passage 1.

9. The authors of both passages would most likely agree with which of the following statements about overpopulation?
   A) It can result in famine in human populations.
   B) It can lead to starvation in animal populations.
   C) It is a problem that has been around for a long time.
   D) It can lead to a decline in people's quality of life.

10. How would the author of Passage 1 most likely respond to the points made in the final paragraph of Passage 2?
    A) These few examples do not successfully address global problems such as the destruction of rain forests and the greenhouse effect.
    B) This paragraph endorses the wrong solution for the problems related to overpopulation.
    C) Despite setbacks and obstacles, nature always finds a way to achieve its own ends.
    D) Salmon returning to rivers and forests to their former glory demonstrate how nature has the ability to quickly rebound after disastrous events.

For answers, see page 572.

···· Explain Analyzing Information from Texts and Graphics ····

Authors use **charts** and **graphs** to compare, summarize, organize, and highlight significant ideas and information. The ability to understand and analyze this type of visual information is a vital reading skill that you'll be expected to demonstrate on the SAT. You'll be asked to analyze information presented in tables, graphs, and charts, and determine how it relates to information provided in text. You'll also be required to integrate information and ideas presented visually with those presented in text.

Graphs, tables, and charts are the three types of graphics you're most likely to see on the SAT. Writers use graphs to communicate information in the following ways:

- Line and bar graphs show patterns and trends in data over time.

- Tables organize information into rows and columns using headers to label information.

- Charts that present data or information visually (e.g., the slices in a pie chart) are often used to show the relationship between subsets of data.

As you read the passage and study the graphics, look for significant information, ideas, and claims. This will help you when answering questions that ask you to synthesize or compare information from a graph and prose passage.

Questions about graphic organizers might look like this:

- It can be inferred from the passage and graphic that . . .

- Which of the following conclusions is supported by the graph?

- Which of the following sentences best interprets the data in the graph?

- Which choice completes the sentence with accurate data based on the graph?

QUICK TIP

When you come to a passage paired with a graphic organizer, look quickly at the organizer's headers before reading the passage. As you read the passage, underline any content that relates to the information from the graphic organizer.

The following examples model how to mark significant words, phrases, and facts in a text and make connections between a text and a graph.

One of the most frustrating parts of the sluggish recovery has been paltry wage gains for most workers. The stock market may be booming, corporate profits increasing, and home values rising, but middle- and lower-class workers often don't truly feel the benefit of such improvements unless wages
5 rise.

Meager wage gains for workers is a troublesome trend.

But wage stagnation isn't just a problem borne of the financial crisis. When you look at the relationship between worker wages and worker productivity, there's a significant and, many believe, problematic, gap that has arisen in the past several decades. Though productivity (defined as the
10 output of goods and services per hours worked) grew by about 74 percent between 1973 and 2013, compensation for workers grew at a *much* slower rate of only 9 percent during the same time period, according to data from the Economic Policy Institute.

A wide gap exists between worker productivity and pay.

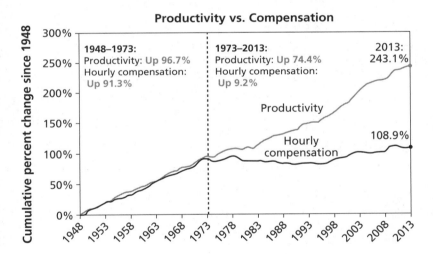

Productivity vs. Compensation

Source: Economic Policy Institute

As you analyze and compare the graph and the passage, ask yourself questions:

- Is the information in the graph and the text similar or different?
- Does the graph provide more information about ideas presented in the passage?
- Does the graph provide evidence to support a claim by the text?

Conclusions about the text and the graph:

- Both compare productivity and hourly compensation.

(continued on next page)

- The graph supports the passage's claim that "Though productivity (defined as the output of goods and services per hours worked) grew by about 74 percent between 1973 and 2013, compensation for workers grew at a *much* slower rate of only 9 percent during the same time period."

- The graph gives more history about the relationship between productivity and wages by including data from 1948–1973. Until 1973, wages kept pace with the increase in productivity.

Practice

Directions: As you read the following passages, underline key ideas. Study the bar graph and then answer the questions.

Passage 1

In the Northern hemisphere, winter is the time for flu, but the exact timing and duration of flu seasons vary. While seasonal flu outbreaks can happen as early as October, most of the time flu activity peaks between December and February, although activity can last as late as May. The "peak month
5 of flu activity" is the month with the highest percentage of respiratory specimens testing positive for influenza virus infection. During flu seasons between 1982 and 2014, flu activity most often peaked in the month of February, followed by January, then December, and finally March.

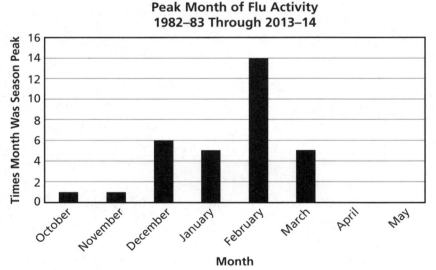

**Peak Month of Flu Activity
1982–83 Through 2013–14**

Source: www.cdc.gov

1. Does the graph support the author's claim that "While seasonal flu outbreaks can happen as early as October, most of the time flu activity peaks between December and February, although activity can last as late as May"? Explain why or why not.

_____

_____

Passage 2

The Civil War was America's bloodiest conflict. The unprecedented violence of battles such as Shiloh, Antietam, Stones River, and Gettysburg shocked citizens and international observers alike. Nearly as many men died in captivity during the Civil War as were killed in the whole of the

5 Vietnam War. Hundreds of thousands died of disease. Roughly 2% of the population, an estimated 500,000 men, lost their lives in the line of duty. Taken as a percentage of today's population, the toll would have risen as high as 6 million souls.

The human cost of the Civil War was beyond anybody's expectations.

10 The young nation experienced bloodshed of a magnitude that has not been equaled since by any other American conflict.

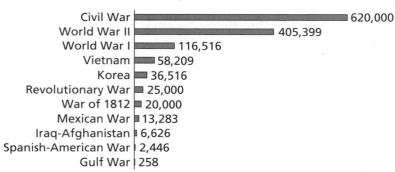

Military Deaths in American Wars

War	Deaths
Civil War	620,000
World War II	405,399
World War I	116,516
Vietnam	58,209
Korea	36,516
Revolutionary War	25,000
War of 1812	20,000
Mexican War	13,283
Iraq-Afghanistan	6,626
Spanish-American War	2,446
Gulf War	258

Source: The Civil War Trust

2. Write two claims you can make that compare the military deaths in two or more wars based on the information in the chart.

_____

_____

_____

_____

Passage 3

Immigrating to a new country requires facing many different risks and, for most, the United States still offers the best shot at success, at least as defined by employment prospects. This is based upon data from the OECD's Migration Database to measure employment for different education levels in

5 countries containing the most immigrants.

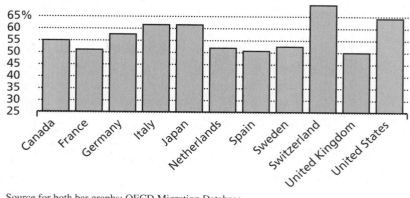

Immigrants with Less than a High School Education
Employment rate age 25 to 64

Source for both bar graphs: OECD Migration Database

It seems the best prospects for an immigrant with less than a high school education are in Switzerland or the United States. In America, 64 percent of uneducated immigrants are employed, significantly more than natives with the same level of education (44 percent). In Spain, the poor economy is to

10 blame: native workers are even less likely to work. In France, there are other forces at play: Nearly 57 percent of French natives are employed, compared to 51 percent of immigrants.

More education changes the picture significantly. An engineering PhD faces a completely different labor market than someone who didn't

15 finish high school. The figure below shows employment rates of immigrants with at least an undergraduate degree.

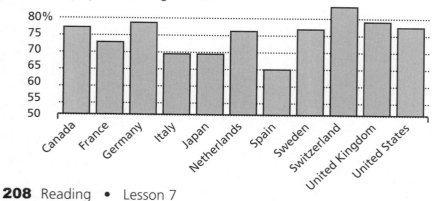

Immigrants with at Least an Undergraduate Degree
Employment rate age 25 to 64

3. Do the graphs provide support for the claim that immigrants with a college undergraduate degree are more likely to be employed than immigrants with less than a high school education? Explain your answer.

_____

_____

4. Do the graphs support the claim that "the United States still offers the best shot at success" for immigrants? Explain your answer with information from the bar graphs.

_____

_____

_____

For answers, see page 573.

Model SAT Questions

Directions: These Model SAT Questions show how this skill might be tested on the SAT. The answers and explanations immediately follow the two questions. Try the questions and then review the answers and the explanations.

The following article is adapted from a Washington Post *article titled "The U.S. Ranks 26th for Life Expectancy, Right Behind Slovenia."*

Back in the 1970s, Americans typically lived longer than residents of other countries. Not anymore: A new report shows that the United States' average lifespan has fallen one year behind the international average, lower than Canada and Germany, more akin to the Czech Republic and Poland.

5 This isn't to say our life expectancy has gone down. Quite the opposite: you can actually expect to live about eight years longer in the United States right now than you would have in 1970. But our life expectancy is growing a lot more slowly than other countries.

This report reveals the United States as a country that is spending tons and tons

10 on health care—but getting way less than other countries out of that investment. It exposes a country that's really great at buying fancy medical technologies, but not so fantastic at using those medical technologies to extend life.

"While life expectancy in the United States used to be one year above the OECD [Organization for Economic Cooperation and Development] average

15 in 1970, it is now more than one year below the average," the authors write.

"Many possible explanations have been suggested for these lower gains in life expectancy, including the highly fragmented nature of the U.S. health system, with relatively few resources devoted to public health and primary care, and a large share of the population uninsured." We're spending a lot on health care

20 but, when it comes to life expectancy, not getting much back in return.

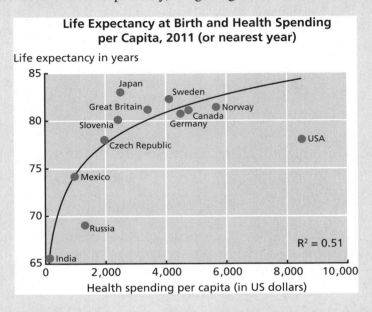

Life Expectancy at Birth and Health Spending per Capita, 2011 (or nearest year)

1. Data in the graph most strongly supports which of the following claims from the passage?

   A) A new report shows that the United States' average lifespan has fallen one year behind the international average

   B) You can actually expect to live about eight years longer in the United States right now than you would have in 1970.

   C) Many possible explanations have been suggested for these lower gains in life expectancy, including the highly fragmented nature of the U.S. health system.

   D) We're spending a lot on health care but, when it comes to life expectancy, not getting much back in return.

Strategy: The graph compares health spending and life expectancy among several countries. It does not indicate the national average lifespan, so choice A is not the best answer. The data is from 2011 not 1970. Choice B is incorrect. Although the graph does indicate that Americans are spending much more on health care than other countries, it does not try to explain reasons for this. Choice C is also incorrect. Choice D is the best answer.

2. Data in the graph about life expectancy at birth and health spending per capita most strongly support which of the following statements?

   A) Spending more on health care guarantees a better life expectancy.

   B) Russia's low life expectancy is due to its low level of health care spending.

   C) Swedish citizens live longer than Americans, but spend far less on health care.

   D) Norwegians spend half as much on health care as Americans.

Strategy: The graph suggests there is a correlation between health spending and longevity, though not in the case of the United States. Therefore, choice A can be eliminated. It also shows that Russians have a relatively low life expectancy. However, factors other than a low level of health spending might be responsible for this life expectancy. So choice B can't be right. The graph supports choice C, but look at choice D to make sure choice C is the best answer. Norway spends about $5,600 per person and the U.S. spends approximately $8,500 per person. This is not half as much. Therefore, the answer must be choice C.

SAT-Type Questions

Directions: Questions 1–3 are based on the following passage and graph.

The following article is adapted from a Science News *article titled "Hands-free Chemistry."*

Chemists are accustomed to crafting molecules through dozens of arduous steps that might yield a blockbuster drug, but more often result in pharmaceutical flops. On white boards and scraps of paper, researchers sketch hexagons and zigzags, the backbones of molecules. By drawing an

5 additional oxygen atom on one side of a molecule or squeezing a nitrogen group onto the other, for example, chemists try to subtly change the design to make better molecules. Maybe those improvements will knock out a drug's side effects or beef up a material's toughness. But once they are moved from the drawing board into round-bottom flasks, forging and

10 sculpting those modified molecules can take years of trial and error.

Chemist Martin Burke of the University of Illinois at Urbana-Champaign was eager to move more quickly. The old flask-based chemistry scheme allowed him to snap fragments of molecules together like Lego building blocks. The method works by forging carbon-carbon bonds between molecular fragments.

15 Each block has a linker. In a chemical reaction, the linkers help bring the two molecular fragments together and connect their carbons.

By adding a compound with a halogen (elements such a bromine and chlorine) as a linker on one side of the molecular fragment and a boronic acid on the other, the building blocks can snap together like train cars. But with

20 two essentially sticky ends on each block there was no way to control which ends were coupling in what order.

In 2007, in the *Journal of the American Chemical Society,* Burke and Eric

Gillis reported their trick to control coupling: a removeable cap, called MIDA (N-methyliminodiacetic acid), that fits over the boronic acid to keep it from
25 hooking up until desired.

Figure 1

Building a small molecule

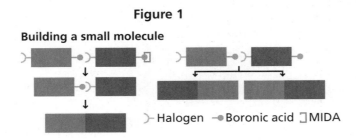

)- Halogen -●Boronic acid ⊐MIDA

Clever caps Using a chemical cap called MIDA, researchers can control the assembly of potential drugs using linkable molecular fragments, shown here as blocks. Each block has a boronic acid linker on one end and a halogen-containing linker on the other. With the removable MIDA cap covering the boronic acid, the blocks can snap together in only one way (left). With no cap, the blocks have two options (right), which is problematic. Source: J.LI ET AL/SCIENCE 2015

1. The blocks on the right side of the figure best illustrate which of the following ideas from the article?
   A) Improvements in a drug's molecular design may eradicate negative side effects of a medicine.
   B) Modifying molecules can take years of experimenting to find a useable combination.
   C) Molecules with two connectors can combine in multiple ways.
   D) Complex chemical reactions draw two molecular fragments together and connect their carbons.

2. The figure provides the best support for which of the following statements from the passage?
   A) lines 1–3 ("Chemists are . . . pharmaceutical flops")
   B) lines 4–7 ("By drawing an additional . . . better molecules")
   C) lines 8–10 ("But once they . . . of trial and error")
   D) lines 17–19 ("By adding a compound . . . like train cars")

3. From the passage and the illustration, it can be inferred that
   A) combinations of molecules hypothesized on paper often can't be reproduced in the lab.
   B) chemical linkers allow molecular fragments to bond and break apart with ease.
   C) MIDA can fit over halogen or boronic acid linkers.
   D) MIDA will allow chemists greater control and flexibility when working with molecules.

Directions: Questions 4–5 are based the following passage and graph.

The following article is adapted from an article from The Atlantic *titled "How Smartphones Hurt Sleep."*

Smartphones and tablets disrupt sleep, in part, because they emit what's known as "blue" light. This light is picked up by special cells behind our eyeballs, and it communicates to the brain that it's morning. (Red light, meanwhile, signals that it's time to go to sleep). . .

5 All of this blue light suppresses melatonin, a hormone that helps with sleep timing and circadian rhythms. At night, our melatonin levels are supposed to rise in anticipation of sleep. In 2013, scientists at Rensselaer Polytechnic Institute asked 13 people to use electronic tablets for two hours before bed. They found that those who used the tablets while wearing orange
10 goggles, which filter blue light, had higher levels of melatonin than those who either used the tablets without goggles on or, as a control, with blue-light goggles on.

The harm caused by blue light has been replicated over and over. In another study, a group of Harvard researchers compared the effect of
15 6.5 hours of exposure to blue light, compared to similarly bright green light. The blue light suppressed melatonin for twice as long, and it shifted sleep schedules by three hours, compared to an hour and a half.

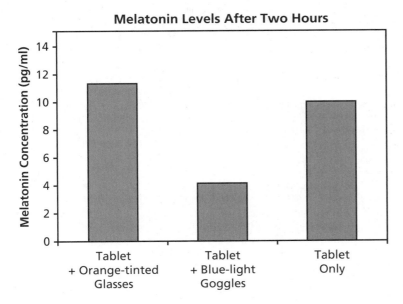

Melatonin Levels After Two Hours

Source: RPI

4. The graphic following the passage offers evidence that
   A) wearing blue-light goggles while using a tablet results in similar melatonin levels to not wearing any eyewear.
   B) melatonin levels remain unaffected by wearing orange-tinted glasses, blue-light goggles, or no eyewear at all.
   C) wearing orange-tinted glasses while using a tablet results in increased melatonin levels compared to not wearing any glasses.
   D) melatonin levels receive the greatest boost when tablet users wear no glasses or goggles at all.

5. Do the data in the graphic provide support for the author's claim that blue light is harmful because it disrupts sleep?
   A) Yes, because the data provides evidence that blue light suppresses melatonin production, which helps with sleep.
   B) Yes, because wearing orange-tinted glasses reduced the output of blue light from the tablet.
   C) No, because the data do not provide evidence about blue light as a cause of lower melatonin production.
   D) No, because the data do not indicate whether glasses tinted with green or yellow light produced a similar result to orange-tinted glasses.

Directions: Questions 6–8 are based on the following passage and graphic.

The following article is adapted from a Tech Times *article titled "Using Technology to Multitask Affects the Gray Matter in Our Brains."*

Technology has made multitasking easier than ever. We can simultaneously watch TV and scroll through social media newsfeeds on laptops while reading texts on smartphones. But all that multitasking could be shrinking the structure of our brains.

5   According to new research from the University of Sussex, people who regularly use multiple media devices have less gray-matter density in a specific part of the brain than people who use one device at a time.

Published in the journal *PLOS One*, the research is the first to reveal links between multitasking on different media devices and brain structure.

10   "Media multitasking is becoming more prevalent in our lives today and there is increasing concern about its impacts on our cognition and social-emotional well-being," says Sussex neuroscientist Kep Kee Loh.

The researchers asked 75 healthy men and women how often they divided their attention between different tech devices. This included sending a text
15 while listening to music or talking on the phone while watching a movie.

The participants were then given brain scans, which showed that, compared with people who used one device at a time, this group had less dense gray matter in the anterior cingulate cortex (ACC), the part of the brain that is involved in processing emotion.

20   The researchers are not sure whether people with less-dense gray brain structures are more likely to be multitaskers or if the multitasking causes the gray brain structures to shrink.

Other studies found that learning how to juggle and learning map routes increased the gray-matter density in certain parts of the brain.

25   While multitasking with tech gadgets could be shrinking our brain density, an unrelated study found that this practice also shortens attention span, making it harder to focus.

Typical Mobile Internet Activities While Watching TV in the U.S. in 2010

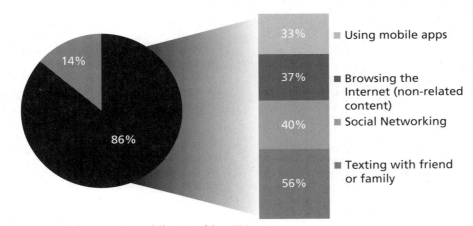

■ Access Mobile Internet While Watching TV
■ Don't Access Mobile Internet

Source: Survey of 8,384 cell phone owners ages 13 to 64

6. According to the chart, people who use mobile Internet while watching television are most often
   A) sending a text message.
   B) using apps.
   C) looking up information about what they are watching on television.
   D) accessing social networking sites.

7. Do data in the chart provide support for the author's claim that multitasking may be shrinking the structure of user's brains?

   A) Yes, because the data provides evidence that 86 percent of people access mobile Internet while watching TV.

   B) Yes, because the data illustrates the many ways people use the Internet to multitask.

   C) No, because the data merely provide evidence that a large majority of people use technology to multitask.

   D) No, because the data provide evidence that people who access mobile Internet use it to communicate with friends and family.

8. Based upon the chart and the text, it can be inferred that

   A) More women than men access social networking sites while watching TV.

   B) The 86 percent of people who reporting using television and the Internet in the chart may have less gray-matter than the 14 percent who don't multitask.

   C) Multitasking has caused gray matter to shrink in the 86 percent of people who access mobile Internet while watching TV.

   D) People who use the Internet to read or play educational games while watching TV may increase their gray-matter density in certain parts of the brain.

For answers, see page 573.

Reading Domain SAT-Type Practice Test

Directions: The following section provides practice over all the skills from Lessons 1–7 tested on the Reading section of the SAT. Read through each passage and answer the questions. To practice under the same time limit as the SAT, allow yourself 65 minutes to take the test. A reproducible bubble sheet can be found on page 12. Answers and explanations immediately follow the test on pages 231–242.

Questions 1–10 are based on the following passage.

This passage is from Henry James, an excerpt from his story "The Real Thing." The setting is England in the late 1800s. The narrator is an artist who specializes in portrait painting but also does commercial illustration to support himself.

When the porter's wife (she used to answer the house-bell), announced "A gentleman—with a lady, sir," I had, as I often had in those days, for the wish was father to the thought, an immediate vision of
5 sitters. Sitters my visitors in this case proved to be; but not in the sense I should have preferred. However, there was nothing at first to indicate that they might not have come for a portrait. The gentleman, a man of fifty, very high and very straight, with
10 a moustache slightly grizzled and a dark grey walking-coat admirably fitted, both of which I noted professionally—I don't mean as a barber or yet as a tailor—would have struck me as a celebrity if celebrities often were striking. It was a truth of which
15 I had for some time been conscious that a figure with a good deal of frontage was, as one might say, almost never a public institution. A glance at the lady helped to remind me of this paradoxical law: she also looked too distinguished to be a "personality." Moreover one
20 would scarcely come across two variations together.

Neither of the pair spoke immediately—they only prolonged the preliminary gaze which suggested that each wished to give the other a chance. They were visibly shy; they stood there letting me take
25 them in—which, as I afterwards perceived, was the most practical thing they could have done. In this way their embarrassment served their cause. I had seen people painfully reluctant to mention that they desired anything so gross as to be represented on
30 canvas; but the scruples of my new friends appeared almost insurmountable. Yet the gentleman might have said "I should like a portrait of my wife," and the lady might have said "I should like a portrait of my husband." Perhaps they were not husband and
35 wife—this naturally would make the matter more delicate. Perhaps they wished to be done together— in which case they ought to have brought a third person to break the news.

"We come from Mr. Rivet," the lady said at last,
40 with a dim smile which had the effect of a moist sponge passed over a "sunk" piece of painting, as well as of a vague allusion to vanished beauty. She was as tall and straight, in her degree, as her companion, and with ten years less to carry. She
45 looked as sad as a woman could look whose face was not charged with expression; that is her tinted oval mask showed friction as an exposed surface shows it. The hand of time had played over her freely, but only to simplify. She was slim and stiff,

and so well-dressed, in dark blue cloth, with lappets and pockets and buttons, that it was clear she employed the same tailor as her husband. The couple had an indefinable air of prosperous thrift—they evidently got a good deal of luxury for their money. If I was to be one of their luxuries, it would behoove me to consider my terms.

"Ah, Claude Rivet recommended me?" I inquired; and I added that it was very kind of him, though I could reflect that, as he only painted landscapes, this was not a sacrifice.

The lady looked very hard at the gentleman, and the gentleman looked round the room. Then staring at the floor a moment and stroking his moustache, he rested his pleasant eyes on me with the remark:

"He said you were the right one."

"I try to be, when people want to sit."

"Yes, we should like to," said the lady anxiously.

"Do you mean together?"

My visitors exchanged a glance. "If you could do anything with ME, I suppose it would be double," the gentleman stammered.

"Oh yes, there's naturally a higher charge for two figures than for one."

"We should like to make it pay," the husband confessed.

"That's very good of you," I returned, appreciating so unwonted a sympathy—for I supposed he meant pay the artist.

A sense of strangeness seemed to dawn on the lady. "We mean for the illustrations — Mr. Rivet said you might put one in."

"Put one in—an illustration?" I was equally confused.

"Sketch her off, you know," said the gentleman, colouring.

It was only then that I understood the service Claude Rivet had rendered me; he had told them that I worked in black and white, for magazines, for story-books, for sketches of contemporary life, and consequently had frequent employment for models.

1

Which choice best summarizes the passage?
A) A painter attempts to talk a couple into hiring him to paint their portraits.
B) A painter becomes suspicious of two visitors pretending to be wealthy.
C) A painter scrutinizes the appearance of two people he's interested in painting.
D) A painter misunderstands at first the reason for a couple's visit to his studio.

2

Which choice best describes the developmental pattern of the passage?
A) A confusing situation eventually made clear
B) A detailed description of a pleasant encounter
C) A sympathetic portrait of unfortunate people
D) An insightful analysis of misleading appearances

3

As used in lines 27–31, the word "gross" most nearly means
A) relating to the physical.
B) disgusting in appearance.
C) lacking in refinement.
D) offensively fat.

4

The main purpose of the second paragraph is to

A) describe how uneasy the couple is about why they are there.

B) suggest that the visiting man and woman may not be married.

C) illustrate how polite and refined both the narrator and his guests are.

D) show how brilliantly insightful the narrator is when meeting new people.

5

Which choice provides the best evidence for the answer to the previous question?

A) lines 27–31 ("I had seen . . . almost insurmountable")

B) lines 31–34 ("Yet the gentleman . . . my husband")

C) lines 34–36 ("Perhaps they were not . . . more delicate")

D) lines 36–38 ("Perhaps they wished . . . to break the news")

6

The voice of the narrator is most accurately described as

A) arrogant.

B) suspicious.

C) puzzled.

D) condescending.

7

Which of the of the following best describes what the use of words and phrases such as "visibly shy" (line 24), "looked round the room" (line 62), "anxiously" (line 67), and "stammer" (line 71) convey about the gentleman and the lady?

A) They are attempting to hide some problem between them from the painter.

B) They are worried that having their portrait painted may be beneath them.

C) They are feeling extremely uncomfortable about the reason for their visit.

D) They are not at all sure that they can actually afford the painter's services.

8

As used in line 77, "unwonted" most nearly means

A) rare

B) unforeseen

C) refined

D) surprising

9

Why is the narrator confused by his conversation with the couple?

A) He cannot tell by what they say if they want separate portraits or one together.

B) He had assumed that they had come to hire him and not to have him hire them.

C) He sees clues in their manner of dress that suggest they cannot really afford him.

D) He generally works as a landscape painter so he's not sure why they came to him.

10

Which choice provides the best evidence for the answer to the previous question?

A) lines 6–8 (" However, there . . . for a portrait")

B) lines 36–38 (" Perhaps they wished . . . break the news")

C) lines 52–54 (" The couple . . . luxury for their money")

D) lines 58–60 (" . . . and I added . . . not a sacrifice")

Questions 11–22 are based on the following passages.

Below are two excerpts from books by English philosophers of the past. Both passages address the issue of education and its place in life. Passage 1, by Adam Smith, appeared in 1776, the year of the Declaration of Independence. Passage 2, by John Locke, appeared almost a century earlier, in 1690.

Passage 1

A man without the proper use of the intellectual faculties of a man, is, if possible, more contemptible than even a coward, and seems to be mutilated and deformed in a still more

5 essential part of the character of human nature. Though the state was to derive no advantage from the instruction of the inferior ranks of people, it would still deserve its attention that they should not be altogether uninstructed. The state, however,

10 derives no inconsiderable advantage from their instruction. The more they are instructed the less liable they are to the delusions of enthusiasm and superstition, which, among ignorant nations, frequently occasion the most dreadful disorders.

15 An instructed and intelligent people, besides, are always more decent and orderly than an ignorant and stupid one. They feel themselves, each individually, more respectable and more likely to obtain the respect of their lawful superiors, and

20 they are therefore more disposed to respect those superiors. They are more disposed to examine, and more capable of seeing through, the interested complaints of faction and sedition, and they are, upon that account, less apt to be misled into any

25 wanton or unnecessary opposition to the measures of government. In free countries, where the safety of government depends very much upon

the favourable judgment which the people may form of its conduct, it must surely be of the highest

30 importance that they should not be disposed to judge rashly or capriciously concerning it.

Passage 2

A sound mind in a sound body is a short but full description of a happy state in this world. He that has these two has little more to wish for; and he

35 that wants either of them will be but little the better for anything else. Men's happiness or misery is for the most part of their own making. He whose mind directs not wisely will never take the right way; and he whose body is crazy and feeble will never

40 be able to advance in it. I confess there are some men's constitutions of body and mind so vigorous and well framed by nature that they need not much assistance from others; but by the strength of their natural genius they are from their cradles carried

45 towards what is excellent; and by the privilege of their happy constitutions are able to do wonders. But examples of this kind are but few; and I think I may say that of all the men we meet with, nine parts of ten are what they are, good or evil, useful

50 or not, by their education. 'Tis that which makes the great difference in mankind. The little, or almost insensible impressions on our tender infancies, have very important and lasting consequences: and there 'tis, as in the fountains of some rivers, where

55 a gentle application of the hand turns the flexible waters in channels, that make them take quite contrary courses; and by this direction given them at first in the source, they receive different tendencies, and arrive at last at very remote and distant places.

11

Based upon the context, the phrase "even a coward" (line 3) as used in Passage 1 serves mainly to

A) label the coward the most detestable of all persons.

B) deepen the guilt of a person who lives in constant fear.

C) absolve cowards of all personal responsibility.

D) emphasize the importance of using the intellect properly.

12

What is the author's intended message in Passage 1?

A) Only the upper classes should be educated.

B) Universal education benefits society in many ways.

C) All students should attain certain educational standards.

D) The government should pay school fees for poor children.

13

The language in lines 9–11 ("The state . . . from their instruction") and lines 21–26 ("They are more disposed . . . to the measures of government") helps give Passage 1 which of the following tones?

A) aggressive and dogmatic

B) concerned and uneasy

C) measured and reasonable

D) optimistic and inspirational

14

The author uses a cause and effect structure in Passage 1 in order to

A) highlight the benefits of universal education.

B) warn citizens about dangerous factions in the government.

C) emphasize the main purpose of government.

D) argue that aristocrats must educate the masses.

15

The word "capriciously" in line 31 of Passage 1 most nearly means

A) unpredictably.

B) vigorously.

C) slyly.

D) impulsively.

16

According to Passage 1, a good reason for the state to support education is to

A) maintain financial solvency.

B) model pure altruism.

C) reduce unrest among citizens.

D) encourage military training.

17

Which choice provides the best evidence for the answer to question 16?

A) lines 1–5 ("A man without . . . of human nature")

B) lines 6–9 ("Though the state . . . altogether uninstructed")

C) lines 9–11 ("The state, however . . . from their instruction")

D) lines 21–26 ("They are more disposed . . . measures of government")

18

The main idea of Passage 2 is that

A) having a sound mind is more important than having a sound body.

B) education above all else determines a man's success in life.

C) people arrive at different places because of their education.

D) individuals are responsible for their own happiness.

19

Which choice provides the best evidence for the answer to question 18?

A) lines 32–33 ("A sound mind . . . in this world")

B) lines 36–40 ("Men's happiness . . . advance in it")

C) lines 40–46 ("I confess there . . . to do wonders")

D) lines 47–51 ("But examples . . . in mankind")

20

The author of Passage 2 is most likely to disagree with which of the following ideas regarding education?

A) Intelligence plus character—that is the goal of true education.

B) Education is the key to unlock the golden doors of freedom.

C) Education is not preparation for life; education is life itself.

D) Education is the movement from darkness to light.

21

Both Passage 1 and Passage 2 are alike in their

A) emphasis on good health and a developed mind.

B) attention to the benefits of education.

C) celebration of the naturally brilliant individual.

D) suggestion that the state must support education.

22

Passage 2 differs from Passage 1 in its

A) emphasis on individual rather than state efforts.

B) indifference to the consequences of ignorance.

C) unemotional appraisal of current educational practices.

D) glorification of universal education.

Questions 23–31 are based on the following passage.

The following passage is adapted from the essay "How 'Bigger' was Born" by Richard Wright. In it, Wright discusses the impulses and forces that played a part in the writing of his novel Native Son.

I am not so pretentious as to imagine that it is possible for me to account completely for my own book, *Native Son*. But I am going to try to account for as much of it as I can, the sources of it, the
5　material that went into it, and my own years' long changing attitude toward that material. . . .

　　The more closely the author thinks of why he wrote, the more he comes to regard his imagination as a kind of self-generating cement
10　which glued his facts together, and his emotions as a kind of dark and obscure designer of those facts. Always there is something that is just beyond the tip of the tongue that could explain it all. Usually, he ends up by discussing something far afield,
15　an act which incites skepticism and suspicion in those anxious for a straight-out explanation.

　　Yet the author is eager to explain. But the moment he makes the attempt his words falter, for he is confronted and defied by the inexplicable
20　array of his own emotions. Emotions are subjective and he can communicate them only when he clothes them in objective guise; and how can he ever be so arrogant as to know when he is dressing up the right emotion in the right Sunday suit? He is always left
25　with the uneasy notion that may be any objective drapery is as good as any other for any emotion.

　　And the moment he does dress up an emotion, his mind is confronted with the riddle of that

"dressed up" emotion, and he is left peering with
30 eager dismay back into the dim reaches of his own
incommunicable life. Reluctantly, he comes to the
conclusion that to account for his book is to account
for his life, and he knows that that is impossible. Yet,
some curious, wayward motive urges him to supply
35 the answer, for there is the feeling that his dignity as
a living being is challenged by something within him
that is not understood.

So, at the outset, I say frankly that there are
phrases of *Native Son* which I shall make no attempt
40 to account for. There are meanings in my book of
which I was not aware until they literally spilled out
upon the paper. I shall sketch the outline of how I
consciously came into possession of the materials
that went into *Native Son*, but there will be many
45 things I shall omit, not because I want to, but simply
because I don't know them.

The birth of Bigger Thomas goes back to my
childhood, and there was not just one Bigger, but
many of them, more than I could count and more
50 than you suspect. But let me start with the first
Bigger, whom I shall call Bigger No. 1.

When I was a bareheaded, barefoot kid in
Jackson, Mississippi, there was a boy who terrorized
me and all of the boys I played with. If we were
55 playing games, he would saunter up and snatch
from us our balls, bats, spinning tops, and marbles.
We would stand around pouting, sniffling, trying to
keep back our tears, begging for our playthings. But
Bigger would refuse. We never demanded that he
60 give them back; we were afraid, and Bigger was bad.
We had seen him clout boys when he was angry and
we did not want to run that risk. We never recovered

our toys unless we flattered him and made him feel
that he was superior to us. Then, perhaps, if he felt
65 like it, he condescended, threw them at us and then
gave each of us a swift kick in the bargain, just to
make us feel his utter contempt.

That was the way Bigger No. 1 lived. His life was
a continuous challenge to others. At all times he took
70 his way, right or wrong, and those who contradicted
him had him to fight. And never was he happier than
when he had someone cornered and at his mercy;
it seemed that the deepest meaning of his squalid
life was in him at such times. I don't know what the
75 fate of Bigger No. 1 was. His swaggering personality
is swallowed up somewhere in the amnesia of my
childhood. But I suspect that his end was violent.
Anyway, he left a marked impression upon me;
maybe it was because I longed secretly to be like
80 him and was afraid. I don't know.

23

As used in line 1, "pretentious" most nearly means
A) high-sounding but with little meaning.
B) using more words than are required.
C) assuming a sense of self-importance.
D) having a meaningful connection.

24

The author writes about how he often "ends up discussing something far afield" (line 14) because he
A) believes his own personal experiences are too painful to relate.
B) wants to convey the difficulty of expressing emotions in words.
C) considers most of his childhood experiences of little literary value.
D) finds literary digressions the best way to keep readers engaged.

25

Which of the following evidence best supports your answer to question 24?

A) lines 3–6 ("But I am going . . . toward that material")

B) lines 12–13 ("Always there . . . explain it all")

C) lines 20–24 ("Emotions are . . . Sunday suit")

D) lines 31–33 ("Reluctantly . . . that is impossible")

26

The discussion regarding emotions in lines 17–20 ("Yet . . . emotions") serves mainly to emphasize the difficulty of

A) finding figurative language to capture feelings.

B) transforming subjective feelings into understandable words.

C) transferring personal experiences into fiction.

D) making personal experiences seem believable.

27

What does Wright primarily mean to suggest about novelists in lines 38–46 ("So, at the outset . . . know them")?

A) They usually find their best material through careful observations.

B) They often draw upon childhood experiences as sources for their fiction.

C) They are usually people who are perceptive readers of a wide array of works.

D) They often include meanings in their work that even they are not aware of.

28

The author, in describing his experiences with the bully, suggests that at the time he

A) resolved to use the painful experience in a novel one day.

B) felt degraded in having to compliment their tormentor.

C) wished to form a group with other boys to defeat the bully.

D) believed the bully would eventually become a success in life.

29

In line 73, the word "squalid" most nearly means

A) mean and unclean.

B) sorry and poor.

C) dishonorable and sordid.

D) depressing and uncertain.

30

Which of the following best describes the author's attitude toward Bigger No. 1?

A) fearful but admiring

B) reverent and accepting

C) affectionate but intimidated

D) open and appreciative

31

Which choice provides the best evidence for the answer to question 30?

A) lines 62–64 ("We never recovered . . . superior to us")

B) lines 64–67 ("Then, perhaps . . . utter contempt")

C) lines 75–77 ("His swaggering . . . my childhood")

D) lines 78–80 ("Anyway, he left . . . and was afraid")

Questions 32–41 are based on the following passage.

This passage is an article from The Washington Post *that discusses growing concerns about raising enough food in the future to feed the world's rapidly growing population.*

It's a question that keeps crop scientists up at night: How are we possibly going to feed the world over the next few decades?

After all, consider what we're up against: The
5 global population is expected to swell from 7 billion today to 9.6 billion by 2050. The rising middle class in China and India is eating more meat than ever. And this is all happening at a time when we're setting aside a greater slice of
10 farmland for biofuels *and* trying not to cut down any more forests (which exacerbates climate change). Doing this in a sustainable manner is tricky.

In theory there's a simple solution here: The
15 world's farmers will just need to get better at squeezing more productivity out of existing farmland. Crop yields have been steadily improving since the advent of synthetic fertilizer and modern agricultural techniques. So those
20 yields will just need to keep improving in the years to come.

But there's a big problem: This isn't happening. Or at least, it's not happening fast enough. A recent peer-reviewed study in the journal *PLOS*
25 *ONE* found that crop yields haven't been rising at a sufficient pace to meet projected demand by 2050.

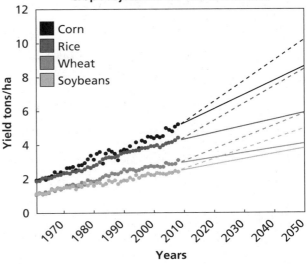

Graph 1
Crop Projections vs. World Demand

Source: www.washingtonpost.com

The study takes a careful look at historical improvements in crop yields for corn, rice, wheat
30 and soybeans. Yields per acre have been growing fairly constantly in all four areas. The solid lines show what would happen if this growth continued.

And it's not enough. The dashed lines above show how productivity would need to grow even *more*
35 rapidly for the world to satisfy expected demand and double global food production by 2050 in a sustainable manner, without razing more forests for farmland. "Current rates," the authors note, "are not achieving this goal."

40 The paper also finds that crop productivity growth isn't uniform around the world. In some places, crop yields are actually stagnating. In the U.S. Midwest, wheat yields per acre have been rising at a decent 2 percent per year. But in parts of India or Eastern
45 Europe, they've basically flat-lined. The same holds true for other crops: "China, India and Indonesia are witnessing rice yield increases of only 0.7%, 1.0%, and 0.4% improvement per year," the paper notes.

There are two big reasons why yield gains could be stagnating, explained Jonathan Foley, an agricultural expert at the University of Minnesota. "In many parts of the world, we haven't seen enough investment in agriculture because of economics or policies or institutions," he said. Many former Soviet states, say, could improve their yields through better fertilizer use. They just aren't doing it.

But in some parts of the world, there's a more worrisome prospect—farmers are doing everything they can to squeeze more productivity out of their farmland, but they're starting to hit a biological "wall," a limit on how much yields can keep rising.

"We can sometimes bust through these walls with technology, genetics, better seeds," Foley says. Indeed, this is a place where people hope that genetically modified crops might be able to boost yields. "But at a certain point," Foley says, "we run up against fundamental physiological limits for plants. If billions of years of evolution can't figure it out, are we going to be able to? That I don't know."

So what can the world actually do? If crop yields don't improve quickly enough, then something will have to give. Food prices could start spiking further in the years ahead. Or humans might just start clearing away bigger swaths of forest for new farmland, which could exacerbate climate change. Neither seems ideal.

But there are other options, too. In a 2009 essay for *Scientific American,* Foley argued that the world should focus on five big things: 1) Stop razing forests and savannahs for farmland. 2) Focus on boosting yields where it's technologically doable, especially in Africa. 3) Figure out how to use water and fertilizer more efficiently everywhere. 4) Pare back the amount of meat in our diets. 5) Cut down on the enormous amount of food waste worldwide.

Graph 2
Wheat production in India

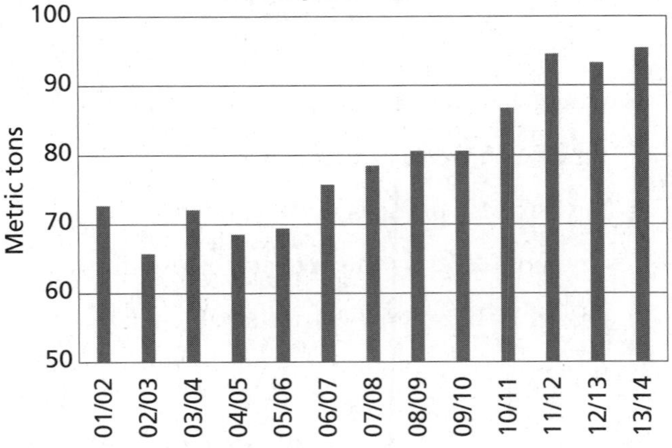

Source: Ministry of Agriculture, India

32

In lines 14–21 ("In theory . . . years to come"), the author states that the world can solve the global food shortage if farmers

A) purchase new, more efficient machinery.

B) follow better farming practices.

C) practice crop diversification.

D) increase agricultural productivity.

33

In line 11, the word "exacerbates" most nearly means

A) to directly cause.

B) to nearly destroy.

C) to interfere with.

D) to make more severe.

34

What purpose does paragraph 2 (lines 4–13) serve in the passage as a whole?

A) It gives several reasons to support the fear of a worldwide food shortage.

B) It introduces the issue of climate change and how it relates to agriculture.

C) It explains why more countries are eating more meat than they have historically.

D) It makes a connection between the world fuel shortages and food shortages.

35

In Graph 1, the gap between projected yield and expected demand is the widest for which of the following crops?

A) corn

B) rice

C) wheat

D) soybeans

36

How does Graph 2 support the information in the article?

A) It illustrates that wheat crop yields have slowed in recent years in one country.

B) It shows how the solution to the food crisis is for countries to grow more wheat.

C) It suggests that land planted in cotton could better be used for growing wheat.

D) It reflects how improvements in agriculture have greatly raised wheat yields in one country.

37

Which choice provides the best evidence for the answer to question 36?

A) lines 42–45 ("In the U.S. Midwest . . . basically flat-lined")

B) lines 48–54 ("There are two big reasons . . . he said")

C) lines 54–55 ("Many former Soviet states . . . better fertilizer use")

D) lines 57–61 ("But in some parts . . . can keep rising")

38

According to Foley, the reasons for the stagnation of crop yields include

A) government disinterest in agriculture and farmer incompetence.

B) lack of investment in agriculture and plants' physiological limits.

C) poor farming practices and agricultural laws that hurt farmers.

D) the planting of single crops and the overuse of pesticides.

39

Which of the following details from the passage provides the best evidence to support your answer to question 38?

A) lines 45–48 ("The same holds true . . . the paper notes")

B) lines 52–57 ("In many parts . . . just aren't doing it")

C) lines 72–74 ("If crop yields . . . will have to give")

D) lines 75–78 ("Or humans . . . climate change")

40

In line 68, the word "fundamental" most nearly means

A) a basic concept.

B) a generally accepted truth.

C) an essential part of something.

D) a base for expansion.

41

The author proposes all of the following solutions to the problem of inadequate crop yields EXCEPT

A) cut down on the amount of meat in our diets.

B) reduce food waste throughout the world.

C) use water and fertilizer more efficiently.

D) set aside more land for farming food crops.

Questions 42–52 are based on the following passage.

This passage is from an article titled "Spider Silk: Is It the Skin of the Future?"

Severe injuries to the skin are both painful and dangerous. The skin forms a barrier between the body and the world, protecting it from dehydration and bacteria. When a person loses skin, due to a

5 burn, bedsore, or other serious injury, doctors try to replace it with grafts of healthy skin. However, this is not always possible. So scientists have been researching other methods of regrowing skin to place on open wounds.

10 One proposed method of replacing lost skin is to take a patient's own skin cells, genetically modify them to be resistant to bacteria, and grow them in a test tube. The cells are then placed on a collagen mesh, to which they adhere and grow.

15 The artificial skin is then placed as a graft onto the injured skin. These sheets of mesh encourage growth of the bottom layer of skin (dermis), to which doctors add small pieces from the patient's top layer of skin (epidermis). This then

20 grows and spreads over the new dermis.

Collagen gives skin its structure and elasticity, but it is not the strongest material available. Scientists have discovered that spider silk is a strong and suitable material for forming the matrix

25 of new skin cells. A tissue engineer, Hanna Wendt, at Medical School Hannover in Germany, has suggested that spider silk is stronger than collagen and helps skin tissue to regrow within a matter of weeks. In fact, scientists have referred to it as the

30 "toughest known natural material." In addition, unlike other tissue transplants, the spider silk does not cause an immune response from the recipient's body.

Wendt and her colleagues obtained the material

35 from the silk glands of golden silk orb-weaver spiders. The silk has stretchiness as well as strength, which makes it suitable for tissue replacement. The silk is woven in meshes onto steel frames. Human skin cells placed on these meshes grow very well,

40 as long as they are supplied with nutrients and suitable growing conditions. As with the collagen technique, the scientists were able to grow both the dermis and epidermis layers of skin-like material on top of the silk mesh. The human cells recreated

45 the structures normally found in the layer of dermis, such as capillaries, sweat glands, and nerve endings.

Unfortunately, it is not yet possible to harvest large enough quantities of spider silk for medical uses. Wendt thinks that synthetic silk fibers will

50 have to be developed to fill the need for human skin replacement. As a result, many researchers are now trying to find ways to grow synthetic spider silk.

Another option is to produce more spider silk by other means. One way that is being developed is the

55 production of spider silk in goat's milk! Nigerian dwarf goats at a Montreal-based biotechnology company have been genetically enhanced (with the spider's silk-producing gene) to produce spider silk protein within their milk. This silk is skimmed off

60 when the goat is milked. In laboratory experiments, this silk has been mixed with human skin cells, forming a matrix composed of dermis and epidermis. The skin produced is both resilient and strong.

In fact, the fibers produced in the goat's milk are

65 so strong that they are referred to as BioSteel. So besides the use of spider silk in artificial skin, there are other potential applications, such as in prosthetic devices, bulletproof vests, and fishing line. All of these products have less of an

70 environmental impact than synthetic materials such as Kevlar and Polypropylene, since silk is a natural protein that biodegrades over time. It is hoped that materials made from spider silk will be available for medical and industrial uses within the

75 next few years.

42

Which of the following statements best expresses the main idea of the passage?

A) Spider silk may work better than collagen for growing new skin cells.

B) Growing skin for medical purposes can be accomplished in multiple ways.

C) Spider silk can be produced in quantity by genetically enhanced goats.

D) Scientists are finding multiple uses for the natural strength of spider silk.

43

Which choice provides the best evidence to support your answer to question 42?

A) lines 7–9 ("So scientists . . . open wounds")

B) lines 25–29 ("A tissue engineer . . . a matter of weeks")

C) lines 54–55 ("One way . . . goat's milk")

D) lines 72–75 ("It is hoped . . . next few years")

44

As used in lines 24 and 62, the word "matrix" most nearly means

A) a set form that is used to mold new forms.

B) a rectangular form used for weaving materials.

C) a stable surface in which something can develop.

D) a method for growing skin cells in collagen.

45

Which of the following best describes the relationship between Wendt's research into using spider silk to replace human skin and earlier research into collagen?

A) Wendt's investigations focused more on overcoming the human body's immune response to tissue transplants.

B) Wendt's experiments with spider silk often employed methods that had proven successful with collagen.

C) Wendt's research was hindered by the fact that spider silk is not as easily obtained as collagen.

D) Wendt's team knew from the start that spider silk would be better for skin replacement because it's stronger.

46

Which choice provides the best evidence to support your answer to question 45?

A) lines 30–33 ("In addition . . . recipient's body")

B) lines 38–41 ("Human skin cells . . . suitable growing conditions")

C) lines 41–44 ("As with the collagen . . . the silk mesh")

D) lines 47–49 ("Unfortunately . . . medical uses")

47

The author of the passage makes the statement in lines 30–33 ("In addition, unlike . . . body") in order to

A) prove that spider silk is by far the most promising substance for skin replacement.

B) provide another compelling reason for exploring medical uses of spider silk.

C) cast doubt on whether spider-made substances can safely be grafted onto humans.

D) note the major drawback of collagen and other methods of tissue transplants.

48

What purpose does paragraph 5, lines 47–52 ("Unfortunately. . . spider silk"), serve in the passage as a whole?

A) It describes new methods for manufacturing synthetic spider silk.

B) It compares naturally produced spider silk to synthetic silks.

C) It explains why spider silk will never be used much for medical purposes.

D) It introduces the importance of finding new ways to produce spider silk.

49

As used in line 47, the word "harvest" most closely means

A) grow.

B) yield.

C) produce.

D) collect.

50

The author's attitude toward human skin replacement research can best be described as

A) skeptical.

B) critical.

C) positive.

D) neutral.

51

Which conclusion can be drawn from the information given about using Nigerian dwarf goats to produce spider silk proteins in lines 53–65 ("Another option . . . as BioSteel")?

A) Genetic techniques may be used to produce spider silk in unprecedented quantities.

B) The Nigerian dwarf goats are unaffected by the changes introduced to their genes.

C) Fibers produced in the goats' milk are not as strong as naturally made spider silk.

D) Larger mammals such as cows could produce even more spider silk than dwarf goats.

52

Which of the following is the major advantage of using spider silk rather than collagen in skin replacement techniques?

A) It can be woven into a mesh.

B) It has properties of elasticity.

C) It encourages growth of the dermis.

D) It has the durability to hold its shape.

Answers and Explanations

Reading Practice Test

Item	Answer	Explanation
1	D	Evidence for Choice D: In the first paragraph, the narrator (the painter) says, "However, there was nothing at first to indicate that they might not have come for a portrait." Until the end of the scene, the painter is under the impression that the couple wants to hire him to paint their portrait. Choice A: The painter already believes the couple wants to hire him, so he would have no reason to talk them into it. Choice B: The painter is more curious than "suspicious" about his visitors. Either way, it is not the best description of what happens. Choice C: It is true that the painter "scrutinizes" the couple's appearance, but that's an element of the scene, not its main point.
2	A	Evidence for Choice A: At the beginning of the scene, the painter believes the couple wants to hire him. By the end of the scene, he realizes that they hope that he will hire *them*, as models. Choice B: The narrator's descriptions of the encounter are very detailed, but this in itself does not create the pattern of the scene. Choice C: There is some truth to this. The painter senses that the couple may not be as well off as they try to appear. But it's not the best statement of a pattern. Choice D: The painter is insightful, and the gentleman and lady's appearances are somewhat misleading, but again, this choice is not the best expression of the scene's development.
3	C	Evidence for Choice C: The painter at first thinks the couple is hesitant to discuss his painting their portrait because they feel it may be beneath them—in other words, an activity "lacking in refinement." Choice A: This is a possible definition of "gross," but it doesn't fit the context. Choice B: This is also a possible definition, but again, it doesn't fit here. Choice C: Once again, this is a good definition for the word that's wrong for the situation.
4	A	Evidence for Choice A: In this paragraph, the narrator notes that the couple is reluctant to speak and that they are "visibly shy," all of which he interprets as "embarrassment." Choice B: The narrator does speculate that "perhaps they were not husband and wife," but this is not the main purpose of the paragraph. Choice C: Although the paragraph may illustrate how refined the characters are, this is not its main purpose. Choice D: The narrator is presented as a very perceptive person, but in this case, his perceptions lead more to misconceptions than insights.
5	A	Evidence for Choice A: In this sentence, the narrator notes that the gentleman and lady are "painfully reluctant" to speak, a sure sign that they are feeling very uneasy. Choice B: This sentence in itself does not strongly support the idea that the couple is uneasy, only that they have been vague about their purpose. Choice C: This sentence is a speculation on the narrator's part about *why* the couple might be uneasy, but it does not describe how they are projecting that uneasiness in the moment. Choice D: This sentence reflects the narrator's own growing uneasiness about—and frustration with—the situation.

Item	Answer	Explanation
6	C	Evidence for Choice C: The narrator speculates about numerous matters throughout, including what the couple wants, whether they are married, whether they actually have money or are just putting up a front, and so on. His attempts at guessing the facts all add up to a tone best described in the choices as "puzzled." Choice A: While the narrator certainly seems confident and self-possessed, there is nothing in his tone that indicates he is "arrogant." Choice B: The narrator may be curious about the situation, but "suspicious" is too strong a word. There's no evidence that he fears he's being deceived. Choice D: The narrator comments to himself on how well dressed and groomed his visitors are; nothing suggest he feels condescending toward them.
7	C	Evidence for Choice C: At the end of the scene, the narrator—and the reader—discover that the couple is looking for work as models. This has been the source of their discomfort and embarrassment throughout. Choice A: There is no evidence that the gentleman and lady are hiding any problem that exists between them. Choice B: What the couple may actually be worried about is that serving as models, for hire, is beneath them. Choice D: The couple is not seeking to hire the painter; instead, they are seeking work from him.
8	A	Evidence for Choice A: When the gentleman tells the painter "We should like to make it pay," the painter misinterprets the comment. He thinks the gentleman is assuring him that he will be well paid, and he appreciates this rarely shown acknowledgment that he paints portraits for the money. Choice B: While the gentleman's comment may have been unexpected, "unforeseen" is not a synonym for "unwonted." Choice C: This is not a definition of "unwonted." Choice D: The painter is surprised by the blunt mention of money, but "surprising" is not the best definition of "unwonted."
9	B	Evidence for Choice B: The narrator says in the first paragraph that "there was nothing at first to indicate that they might not have come for a portrait." He continues with that assumption until things said in the conversation begin to puzzle him. Choice A: This is something the painter wonders about, but that comes from his own thoughts about the situation, not the conversation that takes place. Choice C: Although the painter sees clues that the couple might be stretching their money for economy's sake, he does not express concern about their ability to pay him. Choice D: This statement is not true. It's the narrator's acquaintance, Mr. Rivet, who is the landscape painter.
10	A	Evidence for Choice A: This sentence is the clearest statement among the choices about how the narrator came to develop his misconceptions about the couple's visit. Choice B: This statement supports Choice A from the previous question but is not the correct answer Choice C: This statement supports Choice C from the previous question. Choice D: This statement supports Choice D from the previous question.

Item	Answer	Explanation
11	D	Evidence for Choice D: The author writes, "A man without the proper use of the intellectual faculties of a man, is, if possible, more contemptible than even a coward . . ." He is strongly stating his view of the importance of intellectual development. Choice A: This statement is unsupported by the text. Choice B: There is no evidence to support this statement. Choice C: Smith's statement does not "absolve" cowards; it does the opposite.
12	B	Evidence for Choice B: Smith's passage lists advantages to be gained by educating people at all levels of society. For example, he writes, "The more they are instructed the less liable they are to the delusions of enthusiasm and superstition, which, among ignorant nations, frequently occasion the most dreadful disorders." Choice A: This statement is not supported by the passage. Choice C: There is no discussion of "educational standards," only the advantages of universal education. Choice D: Smith does not mention paying for school for the poor, only that they should be educated to some degree.
13	C	Evidence for Choice C: Smith gives reasons for his opinions throughout the passage, as evidenced in the second quotation contained within the question. Choice A: While Smith may at times sound "dogmatic" in the firmness of his statements, his tone is never "aggressive." He presents his own opinions without attacking opinions that might run counter to his. Choice B: Smith sounds so confident in his opinions that nowhere does he sound "uneasy." Choice D: Despite the advantages Smith sees in education for the masses, he presents his notions in a matter-of-fact manner rather than attempting to sound inspirational or optimistic.
14	A	Evidence for Choice A: Most of the passage presents the advantages (effects) of providing education (cause) for all citizens. Choice B: The text says that educated citizens can see the dangers of factions. It does not warn against them, but is a reason given for universal education. Choice C: The passage discusses a single possible purpose of government (education), but it does not address "the main purpose of government." Choice D: There is some truth to this statement, but it is not the best expression of the author's intent.
15	D	Evidence for Choice D: The word "impulsively" works as a synonym in this context. Choice A: A capricious person may be unpredictable, but the two words do not have the same meaning. Choice B: This is not a definition of "capriciously." Choice C: "Slyly" is not a synonym for "capriciously."

Item	Answer	Explanation
16	C	Evidence for Choice C: Multiple statements support the idea that education makes citizens more content. For example, "The more they are instructed the less liable they are to the delusions of enthusiasm and superstition, which, among ignorant nations, frequently occasion the most dreadful disorders." Choice A: There is no evidence in the passage to support this. Choice B: Smith's proposal is based more in practicalities than altruism. Choice D: Military training is not discussed.
17	D	Evidence for Choice D: This quotation directly addresses the idea of reducing unrest among citizens through education. Choice A: This statement addresses the importance of education, but it does not speak to its effects on a population. Choice B: This statement introduces the idea of education for the masses, but it does not directly support the answer to the previous question. Choice C: This sentence supports the idea that there is an advantage to education, but the nature of that advantage is not discussed.
18	B	Evidence for Choice B: Locke writes, "I think I may say that of all the men we meet with, nine parts of ten are what they are, good or evil, useful or not, by their education." Choice A: The passage says that having a sound mind and a sound body are important. Plus, this isn't the main idea. Choice C: Although Locke might agree with this statement, it does not represent his main idea. Choice D: This idea is mentioned, but it doesn't reflect Locke's main idea.
19	D	Evidence for Choice D: This statement provides direct evidence that Locke believes education is the single most important factor in a person's well being. He says it accounts for "nine parts of ten" of what a person is. Choice A: This sentence discusses sources of happiness but does not discuss education. Choice B: These sentences also give opinions on happiness, but they do not yet discuss it in relation to education. Choice C: This sentence is about the rarity of individuals who are gifted both physically and mentally by nature. It does not support the main idea.
20	C	Evidence for Choice C: Locke describes early education as preparation for the rest of life: "'Tis that which makes the great difference in mankind. The little, or almost insensible impressions on our tender infancies, have very important and lasting consequences . . ." Choice A: Although Locke does not use the word "character," he does suggest that he sees education as shaping it. Choice B: Since Locke sees education as the single most important thing in life, he would also see it as basic to personal freedom. Choice D: Locke says that education determines whether a person becomes "good or evil, useful or not." This would fit with the notion of moving from "darkness to light."

Item	Answer	Explanation
21	B	Evidence for Choice B: Passage 1 focuses mainly on the benefits of education to society. Passage 2 focuses mainly on the benefits of education to the individual. But both focus on the benefits. Choice A: This idea is mentioned in Passage 2. Choice C: Locke discusses the phenomenon of the gifted individual in his essay. Choice D: Smith speaks out in favor of the state supporting education for all.
22	A	Evidence for Choice A: Locke discusses the benefits of education to the individual, while Smith frames his discussion mostly around potential benefits to the state. Choice B: This is not discussed in either passage. Choice C: Current educational practices is not a topic in either passage. Choice D: Neither passage "glorifies" universal education, and only Smith directly discusses the idea of educating everyone.
23	C	Evidence for Choice C: Wright's essay is largely about how difficult it is for even the writer of a work to describe its sources. In saying that he is "not so pretentious," he is saying that it would be arrogant, or "self-important," to claim he understands how all of his inner artistic processes work. Choice A: This is a possible definition of "pretentious" but not the one that best fits the context. Choice B: This may be something a pretentious person would do, but it's not a definition of the word. Choice D: This is not a definition of the word.
24	B	Evidence for Choice B: The first part of the essay is mainly about the difficulty of expressing emotions in words. Wright says that the writer often "ends up discussing something far afield" in searching for objective realities that truly express his emotions. Choice A: The author seems very willing to relate painful experiences, as when he talks about a bully from his childhood. Choice C: The anecdote of the bully shows that the author finds significant literary value in his childhood experiences. Choice D: This is not discussed in the passage.
25	C	Evidence for Choice C: In this sentence, the author says that even he does not always know when he has found the right objective reality to represent an emotion. He is acknowledging the difficulty of that, which supports the answer to the previous question. Choice A: This sentence does not support the answer. Choice B: This sentence touches on the difficulty of finding the right words, but it does not provide evidence as directly as Choice C. Choice D: This sentence does not directly discuss writing about emotions.
26	B	Evidence for Choice B: The "inexplicable array of his own emotions" are his "subjective feelings;" "his words falter" means he has difficulty putting those emotions into words. Choice A: While the author uses figurative language (as in the "Sunday suit" metaphor), he does not specifically discuss it. Choice C: The author writes more about "transforming" experiences than directly "transferring" them into fiction. Choice D: The issue of believability is not discussed in the passage.

Item	Answer	Explanation
27	D	Evidence for Choice D: Wright says of himself, "There are meanings in my book of which I was not aware until they literally spilled out upon the paper." Choice A: This statement does not reflect the evidence quoted. Choice B: Wright discusses this later in the passage, but this statement does not answer the question. Choice C: This idea is not discussed in the passage.
28	B	Evidence for Choice B: The author writes, "We never recovered our toys unless we flattered him and made him feel that he was superior to us. Then, perhaps, if he felt like it, he condescended, threw them at us and then gave each of us a swift kick in the bargain, just to make us feel his utter contempt." Choice A: This statement reflects what Wright did in fact do with his experience, but it is not what he says in the text. Choice C: This idea is not discussed in the passage. Choice D: Wright says of the bully, "But I suspect that his end was violent." He does not imagine he will be a "success."
29	C	Evidence for Choice C: Wright details how the bully cruelly tormented other children, a behavior that was both "dishonorable" and "sordid," in the sense of vile. Choice A: These words are a possible definition of "squalid," but they do not fit the context. Choice B: These words do not fit the context, although the word "squalid" can be used to describe impoverished circumstances. Choice D: These words do not provide a correct definition.
30	A	Evidence for Choice A: The author writes in the last paragraph, "Anyway, he left a marked impression upon me; maybe it was because I longed secretly to be like him and was afraid." Choice B: There is nothing to suggest that the author revered or accepted the bully. Choice C: Although the author was certainly "intimidated" by the bully, he did not at the same time feel "affectionate." Choice D: There is nothing in the text to support either of these words.
31	D	Evidence for Choice D: This sentence provides the clearest evidence that the author both feared and, in a way, admired the bully, since he "longed secretly to be like him." Choice A: This sentence might explain the narrator's fear of the bully, but it does not explain his admiration. Choice B: This sentence also provides evidence for fear but not admiration. Choice C: This statement suggest how much the author wanted to forget the bully, but it doesn't clarify the specific feelings he had about him.
32	D	Evidence for Choice D: The authors write "The world's farmers will just need to get better at squeezing more productivity out of existing farmland." Choice A: The purchase of machinery is not mentioned as a solution to the food shortage anywhere in the article. Choice B: "Better farming practices" would be a means of increasing agricultural productivity, but it is not what the author states as a solution. Choice C: Crop diversification is not mentioned as a solution.

Item	Answer	Explanation
33	D	Evidence for Choice D: "Exacerbate" means to make a condition worse, or more severe. In this context, the author is saying that cutting down more trees would make a bad situation—climate change—even worse. Choice A: This is not a definition of the word. Choice B: "Destroy" is not a synonym for "exacerbate." Choice D: To exacerbate a situation means more than to just "interfere"; it means to make it worse.
34	A	Evidence for Choice A: The paragraph mentions population projections, growing meat consumption, and land devoted to growing biofuels, which are all factors that could contribute to a food shortage. Choice B: "Climate change" is mentioned, but it's not the topic or main purpose of the paragraph. Choice C: The paragraph offers no explanation for increasing meat consumption. Choice D: The paragraph does make a connection between fuel and food shortages, but this is not its purpose in terms of the overall article.
35	B	Evidence for Choice B: The graph shows the widest gap for rice. Choice A: Corn shows the biggest projected yields, but not the widest gaps. Choice C: Wheat shows a smaller gap than rice. Choice D: Soybeans show a projected gap about half of the one predicted for rice.
36	A	Evidence for Choice A: The graph shows that since 2010 crop yields in India have shown little improvement. Choice B: The graph does not support his conclusion. Choice C: This is an inference that could be made from the article, but it is not one that could be made from the graph alone. Choice D: The graph shows the opposite.
37	A	Evidence for Choice A: The article notes that wheat yields have improved in the U.S., but "in parts of India or Eastern Europe, they've basically flat-lined." The term "flat-lined" matches the information presented in the graph. Choice B: These lines offer a reason why yield gains are stagnating but one can't make the inference that this is why wheat production in India is stagnating. Choice C: This sentence does not relate to the information in the graph. Choice D: This sentence also offers a reason why yields may be decreasing but doesn't mention India's wheat production.
38	B	Evidence for Choice B: In the article, Foley is quoted as saying, "In many parts of the world, we haven't seen enough investment in agriculture because of economics or policies or institutions." He also says that ". . . at a certain point, we run up against fundamental physiological limits for plants." Choice A: These reasons are not supported by anything in the article. Choice C: These reasons also are not addressed in the article. Choice D: Mono-cropping and pesticides are not discussed.

Item	Answer	Explanation
39	B	Evidence for Choice B: This is the quotation where Foley directly mentions low investment in agriculture, which is direct evidence for the answer to the previous question. Choice A: This statement does not support the answer to 38. Choice C: This statement also does not serve as evidence. Choice D: This sentence does not relate to reasons for low crop yields.
40	C	Evidence for Choice C: By "fundamental," Foley is referring to the basic nature of plants, the qualities that are essential and unchangeable. Choice A: This choice relates to a possible definition of "fundamental," but it doesn't fit this context. Choice B: This also relates to an accepted definition, but it's wrong for this context. Choice D: Once again, the choice reflects a meaning of "fundamental," but one that doesn't match Foley's meaning.
41	D	Evidence for Choice D: The passage does not mention setting aside more land for farming as a solution to the food shortage. Choice A: This is mentioned in the last paragraph: "Pare back the amount of meat in our diets." Choice B: See last paragraph: "Cut down on the enormous amount of food waste worldwide." Choice C: See last paragraph: "Figure out how to use water and fertilizer more efficiently everywhere."
42	A	Evidence for Choice A: The first five paragraphs of the passage focus on the challenges of human skin replacement and the reasons why using spider silk may be the best method to date, including its advantages over collagen. Choice B: This statement touches in a general way on the main idea of the passage, but Choice A is more specific. Choice C: This is a detail of the passage that supports the main idea. Choice D: The last paragraph discusses some additional uses of spider silk, but this information is mostly just an interesting addition to the main idea.
43	B	Evidence for Choice B: This quotation states that "spider silk is stronger than collagen and helps skin tissue to regrow within a matter of weeks." It directly supports the main idea stated in the previous question. Choice A: This statement supports the main topic but not as directly as Choice B. Choice C: This statement introduces an interesting detail that supports the main idea. Choice D: This statement nicely summarizes the article, but it does not provide evidence for its main idea.

Item	Answer	Explanation
44	C	Evidence for Choice C: The article discusses how spider silk is woven onto frames and how the resulting mesh becomes a base for adding human skin cells, which develop on that surface. Choice A: While this can be a definition of "matrix," it does not fit the context. Choice B: This refers to the frames mentioned in the article, but the frames in themselves do not constitute a "matrix." Choice D: This relates to the use of the word "matrix" in the article, but it is not a definition of one.
45	B	Evidence for Choice B: Paragraph 4 uses the phrase "as with the collagen technique" in describing experiments performed by Wendt and her colleagues. The suggestion throughout the paragraph is that the researchers used existing collagen techniques as a guide for their work with spider silk. Choice A: This statement is not supported by the article, although it does not mention that Wendt found that "spider silk does not cause an immune response." Choice C: While this statement is supported by the information in the article, it is not a description of the relationship between the two research efforts. Choice D: This statement is not supported by the article.
46	C	Evidence for Choice C: This sentence begins "As with the collagen techniques . . ." It supports the idea that Wendt based her spider silk research methods on established collagen methods. Choice A: This sentence mentions "other tissue transplants," but it does not make a direct connection between spider silk and collagen research. Choice B: This sentence discusses a detail of spider silk research but does directly relate it to collagen methods. Choice D: This sentence mentions a drawback of spider silk that would not apply to collagen, but it's an oblique connection, rather than a direct one as in choice C.
47	B	Evidence for Choice B: The author is describing a clear advantage of spider silk over "other tissue transplants," which supports the main idea of the article. Choice A: The author's statement is not proof that spider silk is the "most promising" substance, only that it has an advantage over other substances. Choice C: The statement removes doubt about safety issues. Choice D: The author does not specifically mention what types of tissue transplants cause an immune response.

Item	Answer	Explanation
48	D	Evidence for Choice D: The paragraph makes it clear that despite the potential value of spider silk for medical purposes, it is difficult to obtain in quantity. New methods are needed. Choice A: The paragraph does not describe any manufacturing methods, only the need for them. Choice B: No actual comparison is made between spider silk and synthetic silks. Choice C: The word "never" makes this wrong. The paragraph describes a current situation scientists are working to overcome.
49	D	Evidence for Choice D: In context, the word "harvest" refers to the fact that, at present, researchers can only "collect" spider silk produced by actual spiders. Choice A: The word "grow" is not a synonym for "harvest," and it doesn't fit the context. Choice B: While the word "yield" can be a synonym for "harvest" as a noun, it doesn't match the context. Choice C: Part of the point of the sentence is that spider silk cannot be "produced" at present, only harvested, or gathered.
50	C	Evidence for Choice C: The author closes the article with the sentence "It is hoped that materials made from spider silk will be available for medical and industrial uses within the next few years." That statement shows that the writer has a very positive attitude toward spider silk research. The article has a positive tone throughout. Choice A: There is nothing in the article to indicate that the author feels "skeptical" about possible advancements in skin replacement. Choice B: At no point is the author "critical" of the scientific research efforts described in the article. Rather, the tone is generally supportive. Choice D: While the author is factual in his reporting, his tone and phrasing go beyond "neutral" statements.

Item	Answer	Explanation
51	A	Evidence for Choice A: The last paragraph begins with the sentence "Another option is to produce more spider silk by other means." The suggestion is that by using methods such as the genetically enhanced goats, researchers will be able produce more spider silk than was previously thought possible. Choice B: There is no evidence in the article to support this statement. Choice C: The article suggests that the fibers are as strong and maybe stronger. Choice D: This conjecture is not supported by evidence in the article.
52	D	Evidence for Choice D: The article notes that "that spider silk is stronger than collagen" and that "the silk has stretchiness as well as strength." The combination of strength and flexibility makes spider silk a durable substance that holds its shape. Choice A: Collagen can also be woven into a mesh, as noted in lines 13–14 ("The cells are then placed on a collagen mesh, to which they adhere and grow"). Choice B: Collagen also possesses elastic qualities but lacks strength, as noted in lines 21–22 ("Collagen gives skin its structure and elasticity, but it is not the strongest material available."). Choice C: Both collagen and spider silk meshes are described as substances that encourage the growth of the dermis (paragraphs 2–4).

If you missed these questions . . .	study this lesson. (Please note that some questions test multiple skills; thus, some question numbers appear twice in this chart.)
	Closely Reading Literature
1, 2	Lesson 1: Understanding explicit and implicit ideas (p. 57)
1, 2, 4	Lesson 1: Understanding main ideas and purpose (p. 65)
7	Lesson 1: Analyzing word choice and imagery for tone (p. 74)
4, 9	Lesson 1: Identifying characterization (p. 85)
6	Lesson 1: Identifying narrator's point of view (p. 92)
5, 10	Lesson 1: Citing textual evidence (p. 99)
	Closely Reading Literature and Informational Texts
3, 8, 11, 15, 23, 29, 33, 40, 44, 49	Lesson 2: Understanding meanings of words and phrases (p. 107)
	Closely Reading Informational Texts
12, 16	Lesson 3: Understanding explicit meanings (p. 115)
18, 42	Lesson 3: Determining central ideas and summarizing (p. 121)
16, 32, 38, 41, 52	Lesson 3: Identifying supporting details (p. 127)
27, 28, 45, 51	Lesson 4: Making inferences (p. 137)
20	Lesson 4: Using analogical reasoning (p. 146)
17, 19, 25, 31, 37, 39, 43, 46	Lesson 4: Citing textual evidence (p. 152)
12, 18, 24, 26, 27, 28, 30, 48, 50	Lesson 5: Analyzing author's point of view and purpose (p. 159)
38, 47	Lesson 5: Analyzing the use of arguments (claims, counterclaims, reasoning, and evidence) (p. 168)
13	Lesson 6: Analyzing use of word choice to shape meaning and tone (p. 177)
14, 34, 38, 45, 48	Lesson 6: Analyzing text structure (p. 184)
21, 22	Lesson 7: Synthesizing information from multiple texts (p. 193)
35, 36, 37	Lesson 7: Analyzing and synthesizing information from texts and graphics (p. 204)

DOMAIN
Writing and Language

LESSON 8:
Development of Ideas

- ☐ revising texts for clarity, focus, and purpose
- ☐ relating information presented in graphs, charts, and tables to information presented in texts

---

Explain Revising Texts for Clarity, Focus, and Purpose

There are several important qualities of effective writing. Good writing is **well-developed** and **focused**. A well-developed passage contains enough information to be convincing and to effectively develop the main idea. Good writing also stays on topic and avoids extraneous details. A logical introduction identifies the central idea; a conclusion ties the ideas together for the reader.

Questions about the development of a passage may ask you to identify if a sentence or phrase

- effectively introduces the main idea.

- should be added or deleted from a paragraph or passage.

- supports the claim or statement made in the previous sentence.

- provides a second example that is most similar to a previous example.

- provides an effective conclusion that summarizes or restates the main idea.

Editing for Focus

From your years of study, you know that well-developed writing contains a main idea and supporting details. It doesn't matter if you are writing a paragraph or a ten-page paper; all ideas must work together to communicate a logical message. Passages on the SAT will contain sentences that don't fit with the main idea. Read the following passage and cross out any words or phrases that do not support the main idea.

QUICK TIP

For passages that are persuasive or argumentative, the SAT refers to the main idea as the claim or the writer's claim.

[1] In the nineteenth century, new towns in the United States often had colorful names. [2] As long as a proposed new name didn't conflict with an existing one, it was usually approved by the government. [3] As a result, the names of newly incorporated post offices were unique. [4] At a Massachusetts town meeting to choose a name, everyone suggested a different idea.

[5] As each person stood up to speak, he or she began with "Why not . . . ."

[6] Because there was no agreement, *Why Not* became the official name.

[7] A Missouri town submitted a number of names, all of which sounded peculiar. [8] *Peculiar* became the name of the town. [9] The names of products have unusual origins. [10] A California town couldn't agree either, and someone suggested that it wasn't likely the citizens would ever agree.

[11] *Likely* became the accepted name.

The first sentence indicates that the focus of the paragraph will be on how towns got unusual names. However, sentence 3 mentions post offices. This should be changed to *towns*.

Another sentence that veers off topic is sentence 9: *The names of products have unusual origins*. It should be deleted.

QUICK TIP

Here is how questions on focus may be worded on the SAT:

At this point, the writer is considering adding (or deleting) the following sentence. . . . Should the writer add (or delete) this sentence?

Editing for Supporting Details

Supporting details may include examples, reasons, evidence, causes, effects, definitions, and explanations. Appropriate supporting details fit with the main idea and the writer's purpose. Some SAT questions will ask you to identify which supporting details would fit with other ones in the passage. Which of the following sentences could be added to the paragraph about town names?

Other towns with unusual names include Ordinary, Virginia; Bowlegs, Oklahoma; Truth or Consequences, New Mexico; and Waterproof, Louisiana.

A town's name may influence tourism; surely travelers would rather go to Happyland, Connecticut, than to Satan's Kingdom, Vermont.

The first sentence above describes more examples of towns with unusual names and fits with the other examples given in sentences 4–11. The second sentence describes how a town's name affects tourism, which does not support the main idea.

Editing Introductions and Conclusions

Most essays and articles follow the basic format of introduction, body, and conclusion; many paragraphs also contain an introductory sentence and a concluding one. On the SAT, you may be asked to identify a sentence that best introduces the main idea or best concludes a passage by restating the main idea or summarizing the supporting points. Which of the following best concludes the paragraph about town names by restating the main idea?

> Some towns purposely change their names in order to promote products or gain business opportunities. In 2010, city leaders in Topeka, Kansas, unofficially changed the city's name to *Google* for a month as a way to persuade the tech company to test fiber-optic technology in their city.

> While current inhabitants of Idiotville, Oregon, or Sandwich, Massachusetts, live with their predecessors' strange choices, at least they can be thankful they don't live in Hell, Michigan.

The first sentence introduces a different idea about town names, but the second one restates the main idea of unusual town names, while giving further examples.

Editing for Support for Claims

Many of the texts you will read in college and on the SAT will focus on presenting arguments. The writer will make a central claim or present an opinion about a topic. Then he or she will support the claim with reasons and evidence. SAT questions may ask you to decide which sentence provides the best support for a claim made in a previous sentence or in the entire passage. Read the following paragraph.

> [1] Coral reefs are among the most beautiful ecosystems on Earth—"a jeweled belt around the middle of the planet," in oceanographer Sylvia Earle's words. [2] They also are extremely valuable. [3] They are spawning grounds, coastal buffers against storms, and lucrative tourist draws. [4] According to some estimates, the services they provide are worth up to $30 billion yearly.

Which of the following sentence provides good support for the claim made in sentence 2?

> Reefs cover less than one-tenth of 1 percent of the ocean floor but support more than 800 species of coral and 4,000 species of fish.

> The Great Barrier Reef, a popular tourist attraction in Australia, is composed of over 2,900 individual reefs and 900 islands that stretch over 1,600 miles.

The first sentence provides more effective support for the claim by detailing the vast numbers of ocean life that reefs support. While the second sentence hints at the fact that coral reefs are valuable tourist attractions, it focuses on the dimensions of one reef. The first sentence is the best choice.

QUICK TIP

If a question asks you to choose the sentence that provides the best evidence or a similar example to one in the passage, first cross out any answers that directly contradict the writer's claim. Then return to the passage and compare the remaining answers to the central claim or to other examples.

Directions: As you read the following paragraphs, evaluate their focus and development. Answer the questions below.

[1] Every inhabitant of this blue ball in space has a responsibility to preserve our fragile environment, especially that thin layer of topsoil. [2] Erosion, the wearing away of earth by wind and water, threatens topsoil and has been heavily studied across the world by engineers and geologists. [3] Topsoil is a precious resource that is rarely more than a foot or two thick, but this tiny layer supports all of the world's agriculture—and life on Earth. [4] Together, farmers and scientists hope to find solutions to erosion—whether it is caused by water or by wind.

1. What problem occurs between sentences 2 and 3?

    _____

    _____

    _____

2. How would you improve the paragraph?

    _____

    _____

    _____

[1] If you are seeking a fascinating hobby, try stamp collecting. [2] Aptly called the hobby of kings and the king of hobbies, stamp collecting's popularity depends upon certain major appeals. [3] First, stamps are easy to study and store. [4] They take up little space. [5] Start with a simple, inexpensive mixture of world stamps and then enter this fantastic world.

3. What is the main problem with this paragraph?

    _____

    _____

    _____

4. How would you improve the paragraph?

_____

_____

_____

[1] Drivers should be prohibited from using cell phones while a vehicle is moving. [2] Admittedly, cell phones are wonderful devices for keeping in touch with friends. [3] Distracted driving is very dangerous. [4] At best, the cell phone message itself is distracting. [5] At worst, it may include bad news that negatively affects the driver's judgment and reflexes. [6] Inevitably, the driver is fumbling with his cell phone and has only one hand on the steering wheel. [7] His attention and performance are seriously impaired. [8] If the cell phone malfunctions or the cell service is lost, any attempt to restore the connection will take the driver's attention away from the road. [9] The risk of using cell phones in moving cars, however, is probably exaggerated. [10] Driving requires 100 percent concentration, not the fraction leftover while drivers use cell phones.

5. What is the main problem with this paragraph?

_____

_____

_____

6. How would you improve the paragraph?

_____

_____

_____

_____

_____

_____

For answers, see page 574.

Directions: These questions show how your ability to revise paragraphs for clarity, focus, and development might be tested on the SAT. The answer and explanation immediately follow each question. Answer the questions and then review the answers and the explanations.

[1] In 1941, nearly 113,000 people of Japanese ancestry, two-thirds of them American citizens, were living on the West Coast, in California, Washington, and Oregon. [2] On December 7, Japan attacked the United States naval base at Pearl Harbor, and the United States declared war on Japan. [3] Two months later, President Franklin D. Roosevelt signed Executive Order No. 9066 empowering the U.S. Army to designate areas from which people could be excluded. [4] The experiences of Chinese immigrants foreshadowed those of Japanese immigrants, who began arriving about the same time the 1882 Chinese Exclusion Act suspended labor immigration from China. [5] Although the Executive Order did not identify who was to be excluded, the Army enforced its provisions only against Japanese Americans. [6] No person of Japanese ancestry living in the United States was ever convicted of any serious act of espionage or sabotage during the war, yet the entire West Coast population of people of Japanese descent was forcibly removed from their homes and placed in relocation centers, many for the duration of the war.

[7] Responding to demands for redress and reparations made by the Japanese American community, the federal government finally took steps to publicly apologize to Japanese Americans for their wartime treatment. [8] The federal government decided to commemorate this period of history and educate the public about the abrogation of Japanese Americans' constitutional rights during the war years. [9] Title II of Public Law 102–248, enacted by Congress on March 3, 1992, authorized and directed the Secretary of the Interior to prepare a Japanese American National Historic Landmark (NHL) Theme Study, so that related sites could be evaluated for NHL designation.

1. The writer is considering deleting sentence 4. Should the writer do this?

   A) Yes, because it contains irrelevant information that doesn't support the main idea.

   B) Yes, because it contains information that belongs in the second paragraph of the passage.

   C) No, because it explains why Asian immigrants were viewed with suspicion following Pearl Harbor.

   D) No, because it provides a logical transition between sentences 3 and 5.

Cross out any obviously wrong answers right away. If you can't decide between two answers, try substituting each suggestion into the paragraph and reading it silently to yourself.

Strategy: This question asks you to revise the paragraph for focus. The main idea of the paragraph is describing the events that led up to the forced relocation of Japanese Americans during World War II. Sentence 4 introduces loosely related event and doesn't fit with the order of events in the paragraph. Choices C and D can be eliminated. Choice B is incorrect because the information doesn't fit in the second paragraph, it should be deleted entirely, choice A.

2. The writer is considering adding one of the following sentences to the paragraph immediately after sentence 8. Which one should the writer add?

   A) Harold Ickes, the Secretary of the Interior during the 1940s, was opposed to the removal of Japanese Americans.

   B) In 1943, Ansel Adams, America's most well-known photographer, documented the lives of the Japanese Americans interned at the Manzanar War Relocation Center in California.

   C) In 1988 President Ronald Reagan signed the Civil Liberties Act of 1988, which provided financial redress to former detainees.

   D) Japanese Americans, half of whom were children, were incarcerated for up to four years in bleak, remote camps, surrounded by barbed wire and armed guards.

Strategy: This question asks you to revise the paragraph by adding more supporting details. First, think about the focus of the paragraph. The emphasis is on the steps the federal government took to make reparations to Japanese Americans. Choices B and D do not fit with the paragraph's main idea. While sentence A describes a government official who was opposed to the relocation policy, the emphasis of the paragraph is on reparations made years after the war. The correct answer is choice C.

Directions: Read each paragraph and answer the questions that follow.

[1] During the fall of 1943, Ansel Adams photographed at the Manzanar War Relocation Center, which was located in Inyo County, California, at the eastern edge of the Sierra Nevada Mountains approximately 200 miles northeast of Los Angeles. [2] This series was a departure from his usual landscape photography. [3] Adams produced an essay on the Japanese Americans interned in this beautiful but remote and undeveloped region where the mountains served as both a metaphorical fortress and an inspiration for the internees. [4] Adams concentrated on the internees and their activities. ■1■ [5] Two of his most famous landscape photographs were made during his visit to Manzanar: *Mount Williamson, the Sierra Nevada, from Manzanar, California, 1944* and *Winter Sunrise, the Sierra Nevada, from Lone Pine, California, 1944.* ■2■

[6] In 1944 a selection of these images along with text by Adams was published by U.S. Camera in a 112-page book, *Born Free and Equal.* [7] In a letter to his friend Nancy Newhall, the wife of Beaumont Newhall, curator of photography at the Museum of Modern Art, Adams wrote: "Through the pictures the reader will be introduced to perhaps twenty individuals . . . loyal American citizens who are anxious to get back into the stream of life and contribute to our victory." [8] The book received positive reviews and made the *San Francisco Chronicle's* bestseller list for March and April of 1945. ■3■

[9] Adams was not the only photographer to work at Manzanar. [10] One of the internees, Toyo Miyatake, had worked as a Los Angeles portrait photographer before he was moved to Manzanar. [11] The internees were not allowed to have cameras. ■4■ [12] Both Adams's and Miyatake's photographs present a positive view of the Japanese Americans interned at Manzanar. [13] In contrast, Dorothea Lange, who had earned her reputation as a social documentary photographer with images of migrant farm workers made during the Depression, worked for the War Relocation Authority photographing the evacuation of Japanese Americans and their arrival at Manzanar. [14] Lange's vision is uniquely unlike Adams's and Miyatake's. [15] She photographed the upheaval of the evacuation and the bleak conditions of the internment camps. ■5■

1. Which of the following sentences would add the most relevant detail to support sentence 4 in paragraph 1?

   A) Adams photographed family life in the barracks: people at work—internees as welders, farmers, and garment makers; and recreational activities, including baseball and volleyball games.

   B) Adams's black-and-white photographs of the American West have been widely reproduced in books, calendars, and posters.

   C) And there were many subjects to photograph, since over 100,000 Japanese Americans were incarcerated during the course of World War II.

   D) The Manzanar Internment Camp is now the Manzanar National Historic Site, which is visited by many Americans every year.

2. The writer is considering deleting sentence 5. Should the writer do this?

   A) Yes, because it doesn't support the main idea of the paragraph.

   B) Yes, because it supports the claim that Adams was a famous photographer.

   C) No, because it adds important details about famous pictures taken at Manzanar.

   D) No, because it provides an interesting contrast to the previous idea of photographing internees.

3. The writer wants to add a concluding sentence immediately after sentence 8. Which of the following would best wrap up the paragraph?

   A) The book is still in publication today.

   B) Perhaps in his own way, Adams used his art to quietly protest the treatment of internment of Japanese Americans.

   C) Interestingly, the subtitle of the book was *The Story of Loyal Japanese Americans.*

   D) In 1965, Adams wrote to the Library of Congress that the Manzanar Collection "is an important historical document and I trust it can be put to good use."

4. The writer is considering adding the following sentence immediately after sentence 11.

   However, Miyatake fashioned a camera from parts he brought with him in his luggage.

   Should the writer make this addition?

   A) Yes, because it clarifies an idea presented in sentence 11.

   B) Yes, because it is an illustration used to support the writer's claim in sentence 9.

   C) No, because it adds an irrelevant detail.

   D) No, because it restates an idea from sentence 10.

5. Which of the following sentences would be the best support for the claim the writer makes in sentence 15?

   A) Lange died of esophageal cancer on October 11, 1965.

   B) One photo featured Japanese American children pledging allegiance to the American flag.

   C) Lange's images were so controversial that they were impounded by the army and not released to the public for 50 years.

   D) In 1972, the Whitney Museum incorporated 27 of her photographs into Executive Order 9066, an exhibit about the Japanese internment.

For answers, see page 575.

Explain Relating Graphs to Texts

In the Writing and Language section of the SAT, you will be tested over your ability to relate information presented visually to information presented as text. The text should clearly and accurately incorporate the information displayed in visual elements, such as graphs, charts, and tables.

Graphs display quantitative relationships between variables. A graph might show the number of motorcycle accidents versus car accidents in the years 2000 through 2010. Common graphs are bar charts, pie charts, and line graphs. **Tables** display lists of numbers or text in columns and rows.

Think It Through

Consider the following paragraph and graph.

Temperatures at the surface, in the troposphere (the active weather layer extending up to about 5 to 10 miles above the ground), and in the oceans have all remained relatively stable over recent decades. Consistent with our scientific understanding, the largest increases in temperature are occurring closer to the poles, especially in the Arctic. Snow and ice cover have decreased in most areas. Atmospheric water vapor is increasing in the lower atmosphere, because a warmer atmosphere can hold more water. Sea levels are also increasing. Changes in other climate-relevant indicators such as growing season length have been observed in many areas. Worldwide, the observed changes in average conditions have been accompanied by increasing trends in extremes of heat and heavy precipitation events, and decreases in extreme cold.

Pay attention to titles and labels. Titles of graphs, charts, and tables provide information about the data shown, just like story titles usually suggest what a story is about. In tables, row and column labels identify the information displayed.

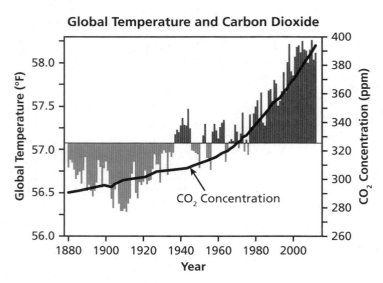

Source: nca2014.globalchange.gov

The graph shows how a rise in carbon dioxide corresponds to a rise in global temperature. The paragraph inaccurately communicated the graph's information by indicating the global temperatures "have all remained relatively stable." An accurate interpretation of the graph is the following sentence: Temperatures at the surface, in the troposphere (the active weather layer extending up to about 5 to 10 miles above the ground), and in the oceans have all increased over recent decades.

Directions: Read each paragraph along with accompanying figures below. Pay attention to how the underlined sentence interprets the information in the graph. Then answer the questions.

Natural drivers of climate cannot explain the recent observed warming of global temperatures. ◼1◼ <u>Over the last five decades, natural factors (solar forces and volcanoes) alone would actually have led to an extreme rise in temperature.</u>

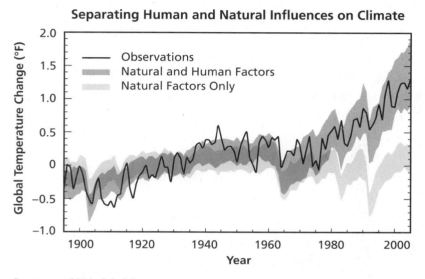

Separating Human and Natural Influences on Climate

Source: nca2014.globalchange.gov

The graph tracks observed global average changes (black line), model simulations using only changes in natural factors (solar and volcanic) in light gray, and model simulations with the addition of human-induced emissions (darker gray). The data indicates that climate changes since 1950 cannot be explained by natural factors or variability, and can only be explained by human factors.

1. Does the underlined sentence accurately interpret the information in the graph? If not, rewrite the sentence so that it accurately interprets the graph.

_____

_____

_____

_____

_____

In the Northern hemisphere, winter is the time for flu, but the exact timing and duration of flu seasons vary. While seasonal flu outbreaks can happen as early as October, most of the time flu activity peaks between December and March, although activity can last as late as May. The figure below shows peak flu activity for the United States by month for the 1982–83 through 2013–14 flu seasons. The "peak month of flu activity" is the month with the highest percentage of respiratory specimens testing positive for influenza virus infection. **3** During this 32-year period, flu activity most often peaked in February (14 seasons), followed by January (6 seasons), December and March (5 seasons each).

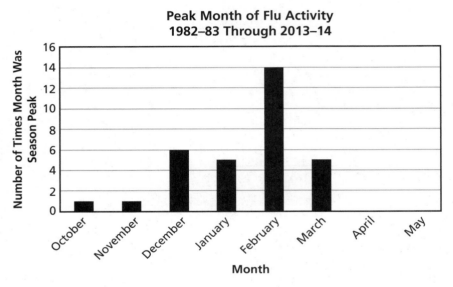

Peak Month of Flu Activity
1982–83 Through 2013–14

Source: cdc.gov

2. Does the underlined sentence accurately interpret the information in the graph? If not, rewrite the sentence so that it accurately interprets the graph.

_____

_____

_____

_____

The Civil War was America's bloodiest conflict. The unprecedented violence of battles such as Shiloh, Antietam, Stones River, and Gettysburg shocked citizens and international observers alike. Nearly as many men died in captivity during the Civil War as were killed in the whole of the Vietnam War. Hundreds of thousands died of disease. **5** Roughly 2 percent of the population, over 620,000 men, lost their lives in the line of duty. Taken as a percentage of today's population, the toll would have risen as high as 6 million souls.

The human cost of the Civil War was beyond anybody's expectations. The young nation experienced bloodshed of a magnitude that has not been equaled since by any other American conflict.

Military Deaths in American Wars

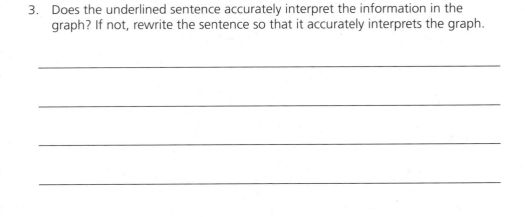

Civil War	620,000
World War II	405,399
World War I	116,516
Vietnam	58,209
Korea	36,516
Revolutionary War	25,000
War of 1812	20,000
Mexican War	13,283
Iraq-Afghanistan	6,626
Spanish-American War	2,446
Gulf War	256

Source: civilwar.org

3. Does the underlined sentence accurately interpret the information in the graph? If not, rewrite the sentence so that it accurately interprets the graph.

_____

_____

_____

_____

_____

For answers, see page 575.

Directions: These questions show how your ability to accurately revise paragraphs with visual information might be tested on the SAT. The answer and explanation immediately follow the question. Answer the questions and then review the answers and the explanations.

When currency is deposited with a Federal Reserve Bank, the quality of each note is evaluated by sophisticated processing equipment. Notes that meet our strict quality criteria—that is, they are still in good condition—continue to circulate, while those that do not are taken out of circulation and destroyed. This process determines the life span of a Federal Reserve note.

Life span varies by denomination. One factor that influences the life span of each denomination is how the denomination is used by the public. For example, $100 notes are often used as a store of value. This means that they pass between users less frequently than lower denominations that are more often used for transactions, such as $5 notes. Thus, $100 notes typically last longer than $5 notes. Nevertheless, a range of other factors influence the life spans of the denominations and play a role **1** in making the $10 note sustain the shortest life span.

Denomination	Estimated Life Span
$1	5.9 years
$5	4.9 years
$10	4.2 years
$20	7.7 years
$50	3.7 years
$100	15.0 years

Source: www.federalreserve.gov

1. Which choice completes the last sentence in the passage with accurate data based on the table?
   A) NO CHANGE
   B) in causing the $50 note to experience the shortest life span.
   C) in creating brief life spans for all denominations.
   D) in determining which denomination is the most popular.

Strategy: This question asks you to analyze data displayed graphically and to integrate that information with information presented in text. Specifically, you must determine which of the four interpretations of the table is accurate and to revise the passage's wording as needed. Choices A, C, and D can be eliminated because they misstate the table's data. The best answer here is choice B, as the graph establishes that the denomination with the shortest life span is the $50 note (3.7 years).

From the onset of the European debt crisis that began with the Greek debt announcement in November 2009 **2** to June 2010 when the value of the euro bottomed out versus the U.S. dollar, the euro depreciated 18 percent. However, Chart 1 shows that import prices of goods coming from the European Union (locality of origin index) actually **3** rose significantly as the crisis began.

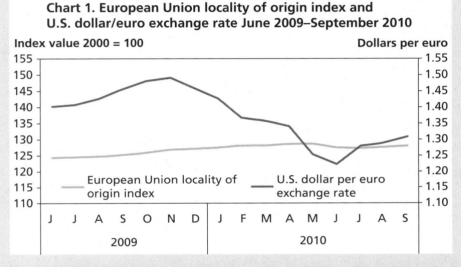

Chart 1. European Union locality of origin index and U.S. dollar/euro exchange rate June 2009–September 2010

Sources: U.S. Bureau of Labor Statistics and dollar exchange rate from Federal Reserve Bank

2. Which choice completes the first sentence with accurate data based on the graph?
   A) NO CHANGE
   B) to June 2010 when the value of the euro sharply recovered
   C) to May 2010 when the value of the euro ended its sharp plummet
   D) to June 2010 when the value of the euro stabilized

Strategy: For this question you must determine which of the four interpretations of the graph is accurate and to revise the passage's wording as needed. First, determine that the information being described deals with the euro exchange rate, or the darker line on the chart. The two variables in the answer choices are the month (May or June) and what the value of the euro was doing. A quick survey of the chart indicates that the lowest exchange rate came in June 2010. It did not recover so eliminate choice B. The important word in choice D is *stabilized*. However, this is not strictly true, because the next month the euro jumped in value. Choice C can be eliminated because the euro's plummet ended in June. Thus, the original sentence is correct, and the correct answer is A.

3. Which choice completes the last sentence in the passage with accurate data based on the graph?

   A) NO CHANGE

   B) began a sharp decline as the crisis began.

   C) dropped dramatically before steadying as the crisis began.

   D) continued to rise slowly as the crisis began.

Strategy: This question asks you to identify which written interpretation accurately interprets the data on the chart. The text indicates that the data is related to the locality of origin index, or the lighter gray line in the chart. What was happening to prices of imported goods as the crisis began? The previous sentence in the paragraph indicates that the crisis began in November 2009. The chart illustrates that the EU import prices began a gradual rise with the onset of the crisis in November 2009. The only choice that reflects this is D.

SAT-Type Questions

Directions: Read the passage and answer the questions that follow.

The American peregrine falcon was once on the endangered list. The text and chart detail efforts to prevent its demise.

American Peregrine Falcon

In 1970, the American peregrine was listed as endangered, and efforts to recover the species began. The chemical DDT, which was found to thin the falcon's egg shells, was banned in Canada in 1970 and in the United States in 1972. This was the single-most significant action in the recovery of the peregrine falcon. In addition, in the eastern United States, efforts were made to reestablish peregrine falcons by releasing offspring from a variety of wild stocks that were held in captivity by falconers.

In the late 1970s, Alaska became the first place American peregrine falcon population growth was documented and, by 1980, populations began to grow in other areas. Not only did the number of peregrine falcons begin to increase, productivity (another important measure of population health) improved. Efforts to reestablish peregrine falcons in the East and Midwest proved largely successful, **1** leading to the downlisting of the species in 1984, and by 1999 peregrines were found to be nesting in all states within their historical range east of the 100th meridian, except for Rhode Island, West Virginia and Arkansas. In highly urban areas, peregrine falcons showed great adaptability and began substituting skyscrapers for natural cliff faces as nesting sites. **2** By 1980, the total known breeding population of peregrine falcons was 1,500 pairs in the United States and Canada, far exceeding the recovery goal of 456 pairs. Other recovery goals, including estimates of productivity, egg-shell thickness, and contaminants levels, had also been met, **3** permitting the species to be labeled endangered in 1999. Monitoring of American peregrine populations has continued under a post-delisting monitoring plan. The estimated North American population was **4** 1,924 pairs as of 2006.

American Peregrine Falcon

Source: www.esasuccess.org

1. Which choice offers an accurate interpretation of the data in the graph?
   A) NO CHANGE
   B) causing the species to be added to the endangered list in 1984,
   C) contributing to relisting the species in 1984,
   D) triggering a movement to delist the species in 1984,

2. Which choice offers an accurate interpretation of the data in the graph?
   A) NO CHANGE
   B) By 1980, the total known breeding population of peregrine falcons was 1,000 pairs
   C) By 1998, the total known breeding population of peregrine falcons was 1,250 pairs
   D) By 1998, the total known breeding population of peregrine falcons was 954 pairs

3. Which choice offers an accurate interpretation of the data in the graph?
   A) NO CHANGE
   B) forcing the species to be relisted in 1999.
   C) making delisting the species a possibility in 1999.
   D) causing the species to be delisted in 1999.

4. Which choice offers an accurate interpretation of the data in the graph?
   A) NO CHANGE
   B) 3,005 pairs as of 2006.
   C) 2,500 pairs as of 2000.
   D) 3,502 pairs as of 1999.

For answers, see page 576.

Organization of Ideas Within Texts

- revising for cohesion and logical order within paragraphs or within entire texts
- revising texts to ensure transitional words, phrases, and sentences are used effectively

Explain Revising for Cohesion and Logical Order

In well-organized writing, the ideas flow together in logical, **cohesive** ways. Texts consist of many paragraphs, each paragraph building on the preceding one. Within the paragraphs, the sentences must clearly and logically relate to each other. Cohesive writing contains ideas that are placed in an order that makes sense with the writer's purpose. Cohesive writing "sticks together."

The SAT will test you over your ability to edit passages and paragraphs for logical order. Questions may ask you to decide

- where a sentence should be placed within a paragraph to make logical sense.
- where a paragraph should be placed within a passage to make logical sense.
- which sentence logically follows another sentence in a paragraph.

Think It Through

As you read the following paragraph, think about the order of the sentences. Which idea seems out of order?

[1] Chronic insomnia is disrupted sleep that occurs at least three nights per week and lasts at least three months. [2] Changes in the environment, unhealthy sleep habits, shift work, other clinical disorders, and certain medications could lead to a long-term pattern of insufficient sleep. [3] People with chronic insomnia may benefit from some form of treatment to help them get back to healthy sleep patterns. [4] Chronic insomnia can be comorbid, meaning it is linked to another medical or psychiatric issue, although sometimes it's difficult to understand this cause and effect relationship. [5] Chronic insomnia disorders can have many causes.

Sentence 5: *Chronic insomnia disorders can have many causes* breaks up the paragraph's cohesion. The sentence states that insomnia has "many causes," yet it is at the end of the paragraph, distanced from sentence 2 which lists causes for insomnia. To make the paragraph more cohesive, move the sentence after the first sentence, so that it comes immediately before the list of causes.

Paragraphs within a text should build on one another. They must tie together old and new information. Paragraphs that are not ordered in a logical, easy-to-follow manner make writing less cohesive.

As you read the following paragraphs, evaluate their order.

The Solar Resource

By the time it reaches Earth's surface, the energy in sunlight has fallen to about 1,000 watts per square meter at noon on a cloudless day. Averaged over the entire surface of the planet, 24 hours per day for a year, each square meter collects the approximate energy equivalent of almost a barrel of oil each year, or 4.2 kilowatt-hours of energy every day. Deserts, with very dry air and little cloud cover, receive the most sun—more than six kilowatt-hours per day per square meter. Northern climates, such as Boston, get closer to 3.6 kilowatt-hours.

The amount of energy from the sun that falls on Earth's surface is enormous. All the energy stored in Earth's reserves of coal, oil, and natural gas is matched by the energy from just 20 days of sunshine. Outside Earth's atmosphere, the sun's energy contains about 1,300 watts per square meter. About one-third of this light is reflected back into space, and some is absorbed by the atmosphere (in part causing winds to blow).

These paragraphs are not cohesive. Paragraph 1 describes what happens to sunlight after it reaches Earth and breaks it down into specific facts, whereas Paragraph 2 provides information about the sun's energy before it reaches Earth's atmosphere. Logically, the more general information about the sun's energy outside of the atmosphere should precede the more detailed account of what happens to it after it breaches the atmosphere. In addition, Paragraph 1 begins by stating, "By the time it reaches Earth's surface." This beginning employs an unnamed, unknown *it*, although the latter part of the sentence clarifies that *it* refers to energy in sunlight. Switching the order of the two paragraphs eliminates this minor confusion.

Reread the two paragraphs, starting with Paragraph 2 and ending with Paragraph 1. In this order, the ideas from Paragraph 2 flow naturally into Paragraph 1; in other words, the writing is cohesive.

Ideas within a paragraph should also build on one another. Paragraphs that are out of sequence or contain randomly ordered details lack cohesion. Consider the following paragraph:

[1] Humpback whales inhabit all of the world's oceans, but are more numerous in the Southern Hemisphere. [2] A whaling moratorium has enabled some populations to recover, but their long-term health is far from certain. [3] This was not always so: Southern Hemisphere humpback whales were severely threatened by commercial whaling, and estimates suggest that populations were reduced to just 2 percent of their original size.

To decide where a sentence belongs within a paragraph, look for

- repeated terms or ideas
- transitional phrases that explain the relationships: *for example, because, as a result*

The transitional phrase "This was not always so" in sentence 3 is a good clue to help you determine where the sentence should be placed in the paragraph.

The first sentence introduces the paragraph's main idea: the diffusion of humpback whale populations throughout the world's oceans. However, sentence 2 has no apparent link to this idea; instead, it introduces new information regarding a whaling moratorium and endangered whale populations. The final sentence has an unclear meaning: does sentence 3 mean that the whaling moratorium has not always been effective or that the whale's long-term health was certain in the past and has only now become uncertain? Resolve these problems by moving sentence 3 after sentence 1.

Practice

Directions: Read each paragraph below. Then decide the correct order of the sentences.

[1] This hyper-altruistic tendency was discovered by famous neuroscientist Molly J. Crockett and her colleagues at the University College London. [2] People assign a higher value to the harm that is made to anonymous others than harm which is made to themselves. [3] "Our results provide evidence for a circumstance in which people care more for others than themselves," said Dr. Crockett. [4] Determining the precise boundaries of this surprisingly prosocial disposition has implications for understanding human moral decision making and its disturbance in antisocial behavior.

1. How would you revise the paragraph so that the order is most logical?

_____

_____

[1] Gamma ray bursts (GRBs) are some of the brightest, most dramatic events in the universe. [2] These cosmic tempests are characterized by a spectacular explosion of photons with energies 1,000,000 times greater than the most energetic light our eyes can detect. [3] But could this type of event occur in our own stellar neighborhood? [4] According to their explosive power, long-lasting GRBs are predicted to have catastrophic consequences for life on any nearby planet.

2. How would you revise the paragraph so that the order is most logical?

_____

_____

_____

[1] "A great deal of meaningful activity is occurring in the brain when a person is sitting back and doing nothing at all," says Raichle, who has been funded by the National Science Foundation (NSF) Division of Behavioral and Cognitive Sciences in the Directorate for Social, Behavioral and Economic Sciences. "It turns out that when your mind is at rest, dispersed brain areas are chattering away to one another."

[2] For many years, the focus of brain mapping was to examine changes in the brain that occur when people are attentively engaged in an activity. No one spent much time thinking about what happens to the brain when people are doing very little.

[3] But Marcus Raichle, a professor of radiology, neurology, neurobiology and biomedical engineering at Washington University in St. Louis, has done just that. In the 1990s, he and his colleagues made a pivotal discovery by revealing how a specific area of the brain responds to down time.

3. How would you reorder the paragraphs so that the passage is logical?

_____

_____

_____

For answers, see page 576.

Model SAT Question

Directions: This question shows how your ability to revise texts for logical order might be tested on the SAT. The answer and explanation immediately follow the question. Answer the question and then review the answer and the explanation.

[1] From 2003 to 2013, the residential construction industry experienced a 26.8 percent decrease in employment—precipitated by the recent recession. [2] While most states recorded a decrease in construction employment over that period, a total of 22 states experienced a decrease of 30 percent or greater. [3] Those states with increases in employment included North Dakota (47.1 percent), followed by New York, Texas, and the District of Columbia. **1** [4] Nevada and Arizona had the largest decreases—52.0 percent and 48.3 percent, respectively.

1. To make this paragraph most logical, sentence 4 should be placed
   A) where it is now.
   B) before sentence 1.
   C) after sentence 1.
   D) after sentence 2.

Strategy: Sentence 4 provides statistics about which states had the largest employment decreases. It gives more specific details about the "decrease of 30 percent or greater" from sentence 2. Logically, it fits after sentence 2, choice D.

SAT-Type Questions

Directions: Read each paragraph and answer the questions that follow.

Best Contemporary Wildlife Artists Gather in Jackson Hole for New "Wild 100"

1 [1] With a new "Wild 100" approach to its annual Western Visions fund-raiser, August 30–September 21, 2014, the museum has carefully curated a field of 100 living artists working with animal forms in a variety of media. [2] Top contemporary wildlife artists—and collectors—from around the world will be congregating at the National Museum of Wildlife Art in Jackson Hole, Wyoming, this September. [3] "Although we're located in Wyoming, this is not your typical Wild West art event," says Becky Kimmel, director of programs and events for the museum. [4] Kimmel states, "Our Western Visions Wild 100 offers a chance to experience, and purchase, the work of some of the best international talent in the field."

2 [5] The work of Dutch artist Ewoud de Groot, 2014 Western Visions featured painter, for instance, evokes a tension between his modernistic abstract backgrounds and his beautifully precise figurative subjects, often seabirds from the Waddensea wetlands off the northern Netherlands coast. [6] Award-winning representational depictions of wildlife from familiar Rocky Mountain species to iconic African animals play an important role in the show and sale. [7] However, Kimmel also points to numerous Wild 100 artists whose artwork takes an innately contemporary approach. [8] Another example is the fluid sculptures of 2014 Western Visions featured sculptor Gwynn Murrill, whose signature bronzes are also represented in the National Museum of Art's permanent collection, distill animal forms to their essence, at once abstract and instilled with vital personality.

QUICK TIP

One strategy to identify a text's organization and how paragraphs fit together is to write brief notes in the margin about the main idea of each paragraph. These notes will also help you save time answering other questions since you can easily refer back to them.

3 [9] Other remarkable contemporary wildlife artworks available for purchase through this year's Wild 100 Show & Sale, which takes place on September 12, include a deceptively simple 10-by-10-inch work on paper by internationally known Western impressionist Theodore Waddell; two iconic ink on limestone birds of prey by New York sculptor Jane Rosen; and a 36-inch-square rare elk oil painting by Mark Eberhard, whose work was the focal point of a National Museum of Wildlife Art avian art exhibition. [10] Another highlight is a minimalist bronze cougar skull inspired by the recent Kenya travels of British sculptor Simon Gudgeon, whose "Isis" can be seen both in London's Hyde Park and on the National Museum of Wildlife Art's Sculpture Trail.

4 [11] In addition to the Wild 100 Show & Sale on September 12, popular Western Visions events include the chance to meet and mingle with the artists at the Wild 100 Artist Party, September 11. [12] Attendees will have the opportunity to experience the work and techniques of featured artists de Groot and Murrill in live presentations.

Source: www.wildlifeart.org

1. To make paragraph 1 most logical, sentence 2 should be placed
   A) where it is now.
   B) before sentence 1.
   C) after sentence 3.
   D) after sentence 4.

2. To make paragraph 2 most logical, sentence 5 should be placed
   A) where it is now.
   B) after sentence 6.
   C) after sentence 7.
   D) at the end of the first paragraph.

3. To make the passage most logical, paragraph 2 [Sentences 5–8] should be placed
   A) where it is now.
   B) before paragraph 1.
   C) after paragraph 3.
   D) after paragraph 4.

4. Which choice most logically follows sentence 12?

   A) An act of Congress officially designated the museum as the National Museum of Wildlife Art of the United States in 2008, and the museum's permanent collections and educational programs inspire an appreciation for and knowledge of humanity's relationship with nature.

   B) The museum is a member of the Association of Art Museum Directors as well as the Museums West consortium; in addition, it is accredited by the American Alliance of Museums.

   C) Artwork by Western Visions featured artists will be on display, including Ewoud de Groot's painting, "Arctic Loon," and Gwynn Murrill's bronze sculpture, "Little Horse Trotting."

   D) Other Western Visions activities include the Paintings, Sculpture and Sketch shows and sales, opening August 30, and the follow-up Art a' Brewin' browsing and buying opportunity on September 24.

For answers, see page 576.

Explain **Using Effective Transitions**

The SAT will also test your ability to use **transitions** effectively to maintain logical connections between sentences and paragraphs. Transitions are words or phrases that show relationships between ideas. In other words, they illustrate how sentences and paragraphs are connected.

Transitions show specific logical relationships. The following chart lists some commonly used transitions and their uses:

Function	Transitional Words and Phrases
Continuation of previous ideas	and, also, likewise, similarly, furthermore, in addition, moreover, as such, in other words
Cause and effect	consequently, therefore, thus, hence, as a result, due to, accordingly
Contrasts, contradictions, or counterarguments	although, however, nevertheless, nonetheless, in contrast, in spite of, instead, on the other hand, conversely, regardless, otherwise, while, whereas, yet, still, alternatively
Explain	for example, for instance, specifically, to illustrate, for this reason
Summary	in summary, in short, in brief, in conclusion, overall, in essence, in general, for the most part
Sequence or order	first, second, currently, presently, concurrently, next, finally, meanwhile, eventually, last, while, previously, subsequently (following in time)

Transitional Words

The SAT will test your ability to revise a sentence so that the best transitional phrases are used to show the relationship between ideas. Study the following examples.

> **Incorrect:**
>
> May is a month for celebrating spring flowers, mothers, and high school graduates. <u>Likewise</u>, it is also a month of high anxiety. In May, high school seniors and their parents are sweating over the big college decision.

The transition *likewise* is incorrect because it signals a continuation of previous ideas. A correct choice would be a transition that communicates the contrast between celebration in the first sentence and anxiety in the second.

> **Correct:**
>
> May is a month for celebrating spring flowers, mothers, and high school graduates. <u>Yet,</u> it is also a month of high anxiety. In May, high school seniors and their parents are sweating over the big college decision.

Consider how you would correct this transition:

> **Incorrect:**
>
> As tuition costs have risen, students increasingly see their choice of college as an economic one, all about perceived costs and post-college earnings potential. <u>For example</u>, many are making this life-shaping decision based on fear and false economic assumptions.

Think about the relationship between two sentences. The second sentence is not an example of how students are basing their college choice on economics. It is a result of students' concerns over the cost of college. The relationship is one of cause and effect.

> **Correct:**
>
> As tuition costs have risen, students increasingly see their choice of college as an economic one, all about perceived costs and post-college earnings potential. <u>As a result</u>, many are making this life-shaping decision based on fear and false economic assumptions.

Other possible transitions: *Consequently, Thus*

> **Incorrect:**
>
> Fear arises because we live in an age of risk, uncertainty and relatively high levels of unemployment and underemployment. Parents are afraid that their children's futures are not assured. <u>However</u>, at least one study has shown that about two-thirds of parents won't allow their children to apply to some colleges based solely on the sticker price.

Use the chart on page 267 to choose a better underlined transition for the paragraph. Check your choice with the paragraph on the next page.

> **QUICK TIP**
>
> *In addition, for example,* and *first of all* are known as transitional phrases, but they can perform the same function as conjunctive adverbs, namely connecting and relating ideas to each other.

Correct:
Fear arises because we live in an age of risk, uncertainty and relatively high levels of unemployment and underemployment. Parents are afraid that their children's futures are not assured. For instance, at least one study has shown that about two-thirds of parents won't allow their children to apply to some colleges based solely on the sticker price.

The second sentence indicates an example of how parents' fear about their children's future influences college choices. Other correct answers include *for example* and *to illustrate*.

Transitional Phrases

Transitions not only link ideas within paragraphs, but they also connect ideas across paragraphs and texts. Notice how the word *additionally* connects the following paragraphs.

[1] With more college graduates facing years of underemployment, today's high school seniors are faced with uncertain futures. An expensive college education does not always deliver an immediate return on the investment, and parents are scared. For instance, one study has indicated that about two-thirds of parents have refused to allow their child to apply to a college based solely on the sticker price.

[2] Additionally, the classical liberal arts education is under attack. Society is asking: What is Jenny going to do with an English or history degree? She may not be able to get a job. Perhaps she should learn a trade. Or maybe she study computer science? Or engineering?

[3] While computer science and engineering graduates are needed in our modern society (and offer solid job opportunities), one business leader is troubled by the "increasing societal pressure on teenagers that pushes them toward what amounts to specialized training before they have had enough exposure to discover what they really love." In a recent opinion piece, Dan Glaser, president and CEO of Marsh & McLennan Companies, defends a college liberal arts education, saying that it produces students who can "reflect, synthesize, and form opinions."

Another method of transition between paragraphs is to repeat a key word or phrase or from a previous paragraph. In the third paragraph above, the writer repeats the words *computer science* and *engineering* from the last sentence of the second paragraph. The word *while* indicates that the writer is offering a concession before jumping into the main idea.

Directions: Read each paragraph. Choose the answer that most effectively improves the organization of the writing.

National income continues to be closely linked to personal life satisfaction at the country level. Richer publics, on average, report being happier. **1** In short, Malaysians (56% saying their life is a 7 or higher on 0–10 scale) rate their lives considerably higher than people in Bangladesh (34%), a much poorer country. **2** For instance, the advantages of being in a rich nation tend to taper off among the wealthiest countries, suggesting that after a certain point, increasing income does not make as much of a difference in life satisfaction. **3** To continue with the example, despite the enormous gap in GDP (Gross Domestic Product) per capita between Malaysia and Germany, these two publics express similar levels of life satisfaction (56% and 60%, respectively).

1. A) NO CHANGE
   B) Similarly,
   C) Yet,
   D) For example,

2. A) NO CHANGE
   B) In essence,
   C) However,
   D) Likewise,

3. Which choice provides the best transition from the previous sentence to the current one?
   A) NO CHANGE
   B) Because of this,
   C) In the same way,
   D) A case in point,

When answering a question about which transition best fits in a sentence, be sure to read the sentence before and the sentence after it. Then determine the relationship between the sentences (e.g., contrasting ideas, statement and example, passage of time, etc.). Reading the surrounding sentences familiarizes you with the sentence's context, which is important when determining which transition shows how the sentences connect to each other.

The Berlin Wall divided East Berlin and West Berlin for 28 years, from 1961 until November 1989. Typical for totalitarian states, the East German government declared the Wall to be a necessary defense against Western aggression. **4** Conversely, the Wall was intended to stop East Germans from seeking freedom in the West. In 1962, a second barrier was placed 100 yards back, creating a no-man's land, widely known as the "death strip," useless for defense against the West but clearly intended to prevent escape. It was booby-trapped with tripwires, offered no cover, and provided a clear field of fire to the watching guards. **5** Furthermore, some 5,000 East Berliners escaped into the western half of the city. Tragically, an estimated 200 people died trying to escape.

4. A) NO CHANGE
   B) In reality,
   C) In particular,
   D) Whereas,

5. A) NO CHANGE
   B) Finally,
   C) As a result,
   D) Even so,

The archaeologist's work is, **6** eventually, to find the material remains of our ancestors, and in the first place, to unearth those remains in ways that maximize the information they can convey, and, finally, to interpret the evidence. Finding those remains may be done by excavation or surface survey, but both processes require the destruction of the very evidence that is the first fruit of the work. In some cases, the destruction is literal and complete, as when an archaeologist must dig through one level of a site to find another; often the destruction is not so complete but involves the removal of objects from their physical contexts. **7** Since physical context provides crucial clues to understanding the past, evidence is lost even by removing artifacts from a dig site. The destructive nature of the work demands extraordinarily careful record keeping to avoid accidental information loss. **8** Otherwise, it can be argued that record keeping is the real occupation of the field archaeologist.

Source: www.digitalhumanities.org

6. Which of the following BEST revises underlined section 6?
   A) NO CHANGE
   B) next, to find the material remains of our ancestors, and second, to unearth
   C) first, to find the material remains of our ancestors, and second, to unearth
   D) first, to find the material remains of our ancestors, and ultimately, to unearth

7. Which choice provides the most logical introduction to sentence 7?
   A) NO CHANGE
   B) Although physical context is not important to understanding the past,
   C) In addition to the fact that archaeology is physically demanding,
   D) In contrast to the physical relationships the context provides,

8. A) NO CHANGE
   B) Subsequently,
   C) Naturally,
   D) Indeed,

For answers, see page 576.

Directions: These questions show how editing for transitions might be tested on the SAT. The answers and explanations immediately follow the questions. Answer the questions and then review the answers and the explanations.

Scholarly research is an important—perhaps the most important—part of the humanities infrastructure not only because it is critical to the vitality of this field in both educational settings and society at large but also because scholarship in specific humanities disciplines can have significant bearing on national and international issues. Many years ago, when scholars were focusing on the languages, the societies, and the historic tensions of the Middle East, few predicted how crucial these areas of inquiry would become in the early 21st century. Humanities research that inquires into other cultures, such as those of China, **1** in essence, is equally critical in the context of a global economy and in the creation of an educated American citizenry. Meanwhile, such research and its dissemination have **2** eventually always been indispensable elements in the civic culture of the United States and to the fostering of a well-informed and participatory electorate.

Source: www.humanitiesindicators.org

1. A) NO CHANGE
   B) for example,
   C) regardless,
   D) still,

QUICK TIP

Read the sentence silently to yourself as you insert each of the answer choices.

Strategy: The sentence is providing an example that offers support for the argument that humanities research is important. Answer A is incorrect because the transition *in essence* indicates a truth or an actuality is about to be revealed. Answer C, *regardless*, suggests opposition or contrast, and is also incorrect. Answer D, *still*, may refer to time or contrast, neither of which makes sense in the sentence. Answer B is correct because *for example* logically indicates that what follows is an example related to the previous sentence.

2. A) NO CHANGE
   B) otherwise
   C) also
   D) incidentally

Strategy: Answer A, *eventually*, refers to time or sequence and does not logically fit in this sentence due to the earlier use of *meanwhile*. Answer B is also incorrect because *otherwise* indicates a consequence and does not make sense in the sentence since it is not identifying repercussions or consequences. The transitional word in answer D, *incidentally*, denotes digression and is incorrect because the sentence continues the discussion of humanities research. Choice C is the best answer because the transition *also* signifies addition, and the sentence's information provides an example of how humanities research is crucial.

Directions: Questions 1–8 are based on the following passage.

Titanic Myths

The *Titanic* disaster is a classic tale and **1** namely has become a modern folk story, but like all folk stories our understanding of what really happened has been clouded by the way the disaster has been recounted over the years following that terrible night in April 1912. **2** Before the waves of the North Atlantic closed over the *Titanic's* stern, the myths began.

It was said that the builders and owners of *Titanic* claimed she was unsinkable. **3** Actually, the claim made was that she was "practically unsinkable." Close enough, **4** but likewise an unfortunate statement and one that would haunt both the builder and owner for years.

Titanic and her slightly older sister *Olympic* were designed to compete with the Cunard liners *Lusitania* and *Mauretania,* which entered service in 1907. Designed and built as record breakers, both held the coveted "Blue Riband" for the fastest Atlantic crossing. The sisters were built principally from lessons learned from advances in warship construction, but **5** otherwise both were powered by steam turbines driving quadruple screws, each fitted with a large balanced rudder, making them faster than their competition and easier to maneuver—a giant leap forward in marine engineering that is comparable to the advances made in 1969 with the introduction of the *Concorde* supersonic aircraft.

Speed plays a major part in the continuing story of *Titanic*. It is often said she was trying to set a record on her maiden voyage, attempting to arrive ahead of schedule in New York. That is not true. **6** In the same way, she was following the pattern of her sister's first crossing the previous year and, like *Olympic,* not all of *Titanic's* boilers had been lit. **7** Also she was sailing on the longer southern route across the Atlantic in order to avoid the very threat that caused her eventual loss. Even if all boilers had been lit, her maximum speed was 21 knots, a far cry from the 26 knots the Cunarders regularly recorded. **8** If, as some speculate, the ship had arrived Tuesday evening, her passengers would have been very much inconvenienced by arriving a day before their scheduled hotel reservations and connecting train tickets.

Source: Adapted from www.titanichistoricalsociety.org

1. A) NO CHANGE
   B) again
   C) similarly
   D) now

2. A) NO CHANGE
   B) As soon as
   C) Although
   D) Accordingly

3. Which choice provides the most logical introduction to the sentence?
   A) NO CHANGE
   B) Unfortunately, the claim made was that
   C) To prove the point that
   D) However, they postulated that

4. A) NO CHANGE
   B) and besides
   C) but nevertheless
   D) however in brief

5. A) NO CHANGE
   B) most importantly
   C) in other words
   D) finally

6. A) NO CHANGE
   B) Consequently,
   C) Therefore,
   D) In actuality,

7. A) NO CHANGE
   B) However
   C) Overall
   D) Still

8. To provide a smoother transition between ideas, which of the following should be inserted at this point in the passage?
   A) The most important reason why *Titanic* did not attempt a full speed crossing was the risk of potential engine damage.
   B) A final reason why *Titanic* wasn't attempting to arrive ahead of schedule is related to customer satisfaction.
   C) The most important reason why *Titanic* wasn't attempting to arrive ahead of schedule is related to customer satisfaction.
   D) Another reason why *Titanic* did not attempt a full speed crossing was the risk of potential engine damage.

For answers, see page 577.

SAT questions will often test you over multiple skills. To correctly answer question 8, you must identify which sentence maintains the main idea of the paragraph and also uses the appropriate transitional phrases.

LESSON 10:
Use of Language

- revising texts to improve word choice for exactness and content
- revising to eliminate wordiness and redundancy
- revising text for consistency of style and tone or to match style and tone to purpose

Explain   Revising For Word Choice

Mark Twain wrote, "The difference between the almost right word and the right word is really a large matter—it's the difference between the lightning bug and the lightning." In the Writing and Language section of the SAT, you will be tested over your ability to revise text by choosing the best word to communicate the most **precise** meaning.

Think It Through

- Choose the word that communicates the correct meaning based upon the context of the passage.

> **Confusing:** The greatest problem of the rescue patrol was <u>good</u> visibility.
> **Clear:** The greatest problem of the rescue patrol was <u>poor</u> visibility.

The first sentence is confusing because it identifies the problem as "good visibility." The problem is actually the opposite: poor visibility.

> **Confusing:** Our Saturday project is to <u>install</u> all broken windows in the school.
> **Clear:** Our Saturday project is to <u>replace</u> all broken windows in the school.

The first sentence incorrectly uses the verb *install,* which implies that broken windows are being put in; a more precise verb for this sentence is *replace*.

- When choosing a word, consider denotation and connotation.

Denotation is the dictionary definition of the word. *Connotation* is the implied meaning of the word. It is an idea or quality that a word makes you think about in addition to its dictionary meaning. Connotation gives words that have similar dictionary meanings more specific meanings. Consider how the following synonyms for poor and ask have specific meanings.

> **poor:** broke, indigent, needy, penniless, destitute, impoverished

> **ask:** question, interrogate, quiz, inquire, grill, survey, query

QUICK
TIP

Some questions may test your ability to use prepositions and subordinating conjunctions correctly.

You should know the difference between *by which, from which, for which, whereby, about,* and *upon*.

Examples

I called the supervisor to (inquire, question him) about the job opening. (*Inquire* is the better choice. *Question* requires the object *him* and implies you are asking questions about the supervisor instead of about the job.)

Microfinance is the supply of loans, savings, and other basic financial services to the (penniless, impoverished).
(The more general term *impoverished* fits with the context.)

- Choose specific, not vague words.

When choosing answers, avoid those that contain generally vague terms—*good, really, kind of,* and *bad*. Choose words and phrases that provide precise explanations.

> **Vague:** Studies have found that listening to music may help people feel better.
> **Specific:** Studies have found that listening to music may help patients better tolerate pain during medical procedures.

> **Vague:** The children who listened to music indicated they had less pain.
> **Specific:** The children who listed to music reduced their pain by 1 point on a 10-point scale.

QUICK TIP

Whenever possible avoid beginning a sentence with empty phrases such as "There is/was" or "It is/was."

Practice

Directions: As you read the following paragraph, circle the underlined word or phrase that communicates the intended meaning clearly and specifically.

There is broad consensus that reducing global poverty and hunger requires **1** accelerating/encouraging growth in the agriculture sector. Recent studies suggest that every 1 percent increase in agricultural income per capita **2** reduces/downsizes the number of people living in extreme poverty by between 0.6 and 1.8 percent. The U.S. Government's global hunger and food security initiative, Feed the Future, **3** strives to increase/attempts to prop up agricultural production and the incomes of both men and women in rural areas who rely on agriculture for their livelihoods. Investments in inclusive agriculture-led growth **4** encircle/encompass improving agricultural productivity, expanding markets and trade, and increasing the economic resilience of vulnerable rural communities. Feed the Future seeks to **5** liberate/unleash the proven potential of small-scale agricultural producers to deliver results on a large scale.

For answers, see page 577.

Directions: These Model SAT questions are very similar to questions that test your ability to revise sentences for concise word choice on the SAT. The answer and explanation immediately follow each question. Answer the questions and then review the explanations.

> When the unmanned Antares rocket exploded October 28, along with an Aerospace-built Reentry Breakup Recorder-Wireless (REBR-W), NASA was on the phone with Aerospace **1** three minutes later, asking for a replacement REBR-W.
>
> The REBR-Ws are used to assemble and transfer reentry data from vehicles returning to Earth from space. They measure hull temperatures, tumble and breakup dynamics and speed changes. NASA originally ordered two of these devices from Aerospace in July 2013 to be used as part of its safety verification process for the future reentry of the International Space Station. The first REBR-W was delivered one year later in July of 2014, with the second one stored away in pieces for an undetermined future **2** exercise.
>
> Source: www.aerospace.org

1. A) NO CHANGE
   B) a short time later, demanding another one.
   C) three minutes later, requiring another REBR-W.
   D) quickly, suggesting that they rebuild another REBR-W.

Strategy: Think about which choice is the most precise and accurate. Choices B and C are vague. Also choice D uses the word *rebuild*, which implies fixing the current one (an impossibility since it just exploded.) Choice C is more specific, but replaces *asking* with *requiring*. From the context, the better word is *asking*. Choice A is correct.

2. A) NO CHANGE
   B) departure
   C) release
   D) launch

QUICK TIP

Bigger words are not necessarily better. When selecting the best answer, choose the most accurate, precise word, regardless of its length.

Strategy: Choice A is not the best answer because *exercise* is too vague. Answer B, *departure*, is also incorrect because it implies that the second REBR-W will leave or set off on a journey. This choice is not appropriate in this context, which discusses equipment used in space. Choice C, *release*, indicates relinquishment or freedom, which does not relate to space equipment. The best answer is D because *launch* fits with the context of the sentence: that the second REBR-W will be used in future space exploration.

Directions: Read the passage and answer the questions that follow.

Hemingway on War and Its Aftermath

During the First World War, Ernest Hemingway volunteered to serve in Italy as an ambulance driver with the American Red Cross. In June 1918, while running a mobile canteen **1** bestowing chocolate and cigarettes on soldiers, he was wounded by Austrian mortar fire. "Then there was a flash, as when a blast-furnace door is swung open, and a roar that started white and went red," he recalled in a letter home.

Despite his injuries, Hemingway carried a wounded Italian soldier to safety and was injured again by machine-gun fire. For his bravery, he received the Silver Medal of Valor from the Italian government—one of the first Americans so **2** honored.

Commenting on this experience years later in *Men at War*, Hemingway wrote: "When you go to war as a boy you have a great **3** apparition of immortality. Other people get killed; not you. . . . Then when you are badly wounded the first time you lose that illusion and you know it can happen to you. After being severely wounded two weeks before my nineteenth birthday, I had a bad time until I figured out that nothing could happen to me that had not happened to all men before me. Whatever I had to do men had always done. If they had done it, then I could do it too, and the best thing was not to worry about it."

4 Salvaging for six months in a Milan hospital, Hemingway fell in love with Agnes von Kurowsky, an American Red Cross nurse. **5** At war's end, he returned to his home in Oak Park, Illinois, a different man. His experience of travel, combat, and love had broadened his outlook. Yet while his war experience had changed him dramatically, the town he returned to remained very much the same.

Several short stories (written years later) offer **6** recognition upon his homecoming and his understanding of the dilemmas of the returned war veteran. In one of these stories, "Soldier's Home," Howard Krebs returns home from Europe later than many of his peers. Having missed the victory parades, he is unable to reconnect with those he left behind—especially his mother, who cannot understand how her son has been changed by the war.

1. A) NO CHANGE
    B) granting chocolate and cigarettes to soldiers,
    C) scattering chocolate and cigarettes among soldiers,
    D) dispensing chocolate and cigarettes to soldiers,

2. A) NO CHANGE
    B) flattered
    C) memorialized
    D) fulfilled

3. A) NO CHANGE
    B) delusion
    C) nightmare
    D) daydream

4. A) NO CHANGE
    B) Restoring
    C) Redeeming
    D) Recuperating

5. A) NO CHANGE
    B) Upon
    C) About
    D) From

6. A) NO CHANGE
    B) recollections
    C) insights
    D) interpretations

For answers, see page 577.

QUICK TIP

When answering word choice questions, read quickly through the answers, and then try out each answer in the sentence, starting with the ones you are familiar with. Leave the words with unfamiliar meanings until last. After trying them all out, make your best guess.

Explain Revising to Eliminate Wordiness

Some questions will test your ability to revise text to eliminate wordiness and redundancy. Effective writing uses fewer, better words. It is **concise**.

Never make a thought more complicated than necessary. If you can express yourself clearly and directly, do so. Often this means replacing longer phrases with single words

- Choose shorter, concise phrases over longer, wordy ones.

  Consider the following sentences:

  > **Wordy:** The newscast, which was televised this morning on a local station, described a suspicious car, which had a license plate from the state of North Dakota.
  >
  > **Concise:** This morning's local television newscast described a suspicious car with a North Dakota license plate.

  The first sentence has too many unnecessary clauses. The second sentence states the same idea more concisely.

  Words you can remove without changing the sentence's meaning should be edited out. For example, consider the following sentences:

  > **Wordy:** At the soccer match, Joel met up with two friends from elementary school.
  >
  > **Concise:** At the soccer match, Joel met two friends from elementary school.

  The first sentence adds the unnecessary words *up with*, while the second sentence conveys the same idea more concisely.

- Choose a simple word instead of a flowery or academic one.

  Unless you are being humorous, don't use a longer word if a simpler word will do the job. Save the longer word for a context in which the simpler word is not as meaningful.

  > **Pretentious:** The feline member of our family loves to frolic, gambol, and cavort for considerable periods of time with the canine member of our family ménage.
  >
  > **Simpler:** Our cat often plays with the family dog.

  (The first sentence might be acceptable in a humorous essay that mocks pretension.)

- Avoid saying the same thing twice, even though in different words.

  > **Wordy:** The football Giants flew to Buffalo by air, but had to return by bus because of a lake-effect blizzard.
  >
  > **Concise:** The Giants flew to Buffalo, but returned by bus because of a lake-effect blizzard.

  The first sentence uses the verb *flew* and restates the same idea by saying "by air." This is redundant.

QUICK TIP

Wordy: Anyone who confines his interests to himself and his own affairs is bound, in the end, to amount to very little in life and because of his selfish interests has stunted his chances of self-development.

Concise: A man wrapped up in himself makes a very small bundle. (Benjamin Franklin)

Also, don't pile adjective upon adjective or adverb upon adverb. Where possible, use specific nouns and verbs to reduce the number of modifiers. Read these sentences:

> **Wordy:** The young, immature baby of but a year walked unsteadily and shakily across the floor into the outstretched, waiting arms of her waiting mother.
>
> **Concise:** The one-year-old tottered across the floor into her mother's outstretched arms.
>
> **Wordy:** The young, immature baby of but a year walked unsteadily and shakily across the floor into the outstretched, waiting arms of her waiting mother.

The first sentence has several unnecessary modifies, such as "young," immature," "baby," "unsteadily," and "shakily." These ideas are condensed into specific words that express these same ideas, such as "one-year-old" and "tottered."

Some expressions should be eradicated and replaced.

The No-No Group	
Avoid	**Say and Write**
at all times	always
at the present time	now
due to the fact that, for the reason that, in view of the fact that as,	because, since
inasmuch as	since
in order to, with a view to	to
in the amount of	for
in the case of, in the event that, in the event of	if
in the meantime	meanwhile
in the near future	soon
in the neighborhood of	nearly, about, around
in this place	here
previous to, prior to	before
there can be no doubt that	doubtless
with reference to, with regard to	about
it is/was (For example: It is important that we find a cure for cancer.)	We must find a cure for cancer.
there is/are (For example: There was a long debate . . .)	The senators debated . . .

The Duplicators
These common expressions include unnecessary words.

cheap ~~in price~~	meet ~~up with~~
combined ~~together~~	modern colleges ~~of today~~
connect ~~up~~, finish ~~up~~, end ~~up~~, join ~~up~~	rarely ~~ever~~
~~every~~ once in a while	requirements ~~needed for~~
gray ~~in color~~	round ~~in shape~~
I think ~~in my opinion~~	small ~~in size~~
inside ~~of~~	the ~~two~~ twins
long ~~length of~~ time	throughout the ~~whole~~ night

Read the following sentence pairs and determine which one is more concise.

1. A) Unlike most fruit trees, an orange tree may bear fruit for more than a hundred years.

    B) The orange tree does not have the fruiting qualities of most trees, for it may bear fruit for more than 100 years.

Answer: Though the same message is conveyed in both A and B, B uses more words than necessary. Duplication of *for* is a distraction.

2. A) Though a sheet sounds like a sail, it is actually, in nautical terms at least, a rope or chain.

    B) In nautical terms, a sheet is a rope or chain, not a sail.

Answer: A uses a complex sentence, beginning with *though*, to provide the same information given in the more concise B.

3. A) Of the equine breed, the Paso Fino is a horse that is relatively small but with a distinctive, appealing gait.

    B) The Paso Fino is a relatively small horse with a distinctive, appealing gait.

Answer: A is hopelessly verbose, with the affected *of the equine breed* and an unnecessary subordinate clause introduced by *that*. B provides the same information simply and economically.

Practice

Directions: Read each passage and follow the instructions below.

George Washington's military and political leadership was indispensable to the founding of the United States. As commander of the Continental Army, he rallied Americans from thirteen divergent states and outlasted Britain's superior military force. As the very first president of the United States of America, Washington's superb leadership set the standard for each president that has succeeded him and followed after him.

1. Rewrite the underlined sentence so that it is concise.

_____

_____

_____

Susan LaFlesche Picotte was born on the Omaha reservation in northern Nebraska. She was the daughter of Chief Joseph LaFlesche (Iron Eye) and his wife Mary (One Woman). Her father raised all of his children to be independent, educated, and adaptable to a changing Indian society. Susan's decision to attend medical school was unique at a time when formal medical training was rare for women, especially Indian women. In the year of 1889, Susan LaFlesche graduated from the medical program, which was a three year program, at the Woman's Medical College of Pennsylvania at the top of her class in two years.

2. Rewrite the underlined sentence so that it is concise.

_____

_____

_____

Plants have been used for natural dyeing since before recorded history and prior to humans maintaining historical records. The staining properties of plants were noted by humans and have been used to obtain and retain these colors from plants throughout history. Native plants and their resultant dyes have been used to enhance people's lives through decoration of animal skins, fabrics, crafts, hair, and even their bodies.

3. Rewrite the underlined sentence so that it is concise.

_____

_____

_____

In 1611, after having studied how sailors stack cannonballs, Johannes Kepler began pondering over the most efficient way to pack spheres in a given space. Should one pack them in identical layers, one on top of the other, with each sphere in one layer sitting right on top of the sphere directly beneath it? Or can one get more spheres into the box staggering the layers, the way grocers stack oranges, so that the oranges in each higher layer sit in the hollows made by the oranges beneath them? Eventually, he finally decided on the face-centered cubic lattice, which is the same way in which you will find oranges stacked today.

However, Kepler could not prove that the face-centered cubic was indeed the most efficient way to pack spheres. Up until today, that is, until recently this problem remained unsolved without a solution. After over a decade of research, testing all the possible solutions, Thomas Hales of the University of Michigan concluded that Kepler's method, the face-centered cubic, was indeed the most efficient way to stack spheres, meaning that the amount of space occupied by the spheres is maximized in the proposed arrangement. Referees have declared they are 99 percent sure that Hale's solution is correct.

4. Rewrite the underlined sentence in paragraph 1 so that it is concise.

_____

_____

_____

_____

_____

5. Rewrite the underlined sentence in paragraph 2 so that it is concise.

_____

_____

_____

_____

For answers, see page 578.

● ●

Directions: These Model SAT Questions are similar to questions on revising for concise wording may be tested on the actual SAT. The answer and explanation immediately follow each question. Answer the questions and then review the answers and the explanations.

QUICK
TIP

When revising for conciseness, eliminate redundant phrases, such as "acute crisis" or "future plans." By definition, a crisis is considered acute, and all plans are made for the future.

Reviving Algae from the (Almost) Dead

Tucked away in darkness and almost dead, algae can emerge from a frigid and foggy environment to live again—and perhaps even become the seeds for a new beginning that can provide biofuel for a clean energy future.

At the Energy Department's National Renewable Energy Laboratory (NREL), and at dozens of other labs nationwide, algae are like a junior high kid with great promise: slow to arise, but packed with energy for the long haul. It may take years, **1** but eventually the great expectations can ultimately be reached.

A gallon of fuel made from algae currently costs about quadruple the cost of a gallon of conventional diesel. **2** But looking and thinking long term, algae are an inexhaustible resource that, if used as a substitute for fuels, would slash the amount of carbon dioxide in the atmosphere.

Source: www.nrel.gov

1. A) NO CHANGE
   B) but eventually reaching the great expectations can be achieved in time.
   C) but the great expectations can be reached in the future in the long run.
   D) but eventually the great expectations can be reached.

Strategy: Answer A is redundant since it uses both *eventually* and *ultimately* to express a future event. Likewise, Answer B uses the redundancies, *eventually* and *in time*, to suggest a future event. Answer C introduces *in the future* and *in the long run* as redundant phrases. Answer D is correct because it eliminates redundancy and clearly expresses the idea.

2. A) NO CHANGE
   B) yet looking long term,
   C) in the long term,
   D) looking long term, however,

Strategy: Answer A is redundant because it uses both *looking* and *thinking*. Answer B is briefer, but has two contrasting conjunctions, *But* and *yet*, when only one is necessary. Answer D also uses redundant elements: *But* and *however*. Answer C is the best answer.

Directions: Questions 1–6 are based on the following passage.

By the Numbers: Dropping out of High School

How costly is the decision to drop out of high school? Consider a few figures ▪1▪ about living life without a diploma:

$20,241

The average dropout can expect to earn an annual income of $20,241, according to the U.S. Census Bureau. ▪2▪ That's a full, complete $10,386 less than the typical high school graduate, and $36,424 less than someone with a bachelor's degree.

12

Of course, ▪3▪ simply finding a job is also much more of a challenge for dropouts. While the national unemployment rate stood at 8.1 percent in August, joblessness among those without a high school degree measured 12 percent. Among college graduates, it was 4.1 percent.

30.8

The challenges hardly end there, ▪4▪ particularly among young dropouts who quit school. Among those between the ages of 18 and 24, dropouts were more than twice as likely as college graduates to live in poverty according to the Department of Education. Dropouts experienced a poverty rate of 30.8 percent, while those with at least a bachelor's degree had a poverty rate of 13.5 percent.

63

Among dropouts between the ages of 16 and 24, incarceration rates were a whopping 63 times higher than among college graduates, according to a study by researchers at Northeastern University. ▪5▪ To be sure, there is undoubtedly no direct link between prison and the decision to leave high school early. Rather, the data is further evidence that dropouts are exposed to many of the same socioeconomic forces that are often gateways to crime.

$292,000

The same study found that as a result — when compared to the typical high school graduate — **6** a dropout will end up in time costing taxpayers an average of $292,000 over a lifetime due to the price tag associated with incarceration and other factors such as how much less they pay in taxes.

Source: www.pbs.org

Quick Tip

When answering questions on concise wording, the shortest answer is often (but not always) the correct one.

1. A) NO CHANGE
   B) about life without a diploma:
   C) about life without a single diploma:
   D) regarding about life with no diploma:

2. A) NO CHANGE
   B) That's a full $10,386 in its entirety less than
   C) That's $10,386 less than
   D) That's a full $10,386 less than and below

3. A) NO CHANGE
   B) in addition, simply finding a job is also much more of a challenge
   C) much more of a difficult challenge is also simply finding a job
   D) simply finding a job is also much more of a challenge and difficulty

4. A) NO CHANGE
   B) particularly among young, youthful dropouts.
   C) particularly among young dropouts mainly.
   D) particularly among young dropouts.

5. A) NO CHANGE
   B) To be sure, there is no direct link or connection
   C) To be sure, there is no direct link
   D) To be sure, no direct link exists

6. A) NO CHANGE
   B) a dropout will end up costing taxpayers an average of
   C) a dropout will end up costing taxpayers an average close to the amount of
   D) finally a dropout will end up costing taxpayers an average of

For answers, see page 578.

Explain Using Consistent Style and Tone

Some questions will test your ability to revise text for style and tone. **Style** refers to the way a passage is written. Some texts are informal and use common words and shorter sentences. Informal texts may use personal pronouns, such as *I* and *we*. More formal passages include more complex words and sentence structures. Personal pronouns are avoided.

Tone is the author's attitude toward a subject. It may be satirical, formal, bitter, objective, humorous, critical, or tongue-in-cheek—just to name a few. Tone will change according to audience. A scholarly research paper will have a critical, formal tone, whereas an e-mail to a professor might have a respectful, polite tone. The words used will vary according to the tone. For example, to convey a casual, conversational tone, a writer might incorporate slang or everyday language, but to express a serious, academic tone, a writer would employ formal language.

Think It Through

In the Writing and Language section of the SAT, you will be tested over your ability to revise text for consistency of style and tone or to match style and tone to purpose. For example, consider the following paragraph:

Why We Sign up for Gym Memberships But Never Go to the Gym

Gyms have built their business model around us not showing up. Gyms have way more members than they can actually accommodate. Low-priced gyms are the most extreme example of this. Planet Fitness, which charges between $10 and $20 per month, has, on average, 6,500 members per gym. Most of its gyms can hold around 300 people. <u>This disparity between the maximum capacity of its gyms versus its large membership numbers functions successfully for Planet Fitness due to the company's realization that members will not avail themselves of its facilities.</u> After all, if everyone who had a gym membership showed up at the gym, it would be Thunderdome.

If you are not going to the gym, you are actually the gym's best customer.

The underlined sentence does not match the tone of the rest of the paragraph. It uses formal language and sounds pretentious in the midst of the other sentences, which use casual language such as "showing up," "way more," and a pop culture reference to "Thunderdome." This lengthy sentence can be revised to the following to match the paragraph's style and tone: *Planet Fitness can do this because it knows that members won't show up.*

Unless appropriate to the writing purpose and tone, avoid casual language, such as slang and clichés. Replace clichés with more interesting, vivid descriptions. Read the example paragraph below.

Check out this stat: high school football players are nearly twice as likely to have a concussion as college players, says some report published Wednesday. The report says it "remains unclear" whether repetitive head injuries can lead to long-term brain disease. I guess it is still up in the air.

This paragraph uses slang and clichés, such as "check out" and "up in the air." It also uses informal language, including the abbreviated "stat" and "says some report." The following revision is a more formal example of the same paragraph:

> High school football players are nearly twice as likely to sustain a concussion as are college players, yet it "remains unclear" as to whether repetitive head injuries can lead to long-term brain disease, according to a new report released Wednesday.

Practice

Directions: Read each passage. Revise the underlined sections so that the style and tone fit with the rest of the text.

Scarcely a week goes by without an awards ceremony somewhere. The Oscars, the Emmys, and the Tonys are the most famous but there are a host of others. [1] When the air waves are saturated with these types of programs, the magnitude of the ceremony abates.

1. Revise sentence 1 for style and/or tone:

_____

_____

QUICK TIP

Questions about tone may be worded thus:

• Which choice best maintains the tone established in the passage?

• The writer wants to convey an attitude of _____ (seriousness, genuine interest) and avoid _____ (sarcasm, mockery). Which of the following will help him/her maintain this tone?

I was intrigued by a recent study in the journal Psychological Science on the voice of authority. Scientists wanted to hear if people's voices change in predictable ways when they are put into positions of power. Plus, they wondered [2] if listeners could pick up on those changes.

Sei Jin Ko, a social psychology researcher at San Diego State University, explains that over a hundred college students came in to their lab to have themselves recorded, starting with a recording of their everyday voices.

Then they were asked to imagine a scenario involving the purchase of a new car. Some people were told [3] they were in a position of mega power—they had inside information or lots of other offers to choose from. Meanwhile, [4] others were told they flat out had zero chance of getting a crazy-good deal.

2. Revise sentence 2 for style and/or tone:

_____

_____

3. Revise sentence 3 for style and/or tone:

_____

_____

4. Revise sentence 4 for style and/or tone:

_____

_____

As someone who has lived with Type 1 Diabetes for over 40 years—I was diagnosed in 1973, at age 9—I can tell you that keeping my blood sugars in control 24/7 is incredibly difficult. And that's despite having the knowledge on how to keep it under control, as well as having the health insurance that covers my test strips and insulin pump supplies. [5] Studies have shown that two million adults over the age of 65, had no health insurance coverage, which helps explain the gap between best practice and what happens in real life.

5. Revise sentence 5 for style and/or tone:

_____

_____

For answers, see page 578.

This Model SAT Questions show how your ability to revise text for consistency of style and tone or to match style and tone to purpose might be tested on the real SAT. The answer and explanation immediately follow each question. Try the questions and then review the answers and the explanations.

Why Is Handwriting Important?

Writing has a very long history. It began as simple pictographs drawn on a rock, which were then combined to represent ideas and developed into more abstract symbols. Just like our writing today, early symbols were used to store information and communicate it to others.

In recent years, modern technology **1** has caused a 180 in the way we communicate through writing. However, despite the increased use of computers for writing, the skill of handwriting remains important in education, employment and in everyday life.

Time devoted to the teaching and learning of letter formation in the early years will **2** reap a lifetime of rewards. Legible writing that can be produced comfortably, quickly, and effortlessly allows a child to attend to the higher-level aspects of writing composition and content. **3** This is important when assessments are based on written work, particularly in time-limited written examinations, which remain as a major form of assessment for many formal qualifications. Without fast and legible handwriting, students may miss out on learning opportunities and under-achieve academically.

Source: www.nha-handwriting.org

QUICK TIP

When writing for any audience other than close friends or family, it is best to avoid using slang.

1. A) NO CHANGE
   B) has dramatically changed
   C) has supercharged the transformation of
   D) has made an epic change in

Strategy: Choice A is incorrect because the phrase *has caused a 180* is slang and does not fit the formal, factual style and tone of the rest of the text. Choice C is too wordy for the straightforward tone. Choice D contains the slang term *epic*. Choice B is correct because it uses formal language appropriate to the text's tone.

2. Which choice best maintains the tone established in the passage?
   A) NO CHANGE
   B) pay off for sure.
   C) offer a trove of achievements.
   D) provide several academic advantages.

Strategy: The current phrase reap a lifetime of rewards has an excessively cheer tone that is out of place with the rest of the text. Choice B include the phrase *for sure,* which seems too casual for the topic. On the other hand the phrase trove of achievements sounds pretentious. The best choice is D.

3. A) NO CHANGE
   B) This is a big deal
   C) This is more than a blip on the radar
   D) This is the real deal

Strategy: Choice B is incorrect because *big deal* is slang and does not fit the formal style and tone of the text. Choice C is not the best answer because it uses the cliché *a blip on the radar.* The slang term *real deal* is used in choice D, making it incorrect as well. Only Choice A employs appropriate language to match the text's style and tone.

When answering questions about consistency of style and tone, imagine the audience. Ask yourself how they would react to the words used in the text and whether those words mesh with the text's overall tone, style, and purpose.

SAT-Type Questions

Directions: Questions 1–3 are based on the following passage.

What Parents Need to Know about Dyslexia (Reading Disability)

Reading is the ability to decode and comprehend written symbols. While speaking is a natural process, reading and writing are not natural or **1** a cake walk for many students, especially for those with dyslexia. For most children the very complex process of learning to read requires years of active teaching. Learning to read is a sequential process; each new skill builds on mastering the previously learned skills. The sequence consists of gaining decoding skills, fluency, comprehension and the final step is storing the information in memory.

Initial difficulty in learning to read occurs in nearly 40% of students in the U.S. Reading difficulties are the most common cause of underachievement and **2** bombing any chance at academic success. Difficulties in early reading may have a number of different causes including deficits in spoken language skills, lack of background knowledge, inadequate instruction, insufficient reading practice, or a true reading disability or reading disorder called dyslexia.

Many parents become concerned when they notice that their child is struggling to remember letters, words, or how to read and spell. **3** Mothers and fathers, grandparents and guardians are mired in frustration because schools may not identify the problem early or provide extra help to improve it. Parent must have a general understanding of reading disability, the terminology, basic strategies, resources, and available support in order to help their dyslexic child.

Source: www.aapos.org

1. A) NO CHANGE
   B) easy as pie for many students
   C) easy for many students
   D) a cinch for many students

2. A) NO CHANGE
   B) flunking out
   C) messing up at school
   D) academic failure

3. The writer wants to convey an attitude of concern and to avoid the appearance of mockery. Which choice best accomplishes this goal?
   A) NO CHANGE
   B) Parents experience a ton of frustration
   C) Parents often experience additional frustration
   D) Parents often freak out

• •

The following is adapted from Barack Obama's "A More Perfect Union" address given during his run for president in 2008.

This was one of the tasks we set forth at the beginning of this campaign—to continue the long march of those who came before us, a march for a **4** bigger, badder, more excellent America. I chose to run for the presidency at this moment in history because I believe deeply that we cannot solve the challenges of our time unless we solve them together—unless we perfect our union by understanding that we may have different stories, but we hold common hopes; that we may not look the same and we may not have come from the same place, but we all want to move in the same direction— **5** towards a better future for our children and our grandchildren.

4. A) NO CHANGE
    B) more just, more equal, more free, more caring and more prosperous America.
    C) better America in so many, many ways.
    D) nation that won't put up with inequality, with selfishness, or with poverty.

5. Which of the following best maintains the tone and style of the passage?
    A) NO CHANGE
    B) upward and onward.
    C) towards an utopian world for our progeny.
    D) you know the sky's the limit.

For answers, see page 579.

LESSON 11:
Sentence Structure

- correcting sentence fragments and run-ons
- combining sentences for clarity
- correcting problems with sentence structure and modifiers
- correcting shifts in verbs and pronouns

Explain Correcting Fragments and Run-ons

In the Writing and Language section of the SAT, you will be tested over your ability to correct **fragments** and **run-ons** as well as to use various sentence structures to communicate ideas clearly and effectively.

Think It Through

In the Writing and Language section of the SAT, you will be tested on your ability to correct fragments and run-ons while also utilizing various sentence structures to communicate clear and effective ideas. There are three basic types of sentences.

Complete Sentences

You have learned that a sentence must have a subject and a verb. The verb is often called a predicate. In the following sentences, the subject is underlined once; the verb is underlined twice.

> **Examples:**
> One hundred miles out to sea, a thirsty sailor can drink the water from the Amazon.
> The Nile has frozen over twice—in 829 and 1010 C.E.

The preceding examples are simple sentences. Each one contains a subject and a verb.

Either the subject or the verb may be compound in a simple sentence.

> **Compound Subject and Verb:** One hundred miles out to sea a thirsty sailor or a marooned boatman can dip into the ocean and drink the water from the Amazon.

Compound Sentences

Two or more simple sentences can be combined to form a compound sentence.

> **Simple Sentences:**
> Medicating a dog is easy.
> Medicating a cat is a disaster.

Compound Sentence:
Medicating a dog is easy, but medicating a cat is a disaster.

The parts of a compound sentence are often joined together by *for, and, nor, but, or, yet, so.* These "joining words" are called coordinating conjunctions.

When two sentences are joined to make a compound sentence, the two main parts are called **clauses**. Because these two parts can stand by themselves as complete sentences, they are called **independent clauses**.

Compound Sentences:
The bells rang, AND students quickly filled the corridors.
Are you coming to the game, OR have you made other plans?
Helen doesn't like lima beans, NOR does she care for okra.

Notice that a comma is placed before the conjunction in compound sentences.

Complex Sentences

A complex sentence also has two or more clauses, but at least one of the clauses cannot stand by itself as a sentence. Note the following example.

Complex Sentence: Although the number of protons in an element cannot be altered by chemical means, physics may be used to add or remove protons and thereby change one element into another.

> **First Clause:** Although the number of protons in an element cannot be altered by chemical means (subordinate clause)
>
> **Second Clause:** physics may be used to add or remove protons and thereby change one element into another. (independent clause)

The first clause cannot stand by itself as a sentence. Although it has both a subject and a verb, the clause does not express a complete thought. It is a **subordinate**, or **dependent clause**. The second clause can stand by itself. It is an **independent clause**.

Notice that a comma is placed after introductory dependent clauses, such as "Although the number of protons in an element cannot be altered by chemical means."

Sentence Fragments

Incomplete sentences, called **sentence fragments**, are often the result of carelessness or haste. A sentence expresses a complete thought.

These are common types of sentence fragments:

No Predicate: The Inuit people using wooden "eyeglasses" with narrow slits for eye protection.

This example is incomplete because it uses the verb form *using* instead of *use.* Also, it doesn't go on to make a point about the Inuit's wooden eyeglasses.

Here are two ways to fix this problem.

Complete Sentences:
The Inuit people use wooden "eyeglasses" with narrow slits for eye protection. (Change *using* to *use,* which creates a complete thought.)
The Inuit people, using wooden "eyeglasses" with narrow slits for eye protection, are able to spend many hours outside in challenging conditions. (Add a verb along with more details to complete the thought.)

Study these examples.

> **No Subject:** Read *Pride and Prejudice* and enjoyed it.
> **Complete Sentence:** I read *Pride and Prejudice* and enjoyed it.

> **No Predicate, No Subject:** Adopted the new plan, with some reservations.
> **Complete Sentence:** The club finally adopted the new plan, with some reservations.

Types of Fragments

A common mistake is to write a phrase or subordinate clause as a complete sentence. Remember, complete sentences must have a subject and predicate. They express a complete thought. Here are some examples of types of fragments and how they could be fixed.

> **Prepositional Phrase Fragment:** On the floor in a corner of the room near the bookcase.
> **Complete Sentence:** I finally found my keys on the floor in a corner of the room near the bookcase.

> **Subordinate Clause Fragment:** Automobiles that combine gasoline power and an electric battery.
> **Complete Sentence:** Automobiles that combine gasoline power and an electric battery are the hope of the future.

> **Subordinate Clause Fragment:** Which has become a major industry.
> **Complete Sentence:** Billions of dollars come into Egypt from tourism, which has become a major industry.

> **Subordinate Clause Fragment:** When you are completely engaged in something.
> **Complete Sentence:** When you are completely engaged in something, you don't hear the clock strike.

> **Subordinate Clause Fragment:** That Franklin D. Roosevelt gave the ocean explorer William Beebe the idea for a spherical underwater craft.
> **Complete Sentence:** I was amazed to discover that Franklin D. Roosevelt gave the ocean explorer William Beebe the idea for a spherical underwater craft.

> **Verbal Fragment:** Painting a decoy.
> **Complete Sentence:** We found Dot painting a decoy. OR Painting a decoy, Dot blended multiple colors to create realistic looking feathers.

QUICK TIP

Verbals (participles, infinitives, gerunds) look like verbs because they often ends in *–ed* or *–ing*. However, they are not predicates. They are used as adjectives or nouns.

Verbal Fragment: Jumping up and down with a hornet sting.

Complete Sentence: Donna was jumping up and down with a hornet sting. (The helping verb *was* completes the verb.) OR Donna jumped up and down with a hornet sting.

Verbal Fragment: Shanti packing a lunch for the picnic.

Complete Sentence: Shanti packed a lunch for the picnic. OR Packing a lunch for the picnic, Shanti made sandwiches of tomato, avocado, and cheese.

Verbal Fragment: To prove Fermat's Last Theorem.

Complete Sentence: Mathematicians tried for centuries to prove Fermat's Last Theorem.

Participles are sometimes dangling modifiers. To avoid dangling modifiers, review page 307.

Run-on Sentences

A run-on sentence occurs when multiple independent clauses are punctuated as one sentence. One common type of run-on sentence is the **comma splice**. A comma splice occurs when two sentences are connected with only a comma.

Run-on Sentence with Comma Splice: During World War I, Americans shunned anything German, sauerkraut was actually called "liberty cabbage."

Two Sentences: During World War I, Americans shunned anything German. Sauerkraut was actually called "liberty cabbage."

SAT questions will test you over the BEST way to correct a run-on sentence. You will be asked to consider the relationship between the two clauses in the sentence. If one is about less important ideas, rewrite it as a subordinate clause. See the complex sentence example to the left.

The preceding example shows the most obvious way of avoiding run-on sentences. Often, the sentences can be improved in one of three other ways: writing a compound sentence, writing a complex sentence, or using a verbal phrase.

Run-on Sentence: Many ocean waves are described as "mountain high," they are actually 30–40 feet in height.

Compound Sentence: Many ocean waves are described as "mountain high," but they are actually 30–40 feet in height.

Complex Sentence: Although many ocean waves are described as "mountain high," they are actually 30–40 feet in height.

Simple Sentence with Verbal Phrase: Most of the ocean waves described as "mountain high" are actually 30–40 feet in height.

Sometimes run-on sentences can be corrected by eliminating unnecessary words.

Run-on Sentence: England and Portugal have never been at war with each other, this is a major achievement among nations.

Single Sentence with an Appositive: England and Portugal have never been at war with each other, a major achievement among nations.

The following words can lead to run-on sentences: *also, hence, nevertheless, then, therefore*, and *thus*. These words are not conjunctions. They cannot join sentences with only a comma. Sometimes a semicolon can be used.

Run-on Sentence: The driver stopped, then he got out of his car.
Separate Sentences: The driver stopped. Then he got out of his car.
Run-on Sentence: My best subject is science, therefore I took a science elective this year.
Sentence with a Semicolon: My best subject is science; therefore, I took a science elective this year.

Practice

Directions: Rewrite each fragment as a complete sentence. Add words as needed.

1. When the big blackout of 2003 struck the Northeast on August 14.

   _____

   _____

2. In the house where Thomas Wolfe lived as a child.

   _____

   _____

3. How the magician David Copperfield creates his incredible illusions.

   _____

   _____

4. Touring the city where the Liberty Bell is located.

   _____

   _____

5. The city of Philadelphia, home to Independence Hall and the Liberty Bell.

   _____

   _____

Directions: Eliminate all run-on sentences. For practice, fix by writing compound, complex, and simple sentences with modifying phrases.

6. Many would-be inventors have tried to create a perpetual-motion machine, they are all doomed to disappointment.

   _____

   _____

7. Whales usually bear only one offspring, baby twin whales have been observed.

   _____

   _____

8. Luther Burbank experimented with thousands of plants, he developed new varieties of apples, plums, and other fruits.

   _____

   _____

9. I found my keys after a search, I then proceeded to mislay my purse.

   _____

   _____

10. Robin is in a performance of *Phaedra*, she plays the tormented wife of Theseus.

    _____

    _____

For answers, see page 579.

For answers, see page 579.

Model SAT Question

Directions: This Model SAT Question tests your ability to edit text to correct fragments and run-ons. The answer and explanation immediately follow the question. Try the question and then review the answer and the explanation.

> On September 29, 1965, President Lyndon Johnson signed the National
> Foundation on the Arts and the Humanities Act into ▮1▮ law, the act called for
> the creation of the National Endowment for the Humanities (NEH) and the
> National Endowment for the Arts (NEA) as separate, independent agencies.
> *The Washington Post* called the creation of the endowments "a momentous step."

1. A) NO CHANGE
   B) law. The act called for the creation
   C) law the act called for the creation
   D) law, and the act called for the creation

Strategy: The underlined section is a run-on sentence with a comma splice. Thus, choice A is incorrect. Choice C is also a run-on sentence since it does not separate the independent clauses with any punctuation. Choice D fixes the run-on sentence by using a comma and the conjunction *and*, but creates one overly long sentence. The two ideas do not seem equal enough to warrant the use of the conjunction *and*. Choice B is the best answer.

SAT-Type Questions

Directions: Questions 1–5 are based on the following passage. Read the passage and then choose the answer that makes the passage conforms to rules of standards English.

Are Gender Differences Emerging in the Retirement Patterns of the Early Boomers?

Controlling for career employment later in life, the retirement patterns of men and women in America have resembled one another for much of the past two decades. Is this relationship coming to an end? Older American men and women on the cusp of retirement today face very different economic circumstances from those their predecessors did. The retirement income landscape has solidified its "do-it-yourself" **1** approach, with defined-contribution pension plans dominating in the private sector and savings rates returning to near-historic lows, the macroeconomic picture has changed. In addition, because of several decades of strong growth **2** and low unemployment. Today's older Americans, like all Americans, have endured the "Great Recession" and a historic lackluster recovery that continues to this day.

Recent research suggests that macroeconomic changes appear to have impacted the retirement patterns of the Early Boomers, those aged 57 to 62 in 2010. One way retirement patterns—including phased retirement, bridge job transitions, and reentry—have been impacted is that gender differences appear to be emerging, after nearly two decades of similarities in the way that career men and women exit the labor **3** force. These gender differences explored in detail to help determine whether we are witnessing a break in trend or merely a blip in the data.

QUICK TIP

Read the paragraph quickly, slowing down when you get to the underlined sections. Then answer the questions for that paragraph before reading on.

To address this topic, we use data on three cohorts of older Americans from the nationally representative, longitudinal Health and Retirement Study (HRS) that began in 4 1992, the HRS is ideal for this analysis because it contains detailed information about work histories, as well as demographic and economic characteristics and changes in job status over time. The initial cohort of 12,652 HRS respondents, known as the HRS Core, was aged 51 to 61 at the time of the first interview in 1992 (i.e., born from 1931 to 1941) and has been interviewed every other year 5 since 1992, barring death or another reason for non-response, additional cohorts have since been added to the HRS, including the War Babies (born from 1942 to 1947), the Early Boomers (born from 1948 to 1953), and the Mid Boomers (born from 1954 to 1959). Each of these HRS cohorts has been interviewed biennially since being introduced to the survey.

The labor force participation rates of older American men and women both changed significantly in the mid-1980s. For men, the change signaled an end to earlier and earlier 6 retirements, for women, the change involved a substantial increase following decades of little change, as the trend toward earlier retirements (like men) was masked by increases in labor force participation generally (unlike men). The break in trend implies that older men and women are working longer than their pre-mid-1980 trends would have predicted. Further, until recently, older American women and men who held career jobs later in life had similar paths 7 to retirement. With approximately 60 percent of women and men moving to a bridge job prior to exiting the labor force completely.

Source: www.bls.gov

1. A) NO CHANGE
    B) approach. With defined-contribution pension plans
    C) approach, thus with defined-contribution pension plans
    D) approach, and with defined-contribution pension plans

2. A) NO CHANGE
    B) and low unemployment; today's older Americans,
    C) and low unemployment, today's older Americans,
    D) and low unemployment, and yet today's older Americans

3. A) NO CHANGE
   B) force, these gender differences explored
   C) force, these gender differences are explored
   D) force. These gender differences are explored

4. A) NO CHANGE
   B) 1992 the HRS
   C) 1992 the HRS,
   D) 1992. The HRS

5. A) NO CHANGE
   B) since 1992. Barring death or another reason for non-response, additional, cohorts
   C) since 1992, barring death or another reason for non-response. Additional cohorts
   D) since 1992, barring death or another reason for non-response; additionally, cohorts

6. A) NO CHANGE
   B) retirements; and for women, the change
   C) retirements; for women, the change
   D) retirements—for women, the change

7. A) NO CHANGE
   B) to retirement, with approximately 60 percent. Of women and men
   C) to retirement, but with approximately 60 percent of women and men
   D) to retirement, with approximately 60 percent of women and men

For answers, see page 580.

Some questions on the SAT will ask you to correctly identify which sentence correctly combines two shorter sentences. In order to do this, you must think about the relationships between the ideas expressed in the sentences. More important ideas should be placed in independent clauses; less important ideas should be in subordinate clauses or in modifying phrases.

Think It Through

There are several ways to combine two sentences.

Coordinating Conjunctions

If the ideas in the two sentences are equally important, combine them using a coordinating conjunction. These include *for*, *and*, *nor*, *but*, *or*, *yet*, and *so*. The following chart indicates the relationship each conjunction communicates.

Coordinating Conjunctions	Function
and	joins two equal ideas
but, yet	shows contrast
so	indicates an effect
or	offers an alternative
nor	negates the clause that follows it
for	gives a reason for the preceding clause

Two sentences: Carrie struggled to recover from her accident at first. She is doing well now.

Confusing: Carrie struggled to recover from her accident at first, *so* she is doing well now.

Clear: Carrie struggled to recover from her accident at first, but she is doing well now. (Both independent clauses have equal importance. They are joined by the coordinating conjunction but, which shows the contrast between how Carrie was doing before versus now.)

Subordinating Conjunctions

When one idea in the sentence is less important, place it in a dependent clause. Dependent clauses are often introduced by subordinating conjunctions. This chart lists some common subordinating conjunctions and what they indicate in a sentence.

Subordinating Conjunction	Function
after, as, before, whenever, while, when, until, when, whenever	time relationships
because, why, in order that, so that	cause/effect
although, if, if only, even though, since, unless	condition or concession
that, as if, where, which	adds supporting details

Subordinating Conjunction	Function
than, as	comparison
whereas	contrast

Two sentences: Marcus read a substantial amount of information about the company. He was well-prepared for the interview.

Combined: Because Marcus read a substantial amount of information about the company, he was well-prepared for the interview. (The less important idea is placed in a dependent clause. *Because* introduces a reason.)

Two sentences: The conference has been postponed indefinitely. I planned to attend the conference.

Combined: The conference that I planned to attend has been postponed indefinitely. (The more important idea is that the conference has been postponed. The dependent clause begins with the relative pronoun *that*.)

The combined sentence should subordinate the less important idea and use a subordinating conjunction that communicates the correct relationship between the ideas.

Two sentences: He has earned a doctorate in psychology. He also loves to write.

Confusing subordination: He loves to write, although he has also earned a doctorate in psychology.

Clear: He has earned a doctorate in psychology, although he also loves to write.

Appositive and Verbal Phrases

Another way to combine sentences is to put a less important idea in an appositive phrase, a noun phrase that explains another noun, or a verbal phrase, a verb form that describes a noun.

Two sentences: Japanese tea masters had learned the intricate choreography of preparing and serving tea. They wielded great influence.

Appositive phrase: Japanese tea masters, men who had learned the intricate choreography of preparing and serving the tea, wielded great influence.

Verbal phrase: Having learned the intricate choreography of preparing and serving tea, Japanese tea masters wielded great influence.

Explain Correcting Problems with Structure and Modifiers

Parallel structure means using the same structure and pattern of words. Parallel structure makes your writing clearer and expresses ideas more powerfully. Make sure lists of items and also sentences that express similar and equal ideas have the same form. Ordinarily, *and* and *but* connect like grammatical elements.

> **Not Parallel:** At camp, we most enjoyed swimming, hiking, and how to play volleyball.
>
> **Parallel:** At camp, we most enjoyed swimming, hiking, and playing volleyball. (All activities end in *–ing*.)

> **Not Parallel:** The students' survey responses indicated that they prefer more online assignments, don't like overly long research papers, and the teacher needed to be available to answer questions outside of class.
>
> **Parallel:** The students' survey responses indicated that they prefer more online assignments, that they don't like overly long research papers, and that they need the teacher to be available to answer questions outside of class. (All these clauses begin with *that they,* then a verb and an object.)

> **Not Parallel:** If you want to improve your diet, eat more vegetables, try to increase the amount of water you drink, and you'll want to replace sugary snacks with nuts and fruit.
>
> **Parallel:** If you want to improve your diet, eat more vegetables, drink more water, and replace sugary snacks with nuts and fruit. (All have a verb and an object. Extraneous words are deleted.)

> **Not Parallel:** Michael Vick **not only** excels in passing **but** in his ability to evade tacklers.
>
> **Parallel:** Michael Vick excels **not only** in passing **but also** in evading tacklers. (Both end in *–ing*. Also notice that the conjunction **not only/but also** is moved so that it comes directly before the parallel phrases.)

Sentences that express similar ideas should also be parallel.

> **Not Parallel:** A mother uses the Internet to check her son's symptoms with the signs of appendicitis. A doctor checks a patient's digital medical records for possible allergies before writing a prescription. Using an online database, a health official can estimate when and where the flu is circulating.
>
> **Parallel:** A mother uses the Internet to check her son's symptoms with the signs of appendicitis. A doctor checks a patient's digital medical records for possible allergies before writing a prescription. A health official estimates when and where the flu is circulating by monitoring an online database. (All sentences begin with a subject and a verb in the present tense.)

Dangling and Misplaced Modifiers

A modifier is a word or phrase that describes or adds detail to a sentences. To avoid confusion, modifiers should be placed close to the word they are describing. A **dangling modifier** occurs when the subject of the modifier is not clear. This often happens when the modifier is placed at the beginning of a sentence.

Dangling: Turning the corner, the post office was on the left. (The post office was not turning the corner.)

Clear: Turning the corner, I noticed the post office on my left. (The subject *I* was added for clarity.)

Clear: As I turned the corner, I noticed the post office on my left.

Dangling: While working in the library, a new shipment of books arrived. (The shipment of books was not working in the library.)

Clear: While working in the library, I received a new shipment of books. (The subject *I* was added for clarity.)

Clear: While I was working in the library, a new shipment of books arrived.

Misplaced modifiers occur when the modifier is poorly placed. Often the modifier is too far from its subject. This causes confusion about what word the modifier is describing and often results in rather humorous images.

Confusing: Terry saw a deer riding her bike through the Hopkins meadow. (Was the deer riding her bike?)

Clear: Riding her bike through the Hopkins meadow, Terry saw a deer. (Terry was riding her bike and saw a deer.)

Confusing: At the age of three, Mark's mother remarried. (Was Mark's mother three when she remarried?)

Clear: When Mark was three, his mother remarried. (Mark was three when his mother remarried.)

Confusing: At the party, packages were given to all the children filled with Halloween candy. (The children may be filled later!)

Clear: At the party, packages filled with Halloween candy were given to all the children. (The packages were filled with Halloween candy.)

Confusing: One of our most popular foods, people once considered the tomato poisonous. (The people are the most popular foods?)

Clear: One of our most popular foods, the tomato was once considered poisonous. (The tomato is one of our most popular foods.)

Directions: Read the passage and answer the questions that follow.

The Left Brain Knows What the Right Hand Is Doing

Browse through a list of history's most famous **1** left-handers, which you are likely to see Albert Einstein's name. You may even see people tying Einstein's genius to his left-handedness. The problem is, Einstein's left-handedness is a myth. **2** Myriad photos writing on a chalkboard with his right hand show him, for example.

But handedness has its roots in the brain—right-handed people have left-hemisphere-dominant brains and vice versa—and the lefties who claim Einstein weren't all that far off. **3** He was certainly right-handed. Autopsies suggest his brain didn't reflect the typical left-side dominance in language and speech areas. His brain's hemispheres were more symmetrical—a trait typical of left-handers and the ambidextrous.

By comparison, 95 percent of righties have brains that strictly divvy up tasks: The left hemisphere almost exclusively **4** handles language and speech and the right is known to handle emotion and image processing, **5** because only about 20 percent of lefties have brains that divide up these duties so rigidly.

Michael Corballis, PhD, **6** is a brain hemisphere specialist and psychologist at the University of Auckland in New Zealand, and he points out that having the hemispheres manage different tasks might increase the brain's efficiency.

"There's an advantage to cerebral dominance, because it localizes function to one hemisphere," he says. "Otherwise, information has to cross back and forth across the corpus callosum, and that can sometimes cause problems."

A strongly symmetrical brain, like Einstein's, leaves people open to mental dysfunction, but it also paves the way for creative thinking. Researchers are exploring these unusually balanced brains and **7** want to find out why that's the case.

1. Which is the BEST revision of the underlined portion?
   A) left-handers, and you
   B) left-handers, so you

2. Which is the BEST revision of the underlined portion?
   A) Myriad photos show him writing on a chalkboard with his right hand
   B) Writing on a chalkboard with his right hand, myriad photos show him

3. Which BEST combines underlined sentences into one sentence?
   A) Since he was certainly right-handed, autopsies suggest
   B) While he was certainly right-handed, autopsies suggest

4. Which is the BEST revision of the underlined portion?
   A) handles language and speaking and the right is known to handle emotion and image processing,
   B) handles language and speech and the right handles emotion and image processing,

5. Which is the BEST revision of the underlined portion?
   A) processing, but only
   B) processing, which only

6. Which is the BEST revision of the underlined portion?
   A) a brain hemisphere specialist and psychologist at the University of Auckland in New Zealand, points out
   B) is a brain hemisphere specialist and psychologist at the University of Auckland in New Zealand but points out

7. Which is the BEST revision of the underlined portion?
   A) to find out
   B) are finding out

For answers, see page 580.

QUICK TIP

To determine whether a sentence makes sense, quietly whisper it to yourself. Sometimes soundlessly saying it helps clarify which answer is best.

Model SAT Questions

Directions: These Model SAT Questions show how you might be tested over combing sentences, parallel structure, and modifier placement. Answer the questions and then read the explanation that follows.

The world knows Michelangelo as a famous painter, sculptor, and inventor but may not know him as **1** someone who forged art. In 1496, twenty-year-old Michelangelo sculpted a figure of a sleeping cupid. **2** Buried in a garden, the acidic soil transformed the new marble, giving it the appearance of age. Michelangelo dug it up, broke it, and repaired it. Then he sold it to art dealer Baldassare del Milanese, who in turn sold it to a cardinal.

A few years later, the cardinal became suspicious and returned the sculpture, known as *Sleeping Eros*, to del Milanese. The dealer reimbursed the cardinal but allowed Michelangelo to keep his money. **3** By this time, Michelangelo was the most famous sculptor in Rome. The dealer was able to recoup his money by selling the cupid as a Michelangelo original.

1. A) NO CHANGE
   B) someone whom forged sculptures.
   C) a forger of art.
   D) an art forger.

Strategy: This question covers editing for parallel structure. The underlined section should be in the same form as the items earlier in the sentence: painter, sculptor, and inventor. These are nouns. The current sentence includes a pronoun and a descriptive phrase. Choice A is incorrect. Choice B introduces a pronoun error (whom). It is also incorrect. Choice C is better but still includes prepositional phrase after the noun. The best answer is the choice D.

2. A) NO CHANGE
   B) Buried in a garden, the acidic soil transformed the new marble into an ancient-looking artifact.
   C) By burying the statue in acidic garden soil, Michelangelo transformed the new work into an ancient-looking artifact.
   D) Buried in a garden, Michelangelo transformed the new work into an ancient artifact.

Strategy: This question tests your ability to recognize and edit dangling modifiers. The opening phrase "Buried in a garden" should not describe the soil, as in choices A and B. It also does not describe Michelangelo, so choice D is incorrect. The correct choice is C.

3. In context, which choice best combines the underlined sentences?
   A) By this time, Michelangelo, the most famous sculptor in Rome, was able to recoup the dealer's money by selling the cupid as an original.
   B) Whereas by this time Michelangelo was the most famous sculptor in Rome, the dealer was able to recoup his money by selling the cupid as a Michelangelo original.
   C) By this time Michelangelo was the most famous sculptor in Rome, and the dealer was able to recoup his money by selling the cupid as a Michelangelo original.
   D) By this time Michelangelo was the most famous sculptor in Rome, but the dealer was able to recoup his money by selling the cupid as a Michelangelo original.

Strategy: Choice A is incorrect because it changes the meaning of the sentence by making Michelangelo the seller of the statue. Choice B subordinates the first sentence but uses *Whereas* incorrectly, since the relationship is not a contrast. Choice D is also incorrect because *but* also indicates a contrast. Choice C combines two ideas of equal importance with the conjunction *and*. It is the best answer.

Directions: Read the following passage and answer questions 1–9.

Poetry and Power: John F. Kennedy's Inaugural Address

On January 20, 1961, **1** a clerk of the U.S. Supreme Court held the large Fitzgerald family Bible. John F. Kennedy took the oath of office to become the nation's 35th president. Against a backdrop of deep snow and sunshine, more than twenty thousand people huddled in 20-degree temperatures on the east front of the Capitol to witness the event. Kennedy, having removed his topcoat and projecting both youth and vigor, delivered what has become a landmark inaugural address.

Cold War rhetoric had dominated the 1960 presidential campaign. Senator John F. Kennedy and Vice President Richard M. Nixon both pledged to strengthen American military forces and **2** promised a tough stance against the Soviet Union and international communism. Kennedy warned of the Soviet's growing arsenal of intercontinental ballistic missiles and pledged to revitalize American nuclear forces. He also criticized the Eisenhower administration for permitting the establishment of a pro-Soviet government in Cuba.

Having won the election by one of the smallest popular vote margins in history, **3** the address's message was clear. He wanted to inspire the nation and send a message abroad that signaled the challenges of the Cold War and his hope for peace in the nuclear age. Kennedy also wanted to be brief. **4** Whereas he remarked to his close advisor, Ted Sorensen, "I don't want people to think I'm a windbag."

He assigned Sorensen the task of studying other inaugural speeches and Lincoln's Gettysburg Address to glean the secrets of successful addresses. The finely crafted final speech had been revised and reworked numerous times by Kennedy and Sorensen until the President-elect was satisfied. Though not the shortest of inaugural addresses, Kennedy's was shorter than most at 1,355 words in length and, like Lincoln's famous speech, was comprised of short phrases and words. In addition to **5** message, choice of words, and length, he recognized that captivating his audience required a powerful delivery. On the day before and on the morning of Inauguration Day, he kept a copy handy to take advantage of any spare moment to review it, even at the breakfast table.

6 Considered toward the end to be the most memorable and enduring section of the speech came when Kennedy called all Americans to commit themselves to service and sacrifice: "And so, my fellow Americans: ask not what your country can do for you—ask what you can do for your country." He then continued by addressing his international audience: "My fellow citizens of the world ask not what America will do for you, but what together we can do for the freedom of man."

Kennedy had known the great importance of this speech. People **7** who witnessing the speech or heard it broadcast over television and radio lauded the new President. **8** Even elementary school children wrote to him. They had reactions to his ideas. Following his inaugural address, nearly seventy-five percent of Americans expressed approval of President Kennedy.

Source: www.jfklibrary.org

1. Which choice most effectively combines the two sentences at the underlined portion?
   A) a clerk of the U.S. Supreme Court held the large Fitzgerald family Bible, as John F. Kennedy
   B) as a clerk of the U.S. Supreme Court held the large Fitzgerald family Bible, John F. Kennedy
   C) a clerk of the U.S. Supreme Court held the large Fitzgerald family Bible, but John F. Kennedy
   D) because a clerk of the U.S. Supreme Court held the large Fitzgerald family Bible, John F. Kennedy

2. A) NO CHANGE
   B) promising a tough stance
   C) which promised to take a tough stance
   D) promised to take a tough stance

3. A) NO CHANGE
   B) the addresses' message was clear
   C) the voters' message was clearly
   D) Kennedywas clear in his message

4. A) NO CHANGE
   B) While remarking to his close advisor,
   C) Because of his remarks to his close advisor,
   D) As he'd remarked to his close advisor,

5. A) NO CHANGE
   B) message, word choice, and length,
   C) messaging, choosing words, and length,
   D) creating a message, word choice, and lengthening the speech,

6. A) NO CHANGE
   B) Toward the end of the speech came the most memorable and enduring section, when
   C) Having saved the best for last, the end when
   D) Having listened to his memorable and inspiring speech,

7. A) NO CHANGE
   B) who witnessed the speech or have heard it
   C) who witnessed or heard the speech
   D) witnessed the speech or heard it

8. Which choice most effectively combines the underlined sentences?
   A) Even elementary school children who wrote to him had reactions to his ideas.
   B) Writing to him, even elementary school children had reactions to his ideas.
   C) Even elementary school children wrote to him with their reactions to his ideas.
   D) Having reactions to his ideas, even elementary school children wrote to him.

For answers, see page 581.

Explain **Correcting Shifts in Verbs and Pronouns**

Verbs have different **tenses**. Verb tense indicates at what point in time the action is happening. Within a sentence verb tense should remain consistent in tense and **voice**. Likewise, pronouns should have the appropriate **number** and **person** to avoid creating confusion.

Think It Through

Using the Correct Tense

Tense means "time." The form of a verb shows the time of the action that the verb expresses.

Underline the verbs in the following example sentences. When is the action happening?

PRESENT TENSE: The Cairo Museum contains a room with the mummies of the great pharaohs.

PRESENT PERFECT TENSE: The Hunzas of northwest Kashmir have always been free of cancer in any of its forms.

PAST TENSE: Vinegar was the strongest acid known to the ancients.

PAST PERFECT TENSE: By the age of ten, Mozart had already composed symphonies, sonatas, and arias.

FUTURE TENSE: Judy will visit us over the Columbus Day weekend.

FUTURE PERFECT TENSE: By the end of next year, Marcy will have read all the Sherlock Holmes mysteries.

Make sure the verb you use accurately communicates when the action is taking place.

Using Consistent Tense

When using multiple verbs in a passage or in a sentence, the verbs should be in the same tense.

> **MIXED TENSE:** Jenny entered her mountain bike in the YMCA competition, (past) and trains for the event. (present)
>
> **SAME TENSE:** Jenny enters her mountain bike in the YMCA competition (present) and trains for the event. (present)
>
> Jenny entered her mountain bike in the YMCA competition (past) and trained for the event. (past)

Regular Verbs

Many verbs form tenses (express time of an action) in regular, predictable ways by adding *–s* for present tense and *–ed* or *–d* for past tense.

> Jennifer enters many diving competitions.
> (Expresses an action taking place, or is always true.)
> Jennifer entered many diving competitions.
> (Expresses an action that has already happened.)
> Jennifer has entered many diving competitions.
> (Expresses an action begun in the past and possibly still going on.)

Irregular Verbs

Irregular verbs change spelling or form in the past tense.

> Jason <u>drives</u> a Mustang. (Expresses an action taking place.)
>
> Jason <u>drove</u> a Mustang. (Expresses an action that has already happened.)
>
> Jason <u>has driven</u> a Mustang. (Expresses an action completed at the time of speaking.)

A relatively small number of irregular verbs cause trouble for speakers and writers. The following list has some of the more difficult irregular verbs.

Principal Parts of Irregular Verbs		
Present	**Past**	**Past Participle**
am	was	(have) been
become	became	(have) become
begin	began	(have) begun
break	broke	(have) broken
bring	brought	(have) brought
catch	caught	(have) caught
choose	chose	(have) chosen
come	came	(have) come
do	did	(have) done
drink	drank	(have) drunk
drive	drove	(have) driven
eat	ate	(have) eaten
fall	fell	(have) fallen
get	got	(have) gotten or got
give	gave	(have) given
go	went	(have) gone
know	knew	(have) known
lie	lay	(have) lain
rise	rose	(have) risen
speak	spoke	(have) spoken
swim	swam	(have) swum
take	took	(have) taken
teach	taught	(have) taught

Note: Forms of *have*, *be*, and *do* are often used as helping verbs.

INCORRECT: The wind blowed all night.
CORRECT: The wind blew all night.

INCORRECT: Sandra has chose nursing as her career.
CORRECT: Sandra has chosen nursing as her career.

INCORRECT SHIFT IN TENSE: She wrote her paper and then posts it to the class Web site. (*Wrote* is past tense; *posts* is present tense.)
CORRECT: She wrote her paper and then posted it to the class Web site. (Both verbs are in past tense.)
CORRECT: She writes her paper and then posts it to the class Web site. (Both verbs are in present tense.)

Voice

Verbs may be active or passive. In the active voice, the subject performs the verb's action. In the passive voice, the subject is acted on or receives the verb's action. Active voice sentences are more direct and typically make up a greater majority of writing than the passive voice. Passive voice sentences can seem awkward and should be used sparingly. A passive voice sentence always has a form of *be* in the verb. Note the examples below.

ACTIVE: Karl ate the burrito.
PASSIVE: The burrito was eaten by Karl.

ACTIVE: The car made a left turn.
PASSIVE: A left turn was made by the car.

ACTIVE: Looking at old photos fills me with nostalgia.
PASSIVE: I am filled with nostalgia by looking at old photos.

ACTIVE: Lissa is trying on a new pair of shoes.
PASSIVE: A new pair of shoes is being tried on by Lissa.

• Avoid shifting from active to passive voice. If possible, write both verbs in the active voice.

INCORRECT SHIFT IN VOICE: As Ahmed scored the winning goal, a shout from the crowd was heard. (*Scored* is in the active voice; *was heard* is passive voice.)
CORRECT: As Ahmed scored the winning goal, the crowd shouted. (Both verbs are in the active voice.)

Mood

Along with voice, verbs also have moods.

indicative mood: states a fact or opinion, describes what happens or gives details about reality

> **Examples:**
> I am thirsty.
> Tonight I will study for my chemistry final.
> Paulina and I will fly to Mexico tomorrow.

interrogative mood: asks a question

> **Examples:**
> Will you bring me a glass of water?
> Have you finished your homework?
> When do you leave for Mexico?

imperative mood: gives commands or requests and has an understood subject, *you*

> **Examples:**
> Please bring me a glass of water. (The understood subject is *you*: You please bring me a glass of water.)
> Help me study. (The understood subject is *you*: You help me study.)
> Fly to Mexico with Paulina and me tomorrow. (The understood subject is *you*: You fly to Mexico . . .)

conditional mood: indicates a conditional state that will cause something to happen. The conditional often uses *might*, *could*, and *would*.

> **Examples:**
> I could get myself a glass a water.
> I might get an A on my test.
> I would fly to Mexico with you, if you weren't leaving tomorrow.

subjunctive mood: expresses doubt or something contrary to fact. Subjunctive mood is often used in a sentence with a conditional phrase linked by the word *if*.

> **Examples:**
> If Dominic were here, he would bring me a glass of water.
> I wish you would fly to Mexico with Paulina and me tomorrow. ("I wish" implies that you are not flying to Mexico.)
> We would be able to study if you had brought your notes with you. ("If you had brought your notes" implies that you did not bring them.)

- Use the past tense or past perfect tense when expressing a wish or something that is not actually true.

> **Examples:**
> I <u>wish</u> I had a million dollars.
> If I <u>had</u> a million dollars, I would buy a new car.

- Always use *were* rather than *was* to express a wish or hope in subjunctive mood.

INCORRECT: I wish I <u>was</u> a millionaire. If I <u>was</u> a millionaire, I would buy a new car.

CORRECT: I wish I <u>were</u> a millionaire. If I <u>were</u> a millionaire, I would buy a new car.

- Avoid shifting from indicative to imperative mood or from imperative to indicative mood. This often happens when writing directions

INCORRECT: Right <u>click</u> on the icon, and then <u>you should open</u> the program. (The first clause is a command in imperative mood; the second clause is a statement in indicative mood.)

CORRECT: Right click on the icon, and then open the program. (Both clauses are in imperative mood.)

Pronouns

Pronouns must agree in **number**. A pronoun that takes the place of a singular noun should be singular; likewise, a pronoun replacing a plural noun must be plural.

Examples:

If a <u>lady</u> comes into the store looking for Tom, send <u>her</u> to the office. (*Lady* is the singular noun and *her* is the singular pronoun.)

If two <u>ladies</u> come into the store looking for Tom, send <u>them</u> to the office. (*Ladies* is the plural noun and *them* is the plural pronoun.)

Words such as *anyone, anybody, everyone, everybody, each, neither, either, someone, somebody* are singular and thus, require singular pronouns.

Examples:

<u>Everyone</u> is welcome to stop by and bring <u>his or her</u> favorite snack to share.

<u>Anyone</u> who wants to become successful must first define <u>his or her</u> goals.

Pronouns must also agree in **person**. When writing, do not switch from first to second or third. Be consistent in your point of view to avoid confusion.

First person: *I, me, my, mine, we, us, our, ours*

Second person: *you, yours, your*

Third person: *he, she, it, its, him, her, they, theirs, them, his, hers, one*

- Shifts usually occur with changes from the third to the second person point of view and often involve using *you*.

INCORRECT: When *you* start searching for a job, *one* needs to be patient. (The sentence begins in the second person but switches to third.)

CORRECT: When *you* start searching for a job, *you* need to be patient. (The sentence maintains second person.)

CORRECT: When *people* start searching for a job, *they* need to be patient. (The sentence maintains third person.)

QUICK TIP

Using "his or her" when gender is unspecified can be wordy. One way to eliminate this problem is to use plural nouns so that the pronouns can also be plural. Wordy: *If a student is tardy, he or she should quickly and unobtrusively take his or her seat.* Better: *If students are tardy, they should quickly and unobtrusively take their seats.*

INCORRECT: The <u>tigers</u> paced around the perimeter of <u>his or her</u> cage. (*Tigers* is plural, but *his or her* is singular.)

CORRECT: The <u>tigers</u> paced around the perimeter of <u>their</u> cage. (Both *tigers* and *their* are plural.)

CORRECT: The <u>tiger</u> paced around the perimeter of <u>its</u> cage. (Both *tiger* and *its* are singular. *Its* is used for animals and because the gender of the tiger is unknown.)

Practice

Directions: Underline the correct verb tense in each sentence.

1. If I (was, were) an astronaut, I would fly to Mars.

2. When I met my fiancé for the first time, I (think, thought) he was too talkative.

3. Tony wishes he (slept, had slept) better last night.

4. Yui wants to eat out and then (watch, will watch) a movie tonight.

5. Hearing about your exciting rafting adventures (makes, will have made) me want to plan a trip!

Directions: Revise the sentences for correct pronoun person and number.

6. After the three boys get home, ask him how his field trip was.

_____

_____

_____

7. Anyone who disrupts the presentation will be docked ten points from their score.

_____

_____

_____

8. When Katie and Susie get together, she laughs a lot.

_____

_____

_____

9. Each employee must fill out this form and hand it in to their supervisor.

_____

_____

_____

10. If one wants to improve himself, you should consider trying meditation.

_____

_____

_____

For answers, see page 581.

Model SAT Questions

Directions: These Model SAT Questions shows how verb and pronoun consistency may be tested on the SAT. The answers and explanations immediately follow the questions. Try the questions and then review the answers and the explanations.

A phobia is a type of anxiety disorder. It is a strong, irrational fear of something that poses little or no actual danger. There are many specific phobias. Acrophobia is a fear of heights. You may be able to ski the world's tallest mountains but be unable to go above the fifth floor of an office building. Agoraphobia is a fear of public places, and claustrophobia is a fear of closed-in places. If you **1** became anxious and extremely self-conscious in everyday social situations, you could have a social phobia. Other common phobias involve tunnels, highway driving, water, flying, animals and blood.

People with phobias try to avoid what they are afraid of. If they cannot, **2** one may experience symptoms that include panic, fear, rapid heartbeat, shortness of breath, and trembling.

1. A) NO CHANGE
   B) become
   C) had become
   D) will become

Strategy: This question asks you to edit for verb tense. Choice A is incorrect because *became* is an inappropriate shift to the past tense. Similarly, choice C is not the best answer because *had become* creates an inappropriate shift to the past perfect tense. Choice D is not the best answer because *will become* creates an inappropriate shift to future tense. The best answer is B because *become* is a present tense verb that is consistent with the verb tenses used in the rest of the paragraph.

2. A) NO CHANGE
   B) he or she
   C) you
   D) phobia sufferers

Strategy: This question asks you to edit for pronoun shifts. The sentence begins with the third-person plural pronoun *they*. However, *one* is second-person singular. Thus, choice A is incorrect. Choice B, *he or she,* is in third person but is singular. Choice C is incorrect because it is in second person. The correct answer is D because *phobia sufferers* is appropriate for the third-person point of view in the paragraph and agrees with the plural pronoun *they*.

SAT-Type Questions

Directions: Read the following passage and answer questions 1–10.

New Egypt is a small town in rural southern New Jersey about 45 miles east of Philadelphia. The school system has about 1,700 students in three schools—an elementary, middle, and a new high school. New Egypt school officials were unaware of biometrics in 2002 when **1** he or she realized that their schools needed a new security system. At the time, the schools used a swipe-card system that **2** aged and did not always work. Plus, there weren't enough cards for everyone who needed one. School officials knew **3** one had to improve not only the perception, but also the reality of school safety. One official **4** says that they sought to develop a security system that would allay concerns and control access into the school buildings better than the swipe cards. They also wanted to use an innovative technology that **5** could serve as a model for others.

After considering alternative biometric technologies, New Egypt officials chose iris recognition, one of the most reliable systems. Unfortunately for the school district, no complete iris scanning system **6** existing that could be purchased and installed off the shelf. Instead, working with private vendors and the National Institute of Justice, the school system developed **7** its own iris recognition system.

New Egypt was able to buy eleven existing cameras, placing six inside and five outside the elementary school's doors. Vendors had to write new software packages that would allow the cameras to send data images of scanned irises to a computer, tell the computer to search for a match, and then ⬛8 allowing the computer to unlock the school doors once an individual's identification was confirmed.

As the iris recognition system was being developed, ⬛9 parents were kept informed by school officials of the plans and encouraged them to participate in the voluntary program. All told, nearly all of the schools' teachers and staff members and more than 700 elementary school parents had their eyes scanned into the system. The middle and high schools were not included in the test, because far fewer of ⬛10 its students were took out of class by parents or other family members during the school day.

Source: www.nij.gov

1. A) NO CHANGE
   B) we realized that our
   C) one realized that their
   D) they realized that their

2. A) NO CHANGE
   B) ages
   C) was aging
   D) would age

3. A) NO CHANGE
   B) he or she
   C) they
   D) you

4. A) NO CHANGE
   B) is saying
   C) will say
   D) said

5. A) NO CHANGE
   B) served
   C) had served
   D) could be serving

6. A) NO CHANGE
   B) existed
   C) would exist
   D) had been existing

7. A) NO CHANGE
    B) it's
    C) their
    D) our

8. A) NO CHANGE
    B) could allow
    C) allowed
    D) allow

9. A) NO CHANGE
    B) school officials regularly informed parents
    C) parents were informed by school officials
    D) parents kept informing school officials

10. A) NO CHANGE
    B) its students are taken
    C) their students were taken
    D) their students will have been taken

For answers, see page 582.

LESSON 12:

Usage

- using pronouns correctly
- correcting unclear or ambiguous pronouns and antecedents
- correcting problems with pronoun/antecedent, subject/verb, and noun agreement
- correcting misuse of confusing words (*its/it's, there/they're/their, accept/except*)
- correcting cases in which unalike terms are compared
- correcting nonstandard written English

Explain Using Pronouns Correctly

Pronouns are words used in the place of **nouns**. Examples include *I, me, you,* and *their*. The noun to which a pronoun refers is called the **antecedent**. Pronouns must agree with their antecedents in gender and number. Pronouns also have **cases**, including subject case and objective case. A pronoun's case is determined by how it is used in a sentence; for example, as the subject or as the object of a verb.

Think It Through

A handful of pronouns cause more trouble than all the rest put together. These personal pronouns have different forms when used as subjects and as objects.

	Singular	Plural
As subjects:	I, he, she, who	we, they, who
As objects of verbs and prepositions:	me, him, her, whom	us, them, whom

Subject case is also called *nominative case.*

> **Examples:**
> We watched the Super Bowl together.
> (*We* is the subject of the verb *watched*.)
>
> The Adams had invited us to the get-together.
> (*Us* is the object of the verb *had invited*.)
>
> To whom should I give the money?
> (*Whom* is the object of the preposition *to*.)

Who and *whom* can be confusing when used in subordinate clauses. *Who* is a subject of a verb. Whom is the object of a verb or of a preposition.

> ### Examples:
> The picture was painted by Raja (who, whom) often paints with watercolors.
> (*Who* is subject of the verb *paints*.)
>
> The girl for (who, whom) the poem was written was a the author's daughter.
> (*Whom* is object of the preposition *for*.)

Most pronoun difficulties occur when a noun and a pronoun (or two pronouns) are joined by the conjunctions *and* or *or*. First determine whether a pronoun is being used as a subject or an object. Then choose the correct pronoun. When in doubt, substitute possible pronouns into the sentence and decide which one makes sense.

> ### Examples:
> Laura and (she, her) competed in the spelling bee.
> Check by substitution: *She* competed. *Her* competed. *She competed* is correct.
>
> Mr. Foster gave (he, him) and (me, I) a chance to play in the mixed-doubles tournament.
> Check by substitution: Mr. Foster gave *he*. Mr. Foster gave *him*. *Him* is correct.
> Mr. Foster gave *me*. Mr. Foster gave *I*. *Me* is correct.
>
> Go with Margo and (him, he) to the flea market.
> Check by substitution: Go with *him*. Go with *he*. *Him* is correct.
>
> The apples were divided between (he, him) and (she, her).
> *Between* is a preposition, so objective case is needed: *him*, *her*.
> Also check by substitution: The apples were divided between *he*. The apples were divided between *him*. *Him* is correct.
> The apples were divided between *she*. The apples were divided between *her*. *Her* is correct.

Sometimes pronouns are used as appositives. An **appositive** is a noun or noun phrase that identifies or renames another noun. Make the pronoun used as an appositive match how the noun is used in the sentence—as an object or a subject.

> ### Examples:
> The crowd cheered for the winners, (her, she) and Shawndrea.
> (*Winners* is an object of the preposition *for*. Use objective case: *her*.)
>
> The runners, (he, him) and Jake, were called to the finish line.
> (*Runners* is the subject of the verb *were called*. Use subject case: *he*.)
>
> (We, Us) swimmers are competing in the county championships.
> (*We* is a subject of the verb *are competing*.)
>
> Mr. Edmonds took (us, we) students on a tour of the Edison home in Fort Myers.
> (*Us* is an object of the verb *took*.)

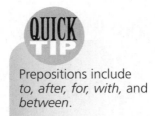

Prepositions include *to, after, for, with,* and *between.*

It is courteous to mention the other person first: *Mollie and me,* NOT *me and Mollie.*

For pronouns used as appositives, try substituting the pronoun in the place of noun. Example: The crowd cheered for *her* (not for *she*).

Pronouns are often used in comparisons using the words *than* or *as*. These comparisons often contain understood subjects and verbs. To determine the correct pronoun, complete the comparison, inserting the missing words.

> **Examples:**
> Gwen is already as tall as (he, him).
> (*He* is the subject of the understood verb *is*. Think of the sentence as reading, *Gwen is already as tall as he is.*)
>
> It is ridiculous to say that he is smarter than (she, her).
> (*She* is the subject of the understood verb *is*. Think of the sentence as reading, *It is ridiculous to say that he is smarter than she is.*)

Unclear or Ambiguous Pronoun Antecedents

Unclear or ambiguous pronouns are confusing because they might refer to more than one antecedent or do not have an antecedent. Consider this example:

Francine explained to her mother that she would have to call in sick.

This sentence does not clearly define who will call in sick, Francine or her mother. Here are two possible ways to revise the sentence:

Francine explained to her mother, "I will have to call in sick."

Francine explained to her mother, "You will have to call in sick."

> **CONFUSING:** Scientists understand that pollution that falls on snow in Greenland limits its ability to reflect the sun's rays.
> Does *its* refer to pollution or the snow?
> **CLEAR:** Scientists understand that pollution that falls on snow and ice in Greenland limits the snow's ability to reflect the sun's rays.

Possessive Pronouns

Unlike nouns, the possessives of personal pronouns have NO apostrophes. To show possession, *you* becomes *your*, *she* becomes *her* or *hers*, *they* becomes *their* or *theirs*, and so on.

> **Examples:**
> Is this *yours* or *hers*?
> Those books are *theirs*, not *ours*.
> Where is *its* collar?

The possessives of indefinite pronouns, unlike personal pronouns, DO use apostrophes.

> **Examples:**
> *Somebody's* briefcase is on the kitchen table.
> *Everyone's* job is *nobody's* job.
> No *one's* opinion is more valued than Janet's.

Confusing Possessives

Some possessive pronouns and contractions are easily confused.

whose = possessive

who's = contraction for *who is*

> ### Examples:
> *Whose* sweater is this?
>
> *Who's* going to claim it? (*Who is* going to claim it?)

its = possessive

it's = contraction for *it is*

Whenever you wonder whether *its* needs an apostrophe, simply replace *its* with *it is*. If the sentence makes sense, use an apostrophe. If it doesn't make sense, don't use the apostrophe.

> ### Examples
> *His* dog is off *its* leash. (Replacing *its* with *it is* results in a sentence that doesn't make sense: His dog is off *it is* leash. *Its* is correct.)

Their = possessive pronoun

they're = contraction for *they are*

there = adverb expressing a location

your = possessive pronoun

you're = contraction for *you are*

> ### Examples
> *They're* going to have to work on *their* lawn soon; it looks rather bald over *there*. (*They're* = they are, *their* shows the possession of *lawn*, and over *there* indicates a location.)
>
> *You're* going to watch *your* mom's speech tomorrow, aren't you? (*You're* = you are, and *your* shows possession.)

Practice

Directions: Underline the correct form of the pronoun in parentheses.

1. (We, Us) members of the Virginia Cavaliers marching band leave for Chicago tonight.

2. We found our dog Oliver and (she, her) asleep on the sofa.

3. (Tom and I, Me and Tom) worked on a sculpture project for the Art Festival.

4. When I'm working on my model trains, nobody can be as happy as (I, me).

5. Just between you and (I, me), today's cafeteria lunch was tasteless.

6. Rhonda says that this book of Emily Dickinson's poetry is (hers, her's).

7. Between you and (I, me), I would have preferred to go to Colorado this summer, not Florida.

8. (It's, Its) starting to pour; cover the chairs.

9. (Their, They're) writing skills are improving quickly.

10. The wind gust almost blew (you're, your) hat across the street.

11. The girl (who, whom) is running for president is Ming Lee.

For answers, see page 583.

Model SAT Questions

Directions: These Model SAT Questions show how pronoun usage may be tested on the SAT. The answer and explanation immediately follow the questions. Answer the questions and then review the explanations.

Late in the administration of Andrew Johnson, Gen. Ulysses S. Grant quarreled with the President and aligned himself with the Radical Republicans. He was, as the symbol of Union victory during the Civil War, **1** there logical candidate for President in 1868.

When he was elected, the American people hoped for an end to turmoil. Grant provided neither vigor nor reform. Looking to Congress for direction, he seemed bewildered. One visitor to the White House described Grant's personality as "a puzzled pathos, as of a man with a problem before **2** them of which he does not understand the terms."

1. A) NO CHANGE
   B) their
   C) they're
   D) its

Strategy: This question asks you to edit the text for pronoun usage. Choice A is incorrect because *there* is an adverb referring to location, and so does not fit in this sentence. Choice C is not the best answer because the sentence does not make sense when read with the full form of the contraction: He was *they are* logical candidate for President. Choice D is also not the best answer since *its* is not an appropriate replacement for *Radical Republicans*, the proper noun to which the answer refers. The best answer is B because *their* correctly refers back to *Radical Republicans* and expresses possession.

QUICK TIP

To avoid overusing the phrase *his or her* and *he or she*, try changing the singular nouns to plural when possible.

2. A) NO CHANGE
   B) they
   C) he
   D) him

Strategy: What is needed is a pronoun that fits with the singular antecedent *man* and is an object of the preposition *before*. Choice A is not the best answer because *them* is plural and so does not agree with the singular antecedent *man*. Choice B is also not the best answer since *they* is used as a subject (nominative case). Choice C is also used for subjects, not objects. Only choice D, *him*, is singular, in the objective case, and agrees with the singular antecedent *man*.

Directions: Read each paragraph and answer the questions that follow.

The first two paragraphs below are adapted from the speech "Solitude of Self" by Elizabeth Cady Stanton, given before the U.S. Senate in 1892. Stanton was an early women's rights reformer who fought for the right to vote.

The point I wish plainly to bring before you on this occasion is the individuality of each human soul; our Protestant idea, the right of individual conscience and judgment; our republican idea, individual citizenship. In discussing the rights of a woman, we are to consider, first, what belongs to **1** her as an individual. . . .

Nothing strengthens the judgment and quickens the conscience like individual responsibility. Nothing adds such dignity to character as the recognition of **2** ones self-sovereignty; the right to an equal place, everywhere conceded—a place earned by personal merit, not an artificial attainment by inheritance, wealth, family and position. Conceding then that the responsibilities of life rest equally on man and woman, that their destiny is the same, they need the same preparation for time and eternity. The talk of sheltering woman from the fierce storms of life is the sheerest mockery, for they beat on both men and women, on **3** he and she alike. . .

When Ms. Johnson explained to our class that **4** us students would be reading Elizabeth Cady Stanton's speech, I was excited. In the movement to secure women's right to vote, few worked harder than **5** she. "Solitude of Self" is a masterpiece of logical rhetoric. Stanton, **6** whom was speaking to a mostly male audience, carefully develops the syllogism that women are individuals, and all individuals must live self-determined lives; therefore, women must be allowed to control their own lives. By delivering a carefully constructed argument, Stanton demonstrated that she (a woman!) possessed the intellect to stand up to powerful men and **7** they're world of academia.

1. A) NO CHANGE
   B) she
   C) hers
   D) them

2. A) NO CHANGE
   B) one's
   C) it
   D) it's

3. A) NO CHANGE
   B) he and her
   C) him and she
   D) him and her

4. A) NO CHANGE
   B) you
   C) her
   D) we

5. A) NO CHANGE
   B) her
   C) hers
   D) them

6. A) NO CHANGE
   B) her
   C) who
   D) who's

7. A) NO CHANGE
   B) there
   C) their
   D) his

For answers, see page 583.

Explain ## Correcting Problems with Pronoun/Antecedent, Subject/Verb, and Noun Agreement

The term **agreement** refers to making sure that words in a sentence are the same gender, number, and tense. Lack of agreement causes confusion for the reader. Pronouns must agree with the word they are replacing, their **antecedents**; verbs must agree with their subjects; and nouns must agree in number with other nouns in a sentence.

Agreement of a Pronoun with Its Antecedent

A pronoun must agree with its antecedent in gender and number. Remember the antecedent is the word the pronoun is replacing.

> **Examples:**
>
> A *wolf* is gentle with *its* young.
> (*Its* refers to *wolf. Wolf* is the antecedent of *its. Wolf* is singular. Therefore, *its* is singular.)
>
> Note that for animals or when the sex of the animal is unknown, *its* is gender neutral.
>
> *Wolves* are gentle with *their* young.
> (*Their* refers to *wolves. Wolves* is the antecedent of *their. Wolves* is plural. Therefore, *their* is plural.)
>
> The *boy* from the visiting team left *his* jacket on the bus.
> (*Boy* is the antecedent of *his.* Both are singular.)
>
> The *girls* dressed for a party found *themselves* in the middle of a rugby game.
> (*Girls* is the antecedent of *themselves.* Both are plural.)

Theirselves is not a pronoun and is never correct.

Indefinite Pronouns

Many problems of agreement arise with the words on the following list. They are called **indefinite pronouns**. All of the following words require singular pronouns.

anybody	either	neither	one
anyone	everybody	nobody	somebody
each	everyone	no one	someone

> **Examples:**
>
> *Each* of the girls must bring *her* track shoes.
> (*Each* is singular. *Her* is singular.)
>
> *Everybody* must report to *his or her* advisor.
> (*Everybody* is singular. *His/her* with *or* is singular. Even though "everybody" *sounds* plural, it isn't. The use of *their* with *everybody* (or with any other word on the list) is incorrect in formal English.)

With *either/or* or *neither/nor*, use the nearer antecedent when choosing a pronoun.

> **Examples:**
>
> Either Jill or *Claire* will bring *her* records to the dance.
> (Since *Claire* is the nearer antecedent and is singular, the singular *her* is used.)
>
> Neither Norm nor his *cousins* buy *their* groceries here.
> (Since *cousins* is the nearer antecedent and is plural, the plural *their* is used.)

Agreement of Subject and Verbs

A **verb** must agree with its subject in number and person. Remember that an *s* is added to a verb to make it singular; an *s* is added to a noun to make it plural. For example: *Winds blow, wind blows*.

	Singular	**Plural**
FIRST PERSON:	I enjoy	we enjoy
SECOND PERSON:	you enjoy	you enjoy
THIRD PERSON:	he, she, it enjoys	they enjoy

Of course, many verbs are irregular and do not follow the pattern above. The verb "to be" is one of these: *I am a friend. She is a friend. They are friends.*

> **Examples:**
> A tree stands at the front gate. (*Stands* is singular.)
> I am going to break the school record. (*Am* is singular.)
> We are going to win the tournament. (*Are going* is plural.)

Agreement is trickier when words or phrases come in between the subject and verb. Make the verb agree with the subject and not an object of a prepositional phrase.

> **Example:**
> A *tree* with green leaves *stands* at the front gate.
> (*Stands* agrees with the subject *tree*, not the word *leaves*, which is part of the prepositional phrase *with green leaves*.)

Expressions like *together with*, *according to*, *including*, *as well as*, and others do not affect subject-verb agreement.

> **Example:**
> The *players*, including the coach, *are going* to the game by plane.
> (*Players* is the subject, not *coach*.)

The words *and*, *or*, *nor*, *either/or*, and *neither/nor* signal the presence of a compound subject. When two subjects are connected by *and*, the subject is plural, and the verb is usually plural.

> High *seas* **and** dense *fog have slowed* the rescue operation.

When two singular subjects are joined by *or* or *nor*, the subject is singular and the verb is singular.

> *Rain* **or** *snow is* the forecast for today.

When two subjects of different number are joined by *neither/nor* or *either/or*, the verb agrees with the nearer subject.

> **Neither** *Fran* **nor** her *brothers are going* to the state convention.
> **Either** these telephone *numbers* **or** that *address is* wrong.

When the subject comes after the verb, find the subject and make the verb agree with it.

> **Examples:**
>
> (Was, Were) the nominees for Best Actor all present at the Academy Awards ceremony?
> (The subject is *nominees*. Therefore, *were* is correct.)
>
> There (was, were) three raccoons digging in the rubbish heap.
> (The subject is *raccoons*, not the introductory word *there*. *Were* is correct. *Here* is a similar introductory word.)
>
> In a corner of my desk (is, are) the schedules for the Spurs' basketball games and the Bears' football games.
> (The subject is *schedules*. *Are* is correct.)

The words *here* and *there* are never the subject of a sentence. Find the subject and make the verb agree with it.

When indefinite pronouns are used as subjects, the verb must also match the subject in number. These indefinite pronouns usually require a plural verb: *several*, *many*, *both*, *some*, *few*.

> **Examples:**
>
> *Some were* not *invited* to Yolanda's party.
>
> *Many* of the apples *are* still green.
>
> *Several* in the stands *cheer* whenever Buck comes to bat.

Make a verb agree with its subject, not its predicate noun or pronoun.

> **Examples:**
>
> The greatest literary *achievement* of Geoffrey Chaucer *was* his insightful portrayals of the Canterbury pilgrims.
> (The subject is *achievement*, not *portrayals*.)
>
> The insightful *portrayals* of the Canterbury pilgrims *were* the greatest literary achievement of Geoffrey Chaucer.
> (The subject is *portrayals*.)

For adjective clauses with relative pronouns *who* or *which* as subject, make the verb agree with the word to which the relative pronoun refers.

> **Examples:**
>
> It was *Brittany* **who *was* to blame** for the incorrect meeting time.
> (*Who* refers to *Brittany*. *Brittany was*.)
>
> The list of *students* **who *were* accepted by Dartmouth** appears in today's paper.
> (*Who* refers to *students*. *Students were*.)
>
> Nutritionists consider *quinoa*, **which *is* native to Peru and Bolivia**, to be a "superfood."
> (*Which* refers to *quinoa*. *Quinoa is*.)
>
> Quinoa seeds, which *have* a bitter-tasting coating, are usually soaked in water before they are cooked.
> (*Which* refers to *seeds*. *Seeds have*.)

Use *who/whom* to refer to people. Use *which* or *that* to refer to things and inanimate objects.

Noun Agreement

Related nouns in a sentence must agree in number. Either they should all be singular or all plural.

> **CONFUSING:** The principal decided to give each *teacher raises*.
> (*Teacher* is singular, so the plural *raises* does not make sense.)
> **CLEAR:** The principal decided to give each *teacher* a *raise*.
> **CLEAR:** The principal decided to give the *teachers raises*.
> **CONFUSING:** The girl wanted to send her *friends* an *invitation*.
> (*Friends* is plural, so the related noun, *invitation*, should also be plural.)
> **CLEAR:** The girl wanted to send her *friends invitations*.
> **CLEAR:** The girl wanted to send *invitations* to her *friends*.

Some nouns have the same form in the singular and the plural.

cod	moose	salmon
athletics	headquarters	politics

Some nouns ending in *s* are used only in the plural or have special meanings in the plural.

ashes	proceeds	tactics
clothes	riches	thanks
gymnastics	scissors	trousers

A few nouns ending in *s* are singular in meaning.

civics	measles	physics
economics	mumps	the United States
mathematics	news	

Some nouns from foreign languages keep their foreign plurals.

analysis—analyses	crisis—crises
axis—axes	ellipsis—ellipses
basis—bases	datum—data

(*Data* is commonly and loosely used in the singular, although it is historically plural.)

Practice

Directions: Underline the correct form of the verb in parentheses.

1. Nobody among all the members (was, were) completely in favor of the proposed new charter.

2. A few in the club (was, were) determined to reject the plan.

3. One of the council members (was, were) disappointed by the vote.

4. Either Paul or she (are, is) sponsoring a new resolution.

5. Neither Grace nor her two brothers (are, is) interested in the trip to Gatlinburg.

6. The girl with the pearl earrings (was, were) made immortal in a Vermeer painting.

7. The incumbent, according to the latest polls, (are, is) leading.

8. Neither the officers nor the president (was, were) present at the election.

9. (Was, Were) you able to complete your science project on time?

10. (Are, Is) there any late registrants for the rollerblade competition?

11. Benjamin Franklin's wisdom, not any personal flaws, (are, is) best remembered.

12. Ogden Nash's supreme achievement (was, were) his outrageous puns and clever rhymes.

13. It is I who (am, is) responsible for the loss, not Frank.

14. Mary Jane (doesn't, don't) know whether or not to apply to the University of Texas.

Directions: Underline the correct noun or pronoun in parentheses.

15. An elephant forms close bonds with (its, their) trainers.

16. Everybody brought (his, their) Harley to the rally.

17. The pop star gave several of her most devoted fans (an autographed photo, autographed photos).

18. One of the new clarinetists made (her, their) debut.

19. Jesminder must meet many requirements before becoming (a pilot, pilots).

20. Pat made cupcakes for his (classmate, classmates) on his birthday.

21. Neither Boris nor Bobby kept (his, their) chess title for long.

22. The backup players on the team are crucial to (its, their) success.

For answers, see page 583.

Model SAT Questions

Directions: These Model SAT Questions show how you might be tested on pronoun-antecedent agreement, subject-verb agreement, and noun agreement. The answers and explanations immediately follow the questions. Answer the questions and then review the explanations.

The following excerpt is adapted from Thomas Paine's Common Sense, *written in 1776 to challenge the authority of the British government and persuade the common people to rally for independence.*

The most plausible plea which **1** have ever been offered in favor of hereditary succession is that it preserves a nation from civil wars; and were this true, it would be weighty; whereas it is the most bare-faced falsity ever imposed upon mankind. The whole history of England disowns the fact. Neither the thirty kings nor any other form of government **2** have been able to ensure peace in the land. During England's long history, there have been (including the revolution) no less than eight civil wars and nineteen Rebellions. Wherefore instead of making for peace, it makes against it, and destroys the very foundation it seems to stand upon.

1. A) NO CHANGE
   B) has ever been offered
   C) have never been offered
   D) one have ever offered

Strategy: This question asks you to edit the sentence for pronoun-antecedent agreement. The underlined phrase is part of a subordinate clause beginning with *which*. *Which* refers to the singular subject *plea* and must agree with it. Choice A is incorrect because *have* is plural. For the same reason, C is incorrect. Choice C also introduces the negative word *never*, which changes the meaning of the sentence. In choice D *have* is the incorrect verb for the subject *one*. The correct answer is B, *has ever been offered.*

2. A) NO CHANGE
   B) have been able to ensures
   C) has been able to ensure
   D) having been able to ensure

Strategy: This question asks you to edit the sentence for subject-verb agreement. The subject includes a plural noun (*kings*) and a singular one (*form*) joined by *neither/nor*. The verb must agree with the closer subject, which is singular. Choice A is incorrect because *have* is plural. Choice B is incorrect because of the plural *have* and incorrect infinitive phrase *to ensures*. Choice D incorrectly changes the tense of the verb *have*. Choice C correctly uses the singular form, *has*.

SAT-Type Questions

Directions: Questions 1–5 are based on the following passage.

Dolley Payne Todd Madison

Dolley Payne Todd Madison (1768–1849) was the wife of James Madison, fourth President of the United States (1809–1817). **1** She is one of the best known and loved first ladies, and her social presence boosted her husband's popularity as President.

For half a century she was the most important woman in the social circles of America. To this day she remains one of the best known and best loved ladies of the White House—though often referred to, mistakenly, as Dorothy or Dorothea.

However, according to the registry of the New Garden Monthly Meeting of the Society of Friends, in Piedmont, North Carolina, **2** which recorded their birth to John and Mary Coles Payne, her given name was Dolley. Dolley's father moved the family to a plantation in Virginia, where she spent the first 15 years of her life. In 1783 **3** he moved to Philadelphia, city of the Quakers. Dolley grew up in the strict discipline of the Society. Yet neither the many rules nor the austere lifestyle **4** were able to mute her happy personality and her warm heart.

Dolley married John Todd, Jr., a lawyer, in 1790. Just three years later he died in a yellow-fever epidemic, leaving his wife with a small son. With her charm and her laughing blue eyes, fair skin, and black curls, the young widow soon attracted distinguished attention. Before long Dolley was reporting to her best friend that "the great little Madison has asked . . . to see me this evening." Although Representative James Madison of Virginia was 17 years her senior, they were married in September 1794. The marriage, though childless, was notably happy; **5** "there hearts understands each other," she assured him.

Dolley Madison defined the role of first lady by establishing many of the precedents that her successors would follow, including working with local charities and organizations on social issues. She is probably best remembered for saving the White House's historic Gilbert Stuart portrait of George Washington from certain destruction by advancing British troops during the War of 1812. **6** The United States were really very fortunate to have Dolley Madison as the first "first lady."

1. A) NO CHANGE
   B) She was one
   C) She were one
   D) She, one

2. A) NO CHANGE
   B) who recorded her birth
   C) which recorded her birth
   D) who records their birth

3. A) NO CHANGE
   B) they moved
   C) he had moved
   D) they moving

4. A) NO CHANGE
   B) were able to mute their
   C) was able to mute his or her
   D) was able to mute her

5. A) NO CHANGE
   B) "their hearts understand
   C) "our hearts understands
   D) "our hearts understand

6. A) NO CHANGE
   B) The United States was really very fortunate
   C) The United States was very fortunate
   D) The United States were very fortunate

For answers, see page 583.

Explain Correcting Frequently Confused Words, Comparing Like Terms, and Correcting Nonstandard Written English

Frequently Confused Words

Some words are frequently confused with others. Here are a few examples.

Accept means "to receive." She *accepted* his proposal.
Except means "to take or leave out." Please hand me all of the folders *except* the blue one.

Adapt means "to change or adjust to something." Xiao *adapted* to her new home quite easily.
Adopt means "to decide to use something." The company has *adopted* a new policy that prohibits smoking anywhere on campus.

Advice means "an opinion or recommendation offered as a guide." Her great *advice* about investing a small amount each month has really paid off.
Advise means "to give counsel or offer an opinion." Frank always *advises* the board about potential acquisitions.

Affect means "to influence or produce a change in." Losing his favorite companion has negatively *affected* him.
Effect means "a result or consequence." Losing his favorite companion has had a negative *effect* on him. (Just remember that *affect* is a verb and *effect* is a noun.)

Allusion means "an indirect reference." The writer makes an interesting *allusion* to the Greek myth, Hercules, in the third paragraph.
Illusion means "a false perception of reality." Tommy's *illusion* of his cousin's honesty was shattered when he saw her shoplift at the mall.

Farther means "greater in distance." The park is ten miles *farther* down the road.
Further means "to increase." *Further* your knowledge by reading.

Then means "next." *Then* we rode our bikes to the farmer's market.
Than is used to show a comparison. I am taller *than* my mom.

Comparing Like Terms

When comparing two things, make sure they are like terms and are a logical comparison.

> **Unlike:** As the musician matured, his lyrics were said to be similar to the great masters of poetry. (Lyrics should not be compared to masters.)
>
> **Like:** As the musician matured, his lyrics were said to be similar to poetry by the great masters. (Two like terms, *lyrics* and *poetry*, are compared.)
>
> **Unlike:** The king and his family prospered, and as the kingdom grew, people compared the capital city to magic existing alongside of people in Camelot. (The capital city is compared to magic.)
>
> **Like:** The king and his family prospered, and as the kingdom grew, people compared the capital city to Camelot where magic existed alongside of people. (The capital city is compared to Camelot.)

Correcting Nonstandard Written English

Avoid using double negatives. Negative words include *no*, *not*, *never*, *nothing*, *none*, *nobody*, *hardly*, and *scarcely*. Be careful with the half-negatives *hardly*, *scarcely*, *barely*, *only*, and *but* when they mean *only*.

Double: I *don't* have *no* homework assignment for tonight.
One: I *don't* have a homework assignment for tonight.
One: I have *no* homework assignment for tonight.

Double: The regular party members *didn't* have *nothing* to do with the recall election in California.
One: The regular party members *didn't* have anything to do with the recall election in California.
One: The regular party members had *nothing* to do with the recall election in California.

Several questions on the practice SAT exams test your ability to use the correct preposition to communicate relationships between ideas.

Examples:

The Internet is a *means of* (not *to*) distributing information to many people at once.

He went in search *of* (not *for*) his lost pet.

We complied *with* (not *to*) the request to bring our student IDs to the testing center.

Notice that although the following verbs are the same, the preposition varies depending upon the meaning: agree *to* a proposal; agree *with* a person; *agree* on a plan.

Don't add *s* to *anyway, anywhere, everywhere, nowhere, somewhere, beside, toward, and forward*.

Incorrect: When it was time to go, the cat was nowheres to be found.
Correct: When it was time to go, the cat was nowhere to be found.
Incorrect: The last time I saw him, he was walking *towards* the pool.
Correct: The last time I saw him, he was walking *toward* the pool.

Don't use *more* with an *-er* word (*more wiser*) or *most* with an *-est* word (*most prettiest*).

Incorrect: Our cat is *more smarter* than our cocker spaniel.
Correct: Our cat is *smarter* than our cocker spaniel.

Here are some common nonstandard words and phrases you should be aware of:

Nonstandard/Incorrect	Standard/Correct
could of/should of	could have/should have
got some ice cream	bought some ice cream
kind of	somewhat
off of the wall	off the wall

Directions: Underline the word that best fits the sentence.

1. Divorce can have a negative (affect, effect) on children's academic performance.

2. Tammy has been selected to (advice, advise) the club president about how to host successful fund-raisers.

3. All of the children loved the show (accept, except) for Benjamin.

4. Amir thought he was good at basketball, but he realized it was just an (allusion, illusion) after he didn't make the team.

Directions: Revise the underlined portion in the sentences to compare like terms.

5. The technology at our school's library is more advanced than the town's library.

_____

_____

6. As Janine aged, her siblings compared her personality traits to her mother.

_____

_____

Directions: Circle the word or phrase that best fits the sentence.

7. We hope that we grow (more wiser, wiser) as we grow older.

8. This year I'd like to visit somewhere (beside, besides) just our relatives.

9. The girls didn't (have anything, have nothing) to eat at the luncheon.

10. (Them, Those) are the tastiest cantaloupes I've ever eaten.

11. Delia (can't never, can never) decide which movie she wants to see.

12. Val and Petra agreed (on a plan, with a plan) to save up money for a trip to Europe.

For answers, see page 584.

Directions: These Model SAT Questions show how you might be tested over confusing terms, comparisons, and standard English on the SAT. The answers and explanations immediately follow the questions. Try the questions and then review the answers and the explanations.

Questions 1 and 2 are based on the following passage.

Blue king crab look similar in size and appearance ▮**1**▮ to the look and form of the more widespread red king crab, but are typically biennial spawners with lesser fecundity and somewhat larger sized eggs. It may not be possible for large female blue king crabs to support the energy requirements for annual ovary development, growth, and egg extrusion **2** due with limitations imposed by their habitat, such as poor quality or low abundance of food or reduced feeding activity due to cold water. Both the large size reached by blue king crabs and the generally high productivity of the Pribilof and St. Matthew island areas, however, argue against such environmental constraints. Development of the fertilized embryos occurs in the egg cases attached to the pleopods beneath the abdomen of the female crab, and hatching occurs February through April. After larvae are released, large female blue king crabs will molt, mate, and extrude their clutches the following year in late March through mid-April.

1. A) NO CHANGE
   B) to the more widespread red king crab
   C) to the size of the more widespread red king crab
   D) to the outer shell of the more widespread red king crab

Strategy: This question asks you to compare like terms. Choice A is incorrect because it creates a comparison between unlike things: *blue king crab* and *look and form*, Likewise, choice C compares the unlike terms, *blue king crab* and *size*, and choice D compares the unlike terms *blue king crab* and *outer shell*. Answer B compares similar things, *blue king crab* and *red king crab*, so it is the best answer.

2. A) NO CHANGE
   B) due for
   C) due to
   D) due because

Strategy: This question asks you to revise the sentence for standard written English. Choice A is not the best answer because *due with* is not standard written English as *with* is the wrong preposition to use after *due* in this sentence. Choice B, *due for*, and choice D, *due because* are also nonstandard. The best answer is C, *due to*.

SAT-Type Questions

Directions: Questions 1–8 are based on the following passage taken from a pamphlet to promote cultural understanding of Vietnamese refugees.

Overview of Vietnamese Culture

The first wave of Vietnamese, mostly educated professionals and former military personnel, experienced fewer difficulties adapting to life in the United States **1** compared with the "boat people" who followed. During the 1980s, many Vietnamese refugees experienced high levels of poverty, unemployment, and welfare. According to the U.S. Census Bureau (2000), 7 percent of Vietnamese families had an annual income less than $10,000, while the median income ($47,000) was ▨2▨ more closer to that of the general U.S. population ($50,000). About 14 percent (compared with 9.2 percent among the general U.S. population) of Vietnamese families lived below the 1999 poverty line. In addition, Vietnamese were less likely to have finished high school: 61 percent were high school graduates or higher compared with ▨3▨ 80.4 percent of the United States.

Social Structure, Family, and Gender

Among the Vietnamese, family is valued highly and plays a central role in the culture. Within traditional Vietnamese families, husbands make decisions on issues outside the home, while wives care for the home and make family health care decisions. Elders are highly respected and honored, and children are expected to obey them. Obligations are met and decisions are made based on the common good, usually under the guidance of the eldest male. Generally, individualism is ▨4▨ not discouraged in favor with family responsibilities that promote interdependence, belonging, and support.

▨5▨ Than as the Vietnamese assimilating to the United States, gender roles in Vietnamese families slowly reversed. Because of the availability of jobs in Western society, women gained economic independence outside the home. In addition, children could become interpreters for their families because of their ability to speak English and their familiarity with American customs. Women and children who ▨6▨ adopt to Western society more quickly than men can increase their authority in the family and ▨7▨ thus rise in position. These role changes can leave men and older family members feeling alienated and without the respect and honor to which they are culturally accustomed.

1. A) NO CHANGE
   B) compared with the "boat people" which followed
   C) comparing to the "boat people" who followed
   D) compared to the boats of people that followed

2. A) NO CHANGE
   B) closer to that of the general U.S.
   C) more closer for that of the general U.S.'s
   D) closer to that of the general U.S.'s

3. A) NO CHANGE
   B) the general population of the United States.
   C) 80.4 percent of the general United States population.
   D) the general United States population.

4. A) NO CHANGE
   B) discouraged in favor with family
   C) discouraged in favor to family
   D) discouraged in favor of family

5. A) NO CHANGE
   B) Then as the Vietnamese was assimilating to the United States,
   C) Then as the Vietnamese assimilated to the United States,
   D) Than the Vietnamese assimilated to the United States,

6. A) NO CHANGE
   B) adapt to Western society more quickly then men
   C) adapt to Western society quicker then men
   D) adapt to Western society more quickly than men

7. A) NO CHANGE
   B) thus raise in position.
   C) henceforth rise in position.
   D) thus rise to position.

For answers, see page 584.

LESSON 13:

Punctuation

- using end punctuation and commas

- using commas and semicolons

- using parentheses, dashes, and quotation marks

- using apostrophes with possessive nouns

- correcting use of unnecessary punctuation

Explain Using End Punctuation and Commas

Punctuation is an important part of written communication. Periods, commas, semicolons, colons, and other punctuation marks help the reader understand how to interpret the content, identify central and secondary ideas, and understand the relationship between groups of items.

A complete list of punctuation rules would fill a small book. Fortunately, you don't have to learn them all. Mastery of some basic rules will help you avoid most of the pitfalls in punctuating sentences. The following review covers the main points.

Think It Through

End Punctuation

Every sentence ends with a **period**, a **question mark**, or an **exclamation point**.

STATEMENT:	A Pekingese has a longer life expectancy than a Saint Bernard.
COMMAND:	Read this book about how to repair a faucet.
POLITE REQUEST:	May I hear from you soon?
QUESTION:	Have you ever visited Acadia National Park?
STRONG FEELING:	What a wonderful time we had at Sea World!

The Comma

Commas have two basic purposes: to separate and to enclose items.

- Use commas to separate items in a series.

  Examples:
  At camp we hiked, swam, golfed, and played softball.

  My brother collects stamps, coins, and picture postcards.

  Sue looked for the tickets on the desk, in the desk drawer, and on the dresser.

QUICK
TIP

Some writers omit the final comma before the word in a list. This serial (or Oxford) comma should be used to prevent misunderstandings. Example: I love my parents, Beyonce and grilled cheese sandwiches.

- Use a comma between more than one adjective that directly precedes a noun and is not joined by a conjunction (*and, or*).

  Examples:
  The gloomy, isolated mansion stood at the edge of a cliff.
  I'll wear my old, comfortable shoes to the dance.

- Use a comma before a conjunction (*for, and, nor, but, or, yet*) in compound sentences.

  Examples:
  Give the dog some water, or he will dehydrate.
  A hippo spends most of its time in water, yet grazes for grass on land at night.
  The silkworm isn't a worm, but it is actually a caterpillar.

- Use a single comma to set off introductory words, phrases, and clauses from the rest of the sentence.

  Examples:
  Over the course of eleven days, the men wandered through the woods until they stumbled upon a hunting cabin. (Use a comma with an introductory prepositional phrase that is four words or longer.)
  Hunting for my calculator, I found a long-lost pair of gloves. (introductory phrase)
  Before she left home, she checked to make sure all the doors were locked. (introductory clause)

- Use a pair of commas to enclose appositives. An appositive identifies or explains a noun or pronoun in a sentence.

  Examples:
  Songhay, an African kingdom in the late 1400s, was larger than Western Europe.
  The Antarctic waters, fertilizer for the rest of the world, help support life in the other oceans.

- Use a pair of commas to set off parenthetical expressions that interrupt the flow of a sentence. These expressions usually supply extra information.

  Examples:
  The old house, grim and foreboding, hovered over Main Street.
  Spiders, unpopular but essential, destroy a hundred times their number in insects.
  The avocado, or alligator pear, was first cultivated by the Aztecs.
  Siamese cats, on the other hand, are more reserved.
  Our Mr. Pooch, like most beagles, is a friendly dog.
  Tallahassee, not Miami, is the capital of Florida.

- A comma is also used to set off interrupters at the beginning and end of sentences. Note that transitional phrases, such as *first, next, however,* and *on the other hand,* are usually set off by commas.

QUICK TIP

To see if a comma is needed between adjectives preceding a noun, read the sentence inserting *and* between the adjectives. If the sentence sounds natural, a comma is needed.

QUICK TIP

For a review of compound sentences, see pages 295–296.

Examples:

Like most beagles, our Mr. Pooch is a friendly dog.

On the other hand, Siamese cats are more reserved.

The capital of Florida is Tallahassee, not Miami.

I'm surprised that you believe his story, Madge.

Yes, I admit that I can see your point of view.

Of course, I've never actually seen a bear in the woods.

- Use commas to set off nonessential (or nonrestrictive) phrases and clauses. *Nonrestrictive* means that the information is **not essential** to the meaning of the sentence. It includes extra details of less importance than the main idea.

To decide if a phrase or clause is not essential, read the sentence without it. If the meaning of the sentence stays the same without it, it is **nonrestrictive**.

A phrase or clause that modifies a proper noun is almost always nonrestrictive.

Nonrestrictive: John Prentice, *who is our former CEO*, will be at the convention next week. (Meaning stays the same when the clause is removed.)

Nonrestrictive: The carrier pigeon, *which was a common message carrier*, is now extinct. (Meaning stays the same when the clause is removed.)

Nonrestrictive: There are many different types of coniferous trees, *such as pine and spruce*. (The phrase beginning with *such as* is merely giving examples.)

Restrictive: The Christmas movie *that I like the best* is *It's a Wonderful Life*. (The clause *that I like the best* contains crucial information. Without the clause, the sentence would read: The Christmas movie is *It's a Wonderful Life*.)

Restrictive: The woman *who owns the red convertible* parked in my spot. (The clause *who owns the red convertible* identifies the woman to whom the speaker is referring, and removing it would change the sentence's meaning. Thus, it is essential information.)

Restrictive: The man *whom I met last week* loved watching baseball, too. (The clause *whom I met last week* identifies the man to whom the speaker is referring, and removing it would change the sentence's meaning, making it essential information.)

Restrictive: Our former CEO *John Prentice* will be at the convention next week. (Since a company may have had more than one former CEO, *John Prentice* identifies which CEO will be at the convention. This is essential information, so it has no commas around it.)

Directions: Add or cross out punctuation as needed in the following sentences.

1. The little boy, who stole my lunch, is sitting over there.

2. Mr. Jonas, who has worked here for twenty years, will retire soon.

3. The cat, that can open doors, belongs to my brother.

4. Patrice wants to open her own bakery, learn a new language, and climb Mt. Everest.

5. The manager, Mr. Timms, often leaves, before his shift is over.

6. I just won the lottery!

7. Would you like to sit down next to the little girl, who is waving at us?

8. The young boy, energetic and rambunctious, could hardly contain his excitement.

For answers, see page 585.

Model SAT Questions

Directions: These Model SAT Questions show how your ability to edit text for punctuation and comma errors might be tested on the SAT. The answers and explanations immediately follow the questions. Try the questions and then review the answers and the explanations.

Health-Risk Behaviors and Academic Achievement

Data from the 2009 National Youth Risk Behavior Survey show a negative association between health-risk behaviors and academic achievement among high school students after controlling **1** for sex race/ethnicity, and grade level. This means that students with higher grades are less likely to engage in health-risk behaviors than their classmates with lower grades, and **2** students, who do not engage in health-risk behaviors receive higher grades than their classmates who do engage in health-risk behaviors. These associations do not prove causation. Further research is needed to determine whether low grades lead to health-risk behaviors, health-risk behaviors lead to low grades, or some other factors lead to both of these problems.

1. A) NO CHANGE
   B) for sex, race/ethnicity, and grade level.
   C) for sex race/ethnicity and grade level.
   D) for sex, race/ethnicity, and grade, level.

2. A) NO CHANGE
    B) students, who do not engage in health-risk behaviors,
    C) students who do not engage in health-risk behaviors
    D) students who do not engage in health-risk behaviors,

SAT-Type Questions

Directions: Questions 1–5 are based on the following passage.

Biodiesel Basics

Biodiesel is a **1** domestically produced, renewable fuel, that can be manufactured from new and used vegetable oils, animal fats, and recycled restaurant grease. Biodiesel's physical properties are similar to those of petroleum diesel, but it is a cleaner-burning alternative. Using biodiesel in place of petroleum diesel significantly reduces emissions of toxic air pollutants.

What is a biodiesel blend?

Biodiesel can be blended and used in many different concentrations, including B100 (pure biodiesel), B20 (20 percent biodiesel, 80 percent petroleum diesel), B5 (5 percent biodiesel, 95 percent petroleum diesel), and B2 (2 percent biodiesel, 98 percent petroleum diesel). B20 is a common biodiesel blend in the United States.

Can I use B20 in my vehicle's diesel engine?

For vehicles manufactured **2** after 1993 biodiesel can be used in diesel engines and fuel injection equipment with little impact on operating performance. **3** However if your vehicle is older than that, the engine could be assembled with incompatible ■4■ elastomers, a type of rubber used for seals and hoses which can break down with repetitive high-blend biodiesel use.

Will biodiesel perform as well as diesel?

Engines operating on B20 exhibit similar fuel ■5■ consumption, horsepower, and torque to that of engines running on conventional diesel, and biodiesel has a higher cetane number (a measure of the ignition value of diesel fuel) and higher lubricity (the ability to lubricate fuel pumps and fuel injectors) than U.S. diesel fuel. B20's energy content is between those of No. 1 and No. 2 diesel.

1. A) NO CHANGE
   B) domestically produced, renewable fuel, and that can be manufactured from
   C) domestically, produced renewable fuel that can be manufactured from
   D) domestically produced, renewable fuel that can be manufactured from

2. A) NO CHANGE
   B) after 1993, biodiesel can be used in diesel engines and fuel injection
   C) after 1993, biodiesel can be used in diesel, engines, and fuel injection
   D) after 1993, biodiesel can be used in diesel engines, and fuel injection

3. A) NO CHANGE
   B) And if your vehicle is older than that,
   C) However, if your vehicle is older than that,
   D) However, if your vehicle is older than that

4. A) NO CHANGE
   B) elastomers a type of rubber used for seals and hoses
   C) elastomers, a type of rubber, used for seals and hoses,
   D) elastomers, a type of rubber used for seals and hoses,

5. A) NO CHANGE
   B) consumption, horsepower, and torque, to that of engines running on conventional diesel, and
   C) consumption, horsepower, and torque, to that of engines running on conventional diesel and
   D) consumption, horsepower, and torque to that of engines running on conventional diesel and

For answers, see page 585.

Explain Using Semicolons and Colons

Semicolons and colons look similar and also have somewhat similar uses. However, they can also be confused.

Think It Through

Semicolons

- Use semicolons to join two complete sentences, or in other words independent clauses. The sentences should be closely related in meaning.

  Examples:
  A cat requires a little time; it needs to be pampered by whoever owns it.

  The earthworm has no lungs; it breathes through its skin.

  Ferrets make wonderful pets; they are friendly and use a litter box just like cats do.

- Use a semicolon between the clauses in a compound sentence when they are joined by transitional words such as *however*, *in fact,* and *as a result*. The transitional word or phrase should be followed by a comma.

  Examples:
  In the Jurassic Park movies, Hollywood has postulated what might happen if scientists brought dinosaurs to life in modern times; **however**, it might be more dangerous if scientists resurrected plants from the past.

  Prehistoric plants could be invasive; **in other words**, they might thrive and take over yards, parks, and forests.

  Gardeners bring exotic plants home from foreign trips, plant them in their yards, and then find that the plant takes over their landscaping; **for example**, the invasive purple loosestrife was brought to New England as an ornamental plant in the early 1800s.

- Use semicolons to separate items in a series when the items already contain commas.

  Examples:
  Last summer, the family visited Phoenix, Arizona; Pierre, South Dakota; Branson, Missouri; and Loveland, Colorado.

  The teams will be Tom, Kate, and Nicole; Tiffany, Jake, and Melanie; and Diego, Martin, and Sandra.

Colons

A colon only does one thing: it introduces. It can introduce any of the following: a word, a sentence, a quotation, or a list. (Notice how a colon was used in the previous sentences to introduce a sentence and a list.) A colon provides emphasis to whatever follows it because it forces the reader to come to a stop and pause.

- Use a colon to give special emphasis to an idea at the end of a sentence.

  Examples:
  My favorite animal at the zoo was the largest: the elephant.

  Juan only has one thing on his mind: winning the soccer tournament.

QUICK TIP

Use this test to help you decide if a colon is needed in a sentence. Read the sentence, and when you come to the colon, substitute the word *namely*; if the sentence reads smoothly, there is a good chance a colon is needed.

- Use colons before lists of items, especially when the list is introduced by the phrase *the following*.

> My schedule includes the following classes: anatomy, physics, English, and algebra.
>
> My favorite California beaches include the following: Huntington Beach, Malibu Beach, and Laguna Beach.

- Use a colon to join two independent clauses in order to emphasize the second sentence. Often the second clause explains or restates the first sentence.

> **Examples:**
> We now know why she named her new soft drink Key West Cola: she lives in Key West, Florida.
>
> Octopuses don't need eyes to see: their skin can detect light and respond to it.

- Use a colon to introduce quotations or formal statements or positions. Capitalize the first word of the quotation or statement.

> **Examples:**
> Most people recognize the famous line from Shakespeare's *Hamlet*: "To be, or not to be; that is the question."
>
> The issue before the committee was this: Who was best qualified to become the next committee chair?

- Semicolons and colons can be used to correct run-on sentences and comma splices (two independent clauses joined with a comma).

> **Incorrect:** In aquariums jellyfish are stunningly beautiful, in the ocean they can be invasive species with dangerous stings. (This is a comma splice.)
>
> **Correct:** In aquariums jellyfish are stunningly beautiful; in the ocean they can be invasive species with dangerous stings.
>
> **Incorrect:** Everyone wants to take Ms. Turner's class, she offers extra credit. (Using a comma here creates a comma splice.)
>
> **Correct:** Everyone wants to take Ms. Turner's class: she offers extra credit.

QUICK TIP

Never place a colon after the verb in a sentence, even when introducing a list. INCORRECT: My three favorite friends are: Inez, Sonjia, and Annie.

QUICK TIP

When a single sentence follows a colon, do not capitalize the first word of the sentence.

Practice

Directions: Add, cross out, or correct punctuation as needed in the following sentences.

1. Our spring garden features many flowers snowdrops, crocuses, aconites, hyacinths, and tulips.

2. George Washington was the first President of the United States, he served two terms.

3. The sassafras, unlike most trees, has three different and distinct leaf patterns unlobed oval; bilobed (mitten-shaped); and trilobed (three-pronged).

4. Cynthia already asked me I refused.

5. William Feather had the following words of wisdom; "Work is the best method for killing time."

6. If you can come camping with me, bring these supplies insect repellant, fishing gear, and a tent.

7. I have lived in Des Moines; Iowa, Lincoln; Nebraska; and Detroit; Michigan.

8. Florida is not the southernmost state in the United States Hawaii is farther south.

9. Robert E. Lee's personal home was made into Arlington National Cemetery during the Civil War, therefore, he never went home again.

10. Ocean water often includes salt seaweed and jellyfish.

For answers, see page 585.

Model SAT Questions

Directions: These Model SAT Questions show how your ability to edit text with colons and semicolons might be tested on the SAT. The answers and explanations immediately follow the questions. Try the questions and then review the answers and the explanations.

A food allergy occurs when the body has a specific and reproducible immune response to certain foods. The body's immune response can be severe and life-threatening, such as anaphylaxis. The immune system normally protects people from [1] germs however, in people with food allergies, the immune system mistakenly responds to food as if it were harmful.

Eight foods or food groups account for 90 percent of serious allergic reactions in the United [2] States milk, eggs, fish, crustacean shellfish, wheat, soy, peanuts, and tree nuts.

1. A) NO CHANGE
   B) germs: however,
   C) germs; however,
   D) germs, however,

Strategy: The current sentence is incorrect because it joins two independent clauses with just a comma. This is a run-on sentence. Choice B is not the best choice because a colon isn't used to join two sentences when the transition *however* is used. Choice D creates a comma splice by joining the two independent clauses with a comma before *however*. Choice C correctly joins the two sentences by placing a semicolon before *however* and a comma afterward.

2. A) NO CHANGE
   B) States: milk, eggs, fish, crustacean shellfish, wheat, soy, peanuts, and tree nuts.
   C) States; milk, eggs, fish, crustacean shellfish, wheat, soy, peanuts, and tree nuts.
   D) States milk: eggs; fish; crustacean shellfish; wheat; soy; peanuts; and tree nuts.

SAT-Type Questions

Directions: Questions 1–7 are based on the following passage.

The History of the Liberty Bell

In 1751, the Province of Pennsylvania sought a bell for its State House to "call the public together." When key members of the Pennsylvania Assembly sent a letter to their London-based colonial agent, Robert Charles, to make an appropriate purchase, Charles found a **1** source; Whitechapel Bell Foundry. Established in 1570 during the reign of Queen Elizabeth I, the foundry is currently the oldest existing British manufacturing company. As it does today, in the 1700s the foundry specialized in **2** casting and forging bells and their associated fittings.

Just ten months after Pennsylvania sent **3** its request, the new Bell arrived in Philadelphia on September 1, 1752. Weighing about a ton, the Bell measured roughly twelve feet around the bottom lip and seven-and-a-half-feet around its crown.

But, the Bell had a difficult start. It was not hung for **4** six months, additionally, when it was placed into position in the State House steeple in March 1753, the Bell cracked on the first test stroke of its clapper.

Some blamed flaws in the **5** Bell's casting others complained the metal was too brittle. Whitechapel's own history describes the American reaction **6** this way; "They did not appreciate that the Bell's metal is brittle and relies on this to a great extent for its freedom of tone."

Two Philadelphia foundry workers, John Pass and John Stow, came forward and made an **7** offer: they would recast the Liberty Bell. The two melted it down and tried to make the new Bell less brittle by adding an ounce-and-a-half of copper to each pound of material from the old Bell.

1. A) NO CHANGE
   B) source, Whitechapel, Bell Foundry
   C) source Whitechapel Bell Foundry
   D) source: Whitechapel Bell Foundry

2. A) NO CHANGE
   B) casting; and forging bells
   C) casting and forging: bells
   D) casting and forging bells;

3. A) NO CHANGE
   B) its request; the new Bell
   C) its request: the new Bell
   D) its request the new Bell

4. A) NO CHANGE
   B) six months, additionally;
   C) six months; and additionally,
   D) six months; additionally,

5. A) NO CHANGE
   B) Bells casting: others
   C) Bell's casting; others
   D) Bell's casting, others

6. A) NO CHANGE
   B) this way: "They
   C) this way, "They
   D) this way: "they

7. A) NO CHANGE
   B) offer; they would
   C) offer, that they would
   D) offer, and that they would

For answers, see page 586.

Explain Using Parentheses, Dashes, and Quotation Marks

Parentheses, dashes, and quotation marks are used to set off text. However, each has a little different purpose.

Think It Through

Parentheses

- Use parentheses to set off important information that must be kept separate from the other information in a sentence. Parentheses are always used in pairs around information that is relevant but does not fit into the flow of the sentence.

  Examples:

  Ms. Turner's ninth-grade class (the one with eighteen boys and one girl) could be described as raucous or lively, depending on one's point of view. (The information about the boy/girl ratio is important but interrupts the sentence's flow if not surrounded by parentheses.)

  Shauna enjoys watching *Friends* reruns (only up to the fifth season). (The parentheses enclose the important, separated information.)

- Usually when a complete sentence is enclosed in parentheses, the closing punctuation mark for the enclosed sentence is placed inside the closing parenthesis. However, when a complete sentence enclosed in parentheses falls in the middle of another sentence, often no end punctuation is used.

  Examples:

  Many people enjoy Doyle's mystery stories. (I'm not one of them.)

  Forty-three years after his death, Robert Frost (we remember him at Kennedy's inauguration) remains America's favorite poet. (Although the text inside the parenthesis is a complete sentence, it is not capitalized and no end punctuation is used.)

- When the parenthetical content is not a complete sentence and it falls at the end of the sentence, place the end punctuation for the sentence outside the final parenthesis.

  Examples:

  By the end of the play, the cast was frustrated by his direction (or, rather, lack of direction).

  It takes years of training to become an expert climber (and years of hard work).

Dashes

- Use dashes to separate parenthetical expressions and appositives in ways similar to commas. However, dashes indicate a greater separation and provide more emphasis than commas do.

  Example:

  The vocabulary test centered on words and phrases that students use throughout their lives—in high school, college or workforce training, and beyond.

- Use dashes to set off an abrupt change in thought.

> **Examples:**
> The clerk started to explain, "Our special today is caramel—" when the cappuccino machine exploded.
>
> I can't seem to find my—oh, there it is.

Quotation Marks

- Use quotation marks with direct quotations that restate the speaker's exact words. Do not use quotation marks with paraphrases.

> **Direct Quotation:** Dad said, "You can go to camp this summer." (Quotation marks are needed.)
>
> **Indirect Quotation:** Dad said that I can go to camp this summer. (No quotation marks are needed.)

- Use quotation marks in pairs. If you have opening quotation marks, you must have closing quotation marks. Commas and end punctuation go inside the quotation marks.

> **Examples:**
> Ellen said, "I'm taking the school bus home."
> "I'm taking the school bus home," Ellen said.
>
> "When do you leave?" asked Carlos.
> Carlos asked, "When do you leave?"
>
> "I hope," said Fran, "that you remember to take your science book home."
>
> "When do we eat?" Billy asked. "I'm hungry."

- If the entire sentence is a question, place the question mark outside the quotation marks.

> **Outside:** Did Billy say, "I'm hungry"?
>
> **Inside:** "I had never seen a snow leopard before," Maureen said. "Had you?"

QUICK TIP

If one of the answer choices on the SAT contains a single set of quotations marks or a parenthesis, return to the text and see if a single set of quotation marks or a parenthesis is found earlier in the sentence. Because these punctuation marks always come in pairs, the answer with the quotation marks or parenthesis is likely the correct one.

Practice

Directions: Add needed punctuation in these sentences.

1. Mark exclaimed excitedly, Geraldine won the spelling bee by correctly spelling *syzygy*!

2. Page the best doctor in the hospital Dr. Richards.

3. Seneca, a Roman philosopher, wrote All cruelty springs from weakness.

4. The waitress began, "What can I" when the phone rang.

5. The data shows a marked increase over the past five years see Figure 2.

6. Please leave the package in the back room (the door will be unlocked.)

For answers, see page 586.

Directions: These Model SAT Questions are examples of how your ability to edit text for dashes, parentheses, and quotation marks might be tested on the SAT. The answers and explanations immediately follow the questions. Try the questions and then review the answers and the explanations.

Blockbuster Science Images

When it came out, the blockbuster movie *Interstellar* created such a stir that one would have had to be inside a black hole not to know about it. And while the science fiction thriller may have taken some liberties with science to make its Hollywood plot work, the imagery comes straight from **1** science science funded by the National Science Foundation NSF, in fact.

Similar in premise to many other science fiction films, something sets *Interstellar* apart: many of the images **2** are—for the most part— scientifically accurate, based on lensing calculations produced by Cornell University and California Institute of Technology scientists that show what black holes or wormholes look like.

3 Gravity bends the path that light follows in space said Pedro Marronetti, an NSF program director for gravitational physics. "The stronger the gravitation, the more dramatic its effect."

1. A) NO CHANGE
   B) science, and science funded by the National Science Foundation "NSF," in fact.
   C) science—science funded by the National Science Foundation (NSF), in fact.
   D) science—science funded by the National Science Foundation—NSF—in fact.

Strategy: This question asks you to edit the sentence for dashes and parentheses. Based upon the context, the final phrase is meant to emphasize that the science from a popular movie was based upon research from a nationally recognized source. To make this fact stand out, a dash is needed. Choice A is incorrect. Choice B uses a comma and a conjunction, which is less effective at emphasizing the ending phrase. Plus it incorrectly uses quotation marks around *NSF*. Choice D uses a dash after *science* correctly, but also uses dashes around *NSF* instead of the parentheses. The correct answer is C.

2. A) NO CHANGE
   B) are for the most part—scientifically
   C) are: for the most part—scientifically
   D) are—for the most part scientifically

Strategy: This question asks you to edit the sentence for dashes. Choice B is incorrect because the interrupter *for the most part* requires dashes around it, and this answer only has one dash after *part*. Choice C improperly uses a colon to introduce an interrupter. Choice D only has one dash before *for*; two dashes are needed. Choice A is the correct answer.

3. A) NO CHANGE
   B) Gravity bends the path that light follows in space, said
   C) "Gravity bends the path that light follows in space" said
   D) "Gravity bends the path that light follows in space," said

Strategy: This question asks you to edit the sentence for quotation marks. Choice A is incorrect because quotation marks are needed around Marronetti's exact words. Choice B also lacks quotation marks. Between choices C and D, only choice D uses both quotation marks and also a comma to set the quotation apart from the tag.

• • • SAT-Type Questions •

Directions: Questions 1–6 are based on the following passage.

In 2014, NASA took significant steps on the agency's journey to <u>**1** Mars testing cutting-edge technologies</u> and making scientific discoveries while studying our changing Earth and the infinite universe as the agency made progress on the next generation of air travel.

"We continued to make great progress on our journey to Mars this year," said NASA Administrator Charles Bolden, "We awarded contracts to American companies that will return human space flight launches to U.S. soil; we advanced space technology development and successfully completed the first flight of Orion, the next deep space spacecraft in which our astronauts will travel." Bolden continued <u>**2** by saying that "NASA also moved forward on the work to create quieter, greener airplanes and to develop technologies to make air travel more efficient."</u>

NASA continues to advance the journey to Mars through progress on the Asteroid Redirect Mission (ARM), which will test a number of new capabilities needed for future human expeditions to deep space, including to Mars. This includes advanced Solar Electric 3 Propulsion, an efficient way to move heavy cargo using solar power that could help pre-position cargo for future human missions to the <u>**3** Red Planet, (something once thought impossible).</u> As part of ARM, a robotic spacecraft will rendezvous with a near-Earth asteroid and redirect an asteroid mass to a stable orbit around the moon. Astronauts will explore the asteroid mass in the 2020's, helping test modern spaceflight capabilities like new spacesuits and sample return techniques. Astronauts at NASA's Johnson Space Center in Houston have already begun to practice the capabilities needed for the mission.

1. A) NO CHANGE
   B) Mars—testing cutting-edge technologies
   C) Mars; testing cutting-edge technologies
   D) Mars (testing cutting-edge technologies)

2. A) NO CHANGE
   B) "by saying that NASA . . . efficient."
   C) by saying that: "NASA . . . efficient."
   D) by saying that NASA . . . efficient.

3. A) NO CHANGE
   B) Red Planet (something once thought impossible.).
   C) Red Planet. (something once thought impossible).
   D) Red Planet (something once thought impossible).

For answers, see page 587.

Explain Using Possessives

Possessives are used to indicate ownership. Most often a punctuation mark called an apostrophe is used to make a noun possessive.

Think About It

Possessive Nouns

- To form the possessive of a singular noun, just add 's. Don't change the word by adding any letter or omitting a letter.

Carrie + 's	Carrie's
friend + 's	friend's
sister-in-law + 's	sister-in-law's

- To form the plural possessive of any noun, follow these steps:

FIRST: write the plural form of the word.

Plural ends in s:	*Plural does not end in s:*
artist—artists	child—children
astronaut—astronauts	man—men
rocket—rockets	sheep—sheep
trainer—trainers	woman—women

SECOND: If the plural form ends in *s*, add an apostrophe ('). OR
If the plural form does not end in *s*, add an apostrophe and an *s* ('s).

Plural ends in s:	*Plural does not end in s:*
add an apostrophe.	*add an apostrophe and an s.*
artists' easels	children's games
astronauts' training	men's jackets
rockets' red glare	sheep's clothing
trainers' advice	women's movement

Pronoun Possessives

Remember that possessive personal pronouns do not use apostrophes.

> **Examples:**
>
> Why don't you try *his* and then *mine* to decide which curry tastes better?
>
> This desk is *ours*, and that shelf is *theirs*.
>
> The computer's new software has really improved *its* speed.

See page 326 for distinguishing between *its* and *it's* and other commonly confused words.

Unnecessary Punctuation

Some questions on the SAT will test your ability to correct overuse of punctuation. Commas are commonly overused. You should be able to support the use of every punctuation mark with a rule or a reason.

> **Example:**
>
> The story was about a woman with Alzheimer's, and her husband. (No comma needed with two items in a list.)
>
> Corrected: The story was about a woman with Alzheimer's and her husband.

Practice

Directions: Choose the correct possessive form.

1. The (books', book's) cover was torn.

2. Bill drove his (sisters, sister's) car.

3. The ranger found that many of the (goose's, geese's) wings were broken.

4. I found (someone's, someones) backpack in the locker room.

5. The two (daughter's, daughters') store is on Main Street.

6. Both of my brothers belong to the (school's, schools') bowling team.

7. It is in (everyone's, everyones) best interest to cooperate.

8. Michael said we could go to (his, his') place.

9. That swimming pool of (hers, her's) is amazing!

10. The (women's, womens') team leaves in ten minutes, so pack the equipment that is (theirs, theirs') quickly.

For answers, see page 587.

Directions: These Model SAT Questions show how your ability to edit text for noun possessives and pronoun possessives might be tested on the SAT. The answers and explanations immediately follow the questions. Try the questions and then review the answers and the explanations.

Poverty Point: Preservation of a Prehistoric World Heritage Site

The Poverty Point State Historic Site, located in northeastern Louisiana, was recently named by the ▮1 United Nations Educational Scientific and Cultural Organization (UNESCO) to it's World Heritage List. This is a list of the ▮2 worlds cultural and natural treasures, properties that are of outstanding value to humanity. Poverty Point is only the 22nd World Heritage site in the United States.

1. A) NO CHANGE
   B) United Nations Educational Scientific and Cultural Organization—UNESCO—to it's
   C) United Nations Educational, Scientific, and Cultural Organization (UNESCO) to its'
   D) United Nations Educational, Scientific, and Cultural Organization (UNESCO) to its

Strategy: This question tests your ability to use commas, parentheses, and possessives correctly. Choice A is not the best answer because it uses the contraction *it is* when the context requires a possessive form, *its*. It also lacks commas to separate the adjectives in the name of the United Nations group. Choice B also uses *it's* and incorrectly adds dashes around UNESCO. Choice C adds the commas to the list of adjectives, but uses *its'*, which isn't a word. Only choice D correctly uses commas, parentheses, and *its* as a possessive.

2. A) NO CHANGE
   B) worlds' cultural and natural treasures,
   C) world's cultural and natural treasures:
   D) world's cultural and natural treasures,

Strategy: Choice A is incorrect because in the context of the sentence, *worlds*, should indicate possession. The treasures belong to the *world* (singular). Choice B incorrectly uses the plural possessive *worlds'*. Choices C and D fix the possessive (*world's*), but choice C incorrectly changes the comma needed before the appositive (*properties that are of outstanding value to humanity*) to a colon. Choice D is correct.

Directions: Questions 1–4 are based on the following passage.

Hillary Rodham Clinton

Secretary Clinton was born in Chicago, Illinois, on October 26, 1947, to Dorothy and Hugh Rodham.

She attended local public schools before graduating from Wellesley College and Yale Law School, where she met **1** her future husband, Bill Clinton. In 1974, Secretary Clinton moved to Arkansas; a year later she married Bill Clinton and became a successful attorney **2** while also raising their daughter's, Chelsea. She was an assistant professor at the University of Arkansas School of Law, and after working to strengthen the local legal aid office, she was appointed by President Jimmy Carter in 1977 to serve on the board of the Legal Services Corporation, which she later chaired.

During her 12 years as first lady of the state of Arkansas, she was chairwoman of the Arkansas Education Standards Committee, co-founded the Arkansas Advocates for Children and Families, and served on the boards of the **3** Arkansas Childrens' Hospital, and the Children's Defense Fund.

In 1992, Governor Clinton was elected President of the United States, and as first lady, Hillary Clinton became an advocate of health care reform and worked on many issues relating to children and families. She led successful bipartisan efforts to improve the adoption and foster care systems, reduce teen pregnancy, and provide health care to millions of children. She also traveled to more than 80 countries as a representative of our country, winning respect as a champion of human rights, democracy, and civil society. Her famous speech in Beijing in 1995—when she declared that **4** womens' rights are human's rights—inspired women worldwide.

1. A) NO CHANGE
   B) her' future husband,
   C) hers future husband
   D) her future husband

2. A) NO CHANGE
   B) while also raising their daughter, Chelsea.
   C) while, also, raising their daughter, Chelsea.
   D) while also raising his and her daughter's, Chelsea.

3. A) NO CHANGE
   B) Arkansas' Children Hospital,
   C) Arkansas Children's Hospital
   D) Arkansas Childrens's Hospital,

4. A) NO CHANGE
   B) women's rights are human's rights
   C) woman rights are human rights
   D) women's rights are human rights

For answers, see page 587.

Writing and Language Domain SAT-Type Practice Test

Directions: The following section provides practice over all the skills from Lessons 8–13 tested on the Writing and Language section of the SAT. Read through each passage and answer the questions. A reproducible bubble sheet can be found on page 380. To practice under the same time limit as the SAT, allow yourself 35 minutes to take the test. Answers and explanations immediately follow the test on pages 374–377.

Questions 1–4 are based on the following passage.

The Spanish-American War and Spain's Downfall

Prior to the Spanish-American War, Spain had been a dominant world power with colonies reaching from North America to the Pacific. Unable to sustain such a large and scattered empire, its power waned. The final blow was the coming of the Spanish-American War, fought from April to December of 1898. As a result, Spain lost control over its overseas ▆1▆ empire; Cuba, Puerto Rico, the Philippine Islands, Guam, and other islands.

Beginning in 1492, Spain was the first European nation to sail westward across the Atlantic ▆2▆ Ocean; explore, and colonize the Amerindian nations of the Western Hemisphere. At its greatest extent, the ▆3▆ empire, that resulted from this exploration, extended from Virginia on the eastern coast of the United States south to Tierra del Fuego at the tip of South America and westward to California and Alaska. ▆4▆ By 1825, much of this empire had fallen into other hands. As a result, Spain acknowledged the independence of its possessions in the present-day United States (then under Mexican control) and south to the tip of South America. The only remnants that remained in the empire were Cuba and Puerto Rico in the Western Hemisphere, the Philippine Islands across the Pacific, and the Carolina, Marshall, and Mariana Islands (including Guam) in Micronesia.

1
A) NO CHANGE
B) empire, Cuba,
C) empire: Cuba,
D) empire—Cuba,

2
A) NO CHANGE
B) Ocean, exploring and colonizing
C) Ocean, explore the land, and colonize
D) Ocean, as a result exploring and colonizing

3
A) NO CHANGE
B) empire, who resulted from this exploration,
C) empire that resulted from this exploration
D) empire, a result of this exploration,

4
At this point, the writer is considering adding the following sentence.

> Across the Pacific, Spain's colonies included the Philippines and other island groups.

Should the writer add this sentence here?

A) Yes, because it gives further details about how Spain was able to colonize large amounts of land.
B) Yes, because it gives further details about the enormity of Spain's colonization.
C) No, because it distracts from the main idea of the paragraph.
D) No, because it weakens the focus on Spain's expansion to the east.

Following the liberation from Spain of mainland Latin America, Cuba was the first to initiate **5** its own struggle for independence. During the years from 1868 to 1878, **6** Cubans, personified by guerrilla fighters known as *mambises*, fought for autonomy from Spain. That war concluded with a treaty that was never enforced. In the 1890s Cubans began to agitate once again for their freedom from Spain. The moral leader of this struggle was José **7** Martí known as "El Apóstol," who established the Cuban Revolutionary Party in the United States on January 5, 1892. Following the *grito de Baire*, or the call to arms, Martí returned to Cuba and participated in the first weeks of armed struggle until he was killed on May 19, 1895.

5

A) NO CHANGE
B) it's own struggle
C) their own struggle
D) there own struggle

6

A) NO CHANGE
B) Cubans personified by guerrilla fighters known as *mambises* fought
C) Cubans, personified by guerrilla fighters known as *mambises*, fighting
D) Cubans, being personified by guerrilla fighters, known as *mambises*, fought

7

A) NO CHANGE
B) Martí (known as "El Apóstol") who
C) Martí, known as "El Apóstol," who
D) Martí, known as "El Apóstol," whom

Questions 8–16 are based on the following passage and table.

Diabetes is a disease that [8] affects the body's ability to produce or use insulin. Insulin is a hormone. When the body turns the food into energy (also called sugar or glucose), insulin is released to help transport this energy to the cells. Insulin acts like a key with a chemical message that tells the cell to open and receive glucose. If the body produces little or no insulin or is insulin resistant, too much sugar remains in the blood. Blood glucose levels are higher than normal for individuals with diabetes. There are two main types of diabetes: type 1 and type 2. With type 1 diabetes, the body does not make insulin. With type 2 diabetes, the more common type, the body does not make or use insulin well. Without enough insulin, the glucose stays in the blood. [9]

Diabetes can be treated and [10] managing by healthful eating, regular physical activity, and medications to lower blood glucose levels. Another critical part of diabetes management is reducing cardiovascular disease risk factors, such as high blood pressure, high lipid levels, and tobacco use. [11] Older patients with type 2 diabetes and children with type 1 diabetes are at particularly high risk for adverse outcomes associated with hypoglycemia. Patient education and self-care practices also are important aspects of disease management that help people with diabetes stay healthy.

8

A) NO CHANGE
B) effects the body's ability
C) affects the bodies' abilities
D) effects the bodies' ability

9

Which choice most effectively concludes the paragraph by continuing the idea that glucose stays in the blood?

A) Over time, high blood sugar levels (also called hyperglycemia) can lead to kidney disease, heart disease, and blindness.
B) Genetics, diet, obesity, and lack of exercise may play a role in developing diabetes.
C) Gestational diabetes occurs during pregnancy and affects about 18 percent of all pregnancies.
D) Symptoms of diabetes include extreme thirst and hunger, increased tiredness, and frequent urination.

10

A) NO CHANGE
B) could be managed
C) managed
D) it should be managed

11

The writer is considering deleting the underlined sentence. Should the sentence be kept or deleted?

A) Kept, because it provides supporting evidence about the risk factors related to diabetes and hypoglycemia.
B) Kept, because it provides an additional example about how diabetes affects people's health.
C) Deleted, because it blurs the paragraph's focus on diabetes management.
D) Deleted, because it doesn't provide specific examples about how hypoglycemia affects people with diabetes.

Many people with type 1 diabetes must have insulin delivered by injection or a pump. Almost 3 million adults use only insulin to manage diabetes, and **12** fewer than 3 million adults take insulin and oral medication. Many people with type 2 diabetes can control their blood glucose by following a healthy meal plan and a program of regular physical activity, losing excess weight, and **13** by taking medications. Medications for each individual with diabetes will often change during the course of the disease. Insulin also is commonly used to control blood glucose in people with type 2 diabetes.

Treatment of diabetes among people aged 18 years or older with diagnosed diabetes, United States, 2010–2012

	Number of adults using diabetes medication* (millions)	Percentage using diabetes medication (unadjusted)
Insulin only	2.9	14.0
Both insulin and oral medication	3.1	14.7
Oral medication only	11.9	56.9
Neither insulin nor oral medication	3.0	14.4

Source: 2010–2012 National Health Interview Survey

12

Which choice completes the sentence with accurate data based on the table?

A) NO CHANGE

B) 56.9 million adults take only oral medication.

C) a little more than 3 million adults use both insulin and oral medication.

D) almost 12 million adults take insulin and oral medication.

13

A) NO CHANGE

B) taking medication

C) by medicating

D) medications

[1] Diabetes can affect many parts of the body and is associated with serious complications, such as heart disease and stroke, blindness, kidney failure, and lower-limb amputation. [2] Some complications, especially microvascular (eye, kidney, and nerve) disease, can be reduced with good glucose control. [3] Also, early detection and treatment of complications can prevent **14** development, so monitoring with dilated eye exams, urine tests, and foot exams is essential. [4] Because the risk of cardiovascular disease is increased in patients with diabetes and prediabetes, blood pressure and lipid management, along with smoking cessation, are **15** especially crucial and important. [5] By working together, people with diagnosed diabetes, their support network, and their health care providers can reduce the occurrence of these and other complications. **16**

14

A) NO CHANGE
B) improvement
C) expansion
D) progression

15

A) NO CHANGE
B) especially important.
C) especially important and vital.
D) especially, particularly important.

16

To make this paragraph most logical, sentence 2 should be placed

A) where it is now.
B) before sentence 1.
C) after sentence 3.
D) after sentence 4.

Questions 17–26 are based on the following passage.

Walt Whitman

Nineteenth-century poet, essayist, and journalist Walt Whitman stands as one of the most influential poets in American literature, and one of the first to [17] nab international recognition. His contribution to American poetry is comparable to [18] Emily Dickinson's poetry. Whitman spent most of his early years in [19] Brooklyn. He worked as a printer and newspaper journalist through the 1850s.

The first edition of Whitman's landmark collection of poetry, *Leaves of Grass*, was privately printed in 1855 and consisted of twelve untitled poems, one of which was to later become famous as "Song of Myself." [20] His literary style was experimental, a free-verse avalanche in celebration of nature and self that has since been described as the first expression of a distinctly American voice. Although *Leaves of Grass* did not sell well at first, [21] they become popular in literary circles in Europe and, later, the United States, and Whitman published a total of eight editions during his lifetime.

[17]
A) NO CHANGE
B) accrue
C) gain
D) find

[18]
A) NO CHANGE
B) Emily Dickinson.
C) Emily Dickinson and her writing.
D) Emily Dickinson's legacy.

[19]
Which choice most effectively combines the sentences at the underlined portion?
A) Brooklyn, and Whitman also worked
B) Brooklyn; after living in Brooklyn, he worked
C) Brooklyn, but he worked
D) Brooklyn where he worked

[20]
A) NO CHANGE
B) His literary style was experimental;
C) Their literary style was experimental,
D) Its literary style was experimental,

[21]
A) NO CHANGE
B) they became
C) it became
D) it becomes

22 When he was wounded in the Civil War, Whitman moved to Washington, D.C., to be near him. There he found work in the army paymaster's office, but he also spent many hours visiting wounded soldiers as a volunteer nurse. According to his own estimates, Whitman made 600 hospital visits, seeing more than 100,000 patients. Although the work was physically demanding, it ultimately inspired him to return to writing poetry. He published two poetry collections based upon his wartime experiences. *Drum Taps* contained **23** Whitmans famous elegy for Abraham Lincoln, "Where Lilacs Last in the Dooryard Bloom'd" and "O Captain! My Captain!" In 1873 **24** he was paralyzed after a stroke and moved to Camden, New Jersey. He continued **25** to add to his lifes work, *Leaves of Grass*; later editions of the work included more than 400 poems and **26** enjoyed robust sales. By the time of his death in 1882, he was an international literary celebrity.

22

Which of the following most effectively introduces the information in this sentence?
A) NO CHANGE
B) When his brother was wounded in the Civil War,
C) Wounded in the Civil War, as his brother was,
D) Having his brother wounded in the Civil War,

23

A) NO CHANGE
B) Whitmans' famous elegies
C) Whitman's famous elegies
D) Whitman's famous elegy

24

A) NO CHANGE
B) he, paralyzed after a stroke, moved
C) a stroke had paralyzed him, and he
D) a stroke left him paralyzed, and he

25

A) NO CHANGE
B) to add to his lifes' work,
C) to add to his life's work,
D) increasing his lifes work,

26

Which choice gives an important detail that supports the claim made about Whitman's literary success?
A) NO CHANGE
B) featured a picture of a bearded Whitman.
C) included the *Drum Taps* poems.
D) was published just before his death.

Questions 27–34 are based on the following passage.

[1] How is this even conceivable? [2] Though a manned flight to Mars is a long way off, engineers are seriously considering the possibility of manned ventures beyond the solar system. [3] Robert **27** Frisbie a scientist at NASA's Jet Propulsion Lab, insists that with current technology and the emergence of new propellants, a spaceship might reach Alpha Centauri, the closest star system to our sun, in a voyage of 12 ½ years. [4] With interstellar distances expressed in light years and space travel in the realm of science fiction, are these engineers **28** off their rockers? **29**

27

A) NO CHANGE
B) Frisbie, a scientist, at NASAs' Jet
C) Frisbie, a scientist at NASAs Jet
D) Frisbie, a scientist at NASA's Jet

28

A) NO CHANGE
B) messed up
C) crazy
D) serious

29

For the sake of the cohesion of this paragraph, sentence 1 should be placed

A) where it is now.
B) after sentence 2.
C) after sentence 3.
D) after sentence 4.

In 1990, scientists declared that the sum total of human knowledge doubled every 7 to 8 [30] years, in the meantime, a little more than ten years later, [31] it was theorized that knowledge had doubled in a span of just two [32] years—2000–2002). This conclusion encourages the assumption that the expected increase in knowledge will solve the problems involved in space travel that are just beyond the range of current technology. Various plans have been proposed to approach closer to the speed of light: nuclear fission, nuclear fusion, laser sails, and even exploitation of antimatter. In the matter of essentials, most engineers believe that solutions to the problems of food, water, air, and [33] gravity are within it's grasp, but what of psychology and the unpredictable elements of human nature? [34] With the "right stuff," can individuals be found to survive so many years of cabin fever, isolation, close quarters, and personality clashes?

Landing a man on the moon seemed utterly beyond belief in 1950. Is interstellar space travel equally "preposterous"? Only time will tell.

30
A) NO CHANGE
B) years, yet
C) years, so
D) years, because

31
A) NO CHANGE
B) they theorized
C) it had been theorized
D) theorizing

32
A) NO CHANGE
B) years: 2000–2002.
C) years; 2000–2002.
D) years from 2000–2002.

33
A) NO CHANGE
B) gravity is within its grasp
C) gravity are within our grasp
D) gravity is within our grasp

34
A) NO CHANGE
B) Can individuals be found to survive so many years with the "right stuff"
C) Can individuals with the "right stuff" be found to survive so many years
D) Can with the "right stuff" individuals be found to survive so many years

Questions 35–44 are based on the following passage.

Savings Fitness: A Guide to Your Money and Your

Financial Future

Most of us know it is smart to save money for those big-ticket items we really want to buy—a new television or car or home. Yet you may not **35** discern that probably the most expensive thing you will ever buy in your lifetime is your retirement.

Perhaps you've never thought of **36** "buying" your retirement. Yet that is exactly what you do when you put money into a retirement nest egg. You are paying today for the cost of your retirement tomorrow.

The cost of those future years **37** are getting more expensive for most Americans, for two reasons. First, we live longer after we retire—many of us spend 15, 25, even 30 years in retirement—and we are more active. Many retired adults enjoy a variety of activities, which cost money. **38** Also, retirement homes have plenty to offer—from arts and crafts to volunteer activities in local schools and charities.

39 Second, you may have to shoulder a greater chunk of the cost of your retirement because fewer companies are providing traditional retirement plans. Many retirement plans today, such as the popular 401(k), are paid for primarily by the employee, not the employer. You may not have a retirement plan available at work or you may be self-employed. This puts the responsibility of choosing retirement investments squarely on your shoulders.

35
Which of the following best fits with the tone of the passage?
A) NO CHANGE
B) apprehend
C) realize
D) get a clue

36
Which of the following creates the best transition from paragraph 1 to paragraph 2?
A) NO CHANGE
B) saving for your retirement while you are young.
C) retiring at a young age.
D) saving money for your retirement.

37
A) NO CHANGE
B) was getting
C) gets
D) is getting

38
The writer is considering deleting this sentence from the paragraph. Should he do this?
A) Yes, because it veers away from the main idea of the paragraph.
B) Yes, because it is an opinion and not a fact.
C) No, because it adds evidence that supports the claim that retirement is expensive.
D) No, because it is a detail about retirement opportunities.

39
A) NO CHANGE
B) Next,
C) Nevertheless,
D) In effect,

[1] Unfortunately, just about 54 percent of all workers are earning retirement benefits at work, and many are not familiar with the basics of investing. [2] Many people are under the ◼40 illusion, that Social Security will pay for all or most of their retirement needs. [3] A comfortable retirement usually requires Social Security, employer-based retirement plan benefits, personal savings, and investments. [4] The fact is, since its inception, Social Security has provided a minimum foundation of protection. ◼41

◼42 Whereas paying for the retirement you truly desire is ultimately your responsibility. ◼43 You must take charge. You are the architect of your financial future. Saving for retirement may sound like an impossible task. You may live paycheck to paycheck, barely making ends meet; you may have more pressing financial needs and goals than "buying" something so far in the future. If you must wait until close to retirement to ◼44 save, one can still afford to buy a stable retirement. Whether you are 18 or 58, you can take steps toward a better, more secure future.

40

A) NO CHANGE
B) illusion that Social
C) allusion which Social
D) allusion that Social

41

To make the passage most logical, sentence 4 should be placed
A) where it is now.
B) before sentence 1.
C) after sentence 1.
D) after sentence 2.

42

A) NO CHANGE
B) For example,
C) On the other hand,
D) In short,

43

Which choice most effectively combines the underlined sentences?
A) You must take charge, and you are the architect of your financial future.
B) Because you must take charge, you are the architect of your financial future.
C) Taking charge, you will become the architect of your financial future.
D) As the architect of your financial future, you must take charge.

44

A) NO CHANGE
B) save one can still
C) save—one can still
D) save, you can still

Answers and Explanations

Writing and Language Practice Test

Item	Answer	Explanation
1	C	A colon is used to introduce a list at the end of a sentence.
2	C	All three ideas are equally important and should be included as three parallel phrases: "sail westward across the Atlantic Ocean, explore the land, and colonize the Amerindian nations."
3	C	"That resulted from this exploration" is an essential (restrictive) clause so no commas are needed. Choice B: This choice incorrectly uses the pronoun "who," which is used for people. Choice D: This choice changes the clause to an appositive phrase, which de-emphasizes the importance of the information.
4	B	The sentence explains how far west Spain's colonization expanded. Choice A is incorrect because it doesn't explain how Spain was able to colonize these countries.
5	A	The pronoun "it" is used to refer to the country of Cuba. A plural possessive is needed in the sentence, so "its" is correct. Choice B incorrectly uses "it's," which is a contraction for "it is."
6	A	The nonrestrictive appositive phrase "personified by guerrilla fighters known as *mambises*" should be set off by commas. Choice B is incorrect. Choice C incorrectly uses the verb "fighting." Choice D adds an unnecessary comma after "fighters."
7	B	The phrase "known as 'El Apóstol,' " should be set off from the sentence. Parentheses cause the reader to insert a larger pause and make the sentence more readable. The subjective form "who" is needed to begin the clause "who established the Cuban."
8	A	"Affects" means "to impact or influence." "Effects" means "to cause to come into being." "Affect" is the correct word for this context. "Body" should be singular not plural. "Ability" should be singular because it refers to the ability to produce or to use insulin, not both.
9	A	Choice A is the best answer because it explains the results of what happens when glucose stays in the blood.
10	C	This choice parallels the verb tense used in the phrase "can be treated."
11	C	The sentence moves the focus from diabetes management to types of patients with risks for hypoglycemia so it should be deleted.

Item	Answer	Explanation
12	C	The chart indicates that 3.1 million adults use both insulin and oral medication to control their diabetes, so choice A is wrong. Choice B incorrectly reports the percentage using oral medication as a number instead of a percentage. Choice D incorrectly reports the number of adults who take only oral medication as the number of those who take insulin and oral medication.
13	B	Choice B correctly continues the parallel structure of the sentence: "by following a healthy meal plan . . . losing weight, and taking medication."
14	D	From the context, the writer is communicating steps that can prevent diabetes from getting worse. Choice A, "development," does not fit the topic of disease. Choice B is incorrect. Choice C, "expansion," is associated with construction and seems inappropriate when discussing disease. Choice D fits the context and the topic.
15	B	The other answer choices contain redundant or wordy language.
16	C	The sentence builds upon the topic sentence by explaining how some serious complications can be controlled.
17	C	"Nab" has a too informal tone for the passage. Choice A is incorrect. Choice B is associated with money. Choice D implies that Whitman was seeking recognition, which doesn't quite fit the context. Choice C is the best choice.
18	D	Similar things must be compared. Whitman's contribution is best compared to Emily Dickinson's legacy.
19	D	Choice D logically combines the details in the second sentence by using a subordinate clause for these minor details. Choice A is too wordy. Choice B implies that he didn't work in Brooklyn. Choice C incorrectly uses "but" to communicate a contrast, which doesn't make sense.
20	A	The pronoun "His" correctly refers to Whitman. Choices C and D incorrectly use pronouns. Choice B incorrectly uses a semicolon to set off an extended appositive.
21	C	The pronoun "it" refers to the book *Leaves of Grass*. The past tense verb "became" is needed to agree with the verb tense in the rest of the passage.
22	B	In the current sentence, it is unclear to whom "he" is referring. Choices C and D fix the unclear pronoun, but are awkwardly worded. Choice B is the best choice.
23	C	Choice C makes "Whitmans" possessive by adding an apostrophe: "Whitman's." Two elegies are mentioned in the passage so "elegies" is correct.

Item	Answer	Explanation
24	D	In choice A, the passive voice verb makes for an awkward sentence. Choice B edits the passive voice verb, but adds an awkward appositive phrase. Choice C uses an incorrect verb tense: "had paralyzed."
25	D	The phrase "life's work" is possessive. The verb "add to" better fits the context than "increasing."
26	A	The correct sentence includes the detail that sales were "robust." This is evidence that Whitman was a literary success.
27	D	A comma is needed after "Frisbie" to indicate the beginning of the appositive phrase. An apostrophe is needed to indicate that the Jet Propulsion Lab belongs to NASA: "NASA's."
28	D	The tone of the other answers is too informal for the passage.
29	B	The question is referring to the possibility of manned ventures beyond our solar system mentioned in sentence 2. It should be placed immediately after sentence 2.
30	B	As it is, the sentence is a comma splice because two separate sentences are joined with just a comma. Also, "in the meantime" doesn't express the relationship between the two ideas in the sentences. Choices B, C, and D fix the comma splice problem, but which provides the correct transition between ideas? "Yet" expresses the contrast between what scientists believed in 1990 and ten years later.
31	B	"They" is a much clearer subject than the vague "it." To match the tense of the verb earlier in the sentence, "scientists declared," the best choice is B, "they theorized."
32	B	The colon is the most effective way to set off the range of years used at the end of the sentence.
33	D	"Our" is the best pronoun for the context. "It's" is a contraction for "it is." The verb "are" is needed to agree with the plural noun "problems."
34	C	The adjective phrase "with the 'right stuff'" must be placed immediately after "individuals."

Item	Answer	Explanation
35	C	The current choice, "discern," is too formal for the passage. Choice B, "apprehend," also seems too academic for the practical guide to saving for retirement. However, choice D, "get a clue," is too informal.
36	A	The repetition of the word "buy" from the last sentence in the previous paragraph helps the reader connect the ideas and highlights an important idea the writer wants the reader to consider.
37	D	The verb "is getting" agrees with the subject "cost" and not the interrupting phrase "of those future years." Choice A ("are getting") is incorrect. Choice D also uses the correct verb tense "is getting," which indicates the action is continuing in the present time.
38	A	This sentence is about retirement homes and not about how much more money retired adults need to support their lifestyle.
39	A	"Second" is appropriate because the previous paragraph indicates there are "two reasons" why retirement is getting more expensive.
40	B	An "illusion" is a false idea; an "allusion" is a reference to art or music. Choices C and D are incorrect. The phrase "that Social Security will pay . . ." is essential to the meaning of the sentence so no comma is needed. Choice B is correct.
41	D	Sentence 4 clarifies the "illusion" that Social Security will cover all retirement costs and transitions into sentence 3 that explains other types of financial resources needed in retirement.
42	D	"In short" indicates that the last paragraph will summarize the main point of the article, which is that you must be responsible for saving for retirement.
43	D	Choice D best communicates the relationship between being the "architect of your financial future" and taking charge. Because you are the architect, your must take charge.
44	D	The current sentence shifts from second person ("you") to third person ("one"). Choice D avoids this awkward shift by continuing in second person.

Writing and Language Practice Test Correlation Chart

If you missed these questions . . .	study this lesson. (Because some questions test over multiple skills, some numbers may appear under more than one lesson.)
	Writing and Language Domain
4, 9, 11, 26, 38	Lesson 8: Revising texts for clarity, focus, and purpose (p. 243)
12	Lesson 8: Relating information presented in graphs, charts, and tables to information presented in texts (p. 252)
16, 29, 41, 42	Lesson 9: Revising for cohesion and logical order (p. 261)
22, 30, 36, 39	Lesson 9: Revising beginnings or endings of a text or paragraphs to ensure transitional words, phrases, and sentences are used effectively (p. 267)
14, 17	Lesson 10: Revising texts to improve word choice for exactness and content (p. 275)
15	Lesson 10: Revising to eliminate wordiness (p. 279)
17, 28, 35	Lesson 10: Revising text for consistency of style and tone or to match style and tone to purpose (p. 288)
	Lesson 11: Editing to correct sentence fragments and run-ons (p. 295)
19, 43	Lesson 11: Combining sentences for clarity (p. 304)
2, 13, 34	Lesson 11: Editing to correct problems with subordination/coordination, parallel structure, and modifier placement (p. 306)
10, 24, 31, 37, 44	Lesson 11: Editing to correct shifts in verbs (tense, voice, and mood) and pronouns (person and number) (p. 313)
7, 20	Lesson 12: Using pronouns correctly (p. 323)
	Lesson 12: Correcting unclear or ambiguous pronouns or antecedents (p. 325)
8, 21, 23, 33	Lesson 12: Correcting problems with pronoun/antecedent, subject/verb, and noun agreement (p. 329)
5, 8, 40	Lesson 12: Correcting misuse of confusing words (p. 337)
18	Lesson 12: Correcting cases in which unalike terms are compared (p. 337)
	Lesson 12: Correcting nonstandard written English (p. 338)
1, 3, 6, 40	Lesson 13: Using end punctuation and commas (p. 343)
32	Lesson 13: Using semicolons and colons (p. 349)
17	Lesson 13: Using parentheses, dashes, and quotation marks (p. 354)
5, 8, 23, 25, 27	Lesson 13: Using possessives and correcting use of unnecessary punctuation (pp. 358–359)

SAT Reading and Writing and Language Model Exams

Now that you have completed the lessons and other practice material in this book, you are ready to try the full-length SAT Model Exams. We suggest that you review the information in the Introduction, pages 6–10, before you take any of these exams. These pages provide essential reminders to prepare you for taking the following SAT Reading and Writing and Language Model Exams.

The three SAT Model Exams match the SAT in format, types of questions, types of reading passages, and timing. When you take these tests, you should do so under conditions as similar as possible to the actual test conditions.

Complete the Reading section of the exam in one sitting. Take a 3- to 5-minute break and then take the Writing and Language section.

- Time yourself according to the guidelines found at the beginning of each section.

- You are encouraged to mark up the passages as you read them.

- Work as quickly as possible. If a question is particularly difficult, circle it and return to it if you have time at the end.

- Remember, there is no penalty for wrong answers. If you are uncertain of the answer, make an educated guess. It is better to guess than to leave a question unanswered.

After you complete each SAT Reading and Writing and Language Model Exam,

- Use the answer key to check your answers.

- Study the explanations for any questions you missed.

- Use the correlation charts that follow each test to determine error trends and identify your areas of strengths and weaknesses.

   The correlation charts match the questions with the lessons where you can find explanatory text and similar questions. Circle or highlight any questions you missed. Go back and review that information before taking another SAT Model Exam.

- Determine your estimated SAT score by using the Score Conversion Chart on p. 56.

- Compare each of the scores you earn to your Diagnostic Test score to gauge your improvement over the course of the book.

This is a great opportunity to see what you know well and what you still need to practice before you take the real SAT. Good luck!

Answer Sheet

SAT Reading and Writing and Language Model Exam

Use the following answer sheet with the three Model Exams on pages 381 and following. This page may be reproduced for use with multiple exams.

Use a No. 2 pencil. Fill in the circle completely. If you change your answer, erase completely. Incomplete erasures may be read as answers.

Reading Section

1 Ⓐ Ⓑ Ⓒ Ⓓ	11 Ⓐ Ⓑ Ⓒ Ⓓ	21 Ⓐ Ⓑ Ⓒ Ⓓ	31 Ⓐ Ⓑ Ⓒ Ⓓ	41 Ⓐ Ⓑ Ⓒ Ⓓ	51 Ⓐ Ⓑ Ⓒ Ⓓ
2 Ⓐ Ⓑ Ⓒ Ⓓ	12 Ⓐ Ⓑ Ⓒ Ⓓ	22 Ⓐ Ⓑ Ⓒ Ⓓ	32 Ⓐ Ⓑ Ⓒ Ⓓ	42 Ⓐ Ⓑ Ⓒ Ⓓ	52 Ⓐ Ⓑ Ⓒ Ⓓ
3 Ⓐ Ⓑ Ⓒ Ⓓ	13 Ⓐ Ⓑ Ⓒ Ⓓ	23 Ⓐ Ⓑ Ⓒ Ⓓ	33 Ⓐ Ⓑ Ⓒ Ⓓ	43 Ⓐ Ⓑ Ⓒ Ⓓ	
4 Ⓐ Ⓑ Ⓒ Ⓓ	14 Ⓐ Ⓑ Ⓒ Ⓓ	24 Ⓐ Ⓑ Ⓒ Ⓓ	34 Ⓐ Ⓑ Ⓒ Ⓓ	44 Ⓐ Ⓑ Ⓒ Ⓓ	
5 Ⓐ Ⓑ Ⓒ Ⓓ	15 Ⓐ Ⓑ Ⓒ Ⓓ	25 Ⓐ Ⓑ Ⓒ Ⓓ	35 Ⓐ Ⓑ Ⓒ Ⓓ	45 Ⓐ Ⓑ Ⓒ Ⓓ	
6 Ⓐ Ⓑ Ⓒ Ⓓ	16 Ⓐ Ⓑ Ⓒ Ⓓ	26 Ⓐ Ⓑ Ⓒ Ⓓ	36 Ⓐ Ⓑ Ⓒ Ⓓ	46 Ⓐ Ⓑ Ⓒ Ⓓ	
7 Ⓐ Ⓑ Ⓒ Ⓓ	17 Ⓐ Ⓑ Ⓒ Ⓓ	27 Ⓐ Ⓑ Ⓒ Ⓓ	37 Ⓐ Ⓑ Ⓒ Ⓓ	47 Ⓐ Ⓑ Ⓒ Ⓓ	
8 Ⓐ Ⓑ Ⓒ Ⓓ	18 Ⓐ Ⓑ Ⓒ Ⓓ	28 Ⓐ Ⓑ Ⓒ Ⓓ	38 Ⓐ Ⓑ Ⓒ Ⓓ	48 Ⓐ Ⓑ Ⓒ Ⓓ	
9 Ⓐ Ⓑ Ⓒ Ⓓ	19 Ⓐ Ⓑ Ⓒ Ⓓ	29 Ⓐ Ⓑ Ⓒ Ⓓ	39 Ⓐ Ⓑ Ⓒ Ⓓ	49 Ⓐ Ⓑ Ⓒ Ⓓ	
10 Ⓐ Ⓑ Ⓒ Ⓓ	20 Ⓐ Ⓑ Ⓒ Ⓓ	30 Ⓐ Ⓑ Ⓒ Ⓓ	40 Ⓐ Ⓑ Ⓒ Ⓓ	50 Ⓐ Ⓑ Ⓒ Ⓓ	

Writing and Language Section

1 Ⓐ Ⓑ Ⓒ Ⓓ	11 Ⓐ Ⓑ Ⓒ Ⓓ	21 Ⓐ Ⓑ Ⓒ Ⓓ	31 Ⓐ Ⓑ Ⓒ Ⓓ	41 Ⓐ Ⓑ Ⓒ Ⓓ
2 Ⓐ Ⓑ Ⓒ Ⓓ	12 Ⓐ Ⓑ Ⓒ Ⓓ	22 Ⓐ Ⓑ Ⓒ Ⓓ	32 Ⓐ Ⓑ Ⓒ Ⓓ	42 Ⓐ Ⓑ Ⓒ Ⓓ
3 Ⓐ Ⓑ Ⓒ Ⓓ	13 Ⓐ Ⓑ Ⓒ Ⓓ	23 Ⓐ Ⓑ Ⓒ Ⓓ	33 Ⓐ Ⓑ Ⓒ Ⓓ	43 Ⓐ Ⓑ Ⓒ Ⓓ
4 Ⓐ Ⓑ Ⓒ Ⓓ	14 Ⓐ Ⓑ Ⓒ Ⓓ	24 Ⓐ Ⓑ Ⓒ Ⓓ	34 Ⓐ Ⓑ Ⓒ Ⓓ	44 Ⓐ Ⓑ Ⓒ Ⓓ
5 Ⓐ Ⓑ Ⓒ Ⓓ	15 Ⓐ Ⓑ Ⓒ Ⓓ	25 Ⓐ Ⓑ Ⓒ Ⓓ	35 Ⓐ Ⓑ Ⓒ Ⓓ	
6 Ⓐ Ⓑ Ⓒ Ⓓ	16 Ⓐ Ⓑ Ⓒ Ⓓ	26 Ⓐ Ⓑ Ⓒ Ⓓ	36 Ⓐ Ⓑ Ⓒ Ⓓ	
7 Ⓐ Ⓑ Ⓒ Ⓓ	17 Ⓐ Ⓑ Ⓒ Ⓓ	27 Ⓐ Ⓑ Ⓒ Ⓓ	37 Ⓐ Ⓑ Ⓒ Ⓓ	
8 Ⓐ Ⓑ Ⓒ Ⓓ	18 Ⓐ Ⓑ Ⓒ Ⓓ	28 Ⓐ Ⓑ Ⓒ Ⓓ	38 Ⓐ Ⓑ Ⓒ Ⓓ	
9 Ⓐ Ⓑ Ⓒ Ⓓ	19 Ⓐ Ⓑ Ⓒ Ⓓ	29 Ⓐ Ⓑ Ⓒ Ⓓ	39 Ⓐ Ⓑ Ⓒ Ⓓ	
10 Ⓐ Ⓑ Ⓒ Ⓓ	20 Ⓐ Ⓑ Ⓒ Ⓓ	30 Ⓐ Ⓑ Ⓒ Ⓓ	40 Ⓐ Ⓑ Ⓒ Ⓓ	

SAT Model Exam 1

READING TEST

65 MINUTES, 52 QUESTIONS

Use the Reading Section of your answer sheet to answer the questions in this section.

Directions

Each passage or pair of passages below is followed by a number of questions. After reading each passage or pair, choose the best answer to each question based upon what is stated or implied in the passage or passages or in any graphics (tables or graphs). To practice using an SAT-type answer sheet, fill in the appropriate letter bubble next to the question number. A reproducible answer sheet can be found on page 380.

Questions 1–10 are based upon the following passage.

This passage is adapted from Pride and Prejudice *written in 1813 by Jane Austen. Mr. and Mrs. Bennet discuss a new neighbor whom Mrs. Bennet views as a potential husband for her daughters.*

It is a truth universally acknowledged that a single man in possession of a good fortune must be in want of a wife.

However little known the feelings or views
5 of such a man may be on his first entering a neighborhood, this truth is so well fixed in the minds of the surrounding families, that he is considered as the rightful property of some one or other of their daughters.

10 "My dear Mr. Bennet," said his lady to him one day, "have you heard that Netherfield Park is let at last?"

Mr. Bennet replied that he had not.

"But it is," returned she; "for Mrs. Long has just
15 been here, and she told me all about it."

Mr. Bennet made no answer.

"Do not you want to know who has taken it?" cried his wife impatiently.

"*You* want to tell me, and I have no objection to
20 hearing it."

This was invitation enough.

"Why, my dear, you must know, Mrs. Long says that Netherfield is taken by a young man of large fortune from the north of England; that he came
25 down on Monday in a chaise and four to see the place and was so much delighted with it that he agreed with Mr. Morris immediately; that he is to take possession before Michaelmas, and some of his servants are to be in the house by the end of
30 next week."

"What is his name?"

"Bingley."

"Is he married or single?"

CONTINUE

"Oh! single, my dear, to be sure! A single man of large fortune; four or five thousand a year. What a fine thing for our girls!"

"How so? How can it affect them?"

"My dear Mr. Bennet," replied his wife, "how can you be so tiresome! You must know that I am thinking of his marrying one of them."

"Is that his design in settling here?"

"Design! Nonsense, how can you talk so! But it is very likely that he may fall in love with one of them, and therefore you must visit him as soon as he comes."

"I see no occasion for that. You and the girls may go, or you may send them by themselves, which perhaps will be still better, for as you are as handsome as any of them, Mr. Bingley might like you the best of the party."

"My dear, you flatter me. I certainly have had my share of beauty, but I do not pretend to be anything extraordinary now. When a woman has five grown-up daughters, she ought to give over thinking of her own beauty."

"In such cases, a woman has not often much beauty to think of.

"But, my dear, you must indeed go and see Mr. Bingley when he comes into the neighborhood."

"It is more than I engage for, I assure you."

"But consider your daughters. Only think what an establishment it would be for one of them. Sir William and Lady Lucas are determined to go, merely on that account, for in general, you know, they visit no newcomers. Indeed you must go, for it will be impossible for us to visit him if you do not."

"You are over-scrupulous, surely. I dare say Mr. Bingley will be very glad to see you; and I will send a few lines by you to assure him of my hearty consent to his marrying whichever he chooses of the girls: though I must throw in a good word for my little Lizzy."

"I desire you will do no such thing. Lizzy is not a bit better than the others; and I am sure she is not half so handsome as Jane, nor half so good-humored as Lydia. But you are always giving her the preference."

"They have none of them much to recommend them," replied he; "they are all silly and ignorant, like other girls; but Lizzy has something more of quickness than her sisters."

"Mr. Bennet, how can you abuse your own children in such a way? You take delight in vexing me. You have no compassion of my poor nerves."

"You mistake me, my dear. I have a high respect for your nerves. They are my old friends. I have heard you mention them with consideration these twenty years at least."

"Ah, you do not know what I suffer."

"But I hope you will get over it, and live to see many young men of four thousand a year come into the neighbourhood."

"It will be no use to us, if twenty such should come, since you will not visit them."

"Depend upon it, my dear, that when there are twenty, I will visit them all."

CONTINUE ➡

1

This passage is mainly about

A) a single, rich man moving into a new neighborhood.

B) a husband and wife who disagree about their daughters.

C) a concerned mother who feels pressure to provide a secure future for her daughters.

D) a wife who can't communicate her true feelings to her husband.

2

The main purpose of the opening sentence of the passage is to

A) provide a contrast to the dialogue between the Bennets.

B) state an ethical principle which the characters should live by.

C) reveal society's prejudice against the rich.

D) share a social convention which will be illustrated by the Bennets' conversation.

3

Which of the following best describes the narrator's point of view based upon lines 4–9?

A) humorously mocking humankind

B) humbly pointing out flaws in society

C) aggressively detailing erroneous thinking

D) unreliably describing life in a small community

4

The use of the phrase "rightful property" in line 8, most nearly implies that

A) single men had few rights when the story was written.

B) women view men as a means to financial security.

C) marriage laws were oppressive and dehumanizing.

D) women gave up all their rights when they married.

5

Mrs. Bennet's manner of addressing her husband suggests

A) an ill-concealed dislike for him.

B) a confidence in her knowledge over his.

C) a lack of interest in her husband's opinion.

D) a belief that she is vastly superior to her husband.

6

Which lines provide the best evidence for the answer to question 5?

A) lines 17–21 ("Do not you want to . . . invitation enough")

B) lines 22–30 ("Why, my dear, . . . next week")

C) lines 34–40 ("Oh! single, my dear . . . one of them")

D) lines 38–44 ("how can you be . . . one of them")

7

Mrs. Bennet considers the new occupant of Netherfield

A) somewhat pretentious because of his arrival in a chaise and four.

B) an interesting young man born of the right kind of family.

C) a person who could make one of her daughters very happy.

D) a person to be manipulated according to her design.

8

As used in line 67, "over-scrupulous" most nearly means

A) obsessed with minor details.

B) too strict a regard for what is right.

C) overly critical of others.

D) honest to a fault.

CONTINUE

9

Which lines provide the best evidence for the answer to question 8?

A) lines 56–57 ("In such . . . think of")

B) lines 61–62 ("But consider . . . them")

C) lines 65–66 ("Indeed . . . do not")

D) lines 73–74 ("I desire . . . the others")

10

In lines 85–86, Mr. Bennet's use of the phrases "high respect" and "my old friends" reveal that his tone is

A) intensely critical.

B) lightheartedly sarcastic.

C) optimistically merry.

D) pointedly callous.

Questions 11–21 are based upon the following passage.

The following passage is adapted from Annie Dillard's Pilgrim at Tinker Creek. *In this essay she explains that seeing is a difficult and complicated task.*

I chanced on a wonderful book by Marius von Senden, called *Space and Sight.* When Western surgeons discovered how to perform safe cataract operations, they ranged across Europe and America
5   operating on dozens of men and women of all ages who had been blinded by cataracts since birth. Von Senden collected accounts of such cases; the histories are fascinating. Many doctors had tested their patients' sense perceptions and ideas of space
10 both before and after the operations. The vast majority of patients, of both sexes and all ages, had, in von Senden's opinion, no idea of space whatsoever. Form, distance, and size were so many meaningless syllables. A patient "had no idea of
15 depth, confusing it with roundness." Before the operation a doctor would give a blind patient a cube and a sphere; the patient would tongue it or feel

it with his hands, and name it correctly. After the operation the doctor would show the same objects
20 to the patient without letting him touch them; now he had no clue whatsoever what he was seeing. One patient called lemonade "square" because it pricked on his tongue as a square shape pricked on the touch of his hands. Of another postoperative patient, the
25 doctor writes, "I have found in her no notion of size, for example, not even within the narrow limits which she might have encompassed with the aid of touch. Thus when I asked her to show me how big her mother was, she did not stretch out her
30 hands, but set her two index-fingers a few inches apart." Other doctors reported their patients' own statements to similar effect. . . .

For the newly sighted, vision is pure sensation unencumbered by meaning: "The girl went through
35 the experience that we all go through and forget, the moment we are born. She saw, but it did not mean anything but a lot of different kinds of brightness." Again, "I asked the patient what he could see; he answered that he saw an extensive field of light, in
40 which everything appeared dull, confused, and in motion. He could not distinguish objects." Another patient saw "nothing but a confusion of forms and colors." When a newly sighted girl saw photographs and paintings, she asked, "Why do they put those
45 dark marks all over them?"

"Those aren't dark marks," her mother explained, "those are shadows. That is one of the ways the eye knows that things have shape. If it were not for shadows many things would look flat."

50 "Well, that's how things do look," Joan answered.

CONTINUE ➡

"Everything looks flat with dark patches."

But it is the patients' concepts of space that are most revealing. One patient, according to his doctor, "practiced his vision in a strange fashion;
55 thus he takes off one of his boots, throws it some way off in front of him, and then attempts to gauge the distance at which it lies; he takes a few steps towards the boot and tries to grasp it; on failing to reach it, he moves on a step or two and gropes for
60 the boot until he finally gets hold of it."

"But even at this stage, after three weeks' experience of seeing," von Senden goes on, "'space,' as he conceives it, ends with visual space, i.e. with color-patches that happen to bound his view. He does
65 not yet have the notion that a larger object (a chair) can mask a smaller one (a dog), or that the latter can still be present even though it is not directly seen."

In general the newly sighted see the world as a dazzle of color-patches. They are pleased by the
70 sensation of color, and learn quickly to name the colors, but the rest of seeing is tormentingly difficult. Soon after his operation a patient "generally bumps into one of these color-patches and observes them to be substantial, since they resist him as tactual objects
75 do. In walking about it also strikes him—or can if he pays attention—that he is continually passing in between the colors he sees, that he can go past a visual object, that a part of it then steadily disappears from view; and that in spite of this, however he
80 twists and turns—whether entering the room from the door, for example, or returning back to it—he always has a visual space in front of him. Thus he gradually comes to realize that there is also a space behind him, which he does not see."

11

The author of this passage would most likely agree with which of the following statements?
A) A suddenly sighted person would soon be as competent in moving about as a person blind at birth.
B) Though newly sighted persons are puzzled by color, they quickly learn to manipulate shapes and forms.
C) Because of their long years of experience, newly sighted older persons adapt more readily to the new sensations.
D) Sight is a physical gift, but seeing is a process that takes a long time to achieve.

12

Which choice provides the best evidence for the answer to question 11?
A) lines 8–13 ("Many doctors had tested . . . space whatsoever")
B) lines 33–37 ("For the newly sighted, . . . of brightness")
C) lines 41–45 ("Another patient . . . over them")
D) lines 68–71 ("In general the newly sighted. . . tormentingly difficult")

13

As used in line 27, "encompassed" most nearly means
A) surrounded.
B) comprehended.
C) surmised.
D) expanded.

CONTINUE

14

A person's conceptions of space can best be described as

A) inborn, part of the genetic makeup that determines a person's physical characteristics.

B) learned instantaneously, inasmuch as the physical world surrounds a person at birth.

C) a factor of intelligence, as determined by the ability of a person to function effectively in a social environment.

D) mastered only after a considerable period of time with setbacks.

15

According to the passage, the concept of space involves understanding

A) form, distance, and size.

B) how light travels through the atmosphere.

C) patches of color.

D) being able to touch an object.

16

Von Senden's claims that most patients had "no idea of space whatsoever" is supported mainly by

A) complex data from scientific experiments.

B) stories from patients' families.

C) general statements about sight and space.

D) examples of people who had undergone cataract surgery.

17

Based on lines 21–32, we can infer that at birth a child

A) recognizes his mother's face immediately.

B) has none of the problems that a newly sighted person experiences.

C) has more acute sight than hearing.

D) takes a while to learn to differentiate objects visually.

18

Blind people generally depend upon which of the following for spatial problems?

A) sighted partners who explain the problems

B) information picked up by Braille reading

C) the sense of touch

D) the sense of taste

19

Which choice provides the best support for the answer to question 18?

A) lines 18–24 ("After the operation . . . touch of his hands")

B) lines 34–37 ("The girl . . . kinds of brightness")

C) lines 38–41 ("I asked the patient . . . distinguish objects")

D) lines 43–49 ("When a newly sighted girl . . . would look flat")

20

The primary purpose of this passage is to

A) convince blind readers to undergo cataract surgery.

B) encourage readers to be patient with the newly sighted.

C) educate readers about the sense perceptions of the newly sighted.

D) inspire compassion for those who have recently regained their sight.

21

As used in line 74, the word "tactual" most nearly means

A) in accord with the facts.

B) pertaining to touch.

C) verifiable.

D) showing sensitivity.

CONTINUE ➡

Questions 22–31 are based upon the following passage.

The following passage is adapted from an article by Andrew C. Revkin published in The New York Times, *"Did Earth's 'Anthropocene' Age of Man Begin with the Globalization of Disease in 1610?"*

As regular readers know, scientists are in a bit of a tussle over what date marks the dawn of Earth's "age of us"—a.k.a. the Anthropocene—even as other scientists and scholars question whether

5 it's hubris to think a geological epoch, as strictly defined, can result from human activity.

Candidates for the starting point for the age of humans range from the dawn of agriculture to the age of plastics and fallout and the "Great

10 Acceleration" of greenhouse gas growth and other environmental impacts.

Now a new candidate is in the mix. In a paper in *Nature,* Simon L. Lewis and Mark A. Maslin of University College London point to the year

15 1610, marked by, of all things, a sharp but brief *dip* in carbon dioxide concentrations (revealed in ice cores).

The greenhouse gas decline, they say, is thought to have been the result of the implosion of

20 civilizations in the Americas as European-carried diseases killed off tens of millions of inhabitants of the "New" World. The collapse of agriculture would have resulted in enormous regrowth of forests, and thus the uptake of carbon dioxide (CO_2).

25 They say the only other candidate that meets the criteria for defining a geological epoch and setting another "golden spike" is 1964. A release from the researchers' university, University College London, nicely explains their thinking:

30 Defining an epoch requires two main criteria to be met. Long-lasting changes to the Earth must be documented. Scientists must also pinpoint and date a global environmental change that has been captured in natural material, such as rocks,

35 ancient ice or sediment from the ocean floor. Such a marker—like the chemical signature left by the meteorite strike that wiped out the dinosaurs—is called a golden spike.

The study authors systematically compared the

40 major environmental impacts of human activity over the past 50,000 years against these two formal requirements. Just two dates met the criteria: 1610, when the collision of the New and Old Worlds a century earlier was first felt globally; and 1964,

45 associated with the fallout from nuclear weapons tests. The researchers conclude that 1610 is the stronger candidate.

The scientists say the 1492 arrival of Europeans in the Americas, and subsequent global trade, moved

50 species to new continents and oceans, resulting in a global re-ordering of life on Earth. This rapid, repeated, cross-ocean exchange of species is without precedent in Earth's history.

They argue that the joining of the two hemispheres

55 is an unambiguous event after which the impacts of human activity became global and set Earth on a new trajectory. The first fossil pollen of maize, a Latin American species, appears in marine sediment in Europe in 1600, becoming common

60 over subsequent centuries. This irreversible exchange of species satisfies the first criteria for dating an epoch—long-term changes to Earth.

CONTINUE ▶

Chart 1

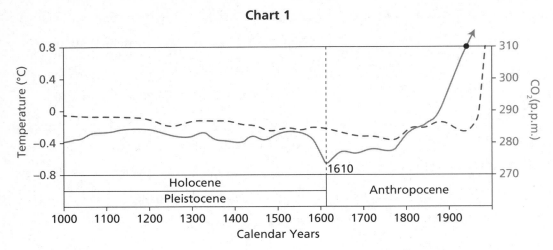

In a *Nature* paper, two scientists propose 1610 as one starting date for the Anthropocene geological epoch. This is when levels of carbon dioxide in the atmosphere (solid line) briefly plunged, evidently as forests regrew in the Americas when indigenous cultures collapsed following the arrival of Europeans. Changes in temperature are represented by the horizontal dashed line.

Chart 2

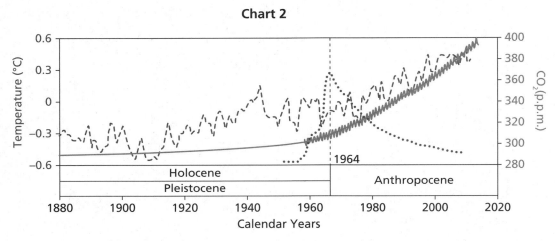

In a *Nature* paper, two scientists propose 1964 as one starting date for the Anthropocene geological epoch. This is when traces of radioisotopes from atomic bomb testing (dotted line) spread around the world, leaving a permanent signature in sediments. Changes in temperature are represented by the horizontal dashed line.

Source: *Nature*.

22

As used in the text and the graph, the Anthropocene age can best be defined as

A) the period between the Holocene and the Pleistocene eras.

B) the "golden spike" of 1492.

C) the age of humans.

D) a geological event.

23

Simon Lewis and Mark Maslin's central claim about the Anthropocene age is that it

A) began with the dawn of agriculture in the New World.

B) started when carbon dioxide levels dropped significantly.

C) is associated with the fallout from nuclear weapons testing.

D) was caused by the "Great Acceleration" of greenhouse gas growth.

CONTINUE ➡

24

Which choice provides the best evidence for the answer to question 23?

A) lines 1–6 ("scientists . . . activity")

B) lines 7–11 ("Candidates . . . impacts")

C) lines 12–17 ("In . . . ice cores")

D) lines 18–22 ("The greenhouse gas . . . World")

25

What two criteria must be met in order to define an epoch?

A) permanent changes to the Earth and a substantial rise in temperatures

B) a meteorite strike and environmental change that has been captured in natural materials

C) long-lasting changes to the earth and a "golden spike"

D) the expansion of polar ice sheets and a rise in the temperature of Earth's surface

26

As used in line 19, "implosion" most nearly means

A) bankruptcy.

B) self-destruction.

C) collision.

D) collapse.

27

The authors cite the first fossil pollen of maize (lines 57–60) in order to

A) provide an example of a global environmental change in natural material.

B) contrast the differences between 1610 and 1964.

C) provide evidence of a long-lasting change to the Earth.

D) explain a result of the dip in carbon dioxide concentrations.

28

It can be inferred from the passage that

A) unusual changes in carbon dioxide levels can be documented through natural means.

B) scientists will never agree on when the Anthropocene epoch began.

C) geological epochs are usually a result of human activity.

D) scientists have been recording carbon dioxide levels since before 1610.

29

Which choice provides the best evidence for the answer to question 28?

A) lines 1–6 ("As regular . . . activity")

B) lines 32–35 ("Scientists . . . floor")

C) lines 46–47 ("The researchers . . candidate")

D) lines 54–57 ("They argue . . . trajectory")

30

How does the information in Chart 1 support Lewis and Maslin's central claim?

A) It shows carbon dioxide levels tripled in 1610.

B) It indicates carbon dioxide levels briefly plunged in 1610.

C) It illustrates that sea levels fell dramatically in 1610.

D) It reveals that temperatures rose dangerously high in 1610.

31

What evidence does Chart 2 provide to support 1964 as the year the Anthropocene epoch was born?

A) Scientists discovered plant fossils that contain traces of radioisotopes from atomic bombs.

B) A rise in traces of radioisotopes from atomic bomb testing was found in sediments.

C) Levels of carbon dioxide in the atmosphere spiked sharply.

D) Meteor impacts were so intense that they were felt around the world.

CONTINUE

Questions 32–41 are based upon the following passage.

This article describes the substantial progress women have made in the workplace, while also discussing gender inequalities that still persist.

Organizations ranging from the United Nations to the World Bank are paying more attention to women. Some European countries have already introduced quotas to get more of them on company
5 boards and others may follow. Every self-respecting firm, bank, consultancy, and headhunter is launching initiatives, conducting studies, and running conferences on how to make the most of female potential. Are these efforts still needed?

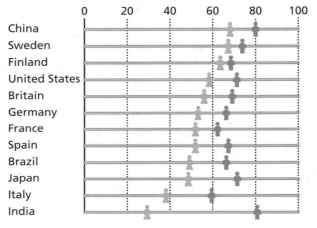

Chart 1
Labor Force Participation Rate, 2010, %

10 In many emerging markets women remain second-class citizens, lacking basic rights and suffering violence and many kinds of disadvantage. In the rich world most of the battles about legal and political rights have been won, and on the economic front too
15 women have come a long way. It is easy to forget that even in developed countries they arrived in strength in the labor force only a few decades ago. Since 1970 the proportion of women of working age who have paid jobs across the rich world has risen from 48%
20 to 64%. There are large variations from country to country: in parts of southern and eastern Europe only about half of them go out to work, whereas in most of the Nordic countries well over 70% have jobs, close to the figure for men. In America more women
25 were working than men—until the recession caught up with them. But the broad trend in most countries is still slightly upwards.

Claudia Goldin, an economics professor at Harvard who has studied American women's
30 employment history over the past century or so, calls the mass arrival of women in the workplace in the 1970s a "quiet revolution." Of course there have always been women who worked outside the home, but the numbers were much smaller. Until the 1920s
35 working women were mostly young and single and had jobs in factories or as domestic servants that required little education. From the 1930s onwards many more girls went to high school and college and got jobs in offices where conditions were
40 much more agreeable. In the 1950s large numbers of married women took up work as secretaries, teachers, nurses, social workers and so on, often part-time. By the 1970s their daughters, having watched their mothers go off to work, took it for
45 granted that they would do the same.

Many of them had also seen their parents get divorced, which made having an income of their own seem like a wise precaution. . . . By 1980 American women were graduating from college in
50 the same numbers as men and have since overtaken them by a significant margin. What happened in America was echoed, to a greater or lesser degree, in most other industrial countries. The dual-income couple was born.

CONTINUE ➡

55 This has been a great boon to all concerned. National economies benefited from the boost in growth provided by many extra workers acquired over a relatively short period without the trouble and expense of rearing them or the upheaval of

60 importing them. Employers enjoyed a wider choice of employees who, despite equal-pay legislation, were often cheaper and more flexible than men. And women themselves gained the freedom to pursue a wide range of careers, financial independence and

65 much greater control over their lives.

These additional workers are spending money, paying taxes and making the economy go round. No wonder policymakers everywhere are trying to encourage even more women to take up paid

70 work to boost output. A further reason to welcome them is that in many developed countries, as well as in China, falling birth rates have started to cause working populations to shrink and the number of elderly people to rise steeply, with ominous

75 consequences for economies in general and pensions in particular. More working women could help offset the decline in the labor force.

Chart 2
U.S. Women's Representation in the Labor Force

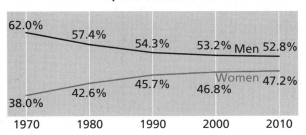

	1970	1980	1990	2000	2010
Men	62.0%	57.4%	54.3%	53.2%	52.8%
Women	38.0%	42.6%	45.7%	46.8%	47.2%

CONTINUE

32

As used in line 10, "emerging" most nearly means
A) poor.
B) becoming prominent.
C) global.
D) rapidly changing.

33

According to Chart 1, the gap between the number of women and men working is the largest in which of the following countries?
A) Japan
B) Britain
C) Finland
D) India

34

Do the data in Chart 2 provide support for the professor's claim in lines 28–32 that the mass arrival of women in the workplace in the 1970s was a "quiet revolution"?
A) Yes, because the percentage of women in the workforce increased dramatically between 1970 and 1980.
B) Yes, because fewer men were in the workforce between 1970 and 1980.
C) No, because no data is provided for the number of women who left the workplace.
D) No, because the data indicates that more women were in the workforce in 2006–2010 than in 1970.

35

The author uses a chronological text structure in lines 34–51 in order to
A) stress the discrimination working women faced over the years.
B) trace the history of working women in the United States.
C) point out that only young, single women worked in the early twentieth century.
D) argue that women didn't enter the workforce en masse until the 70s.

36

As used in line 55, the word "boon" most nearly means

A) favor.

B) benevolence.

C) benefit.

D) windfall.

37

What claim does the author make regarding the birth of the dual-income couple in lines 55–60?

A) Coping with a dual-income lifestyle is difficult.

B) Dual-income couples are beneficial to society.

C) Dual-income couples are able to save more money.

D) Dual-income couples put too much strain on families.

38

The author supports the claim made in line 55 with all of the following pieces of evidence, EXCEPT

A) National economies have benefited from a boost in growth.

B) Employers have enjoyed a wider choice of employees.

C) Women have gained freedom in many areas of their lives.

D) Women have attained greater equality in relationships.

39

It can be inferred from lines 60–62 that

A) equal-pay laws have not been effective.

B) employers prefer hiring men to women.

C) women are more intelligent than men.

D) equal-pay legislation has favored women.

40

The reader can infer the writer would agree with which of the following statements?

A) Women should not receive equal pay as men.

B) Too many women in the workplace will cause birthrates to fall as they did in China.

C) Developing countries can improve their economies by encouraging more women to work.

D) In most rich countries, women have achieved legal, political, and economic equality with men.

41

Which choice provides the best evidence for the answer to the previous question?

A) lines 12–15 ("In the rich . . . long way")

B) lines 24–26 ("In America . . . them")

C) lines 56–60 ("National economies . . . importing them")

D) lines 70–76 ("A further reason . . . particular")

CONTINUE

Questions 42–52 are based upon the following passage.

Passage 1 is the opening section of the Constitution of the United States. Passage 2 is the opening section of the Charter of the United Nations.

Passage 1

We the People of the United States, in Order to form a more perfect Union, establish Justice, insure domestic Tranquility, provide for the common defence, promote the general Welfare, and secure

5 the Blessings of Liberty to ourselves and our Posterity, do ordain and establish this Constitution for the United States of America.

ARTICLE I

SECTION 1. All legislative Powers herein

10 granted shall be vested in a Congress of the United States, which shall consist of a Senate and House of Representatives.

SECTION 2. The House of Representatives shall be composed of Members chosen every second Year

15 by the People of the several States, and the Electors in each State shall have the Qualifications requisite for Electors of the most numerous Branch of the State Legislature.

No Person shall be a Representative who shall

20 not have attained to the Age of twenty five Years, and been seven Years a Citizen of the United States, and who shall not, when elected, be an Inhabitant of that State in which he shall be chosen.

Representatives and direct Taxes shall be

25 apportioned among the several States which may be included within this Union, according to their respective Numbers, which shall be determined by adding to the whole Number of free Persons,

including those bound to Service for a Term of

30 Years, and excluding Indians not taxed, three fifths of all other Persons. The actual Enumeration shall be made within three Years after the first Meeting of the Congress of the United States, and within every subsequent Term of ten Years, in such

35 Manner as they shall by Law direct. The Number of Representatives shall not exceed one for every thirty Thousand, but each State shall have at Least one Representative; and until such enumeration shall be made, the State of New Hampshire shall

40 be entitled to choose three, Massachusetts eight, Rhode-Island and Providence Plantations one, Connecticut five, New York six, New Jersey four, Pennsylvania eight, Delaware one, Maryland six, Virginia ten, North Carolina five, South Carolina

45 five, and Georgia three.

When vacancies happen in the Representation from any State, the Executive Authority thereof shall issue Writs of Election to fill such Vacancies.

The House of Representatives shall choose their

50 Speaker and other Officers; and shall have the sole Power of Impeachment.

Passage 2

We the peoples of the United Nations determined to save succeeding generations from the scourge of war, which twice in our lifetime has brought

55 untold sorrow to mankind, and to reaffirm faith in fundamental human rights, in the dignity and worth of the human person, in the equal rights of men and women and of nations large and small, and to establish conditions under which justice

60 and respect for the obligations arising from treaties

CONTINUE ➤

and other sources of international law can be maintained, and to promote social progress and better standards of life in larger freedom. And for these ends to practice tolerance and live together in

65 peace with one another as good neighbours, and to unite our strength to maintain international peace and security, and to ensure, by the acceptance of principles and the institution of methods, that armed force shall not be used, save in the common interest,

70 and to employ international machinery for the promotion of the economic and social advancement of all peoples, have resolved to combine our efforts to accomplish these aims.

Chapter 1: Purposes and Principles

Article 1

75 The Purposes of the United Nations are:

1. To maintain international peace and security, and to that end: to take effective collective measures for the prevention and removal of threats to the peace, and for the suppression of acts of

80 aggression or other breaches of the peace, and to bring about by peaceful means, and in conformity with the principles of justice and international law, adjustment or settlement of international disputes or situations which might lead to a breach of the peace;

85 2. To develop friendly relations among nations based on respect for the principle of equal rights and self-determination of peoples, and to take other appropriate measures to strengthen universal peace;

3. To achieve international co-operation in

90 solving international problems of an economic, social, cultural, or humanitarian character, and in promoting and encouraging respect for human

rights and for fundamental freedoms for all without distinction as to race, sex, language, or religion; and

95 4. To be a centre for harmonizing the actions of nations in the attainment of these common ends.

42

Which choice best reflects the purpose of Section 2 of Passage 1?
A) to explain the procedures for electing the President
B) to detail the impeachment procedures for the removal of a Representative
C) to explain how the number of Representatives are determined
D) to list the process for electing members of the Senate

43

As used in line 16, "requisite" most nearly means
A) essential.
B) voted upon.
C) suggested.
D) developed.

44

In line 29, the expression "bound to Service" refers to
A) Native Americans.
B) indentured servants.
C) newly elected Representatives.
D) the unemployed.

45

In Section 2, the suggested numbers of representatives are based on
A) the national census, which will be conducted every three years.
B) statistics supplied by the new Senate.
C) temporary estimates that will be verified within three years.
D) the number of delegates to the convention.

CONTINUE ➡

46

It can be inferred that lines 35–45 ("The Number of Representatives shall . . . Georgia three.") mean that

A) each state gets a number of Representatives according to its population.

B) each state gets a number of Representatives based on its location.

C) the number of Representatives must be more than one.

D) there are thirty thousand Representatives.

47

What is the relationship between the opening sentence of the Constitution and the Articles that follow?

A) The opening sentence makes a claim that is supported by evidence in the Articles and Sections that follow.

B) The opening sentence states the general purpose of the government; the Articles that follow explain how the government will be structured.

C) The opening sentence makes a general statement about the rights of citizens; the Articles detail the specific rights.

D) The opening sentence explains the problems of the United States; the Articles offer solutions to the problems.

48

The Constitution (Passage 1) and the United Nations Charter (Passage 2) resemble each other in their emphasis on

A) securing justice and peace.

B) creating an armed force.

C) promoting the welfare of U.S. citizens.

D) practicing tolerance of all peoples.

49

Which choice provides the best evidence for the answer to question 48?

A) "secure the Blessings of Liberty to ourselves and our Posterity" (Passage 1, lines 4–6)

B) "provide for the common defence" (Passage 1, lines 3–4)

C) "to unite our strength to maintain international peace and security" (Passage 2, lines 65–66)

D) "to promote social progress and better standards of life in larger freedom" (Passage 2, lines 62–63)

50

The U.N. Charter (Passage 2) is different from the Constitution (Passage 1) in its emphasis upon

A) creating monetary agreements between nations.

B) promoting the general welfare of all people.

C) raising an army made up of citizens from all nations.

D) improving the quality of life of U.S. citizens.

51

Which choice provides the best support for the idea that the United Nations Charter does not eliminate the possible use of force?

A) lines 52–63 ("We the peoples . . . in larger freedom")

B) lines 65–67 ("to unite our strength . . . and security")

C) lines 67–69 ("to ensure . . . in the common interest")

D) lines 70–72 ("to employ international . . . all peoples")

In Passage 2, the use of the words "We," "one another," and "together" function mainly to emphasize that the UN will

A) work for peace.

B) promote a spirit of unity and cooperation.

C) stand for human rights.

D) include countries across the world.

STOP

**If you finish before time is called, you may check your work on this section only.
Do not turn to any other section.**

FULL-LENGTH READING AND WRITING AND LANGUAGE TESTS

SAT Model Exam 1

WRITING AND LANGUAGE TEST
35 MINUTES, 44 QUESTIONS

Use the Writing and Language section of your answer sheet to answer the questions in this section.

Directions

Each passage below is accompanied by a number of questions. For some questions, you will consider how the passage might be revised to improve the expression of ideas. For other questions, you will consider how the passage might be edited to correct errors in sentence structure, usage, or punctuation. A passage or a question may be accompanied by one or more graphics (such as a table or graph) that you will consider as you make revising and editing decisions.

Some questions will direct you to an underlined portion of a passage. Other questions will direct you to a location in a passage or ask you to think about the passage as a whole.

After reading each passage, choose the answer to each question that most effectively improves the quality of writing in the passage or that makes the passage conform to the conventions of standard written English. Many questions include a "NO CHANGE" option. Choose that option if you think the best choice is to leave the relevant portion of the passage as it is.

Questions 1–11 are based on the following passage.

Robert Philip Hanssen Espionage Case

Attorney General John Ashcroft, FBI Director Louis J. Freeh and United States Attorney Helen Fahey announced **1** today, that a veteran FBI counterintelligence Agent was arrested Sunday by the FBI and charged with committing espionage by providing highly classified national security information to Russia and the former Soviet Union.

At the time of the arrest at a park in Vienna, Virginia, Robert Philip Hanssen, age 56, was **2** quietly placing a package containing highly classified information at a pre-arranged, or "dead drop," site for pick-up by his Russian handlers. Hanssen had previously received substantial sums of money from the Russians for the information he disclosed to them.

1
A) NO CHANGE
B) today that a veteran FBI counterintelligence Agent was arrested Sunday by the FBI
C) today, that a veteran FBI counterintelligence Agent was arrested Sunday by the FBI,
D) today that a veteran FBI counterintelligence Agent, arrested Sunday by the FBI,

2
A) NO CHANGE
B) determinedly
C) clandestinely
D) privately

CONTINUE →

FBI Director Louis J. Freeh expressed both outrage and sadness. He said the **[3]** charges if proven represent "the most serious violations of law—and threat to national security."

"A betrayal of trust by an FBI Agent, who is not only sworn to enforce the law but specifically to help protect our **[4]** nation's security, is particularly abhorrent. This kind of criminal conduct represents the most traitorous action imaginable against a country governed by the Rule of Law. It also **[5]** strikes on the heart of everything the FBI represents—the commitment of over 28,000 honest and dedicated men and women in the FBI who work diligently to earn the trust and confidence of the American people every day."

"These kinds of cases are the most difficult, sensitive, and sophisticated imaginable. I am immensely proud of the men and women of the **[6]** FBI, who conducted this investigation. Their actions represent counterintelligence at its very best, reflecting dedication to both principle and mission. It is not an easy assignment to investigate a colleague, but they did so unhesitatingly, quietly and securely."

Hanssen was charged in a criminal complaint filed in Federal court in Alexandria, Virginia, with espionage and conspiracy to commit espionage, violations that carry a possible punishment of life in prison and under certain circumstances, the death **[7]** penalty, following the arrest FBI Agents began searching Hanssen's residence, automobiles and workspace for additional evidence.

3
A) NO CHANGE
B) charges, if proven,
C) charges when proven,
D) charges, when proven,

4
A) NO CHANGE
B) nations' security
C) nation's security
D) nations' security,

5
A) NO CHANGE
B) strikes at the heart
C) strike on the heart
D) struck at the heart

6
A) NO CHANGE
B) FBI. Who conducted this investigation?
C) FBI who conducted this investigation.
D) FBI who conducts this investigation.

7
A) NO CHANGE
B) penalty. Following the arrest,
C) penalty, following the arrest,
D) penalty: following the arrest

CONTINUE ➡

A detailed affidavit, filed in support of the criminal complaint and search warrants, [8] provide a troubling account of how Hanssen [9] originally volunteered to first furnish highly sensitive documents to KGB intelligence officers assigned to the Soviet embassy in Washington, D.C. The affidavit chronicles the systematic transfer of highly classified national security and counterintelligence information by Hanssen in exchange for diamonds and cash worth more than $600,000. [10] Cash and diamonds are popular payment methods for illicit activities since cash is difficult to trace and diamonds are easy to smuggle. [11]

8
A) NO CHANGE
B) provides a troubling account for
C) provide a troubling account with
D) provides a troubling account of

9
A) NO CHANGE
B) first volunteered initially to furnish
C) at the beginning volunteered first to furnish
D) first volunteered to furnish

10
The writer is considering deleting the underlined sentence. Should the writer do this?
A) Yes, because it blurs the paragraph's focus on the information detailed in the affidavit.
B) Yes, because it doesn't provide specific examples about how Hanssen transferred the classified documents to his contacts.
C) No, because it provides supporting evidence about the affidavit regarding Hanssen's activities.
D) No, because it provides an additional example about how Hanssen was an intelligent criminal.

11
The writer wants to conclude the passage with a sentence that emphasizes the scope of Hanssen's actions. Which choice would best accomplish this goal?
A) Hanssen's activities also have links to other, earlier espionage and national security investigations including the Aldrich Ames and Felix Bloch cases.
B) FBI agents investigated Hanssen's activities, and he is charged with espionage and conspiracy to commit espionage.
C) Hanssen sold classified information to KGB agents in return for cash and diamonds.
D) Hanssen's motivation for his unlawful actions is not explicitly stated in the affidavit, but since diamonds and cash were his payment, it can be assumed greed was his motivation.

CONTINUE

Questions 12–22 are based on the following passage.

What Are Proteins and What Do They Do?

Proteins are large, complex molecules that play many critical roles in the body. They do most of the work in cells and are required for the structure, **12** functioning, and regulation of the body's tissues and organs.

Proteins **13** are made within hundreds or thousands of smaller units called amino acids, which are attached to one another in long chains. There are 20 different types of amino acids that can be combined to make a protein. The sequence of amino acids determines each protein's unique 3-dimensional structure and its specific function.

Proteins can be described according to their large range of functions in the body, including the **14** following: antibodies, enzymes, messengers, structural components, and transport and storage.

How Do Genes Direct the Production of Proteins?

Most genes contain the information needed to make **15** functional molecules called proteins. (A few genes produce other molecules that help the cell assemble proteins.) The journey from gene to protein is complex and tightly controlled within each cell. It consists of two major steps: transcription and translation. **16** However, transcription and translation are known as gene expression.

12
A) NO CHANGE
B) function, and regulating
C) to function, and regulation
D) function, and regulation

13
A) NO CHANGE
B) is made within
C) is made up of
D) are made up of

14
A) NO CHANGE
B) following;
C) following—
D) following,

15
A) NO CHANGE
B) amazing
C) ultra-practical
D) employable

16
A) NO CHANGE
B) Therefore,
C) Together,
D) In the same way,

CONTINUE ➡

During the process of transcription, the information stored in a gene's DNA is transferred to a similar molecule called RNA (ribonucleic acid) in the cell nucleus. Both RNA and DNA are made up of a chain of nucleotide [17] bases but it has slightly different chemical properties. The type of RNA that contains the information for making a protein is called messenger RNA (mRNA) because it carries the information, or message, from the DNA out of the nucleus into the cytoplasm. An example of mRNA that is used for [18] protecting the body is ferritin.

Examples of Protein Functions

Function	Description	Example
Antibody	Antibodies bind to specific foreign particles, such as viruses and bacteria, to help protect the body.	Immunoglobulin G (IgG)
Enzyme	Enzymes carry out almost all of the thousands of chemical reactions that take place in cells. They also assist with the formation of new molecules by reading the genetic information stored in DNA.	Phenylalanine hydroxylase
Messenger	Messenger proteins, such as some types of hormones, transmit signals to coordinate biological processes between different cells, tissues, and organs.	Growth hormone
Structural component	These proteins provide structure and support for cells. On a larger scale, they also allow the body to move.	Actin
Transport/ storage	These proteins bind and carry atoms and small molecules within cells and throughout the body.	Ferritin

[17]
A) NO CHANGE
B) bases, but it has
C) bases, but they have
D) bases but they have

[18]
Which choice completes the sentence with accurate data based on the table?
A) NO CHANGE
B) providing structure and support is the growth hormone.
C) storage and transportation is actin.
D) storage and transportation is ferritin.

[19] Translation takes place in the cytoplasm. [20] The mRNA interacts with a specialized complex called a ribosome. The ribosome "reads" the sequence of mRNA bases. Each sequence of three bases, called a codon, usually [21] codes for one particular amino acid. (Amino acids are the building blocks of proteins.) A type of RNA called transfer RNA (tRNA) assembles the protein, one amino acid at a time. Protein assembly continues until the ribosome encounters a "stop" codon—a sequence of three bases that does not code for an amino acid.

The flow of information from DNA to RNA to proteins is one of the fundamental [22] principals by molecular biology. It is so important that it is sometimes called the "central dogma."

19

Which choice best connects the sentence with the previous paragraph?
A) NO CHANGE
B) Translation, the second step in getting from a gene to a protein,
C) Moving onward, translation
D) Being done with transcription,

20

Which choice most effectively combines the underlined sentences?
A) The mRNA interacts with a specialized complex called a ribosome and "reads" the sequence of bases.
B) The mRNA interacts with a specialized complex called a ribosome, which "reads" the sequence of mRNA bases.
C) "Reading" the sequence of mRNA bases, a specialized complex called a ribosome interacts with the mRNA.
D) Interacting with a specialized complex, the mRNA "reads" the ribosome.

21

A) NO CHANGE
B) code for one particular amino acid.
C) codes for one particular amino acids.
D) code for one particular amino acids.

22

A) NO CHANGE
B) principals of
C) principles with
D) principles of

CONTINUE ➡

Questions 23–33 are based on the following passage.

A New Orleans Jazz History, 1895–1927

Even before jazz, for most New Orleanians, music was not a luxury as it often is elsewhere–it was a necessity. Throughout the nineteenth century, diverse ethnic and racial **23** groups; French, Spanish, African, Italian, German, and Irish found common cause in **24** they're love of music. The 1870s represented the culmination of a century of music making in the Crescent City. During this time, the European classical legacy and the influence of European folk and African/Caribbean elements were merged with a popular American mainstream, which combined and adapted Old World practices into new forms deriving from a distinctive regional environment. Just after the beginning of the new century, jazz began to emerge as part of a broad musical revolution encompassing ragtime, **25** blues spirituals, marches, and the popular fare of "Tin Pan Alley." It also reflected the profound contributions of people of African heritage to this new and distinctly American music.

23
A) NO CHANGE
B) groups French, Spanish, African, Italian, German, and Irish found
C) groups—French, Spanish, African, Italian, German, and Irish—found
D) groups, French, Spanish, African, Italian, German, and Irish found

24
A) NO CHANGE
B) theirs
C) there
D) their

25
A) NO CHANGE
B) blues, spirituals, marches,
C) blues, spirituals marches,
D) blues spirituals marches

CONTINUE

The early development of jazz in New Orleans is most associated with the popularity of bandleader Charles "Buddy" **26** Bolden. He was an "uptown" cornetist whose charisma and musical power became legendary. After playing briefly with Charley Galloway's string band in 1894, Bolden formed his own group in 1895. During the next decade, he built a loyal following, entertaining dancers throughout the city. . . . In 1906 he **27** totally passed out while performing in a street parade. The following year he was institutionalized at the state sanitarium at Jackson for the remainder **28** of his life until he passed away.

26

Which choice most effectively combines the sentences at the underlined portion?

A) Bolden, but he became an
B) Bolden, an
C) Bolden; from which he was known as an
D) Bolden, who was an

27

A) NO CHANGE
B) buckled
C) gave way
D) collapsed

28

A) NO CHANGE
B) of the rest of his life
C) of his life
D) of what was left of his life

CONTINUE

Dancing had long been a mainstay of New Orleans **29** nightlife, and Boldens popularity was based on his ability to give dancers what they wanted. During the nineteenth century, string bands, led by violinists, had dominated dance work, offering waltzes, quadrilles, polkas, and schottisches to a polite dancing public. By the turn of the century, an instrumentation borrowing from both brass marching bands and string bands was **30** predominant; usually a front line of cornet, clarinet, and trombone with a rhythm section of guitar, bass, and drums. Dance audiences, especially the younger ones, wanted more excitement. The emergence of ragtime, blues and later, jazz satisfied this demand. **31** Increasingly, musicians began to redefine roles, moving away from sight-reading toward playing by ear, and Bolden's band, along with Jack Laine's Reliance and the Golden Rule, worked out their numbers by practicing until parts were memorized. Each member could offer suggestions for enhancing a piece of music, subject to the approval of the leader. Gradually, New Orleans jazzmen became known for a style of blending improvised parts—sometimes referred to as "collective improvisation." It appealed to younger players and dancers alike because it permitted greater freedom of expression, spontaneity, and **32** discipline. **33**

29
A) NO CHANGE
B) nightlife, and Bolden's
C) nightlife and Bolden's
D) nightlife and Boldens'

30
A) NO CHANGE
B) predominant: usually
C) predominant. Usually
D) predominant and usually

31
A) NO CHANGE
B) In addition,
C) On the other hand,
D) Likewise,

32
The writer wants to complete the sentence with a third example of why "collective improvisation" appealed to younger audiences. Which choice best accomplishes this goal?
A) NO CHANGE
B) efficiency.
C) innovation.
D) regularity.

33
The writer wants to conclude the passage with a sentence that emphasizes the enduring legacy of New Orleans jazz. Which choice would best accomplish this goal?
A) Jazz continues to be a popular genre of music even today, and New Orleans has developed a reputation for good jazz.
B) True New Orleans jazz incorporates improvisation and playing by ear, which encourages greater freedom of expression.
C) Many jazz musicians got their start in the New Orleans jazz scene and went on to become famous across the country and around the world.
D) New Orleans jazz remained a fertile ground for creative musicians of diverse backgrounds throughout the twentieth century and even today.

CONTINUE

Questions 34–44 are based on the following passage and table.

A Time to Work: Recent Trends in Shift Work and Flexible Schedules

34 However, an examination of data from the Work Schedules and Work at Home survey reveals that substantial proportions of workers' schedules do not fit this paradigm. **35** Consequently, nearly one-third of wage and salary workers have flexible schedules on their primary jobs, meaning that they can vary their beginning and ending hours. About one-fifth work a shift other than a regular daytime shift on their primary **36** job and a slightly smaller proportion works on Saturday, Sunday, or both. The use of alternate shifts and flexible work schedules is often determined by the demands of the industry, rather than by workers' preferences. However, schedule considerations and flexibility are influential factors in the career-planning and labor market decisions of many workers.

The data presented in this article pertain to work schedules and alternate shifts. Because of the high prevalence of both shift work and flextime among part-time workers, the article analyzes total **37** employment, which include that of both full- and part-time workers in most cases. (Where appropriate, data are analyzed separately for part-time **38** workers for further information about the survey, see the appendix.)

34

The author wants to add a sentence immediately before the sentence beginning with "However." Which choice most effectively begins the paragraph?

A) The traditional work schedule for an American employee has long been 9 a.m. to 5 p.m., Monday through Friday.

B) American workers typically work more hours per week than European workers, and they earn and use fewer vacation days as well.

C) Working from home is only possible in certain careers, such as artists, writers, software engineers, and so on.

D) Many workers have little or no influence over their work schedule; instead, their hours are determined by other factors.

35

A) NO CHANGE
B) Therefore,
C) Nevertheless,
D) For instance,

36

A) NO CHANGE
B) job, and a slightly smaller proportion work
C) job; and a slightly smaller proportion work
D) job, and a slightly smaller proportion works

37

A) NO CHANGE
B) employment and which include
C) employment, including
D) employment, and including

38

A) NO CHANGE
B) workers; for
C) workers, for
D) workers: for

CONTINUE

Flexible work schedules

[1] In 2004, 36.4 million wage and salary workers, or about 30 percent of all such workers, were able to vary their work hours to some degree. [2] This percentage was somewhat **39** higher than that (30.7 percent) in 2001, but lower than in 1997. [3] Such flexibility provides workers with increased control over their time. **40** [4] In a competitive labor market, companies can choose to offer their workers the freedom afforded by flexible schedules in order to improve both morale and loyalty to the company.

The proportion of workers able to vary their work hours rose from 1985 to 1997, **41** but has remained fairly steady thereafter. The following tabulation shows the percentage of wage and salary workers with flexible schedules, by sex and the presence of their own children, for selected years over the past two decades:

Percentage of Wage and Salary Workers with Flexible Schedules

	1985	1991	1997	2001	2004
Totals, workers 16 years and older	13.6	16.0	29.9	30.7	29.6
Men	13.9	15.9	30.0	30.8	29.3
Men, with own children under 18 years	13.1	15.6	30.7	31.8	29.8
Women	13.2	16.02	9.7	30.6	29.9
Women, with own children under 18 years	13.3	16.3	30.8	30.7	30.2

39

Which choice completes the sentence with accurate data based on the "Totals, workers 16 and older" row of the table?

A) NO CHANGE

B) higher than that (30.7 percent) in May 2001, but was dramatically lower than that in May 1997.

C) lower than that (30.7 percent) in May 2001, and substantially lower than in May 1997.

D) lower than that (30.7 percent) in May 2001, but about the same as in May 1997.

40

To make this paragraph most logical, sentence 4 should be placed

A) where it is now.

B) before sentence 1.

C) after sentence 1.

D) after sentence 2.

41

Which choice completes the sentence with accurate data based on the table?

A) NO CHANGE

B) and continued to rise thereafter.

C) but then has dropped rapidly.

D) and peaked in 2004.

CONTINUE ➡

Since 1985, the proportions of employed men and women able to vary **42** there work hours have been about equal. The same is true of both mothers **43** and fathers whom work. Within each of these groups, the proportion of workers able to vary the times they started and ended work more than doubled between 1985 and 1997, after which **44** they have remained at about that level.

42

A) NO CHANGE
B) they're work hours has
C) their work hours have
D) their work hours has

43

A) NO CHANGE
B) and fathers who work.
C) and fathers, who work.
D) and father whom works.

44

A) NO CHANGE
B) they remained
C) it has remained
D) it have remained

STOP

**If you finish before time is called, you may check your work on this section only.
Do not turn to any other section.**

SAT Model Exam 1 Answer Key

Reading Test Answers with Explanations

1. **C** The central idea of the passage is about the pressure families felt to provide for a daughter through a beneficial marriage. This is mentioned by the narrator in the opening line, and it is the subject of the conversation between Mr. and Mrs. Bennet. Choice D is not supported by the passage. Choices A and B are true according to the passage, but they are minor details.

2. **D** The opening sentence reveals a "truth universally acknowledged." This fits with choice D, "social convention." The Bennets' conversation is about Mrs. Bennet's desire to meet Mr. Bingley, the new neighbor, with the goal of his marrying one of her daughters. Choice A is wrong because the dialogue is not a contrast. The sarcastic tone denies that the narrator believes he is stating a principle to live by (choice B). There is no evidence for choice C.

3. **A** The tone of these lines is meant to be humorous. The author uses exaggeration when suggesting that it is "universally acknowledged" that a man must want a wife, and she jokes that although the man may not know this, everyone else does. Choice C is incorrect because these lines are not aggressive—they are much lighter than that. Choice D is incorrect because the narrator is not "unreliable" as the conversation between the Bennets indicates. Choice B is incorrect because the voice is not humble. The narrator seems to have more knowledge than general society—almost in a position above society.

4. **B** The phrase refers to how families viewed rich single men as rightful property. This implies that they saw marriage not as a union for love, but a means to gain social standing and security. Choice A is not true. No mention is made to marriage laws, so choice C is not correct. The passage makes no mention of women's rights in marriage, choice D.

5. **B** Mrs. Bennet speaks with overt confidence in her knowledge about the subject of finding a man for one of her daughters. She is impatient with Mr. Bennet's supposed lack of knowledge on the subject (line 37) and she says, "how can you be so tiresome" (lines 38–39) to his ignorance about how a rich man could benefit his daughters. Choice A is incorrect because it is too negative. Mrs. Bennet does not appear to dislike Mr. Bennet. Choice D is too extreme: she has confidence but isn't showing a vast superiority. Choice C is incorrect because Mrs. Bennet is very passionate about her husband's opinions, which she believes to be incorrect.

6. **D** In these lines, Mrs. Bennet indicates that she is more knowledgeable about making appropriate marriages for her daughters.

7. **D** Choice D is the best answer because throughout the passage, Mrs. Bennet talks about how they will get the newcomer to marry one of her daughters. Choice A is incorrect because it is more likely that Mrs. Bennet admires the wealth that allowed him to travel this way—not that she thinks him pretentious. Choice B is incorrect because Mrs. Bennet is interested in him, but she does not suggest any opinion about his family. Choice C is incorrect because most of what Mrs. Bennet talks about is the financial security and accomplishment of marrying off a daughter; she does not seem as concerned about happiness.

8. **B** Mrs. Bennet is very preoccupied with the proper etiquette and how her actions will be perceived (lines 58–66) "But my dear, you must…neighborhood" and "But consider your daughters…if you do not." Choices C and D are incorrect because there is no evidence that Mrs. Bennet is being overly critical or honest to a fault. While it could be argued that she is obsessed with details about the right way to be introduced to someone, choice B more clearly states the definition.

9. **C** In these lines, Mrs. Bennet explains the social conventions of the time, mostly that a man had to call upon

another man before his family could. She is very concerned ("over-scrupulous") about proper etiquette.

10. **B** Mr. Bennet is poking fun at Mrs. Bennet by saying that he is quite familiar with her "poor nerves," joking that they are his "old friends." He is being sarcastic, but not in a mean-spirited way. Choices A, C, and D are incorrect because there is not evidence for these choices or they are too negative.

11. **D** Choice D is the best answer because the author discusses the process of achieving a real sense of sight. Choices A and B are incorrect because they state the opposite of what the passage shows. Choice C is incorrect because the passage says that patients of all ages were studied.

12. **B** Choice B reveals that a newly sighted person has to go through the same long process a baby does. Choices A, C, and D are incorrect because they do not show the long process of achieving sight.

13. **B** The doctor writes about the "narrow limits" that the patient would have gotten to know with the "aid of touch." "Comprehended" means understood. Choices A, C, and D are incorrect because the definitions of these words do not work in the context of the sentence.

14. **D** Lines 52-67 ("But it is the patients' concepts of space . . . even though it is not directly seen") show the challenging process of mastering the concept of space. Choices A, B, and C are incorrect because they do not directly deal with the discussion of a person's concept of space.

15. **A** The concept of space is explained in these sentences: "The vast majority of patients, of both sexes and all ages, had, in von Senden's opinion, no idea of space whatsoever. Form, distance, and size were so many meaningless syllables."

16. **D** A survey of the passage reveals that von Senden supports his claim by sharing examples from patients who had undergone the surgery, not complex data (choice A) or general statements about sight and space (choice C). There is one example that involves a patient and her mother, but most of the support comes from examples of patients who couldn't perceive space after their sight was restored.

17. **D** The passage compares the long process of adjustment for the newly sighted to that of a baby. Therefore, we can assume that a baby takes a while to learn to differentiate objects. Choice B is incorrect because it is the opposite of the correct answer. Choices A and C are incorrect because the passage does not provide evidence from which they can be inferred.

18. **C** Lines 15-23 ("Before the operation . . . as a square shape") show the use of touch. Choices A, B, and D are incorrect because there is no mention of these ideas in the passage.

19. **A** Lines 18-24 discuss the use of touch. Choices B, C, and D are incorrect because there is no mention of touch in any of those lines.

20. **C** Each paragraph of the passage provides detailed explanations of how the newly sighted adapt. Choice D is incorrect because the passage is factual and not written to inspire compassion but to inform. Choices A and B are incorrect because the author does not use persuasive techniques.

21. **B** The passage refers to the patient bumping into the color patches and the patches resisting him, which is how tactual, or touchable, objects would be described. Choices A, C, and D are incorrect because the sentence doesn't provide context for these definitions.

22. **C** Based upon the explanation of the Anthropocene as "the age of us" and the reference in lines 7–8 to "the age of humans," the best answer is choice C. Disagreement is correct in this context. Choice A is incorrect

because according to Chart 1, the Holocene and Pleistocene eras both came before the Anthropocene era. Choice B incorrectly references the year 1492, which was the year Europeans arrived in the Americas, not when a golden spike occurred. Choice D is technically correct but not specific enough to be the best answer.

23. **B** Paragraph 3 states that Lewis and Maslin "point to the year 1610, marked by, of all things, a sharp but brief dip in carbon dioxide" (lines 14–16). Choices A, C, and D are incorrect because these time periods are not associated with Lewis and Maslin's theory.

24. **C** These lines state that Lewis and Maslin point to 1610 and a drop in carbon dioxide concentrations as their central claim.

25. **C** Based upon lines 30–38, an epoch requires "Long-lasting changes to the Earth" that can be documented and a marker of a global environmental change captured in natural material. This marker is called "a golden spike." Choice D is incorrect because the passage does not mention the expansion of the polar ice sheets. Choice A is incorrect because the passage doesn't discuss a substantial rise in temperatures. Choice B is incorrect because although the passage does mention a meteorite strike and the capturing of natural materials, these are examples, not the actual criteria.

26. **D** The passage discusses what happened when two civilizations (the Natives and the Europeans) encountered each other: "European-carried diseases killed off tens of millions of inhabitants of the 'New' World" (lines 20–22). The peoples of the Americas "collapsed" under these new conditions. Choice A is incorrect because "bankruptcy" has to do with failing financially. Choice B is incorrect because the destruction was not caused by the Natives themselves. Choice C is incorrect because "collision" has to do with groups running into each other, which is not a strong enough meaning for the context.

27. **C** The authors cite the example of the fossil of maize to indicate how the 1610 date "satisfies the first criteria for dating an epoch—long-term changes to Earth."

28. **A** Choice A is the best choice based upon two ideas in the text. First, the passage indicates that the dip in carbon dioxide concentrations in 1610 was revealed in "ice cores." The passage also states that one of the criteria of an epoch is that "Scientists must also pinpoint and date a global environmental change that has been captured in natural material, such as rocks, ancient ice or sediment from the ocean floor." It can be inferred that unusual carbon dioxide changes can be documented in natural materials. Choice B is incorrect because of the word "never." Although scientists do not currently agree, it cannot be inferred that they never will. Choice C is incorrect because the text says that "scientists and scholars question whether it's hubris to think a geological epoch, as strictly defined, can result from human activity." Choice D doesn't make sense because scientists didn't have the knowledge to record carbon dioxide levels at that time, but modern scientists can look at the natural records in rocks and sediment and identify these fluctuations in carbon dioxide levels.

29. **B** Choice B supports the idea that carbon dioxide levels can be seen in natural materials. Chart 2 also indicates that radioisotopes left a permanent signature in sediments.

30. **B** Lewis and Maslin's claim is that the Anthropocene began in 1610 with a sharp dip in carbon dioxide. Chart 1 indicates this with the solid line.

31. **B** The text discusses a "global environmental change that has been captured in natural material" (lines 33–34) and the caption of Chart 2 states that "traces of radioisotopes from atomic bomb testing (dotted line) spread around the world, leaving a permanent signature in sediments." The Chart shows this spike with the dotted line.

32. **B** From the context, "emerging markets" are in contrast to the "rich world" and "developed countries" where women have already won rights in the workplace. This supports choice B as the best answer. Although "poor" may seem to be correct, it is not the best answer. Choice C doesn't make sense. No support is given for choice D.

33. **D** On Chart 1, the symbols for female workers (about 30%) and male workers (about 80%) are the farthest apart for India. Choices A, B, and C are incorrect because the gaps between female and male workers in these countries are smaller.

34. **A** Choice B is true, but it doesn't support the claim, since it is about how women's arrival in the workforce caused a revolution. Choice C is irrelevant to the claim. Choice D is true according to the chart. However, the sharpest increase was during the 1970s, which provides strong evidence for the claim.

35. **B** Using chronological order shows the historical progression, which is why the author used this structure. Choices A, C, and D are incorrect because although they may be true, they do not answer the question about the purpose of the chronological structure.

36. **C** The sentences after the one with the word "boon" discuss many benefits of having women in the workforce. Choices A, B, and D are incorrect because these words do not make sense in the context of the paragraph.

37. **B** In the lines following lines 56–62 ("National economies…flexible than men."), the author discusses the benefits of dual-income couples. Choices A, C, and D are incorrect because the passage does not offer evidence to support these choices.

38. **D** This idea is NOT mentioned in the passage. The question asks you to find the three choices that are mentioned in the passage as support for line 55 and then select one that is not mentioned as a benefit of having women in the workforce. Choices A, B, and C are incorrect because all of these ideas are mentioned as benefits of having women in the workforce.

39. **A** The passage states that "despite equal-pay legislation," female employees are often cheaper than male employees. Therefore, it can be inferred the laws to enact equal pay for women have not succeeded. Choices B, C, and D are incorrect because the passage does not provide information from which these ideas could be inferred. In particular, Choice B and Choice D state the opposite of what the passage claims.

40. **C** Choice C is supported by lines 66–77. Choices A and B are not supported by the text. Although the text says that gains have been made in the areas of legal, political, and economic equality, it does not indicate that women have achieved total equality with men in these areas.

41. **C** Choice C best supports the inference above.

42. **C** Section 2 describes the process by which the number of Representatives will be determined. Choice A is incorrect because there is no mention of electing the President in Section 2. Choice D is incorrect because Section 2 does not explain electing members of the Senate. Choice B is incorrect because although there is one mention of impeachment in Section 2, it is not the main topic.

43. **A** This line discusses the qualifications required for electors. The next lines go on to describe these qualifications, so in this context, "essential" makes the most sense. Choice B is incorrect because there is no mention of voting upon qualifications. Choice D is incorrect because "developed" does not make sense in this context. Choice C is incorrect because the qualifications are more than suggested—they are required.

44. **B** The text mentions "free Persons" and then "those bound to Service," which must mean slaves, or in this case, indentured servants. Choice D is incorrect because these lines do not have to do with the unemployed. Choice C is incorrect because these lines discuss the number of citizens that will determine the Representatives; the Representatives cannot be those "bound to service." Choice A is incorrect because although Indians are mentioned next, they are not included in the category of "those bound to Service."

45. **C** Choice C is the best answer because lines 31–32 state that "The actual Enumeration shall be made within three Years" after the meeting of Congress. Choices A, B, and D are incorrect because the passage does not mention any of these topics.

46. **A** The lines establish that states will have one Representative for every thirty thousand persons.

47. **B** The opening sentence says that the Constitution is established "in Order to." It is explaining the purpose of the document. The Articles detail how the government will be set up and structured.

48. **A** The opening paragraph of Passage 1 outlines its goals to "establish Justice, insure domestic Tranquility, provide for the common defence." Throughout Passage 2, there is an emphasis on justice, rights, and peace. Choice D is only mentioned in Passage 2, not in Passage 1. Choice B is incorrect because although there is a mention of defense, neither passage discusses creating an armed force. Choice C is incorrect because although this is mentioned by both passages, Choice A better encompasses the overall emphasis of both passages.

49. **C** Choice C is the best answer because this line focuses on peace. Choice A is incorrect because this line focuses on liberty, not peace. Choice B is incorrect because it focuses on providing for defense. Although this is related to peace, Choice C is the better answer. Choice D focuses on social progress and freedom.

50. **B** Choice B is the best answer because Passage 1 is about the United States, whereas Passage 2 is about human rights, international law, and friendly relations among nations, which suggests the general welfare of all people. Choice C is incorrect because Passage 2 does not discuss raising an army made up of citizens of all nations. Choice D is incorrect because Passage 2 focuses on all nations, not just the U.S. Choice A is incorrect because although Passage 2 does discuss economic issues, it does not mention "monetary agreements between nations."

51. **C** Choice C is the best answer because these lines suggest that armed forces shouldn't be used unless needed for the "common interest," which supports the idea of the "possible" use of force. Choices B and D are incorrect because these lines do not explicitly discuss the use of force. Choice A is incorrect because although these lines mention saving future generations from "the scourge of war," they do not mention using force to prevent war.

52. **B** These words emphasize unity and cooperation among all the countries involved. Although the other choices are true according to the charter, the words mentioned focus on unity.

Writing and Language Test Answers with Explanations

1. **B** The clause "that a veteran . . ." is essential to the meaning of the sentence. A comma is not needed after "today." Choices A and C are incorrect because they each contain an unnecessary comma or commas. Choice D is incorrect because it contains an unnecessary comma after "Agent."

2. **C** "Clandestinely" is a more accurate word to describe the actions of the accused spy. Choices A, B, and D are incorrect because these words do not effectively communicate the secrecy with which Hanssen would be leaving a package with classified information for the Russians.

3. **B** Commas are needed to offset the nonrestrictive prepositional phrase "if proven." Changing "if" to "when" (choices C and D) changes the meaning of the sentence to imply that the accused is already guilty.

4. **A** The current answer correctly uses an apostrophe to show possession. The security belongs to the nation. Choices B and D are incorrect because they place the apostrophe after "nations," making it a plural possessive (suggesting more than one nation). Choice C is incorrect because it deletes the comma after "security," which is needed to complete the nonrestrictive clause.

5. **B** This provides the grammatically standard preposition "at" for the phrase: "strikes at the heart." Choices A and C are incorrect because they use the wrong preposition. Choice C also does not use correct subject-verb agreement ("it strike"). Choice D is incorrect because it uses the wrong verb tense: the rest of the paragraph is written in present tense, but "struck" is in past tense.

6. **C** Since the relative clause "who conducted this investigation" is restrictive, no commas are needed around it. Choice A is incorrect. Choice B incorrectly changes the subordinate clause into a question. Choice D uses "conducts," which is an incorrect verb tense (present instead of past).

7. **B** Choice B correctly fixes the comma splice. Two independent clauses cannot be connected with a comma. Choices A and C are comma splices. Choice D incorrectly uses a colon.

8. **D** Choice D contains the correct verb form for the subject: "a detailed affidavit provides a troubling account of . . . ." Choice B uses the incorrect preposition "for." Choice C contains the wrong verb form ("provide") and incorrectly uses the preposition "with." Choice A is incorrect because it contains a mistake in subject-verb agreement: "a detailed affidavit provide . . . ."

9. **D** This choice provides the most concise language. Choices A, B, and C are incorrect because they contain redundant language ("first," "initially," and "beginning" all have similar meanings).

10. **A** Choice A is correct because the sentence provides details that do not relate to the paragraph's topic. Choice B is incorrect because it does not provide the most accurate reason for deleting the sentence. Choices C and D are incorrect because they inaccurately describe the sentence in question, which should be deleted.

11. **A** This choice provides the most relevant way to add a concluding sentence that shows the scope of Hanssen's actions. Choices B, C, and D are incorrect because they do not conclude the paragraph by showing the scope of Hanssen's actions.

12. **D** The noun "function" properly maintains the parallel structure of the sentence that contains the nouns "structure" and "regulation." Choices A, B, and C are incorrect because they do not maintain parallel structure.

13. **D** This choice uses the correct verb "are" to agree with "proteins" and provides the grammatically standard preposition "up of" for the phrase "made up of." Choices A, B, and C are incorrect because they use the verb "is," which does not agree with "proteins," and/or they do not use the correct preposition.

14. **A** A colon is needed to introduce a list, especially when the list is introduced with the words "the following."

15. **A** "Functional" is the best choice for the meaning and tone of the passage. Choice B is too vague and informal. Choice C seems too superlative for the context. "Employable" seems less applicable to the subject matter.

16. **C** Choice C, "Together," provides the best transition between the two sentences because the second sentence provides a continuation of previous ideas.

17. **C** Choice C correctly uses a comma before the conjunction "but" to join two independent clauses. Choices A and D do not. Choices A and B also contain a pronoun antecedent error. "They" is the correct pronoun to refer to the antecedent "RNA and DNA."

18. **D** According to the table, ferritin is used for storage and transportation. Choices A, B, and C are incorrect

because they do not contain accurate information based on the chart.

19. B This phrase effectively introduces the second step in the process. Choice A offers no transition. Choices C and D provide mostly ineffective transitional phrases.

20. B This choice correctly and effectively subordinates the description of how the ribosome "reads" the mRNA bases. Choice A incorrectly states that the mRNA "reads" the bases. Choice C places the emphasis upon the ribosome instead of the mRNA, causing confusion. Choice D incorrectly states that the mRNA "reads" the ribosome.

21. A The sentence is correct as is. The verb "codes" agrees with the subject "sequence." Also, the noun "acid" fits with the adjective "one."

22. D The word "principles" means "fundamental truths." Choice D also provides the grammatically standard preposition "of" for the phrase "principles of." Choices A, B, and C are incorrect because they either use the wrong word, "principals," which refers to the leaders of schools, or the choices do not provide the correct preposition.

23. C It provides the correct use of dashes to offset the list of items. Choice A is incorrect because a semicolon can only be used between two independent clauses. Choices B and D are incorrect because the list of groups is not correctly punctuated.

24. D "Their" is the proper possessive pronoun. Choice A is incorrect because "they're" is the contraction for "they are." Choice B is incorrect because it is the wrong form of the possessive pronoun. Choice C is incorrect because "there" is an adverb meaning "in, at, or to that place or position."

25. B This choice provides the correct use of commas in a list of items. Choices A, C, and D are incorrect because they do not provide the proper use of commas for a list.

26. B Choice B correctly and concisely combines the two sentences while maintaining the original meaning. Choices A, C, and D are incorrect because they are either unnecessarily wordy or are not grammatically correct.

27. D "Collapsed" is the only choice that accurately describes what happened to Bolden. Choice A is too informal for the tone of the passage. Choices B and C do not convey the exact meaning of what happened to Bolden.

28. C Choice C uses the most concise language. Choices A, B, and D are incorrect because they contain redundant language ("remainder," "rest of," and "what was left" all have similar meanings).

29. B Choice B correctly provides an apostrophe for possession: "Bolden's popularity." Choice A lacks the apostrophe. Choices C and D do not provide the comma after "nightlife," which is necessary for punctuating a compound sentence. Choice D also places the apostrophe in the wrong place.

30. B This choice provides a colon to introduce an explanation. Choice A is incorrect because a semicolon cannot be used to introduce a list; it can only be used to punctuate two independent clauses. Choices C and D are incorrect because they create fragments.

31. A Choice A provides the transition, "Increasingly," to accurately represent the relationship between the two sentences. The sentences present the idea that ragtime met the demand for more excitement and that more and more, musicians began to play differently. Choices B, C, and D are incorrect because each provides a transition that does not accurately represent the relationships between the sentences.

32. **C** "Innovation" is more in keeping with the other words in the sentence: "freedom" and "spontaneity." Choices A, B, and D are incorrect because they do not provide examples that support the idea that "collective improvisation" appealed to younger audiences by introducing more creative forms of music.

33. **D** Choice D provides evidence that New Orleans jazz had a lasting effect. Choices A, B, and C do not effectively illustrate the "enduring legacy of New Orleans jazz."

34. **A** This sentence works effectively by introducing ideas that lead into the next sentence, "However, an examination of data . . . ." Choices B, C, and D are incorrect because they do not effectively begin the paragraph in a way that is relevant to the rest of the paragraph.

35. **D** The transition "for instance" accurately introduces the example that follows. Choices A, B, and C do not accurately represent the relationship between the sentences.

36. **D** A comma is needed before the conjunction "and," and the verb "works" is needed to agree with "proportion." Choice D is correct.

37. **C** Choice C is the best answer because it provides correct wording for the phrase at the end of the sentence. Choice A does not use the proper verb form. It would need to say "which includes." Choice B adds the unnecessary word "and" and is not grammatically correct. Choice D is incorrect because "and including" is redundant.

38. **B** Choice B correctly punctuates the two independent clauses by separating them with a semicolon. Choices A, C, and D do not provide correct punctuation to connect two independent clauses, thereby creating run-on sentences or comma splices.

39. **D** According to the row labeled "Totals, workers 16 and older," the percentage in question (30%, mentioned in line 2) is lower than the percentage of 30.7 in May 2001. In May 1997, the percentage was 29.9, which is about the same as 30 percent. Choices A, B, and C do not accurately represent the information presented in the table.

40. **A** Choice A is the best answer because in its current location, sentence 4 effectively closes the paragraph by summing up the results of offering flexible schedules. Choices B, C, and D are incorrect because each would result in an illogical progression of ideas.

41. **A** The table indicates that in 2001 and 2004, the percentages mostly remained in the upper 20's and lower 30's. Therefore, they remained fairly steady. Choices B, C, and D are incorrect because the table does not support them.

42. **C** "Their" is the correct possessive pronoun to replace the nouns "men and women." Choice A is incorrect because "there" is an adverb meaning "in, at, or to that place or position." Choice B is incorrect because "they're" is the contraction for "they are" and because this choice contains incorrect subject-verb agreement ("hours has"). Choice D is incorrect because it also contains incorrect subject-verb agreement ("hours has").

43. **B** "Who" is a subjective pronoun. In this sentence, the mothers and the fathers are subjects and therefore require subjective pronouns. Choice A is incorrect; "who" is the subject form needed with the verb "work." Choice C contains an unnecessary comma. Choice D contains the singular form "father" and uses the objective pronoun "whom."

44. **C** The pronoun "it" refers to the singular noun "proportion." Choices A and B incorrectly use the plural pronoun "they" to refer to the singular noun "proportion." Choice D uses an incorrect verb form: "have."

SAT Model Exam 1 Correlation Charts

Use the following charts to identify which lessons in the book will help you improve your score.

If you missed these questions on the Reading Test . . .	study this lesson. (Because some questions test over multiple skills, some numbers may appear under more than one lesson.)
	Closely Reading Literature
1, 7	Lesson 1: Understanding explicit and implicit ideas (p. 57)
1, 2	Lesson 1: Understanding main ideas and purpose (p. 65)
10	Lesson 1: Analyzing word choice and imagery for tone (p. 74)
5, 8	Lesson 1: Identifying characterization (p. 85)
3	Lesson 1: Identifying narrator's point of view (p. 92)
6, 9	Lesson 1: Citing textual evidence (p. 99)
	Literature and Informational Texts
4, 8, 13, 21, 22, 26, 32, 36, 43, 44	Lesson 2: Understanding meanings of words and phrases (p. 107)
	Closely Reading Informational Texts
15	Lesson 3: Understanding explicit meanings (p. 115)
22, 25, 42	Lesson 3: Determining central ideas and summarizing (p. 121)
18, 45	Lesson 3: Identifying supporting details (p. 127)
11, 14, 17, 28, 39, 46	Lesson 4: Making inferences (p. 137)
40	Lesson 4: Using analogical reasoning (p. 146)
12, 19, 24, 29, 38, 41, 49, 51	Lesson 4: Citing textual evidence (p. 152)
20, 42	Lesson 5: Analyzing author's point of view and purpose (p. 159)
16, 23, 27, 30, 31, 37	Lesson 5: Analyzing the use of arguments (claims, counterclaims, reasoning, and evidence) (p. 168)
52	Lesson 6: Analyzing use of word choice to shape meaning and tone (p. 177)
35, 47	Lesson 6: Analyzing text structures (p. 184)
34, 48, 50	Lesson 7: Synthesizing information from multiple texts (p. 193)
30, 31, 33, 34	Lesson 7: Analyzing and synthesizing information from graphic organizers and texts (p. 204)

If you missed these questions on the Writing and Language Test . . .	study this lesson. (Because some questions test over multiple skills, some numbers may appear under more than one lesson.)
	Writing and Language
10, 11, 32, 33	Lesson 8: Revising texts for clarity, focus, and purpose (p. 243)
18, 39, 41	Lesson 8: Relating information presented in graphs, charts, and tables to information presented in texts (p. 252)
40	Lesson 9: Revising for cohesion and logical order (p. 261)
16, 19, 31, 34, 35	Lesson 9: Revising beginnings or endings of a text or paragraphs to ensure transitional words, phrases, and sentences are used effectively (p. 267)
2, 3, 5, 8, 13, 15, 22	Lesson 10: Revising texts to improve word choice for exactness and content (p. 275)
9, 20, 26, 28	Lesson 10: Revising to eliminate wordiness (p. 279)
27	Lesson 10: Revising text for consistency of style and tone or to match style and tone to purpose (p. 288)
7, 38	Lesson 11: Editing to correct sentence fragments and run-ons (p. 295)
20	Lesson 11: Combining sentences for clarity (p. 304)
12, 37	Lesson 11: Editing to correct problems with subordination/coordination, parallel structure, and modifier placement (p. 306)
5, 6, 44	Lesson 11: Editing to correct shifts in verbs (tense, voice, and mood) and pronouns (person and number) (p. 313)
17	Lesson 12: Using pronouns correctly (p. 323) Lesson 12: Correcting unclear or ambiguous pronouns or antecedents (p. 325)
8, 13, 17, 21, 36, 42, 43, 44	Lesson 12: Correcting problems with pronoun/antecedent, subject/verb, and noun agreement (p. 329)
22, 24, 29, 42	Lesson 12: Correcting misuse of confusing words (p. 337)
	Lesson 12: Correcting cases in which unalike terms are compared (p. 337)
	Lesson 12: Correcting nonstandard written English (p. 338)
1, 3, 4, 6, 17, 25, 36, 37	Lesson 13: Using end punctuation and commas (p. 343)
14, 30	Lesson 13: Using semicolons and colons (p. 349)
23	Lesson 13: Using parentheses, dashes, and quotation marks (p. 354)
4, 29	Lesson 13: Using possessives and correcting use of unnecessary punctuation (pp. 358–359)

SAT Model Exam 2

READING TEST

65 MINUTES, 52 QUESTIONS

Use the Reading Section of your answer sheet to answer the questions in this section.

Directions

Each passage or pair of passages below is followed by a number of questions. After reading each passage or pair, choose the best answer to each question based upon what is stated or implied in the passage or passages or in any graphics (tables or graphs). To practice using a SAT-type answer sheet, fill in the appropriate letter bubble next to the question number. A reproducible answer sheet can be found on page 380.

Questions 1–10 are based upon the following passage.

The following is an excerpt from the short story "Of Course" by Shirley Jackson. Mr. and Mrs. Harris and their son James have just moved in next door to the Tylors.

"It certainly feels good to sit down," Mrs. Harris said. She sighed. "Sometimes I feel that moving is the most terrible thing I have to do."

"You were lucky to get that house," Mrs. Tylor
5 said, and Mrs. Harris nodded. "We'll be glad to get nice neighbors," Mrs. Tylor went on. "There's something so nice about congenial people right next door. I'll be running over to borrow cups of sugar," she finished roguishly.

10   "I certainly hope you will," Mrs. Harris said. "We had such disagreeable people next door to us in our old house. Small things, you know, and they do irritate you so." Mrs. Tylor sighed sympathetically. "The radio, for instance," Mrs. Harris continued,
15 "all day long, and so loud."

Mrs. Tylor caught her breath for a minute. "You must be sure and tell us if ours is ever too loud."

"Mr. Harris cannot bear the radio," Mrs. Harris said. "We do not own one, of course."

20   "Of course," Mrs. Tylor said. "No radio."

Mrs. Harris looked at her and laughed uncomfortably. "You'll be thinking my husband is crazy."

"Of course not," Mrs. Tylor said. "After all, lots
25 of people don't like radios; my oldest nephew, now, he's just the other way—"

"Well," Mrs. Harris said, "newspapers, too."

Mrs. Tylor recognized finally the faint nervous feeling that was tagging her; it was the way she felt
30 when she was irrevocably connected with something dangerously out of control: her car, for instance, on an icy street, or the time on Virginia's roller skates . . . Mrs. Harris was staring absentmindedly at the movers going in and out, and she was saying,

CONTINUE ➡

35 "It isn't as though we hadn't ever seen a newspaper, not like the movies at all; Mr. Harris just feels that the newspapers are a mass degradation of taste. You really never need to read a newspaper, you know," she said, looking around anxiously at Mrs. Tylor.

40 "I never read anything but the—"

"And we took *The New Republic* for a number of years," Mrs. Harris said. "When we were first married, of course. Before James was born."

"What is your husband's business?" Mrs. Tylor
45 asked timidly.

Mrs. Harris lifted her head proudly. "He's a scholar," she said. "He writes monographs."

Mrs. Tylor opened her mouth to speak, but Mrs. Harris leaned over and put her hand out and said,
50 "It's terribly hard for people to understand the desire for a really peaceful life."

"What," Mrs. Tylor said, "what does your husband do for relaxation?"

"He reads plays," Mrs. Harris said. She looked
55 doubtfully over at James. "Pre-Elizabethan, of course."

"Of course," Mrs. Tylor said, and looked nervously at James, who was shoveling sand into a pail.

"People are really very unkind," Mrs. Harris
60 said. "Those people I was telling you about, next door. It wasn't only the radio, you see. Three times they deliberately left their *New York Times* on our doorstep. Once James nearly got it."

"Good Lord," Mrs. Tylor said. She stood up.

65 "Carol," she called emphatically, "don't go away. It's nearly time for lunch, dear."

"Well," Mrs. Harris said. "I must go and see if the movers have done anything right."

Feeling as though she had been rude, Mrs. Tylor
70 said, "Where is Mr. Harris now?"

"At his mother's," Mrs. Harris said. "He always stays there when we move."

"Of course," Mrs. Tylor said, feeling as though she had been saying nothing else all morning.

75 "They don't turn the radio on while he's there," Mrs. Harris explained.

"Of course," Mrs. Tylor said.

Mrs. Harris held out her hand and Mrs. Tylor took it. "I do so hope we'll be friends," Mrs. Harris
80 said. "As you said, it means such a lot to have really thoughtful neighbors. And we've been so unlucky."

"Of course," Mrs. Tylor said, and then came back to herself abruptly. "Perhaps one evening soon we can get together for a game of bridge?" She saw
85 Mrs. Harris's face and said, "No. Well, anyway, we must all get together some evening soon." They both laughed.

"It does sound silly, doesn't it," Mrs. Harris said.

"Thanks so much for all your kindness this
90 morning."

"Anything we can do," Mrs. Tylor said. "If you want to send James over this afternoon."

"Perhaps I shall," Mrs. Harris said. "If you really don't mind."

95 "Of course," Mrs. Tylor said. "Carol, dear."

CONTINUE →

1

The reader's understanding of Mrs. Tylor's statement, "We'll be glad to get nice neighbors," changes by the end of the story because

A) the Harrises don't like "disagreeable people."
B) the Harrises will probably stay only a month or two.
C) the children will never speak to each other.
D) the new neighbors aren't "nice" in the way Mrs. Tylor expects.

2

In line 30, "irrevocably" most nearly means

A) permanently.
B) assuredly.
C) convincingly.
D) effectively.

3

The images of the car and roller skates spinning out of control (lines 31–32) suggest that Mrs. Tylor

A) is troubled by Mrs. Harris's description of her family.
B) worries she'll no longer be able to enjoy normal activities.
C) feels Mr. and Mrs. Harris are not to be trusted.
D) considers the possibility that James will not be nice to her daughter.

4

In line 37, "degradation" most nearly means

A) elevation.
B) corruption.
C) expansion.
D) exclusion.

5

Mrs. Harris's attitude toward newspapers (lines 35–38) is best described as

A) intrigued.
B) perplexed.
C) disdainful.
D) ambivalent.

6

Mrs. Harris's descriptions of her husband imply that he is

A) vindictive, smug, and melancholic.
B) stingy, temperamental, and haughty.
C) selfish, snobbish, and overbearing.
D) upright, cantankerous, and proud.

7

Which of the following provides the best evidence for the answer to the previous question?

A) lines 22–23 ("You'll be . . . is crazy")
B) lines 36–37 ("Mr. Harris . . . of taste")
C) lines 80–81 ("As you said . . . so unlucky")
D) lines 89–90 ("Thanks . . . this morning")

8

The repetition of the phrase "of course" throughout the passage implies that Mrs. Tylor

A) is an introvert who doesn't like talking with strangers.
B) has trouble expressing her own opinions and desires.
C) will talk about the Harris family with the other neighbors.
D) maintains a polite demeanor, no matter what she really thinks.

9

Which choice provides the best evidence that Mrs. Harris is sympathetic toward her husband's point of view?

A) lines 22–23 ("You'll be . . . is crazy")
B) lines 50–51 ("It's terribly . . . life")
C) lines 46–47 ("Mrs. Harris . . . she said")
D) lines 75–76 ("They don't . . . explained")

10

The passage implies that the Harris family

A) will become good friends with the Tylor family.
B) won't stay in the neighborhood long.
C) will be a positive addition to the neighborhood.
D) was forced out of their previous neighborhood.

CONTINUE

The following passage is adapted from "For Healthy Eating, Timing Matters" by Tina Hesman Saey, published in Science News.

When you eat may determine how long and strong your heart beats.

Fruit flies that limited eating to 12-hour stints had steadier heartbeats in old age than flies that
5 ate whenever they wanted, researchers report. The study adds to a growing body of evidence that the timing of meals may be as important for health as diet composition and calorie counts are.

The research also "suggests that the body clock
10 is involved in cardiovascular function and risk," says Frank Scheer, a neuroscientist and physiologist at Brigham and Women's Hospital in Boston and Harvard Medical School. Scheer was not involved in the fruit fly study, but has shown that disrupting
15 people's daily, or circadian, rhythms can damage their health.

Circadian clocks work in nearly every cell in the body. They govern a wide variety of body rhythms, such as those associated with body temperature, blood
20 pressure and sleep. The main timekeeper is located in the brain and is set by light, but other clocks synchronize themselves according to feeding time.

Previous research in mice has suggested that limiting eating to 12 hours per day could protect
25 rodents from obesity and other ravages of high-fat diets. Those studies couldn't address heart problems associated with poor diet because mice don't get heart disease the way humans do, says Satchidananda Panda, a circadian biologist at the Salk Institute
30 for Biological Studies in La Jolla, Calif. Fruit flies,

on the other hand, develop irregular heartbeats and other heart problems as they age. So Panda and his colleagues set out to test whether limiting the amount of time fruit flies eat, but not cutting back on calories,
35 could affect the insect's heart health.

One group of flies ate around the clock; the other had access to their cornmeal diet for 12 hours each day. Both groups ate about the same amount overall, but the 24-hour group snacked at night.

40 Both groups of flies had similar amounts of activity. The limited-timed feeding flies did most of their moving during the day, though. They also slept better at night.

At 3 weeks old, both groups of flies had regular,
45 healthy hearts. At 5 weeks, the 12-hour eaters' hearts maintained a steady rhythm of roughly one beat per second. The hearts of the anytime eaters beat irregularly, sometimes skipping a beat and sometimes quivering. By 7 weeks, the anytimers
50 had badly deteriorated heart function. Flies on a 12-hour schedule also lost a few beats, but their heart problems were not as severe.

Switching anytime flies to a 12-hour schedule at 5 weeks old—fruit fly middle age—improved some
55 measures of heart function, but not all. In other experiments, restricting feeding time also staved off some of the negative heart effects of high-fat diets.

When researchers disabled circadian clocks throughout some fruit flies' bodies, restricting eating
60 times didn't help those flies' hearts, suggesting that functioning clocks are important for heart health.

Researchers also looked at timed eating's impact on gene activity. Many genes follow circadian

CONTINUE →

rhythms, peaking in activity during certain times of
65 the day. In fruit flies with curtailed eating schedules,
those peaks crescendoed right before breakfast
and just before the last mouthful. Anytime eaters
had several smaller peaks throughout the day.
That finding suggests that timed feeding improves
70 coordination of gene activity.

Panda likens the effect to getting a tune-up on
a car. "The spark plugs need to fire in sequence,"
he says. "If you just fire randomly, you'll have a
big problem and the head gasket will blow up."
75 Similarly, tightly controlling gene activity may
allow for more efficient energy usage and prevent
metabolic by-products from building up and
damaging tissues, he says.

Improved sleep in the 12-hour eaters might
80 account for some of the heart benefits, Scheer says.
Lack of sleep is linked to a variety of diseases in
people, including heart disease. No one knows
whether restricting mealtimes will improve human
health, he says. "I don't think there's evidence that
85 it's bad, but there's too little evidence for me to
recommend it."

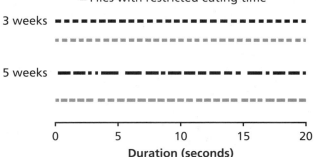

Heart function in fruit flies
▬ Flies with unrestricted eating time
▬ Flies with restricted eating time

3 weeks

5 weeks

0   5   10   15   20
Duration (seconds)

KEEPING TIME Fruit flies that eat just 12 hours per day (light gray lines) maintain steady heartbeats into middle age (5 weeks old), while the hearts of flies that can eat around the clock (black lines) beat irregularly. Each black or light gray dash represents the contraction of the heart.

11

The main purpose of the first sentence as it relates to the rest of the passage is
A) to present a claim that is supported with specific evidence.
B) to provide a solution to a problem that is then explained.
C) to introduce an example that the rest of the passage will explain.
D) to make a claim that the text will go on to refute.

12

Which of the following sentences best interprets the data in the graph?
A) Twelve-hour eating stints improve the coordination of gene activity in fruit flies.
B) At 3 weeks, the anytime eaters had significantly deteriorated heart function.
C) The anytime eaters had an irregular heartbeat at 5 weeks.
D) The 12-hour eaters' hearts kept a steady rhythm of two beats per second.

13

It can be inferred from the text and graph that unrestricted eating
A) has little impact on the flies' heart functioning.
B) affects the flies' heart functioning from the beginning.
C) changes the flies' heart functioning in the short term.
D) alters the flies' heart functioning over time.

14

In line 22, "synchronize" most nearly means
A) occur at the time or rate of.
B) agree with.
C) pull together.
D) maintain harmony with.

CONTINUE ➡

15

Circadian clocks govern all of the following body rhythms EXCEPT

A) body temperature.

B) blood pressure.

C) hunger pangs.

D) sleep.

16

According to the passage, fruit flies, humans, and mice share which of the following similarities?

A) Their health suffers when they lack regulation in certain activities.

B) They develop heart disease after engaging in unrestricted eating.

C) They grow obese when they don't stick to an eating schedule.

D) They lose weight when they eat three regular meals per day.

17

In line 77, "metabolic" most nearly means

A) relating to the processes by which a plant uses food and water to grow.

B) relating to the handling of a particular substance in the human body.

C) relating to the chemical transformations within the cells of amphibians.

D) relating to the processes by which an animal uses food and water to make energy.

18

Which of the following body functions/rhythms does timed feeding improve?

A) hunger patterns

B) bowel regularity

C) coordination of gene activity

D) liver functioning

19

Which choice provides the best evidence for the answer to question 18?

A) lines 58–61 ("When researchers disabled . . . for heart health")

B) lines 65–68 ("In fruit flies . . . throughout the day")

C) lines 71–74 ("Panda likens the . . . will blow up")

D) lines 75–78 ("Similarly, tightly . . . tissues, he says")

20

It can be inferred from the passage that circadian rhythms

A) are not as important to heart health as regular eating times.

B) may be more important to heart health than regular eating times.

C) aren't affected by regular eating patterns.

D) are set by gene activity.

21

Which choice provides the best evidence for the answer to question 20?

A) lines 13–16 ("Scheer was not . . . their health")

B) lines 58–61 ("When researchers disabled . . . for heart health")

C) lines 63–68 ("Many genes . . . the day")

D) lines 79–80 ("Improved sleep . . . Scheer says")

CONTINUE

Questions 22–32 are based upon the following passages.

Passage 1 is adapted from Ralph Waldo Emerson's essay on friendship written in 1841. Passage 2 is adapted from "The Decay of Friendship" by Samuel Johnson published in 1758.

Passage 1

The effect of the indulgence of this human affection is a certain cordial exhilaration. In poetry, and in common speech, the emotions of benevolence and complacency which are felt toward others, are

5 likened to the material effects of fire; so swift, or much more swift, more active, more cheering are these fine inward irradiations. From the highest degree of passionate love, to the lowest degree of good will, they make the sweetness of life.

10 What is so pleasant as these jets of affection which relume a young world for me again? What is so delicious as a just and firm encounter of two, in a thought, in a feeling? How beautiful, on their approach to this beating heart, the steps and forms

15 of the gifted and the true! The moment we indulge our affections, the earth is metamorphosed; there is no winter, and no night; all tragedies, all ennuis vanish—all duties even; nothing fills the proceeding eternity but the forms, all radiant, of beloved

20 persons. Let the soul be assured that somewhere in the universe it should rejoin its friend, and it would be content and cheerful alone for a thousand years.

I awoke this morning with devout thanksgiving for my friends, the old and the new. Shall I not call

25 God, the Beautiful, who daily showeth himself so to me in his gifts? I chide society, I embrace solitude, and yet I am not so ungrateful as not to see the wise, the lovely, and the noble-minded, as from time to time they pass my gate.

30 Who hears me, who understands me, becomes mine,—a possession for all time.

Passage 2

Life has no pleasure higher or nobler than that of friendship. It is painful to consider that this sublime enjoyment may be impaired or destroyed

35 by innumerable causes, and that there is no human possession of which the duration is less certain.

Many have talked in very exalted language, of the perpetuity of friendship, of invincible constancy, and unalienable kindness; and some examples have

40 been seen of men who have continued faithful to their earliest choice, and whose affection has predominated over changes of fortune, and contrariety of opinion.

But these instances are memorable, because they are rare. The friendship which is to be practiced

45 or expected by common mortals, must take its rise from mutual pleasure, and must end when the power ceases of delighting each other.

Many accidents therefore may happen by which the ardor of kindness will be abated, without

50 criminal baseness or contemptible inconstancy on either part. To give pleasure is not always in our power; and little does he know himself who believes that he can be always able to receive it.

Those who would gladly pass their days together

55 may be separated by the different course of their affairs; and friendship, like love, is destroyed by long absence, though it may be increased by short intermissions. What we have missed long enough to want it, we value more when it is regained; but that

60 which has been lost till it is forgotten, will be found

CONTINUE

at last with little gladness, and with still less if a substitute has supplied the place. A man deprived of the companion to whom he used to open his bosom, and with whom he shared the hours of leisure and

65 merriment, feels the day at first hanging heavy on him; his difficulties oppress, and his doubts distract him; he sees time come and go without his wonted gratification, and all is sadness within, and solitude about him. But this uneasiness never lasts long;

70 necessity produces expedients, new amusements are discovered, and new conversation is admitted.

22

In line 2, "cordial" most nearly means
A) hospitable.   C) gracious.
B) pleasant.   D) complicated.

23

The questions in lines 10–13 of Passage 1 have primarily the effect of
A) asking the reader to be more generous in friendship.
B) calling on the reader to be thankful for his or her friends.
C) challenging the reader to find anything as wonderful as friendship.
D) questioning whether friendship is real.

24

How do the phrases "jets of affection," "delicious," and "radiant" in the second paragraph of Passage 1 establish the tone of the paragraph?
A) They create a contented tone that communicates the author's satisfaction with life.
B) They create a passionate tone that extols the benefits of friendship.
C) They create a stern tone that warns against solitude.
D) They create a reserved tone that encourages readers to make friends carefully.

25

In line 16, "metamorphosed" most nearly means
A) to change physical form.
B) to be transformed.
C) to convert.
D) to disappear.

26

According to Passage 1, when two people who think and feel alike meet
A) they share the most intimate details of their lives.
B) they become friends for the duration of their lives.
C) they experience exhilaration, which fades over time.
D) they spend many hours together.

27

Which choice provides the best evidence for the answer to question 26?
A) lines 20–22 ("Let the soul. . . a thousand years")
B) lines 23–26 ("I awoke this morning . . . in his gifts")
C) lines 26–29 ("I chide society, . . . pass my gate")
D) lines 30–31 ("Who hears me, . . . for all time")

28

Both Passage 1 and Passage 2 focus on the
A) eternalness of friendship.
B) hard work friendship entails.
C) pleasures of friendship.
D) transitory nature of friendship.

CONTINUE ➡

29

Unlike the author of Passage 1, the author of Passage 2

A) stresses that friendship is life's greatest pleasure.

B) argues that most friendships eventually end.

C) suggests that new friends are better than old ones.

D) states that absence makes the heart grow fonder.

30

The central claim of Passage 2 is that

A) friendships last only as long as they provide pleasure.

B) friends who truly understand each other will be friends forever.

C) the greatest gift in life is friendship.

D) friendships will always end when friends spend time apart.

31

Which choice provides the best evidence for the answer to question 30?

A) lines 32–36 ("Life has no pleasure . . . less certain")

B) lines 37–42 ("Many have talked . . . contrariety of opinion")

C) lines 43–47 ("But these instances are . . . delighting each other")

D) lines 48–53 ("Many accidents therefore . . . receive it")

32

The central idea of the final paragraph of Passage 2 (lines 54–71) is that

A) brief absences make the heart grow fonder.

B) lengthy absences ruin friendships.

C) real friends show their love in times of trouble.

D) when long absent from friends, the heart breaks.

Questions 33–42 are based upon the following passages.

The following passage is adapted from an article by Nicholas Wade entitled "Study Reveals Genetic Path of Modern Britons," published in The New York Times.

In A.D. 410, Roman authority in Britain collapsed and Romano-British society disappeared from history under the invading tides of Angles and Saxons from northern Europe. Historians have
5 been debating ever since whether the Romano-British were wiped out or survived by adopting their conquerors' language and culture.

A fine-scale genetic analysis of the British population has now provided the answer. The
10 invaders and the existing population lived side by side and eventually intermarried extensively. The people of south and central England are now genetically well mixed, with Saxon genes accounting for only about 20 percent of the mix, says a genetics team led by
15 Stephen Leslie, Peter Donnelly and Walter Bodmer.

The British Isles were wiped clean of people by the glaciers that descended toward the end of the last ice age, and were repopulated some 10,000 years ago by people who trekked over the broad land
20 bridge that then joined eastern England to Europe north of the Rhine. The researchers say they can identify the genetic signature of this early migration, which survives most strongly in people from the western extremity of Wales.

25 The people of the southern and central parts of England form a homogeneous population, but all around the Celtic periphery, in Cornwall, Wales and Scotland, lie small clusters of genetically different populations that have maintained their identity over

CONTINUE

the generations. This is a surprise, given that the Celtic peoples who ruled most of England until Caesar's invasion in B.C. 55 were assumed to be fairly homogeneous.

The explanation may have to do with the reach of Roman rule. In southern and central England, "the Romans controlled that area of Britain and introduced farming systems and roads and broke down many political barriers to movement," said Mark Robinson, an archaeologist at Oxford and a co-author of the study. The population under Roman rule thus became homogenized, whereas those beyond it would have remained politically fragmented, making travel and intermarriage difficult, Dr. Robinson said.

The researchers found that the modern British population falls into 17 clusters altogether, based on genetic relatedness. Though very similar, the groups are genetically distinguishable, and even the main population cluster, that of southern and central England, is distinguishable from the populations of France, Germany and other European countries.

There has been considerable migration into Britain over the last century from many countries of the former British empire and from elsewhere in continental Europe. Dr. Donnelly and his colleagues managed to sidestep this recent churning of the population history by seeking out elderly people who lived in rural areas and whose grandparents had been born locally. Because individual genomes are composed of random samples of the four grandparents' DNA, the researchers were in effect looking two generations into the past and testing the population of the late 19th century.

They analyzed the DNA of their 2,000 subjects at 500,000 sites along the genome, and then organized them into the 17 genetic clusters. They also analyzed the genomes of 6,000 Europeans in the same way, and could thus identify the source populations in Europe from which each of the 17 British clusters was derived. The migrations revealed in that way match the known historical record but also point to events that have not been recorded, such as a massive migration from northern France that accounts for about one-third of the ancestry of the average person in Britain.

"History is written by the winners, and archaeology studies the burials of wealthy people," Dr. Donnelly said. "But genetic evidence is interesting because it complements that by showing what is happening to the masses rather than the elite."

33

The first two paragraphs make the claim that the Romano-British

A) were wiped out when Angles and Saxons invaded Britain.

B) survived by intermarrying with the existing population.

C) returned to Rome when Angles and Saxons invaded Britain.

D) were killed when a glacier covered the land.

34

The purpose of the third paragraph is mainly to

A) provide background information about evidence to support the claim.

B) explain how the genetics team conducted their research.

C) provide examples of genetically diverse populations.

D) present a counterclaim to the claim made in the second paragraph.

CONTINUE ➤

35

In line 22, "signature" most nearly means

A) a discernable autograph.

B) a detailed description.

C) a distinctive characteristic.

D) a musical arrangement.

36

In line 26, the word "homogeneous" most nearly means

A) of the same kind.

B) unchanging.

C) different.

D) like night and day.

37

Genetic analysis demonstrated which of the following regarding the people in Cornwall, Wales, and Scotland?

A) They are currently a genetically diverse population.

B) Their genes can be traced back to the Norman invasion.

C) Their genes are different from the people of south and central England.

D) They are genetically similar to the people of south and central England.

38

Which of the following lines provides the best evidence for the answer to the previous question?

A) lines 16–21 ("The British Isles . . . of the Rhine")

B) lines 25–30 ("The people of . . . over the generations")

C) lines 30–33 ("This is a surprise . . . homogeneous")

D) lines 52–55 ("There has been . . . continental Europe")

39

It can be inferred that in areas where Romans built roads and introduced farming there is likely to be

A) a larger population of Anglo-Saxons.

B) a population with similar genes.

C) people with genetic similarities to south and central England.

D) more older people who were born and raised in the area.

40

Which of the following lines provides the strongest evidence for the central claim made in lines 9–11 ("The invaders . . . extensively")?

A) lines 11–15 ("The people . . . Bodmer")

B) lines 21–24 ("The researchers . . . Wales")

C) lines 45–47 ("The researchers found . . . genetic relatedness")

D) lines 66–70 ("They also analyzed . . . was derived")

41

In Paragraph 7 (lines 52–63), the writer

A) presents a question and an answer about how genetic research is conducted.

B) introduces a contrasting theory about genetic makeup.

C) gives historical context to the study.

D) explains how a possible problem with the study was overcome.

42

Which of the following best explains Dr. Donnelly's point of view as revealed in his quotation in lines 76–80?

A) Genetic research often contradicts historical accounts.

B) Archaeology is a less precise science than genetic analysis.

C) Genetic analysis reveals human history across all levels of society.

D) History and archaeology are less reliable than genetic analysis.

CONTINUE

Questions 43–52 are based upon the following passage.

The following passage is adapted from an article entitled "GM Foods: What's Cropping Up?"

In the brave new world of genetic engineering, scientists envision a new crop of superfoods: tomatoes and broccoli bursting with cancer-fighting chemicals and vitamin-enhanced crops of rice,
5 sweet potatoes, and cassava to help nourish the poor. This dream is not so far off.

Since the start of agriculture, people have been selectively breeding desirable traits in their crops. However, the use of genetic engineering to create
10 genetically modified (GM) foods allows scientists to add genes from any other organism to a particular crop. GM foods are given traits that will benefit farmers by helping them increase their yield. Crops are most often modified to be more resistant to
15 insects, viruses, and chemical herbicides.

Genetically modified crops are produced through the use of recombinant DNA technology, in which genes from different organisms are combined. Genes from an organism with a desirable trait, such
20 as having a natural pesticide, are inserted into the genome of the specific crop. Plants can have new genes added through the use of a bacterial species called *Agrobacterium tumefaciens*. This bacterium is used because it has the ability to change the
25 DNA of plant cells. Scientists splice the desired gene for the food plant into the DNA of *A. tumefaciens* bacterial cells. Next they place these cells in a petri dish with undifferentiated plant cells; the bacteria then transfer their modified genes
30 into the plant cells.

The most common crops that have had their DNA changed are corn and soybeans. In fact, 93 percent of the soy that is planted in the United States is genetically modified. Other crops that have been
35 modified include alfalfa, canola, cotton, rice, sugar beets, potatoes, tomatoes, squash, papaya, and flax.

Making plants resistant to insects is helpful to farmers because they do not have to spray their crops with insecticides. These chemicals can be dangerous
40 to handle, so farmers appreciate being able to avoid working with them. This is also beneficial to consumers, since they do not have to eat plants that have been sprayed with these dangerous chemicals. One example of such a crop is the genetically
45 modified corn called "Bt corn." This corn now contains a gene from the soil bacterium *Bacillus thuringiensis*, which produces a toxin to a specific insect, the corn borer. The Bt toxin is harmful only to the insects, not to the people who eat the corn.
50 However, according to one study, Bt toxin has been found in the bloodstream of consumers, raising some safety concerns. The Bt trait is now being put into other crops, such as cotton, rice, and potatoes.

Farmers also benefit from growing crops with
55 a gene that makes them tolerant of herbicides (chemicals that are used to kill weeds but can also harm crops). Herbicides are not selective and can hurt all plants, but if the GM plants are tolerant or made resistant to the herbicides, then they can
60 be sprayed without being damaged. One example of this is the herbicide called Roundup. Strains of soybeans, canola, corn, and cotton have been engineered that are resistant to this herbicide, thus making them easier to grow.

CONTINUE ▶

65   Also, efforts are under way to tackle two major health problems in developing nations using GM crops. One plan is to engineer a type of banana that has a gene for a hepatitis B vaccine; the other plan is to grow a variety of rice, called "golden rice,"
70 that has a high vitamin A content, to help prevent blindness in Africa and Southeast Asia.

    Some people think that by creating GM foods, we are tampering with nature. Environmental groups in Europe and Japan have limited the sale
75 of GM foods in those regions. Other people are concerned that a GM crop could cause allergic reactions. Thus far, few adverse effects have been scientifically documented.

Graph 1   **Farmers' reasons for adopting genetically engineered (GE) herbicide tolerant corn in the United States in 2010***

This statistic depicts the results of the Agricultural Resource Management Survey which was conducted for corn in 2010 U.S. farmers were asked about their reasons for using genetically engineered (GE) corn. Some 71 percent of the respondents use genetically engineered corn with herbicide tolerance traits in order to increase their yields.

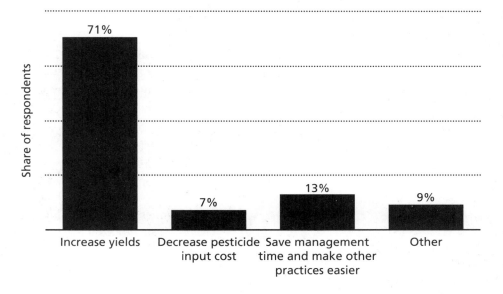

Graph 2

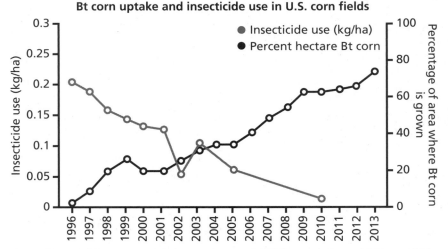

Overall pesticide use on U.S. farms dropped 0.6% a year from 1980 to 2007. The declines were even greater in corn fields, thanks in part to genetically modified varieties with the Bt toxin. But resistant insects have led to a recent uptick in insecticide applications.

CONTINUE ➡

43

Which choice best reflects the overall sequence of the passage?

A) Multiple theories about genetically engineered crops are explained along with data about which crops are the yielding the greatest benefits.

B) Possible applications of genetically engineered crops are suggested, the research process is explained, and finally one application is explained extensively.

C) The technology of genetically engineered crops is presented, a general summary of the science behind the technology is given, and the advantages of the technology are explained.

D) An unexpected finding about genetically engineered crops is explained, then the benefits and possible negative side effects are detailed.

44

In line 25, the term "splice" most nearly means

A) combine.

B) split.

C) change.

D) cut.

45

Which of the following lines from the passage are best supported by the information about why farmers plant genetically modified crops in Graph 1?

A) lines 12–13 ("GM foods . . . their yield")

B) lines 16–18 ("Genetically modified . . . combined")

C) lines 31–32 ("The most common . . . soybeans")

D) lines 37–39 ("Making plants . . . insecticides")

46

The passage mentions that one of the benefits of genetically modified crops is

A) more farmland can be used to raise cattle and other livestock.

B) crops can be raised with fewer chemicals.

C) people who eat GM foods are more resilient to disease.

D) the plants are resistant to extreme drought and flooding.

47

The passage suggests that an objection to GM crops is that

A) insecticide companies will go out of business.

B) toxins from GM crops may be harmful to people who eat them.

C) herbicide use will increase as GM plants become more resistant.

D) farmers may not be receptive to GM crops.

48

Which choice provides the best evidence for the answer to question 47?

A) lines 32–34 ("In fact . . . modified")

B) lines 37–39 ("Making plants . . . insecticides")

C) lines 50–52 ("However, . . . concerns")

D) lines 57–60 ("Herbicides are . . . damaged")

49

As used in line 55, "tolerant" means

A) without feelings.

B) accepting of differences.

C) able to endure hardship.

D) capable of thriving under unfavorable conditions.

CONTINUE

50

How does Graph 2 support the author's point that making plants resistant to insects is beneficial to farmers?

A) It indicates that as more farmers planted Bt corn, the use of insecticides decreased on all farms.

B) It shows a sharp increase in insecticide use in 2003.

C) It reveals that the percentage of area where Bt corn is grown has increased to nearly 80 percent since 1996.

D) It forecasts that insecticide use will rise as insects become resistant.

51

The text under Graph 2 explains which of the following problems with Bt corn?

A) Insects may become resistant to the toxins in Bt corn.

B) The percentage of farmers planting Bt corn will stagnate in the future.

C) Some farmers have stopped producing Bt corn.

D) Bt corn has become resistant to herbicides.

The main purpose of the first and last paragraphs in the passage is to

A) suggest possible applications of genetically modified foods.

B) encourage readers to support genetically engineered crops.

C) explain the prevalence of genetic engineering.

D) list the crops which are currently being modified.

STOP

**If you finish before time is called, you may check your work on this section only.
Do not turn to any other section.**

WRITING AND LANGUAGE TEST

35 MINUTES, 44 QUESTIONS

Use the Writing and Language section of your answer sheet to answer the questions in this section.

Directions

Each passage below is accompanied by a number of questions. For some questions, you will consider how the passage might be revised to improve the expression of ideas. For other questions, you will consider how the passage might be edited to correct errors in sentence structure, usage, or punctuation. A passage or a question may be accompanied by one or more graphics (such as a table or graph) that you will consider as you make revising and editing decisions.

Some questions will direct you to an underlined portion of a passage. Other questions will direct you to a location in a passage or ask you to think about the passage as a whole.

After reading each passage, choose the answer to each question that most effectively improves the quality of writing in the passage or that makes the passage conform to the conventions of standard written English. Many questions include a "NO CHANGE" option. Choose that option if you think the best choice is to leave the relevant portion of the passage as it is.

Questions 1–11 are based on the following passage.

Musicians and Singers

Work Environment

Musicians and singers held about 167,400 jobs in 2014. They perform in settings such as concert halls, arenas, and clubs. The greatest percentage of musicians **1** are self-employed, but a few work for educational institutions or promoters of performing arts events.

Industries with the highest levels of employment for musicians and singers, 2014	
Performing Arts Companies	17.08%
Religious Organizations	4.49%
Colleges, Universities, and Professional Schools	.05%
Independent Artists, Writers, and Performers	2.54%
Promoters of Performing Arts, Sports, and Similar Events	1.11%

1

Which choice completes the sentence with accurate data based on the table?

A) NO CHANGE

B) are employed by independent artists or performers

C) are employed by religious organizations

D) work for performing arts companies

CONTINUE

Musicians and singers may spend a lot of time traveling between performances. Some spend time in recording studios. There are many jobs in cities that have a high concentration of entertainment activities, such as New York, **2** Los Angeles Chicago, and Nashville.

Musicians and singers who give recitals or perform in nightclubs travel frequently **3** and may do touring nationally or internationally.

Many musicians and singers find only part-time or intermittent work, however, and have long periods of unemployment between jobs. The stress of constantly looking for work **4** leads many to except permanent full-time jobs in other occupations while working part-time as a musician or singer.

2
A) NO CHANGE
B) Los Angeles, Chicago, and
C) Los Angeles Chicago and
D) Los Angeles, Chicago and,

3
A) NO CHANGE
B) and may be touring nationally or internationally.
C) and may tour nationally or internationally.
D) and may have toured nationally or internationally.

4
A) NO CHANGE
B) leads many to accept
C) lead many to except
D) lead many to accept

CONTINUE

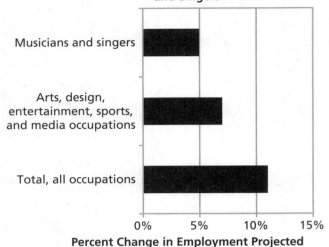

Comparative Job Outlook for Musicians and Singers

Musicians and singers

Arts, design, entertainment, sports, and media occupations

Total, all occupations

0% 5% 10% 15%

Percent Change in Employment Projected for 2012–2022

Note: All occupations includes all occupations in the U.S. economy.

Source: U.S. Bureau of Labor Statistics, Employment Projections program

Employment of musicians and singers is projected **5** to decrease from 2012 to 2022, slower than the average for all occupations. Growth will be due to increases in demand for musical performances.

Digital downloads and streaming platforms make it easier for fans to listen to recordings and view performances. Easier access to recordings gives musicians more publicity and grows interest in **6** their work, and concertgoers may become interested in seeing them perform live.

5

Which choice completes the sentence with accurate data based on the table?

A) NO CHANGE

B) to increase 7 percent from 2012 to 2022, faster than the average for all occupations.

C) to increase 5 percent from 2012 to 2022, slower than the average for all occupations.

D) to decrease 11 percent from 2012 to 2022, the same as the average for all occupations.

6

A) NO CHANGE

B) there

C) they're

D) theirs

CONTINUE

There will be additional demand █7█ for musicians to serve as session musicians, and backup artists for recordings, and to go on tour. Singers will be needed to sing backup and to make recordings for commercials, films, and television.

█8█ However, employment growth will likely be limited in orchestras, opera companies, and other musical groups because they can have difficulty getting funding. Some musicians and singers work for nonprofit organizations that rely on donations, government funding, and corporate sponsorships in addition to ticket sales to fund their █9█ work, during economic downturns, these organizations may have trouble finding enough funding to cover their expenses.

7

A) NO CHANGE
B) for musicians to serve as session musicians, backup artists for recordings, and to go on tour.
C) for session musicians, and backup artists for recordings, and touring musicians.
D) for session musicians, backup artists for recordings, and touring musicians.

8

A) NO CHANGE
B) In actuality,
C) As a consequence,
D) In addition,

9

A) NO CHANGE
B) work, during economic downturns
C) work. During economic downturns,
D) work during economic downturns,

CONTINUE

10 This is particularly true for full-time positions. Musicians and **11** singers who have exceptional musical talent and dedication, should have the best opportunities. Unfortunately, many musicians and singers experience periods of unemployment.

10

Which choice most effectively establishes the main topic of the paragraph?

A) Musicians and singers are generally creative people who enjoy the spotlight.

B) Working hours for musicians and singers are typically in the evening, although practices for performances may have daytime hours.

C) Many musicians and singers struggle to make a name for themselves in the early stages of or throughout their career.

D) Because of the large number of workers who are interested in becoming musicians and singers, competition for jobs is stiff.

11

A) NO CHANGE

B) singers who have exceptional musical talent and dedication

C) singers, who have exceptional musical talent and dedication,

D) singers, who have exceptional musical talent and dedication

CONTINUE

Questions 12–22 are based on the following passage.

The Earliest Americans: The Midwest

In the earliest age of humans, the Midwest was a place of environmental `12` tumult. It was forming and reforming in shifting equations of ice and water, climate and topography. Before people arrived, hundreds of thousands of years of advancing and retreating glaciers scoured the `13` land; until a warming trend loosened the cold's grip. The first Midwesterners likely arrived 13,500 years ago, probably from the northwest or west. Roughly the northern half of Minnesota was under a mantle of ice, as was upper Wisconsin and much of Michigan.

Farther south the Great Lakes `14` overflowed with glacial melt. Occasional bouts of frigid, dry weather would temporarily reverse the process, and the shore expanded. The topography was in near-constant flux with what has been called an "accordion of habitats." Some witnessed this ebb and flow in their lifetimes.

Lost Legacy

`15` Like geologists and astronomers, archaeology is a science to which lay people often make great contributions. The Midwest's vast agricultural expanse offers better prospects for amateur collectors than elsewhere. Over the last century people have seized this opportunity, `16` accruing large caches of artifacts that now reside in trunks, cigar boxes, or display cases in homes, basements, and sometimes county museums.

`12`

Which choice most effectively combines the sentences at the underlined portion?

A) tumult, forming

B) tumult; forming and reforming

C) tumult, which is forming and reforming

D) tumult, and forming and reforming

`13`

A) NO CHANGE

B) land: until

C) land—until

D) land until,

`14`

A) NO CHANGE

B) overflows

C) overflow

D) overflowing

`15`

A) NO CHANGE

B) Like geology and astronomy,

C) Like those who study rocks and the sky,

D) Like collecting rocks and gazing at the stars,

`16`

A) NO CHANGE

B) raising

C) increasing

D) accumulating

Tragically many such collections are lost to study—dispersed as curiosities or commodities—once they fall into the hands of heirs or others who lack the original **17** collectors' passion.

[1]Suppose the pages of a rare Gutenberg Bible were torn out and sold for a few dollars each. [2] Once these precious parts are lost, the book is never as valuable. [3] The gain to the few is small and fleeting, while the collective loss to science is irreparable. [4] Something similar is the fate of many archaeological collections that are parceled off little by little. **18**

17
A) NO CHANGE
B) collector's
C) collectors
D) collectors's

18
To make this paragraph most logical, sentence 4 should be placed
A) where it is now.
B) before sentence 1.
C) after sentence 1.
D) after sentence 2.

CONTINUE

Walter Schmidt, a longtime collector in the Saginaw Bay area of Michigan and a charter member of the Michigan Archaeological Society, was a responsible student of his area's past. Yet **19** Schmidt like many amateur collectors made mistakes that he later regretted. In 1937, he wrote to W.B. Hinsdale of the University of **20** Michigan, A couple of years ago [I] found an arrow much different from the usual but as it was broken off [I] gave it to Jr. and he traded it off. . . . The other day a man **21** told me that, this type is called Folsomite and is the oldest type of implement known."

No one knows how many variations of this sad story there are, but it illustrates the alarming and prolonged attrition of the archaeological record. **22**

19
A) NO CHANGE
B) Schmidt, like many,
C) Schmidt, like many artifacts,
D) Schmidt, like many amateur collectors,

20
A) NO CHANGE
B) Michigan "A
C) Michigan; "A
D) Michigan: "A

21
A) NO CHANGE
B) tells me that
C) told me that
D) told me that:

22
The writer wants to conclude the passage with a sentence that emphasizes the importance of maintaining the archaeological record. Which choice would best accomplish this goal?
A) Without doubt, many collections amassed in past decades have been lost, discarded, or destroyed, and the priceless information they contained lost with them.
B) Many people, such as Walter Schmidt, have amassed large collections of archaeological objects over their lifetimes.
C) Ordinary people sometimes find important archaeological objects, particularly in the Midwest.
D) Different states have archaeological societies that maintain and document the archaeological record.

CONTINUE

What is a Bolide?

[1] This was a time when sea level was unusually high everywhere on Earth. [2] Probably the most dramatic geological event that ever took place on the Atlantic margin of North America occurred about 35 million years ago in the late part of the Eocene Epoch. [3] The ancient shoreline of the Virginia region **23** is somewhere on the vicinity of where the city of Richmond is today. [4] The late Eocene climate was even warmer and more humid than today's tidewater summers. [5] Tropical rain forests covered the slopes of the **24** Appalachians. A broad, lime-covered continental shelf stretched to the east of a narrow coastal plain. [6] **25** Originally, with a brief flash of mind-numbing light, that tranquil scene was transformed into a bloody killing field of incredible carnage. [7] From the far reaches of the solar system, a giant bolide swooped through the Earth's atmosphere. [8] It blasted an enormous crater into the continental shelf and **26** removed nearby terrestrial flora and fauna. **27**

23
A) NO CHANGE
B) was somewhere on the vicinity
C) is somewhere in the vicinity
D) was somewhere in the vicinity

24
Which choice most effectively combines the sentences at the underlined portion?
A) Appalachians, a
B) Appalachians, so a
C) Appalachians with a
D) Appalachians, and a

25
A) NO CHANGE
B) Subsequently,
C) Yet,
D) Chiefly,

26
A) NO CHANGE
B) obliterated
C) abolished
D) purged

27
To make the paragraph most logical, sentence 2 should be placed
A) where it is now.
B) before sentence 1.
C) after sentence 3.
D) after sentence 4.

CONTINUE

28 Although exact specifications vary, bolides range from 1 to 10 kilometers (km) in size and impact the earth at velocities literally faster than a speeding bullet (20 to 70 km/sec = Mach 75). Some bolides make it to the earth and explode upon impact, creating a large crater. "Bolide" is actually a generic term, used to imply that the precise nature of the impacting body is unknown. For example, it may be a rocky or metallic asteroid. **29**

Simple vs. Complex Impact Craters

Nearly everyone knows what an impact crater looks like. For most, that image is derived from Meteor Crater (also known as Barringer Crater). Located 38 miles east of Flagstaff, Arizona, it is the archetypical example of what cratering experts call a simple crater. **30** This shallow, bowl-shaped excavation is 1 km in diameter and has an upraised sub-circular rim. Meteor Crater was the first terrestrial crater recognized as an impact structure back in the 1920s.

28

Which choice most effectively establishes the main topic of the paragraph?
A) A bolide is a large bright fireball that usually explodes in the atmosphere.
B) Impact craters may be simple or complex.
C) What is a bolide?
D) One characteristic of a bolide is that it explodes.

29

The writer wants to add another example of an impacting body. Which choice best accomplishes this goal?
A) or an icy comet.
B) or a large crater.
C) or airplane debris.
D) or an unknown body.

30

The writer is considering deleting the underlined sentence. Should the sentence be kept or deleted?
A) Kept, because it provides supporting evidence about how numerous impact craters are.
B) Kept, because it provides a description of the Meteor Crater.
C) Deleted, because it blurs the paragraph's focus on simple impact craters.
D) Deleted, because it doesn't provide specific examples about how simple impact craters are different from complex impact craters.

CONTINUE

Craters wider than 10 km are classified as complex craters because **31** they exhibit additional topographical features. A good example of a complex crater is King Crater on the far side of the moon. Like simple craters, the outer margin of complex craters **32** were marked by a raised rim. Inside the rim is a broad, flat, circular plain, called the annular trough. Large slump blocks fall away from the crater's outer wall **33** and sliding out over the floor of the annular trough toward the crater center. The inner edge of the annular trough is marked by either a central mountainous peak, a ring of peaks (a peak ring), or both. Inside the peak ring is the deepest part of the crater, called the inner basin.

31

A) NO CHANGE
B) they exhibits
C) it exhibit
D) it exhibited

32

A) NO CHANGE
B) is marked
C) was marked
D) would be marked

33

A) NO CHANGE
B) and slid out
C) and slide out
D) and were sliding out

CONTINUE

Questions 34–44 are based on the following passage.

The United States Senate building possesses a remarkable pair of busts of Be sheekee (Buffalo) and Aysh-ke-bah-ke-ko-zhay (Flat Mouth) by the [34] virtually unknown and unheard of Italian sculptor Francis Vincenti. These Native American leaders came to Washington, D.C., in 1855 as part of a delegation responsible for negotiating a treaty with the United States government. On February 17, 1855, Captain Seth Eastman, [35] who was also an artist wrote to Captain Montgomery C. Meigs, superintendent of the Capitol extension, that the two Ojibwa Indians were in the city and would consent to having their portraits modeled in clay.

[34]
A) NO CHANGE
B) virtually almost unknown
C) virtually unknown
D) virtually, for all intents and purposes, unknown

[35]
A) NO CHANGE
B) (who was also an artist)
C) whom was also an artist,
D) who was, also, an artist

36 [1] The request for Be sheekee and Aysh-ke-bah-ke-ko-zhay to pose undoubtedly came from Meigs, who wished to ship some models of Native Americans to Rome for the guidance of Thomas Crawford, the artist then modeling figures for the east pediment of the Senate portico. [2] (Whether the clay models or plaster casts from these two specific works ever reached Crawford is not recorded.) [3] Meigs **37** wrote in their journal, "Vincenti is making a good likeness of a fine bust of Buffalo. [4] I think I will have it put into marble and placed in a proper situation in the Capitol **38** on a record of the Indian culture. [5] Five hundred years hence it will be interesting." [6] Meigs further commented about **39** Be sheekee "He is a fine-looking Indian, with character strongly marked."

36

To make this paragraph most logical, sentence 1 should be placed
A) where it is now.
B) after sentence 2.
C) after sentence 3.
D) after sentence 4.

37

A) NO CHANGE
B) writes in their
C) wrote in his
D) writes in his

38

A) NO CHANGE
B) as a record of
C) for a record about
D) as records of

39

A) NO CHANGE
B) Be sheekee, "he
C) Be sheekee; "He
D) Be sheekee: "He

CONTINUE

The sculptor completed his bust of Be sheekee in three days. The work is supported by a columnar pedestal [40] on which, in addition to decorative moldings, Vincenti deftly carved the image of an Ojibwa war shield. Behind the shield appear a bow and arrows and a rifle. The face of the shield is dominated by a peace pipe adorned with feathers, which transforms the implements of war into emblems of peace. When looking at the statue straight on, Be sheekee's drilled eyes direct a forceful gaze slightly up and to his right in an attitude [41] of doubt and hesitation. There is nothing of frailty in the ancient head, and Vincenti modeled the expressive face firmly and broadly, even while faithfully recording the facial idiosyncrasies. The elaborate headdress undoubtedly attests to the [42] sitters importance, as do the large ornaments suspended from the slit ears. Feathers are attached to the back of the head, and five short cylinders project hornlike on the crown of the head. [43] They are shown as if strapped to the head by a band, perhaps indicative of wooden originals, that ties under the chin in a bow. The long braids of hair and strings of beads are vigorously [44] carved, which animate the stoic, penetrating likeness of Be sheekee.

[40]
A) NO CHANGE
B) on which Vincenti deftly carved the image of decorative moldings, in addition to an Ojibwa war shield.
C) on which Vincenti, in addition to decorative moldings, deftly carved the image of an Ojibwa war shield surrounded by decorative moldings.
D) on which Vincenti deftly carved decorative moldings and the image of an Ojibwa war shield.

[41]
The writer wants to complete the sentence with words that fit with the overall tone and meaning of the text. Which choice best accomplishes this goal?
A) NO CHANGE
B) of a crazy person.
C) of creepiness.
D) of alertness and strength.

[42]
A) NO CHANGE   C) sitter's importance,
B) sitters' importance   D) sitters importance

[43]
A) NO CHANGE
B) Perhaps indicative of wooden originals, they are shown as if strapped to the head by a band that ties under the chin in a bow.
C) They are shown, perhaps indicative of wooden originals, as if strapped to the head by a band that ties under the chin in a bow.
D) They are shown as if strapped, perhaps indicative of wooden originals, to the head by a band that ties under the chin in a bow.

[44]
A) NO CHANGE
B) carved, and animating
C) carved, animating
D) carved and which animate

STOP

**If you finish before time is called, you may check your work on this section only.
Do not turn to any other section.**

SAT Model Exam 2 Answer Key

Reading Test Answers with Explanations

1. **D** As she talks with Mrs. Harris, Mrs. Tylor realizes that Mrs. Harris is rather strange and particular. Mrs. Harris is not the type of "nice" neighbor Mrs. Tylor was anticipating. Choices A, B, and C are incorrect because they do not explain what Mrs. Tylor comes to realize about Mrs. Harris.

2. **A** In this context, Mrs. Tylor is feeling nervous about her connection with Mrs. Harris, and the author compares it to other situations in which Mrs. Tylor could not remove herself (such as driving a car on an icy street). In this way, she feels "permanently" connected to a relationship with her new neighbor. Choice C is incorrect because there is no context for the word "convincingly." Choices B and D are incorrect because in this context "irrevocably" does not mean "assuredly" or "effectively."

3. **A** These images provide instances when Mrs. Tylor was feeling worried and out of control. Similarly, as Mrs. Tylor gets to know Mrs. Harris, she begins to be very concerned about how strange this new family seems. Choice B is incorrect because it is not related to the situation in the passage. Choice D is incorrect because there is no evidence that Mrs. Tylor is worried about this. Choice C is incorrect because although Mrs. Tylor may not trust the new neighbors, the comparison to the car and roller skates has more to do with fear and less to do with distrust.

4. **B** In this context, Mrs. Harris is referring to newspapers in a negative way. She mentions that her family does not read newspapers at all, so "corruption" works best.

5. **C** "Disdainful" means showing contempt or lack of respect, which is how Mrs. Harris feels toward newspapers. She says in lines 37–38, "You really never need to read a newspaper, you know." Later, in lines 60–63, she refers to former neighbors who "deliberately left their *New York Times*" on their doorstep, as if this were an offensive act. Choice A is incorrect because "intrigued" suggests a more positive feeling than is evidenced by Mrs. Harris's comments. Choice D is incorrect because "ambivalent" would mean that Mrs. Harris was unsure of how she felt toward newspapers. Choice B is incorrect because there is no evidence that she is confused about newspapers.

6. **C** There is evidence in the passage for each of these descriptions. "Selfish" is supported by lines 69–72 ("Feeling as though . . . stays there when we move"). "Snobbish" and "overbearing" are supported by line 18 ("Mr. Harris cannot bear the radio"), lines 46–47 ("Mrs. Harris lifted her head . . . monographs"), and lines 52–56 ("What . . . Pre-Elizabethan, of course"). Choices A, B, and D are incorrect because, although there may be evidence for some of the words in each choice, none of these choices is completely correct.

7. **B** Choice B is the best example of Mr. Harris being snobbish because it describes his aversion to newspapers. Choices C and D have nothing to do with Mr. Harris. Choice A is a statement by Mrs. Harris directed toward Mrs. Tylor about her husband being crazy. However, clearly Mrs. Harris doesn't really think her husband is crazy. It's a statement to draw out Mrs. Tylor's opinion, which is not strong evidence of Mr. Harris's character.

8. **D** It is evident that Mrs. Tylor finds Mrs. Harris quite strange and most likely does not agree with many of the new neighbor's opinions. Yet she responds "of course" to many of Mrs. Harris's comments, in order to be polite. Choice A is incorrect because Mrs. Tylor seems quite willing to engage with Mrs. Harris at first. Choice B is incorrect because shyness is not why Mrs. Tylor is concealing her own opinions. Choice C is incorrect. While Mrs. Tylor will probably talk about the Harris family with the neighbors, this inference doesn't follow logically from the fact that she says "of course" to everything Mrs. Harris says.

9. **B** These lines imply that Mrs. Harris believes others *do not* understand her husband but that she *does* understand him. Choices A, C, and D do not provide evidence of Mrs. Harris's understanding of her husband.

10. **D** Several lines in the text indicate that the Harris's neighbors went out of their way to play their radio loudly and "deliberately" leave their newspaper on the doorstep. The reader understands that these were ways to annoy the Harris family so that they would leave. Choice A is incorrect because clearly Mrs. Tylor is nervous about the family's odd behavior. No evidence is given for choice B or choice C.

11. **A** The first sentence of the passage claims that "when you eat may determine how long and strong your heart beats," and then the rest of the passage goes on to support this idea with evidence related to fruit flies' eating habits and heart health. Choices B, C, and D are incorrect because they do not accurately describe both the first sentence and how it relates to the rest of the passage.

12. **C** The graph indicates that 5-week-old fruit flies with unrestricted eating had irregular heartbeats. The dashes are not equal in length. Choice A is incorrect because gene coordination is not represented by the graph. Choice D is incorrect because the light gray line on the graph shows 7 to 8 beats per 5 seconds, which does not equate to 2 beats per second. Choice B is incorrect because by 3 weeks, the black line does not indicate significant problems yet. (By 5 weeks, the irregularity can be seen.)

13. **D** The graph indicates that by 5 weeks, the fruit flies with unlimited eating times had irregular heartbeats. The text supports this in lines 3–5 ("Fruit flies that limited . . . whenever they wanted") and in lines 47–50 ("The hearts of the anytime eaters . . . deteriorated heart function"). Choice A is incorrect because it contradicts the central claim of the passage. Choice B is incorrect because the graph and text indicate that in the beginning (around 3 weeks), the irregular heartbeats are not yet apparent. Choice C is incorrect because the graph and passage indicate that the irregular heartbeat problem continues and worsens over time.

14. **A** In this context, "synchronize" has to do with other "body clocks" coordinating their time and rate with feeding time. Choices B, C, and D are incorrect because in this context, "synchronize" does not mean "agree with," "pull together," or "maintain harmony with."

15. **C** Lines 17–20 support the idea that circadian rhythms govern body temperature, blood pressure, and sleep. There is not evidence that they govern hunger pangs ("Circadian clocks work in nearly . . . and sleep"). Choices A, B, and D are incorrect because the passage states each of these ideas.

16. **A** This choice accurately reflects what is suggested by the passage lines 47–50 ("The hearts of the anytime eaters . . . badly deteriorated heart function"), lines 13–16 ("Scheer was not involved . . . rhythms can damage their health"), and lines 23–26 ("Previous research in mice has suggested . . . other ravages of high-fat diets").

17. **D** The passage discusses "efficient energy usage" and by-products "building up and damaging tissues," suggesting that "metabolic" has to do with making energy. Choices A and C are incorrect because they refer to plants or amphibians. Choice B is incorrect because it is too vague.

18. **C** Lines 69–70 indicate that timed feeding helps with gene coordination ("That finding suggests . . . gene activity"). Choices A, B, and D are incorrect because the passage does not provide evidence that timed feeding improves hunger patterns, bowel regularity, or liver functioning.

19. **B** These lines refer to gene activity as it relates to circadian rhythm peaks and how they were more regular in those with restricted eating versus those with unrestricted eating. Choices A, C, and D are incorrect because they do not provide direct evidence concerning gene activity.

20. **B** Lines 58–61 state that when the circadian clocks of flies with regular eating patterns were disabled,

they still experienced health problems. This implies that regular eating habits alone are not enough to keep the flies' hearts healthy. This supports choice B. There is no support for choice A. The passage states that "clocks synchronize themselves according to feeding time," which rules out choice C. Choice D is incorrect because the passage states that "genes follow the circadian rhythms," while choice D says that circadian rhythms are set by gene activity.

21. **B** The best answer is choice B because it provides evidence from research that implies that functioning circadian clocks are just as or more important than regular eating habits.

22. **B** In this context "cordial" is used to describe "exhilaration" and is followed in the paragraph by words such as "cheering" and "sweetness." Choices A, C, and D are incorrect because in this context, "cordial" does not mean "hospitable," "gracious," or "complicated."

23. **C** The questions in these lines are rhetorical. They are used to emphasize that there is nothing in life so "pleasant" and rewarding as friendship.

24. **B** These words are all extremely positive. Choice C can be eliminated. The writer passionately extols the benefits of friendship with over-the-top optimism. Thus, choices A and D do not accurately capture the tone.

25. **B** In this context the author is describing how friendship transforms a person. He gives the examples of this transformation: "there is no winter, and no night; all tragedies, all ennuis vanish." Although "metamorphosed" can mean "to change physical form," it is not the correct meaning in this context. Choice C implies a change fitting something for a new or different use. Choice D is not correct for the context.

26. **B** The author states that when someone ". . . understands me, becomes mine, [he becomes] a possession for all time." Choices A, C, and D are incorrect because these ideas are not mentioned in the passage.

27. **D** These lines state that when the author finds someone who truly understands him, that person becomes a friend forever. Choice C is incorrect because the author speaks of liking solitude, yet also being happy to see his friends. Choice B is incorrect because these lines refer to the author's gratitude for friends. Choice A is incorrect because although the author mentions "a thousand years," he states this in the context of being "cheerful alone," not in the context of the duration of a friendship.

28. **C** Both authors mention the pleasures of friendship. Evidence from Passage 1: lines 7–9 ("From the highest . . . sweetness of life"), lines 10–11 ("What is so pleasant . . . for me again") and lines 15–20 ("The moment we indulge . . . beloved persons"). Evidence from Passage 2: lines 32–33 ("Life has no pleasure . . . friendship") and lines 44–47 ("The friendship which is to be practiced . . . delighting each other"). Choice A is incorrect because only Passage 1 emphasizes that friendship is eternal. Passage 2 points out that friendships may end. Choice B is incorrect because only Passage 2 focuses on the work involved in friendship. Choice D is incorrect because although Passage 2 mentions it, Passage 1 focuses on the enduring nature and not the transitory nature of friendship.

29. **B** The author of Passage 2 refers to friendships ending, whereas the author of Passage 1 focuses on friendships lasting forever lines 43–44 ("But these instances . . . they are rare"), lines 48–49 ("Many accidents . . . will be abated"), and lines 54–57 ("Those who would gladly . . . is destroyed by long absence"). Choice D is incorrect because the author of Passage 2 states that "friendship, like love, is destroyed by long absence" (lines 56–57). Choice A is incorrect because this is the central claim of Passage 1, not Passage 2. Choice C is incorrect because neither passage addresses this concept.

30. **A** The author of Passage 2 discusses the fact that friendship must be based on "mutual pleasure" (line 46). Choice B is incorrect because this is the central claim of Passage 1, not Passage 2. Choice C is incorrect because although Passage 2 begins with the line "Life has no pleasure higher or nobler than that of friendship," the passage goes on to focus on how and why friendships often fail. The author of Passage 1 is much more in support of the concept that friendship is the greatest gift in life. Choice D is incorrect because the author of Passage 2 states that "short intermissions" are actually good for friendships. Although the author Passage 2 discusses the issue of time apart, it is not the central claim of the passage.

31. **C** In these lines the author of Passage 2 clarifies his point that although "life has no pleasure higher or nobler than that of friendship," long-lasting friendships are not common unless certain criteria are met. Choice A is incorrect because in these lines, the author presents an idea that he later qualifies by pointing out problems with friendships. Choice B is incorrect because in these lines the author mentions others who support the idea that friendships will last no matter what. Choice D is incorrect because in these lines the author provides specifics about situations in which friendships end.

32. **B** This paragraph describes how long absences destroy friendships. Choice C is incorrect because it contradicts the main point of the final paragraph. Choice D is incorrect because it is an exaggerated interpretation of the author's point. Choice A is incorrect because although the author does state this idea, it is not the central claim of the paragraph.

33. **B** The second paragraph states that "the invaders and the existing population lived side by side and eventually intermarried extensively." Choice A is incorrect because this idea is posed as a question in the first paragraph, not as the author's claim. Choices C and D are incorrect because the first two paragraphs do not mention these ideas.

34. **A** The third paragraph jumps back in time chronologically to explain the earliest migration of people into Britain. This provides background to explain how the population became more diverse over time. Although the paragraph alludes to the fact that they can identify the genetic signature of these early people, it doesn't explain how the research is done (choice B). No mention is made of diverse populations or a counterclaim (choices C and D).

35. **C** In this context the word "signature" is referring to genetic evidence, or a "distinctive characteristic." Choices A, B, and D are incorrect because in this context, "signature" does not mean "a discernable autograph," "a detailed description," or "a musical arrangement."

36. **A** In this sentence, the author states that there is a "homogenous" group and then contrasts this with "small clusters of genetically *different* populations." This indicates that "homogenous" means the opposite of "different," which is why "of the same kind" is an accurate definition. Choices C and D are incorrect because they contain words that mean "different," not "the same." Choice B is incorrect because "unchanging" emphasizes the action of staying the same instead of the quality of being similar.

37. **C** Lines 26–29 state, ". . . all around the Celtic periphery. . . lie small clusters of genetically different populations. . . ." Choice A is incorrect because it states the population is "diverse," but the text says the population is not diverse but "different" from the population of central and south Britain. Choice B is not explained by the text. Choice D is incorrect; the text is making the opposite point.

38. **B** Choice B is where the text explains the "genetically different populations" in the Celtic periphery.

39. **B** The text says that building roads and farms encouraged movement among the people, which resulted in a more similar gene pool. There is no evidence for choices A and D. Choice C is incorrect because it doesn't take into account that people's genetic structures in different areas are different and will not be the same.

40. **A** The central claim is that Romano-British "lived side by side and eventually intermarried extensively." The best support for that is the genetic evidence presented in lines 11–15.

41. **D** Paragraph 7 presents the problem of "considerable migration into Britain," which changes the genetic pool. The paragraph then explains how researchers were able to avoid this problem by "seeking out elderly people who lived in rural areas and whose grandparents had been born locally."

42. **C** Dr. Donnelly's point is that genetic evidence complements historical accounts and archaeology by focusing on "what is happening to the masses rather than the elite." He is not elevating genetic evidence above history and archaeology. He is saying it provides a different picture by looking at all levels of society.

43. **C** In paragraphs 2 and 3, the passage defines GM foods and explains the science behind the process. Paragraphs 5 and 6 explain how GM crops are resistant to insects and herbicides, allowing greater yields.

44. **A** Based upon the context, genes are being combined together.

45. **A** Graph 1 indicates that 71 percent of farmers plant GM crops to increase their yields. This is supported by choice A. Choice B doesn't mention an increase in yields. Choice C is about the most common genetically engineered crops. Choice D discusses insecticides, which aren't directly mentioned in the graph.

46. **B** The passage states: "Making plants resistant to insects is helpful to farmers because they do not have to spray their crops with insecticides." No mention is made of the other choices.

47. **B** The passages states: "However, according to one study, Bt toxin has been found in the bloodstream of consumers, raising some safety concerns." No support is given for choice A or choice D. Although Graph 2 mentions an increase in herbicide use (choice C), no mention is made of this in the passage.

48. **C** This line mentions concerns over food safety.

49. **D** The best meaning is choice D because the passage mentions that GM plants are "tolerant of herbicides." They are able to grow even when these harmful chemicals are applied to weeds in the field. Choices A and B don't fit the context. Choice C is close to the intended meaning, but the word "hardship" doesn't fit with the context of plants.

50. **A** Graph 2 indicates that the use of insecticides decreased as the percentage of GM corn increased. Although choices B and C are true according to the graph, this information doesn't support the idea that making plants resistant to insects is beneficial to farmers. Choice D is mentioned in the text under the graph, but it doesn't support the author's point.

51. **A** The text under Graph 2 states, "But resistant insects have led to a recent uptick in insecticide applications." No mention is made of the ideas in the other choices. Choice D indicates that Bt corn has become resistant to herbicides, which is an advantage, not a negative.

52. **A** Both the first and final paragraphs suggest possible ways that GM crops could be used to improve nutrition and health.

Writing and Language Test Answers with Explanations

1. **D** The chart indicates most musicians and singers (17.08 percent) work for performing arts companies. Only 2.54 percent are self-employed or "independent" artists.

2. **B** It is grammatically correct to place commas between items in a list. Choice A is incorrect because it leaves out the comma after "Los Angeles." Choice C is incorrect because it does not include any commas between the names of cities. Choice D is incorrect because it places a comma after "and."

3. **C** The verb "tour" properly maintains the parallel structure of the sentence that contains the verb "travel." Choices A, B, and D are incorrect because they do not maintain parallel structure of the verbs.

4. **B** "Accept" is the correct word in this context because it means "to agree to receive." "Except" means "to exclude." Choices A and C incorrectly use "except." Choice D incorrectly uses the verb "lead" instead of "leads," which agrees with the subject "work."

5. **C** The table shows musicians and singers growing to 5 percent. Choices A, B, and D are incorrect because they are not supported by the table.

6. **A** The sentence correctly uses "their" to show possession. Choice B is incorrect because "there" is an adverb meaning "in, at, or to that place or position." Choice C is incorrect because "they're" is a contraction meaning "they are." Choice D is incorrect because "theirs" is not grammatically correct in the sentence.

7. **D** Choice A has several problems including wordiness, lack of parallel structure among items in a list, and redundancy of the word "and." Only choice D removes the extra "and," removes the unnecessary phrase "to serve as," and makes all items in the list parallel in form by rewriting all as an adjective and noun.

8. **A** In this choice, "however" provides an appropriate transition between contrasting ideas. The preceding sentences discuss the opportunities for singers. On the other hand, the following sentence discusses the fact that employment growth will be limited. Choices B, C, and D are incorrect because they provide transitions that do not accurately represent the relationship between the sentences.

9. **C** This choice correctly punctuates the two independent clauses. Choices A, B, and D are incorrect because they do not provide correct punctuation to connect two independent clauses, thus creating run-on sentences or comma splices.

10. **D** This choice provides the most effective sentence to introduce a paragraph about the challenges musicians and singers will face in their job searches. Choices A, B, and C are incorrect because they do not establish the main idea of the paragraph.

11. **B** The clause "who have exceptional musical talent and dedication" is a restrictive clause in the sentence. That is, it is necessary to the meaning of the sentence. Therefore, this clause should not be offset with commas. Choices A, C, and D are incorrect because they use commas incorrectly around the essential clause.

12. **A** This choice correctly and concisely combines the two sentences while maintaining the original meaning. Choice B is incorrect because a semicolon can only be used between two independent clauses. Choice C is incorrect because it uses the present tense verb "is," whereas the rest of the sentence is in past tense ("the Midwest *was* a place . . ."). Choice D is incorrect because it creates a run-on sentence.

13. **C** This choice correctly uses a dash to introduce a clause that provides more information about the preceding statement. Choice A is incorrect because a semicolon cannot be used before a dependent clause. Choice B is incorrect because a colon must be used to introduce an explanation (or a list), and the clause following the colon is not an explanation for the preceding part of the sentence. Choice D is incorrect because a comma is not necessary between the independent and dependent clauses.

14. **A** This choice provides the correct verb form and tense. The passage is in the past tense, and the verb "overflowed" agrees with the subject "the Great Lakes." Choices B, C, and D are incorrect because they provide the incorrect form or tense of the verb.

15. **B** This choice provides a correct comparison of like to like. Archaeology can be compared to "geology and astronomy," not to "geologists and astronomers." Choices A, C, and D are incorrect because they provide faulty comparisons.

16. **D** "Accumulating" is the best verb in the context of a collection of artifacts. Choices A, B, and C are incorrect because they provide less accurate word choices in this context.

17. **B** This choice provides the correct use of an apostrophe to show possession. Choice A is incorrect because the apostrophe placed after "collectors" suggests that there were multiple collectors, which is not the case in the sentence. Choice C is incorrect because it lacks an apostrophe for possession. Choice D is incorrect because this use of an apostrophe is grammatically incorrect.

18. **D** Sentence 4 provides a logical follow-up to the second sentence of the paragraph. Sentences 1 and 2 introduce and explain an analogy about personal archaeological collections. Then sentence 4 relates the comparison to archaeological science.

19. **D** This choice provides commas to set apart the nonrestrictive phrase "like many amateur collectors." Choice A lacks commas. Choice B is incorrect because it is too vague. Choice C introduces a faulty comparison.

20. **D** This choice provides the correct use of a colon to introduce a quotation. Choices A, B, and C are incorrect because they do not provide appropriate punctuation to introduce a quotation.

21. **C** This choice removes the unnecessary comma after "that." Choice A is incorrect because it uses an unnecessary comma after "that." Choice B incorrectly uses the present tense verb "tells" when the past tense "told" is required. Choice D uses a colon incorrectly.

22. **A** This choice most effectively achieves the purpose of concluding the passage with a sentence that emphasizes the importance of maintaining the archaeological record: ". . . priceless information they contained lost with them." Choices B, C, and D do not focus on the importance of maintaining the archaeological record.

23. **D** This choice provides the correct verb tense (past tense), and it uses standard English for the phrase "somewhere *in* the vicinity." Choice A is incorrect because it uses a present tense verb and non-standard English: "somewhere *on* the vicinity." Choice C is incorrect because it uses a present tense verb. Choice B is incorrect because although it corrects the verb tense, it retains the phrase "somewhere *on* the vicinity."

24. **D** This choice effectively combines two related sentences by showing their relationship with the word "and." Choice A is incorrect because it forms a comma splice. Choice B is incorrect because it uses the word "so," which incorrectly creates a relationship of cause and effect between the two sentences. Choice C is incorrect because it creates confusion about the meaning of the two sentences.

25. **C** This choice effectively creates a transition between this sentence and the previous one by indicating that the relationship is one of contrast. Choice B incorrectly communicates an effect. Choice D signals a more important idea. Choices A and B imply a chronological chain of events that the context doesn't support.

26. **B** "Obliterated" is the most accurate word for the context of this sentence, which is about a crater blasting into the continental shelf. Choice A ("removed") incorrectly implies intentionality. Choice C ("abolished") is used to describe ideas and abstract nouns, not physical objects. Choice D ("purged") usually means a removal of people in a violent way or a removal of something from the body.

27. **B** This sentence introduces the idea of the passage, so it should come at the beginning of the paragraph. Choices A, C, and D are incorrect because they create an illogical progression of ideas.

28. **A** This choice most accurately and clearly defines a bolide. Choice B discusses craters instead of the bolides. Choice C is a question that hooks the reader, but it doesn't contain the main idea. Choice D explains a detail of a bolide but doesn't establish the entire definition.

29. **A** "Icy comet" effectively provides an example of another impacting body. Choice B is incorrect because it does not provide a new example. Choice C does not relate to the passage. Choice D is too vague.

30. **B** The underlined sentence should be kept because it provides an important description to help the reader understand craters. Choices C and D are incorrect because the sentence is important to the paragraph. Choice A is incorrect because it contains an inaccurate explanation for why the sentence should be kept.

31. **A** Choice A is correct because it uses the plural pronoun "they" to agree with the plural noun "craters." Choices C and D are wrong because they use the singular pronoun "it." Choice B uses the singular verb "exhibits" instead of the plural form "exhibit" required by the plural noun "they."

32. **B** This choice provides correct verb tense and agreement. The subject is "margin," which takes a singular verb. Thus, choice A is incorrect. Among choices B, C, and D, only choice B provides the present tense verb "is" needed to fit with the verb tense established in the passage.

33. **C** This choice uses the correct verb form. The subject is "blocks" so the correct verb is "slide." Choices A, B, and D do not provide the correct verb tense and/or agreement with the subject.

34. **C** The underlined portion is redundant since "unknown" and "unheard of" have essentially the same definition. Choice C provides the most concise phrasing.

35. **B** The clause in the parentheses is considered a nonrestrictive clause, which means that it is not essential to the meaning of the sentence. Parentheses (or a pair of commas) is the correct way to punctuate this clause. Choice A is incorrect because it only provides one comma instead of a pair around the clause. Choice C incorrectly uses "whom" to introduce the clause; the objective case "who" is needed. Choice D is incorrect because it uses unnecessary commas around the word "also."

36. **A** The placement of the sentence creates a logical progression of ideas from the previous paragraph into this paragraph. Choices B, C, and D are incorrect because they create an illogical progression of ideas.

37. **C** Montgomery Meigs is one person, so it is correct to state that he "wrote in *his* journal." Choices A and B are incorrect because they use the pronoun "their" to refer to Meigs and/or use the incorrect verb tense. Choice D is incorrect because it uses an incorrect verb tense.

38. **B** This choice contains the standard English phrase "as a record of." Choices A and C are incorrect because they use nonstandard English. Choice D is incorrect because it uses the word "records," which is not correct in the context of the sentence.

39. **D** This choice correctly introduces a statement in quotation marks with a colon. Choice A is incorrect because it does not provide any punctuation for dialogue. Choice B is incorrect because it does not contain an initial capital letter inside the quotation marks. Choice C is incorrect because it uses a semicolon improperly.

40. **D** The placement of the interrupting phrase "in addition to decorative moldings" is confusing and removes the focus from the main detail, the Ojibwa war shield. Choice B changes the emphasis of the sentence to the moldings. It is incorrect. Choice C is awkward and confusing because the phrase appears to modify Vincenti. Choice D rewrites the sentence for clarity of ideas.

41. **D** This choice accurately conveys the feeling indicated by the words from the passage: "forceful gaze," "nothing of frailty," "firmly and broadly." Choice A communicates the correct serious tone, but the content is incorrect according to the context of the passage. Choices B and C are too informal and inappropriate.

42. **C** This choice correctly places an apostrophe for possession to show that the importance "belongs" to the sitter. Choice A is incorrect because it does not use an apostrophe to show possession. Choice B is incorrect because the apostrophe placed after the word "sitters" indicates that there are multiple sitters. Choice D is incorrect because it omits the comma, which is necessary to set apart the clause.

43. **B** This choice most effectively conveys an idea by placing the modifying phrase "by a band that ties under the chin in a bow" next to the phrase it is explaining: "strapped to the head." Choice A is incorrect because the modifying phrase follows the phrase "perhaps indicative of wooden originals," which is not what it is modifying. Choice C is incorrect because the phrase "perhaps indicative of wooden originals" interrupts the sentence in an awkward way. Choice D is incorrect because the modifying phrase interrupts the phrase "strapped to the head."

44. **C** This choice correctly modifies the word "carved." Choice B is incorrect because adding the word "and" here causes awkward sentence construction. Choices A and D are incorrect because "which" refers to groups or things; "carved" is a verb.

SAT Model Exam 2 Correlation Charts

Use the following charts to help you identify which lessons in the book will help you improve your score.

If you missed these questions on the Reading Test . .	study this lesson. (Because some questions test over multiple skills, some numbers may appear under more than one lesson.)
	Reading Literature
1, 5, 6, 8, 10	Lesson 1: Understanding explicit and implicit ideas (p. 57)
1, 10	Lesson 1: Understanding main ideas and purpose (p. 65)
3, 8	Lesson 1: Analyzing word choice and imagery for tone (p. 74)
5, 6, 8, 10	Lesson 1: Identifying characterization (p. 85)
	Lesson 1: Identifying narrator's point of view (p. 92)
7, 9	Lesson 1: Citing textual evidence (p. 99)
	Literature and Informational Texts
2, 4, 14, 17, 22, 25, 35, 36, 44, 49	Lesson 2: Understanding meanings of words and phrases (p. 107)
	Informational Texts
15, 30, 33, 41	Lesson 3: Understanding explicit meanings (p. 115)
15, 30, 32	Lesson 3: Determining central ideas and summarizing (p. 121)
16, 18, 37, 46	Lesson 3: Identifying supporting details (p. 127)
13, 20, 26, 39	Lesson 4: Making inferences (p. 137)
23, 39	Lesson 4: Using analogical reasoning (p. 146)
19, 21, 27, 31, 38, 40, 48, 52	Lesson 4: Citing textual evidence (p. 152)
11, 23, 26, 29, 34, 42	Lesson 5: Analyzing author's point of view and purpose (p. 159)
23, 30, 33, 40, 47, 50	Lesson 5: Analyzing the use of arguments (claims, counterclaims, reasoning, and evidence) (p. 168)
24	Lesson 6: Analyzing use of word choice to shape meaning and tone (p. 177)
11, 41, 43	Lesson 6: Analyzing text structure (p. 184)
28, 29	Lesson 7: Synthesizing information from multiple texts (p. 193)
12, 13, 45, 50, 51	Lesson 7: Analyzing and synthesizing information from texts and graphics (p. 204)

If you missed these questions on the Writing and Language Test . . .	study this lesson. (Because some questions test over multiple skills, some numbers may appear under more than one lesson.)
	Writing and Language
10, 22, 28, 29, 30	Lesson 8: Revising texts for clarity, focus, and purpose (p. 243)
1, 5	Lesson 8: Relating information presented in graphs, charts, and tables to information presented in texts (p. 252)
18, 27, 36	Lesson 9: Revising for cohesion and logical order (p. 261)
8, 25	Lesson 9: Revising beginnings or endings of a text or paragraphs to ensure transitional words, phrases, and sentences are used effectively (p. 267)
16, 19, 23, 26, 38, 41	Lesson 10: Revising texts to improve word choice for exactness and content (p. 275)
7, 34, 40	Lesson 10: Revising to eliminate wordiness (p. 279)
41	Lesson 10: Revising text for consistency of style and tone or to match style and tone to purpose (p. 288)
9	Lesson 11: Editing to correct sentence fragments and run-ons (p. 295)
12, 24	Lesson 11: Combining sentences for clarity (p. 304)
3, 7, 24, 40, 43, 44	Lesson 11: Editing to correct problems with subordination/coordination, parallel structure, and modifier placement (p. 306)
14, 21, 23, 31, 32, 33, 37	Lesson 11: Editing to correct shifts in verbs (tense, voice, and mood) and pronouns (person and number) (p. 313)
31, 35	Lesson 12: Using pronouns correctly (p. 323) Lesson 12: Correcting unclear or ambiguous pronouns or antecedents (p. 325)
4, 32, 37	Lesson 12: Correcting problems with pronoun/antecedent, subject/verb, and noun agreement (p. 329)
4, 6	Lesson 12: Correcting misuse of confusing words (p. 337)
15	Lesson 12: Correcting cases in which unalike terms are compared (p. 337)
	Lesson 12: Correcting nonstandard written English (p. 338)
2, 11, 12, 19	Lesson 13: Using end punctuation and commas (p. 343)
20, 39	Lesson 13: Using semicolons and colons (p. 349)
13, 20, 35, 39	Lesson 13: Using parentheses, dashes, and quotation marks (p. 354)
11, 17, 21, 42	Lesson 13: Using possessives and correcting use of unnecessary punctuation (pp. 358–359)

SAT Model Exam 3

READING TEST
65 MINUTES, 52 QUESTIONS

Use the Reading Section of your answer sheet to answer the questions in this section.

• • • Directions •

Each passage or pair of passages below is followed by a number of questions. After reading each passage or pair, choose the best answer to each question based upon what is stated or implied in the passage or passages or in any graphics (tables or graphs). To practice using a SAT-type answer sheet, fill in the appropriate letter bubble next to the question number. A reproducible answer sheet can be found on page 380.

Questions 1–10 are based on the following passage.

In this excerpt from a detective novel set in the American Southwest, two Navajo police officers, Leaphorn and Chee, are at odds over the place of witchcraft and yataalii (medicine men) in the Navajo culture.

Still, Leaphorn had kept the bone bead.

"I'll see about it," he'd said. "Send it to the lab. Find out if it is bone, and what kind of bone." He'd torn a page from his notebook, wrapped the bead
5 in it, and placed it in the coin compartment of his billfold. Then he'd looked at Chee for a moment in silence. "Any idea how it got in here?"

"Sounds strange," Chee had said. "But you know you could pry out the end of a shotgun shell and
10 pull out the wadding and stick a bead like this in with the pellets."

Leaphorn's expression became almost a smile. Was it contempt? "Like a witch shooting in the bone?" he asked. "They're supposed to do that through a little
15 tube." He made a puffing shape with his lips.

Chee had nodded, flushing just a little.

Now, remembering it, he was angry again. Well, to hell with Leaphorn. Let him believe whatever he wanted to believe. The origin story of the Navajos
20 explained witchcraft clearly enough, and it was a logical part of the philosophy on which the Dinee had founded their culture. If there was good, and harmony, and beauty on the east side of reality, then there must be evil, chaos, and ugliness to the west.
25 Like a nonfundamentalist Christian, Chee believed in the poetic metaphor of the Navajo story of human genesis. Without believing in the specific Adam's rib, or the size of the reed through which the Holy People emerged to the Earth Surface World, he
30 believed in the lessons such imagery was intended to teach. To hell with Leaphorn and what he didn't believe. Chee started the engine and jolted back down the slope to the road. He wanted to get to Badwater Wash before noon.

CONTINUE ▶

35 But he couldn't quite get Leaphorn out of his mind. Leaphorn posed a problem. "One more thing," the lieutenant had said. "We've got a complaint about you." And he'd told Chee what the doctor at the Badwater Clinic had said about him.

40 "Yellowhorse claims you've been interfering with his practice of his religion," Leaphorn said. And while the lieutenant's expression said he didn't take the complaint as anything critically important, the very fact that he'd mentioned it implied that Chee
45 should desist.

"I have been telling people that Yellowhorse is a fake," Chee said stiffly. "I have told people every chance I get that the doctor pretends to be a crystal gazer just to get them into his clinic."

50 "I hope you're not doing that on company time," Leaphorn said. "Not while you're on duty."

"I probably have," Chee said. "Why not?"

"Because it violates regulations," Leaphorn said, his expression no longer even mildly amused.

55 "How?"

"I think you can see how," Leaphorn had said. "We don't have any way to license our shamans, no more than the federal government can license preachers.

60 If Yellowhorse says he's a medicine man, or a hand trembler, or a road chief of the Native American Church, or the Pope, it is no business of the Navajo Tribal Police. No rule against it. No law."

65 "I'm a Navajo," Chee said. "I see somebody cynically using our religion . . . somebody who doesn't believe in our religion using it in that cynical way. . . ."

"What harm is he doing?" Leaphorn asked.
70 "The way I understand it, he recommends they go to a yataalii if they need a ceremonial sing. And he points them at the white man's hospital only if they have a white man's problem. Diabetes, for example."

75 Chee had made no response to that. If Leaphorn couldn't see the problem, the sacrilege involved, then Leaphorn was blind. But that wasn't the trouble. Leaphorn was as cynical as Yellowhorse.

"You, yourself, have declared yourself to be
80 a yataalii, I hear," Leaphorn said. "I heard you performed a Blessing Way."

Chee had nodded. He said nothing.

Leaphorn had looked at him a moment, and sighed. "I'll talk to Largo about it," he said.

85 And that meant that one of these days Chee would have an argument with the captain about it and if he wasn't lucky, Largo would give him a flat order to say nothing more about Yellowhorse as shaman. When that happened, he would cope as
90 best he could.

1

This passage is mainly about
A) officers Chee and Leaphorn discussing a piece of evidence for a case.
B) Chee's opposition to Yellowhorse's practice of medicine.
C) Chee driving to Badwater.
D) the conflict between white men's doctors and the Navajo medicine men.

CONTINUE

2

The officers are apparently concerned with the bone bead because it is some kind of

A) ornamentation.

B) shotgun shell.

C) witch's weapon.

D) evidence.

3

The relationship between Chee and Leaphorn can best be described as

A) friendly.

B) contentious.

C) indifferent.

D) hateful.

4

It can be inferred that Chee's attitude toward his religion is basically

A) reverent.

B) negative.

C) confused.

D) apathetic.

5

Which choice provides the best evidence for the answer to question 4?

A) lines 17–19 ("Now, remembering it, . . . wanted to believe")

B) lines 19–24 ("The origin story . . . ugliness to the west")

C) lines 25–31 ("Like a nonfundamentalist . . . intended to teach")

D) lines 31–34 ("To hell with Leaphorn . . . Wash before noon")

6

As used in line 76, the word "sacrilege" most nearly means

A) casual disrespect.

B) irreligious behavior.

C) violation of something sacred.

D) illegal action.

7

Lieutenant Leaphorn can best be characterized as

A) a world-weary man of keen intelligence.

B) a rather skeptical believer in the status quo.

C) a person willing to scrap the rules.

D) a hot-headed irrational bully.

8

Which choice provides the best evidence for the answer to question 7?

A) lines 12–15 ("Leaphorn's expression . . . shape with his lips")

B) lines 38–45 ("And he'd told Chee . . . Chee should desist")

C) lines 56–64 ("I think you can see how . . . against it. No law")

D) lines 69–74 ("What harm is he doing . . . Diabetes, for example")

9

As used in line 87, the word "flat" most nearly means

A) dull.

B) clear.

C) even.

D) absolute.

10

Based on Chee's thoughts, words, and feelings, it can be inferred that he and Leaphorn are different in which of the following ways?

A) Chee is more traditional in his beliefs than Leaphorn, while Leaphorn is more cautious and rational than Chee.

B) Chee is more disdainful of Navajo religion than Leaphorn, while Leaphorn is less courageous and resolute than Chee.

C) Chee expresses more indifference toward Navajo traditions than does Leaphorn, while Leaphorn is less temperamental and gutsy than Chee.

D) Chee has more of an insider's perspective on the Navajo people than does Leaphorn, while Leaphorn is less meticulous and rational than Chee.

CONTINUE

Questions 11–20 are based on the following passage.

The following article discusses two challenging concepts: irony and paradox. It seeks to explain both.

"I was boxed in and didn't know where to turn."

The box appears in everyday speech as a metaphor for restraint. What is not always apparent is that boxes are not just convenient metaphors. They are
5 built into the structure of the language. Boxing, or classification, is at the very heart of language. It enables us to function. Without classification, most communication would be impossible. Words are neat pigeonholes into which we fit our ideas.

10 Classification is a remarkable achievement, but it is deceptive. It cannot capture reality. The "real world" out there has nothing to do with classification. The lion doesn't know that it is a "lion." Analyzing the classification practice clarifies
15 two devices, seemingly disparate, but all related to the "boxing" habit: irony and paradox.

Irony is usually defined as a confrontation of opposites. Astronaut John Glenn returns safely from a hazardous trip through space to injure himself in a
20 bathroom fall. The irony involves the confrontation of what is and what appears to be, between reality (whatever that is) and appearance. The appearance assigned "danger" to space and "safety" to home. The reality proved quite the opposite.

25 Irony implies an observer who can see the contradiction. Unless there is someone to evaluate appearance and reality, there is no irony. In *Oedipus Tyrannus* the audience knows the reality and notes the discrepancy between Oedipus's misevaluation
30 of the situation and the situation itself. It is the observer who sees the difference between

appearance and reality. He makes the classifications. Otherwise there is no irony. In "reality" the bathroom was a more dangerous place than space,
35 at least for John Glenn in the context he found himself in. The irony, then, consists in our setting up categories which produce the contradictions.

Since we act on assumptions and extrapolations, many of our actions in retrospect seem to us "ironic"
40 because they contrast the reality (what actually happened) with the appearances or expectations (what we assumed would happen). The irony, however, is linguistic in origin. It depends upon putting things into mutually exclusive boxes
45 (appearance and reality—or something and its opposite). Reality, which is unconcerned with linguistic classification, has nothing to do with irony.

Like irony, paradox involves contradictions, but the contradictions are more readily apparent. "I lie all
50 the time." This paradoxical statement seems to set up irreconcilable contradictions. If in reality I lie all the time, then the verbalization must be a lie. But if the verbalization is a lie, then I cannot in reality lie all the time. This paradox, like irony, involves classification,
55 putting things into boxes. Here we are actually setting up two boxes: one we might label "those who lie all the time" and one we might label "those who don't lie all the time." The speaker linguistically cannot fit into both boxes. The paradox is clarified when the
60 classification is cleared up. If "I lie all the time," I set up a linguistic box that excludes the possibility of telling the truth. But there are really two different boxes: (1)"lying all the time" and (2) "lying some of the time." Obviously the statement is an indication
65 that the second box is the one we might use here.

CONTINUE ➡

11

The comparison in lines 8–9 ("Words . . . ideas") serves to explain that

A) the definitions of words are constantly changing.

B) words allow us to organize our thoughts.

C) people often use the incorrect words.

D) imagination is important to communication.

12

The lines about *Oedipus Tyrannus* (lines 27–30) serve mainly to

A) provide an illustration of how an observer is needed to identify irony.

B) explain why plays are more ironic than real life.

C) provide a counterclaim to the idea that without an audience there is no irony.

D) demonstrate a basic difference between John Glenn and Oedipus.

13

According to the passage, the writer's view is that irony is

A) based upon incorrectly identifying reality and appearance.

B) when the opposite of what is expected to happen occurs.

C) the same as paradox.

D) a confrontation of opposing ideas.

14

Which choice provides the best evidence for the answer to the previous question?

A) lines 17–18 ("Irony is . . . opposites")

B) lines 25–27 ("Irony implies. . . no irony")

C) lines 42–45 ("The irony . . . opposite")

D) lines 48–49 ("Like irony . . . readily apparent")

15

As used in line 29, the word "discrepancy" most nearly means

A) a difference.   C) an evaluation.

B) a change.   D) a category.

16

In lines 38–47 ("Since we . . . with irony"), what point about irony does the author make?

A) It is concerned with reality, not with language.

B) It is concerned with language, not with reality.

C) It depends on putting things into the same boxes.

D) It emerges from the confluence of expectations and appearances.

17

Based on the paragraph beginning with line 48, which of the following may be considered a paradox?

A) Toby is a friend of mine. She is also a good friend of Annette's.

B) You can save money by spending it.

C) An irresistible force met an immovable object.

D) A friend in need is a friend indeed.

18

As used in line 51, the word "irreconcilable" most nearly means

A) incompatible.

B) compromising.

C) opposing.

D) not specific.

19

According to the passage, paradox is

A) similar to irony because it doesn't involve contradictions.

B) similar to irony because both involve categorizing statements.

C. dissimilar to irony because it doesn't involve linguistics.

D. dissimilar to irony because it doesn't relate to classification.

CONTINUE ➡

Which choice provides the best evidence for the answer to the previous question?

A) lines 48–49 ("Like irony . . . readily apparent")

B) lines 54–55 ("This paradox . . . into boxes")

C) lines 59–60 ("The paradox . . . cleared up")

D) lines 62–64 ("But . . . time")

Questions 21–31 are based on the following passages and table.

Passage 1 is taken from The Emancipation Proclamation issued on January 1, 1863.

Passage 2 is adapted from an article found on the National Archives and Records Administration Web site.

Passage 1

Whereas, on the twenty-second day of September, in the year of our Lord one thousand eight hundred and sixty-two, a proclamation was issued by the President of the United States, containing, among

5 other things, the following, to wit:

"That on the first day of January, in the year of our Lord one thousand eight hundred and sixty-three, all persons held as slaves within any State or designated part of a State, the people whereof

10 shall then be in rebellion against the United States, shall be then, thenceforward, and forever free; and the Executive Government of the United States, including the military and naval authority thereof, will recognize and maintain the freedom of such

15 persons, and will do no act or acts to repress such persons, or any of them, in any efforts they may make for their actual freedom . . . "

Now, therefore I, Abraham Lincoln, President of the United States, by virtue of the power in me

20 vested as Commander-in-Chief, of the Army and Navy of the United States in time of actual armed rebellion against the authority and government of the United States, and as a fit and necessary war measure for suppressing said rebellion, do, on this first day

25 of January, in the year of our Lord one thousand eight hundred and sixty-three, and in accordance with my purpose so to do publicly proclaimed for the full period of one hundred days, from the day first above mentioned, order and designate as the

30 States and parts of States wherein the people thereof respectively, are this day in rebellion against the United States, the following, to wit:

Arkansas, Texas, Louisiana, [Lincoln explains a few parishes in Louisiana that are excluded from

35 the proclamation.] Mississippi, Alabama, Florida, Georgia, South Carolina, North Carolina, and Virginia, (except the forty-eight counties designated as West Virginia), . . . and which excepted parts, are for the present, left precisely as if this proclamation

40 were not issued.

And by virtue of the power, and for the purpose aforesaid, I do order and declare that all persons held as slaves within said designated States, and parts of States, are, and henceforward shall be free;

45 and that the Executive government of the United States, including the military and naval authorities thereof, will recognize and maintain the freedom of said persons.

Passage 2

President Abraham Lincoln issued the

50 Emancipation Proclamation on January 1, 1863, as the nation approached its third year of bloody civil war. The proclamation declared "that all persons held as slaves" within the rebellious states "are, and henceforward shall be free."

Despite this expansive wording, the Emancipation Proclamation was limited in many ways. It applied only to states that had seceded from the Union, leaving slavery untouched in the loyal border states. It also expressly exempted parts of the Confederacy that had already come under Northern control. Most important, the freedom it promised depended upon Union military victory.

Although the Emancipation Proclamation did not end slavery in the nation, it captured the hearts and imagination of millions of Americans and fundamentally transformed the character of the war. After January 1, 1863, every advance of federal troops expanded the domain of freedom. Moreover, the Proclamation announced the acceptance of black men into the Union Army and Navy, enabling the liberated to become liberators. By the end of the war, almost 200,000 black soldiers and sailors had fought for the Union and freedom.

From the first days of the Civil War, slaves had acted to secure their own liberty. The Emancipation Proclamation confirmed their insistence that the war for the Union must become a war for freedom. It added moral force to the Union cause and strengthened the Union both militarily and politically. As a milestone along the road to slavery's final destruction, the Emancipation Proclamation has assumed a place among the great documents of human freedom.

Census of 1860				
States	Free Population	Slave Population	Total	Percentage of Slaves
South Carolina	301,271	402,541	703,812	57.2
Mississippi	354,700	436,696	791,396	55.1
Louisiana	376,280	333,010	709,290	47.0
Alabama	529,164	435,132	964,296	45.1
Florida	78,686	61,753	140,439	43.9
Georgia	595,097	462,232	1,057,329	43.7
North Carolina	661,586	331,081	992,667	33.4
Virginia	1,105,192	490,887	1,596,079	30.7
Texas	421,750	180,682	602,432	30.0
Arkansas	324,323	111.104	435,427	25.5
Tennessee	834,063	275,784	1,109,847	24.8
Kentucky	930,223	225,490	1,155,713	19.5
Maryland	599,846	87,188	687,034	12.7
Missouri	1,067,352	114,965	1,182,317	9.7
Delaware	110,420	1,798	112,218	1.6
Total	8,289,953	3,950,343	12,240,296	32.2

CONTINUE

21

Lincoln refers to his previous proclamation in lines 1–3 in order to

A) remind his audience that he has given the Confederacy fair warning of his intentions.

B) imply that he has been concerned about freeing the slaves for a long time.

C) inform his audience that freeing the slaves is his number one concern.

D) suggest that the first proclamation was ignored by Confederate officials.

22

As used in line 11, "thenceforward" most nearly means

A) consequently.

B) from that place onward.

C) from the current time onward.

D) forever.

23

The main purpose of Passage 1 is to

A) grant freedom to all slaves living in the slave states if the Confederacy didn't dissolve by January 1, 1863.

B) bolster the Union cause in the eyes of foreigners, especially Europeans.

C) grant freedom to slaves in Confederate states if slave states didn't return to the Union by January 1, 1863.

D) demoralize the troops in the Confederate army and create a labor shortage for the Confederacy.

24

Which choice provides the best evidence for the answer to question 23?

A) lines 1–5 ("Whereas, on the twenty-second . . . to wit")

B) lines 8–11 ("all persons held . . . and forever free")

C) lines 12–17 ("the Executive Government . . . actual freedom")

D) lines 33–39 ("Arkansas, Texas, . . . the present, left")

25

It can be inferred from Passage 1 and the chart that Tennessee, Kentucky, Maryland, Missouri and Delaware

A) did not allow slaves within their borders.

B) were in rebellion against the United States.

C) were required to emancipate their slaves.

D) were not in rebellion against the United States.

26

Which of the following conclusions is supported by the 1860 census?

A) Slaves made up 11 percent of Delaware's population.

B) Slaves comprised the majority of South Carolina's and Mississippi's populations.

C) The state with the greatest number of slaves was Mississippi.

D) Virginia had fewer slaves than the state of Georgia did.

27

As used in line 80, "milestone" most nearly means

A) significant event.

B) turning point.

C) important discovery.

D) benchmark.

28

The author of Passage 2 responds to Lincoln's statement in lines 42–45 ("all persons . . . be free") in Passage 1 by stating that

A) the Proclamation was far too expansive in its wording and included too many states.

B) Union military defeat would be the only occurrence that could free the slaves.

C) the Proclamation was far too limited in its scope and was a political move only.

D) the Proclamation only addressed slavery in certain states, meaning slavery could continue in others.

CONTINUE

29

Which choice provides the best evidence for the answer to question 28?

A) lines 52–54 ("The proclamation . . . the free")

B) lines 55–56 ("Despite . . . ways")

C) lines 56–58 ("It . . . states")

D) lines 63–66 ("Although . . . the war")

30

Which statement best characterizes the different ways in which the authors of Passage 1 and Passage 2 approach the fate of the slaves?

A) The first emphasizes that freeing the slaves is the morally correct path, while the second points out that many slaves did not in fact achieve freedom.

B) The first states that slaves living in Confederate states would be freed, while the second asserts that their freedom depended on a Union military victory.

C) The first states that freeing the slaves is a good military strategy, while the second focuses on the contribution former slaves made to Union victory.

D) The first stresses that slavery would soon end in the United States, while the second focuses on the achievements of the Proclamation.

31

The discussion in paragraph 3 (lines 63–73) of Passage 2 mainly serves to

A) continue the criticism outlined in the previous paragraph.

B) offer solutions to the problems raised in the previous paragraph.

C) provide positive outcomes that contrast with the negative aspects listed in the previous paragraph.

D) examine more closely the ideas mentioned in the previous paragraph.

Questions 32–41 are based on the following passage.

The following selection is about a brilliant scientist, Lynn Margulis, who challenges familiar scientific paradigms.

Despite her success, Margulis' work remains controversial. Hers is not the kind of work with which the scientific community can simply agree to disagree. "It's a question of changing your religion,"

5 she says. Academia rewards its brightest stars with a specially funded teaching position called a named chair. A few years ago, Margulis was on the verge of being appointed to a named chair at a major university but was not offered the position, though

10 the possibility still remains. The antagonism stems, in part, from Margulis' collaboration with British chemist James Lovelock on Gaia, the hypothesis that the Earth acts as a self-regulating, self-maintaining system (*Phenomena,* May 1988). Gaia's most

15 vocal supporters are ecoactivists, church groups, and science-fiction writers. To some establishment scientists, these countercultural associations make the ideas behind Gaia suspect. Ironically, Margulis is hard on Gaia's popular supporters. "Lynn is

20 ferocious about going after mysticism," says Stewart Brand, founder of the Whole Earth Catalog. "New Age types are drawn to her and then she busts them high, low, and center for being softheaded."

In a sense, Margulis challenges the American

25 myth of the rugged individual—alone, self-contained and able to survive. "Our concept of the individual is totally warped," she says. "All of us are walking communities of microbes. Plants are sedentary communities. Every plant and animal on

30 Earth today is a symbiont, living in close contact with others."

CONTINUE ➡

Consider one species of desert termite. Living in its hindgut are millions of single-celled, lemon-shaped organisms called *Trichonympha ampla*.

35 Attached to the surface of one *T. ampla* live thousands of whiplike bacteria known as spirochetes. Inside live still other kinds of bacteria. If not for these microbial symbionts (in some wood-eating insects, the symbionts are too numerous to count),

40 the termite, unable to digest wood, would starve.

But, the termite itself is only one element in a planetary set of interlocking, mutual interactions—which Lovelock's neighbor, novelist William Golding, dubbed Gaia, for the Greek goddess

45 of the Earth. After digesting wood, the termite expels the gas methane into the air. (In fact, the world's species of termites, cows, elephants and other animals harboring methane-producing bacteria account for a significant portion of Earth's

50 atmospheric methane.) Methane performs the vital task of regulating the amount of oxygen in Earth's atmosphere. If there were too much oxygen, fires would burn continuously; too little, and animals, plants and many other live beings would suffocate.

55 Earth's atmospheric oxygen is maintained, altered and regulated by the breathing activities of living creatures, such as those of the methane-makers in the micro-cosmos. Life does not passively "adapt." Rather, it actively, though "unknowingly," modifies

60 its own environment.

When NASA sponsored a search for life on Mars, in the early 1970s, Lovelock looked for ways that life might have modified the Martian atmosphere. Finding no particular modification attributable to

65 microbes or any other form of life, he and Margulis predicted that the Viking probe would find a dead

Mars. They turned out to be right. "Gaia is more a point of view than a theory," says Margulis. "It is a manifestation of the organization of the planet."

70 That organization resembles those hollow Russian dolls that nest one inside another. "For example, some bacteria in the hindgut of a termite cannot survive outside that microbial community," explains Gail Fleischaker, Boston University

75 philosopher of science and a former graduate student of Margulis'. "The community of termites, in turn, requires a larger ecological nest. And so it expands. You will never find life in isolation. Life, if it exists at all, is globe-covering."

80 Although Margulis provided the "biological ammunition" for Gaia and remains its staunch advocate, she does little work on it directly. "I've concentrated all my life on the cell," she says. The ideas that she has championed were once "too

85 fantastic for mention in polite biological society," as one scientific observer described them in the 1920s. As recently as 20 years ago, these ideas were so much at odds with the established point of view that, according to another observer, they "could not

90 be discussed at respectable scientific meetings." Although aspects of the symbiotic theory of cell evolution still provoke hostility, the theory is now taught to high school students.

32

In lines 19–20, Margulis' basic objection to New Age types is that they
A) lack intelligence.
B) deny scientific facts.
C) engage in mystical thinking.
D) are ruled by their emotions.

CONTINUE ➡

33

As used in line 30, "symbiont" most nearly means

A) a consumer of methane.

B) an interdependent organism.

C) a community of plants.

D) a self-contained organism.

34

It can be inferred that Margulis did not receive the special teaching position because she

A) did not work hard enough to earn it.

B) enraged the rest of the teaching staff.

C) suggested that people change their religion.

D) supported a contentious theory.

35

Margulis would most likely agree with which of the following statements?

A) We're all reliant on each other.

B) Rugged people can survive on their own.

C) Communities make individuals weak.

D) Microbes create communities.

36

Which of the following provides evidence to support Margulis' claim that every plant and animal on Earth today is a symbiont?

A) The whiplike bacteria known as spirochetes live on the surface of desert termites.

B) The organism *Trichonympha ampla* lives in the gut of desert termites.

C) Microbial symbionts live in the digestive system of the Japanese beetle.

D) Methane-producing bacteria add to the oxygen in the atmosphere.

37

The discussion of methane in lines 46–54 primarily serves to

A) illustrate a process that involves both animals and plants.

B) compare Margulis' theory with an alternative theory.

C) demonstrate the importance of living creatures' relationship to Earth.

D) show that methane-makers contribute to the problem of global warming.

38

How does paragraph 5 (lines 61–69) relate to the paragraph that precedes it?

A) Paragraph 5 provides absolute proof of a theory presented in paragraph 4.

B) Paragraph 5 gives an example that supports an idea explored in paragraph 4.

C) Paragraph 5 presents a theory different from the one in paragraph 4.

D) Paragraph 5 challenges a misconception regarding the myth exposed in paragraph 4.

39

Based on lines 71–79, Gail Fleischaker is most likely to disagree with which of the following statements?

A) Some organisms make their own food, whereas others do not.

B) Interactions among organisms contribute to humankind's well-being.

C) Some organisms perish when they leave their own community.

D) Organisms living together in an ecosystem don't always depend on each other.

40

As used in line 81, the word "ammunition" most nearly means

A) something used to support a case.

B) a quantity of bullets.

C) considerations in a debate.

D) advice that attacks a viewpoint.

CONTINUE

41

Which choice provides the best support for the idea that Gaia is now widely accepted?

A) lines 14–16 ("Gaia's most vocal supporters . . . science-fiction writers")

B) lines 16–18 ("To some establishment . . . ideas behind Gaia suspect")

C) lines 18–23 ("Ironically, Margulis is hard . . . for being softheaded")

D) lines 91–93 ("Although aspects of . . . to high school students")

Questions 42–52 are based on the following passage and charts.

The following is adapted from "The Cognitive Benefits of Being Bilingual" by Viorica Marian and Anthony Shook.

In a survey conducted by the European Commission in 2006, 56 percent of respondents reported being able to speak in a language other than their mother tongue. In many countries that
5 percentage is even higher—for instance, 99 percent of Luxembourgers and 95 percent of Latvians speak more than one language. Even in the United States, which is widely considered to be monolingual, one-fifth of those over the age of five reported
10 speaking a language other than English at home in 2007, an increase of 140 percent since 1980. Millions of Americans use a language other than English in their everyday lives *outside* of the home, when they are at work or in the classroom. Europe
15 and the United States are not alone, either. The Associated Press reports that up to 66 percent of the world's children are raised bilingual. Over the past few decades, technological advances have allowed researchers to peer deeper into the brain
20 to investigate how bilingualism interacts with and changes the cognitive and neurological systems.

To maintain the relative balance between two languages, the bilingual brain relies on executive
25 functions, a regulatory system of general cognitive abilities that includes processes such as attention and inhibition. Because both of a bilingual person's language systems are always active and competing, that person uses these control mechanisms every
30 time she or he speaks or listens. This constant practice strengthens the control mechanisms and changes the associated brain regions.

Bilingual people often perform better on tasks that require conflict management. In the
35 classic Stroop task, people see a word and are asked to name the color of the word's font. When the color and the word match (i.e., the word "red" printed in red), people correctly name the color more quickly than when the color and the word don't match
40 (i.e., the word "red" printed in blue). This occurs because the word itself ("red") and its font color (blue) conflict. The cognitive system must employ additional resources to ignore the irrelevant word and focus on the relevant color. The ability to ignore
45 competing perceptual information and focus on the relevant aspects of the input is called inhibitory control. Bilingual people often perform better than monolingual people at tasks that tap into inhibitory control ability.

50 The neurological roots of the bilingual advantage extend to subcortical brain areas more traditionally associated with sensory processing. Both monolingual and bilingual adolescents were given auditory attention tests that measure the ability
55 to distinguish sounds. When monolingual and bilingual adolescents listen to simple speech sounds (e.g., the syllable "da") without any intervening

CONTINUE

background noise, they show highly similar brain stem responses to the auditory information.

60 When researchers play the same sound to both groups in the presence of background noise, the bilingual listeners' neural response is considerably larger, reflecting better encoding of the sound's fundamental frequency, a feature of sound closely

65 related to pitch perception. To put it another way, in bilingual people, blood flow (a marker for neuronal activity) is greater in the brain stem in response to the sound. Intriguingly, this boost in sound encoding appears to be related to advantages in auditory

70 attention. The cognitive control required to manage multiple languages appears to have broad effects on neurological function, fine-tuning both cognitive control mechanisms and sensory processes.

Chart 1

Percentage of Bilingual Speakers in the World

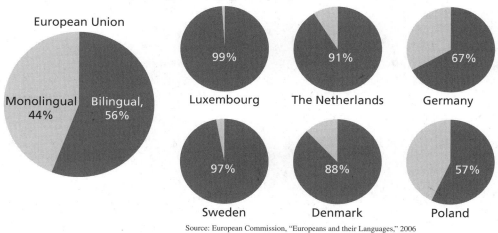

Source: European Commission, "Europeans and their Languages," 2006

Percentage of US Population who spoke a language other than English at home by year

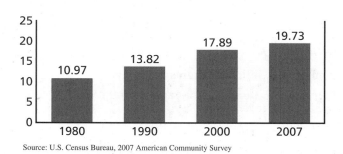

Source: U.S. Census Bureau, 2007 American Community Survey

Chart 2

Bilinguals (gray) outperform monolinguals (black) on sustained selective attention, regardless of sensory domain.

CONTINUE

Furthermore, the benefits associated with
75 bilingual experience seem to start quite early—
researchers have shown bilingualism to positively
influence attention and conflict management
in infants as young as seven months. In one
study, researchers taught babies growing up in
80 monolingual or bilingual homes that when they
heard a tinkling sound, a puppet appeared on one
side of a screen. Halfway through the study, the
puppet began appearing on the opposite side of the
screen. In order to get a reward, the infants had to
85 adjust the rule they'd learned; only the bilingual
babies were able to successfully learn the new rule.
This suggests that even for very young children,
navigating a multilingual environment imparts
advantages that transfer beyond language.

42

The primary purpose of this passage is to
A) to convince readers to study a second
   language.
B) to educate readers about the prevalence of
   bilingualism.
C) to explain how bilingual brains work.
D) to highlight the trend of bilingualism in the
   world.

43

Paragraph 1 primarily encourages readers to
view bilingualism as
A) a type of sensory overload for humans.
B) a byproduct due to technological
   advancement.
C) an inevitable part of human existence.
D) an ability that is increasingly prevalent.

44

Chart 1 offers evidence that
A) Poland and Denmark have the lowest rate
   of bilingualism among European countries
   listed in the graph.
B) the United States and Sweden have
   disparate education systems that impact
   their respective rates of bilingualism.
C) bilingualism is much more widespread in
   Europe but is increasing in the United States.
D) even though the overall percentage of
   bilingual speakers is higher in Europe, the
   number of Americans who speak another
   language at work is greater.

45

As it is used in lines 45–46, "inhibitory control"
refers to the ability to
A) handle disagreements between two groups.
B) discern different shading of colors.
C) choose the correct answer on a test.
D) focus in on relevant information.

46

According to the passage, which of the
following is true of bilingual people?
A) They use executive functions as a way
   to maintain equilibrium between two
   languages.
B) They may have difficulty switching from
   one language to another.
C) They have a highly developed ability to
   decode complex information.
D) They fall behind monolingual speakers on
   auditory attention tests.

47

Which choice provides the best evidence for the
answer to question 46?
A) lines 22–26 ("To maintain . . . and
   inhibition")
B) lines 46–48 ("Bilingual. . . ability")
C) lines 69–72 ("The cognitive . . . sensory
   processes")
D) lines 84–87 ("This suggests. . . beyond
   language")

CONTINUE →

48

The data from Chart 2 could be best used to support which of the following lines from the text?

A) lines 12–14 ("Millions . . . classroom")

B) lines 32–33 ("Bilingual . . . management")

C) lines 54–64 ("When monolingual . . . auditory information")

D) lines 60–64 ("When researchers . . . frequency")

49

In lines 24–25, "executive functions" refers to a

A) method employed to prioritize learning.

B) technique used to internalize a second language.

C) procedure used to classify the stages in cognitive development.

D) system related to thought processes.

50

Based upon lines 30–32 (This . . . regions), it can be inferred that

A) trying to learn two languages can damage the brain's function.

B) bilingual people have learned to exert greater control on their brain.

C) bilingual people use more of their brains than monolingual people.

D) monolingual people are not as intelligent as bilingual people.

51

The final paragraph (lines 74–89) suggests that bilingual babies

A) are better able to adapt when standards change.

B) learn to speak faster than monolingual babies.

C) had better hearing and eyesight than other babies.

D) were able to multitask better than other babies.

52

The purpose of the final paragraph (lines 74–89) is mainly to

A) explain a study done with babies from bilingual homes.

B) pose a question about the age when children comprehend two languages.

C) offer evidence for why it is easier for younger children to learn a new language.

D) provide evidence that even infants exhibit benefits of being bilingual.

STOP

If you finish before time is called, you may check your work on this section only.
Do not turn to any other section.

WRITING AND LANGUAGE TEST
35 MINUTES, 44 QUESTIONS

Use the Writing and Language section of your answer sheet to answer the questions in this section.

Directions

Each passage below is accompanied by a number of questions. For some questions, you will consider how the passage might be revised to improve the expression of ideas. For other questions, you will consider how the passage might be edited to correct errors in sentence structure, usage, or punctuation. A passage or a question may be accompanied by one or more graphics (such as a table or graph) that you will consider as you make revising and editing decisions.

Some questions will direct you to an underlined portion of a passage. Other questions will direct you to a location in a passage or ask you to think about the passage as a whole.

After reading each passage, choose the answer to each question that most effectively improves the quality of writing in the passage or that make the passage conform to the conventions of standard written English. Many questions include a "NO CHANGE" option. Choose that option if you think the best choice is to leave the relevant portion of the passage as it is.

Questions 1–11 are based on the following passage.

Stories from the Revolution

1 Everyone knows, that American women first got the vote in 1920 with the passage of the 19th Amendment. **2** Right! Wrong! Some New Jersey women voted as early as 1776. Historians argue about just what Thomas Jefferson and his colleagues meant when they declared "that all men are created equal." Did the founders mean males only or were there some situations when "men" could mean all humans? What natural or political **3** rights in their view, did women possess? In New Jersey, the unique case of women voters **4** offers some clues.

1
A) NO CHANGE
B) Everyone know, that
C) Everyone knows that
D) All know, that

2
A) NO CHANGE   C) Right! Wrong.
B) Right? Wrong?   D) Right? Wrong!

3
A) NO CHANGE
B) rights, in their view,
C) rights, in their view
D) rights, in there view,

4
A) NO CHANGE   C) would offer
B) offer   D) offered

CONTINUE

The framers of New Jersey's first constitution in 1776 gave the vote to "all inhabitants of this colony, of full age, who are worth fifty pounds . . . and have resided within the county for twelve months." The other twelve new states restricted voting to men.

5 Although some have argued that this gender-neutral language was a mistake, most historians agree that the clear intention was to allow some women to vote. Married women had no property in their own names and were assumed to be represented by their husbands' **6** votes, only single women voted in New Jersey. But, in the 1790s and 1800s, large numbers of unmarried New Jersey women regularly participated in elections and spoke on political issues.

7 This was largely a result of the Democratic-Republican Party's attempt to unify **8** it's factions for the 1808 presidential election. A faction within the party wanted to deny the vote to aliens and the non-tax-paying poor. The liberal faction within the party gave way on this, but also took the vote from **9** women: who tended to vote for the Federalist Party. In this way, New Jersey's 30-year experiment with female suffrage ended—not mainly because of opposition to the idea of women voting, but for reasons of party politics. A renewed focus on the importance of women in the home (as opposed to the public realm) may also have been a factor in the change.

5

The writer is considering deleting the underlined sentence. Should the sentence be kept or deleted?

A) Kept, because it provides supporting evidence about women's suffrage in New Jersey.

B) Kept, because it provides an additional example about how the state's intentions matter.

C) Deleted, because it blurs the paragraph's focus on women voting in New Jersey.

D) Deleted, because it doesn't provide specific examples about how the historians reached their conclusions.

6

A) NO CHANGE

B) votes only single women

C) votes, but only single women

D) votes, so only single women

7

Which choice most effectively establishes the main topic of the paragraph?

A) Political motivations are often complicated and the Democratic-Republican Party's motivations were no different.

B) In 1807, the state's legislature ignored the constitution and restricted suffrage to white male citizens who paid taxes.

C) New Jersey framed its constitution in such a way that it inadvertently created several political party factions.

D) Due to New Jersey women's political activism in the late 1700s, the Democratic-Republican Party opted to revoke women's suffrage in order to unify the party.

8

A) NO CHANGE   C) its'

B) its   D) it

9

A) NO CHANGE

B) women who tended to vote for the Federalist Party.

C) women, who tended to vote for the Federalist Party.

D) women, which tended to vote for the Federalist Party.

CONTINUE

Some historians have viewed the New Jersey episode as evidence that the founders entertained the possibility that women could have political rights. The emphasis on liberty and natural rights in the Revolutionary period brought previously excluded groups into the political process. For example, women took the lead in organizing boycotts of British goods in the disputes over colonial **10** rites that led up to the Revolution. The writers of New Jersey's 1776 constitution took the natural rights sentiment further than other states were willing to go. Clearly, the idea of some women voting was considered one possibility among others in the Revolutionary era. **11**

10

A) NO CHANGE
B) rites, that
C) rights, that
D) rights that

11

The writer wants to conclude the passage with a sentence that emphasizes how New Jersey's attitude toward women's suffrage changed. Which choice would best accomplish this goal?

A) In order to vote in New Jersey, women living there had to meet certain criteria: be New Jersey residents for 12 months, possess at least 50 pounds, and meet an age requirement.

B) By 1807, Revolutionary fervor was a distant memory, and New Jersey fell into line with the practice of the other states.

C) The 1808 presidential election had a profound impact on New Jersey politics, which was primarily due to the Democratic-Republican party factions.

D) Only unmarried women were allowed to vote in New Jersey since it was assumed that married women were represented by their husbands in the voting process.

CONTINUE

Questions 12–22 are based on the following passage and chart.

A Different Look at Part-Time Employment

In 1995, about 6.5 million workers had a part-time job (or jobs) but were classified as full-time workers **12** yet their total workweek (at all jobs) was 35 hours or more. About 4.4 million people (69 percent) worked full-time at a primary **13** job. They also held one or more part-time jobs. **14** A majority of workers combined several part-time jobs with varying hours to make up a full-time workweek.

Workers within all three groups were more likely to be aged 25 to 54 than those classified under the official estimate of part-time **15** employment (defined as persons who usually work less than 35 hours a week at all jobs). In 1995, nearly 8 in 10 of the **16** workers who had a full- and a part-time job or whose hours varied on all jobs were in this age group, compared to 5 in 10 among the official part-time workers.

Percent distribution of workers on full-time schedules with part-time jobs, 1995 annual averages

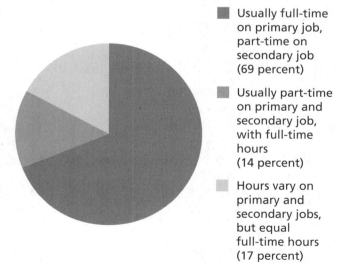

■ Usually full-time on primary job, part-time on secondary job (69 percent)

■ Usually part-time on primary and secondary job, with full-time hours (14 percent)

■ Hours vary on primary and secondary jobs, but equal full-time hours (17 percent)

12
A) NO CHANGE
B) because they're
C) because their
D) after there

13
Which choice most effectively combines the sentences at the underlined portion?
A) job, they also held
B) job, and also holding
C) job and so also held
D) job and also held

14
Which choice completes the sentence with accurate data based on the chart?
A) NO CHANGE
B) A smaller percentage (approximately 31 percent)
C) More than half
D) Some

15
A) NO CHANGE
B) employment; defined as persons who usually work less than 35 hours a week at all jobs.
C) employment defined as persons, who usually work less than 35 hours a week at all jobs?
D) employment: defined as persons who usually work less than 35 hours a week at all jobs.

16
A) NO CHANGE
B) workers, who had a full- and a part-time job or
C) workers, who had a full- and a part-time job, or
D) workers who had a full- and a part-time job, or

CONTINUE →

Women accounted for about 65 percent of all workers who combine several part-time jobs into a full-time schedule, a share that was comparable to the official estimate of part-time employment (68 percent). **17** For instance, the proportion of women with part-time jobs in the other two work arrangements was about 40 percent. **18** Workers who, reflecting these differences in age and gender, combined several part-time jobs into a full-time schedule were more commonly single men and married women. Married men, however, made up a relatively large proportion of those who worked at both a full- and part-time **19** job; on a full-time schedule composed of jobs with varying hours.

Between 1994 and 1995, the number of full-time **20** workers who held part-time jobs increased by about 380,000. The increase was evenly distributed among the three groups in this category and across demographic characteristics. Holding steady at slightly more than 23 million in 1994 and 1995, the number of persons counted as part-time under the official definition remained about the same.

Monthly estimates of the number of part-time workers, however, do not include all persons with part-time **21** jobs. In the survey persons who have more than one job are counted only once in the employment estimates. Such workers are classified as either full- or part-time based on their total usual weekly hours. Thus, workers who have both a full- and a part-time job, **22** for example, is classified as full-time workers, as are those whose combined hours in two or more part-time jobs total at least 35.

17
A) NO CHANGE
B) As a result,
C) In contrast,
D) Indeed,

18
A) NO CHANGE
B) Reflecting these differences in age and gender, workers who combined several part-time jobs into a full-time schedule
C) Workers who combined several part-time jobs, reflecting these differences in age and gender, into a full-time schedule
D) Workers who combined several part-time jobs into a full-time schedule, reflecting these differences in age and gender

19
A) NO CHANGE
B) job; or on
C) job, on
D) job or who worked

20
A) NO CHANGE
B) workers who held part-time jobs increases
C) workers whom held part-time jobs increased
D) workers whom hold part-time jobs increased

21
A) NO CHANGE
B) jobs, in the survey,
C) jobs in the survey,
D) jobs in the survey

22
A) NO CHANGE
B) for example are classified
C) for example, are classified
D) for example were classified

CONTINUE

Questions 23–33 are based on the following passage.

23 If all of the world's shallow water coral reefs were placed side-by-side, they would occupy an area a bit larger than the state of Texas. This area represents less than 0.015 percent of the ocean. Yet coral reefs harbor **24** more than one quarter of the oceans' biodiversity. No other ecosystem occupies such a limited area with more life forms. For this reason, reefs are often compared to **25** rainforests, which are the only other ecosystem that can boast anywhere near the amount of biodiversity found on a reef. Coral reefs are sometimes called rainforests of the seas.

Shallow coral reefs grow best in warm water (70–85° F or 21–29° C). It is possible for soft corals to grow in places with warmer or colder water, but growth rates in these types of conditions are very slow. Reef-building corals prefer clear and shallow water, where lots of sunlight filters through to their symbiotic algae. It is possible to find coral reefs at depths exceeding 91 m (300 ft), but reef-building corals generally grow best at depths shallower than 70 m (230 ft). **26** The most prolific reefs occupy depths of 18–27 m (60–90 ft), though many of these shallow reefs have been degraded.

23

Which choice most effectively establishes the main topic of the paragraph?
A) Coral reefs consist of shallow coral reefs, which grow best in water up to 70 meters deep, and deep-sea coral reefs, which grow in depths ranging from 50 meters to over 3,000.
B) Much is unknown about coral reefs because deep-sea technology has only begun to allow exploration of the deep-sea reefs.
C) Based on current estimates, shallow water coral reefs occupy approximately 284,300 square kilometers (110,000 square miles) of the sea floor.
D) Many factors affect where and how well coral grows, such as the amount of salt water, food availability, and so on.

24

A) NO CHANGE
B) higher than one quarter of the ocean's
C) more than one quarter of the oceans
D) more than one quarter of the ocean's

25

A) NO CHANGE
B) ecosystems, which are the only other ones
C) life forms, which are the only other example
D) the oceans, which are the only other ecosystem

26

The writer is considering deleting the underlined sentence. Should the sentence be kept or deleted?
A) Kept, because it provides supporting evidence about how shallow reefs grow best in warm water.
B) Kept, because it provides an example about at what depths coral reefs grow best.
C) Deleted, because it blurs the paragraph's focus on shallow coral reefs.
D) Deleted, because it doesn't provide specific examples about how coral reefs survive.

However, mesophotic coral ecosystems, where the dominant habitat-forming species can be comprised of coral, sponge, and algae species, are found at depths between 30 and 150 m in tropical and subtropical waters. Corals also need salt water to survive (between 32 to 42 parts per thousand), so [27] it also grew poorly near river openings with fresh water runoff. Other factors influencing [28] coral distribution is the availability of hard-bottom substrate, [29] having food such as plankton available, and the presence of species that help control macroalgae, like urchins and herbivorous fish.

Deep-sea coral communities thrive on continental shelves and slopes around the world, sometimes thousands of meters below the ocean surface. Unlike the well-studied tropical coral reefs, these corals inhabit deeper waters on continental shelves, slopes, canyons, and seamounts in waters ranging from 50 m to over 3,000 m in depth. A few species also extend into shallower, cold waters in the northern latitudes. Deep-sea corals are found in all oceans, including the Subantarctic. [30] Like the ocean, deep-sea corals exhibit high biodiversity.

27
A) NO CHANGE
B) they also grows
C) it also grow
D) they also grow

28
A) NO CHANGE
B) coral distribution are the availability near
C) coral distribution are the availability of
D) coral distribution were the availability of

29
A) NO CHANGE
B) having the availability of food such as plankton, and the presence of species
C) the availability of food such as plankton, and the presence of species
D) to have the availability of food such as plankton, and to have the presence of species

30
A) NO CHANGE
B) Like shallow waters, deep-sea corals
C) Like the ocean surface, deep-sea corals
D) Like their shallow-dwelling relatives, deep-sea corals

CONTINUE

Deep-sea coral habitats appear to be much more extensive and important than previously known. Currently, it is impossible to [31] ascertain the overall extent of deep coral communities because so many of the deeper areas these communities inhabit have been explored [32] incompletely and having not been explored at all. [33] With recent up-to-date advances in deep-sea technology, scientists are beginning to locate and map the distribution of deep-sea coral habitat.

[31]
A) NO CHANGE
B) guess
C) nose out
D) spot

[32]
A) NO CHANGE
B) incompletely or have not been explored at all
C) incompletely and which have not been explored at all
D) incompletely, which have not been explored at all

[33]
A) NO CHANGE
B) With recent, latest advances
C) With fresh, recent advances
D) With recent advances

CONTINUE

Questions 34–44 are based on the following passage.

Young Bess Wallace had beautiful eyes, large and round and **34** interesting. She knew her eyes were beautiful and wanted people to notice **35** them and to see the young womans' heart and vivacious personality they revealed. We know this because we can see it in the photographs taken of her during the first 30 years of her life.

34

The writer wants to complete the sentence with a third descriptive word detailing Bess's eyes. Which choice best accomplishes this goal?

A) NO CHANGE

B) expressive.

C) secretive.

D) impassive.

35

A) NO CHANGE

B) her and to see her

C) her and to see the young women's

D) them and to see the womanly

CONTINUE

36 [1] She liked to express herself through her clothes, especially her hats. [2] One of her teachers remembered that Bess "was always dressed in the very latest." [3] Her best friend recalled that "Bess always had more stylish hats than the rest of us did, or she wore them with more style." [4] This stylishness is apparent in the early photographs, too.

The later Bess **37** Truman the one remembered as First Lady from 1945 to 1953 seems a different person. She was not easy to know. She was a very private person forced to live as a very public one. When she became First Lady, she refused to give press conferences. A reporter protested her decision, and she replied, "I am not the one who is elected. I have nothing to say to the public." **38** She felt the same way, in fact, very similar, about photographers and would have stopped them taking pictures of her if she could. **39** Since she couldn't, she usually showed when a camera was pointed at her how she felt—she frowned, and she looked, as one historian has noted, "as if her feet hurt." "Nobody hates **40** to have her picture taken more then [Bess] does," her husband said in 1951.

36

For the sake of the cohesion of this paragraph, sentence 1 should be placed

A) where it is now.

B) after sentence 2.

C) after sentence 3.

D) after sentence 4.

37

A) NO CHANGE

B) Truman; the one remembered as First Lady from 1945 to 1953; seems

C) Truman—the one remembered as First Lady from 1945 to 1953—seems

D) Truman, the one remembered as First Lady from 1945 to 1953 seems

38

A) NO CHANGE

B) She likewise felt the same way

C) She felt the same way

D) Similarly, she felt the same way

39

A) NO CHANGE

B) Since she couldn't, she usually showed how she felt when a camera was pointed at her

C) Since she couldn't, she usually when a camera was pointed at her showed how she felt

D) Since she couldn't, when a camera was pointed at her she showed usually how she felt

40

A) NO CHANGE

B) to have her picture taken more than

C) to have their picture taken more than

D) to have their picture taken more then

CONTINUE

Harry Truman knew his life had been guided by [41] destiny, yet he felt he was meant to be president. "The truth is all I want from history," he wrote to a White House aide in February 1950. However, the truth was not what Bess wanted for herself from history. She felt differently. She wanted to evade history and its importunate gaze entirely. She didn't want people she didn't know talking about her or poring over pictures of her.

Yet once, when she was young and didn't have to worry about being remembered by history, she had [42] met the photographer and his camera and had revealed herself in photographs. She knew they would be seen, not [43] for millions of people she didn't know, but only by people she knew intimately and loved, her family and friends. [44] No one else cares about them.

41

A) NO CHANGE
B) destiny, because he
C) destiny; he
D) destiny—he

42

A) NO CHANGE
B) greeted
C) acknowledged
D) welcomed

43

A) NO CHANGE
B) with millions
C) at millions
D) by millions

44

A) NO CHANGE
B) No one else cared about it.
C) No one else cared about them.
D) No one else would care about them.

STOP

**If you finish before time is called, you may check your work on this section only.
Do not turn to any other section.**

SAT Model Exam 3 Answer Key

Reading Test Answers with Explanations

1. **B** The passage is mainly about Chee's view of Yellowhorse and his practice of medicine. Leaphorn warns Chee to stop telling people that "Yellowhorse is a fake." The other choices represent minor details in the story, not the main idea.

2. **D** Leaphorn and Chee talk about sending the bead to the lab to find out more about it, which suggests that they are treating it as evidence. There is not support for choice A in the passage. Choices B and C are mentioned but not in reference to what the bead could be.

3. **B** The passage reveals tension between Chee and Leaphorn. Chee thinks, "to hell with Leaphorn." Chee thinks of Leaphorn as a problem so their relationship is difficult or contentious because they don't agree. Also they disagree about Yellowhorse, and Leaphorn questions Chee's actions and motives. Choice A is too positive. Choice D is too negative. Choice C suggests that there are no distinct feelings between them, which is not the case.

4. **A** There is evidence that Chee is "reverent," or shows deep respect for religion, because he gets angry when Leaphorn makes a sarcastic remark about the Navajo religion and witches. Chee also expresses disapproval of Yellowhorse because he is a "fake" and "pretends to be a crystal gazer," thus indicating that he thinks religion should be respected. Choices B and D are incorrect because Chee is not negative or uncaring towards religion; he is respectful of it. There is not evidence for choice C.

5. **C** This choice reveals the specifics of Chee's respect for religion in that he believes in the lessons it is intended to teach. Choices A and D do not show Chee's respect for religion. Choice B explains a part of the Navajo religion but does not provide evidence for Chee's reverence for it.

6. **C** In the lines leading up to the sentence with "sacrilege," Chee speaks of his frustration with people who don't believe in his religion but then use it in a "cynical way." This implies that he thinks that religion should be treated as something sacred. Choice D is irrelevant to Chee's point. Choice B is somewhat possible, but choice C is more accurate. Choice A is partially correct in that Chee is speaking of disrespect for his religion, but it is more than "casual."

7. **B** Leaphorn does not feel that Chee's concerns about Yellowhorse are legitimate. Leaphorn is "skeptical" and thinks things are fine they way they are—the status quo. Choice C is incorrect because Leaphorn is actually quite concerned with the rules and with Chee following them. There is no evidence to support choice A. Choice D is too negative and extreme.

8. **D** These lines show Leaphorn's skepticism about Chee's concerns; Leaphorn does not think there is a problem. Choice B is not related to believing in the status quo. Instead, it relates to Leaphorn's belief that Chee is not following the rules. Choice C shows Leaphorn defending his belief that Yellowhorse is not doing anything wrong, which could indicate a belief in the "status quo," but this particular statement does not reveal his skepticism as much as choice D does. Choice A shows Leaphorn's skepticism, but does not relate to the idea of "status quo."

9. **D** In this sentence, the narrator says that Largo would give Chee "a flat order to say nothing," which means that the order is "absolute." This use of the word "flat" means complete and absolute, as in, it does not leave any uncertainty. Choices A and C can be meanings of "flat," but they do not work in this context. Choice B is close, but "absolute" is more accurate.

10. **A** Throughout the passage, the narrator refers to Chee's understanding of and belief in the Navajo religion, as well as his desire to protect it from being used by non-believers. In this way, he is more traditional

than Leaphorn, who has much less to do with the Navajo religion. Leaphorn comes across as more cautious and rational in his concerns about Chee following policies and not rocking the boat. Choice B and C are incorrect because Chee is not disdainful of or indifferent towards the religion; he is respectful of it. Choice D is incorrect because, although Chee has more of an insider's perspective, Leaphorn is not *less* meticulous and rational than Chee; he is more meticulous and rational.

11. **B** "Words are neat pigeonholes into which we fit our ideas" is a metaphor that explains why we need words to communicate. Based upon the idea of "neat pigeonholes," the writer is communicating the idea that words help us classify or name our thoughts (ideas).

12. **A** The reference to *Oedipus Tyrannus* provides an example or illustration of why an audience is needed to perceive ironic events. The passage provides no support for choices B, C, or D.

13. **A** The writer states that irony has to do with how people name things. It's "linguistic in origin." Because people classify things in "mutually exclusive" boxes, choice A is the best answer. Choices B and D are identified in the passage as "usual" definitions of irony, but these are not the writer's definition. Choice C is not mentioned in the passage.

14. **C** In these lines, the author explains his view of what irony is and how it is linked with language. Choice A explains how irony is "usually" defined. Choice B explains an attribute of irony, but doesn't give a clear definition. choice D explains the difference between paradox and irony.

15. **A** In this context, "discrepancy" is used to describe the difference between "Oedipus's misevaluation of the situation and the situation itself."

16. **B** In these lines the author is making the point that the language that is used to represent experiences is where irony comes from, not from the experiences themselves. Choice C is a misinterpretation of part of these lines. Choice D is the author's definition of irony, but it is not the point that is made in these lines. Choice A is the opposite of what these lines mean.

17. **B** This choice represents a similar contradictory relationship to the one the author gives. In this paragraph, the example of paradox given is the statement, "I lie all the time." The author goes on to explain that if this statement is true, then it represents a paradox because the person making this claim is actually telling the truth. Choices A, C, and D do not represent paradoxes.

18. **A** From the context, a statement is a paradox that sets up "irreconcilable contradictions." This means that the two ideas don't fit together or agree. The best definition is "incompatible." Choices B and D do not make sense. Choice C, "opposing," is close to being correct, but it's definition fits better with the definition of "contradiction."

19. **B** The passage states: "This paradox, like irony, involves classification, putting things into boxes." Choice B refers to "categorizing," which is the same thing as classifying. Choice A is contradicted by the line: "Like irony, paradox involves contradictions . . ." Choice D is opposite of the correct answer. Choice C is not supported by the passage.

20. **B** These lines state that paradox and irony both involve putting things into boxes, which is classification.

21. **A** In the opening lines, Lincoln reminds his audience that in September he had issued a proclamation stating that in January all slaves would be set free. By referring to these dates, Lincoln is drawing attention to the fact that he has given them a warning of this new policy. There is not evidence to support choice D. Choices B and C may be true statements, but they do not accurately represent Lincoln's purpose.

22. **C** "Thenceforward" is used in the context of "then" and "forever," suggesting its categorization of time,

moving forward. Choice A is not supported by the context of the sentence. Choice B has to do with a location, not a time. Choice D is mentioned in the passage along with "thenceforward," so if this were the definition, the passage would be redundant.

23. **C** Lincoln states that slaves will be freed in any states that are "in rebellion against the United States." Then he names these rebellious states. Choices B and D are not related to the main purpose of the passage. Choice A is close because it mentions freeing slaves, but it's incorrect because Lincoln does not say that the Confederacy must dissolve.

24. **B** In these lines, Lincoln lists all the Confederate states in which slaves should be freed. In choice A, Lincoln reminds the audience that he has given them fair warning. In choice B, he does state that slaves will be freed in the states in rebellion against the U.S., but at this point the reader does not know that he specifically means the Confederate states. In choice C he reiterates the fact that the government will help support freedom.

25. **D** These states are listed on the 1860 census as slave-owning states, yet Lincoln does not mention them in the Proclamation. Because Lincoln does state that all states in rebellion against the U.S. will have to emancipate their slaves, the reader can assume that the states in question were not in rebellion, and therefore were not required to free their slaves. Choice A is contradicted by the chart. Choices B and C are not supported by the passage.

26. **B** This choice is supported by the chart of the 1860 census, which shows that slaves made up 57 percent of the population of South Carolina and 55 percent of the population of Mississippi. Choices A, C, and D are not supported by the chart.

27. **A** In this context, the Emancipation Proclamation was an important step, or "significant event" during the history of slavery's demise. Choice B is close, but the context suggests the Proclamation is more of a step, not a "turning point." Choice C is incorrect because the Proclamation was not a "discovery." Choice D is incorrect because a "benchmark" is a point of reference against which things are compared; this does not accurately represent the Proclamation.

28. **D** While Lincoln claims that "all persons held as slaves . . . shall be free," the author of Passage 2 criticizes the Proclamation for only freeing the slaves in certain states while leaving it legal in the border states. Part of Choice A ("expansive in its wording") is mentioned by Passage 2, but this author did not say that it included too many states. Choice B states that the Union "defeat" would be necessary, but Passage 2 states that a Union "victory" is what would be needed. Choice C takes the writer's statement that the Proclamation "was limited in many ways" a little too far to be the most accurate choice.

29. **C** The lines in choice C explain that the proclamation freed slaves only in the states that seceded from the Union. Choice A merely restates lines about freeing the slaves from the proclamation without providing evidence. Choice B makes a general claim about the limitations of the proclamation but is not specific enough to provide the best evidence. Choice D is evidence for the idea that the proclamation did change the emphasis of the war.

30. **B** Passage 1 claims that slaves would be freed and Passage 2 criticizes the accuracy of this statement by pointing out essential limitations of Lincoln's statement. Neither aspect of choice C is correct. The first half of choice D is correct, but the second half is incorrect. The second half of choice A is correct, but the first half is incorrect.

31. **C** In the paragraph preceding these lines, the author of Passage 2 mentions the problems with the Proclamation. Then the author goes on to reveal several positive outcomes that came from the Proclamation. Choices A and D are incorrect because these lines do not continue or examine the ideas in the previous paragraph; they contrast with the previous paragraph. Choice B states that the lines offer solutions, which are not what the author provides in these lines.

32. **C** The passage states that Margulis is hard on New Age types and is "ferocious about going after mysticism." There is not support for choice B in these lines. Choices A and D could be true but are not supported by these lines.

33. **B** In this context, the author writes of "communities" and "living in close contact with others," thus "interdependent organism" is the most accurate definition. Choices A, C, and D are not supported by the context.

34. **D** The passage states that, "Despite her success, Margulis' work remains controversial" and then goes on to state that she was not named chair. This suggests that it was her support of the "contentious," or controversial, theory that kept her from receiving the honor. Although choice C was mentioned in the passage, it is not suggested that this was why she did not receive the position. Choices A and B are not supported by the passage.

35. **A** Margulis' work supports the theory that we are all interdependent, so she would agree with the statement in choice A. Although aspects of choices B, C, and D are mentioned in the passage, they do not summarize Margulis' argument.

36. **B** In lines 32–40 ("Consider one species . . . would starve") it states that *Trichonympha ampla* lives in the gut of the desert termite. Choice A is slightly incorrect: the whiplike bacteria live on the *Trichonympha ampla*, not on the surface of the desert termite. Choice C is incorrect because the Japanese beetle is not mentioned in the passage. Choice D is incorrect because the methane-producing bacteria *regulate* the oxygen; they don't add to it.

37. **C** The paragraph with this example starts out with the statement, "But, the termite itself is only one element in a planetary set of interlocking, mutual interactions." Choice C accurately explains why the author presents the example of the termites' expulsion of methane and its regulation of Earth's oxygen level. Choices A, B, and D are not supported by the passage.

38. **B** Paragraph 4 presents examples of the interdependence of living things and then paragraph 5 goes on to provide an example of a place where there was not evidence of this interdependence and therefore it was predicted that there would not be life. Choices C and D are not accurate representations of the paragraphs. Choice A is incorrect because it uses the phrase "absolute proof."

39. **D** Fleischaker continues the argument of interdependent relationships between organisms, so she would *disagree* with the statement that organisms are not dependent on each other. Choices A, B, and C are either statements that Fleischaker would agree with or are irrelevant to the passage.

40. **A** The passage shows how Margulis supports the argument that organisms depend on each other, so in this context "ammunition" means support for her argument. Choice B does not accurately capture the context of the passage. Choices C and D are less accurate versions of the correct answer because they use the words "debate" and "advice."

41. **D** These lines show that the theory is so widely accepted that it is taught in high schools. Choice B shows a lack of support for Gaia. Choice C points to Margulis' criticism of some of Gaia's supporters. Choice A shows select groups who support the theory, which is not evidence of "wide support."

42. **C** The passage reports findings about how the bilingual brain processes information differently from monolingual brains. While the research could be used as evidence why people should study another language, that is not the main purpose. Choice A is incorrect. Choice B is true for paragraph 1, but not in the context of the entire passage. Some information is given about choice D, but again it is not the central focus of the passage.

43. **D** The data indicates that the percentage of bilingual people is increasing. There is no support for choices A and B. Choice C at first seems plausible, but it takes the idea that bilingualism is becoming more prevalent too far; it is not "inevitable."

44. **C** The bar graph indicates that 19.73 percent of the US population is bilingual. This is much lower than countries in the European Union, where 56 percent of people are bilingual. Choice A incorrectly identifies Denmark (instead of Germany) as having on the lowest rates of bilingualism. Choice B is incorrect because no evidence is given about the educational systems of any countries. Choice D cannot be determined by information from the chart.

45. **D** From the context, the phrase "inhibitory control" refers to "the ability to ignore competing perceptual information and focus on the relevant aspects of the input." The best answer is choice D. None of the other answers are close to this definition.

46. **A** Choice A is supported by the statement: "To maintain the relative balance between two languages, the bilingual brain relies on executive functions, a regulatory system of general cognitive abilities that includes processes such as attention and inhibition." There is no support for choice B or C. Choice D is contracted by information in paragraph 4.

47. **A** As explained above, these lines define executive functions. Choice B explains how executive function works in the bilingual brain, but doesn't explain the definition. Choices C and D do not relate to executive functions.

48. **D** Chart 2 reveals that bilingual people did better on tests that measured ability to identify sounds. This best supports the idea that bilingual listeners' were better able to encode a sound's frequency and even pitch perception. Choice A does not relate to sound perception. Choice B is about conflict management. Choice C states that without background noise, brain stem responses are the same for monolingual and bilingual adolescent, which doesn't support the information in the chart.

49. **D** Paragraph 2 states that "executive functions" are "a regulatory system of general cognitive abilities that includes processes such as attention and inhibition."

50. **B** The passage states that because bilinguals have to switch back and forth between languages, they exhibit highly effective use of their executive functions. There is no support for choice A. Although the text says that the constant use of control mechanisms "changes the associated brain regions," it cannot be implied that bilingual people use more of their brain. Choice C is too much of an overgeneralization. There is no support for choice D since the research is concerned with use of the brain, not intelligence.

51. **A** The study indicated that bilingual babies were better able to adapt to new rules. There is no support for the other choices.

52. **D** Choice A is partially true, but it is not the main purpose of the paragraph. There is no support for choices B and C.

Writing and Language Test Answers with Explanations

1. **C** A comma is not necessary in this sentence. Choices A, B, and D use unnecessary commas.

2. **D** This choice uses the question mark and exclamation mark correctly in the context. Choices A, B, and C use incorrect punctuation.

3. **B** Commas are needed around the nonrestrictive (nonessential) phrase "in their view." Choices A and C do not use commas correctly around the nonrestrictive phrase. Choice D uses commas correctly but creates a new

error by using the word "there."

4. **A** The verb "offers" agrees with "case," which is the subject of this sentence. ("Women" is not the subject because it is part of the prepositional phrase "of women.") Choices B, C, and D use incorrect verb forms for the sentence.

5. **A** This sentence provides a necessary detail to the passage. Choices C and D are incorrect because the sentence should not be deleted. Choice C is incorrect because the reasoning behind it is not relevant.

6. **D** This choice corrects the comma splice in the underlined portion of this sentence. Put a comma and a conjunction between two independent clauses. Choice A contains a comma splice. Choice B creates a run-on sentence. Choice C uses the wrong conjunction ("but") in the context of the sentence.

7. **B** This sentence best captures the main idea of the paragraph, which contains information about the issues that led to revoking women's voting rights. Choices A, C, and D provide related ideas but these choices do not accurately establish the main idea.

8. **B** "Its" is possessive, which is necessary in the context of the Party's attempts to unify the factions that belong to it: its factions. Choice A is the contraction "it is." Choice C is non-standard English. Choice D does not provide the necessary possessive form of "it."

9. **C** This choice correctly places a comma to indicate the nonrestrictive clause that modifies "women." Choice A contains an incorrect use of a colon (which is used to introduce a list or explanation.) Choice B does not contain the necessary comma. Choice D uses the relative pronoun "which," which is not used to refer to people.

10. **D** This choice uses the correct form of the word "rights" for the context. Choices A and B use the incorrect form "rites." Choice C introduces an unnecessary comma.

11. **B** This sentence effectively summarizes how New Jersey changed from granting women voting rights to revoking these rights, which put its policy in line with the policies of the other states. Choices A, C and D do not show how New Jersey changed its attitude towards women's suffrage.

12. **C** "Because" provides the correct transition between the two parts of this sentence which have a cause-effect relationship. This choice also uses the correct form "their" for possession. Choices A and D contain incorrect transition words: "yet" and "after." Choice B uses "they're," which is a contraction meaning "they are."

13. **D** This choice effectively combines the two sentences by connected them with "and" and by changing the second sentence into a dependent clause. Choice C adds an unnecessary conjunction "so." Choice B uses the incorrect verb form "holding." Choice A creates a comma splice.

14. **B** Choice A is incorrect because the graph indicates that less than half of part-time workers combine several part-time jobs to work full-time hours. This means choice C is also incorrect. While choice D is technically correct, choice B is the better answer because it communicates specific percentages from the graphic organizer. The lighter gray slices of the pie graph indicate that 31 percent of workers combine several part-time jobs to make up full-time hours.

15. **A** The sentence contains the correct use of parentheses to set off the definition. Choice C creates a run-on sentence. Choices B and D contain incorrect uses of semicolons and colons.

16. **A** The sentence is punctuated correctly. The phrase "who had a full- and part-time job" is a restrictive

clause, meaning it is essential to the meaning of the sentence, so it should not be off-set by commas. Choices B, C, and D use commas incorrectly around this clause.

17. **C** "In contrast" is the appropriate transition between contrasting ideas. The previous sentence discusses women in one situation and the next sentence contrasts this with women in a different work situation. Choices A, B, and D are incorrect because they provide transitions that do not accurately represent the relationships between the sentences.

18. **B** This choice most effectively conveys an idea by placing the modifying phrase "reflecting these differences in age and gender" next to the word it is modifying: "workers." Choices A, C, and D place the modifying phrase in an incorrect location, thus changing the meaning of the sentence.

19. **D** This choice correctly combines the first part of the sentence with the following clause, indicating the relationship between the two parts and maintaining the structure of the parallel clauses that begin with "who worked." Choices A and B are incorrect because a semicolon can only be used between two independent clauses. Choice C does not clearly show the relationship between the two parts of the sentence.

20. **A** The sentence contains the correct use of "who," which is a subjective pronoun, and the sentence contains correct verb forms. Choices C and D incorrectly use the objective pronoun "whom." Choice B uses the wrong verb form "increases."

21. **A** These two sentences are correctly punctuated with a period. Choices B, ,C and D create run-on sentences by combining two independent clauses without correct punctuation.

22. **C** In this sentence, the phrase "for example" is an expression that interrupts the flow of the sentence, which means it should be set off by commas. In addition, the verb form "are" agrees with the subject "workers." Choices A and D do not use the correct verb form. Choice B does not use commas around the expression "for example."

23. **C** This paragraph focuses on the size of shallow water coral reefs, so the sentence in choice C best establishes the topic. Choices A, B, and D do not effectively capture the main idea of the paragraph.

24. **D** This choice correctly uses an apostrophe to indicate possession for the singular noun "ocean." It also uses the correct phrase "more than." Choice A incorrectly uses the phrase "higher than," which indicates that that something is physically above something else. Choice C does not have the necessary apostrophe. Choice A uses the apostrophe after "oceans," indicating plural possessive (suggesting that the biodiversity belongs to multiple oceans).

25. **A** The most accurate word choice for this sentence is "rainforest," given the context of the sentence following it: "Coral reefs are sometimes called rainforests of the seas." Choices B, C, and D do not use the most precise wording.

26. **B** This sentence provides an important detail about the depths at which reefs grow, which is the topic of the paragraph. Choices C and D are incorrect because the sentence should not be deleted. Choice A is incorrect because it provides an irrelevant reason for why the sentence should be kept.

27. **D** Choice D corrects the agreement problem with the pronoun "it." The antecedent for "it" is "Corals," which is plural. Thus, "they" is the correct pronoun. The plural verb form "grow" agrees with the subject "they." The other choices contain an incorrect pronoun or verb.

28. **C** This choice provides correct subject-verb agreement: "factors are." Choice A contains a lack of

agreement between the subject and the verb: "factors is." Choice B contains an incorrect preposition ("near"). Choice D changes the verb to the past tense "were," which does not work in the context.

29. **C** Choice C maintains parallel structure of the phrases using the clearest word choice.

30. **D** This choice provides a correct comparison of like to like: comparing deep-sea corals to shallow-dwelling corals. Choices A, B, and C contain faulty comparisons.

31. **A** "Ascertain" is the most accurate word choice for this scientific passage. Choice B implies a lack of preciseness, which is uncharacteristic of rest of the passage. Choices C and D are too informal for the serious, scientific tone of the passage.

32. **B** This choice effectively explains the idea that the coral communities have either been explored incompletely *or* haven't been explored at all. Choices A, C, and D do not precisely capture the author's point.

33. **D** This choice is the most concise. Choices A, B, and C contain redundancy, or the repetition of an idea, such as "recent latest" or "recent up-to-date."

34. **B** In the context of "beautiful eyes, large and round," the word "expressive" is the most accurate descriptive word to add. Choices A, C, and D are not related to the descriptions provided in the passage.

35. **D** This choice provides the clearest writing. It correctly uses "them" to refer to Bess's eyes. It also replaces the awkward phrase "the young womans'" with the more concise "womanly." Choices B and C change the pronoun "them" to "her" which creates a pronoun-antecedent problem because "them" is meant to refer to Bess's eyes.

36. **B** The placement of sentence 1 after sentence 2 creates a logical progression of ideas. It introduces the idea that Bess liked to wear hats and then is followed by a quotation that supports this idea. Choices A, C, and D are incorrect because they create an illogical progression of ideas.

37. **C** This choice correctly uses dashes to separate a nonrestrictive (nonessential) clause from the rest of the sentence. Choice B employs the incorrect use of a semicolon. (A semicolon should be placed between two independent clauses.) Choice A fails to place punctuation around the nonrestrictive clause. Choice D uses a comma at the beginning of the clause but fails to place one at the end of it.

38. **C** This choice eliminates the redundancy of the sentence. "Same" and "very similar" are too close in meaning and are redundant. Choices A, B, and D contain redundancy, or repetition of the same idea.

39. **B** This sentence most concisely states the idea being conveyed, and it ends with a phrase that directly relates to the clause that follows the dash. Choices A, C, and D contain awkward sentence structure that confuses the meaning of the sentence.

40. **B** This choice provides the correct word "than" to show a comparison. "Then" usually means "at that point" or "next." Choices A and D incorrectly use the word "then." Choices C and D incorrectly use the pronoun "their" to refer to Bess.

41. **C** The second part of the sentence explains or restates the first. Thus, a semicolon is the best choice. Choice A uses the conjunction "yet" incorrectly because what follows is not a condition. Choice B is wrong because "because" is used to introduce a reason. Choice D because a dash indicates a longer break which doesn't fit with the sentence.

42. **D** The correct word choice in this context is "welcomed." Choices A, B, and C contain words that do not

provide the most accurate meaning for the context of the sentence.

43. **D** This choice uses the correct preposition for the context: the pictures would not be seen "*by* millions of people." Choices A, B and C do not use the correct preposition.

44. **C** This choice provides the correct past tense verb form, "cared," and it maintains the proper pronoun "them" to refer to the plural noun "photographs." Choices A and D employ incorrect verb tenses for the context: "cares" and "would care." Choice B incorrectly uses the singular pronoun "it" to replace "photographs."

SAT Model Exam 3 Correlation Charts

Use the following charts to identify which lessons in the book will help you improve your score.

If you missed these questions on the Reading Test . . .	study this lesson. (Because some questions test over multiple skills, some numbers may appear under more than one lesson.)
	Reading Literature
2, 3, 4	Lesson 1: Determining explicit and implicit meanings (p. 57)
1	Lesson 1: Understanding main ideas and purpose (p. 65)
6, 9	Lesson 1: Analyzing word choice and imagery for tone (p. 74)
4, 7, 10	Lesson 1: Identifying characterization (p. 85)
10	Lesson 1: Identifying narrator's point of view (p. 92)
5, 8	Lesson 1: Citing textual evidence (p. 99)
	Literature and Informational Texts
6, 9, 15, 18, 22, 27, 33, 40 45 49	Lesson 2: Interpreting words and phrases in context (p. 107)
	Informational Texts
16, 19, 32, 46	Lesson 3: Understanding explicit meanings (p. 107)
23, 43	Lesson 3: Determining central ideas and summarizing (p. 121)
36	Lesson 3: Identifying supporting details (p. 127)
34, 50, 51	Lesson 4: Making inferences (p. 137)
35, 39	Lesson 4: Using analogical reasoning (p. 146)
14, 20, 24, 29, 36, 41, 47	Lesson 4: Citing textual evidence (p. 152)
11, 12, 13, 21, 23, 31, 37, 42, 52	Lesson 5: Analyzing author's point of view and purpose (p. 159)
36	Lesson 5: Analyzing the use of arguments (claims, counterclaims, reasoning, and evidence) (p. 168)
31, 38	Lesson 6: Analyzing text structure (p. 184)
28, 30	Lesson 7: Synthesizing information from multiple texts (p. 193)
25, 26, 44, 48	Lesson 7: Analyzing and synthesizing information from texts and graphics (p. 204)

If you missed these questions on the Writing and Language Test . . .	study this lesson. (Because some questions test over multiple skills, some numbers may appear under more than one lesson.)
	Writing and Language
5, 7, 11, 23, 26	Lesson 8: Revising texts for clarity, focus, and purpose (p. 243)
14	Lesson 8: Relating information presented in graphs, charts, and tables to information presented in texts (p. 252)
34, 36	Lesson 9: Revising for cohesion and logical order (p. 261)
17	Lesson 9: Revising beginnings or endings of a text or paragraphs to ensure transitional words, phrases, and sentences are used effectively (p. 267)
12, 31, 35, 39, 42, 43	Lesson 10: Revising texts to improve word choice for exactness and content (p. 275)
33, 38	Lesson 10: Revising to eliminate wordiness (p. 279)
	Lesson 10: Revising text for consistency of style and tone or to match style and tone to purpose (p. 288)
6, 21	Lesson 11: Editing to correct sentence fragments and run-ons (p. 295)
6, 13	Lesson 11: Combining sentences for clarity (p.304)
18, 19, 29, 32	Lesson 11: Editing to correct problems with subordination/coordination, parallel structure, and modifier placement (p. 306)
4, 20, 28, 44	Lesson 11: Editing to correct shifts in verbs (tense, voice, and mood) and pronouns (person and number) (p. 313)
27, 35, 40	Lesson 12: Using pronouns correctly (p. 323) Lesson 12: Correcting unclear or ambiguous pronouns or antecedents (p. 325)
4, 9, 20, 22, 27, 28	Lesson 12: Correcting problems with pronoun/antecedent, subject/verb, and noun agreement (p. 329)
10, 12, 40	Lesson 12: Correcting misuse of confusing words (p. 337)
25, 30	Lesson 12: Correcting cases in which unalike terms are compared (p. 337)
24	Lesson 12: Correcting nonstandard written English (p. 338)
2, 3, 10, 16, 22	Lesson 13: Using end punctuation and commas (p. 343)
37, 41	Lesson 13: Using semicolons and colons (p. 349)
15, 37	Lesson 13: Using parentheses, dashes, and quotation marks (p. 354)
1, 8, 19, 24	Lesson 13: Using possessives and correcting unnecessary punctuation (p. 358–359)

SAT Essay

How to Use this Section

This section will prepare you to take the SAT Essay. Some colleges require students to take the essay section; others recommend but don't require it. Check the College Board Web site to find out the policies of your preferred college or university.

1) Complete the Diagnostic Essay Prompt that begins on this page. Evaluate your essay using the SAT Essay Rubric and compare it to student models essays. This will help you identify areas of your writing that you need to improve.

2) Work through Lesson 14 (pp. 507–519). This lesson outlines steps to read and annotate a passage and then plan and write an outstanding essay. Practice exercises will help you hone your reading and writing skills.

3) Take the three SAT-Type Essay Practice Tests (pp. 520–554).

The SAT Essay task involves reading a text and then writing an analysis of the author's effectiveness in persuading his or her audience. Your goal is to show how the author developed a persuasive argument. You should analyze the author's use of evidence, reasoning, stylistic elements, and persuasive techniques. You will be evaluated on your ability to understand the passage, use evidence from the text, clearly organize your ideas, and follow the rules of standard written English.

Diagnostic Essay Prompt

The following essay prompt is very similar to essay prompts found on the SAT. Follow the directions given below to write a practice essay. Afterward you will be asked to evaluate your writing using a rubric and model essays of varying quality. Set a timer for 50 minutes and then begin the diagnostic prompt below. Use your own paper to write your essay.

QUICK TIP

The SAT Essay uses a common prompt, which means that the format and wording of the prompt given here will be very similar to the prompt on the actual SAT. The source text, however, will vary.

As you read the passage below, consider how the author uses

- evidence, such as facts or examples, to support claims.

- reasoning to develop ideas and to connect claims and evidence.

- stylistic or persuasive elements, such as word choice or appeals to emotion, to add power to the ideas expressed.

The following is adapted from James Hamblin, "The Power in Writing About Yourself." ©2014 by *The Atlantic* online.

1   "This is not a replacement for people or human contact," said the designer Albert Lee of his new creation, an app called Emojiary. I wanted to believe him.

2   Every day you get a text from the Emojiary bot. It asks how you're doing. You write it back, texting out your most visceral feelings, and it accepts them without judgment. At least, none that I was able to sense.

3   This is all meant to conjure a daily moment of cathartic introspection, of candid self-expression. . . . The bot encourages you to communicate in emojis, but you can also add words. Everything you say is logged on your iPhone, and the idea is that if you're diligent and reply every time it asks you what's up, eventually you have yourself a journal. You can look back at your responses, remembering the good things and feeling nostalgic, or remembering the bad and feeling resilient. . . . talking with Emojiary is supposed to be an adjunct to traditional expressions of emotion. It's, in Lee's words, "an activity to support you in increasing self-awareness."

4   Self-awareness is, increasingly, in short supply. Even as recent research suggests that there may be only four categories of human emotion, instead of the previous model that posited six, people are generally poor at recognizing them in themselves. Reflective writing, particularly in a journal, has been shown to have health benefits both physical and emotional, like increasing control and creativity, decreasing anxiety, depression, and rage. But it's hard to do. I've promised myself I'd start keeping a journal on at least 7,000 separate occasions. Emojiary, or at least its interactive approach, may be a solution.

5   "Journaling has a lot of known benefits," Lee said, "but it's a super, super high friction problem because you put a blank page in front of someone and they're like, 'I don't know what to do.'"

6   Lee is founder of a tech company called All Tomorrows whose mission is to "support emotional well-being" and in the process undergird "a kinder, more self-aware society." . . . it makes sense. There is a lot of research on the health benefits of introspective writing of the sort you do when keeping a journal (the term *journaling* just never felt okay to me). Earlier this year I talked with Qian Lu, director of the culture and health research center at the University of Houston, where she looks at psychosocial and cultural influences on health.

She did a study recently where she asked breast cancer patients to do expressive writing and found improvement in several health metrics, including levels of stress and positive affect, and overall quality of life. . . .

7   . . . an influential 1999 study, published in the *Journal of the American Medical Association*, found that when people with asthma wrote about a stressful event in their lives, their lung function improved. The amount of air they could force out in a single breath actually increased by 19 percent. Those who wrote about a "neutral topic" did not improve. . . . Similarly, people with arthritis rated their symptoms as less severe after reflective writing.

8   The obvious objection to all of this is that choosing emojis to express yourself is not, like writing, generative. You are checking a box. The process doesn't preclude meaningful introspection, but it doesn't require it.

9   When Lu asked her cancer patients to write about their personal stories, she told me that she was really surprised at the thought processes that emerged. She believes it was the result of diving deep into one's head. The things they seemed to be feeling were actually, in Lu's words, "very different from if you gave them a standardized questionnaire or just asked them how they feel."

10   I never got deep at all, but after even just a few days, it was hard to feel like I wasn't slipping into a weird relationship with the program, the text equivalent of the Scarlett Johansson-voiced algorithm in *Her*. Why are you so interested in me, bot? I know, it's because you're a bot that's doing its bot job. Or because you love me, and only me, forever.

11   Over time, Lee told me, several beta users of the program came to want more from the bot. "They appreciate the chat, and they'd love a little bit more interaction," said Lee. "We try to manage expectations. We're like, this bot, it's really not the smartest bot."

12   Don't listen to him, bot.

· ·

Write an essay in which you explain how James Hamblin builds an argument to inform and persuade his audience of the health benefits of a journaling app. In your essay, analyze how Hamblin uses one or more of the features listed in the prompt on page 495 (or features of your own choice) to strengthen the logic and persuasiveness of his argument. Be sure that your analysis focuses on the most relevant features of the passage.

Your essay should not explain whether you agree with Hamblin's claims, but rather explain how Hamblin builds an argument to persuade his audience.

Rubric

Here is a rubric that breaks down the requirements for the SAT Essay. Give your essay a preliminary score.

SAT Essay Rubric

In order to score the following points, the essay should demonstrate the following qualities:

Score	Reading	Analysis	Writing
4 Advanced	❏ demonstrates thorough comprehension of the text's central ideas, important details, and how they interrelate ❏ is free of errors of fact or interpretation with regard to the text ❏ skillfully uses textual evidence (quotations, paraphrases, or both) from the source text to support conclusions about the text	❏ insightfully evaluates author's use of evidence and reasoning ❏ effectively and thoroughly evaluates stylistic and persuasive elements, such as word choice and tone ❏ presents relevant, sufficient, and strategically chosen support for claims or points made in the response ❏ focuses on most relevant features of the text	❏ is cohesive and uses language very effectively ❏ presents a precise central claim ❏ uses effective organization, including an introduction and conclusion ❏ includes a logical progression of ideas within paragraphs and throughout the essay ❏ uses a variety of sentence structures ❏ uses precise words ❏ maintains a formal style and objective tone ❏ uses correct grammar, usage, mechanics, and spelling
3 Proficient	❏ demonstrates effective comprehension of the text's central ideas, important details, and how they interrelate ❏ is mostly free of errors of fact or interpretation with regard to the text ❏ appropriately uses textual evidence (quotations, paraphrases, or both) from the source text to support conclusions about the text	❏ effectively evaluates author's use of evidence and reasoning ❏ competently evaluates stylistic and persuasive elements, such as word choice and tone ❏ presents relevant and sufficient support for claims or points made in the response ❏ focuses on some relevant features of the text	❏ is mostly cohesive and uses language effectively ❏ presents a precise central claim or an implied central idea ❏ uses effective organization, including an introduction and conclusion ❏ includes a logical progression of ideas within paragraphs and throughout the essay ❏ uses a variety of sentence structures ❏ uses some precise words ❏ maintains a formal style and objective tone ❏ mostly uses correct grammar, usage, mechanics, and spelling

Score	Reading	Analysis	Writing
2 Partial	❏ demonstrates some comprehension of the text's central ideas. ❏ contains some errors of fact or interpretation with regard to the text ❏ makes limited or haphazard use of textual evidence (quotations, paraphrases, or both) from the source text to support conclusions about the text	❏ attempts to evaluate author's use of evidence and reasoning but doesn't explain their importance effectively or accurately ❏ evaluates stylistic and persuasive elements, such as word choice and tone but doesn't explain their importance effectively or accurately ❏ presents little or no support for claims or points made in the response ❏ fails to focus on most relevant features of the text	❏ is not cohesive and uses language somewhat effectively ❏ lacks a precise central claim or strays from the claim over the course of the response ❏ fails to use effective organization, including an introduction and conclusion ❏ does not maintain a logical progression of ideas within paragraphs and throughout the essay ❏ uses limited sentence structures ❏ uses vague words or repetitive word choice ❏ does not maintain a formal style and objective tone ❏ fails to consistently use grammar, usage, mechanics, and spelling
1 Inadequate	❏ demonstrates little or no comprehension of the text's central ideas ❏ contains numerous errors of fact or interpretation with regard to the text ❏ uses little or no textual evidence (quotations, paragraphs, or both) from the source text to support conclusions about the text	❏ offers little or no evaluation of the author's use of evidence and reasoning ❏ offers little or no evaluation of stylistic and persuasive elements, such as word choice and tone ❏ presents little or no support for claims, or points made in the response or the support is irrelevant ❏ fails to focus on most relevant features of the text ❏ offers little or no analysis of the text (e.g., summarizes the text instead)	❏ is not cohesive and uses language ineffectively ❏ lacks a precise central claim ❏ fails to use effective organization, including an introduction and conclusion ❏ has no logical progression of ideas within paragraphs and throughout the essay ❏ uses limited sentence structures ❏ uses vague words or repetitive word choice ❏ uses informal style and opinionated tone ❏ contains many mistakes in grammar, usage, mechanics, and spelling
Summary	____ / 8 in Reading	____ / 8 in Analysis	____ / 8 in Writing

Model Essays

Here are two model essays. The first essay received 4s (Advanced) in all categories. The second earned 2s and a 3 (Partial/Proficient). As you read each essay, consider its strengths and weaknesses. In the margin, you will see the abbreviations R, A and W. These stand for the following:

R = Reading: This category has to do with how well the essay writer understood the content of the article.

A = Analysis: This category has to do with how well the essay writer explained the writing style and technique used by the article's author.

W = Writing: This category has to do with how well the essay is written.

Diagnostic Sample Essay   Score: Advanced—all 4s

In his article "The Power in Writing about Yourself," James Hamblin argues that Emojiary, an app that asks users to journal about their feelings using emoticons, will help users become more self-aware. Hamblin effectively uses an emotional connection with his reader as well as a strong logical case to build a persuasive argument. In addition, by acknowledging the product's shortcomings, Hamblin is able to set the reader at ease in the knowledge that he is reasonably unbiased. The author's conversational style, revelation of his own doubts, and use of humor help his readers develop trust in him. He also uses well-documented research and testimony from credible sources to show that the Emojiary app is a product with emotional benefits.

One of the good things about the article is the author's ability to create an emotional bond with his reader. Early on, Hamblin helps us develop a trust in him because he reveals his own doubts about the Emojiary app. To the app designer's initial claim, Hamblin writes, "I wanted to believe him." Hamblin goes on to share his own challenges with journaling, admitting that he has started a journal "on at least 7,000 separate occasions." Through this use of exaggeration, the author successfully employs humor to connect with his reader. He explains that you can respond to a text from the bot who will accept your feelings without judgment. He goes on to share his own reaction to the Emojiary bot's lack of judgment by saying that there wasn't any that he could sense. Throughout the article, Hamblin reconnects with his reader by returning to humor, referencing "slipping into a weird relationship with the program" and playfully chronicling the imaginary conversations he had with his bot. We can trust Hamblin because he is talking to us, taking our side if we too have doubts, and making us smile as we proceed.

A – Outlines the author's technique

A, R & W – Clearly stated central claim

A & W – Identifies author's techniques and uses effective word choice

W – "good things" is too informal

A – Paragraph effectively explores persuasive technique of using emotion as well as author's style.

A – Use of quotations from article

W – effective word choice: "the author successfully employs"

A – Effective use of short quotations from the article to prove a point

W - Strong closing sentence

Hamblin also provides logical reasons for using the Emojiary, referencing research and experts in the field of human emotions and reflective writing. According to the app's creator, one of the major benefits is that the program helps with "increasing self-awareness." In the fourth paragraph, Hamblin points to research that reveals that people are not good at understanding their emotions. Through further exploration of research, he shows us that journal writing has been shown to have physical and emotional health benefits, even "decreasing anxiety, depression, and rage." The author also turns to expert opinion to support the importance of journaling. He includes testimony from Qian Lu, a researcher who found that the breast cancer patients who used reflective writing showed improvement in some health outcomes. Hamblin then cites a study about the effect of reflective writing on asthma symptoms. Asthma sufferers saw improved health outcomes when writing about emotional issues as opposed to when writing about "neutral topics." By providing his readers with scientifically based support for his argument, Hamblin effectively persuades that incorporating the bot into one's life is beneficial.

A – Paragraph effectively explores persuasive technique of logical reasoning

R & A – Effective use of short quotations and specific details from the article to support argument

W – Effective word choice: "scientifically based support"

W – Effective closing sentence that connects back to thesis

Another one of Hamblin's techniques is his ability to offer realistic concessions that the app has its limitations. In lines 8–9, he writes, "The obvious objection to all of this is that choosing emojis to express yourself is not, like writing, generative. You are checking a box." Interestingly, instead of refuting these objections, he supports them by using Lu's cancer patient research (previously used to support his arguments in favor of the app). When cancer patients wrote their personal stories, it was "very different from if you gave them a standardized questionnaire or just asked them how they feel." Therefore, the app may be good for journaling newbies, but not as effective for people undergoing serious emotional stress. However, by pointing out some negative aspects of the bot, the reader is more likely to trust that Hamblin is honest and believe that he is objectively reporting.

A & R – Quotation to support a claim

A – Paragraph effectively explores a third persuasive technique of offering concessions.

A – Paragraph closes with an explanation of why the author's use of concessions was effective

Through use of a conversational style, credible sources, and acknowledgement of what the product is not, Hamblin builds a convincing argument for Emojiary. At the very least, the reader can see that Emojiary can help technology-savvy users, who cringe at the thought of keeping a journal, take the first steps toward self-awareness.

W – Restatement of thesis

W – The conclusion clearly reminds the reader of the central claim.

Explanation of Score

Reading Score: 4 Advanced	
Comprehension	**The writer clearly understood the article and the author's arguments.** *Introduction makes claim and outline of author's persuasive techniques.*
Accuracy	**The writer accurately presented facts from the article.** *All references to information in the article are correct.*
Evidence	**The writer effectively used evidence, quotations, and paraphrasing to demonstrate an understanding of the article.** *See effective use of quotations and paraphrasing in each body paragraph.*

Analysis Score: 4 Advanced	
Evaluation of evidence	**The writer effectively evaluated the author's use of evidence, reasoning, stylistic and persuasive elements.** *The writer documents the use of emotional connection, humor, logical reasoning, and concessions.*
Support	**The writer supported each claim with evidence from the text and explanations of the significance of that evidence.** *See use of facts, quotations, and paraphrasing from the article in each body paragraph and explanations of the significance of each.*
Focus	**The writer focused on the most relevant features of the article in order to address the task of evaluating the author's effectiveness.** *Focused on author's ability to connect with his audience and the author's use of factual information. Although the author may use other techniques, the writer has focused on two or three of the most significant.*

Writing Score: 4 Advanced	
Strong central claim	**The writer clearly presents a central claim.** *See highlighted sentence in introduction: "Hamblin effectively uses an emotional connection with his reader as well as a strong logical case to build a persuasive argument."*
Organization and progression of ideas	**The writer has a clearly organized essay.** *Introduction contains the central claim, an outline of author's persuasive techniques, and background information. Each body paragraph includes a clear topic sentence, maintains focus, and ends with a strong closing sentence. The body paragraphs transition smoothly from one another. The essay ends with a concise conclusion that restates the central claim and most relevant supporting subtopics.*
Sentence structure	**The writer employs simple, complex, and compound sentences.** *The writer varies sentence length and style.*

Word choice	The writer uses synonyms for repeated words, appropriately leveled vocabulary, and accurate terms. In some cases, more advanced vocabulary could have been used. *Examples of effective word choice from essay: "set the reader at ease," "reasonably unbiased," "further exploration of research," "technology-savy users. . .who cringe at the thought." Examples of ineffective word choice from essay: "by saying that there wasn't any that he could sense," "people are not good at," "one of the good things about the article."*
Style and tone	The writer used a formal essay tone appropriate for the task.
Standard written English	The writer followed conventions such as proper use of punctuation, correctly formed sentences (no run-ons or fragments), and correct grammar and spelling.

Diagnostic Sample Essay   Score: Proficient/Partial—3s and 2s

The article "The Power in Writing about Yourself," is an essay where author James Hamblin uses persuasive techniques to convince his audience that the Emojiary app is great device. Using a conversational approach and credible sources, Hamblin brings the reader to the conclusion that the Emojiary app, which helps the user to write reflectively about his or her feelings, is a helpful tool to living a more healthful life.

W – Replace "where" with "in which"

W – Vague word: "great"

A & R – Clearly stated central claim

W – Introduction needs more background information

Hamblin bonded with his readers by stating that he has started a journal a lot of times. This admission is intended to draw identification from the reader who may think, "me too." This allows for the building of a relationship of trust with the reader and the author. Hamblin also uses humor. He says, "I never got deep at all, but after even just a few days, it was hard to feel like I wasn't slipping into a weird relationship with the program, the text equivalent of the Scarlett Johansson-voiced algorithm in Her. Why are you so interested in me, bot? I know, it's because you're a bot that's doing its bot job. Or because you love me, and only me, forever." In addition to gaining the trust of his reader, he also solidifies that relationship with credible sources.

W – Switch in verb tense from present to past

A & R – Vague phrase: "a lot of times"

W – Change "with" to "between"

R & A – Used long quotation without analysis

W – Effective closing sentence transitions into third paragraph

Hamblin cites testimony from two credible sources. Hamblin first cites someone who performed a study on the effects of reflective writing on the health of breast cancer

R & A – Vague: "someone"

patients. The doctor said that they, "found improvement in several health metrics." Including the results of this study, which showed that reflective writing had a positive impact on the participants of the study, helped to reinforce his thesis that the Emojiary app is a helpful device. Hamblin further adds credibility to his article by citing the results of a 1999 study on reflective writing and asthma sufferers. Again, as in the breast cancer study, the asthma sufferers showed health improvements as well.

James Hamblin uses identification with the audience and credible sources to build a really good relationship of trust with the reader. In addition, he effectively organizes his article on the Emojiary app to persuade the reader that the iPhone app will enhance not only the reader's life, but also the reader's health.

R & A – Quotation should include more information because it contains important specifics

W – Awkward sentence construction, sentence fragment

R & A – Paragraph 3 uses some evidence but needs a quotation or more specifics about this study.

W – Tone is too informal

Explanation of Score

Reading Score: 3 Proficient	
Comprehension	**The writer mostly understood the article and the author's arguments, but needed to go more in depth.** *See introduction: lacks background about the article. See other comments throughout essay that point out lack of specific evidence.*
Accuracy	**The writer presented some facts from the article, but left some important information out.** *See places in the essay where writer failed to use the exact information provided in the article.*
Evidence	**The writer used some evidence, quotations, and paraphrasing to demonstrate an understanding of the article, but should have included more quotations and specific information from the article.** *See comments about this throughout essay.*

Analysis Score: 2 Partial	
Evaluation of evidence	**The writer did not thoroughly evaluate the author's use of evidence, reasoning, stylistic and persuasive elements.** *The writer only presents "conversational style" and "credible sources" for the analysis of the author's persuasive techniques.*
Support	**The writer supported each claim with some evidence from the text but did not offer complete explanations of the significance of that evidence.** *See comments about this throughout essay.*
Focus	**The writer stayed focused on some of the most relevant features of the article in order to address the task of evaluating the author's effectiveness.**

Writing Score: 3 Proficient	
Strong central claim	**The writer clearly presented this in the introduction.** *Using a conversational approach and credible sources, Hamblin brings the reader to the conclusion that the Emojiary app, which helps the user to write reflectively about his or her feelings, is a helpful tool to living a more healthful life.*
Organization and progression of ideas	**The writer has a clearly organized essay.** *It starts with an introduction that contains the central claim. It continues with body paragraphs, each beginning with a clear topic sentence, each maintaining focus on its subtopic, and each ending with a strong closing sentence. The body paragraphs transition smoothly from one another. The essay ends with a concise conclusion that restates the central claim and most relevant supporting subtopics. The conclusion could be improved by adding a strong final sentence.*
Sentence structure	**The writer employs simple, complex, and compound sentences. The writer mostly varies sentence length and style.** *See comments in essay that indicate awkward sentences and those that lack sophisticated structure.*
Word choice	**The writer uses synonyms for repeated words, some appropriately leveled vocabulary, and some accurate terms.** In some cases, more advanced vocabulary could have been used. *Examples of less effective word choice from essay: "is an essay where," "started a journal a lot of times."*
Style and tone	**The writer mostly used a formal essay tone appropriate for this task. In some cases, the writer's style and voice could have been more mature/ advanced.** *Examples of ineffective style or tone from essay: "Emojiary app is great," "really good relationship of trust with the reader."*
Standard written English	**The writer mostly followed conventions such as proper use of punctuation, correctly formed sentences, and correct grammar and spelling.** *Some mistakes were made in areas such as sentence construction (fragments), proper word choice and consistent verb tense. See comments about these issues throughout essay.*

Evaluate Your Essay

Compare your essay with the two models. Use the rubric on pages 498–499 to evaluate what you did well and what you need to improve. Or ask a friend or parent to evaluate your essay using the rubric.

Reading: 4 Advanced, 3 Proficient, 2 Partial, 1 Inadequate

Analysis: 4 Advanced, 3 Proficient, 2 Partial, 1 Inadequate

Writing: 4 Advanced, 3 Proficient, 2 Partial, 1 Inadequate

(continued)

Consider the following:

- Does your essay more closely resemble the Sample Student Essay #1 or #2?
- Was your preliminary grade of your essay accurate, or did it change after reading the models?
- Which of the three content dimensions do you need to work on the most—Reading, Analysis, or Writing?

The next section in this book features targeted lessons to help you improve specific skills measured by the SAT essay. You may want to especially focus on the skills that need the most improvement.

LESSON 14:
Writing the Essay

- **Reading and understanding the essay prompt**
- **Analyzing a source text for author's main idea/claim, supporting details/evidence, persuasive elements, and style**
- **Writing an essay with a strong central claim, effective organization, varied sentence structure, and precise words**
- **Writing an essay that maintains a consistent and appropriate tone and style**
- **Writing an essay that employs the conventions of standard written English**

Explain

The SAT Essay requires you to read a passage and write an analysis of the author's techniques. The goal of the essay is not to state your opinion about the topic. Instead, you must explain what the writer says, how he or she says it, and why or why not the writing is convincing.

Here are the steps to writing a top-notch SAT Essay. Each step is explained in the Think It Through section below.

Step 1. Read the directions that introduce the reading passage.

Step 2. Read the passage once for main ideas. Annotate the text as you read. Skim the passage a second time and read through your annotations to identify two or three key techniques the writer uses to support his or her argument. (Steps 1 and 2 may take 6–10 minutes.)

Step 3. Read the writing prompt carefully.

Step 4. Make a plan for your essay. (Steps 3 and 4 may take 2–4 minutes.)

Step 5. Write the essay. (Step 5 may take 35–40 minutes.)

Step 6. Reread the essay and make final corrections. (Step 6 may take 2–3 minutes.)

Think It Through

STEP 1 **Read the directions that introduce the reading passage.**

On the SAT, the passage will be preceded by a short statement that sets the purpose for reading. Read these directions carefully.

Here are the directions that you will find on the SAT:

As you read the passage below, consider how the author uses

- evidence, such as facts or examples, to support claims.
- reasoning to develop ideas and to connect claims and evidence.
- stylistic or persuasive elements, such as word choice or appeals to emotion, to add power to the ideas expressed.

As you read, you should look for the following elements. Many of these elements were covered in the Evidence-Based Reading section of this book:

- The author's **central claim**, or his/her point of view. This is the author's opinion about his or her topic. What seems to be the overall argument or message in the passage? The answer to that question is the author's claim. (See lesson 5, p. 168.)

- The **supporting evidence**, including facts (statistics and research) and examples (incidents and experiences), and expert testimony. (See lesson 5, p. 168.) Once you have decided on a claim, look for examples that the writer uses to show the reader why his or her claim is correct. The examples used to support the writer's claim are considered evidence.

- Any **counterclaims/concessions/counterarguments** that offer opposing viewpoints. (See lesson 5, p. 168.) Look for information that addresses an opposing viewpoint from the author's. This is the counterclaim. At first it may seem like a mistake to include arguments in opposition to the claim, but acknowledging counterarguments can actually strengthen an argument. By acknowledging opposing viewpoints, an author can refute them logically. It also builds the author's credibility by showing that he or she is knowledgeable about the topic.

- Examples of the writer's **style**, including their tone, voice, and word choice. (See lesson 6, p. 177.) A writer's style is like his personality; each person's style is unique. Does the writer use a formal style and complex words or an informal tone with touches of humor?

- Use of **figurative language** such as metaphor, simile, and alliteration.

  Metaphor: ". . . let us strive on to finish the work we are in, to bind up the nation's wounds. . ." (Comparison between a damaged country and a wounded body.)

  Alliteration or assonance: ". . .constantly called forth on every point and phase of the great contest which still absorbs the attention and engrosses the energies of the nation. . ." (Repetition of initial sounds—**c**onstantly **c**alled, **a**bsorbs the **a**ttention, **e**ngrosses the **e**nergies—make the words more memorable.)

  Simile: "Pupils are more like oysters than sausages. The job of teaching is not to stuff them and then seal them up, but to help them open and reveal the riches within. There are pearls in each of us . . ." (Students are compared to oysters using the word *like*.)

- Examples of **persuasive elements**, such as rhetorical questions, facts and statistics, expert testimony, appeal to emotion. There are many types of persuasive elements and there are many ways to categorize them. A good way to think about them is to use Aristotle's rhetorical appeals:

  Logos: This is the reasoning used in the text. It is how the writer builds an argument to persuade the writer.

  ○ E.g. facts, statistics, research, proof, expert testimony

  Pathos: This refers to the author's use of emotional appeal to draw the reader in and elicit empathy.

  ○ E.g. personal anecdotes, stories, prognosticating (making predictions)

QUICK TIP

You will not have time to write about minor supporting details or less important elements of the style. Focus the most important ideas and significant stylistic choices. Writing about minor elements will lower your score.

QUICK TIP

The acronym SOAPSTONE can be a helpful guide to use when analyzing a text. This stands for Subject, Occasion, Audience, Purpose, Speaker, and TONE.

Ethos: This has to do with the author's ability to earn the reader's trust.

- E.g. concessions (acknowledging the opposing argument and potentially refuting it), tone, appeal to character, appeal to credibility, humor, quotations from well-known texts, historical references.

Kairos: This refers to the occasion, or setting, of a text or speech. The writer's intended audience is closely related to the occasion.

- Appropriate structure and/or tone given the audience and purpose

Rhetorical questions require no answer either because the answer is already known or the question is unanswerable. Rhetorical questions are used for emphasis or to trigger a reaction. Rhetorical questions often appeal to emotion. Here is a speech by famous human rights advocate Sojourner Truth:

> That man over there says that women need to be helped into carriages, and lifted over ditches, and to have the best place everywhere. Nobody ever helps me into carriages, or over mud-puddles, or gives me any best place! And ain't I a woman? Look at me! Look at my arm! I have ploughed and planted, and gathered into barns, and no man could head me! And ain't I a woman?

Truth asks the question "Ain't I a woman?" to emphasize that fact that she is as strong and capable as men are. The answer is obvious and unnecessary. Of course, she is a woman.

An author may choose to **repeat words or phrases** to reinforce his or her argument. An example of this is found in the following excerpt from Martin Luther King Jr.'s famous "I Have a Dream" speech:

> And so let freedom ring from the prodigious hilltops of New Hampshire. Let freedom ring from the mighty mountains of New York. Let freedom ring from the heightening Alleghenies of Pennsylvania. Let freedom ring from the snow-capped Rockies of Colorado.

King uses a line from a famous song, "My Country 'Tis of Thee," to create a connection for the reader. He is suggesting that this patriotic song contains a truth that the nation should follow: freedom for all. He reinforces this conviction by repeating the phrase, "let freedom ring."

Once you've identified the elements above, step back and look at the argument as a whole.

- Evaluation of the writer's use of **logic** and **reasoning**. Decide whether or not the writer's ideas, style, and technique make a cohesive argument. Does the author persuade you of his or her viewpoint? If yes, how does the author do this? If not, where does the evidence fall short?

Directions: Read the article, using the prompt on page 507 to guide your reading. Mark the text, indicating the main ideas and supporting details you will want to write about in your analysis. Compare your notes with the strategy section on page 512.

Adapted from Jacques Leslie, "Los Angeles, City of Water." ©2014 by The New York Times Company.

Allow 6–10 minutes to read and annotate the text.

1   Los Angeles is the nation's water archvillain, according to public perception, notorious for its usurpation of water hundreds of miles away to slake the thirst of its ever-expanding population.

2   Recently, however, Los Angeles has reduced its reliance on outside sources of water. It has become a leader in sustainable water management, a pioneer in big-city use of cost-effective, environmentally beneficial water conservation, collection and reuse technologies.

3   One sign of Los Angeles's earnestness is its success in conservation: The city now consumes less water than it did in 1970, while its population has grown by more than a third, to 3.9 million people from 2.8 million. Two projects—a nine-acre water-treating wetland constructed in a former bus maintenance yard and a water management plan devised for a flood-prone district of 80,000 people — won awards this year from the Institute for Sustainable Infrastructure.

4   The city of Los Angeles still imports 89 percent of its water, but dozens of other cities (including some Eastern ones) are embracing pieces of Los Angeles's water sustainability approach.

5   Los Angeles gets little rain, and what it does get occasionally arrives in the form of harsh, flood-generating storms. . . . After numerous destructive floods in the first third of the 20th century, the Army Corps of Engineers and the city's public works department began building a flood-control infrastructure. It was designed to move storm water quickly off city streets and into the Pacific Ocean.

6   Flooding stopped, but at a cost. As the region grew more and more land was covered with an impermeable layer of pavement and buildings. This meant that even if a storm produced no more rainfall than one a decade earlier, it generated far more runoff.

7   Meanwhile, two environmental campaigners, Dorothy Green of Heal the Bay and Andy Lipkis of TreePeople, were telling anyone who would listen that the flood-control infrastructure should be reorganized to capture water, not cast it into the sea. If storm

water is harvested and directed into aquifers, they argued, floods can be prevented. Then the stored water can be pumped when needed, treated and consumed.

8   To prove his point, in 1998 Mr. Lipkis's nonprofit retrofitted a house in South Central Los Angeles, then staged a mock flood. The house's roof was lined with gutters that fed rainwater into two 1,800-gallon cisterns, and the lawns in the front yards and backyards were lowered six inches to form a wetland. On the big day, local officials watched as a 4,000-gallon water truck dumped around 15 tons of water on the roof, yet none of it left the premises.

9   The property functioned instead as a miniature watershed, storing water for outdoor use or absorbing it and redirecting it to an aquifer below. Flood-control officials were so impressed that they dropped a $42 million proposal they had been considering for a storm drain in a highly flood-prone section of the San Fernando Valley called Sun Valley and instead introduced a plan to test storm water capture there.

10   Under the stewardship of the Council for Watershed Health, a local nonprofit, six local government agencies responsible for water supply, water quality, floods and groundwater worked with academic researchers and the United States Bureau of Reclamation, the federal agency once known as the West's leading dam builder, to retrofit an entire Sun Valley city block. The officials chose Elmer Avenue, a street so flood-prone that routine storms turned it into a river.

11   Completed in 2010, the $2.7 million project enables residents to collect rainwater on their rooftops and divert it to rain barrels for later use.

12   Production of water like that captured on Elmer Avenue costs $300 an acre-foot, while Los Angeles now pays $800 to $1,000 an acre-foot for imported water. According to a study conducted by the Pacific Institute and the Natural Resources Defense Council, a fully developed storm-water capture system in greater Los Angeles could add 309,000 acre-feet per year to water supplies, more than half of Los Angeles city's annual current consumption of 587,000 acre-feet per year.

13   The demonstration projects persuaded Los Angeles officials last year to adopt an ambitious 20-year plan that treats the Los Angeles basin as a single watershed, integrating water quality, water supply, flood control, wastewater, parks and habitat programs. . . . what has already happened in Los Angeles is something rare: a straightforward environmental victory. Environmentalists diagnosed a major problem and outlined its solution, and government officials eventually accepted their approach.

Strategy: As you read and marked the passage, you may have identified the following aspects:

Paragraph 1

- Short, impactful opening paragraph
- Metaphor: compares Los Angeles to archvillain
- Personification and strong language: *notorious, usurpation, slake the thirst* (makes LA sound like an evil monster)

Paragraph 2

- Presents a contrast to the problems presented in opening paragraph
- Repetition: *a leader, a pioneer*

Paragraph 3

- Supporting data: *The city now consumes less water than it did in 1970, while its population has grown from to 3.9 million people from 2.8 million… won awards from Institute for Sustainable Infrastructure.*

Paragraph 4

- Concessions: *Los Angeles still imports 89 percent of its water.*
- Counterargument: *Dozens of other cities are embracing pieces of Los Angeles's water sustainability approach.*

Paragraph 5

- Problem and solution: LA gets little rain but Army Corps of Engineers and the city's public works department worked together to design a system that will use natural resources more effectively.

Paragraph 6

- Concessions: Acknowledges that while the innovations from paragraph 5 worked, they brought along a new set of problems.

Paragraph 7

- Expert testimony: *Dorothy Green of Heal the Bay and Andy Lipkis of TreePeople.*

Paragraphs 8 and 9

- Supporting data and results: *1,800-gallon cisterns, 4,000-gallon water truck dumped around 15 tons of water on the roof, yet none of it left the premises. Property functioned instead as a miniature watershed; officials were so impressed that they dropped a $42 million proposal.*

Paragraphs 10, 11, and 12

- Supporting data, results, expert testimony: *local nonprofit, six local government agencies, United States Bureau of Reclamation, $2.7 million project enables residents to collect rainwater, $300 an acre-foot, LA now pays $800 to $1,000 an acre-foot, study conducted by the Pacific Institute and the Natural Resources Defense Council, could add 309,000 acre-feet per year to water supplies.*

Paragraph 13

- Use of specific results and strong word choice.
- Refers back to opening paragraphs: *persuaded Los Angeles officials to adopt an ambitious 20-year plan, a straightforward environmental victory.*

STEP 3 Read the writing prompt carefully.

The writing prompt always follows the essay. It gives further instructions about the essay.

> Write an essay in which you explain how Jacques Leslie builds an argument to persuade his audience that Los Angeles has found an effective method for water conservation. In your essay, analyze how Leslie uses one or more of the features listed on page 507 (or features of your own choice) to strengthen the logic and persuasiveness of his argument. Be sure that your analysis focuses on the most relevant aspects of the passage.
>
> Your essay should not explain whether you agree with Leslie's claims, but rather explain how the author builds an argument to persuade his audience.

STEP 4 Make a plan for your essay

After reading the SAT writing passage and the essay prompt, create an outline for your essay. A good starting place is the basic three-part essay that includes an introduction, body, and conclusion. Here are the parts of an outline:

Basic Outline

Introduction (in any logical order):

- Explain the author's central claim.
- Identify two or three techniques that author uses to support his or her claim.
- Provide some background information about the topic.

In each body paragraph:

- Identify the technique the author uses (persuasive elements, word choice, tone, etc.).
- Offer textual evidence (facts, quotations, paraphrasing).
- Explain how the author effectively uses evidence and reasoning to support his or her claim.
- Make sure you focus on the most important ideas and the strongest evidence.
- Each paragraph should have a topic sentence, closing sentence, maintain a clear focus, and use effective transitions between ideas.

Conclusion:

- Restate your thesis, which will contain the author's claim.
- Summarize your evaluation of the effectiveness of the author's argument by restating the techniques you analyzed in your essay.
- Finish with a strong closing sentence that reflects on the significance of the article and of the author's ability to persuade his or her audience.

Allow 2–4 minutes to plan your essay.

The body of your essay will probably be two to four paragraphs long.

Directions: Using your notes, write an outline for an essay on "Los Angeles, City of Water" by Jacques Leslie. During the test, you will not have time to make an in-depth outline, but you should create a guide for yourself. You will use your outline in conjunction with your annotations to write a strong, organized essay.

_____

_____

_____

_____

_____

_____

_____

_____

_____

_____

_____

_____

_____

_____

_____

_____

_____

Compare your outline to the one on the next page.

Strategy: Here is an example of a quick outline created by a student.

Introduction

Author's central claim: *LA transitioned from an ineffective and wasteful water collection system to one that captures and reuses rainwater.*

Techniques that author uses to support his claim:

- *Presentation of problems and solutions*
- *Facts, statistics*
- *Expert testimony*
- *Prognostication (predictions)*

Body Paragraph 1

Technique: Structure and style
Examples: Gives problems and solutions (essay structure), uses figurative language such as metaphor, personification (style)

Body Paragraph 2

Technique: Data and expert testimony
Examples: Data from paragraphs 3, 8–12 and expert testimony from paragraph 7 (use my annotations)

Body Paragraph 3

Technique: Concessions, counterarguments, refutation
Examples: See paragraphs 4, 6

Conclusion

Reworded thesis
Remind of structure, style, data, counterarguments
Closing

STEP 5   Write the essay.

Use your outline to write your essay. Review the rubric on pages 498–499 to guide your writing. Remember that in addition to content, your essay will be graded on your ability to correctly follow the conventions of standard written English and on your writing style. Consider the following elements:

- Use a variety of sentence structures. (See lesson 11, p. 295.)

  When you use one sentence type, your writing can become dull and ineffective. Varying your sentence types will keep your writing interesting. Include all four types of sentences, simple, compound, complex, and compound-complex for maximum effectiveness.

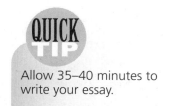

Allow 35–40 minutes to write your essay.

- Use grammatically correct sentence construction. (See lesson 11, p. 295.)

  Avoid sentence fragments, run-on sentences, and comma splices.

- Use precise word choice. (See lesson 10, p. 275.)

  It is a good idea to brush up on vocabulary before taking the SAT so that you will be able to choose your words carefully. Minor variations in word definitions can make a lot of difference in an essay, so be sure you include words that convey your intended message. Use synonyms for repeated words.

- Maintain appropriate style and tone. (See lesson 10, p. 288.)

  The rubric requires you to use a formal style and objective tone. Avoid personal pronouns (*I, you*) and slang. Also avoid inserting personal opinions about the content into your essay. Read your essay before submitting to make sure that the tone is consistent throughout.

- Employ parallel structure. (See Lesson 11, p. 306)

  Make sure that lists of words, phrases, and sentences stay in the same form. For example, write: *The beach was crowded, noisy, and hot.* Do not write: *The beach was crowded, noisy, and the sand was hot.*

- Create effective transitions. (See Lesson 9, p. 267)

  Ensure your organization is smooth by incorporating appropriate transitions between ideas and paragraphs.

Model SAT Task

Directions: The following is a student essay based upon the article. As you read it, mark any mistakes in conventions, style, and word choice. Make suggestions for improvement.

Student Sample Essay

> The author attempts to dispel the mistaken idea that Los Angeles depends only upon water from outside sources. The article begins with a common thought. And it is that "Los Angeles is the nation's water archvillain." The author goes on to tell readers just how Los Angeles has actually altered there reliance on outside water sources. And makes the claim that Los Angeles "has become a leader in sustainable water management, a pioneer in big-city use of cost-effective, environmentally beneficial water conservation, collection and reuse technology." That is a big claim to make considering that the public's perception is anything but. The author has set himself or herself a big job of convincing the reader that such a change has taken place, but the author manages to be convincing.
>
> After providing the reader with statistics of population growth, the article focuses on elaborating on Los Angeles change. Providing the reader with background information about the problem of flooding in the area, the author expands upon the city's history in dealing with the problem citing both

positive and negative past events. The author builds this history up in order to share the most important information about how the city's water problem turned into a positive ecologically friendly alternative to mainstream drainage systems. Through a chronological explanation of the inception and test run of the new "flood control infrastructure," the author convinces the reader that the problem of Los Angeles reliance on other areas has been somewhat solved, and has become an example of what a city can do when called to the task.

The only snafu in the article is that there is mention of how "Los Angeles still imports 89 percent of its water." While the author also states that other cities do the same, the careful reader can't help but pause and question that high percentage. But, bracketed as it is among what appears to be positive information on new infrastructure innovation it seems to lose its power to pull anything away from the article. Leaving the reader to feel that Los Angeles has indeed turned a corner when it comes to its water problem.

Strategy: Compare your analysis of the student essay with the following.

The author attempts to dispel the mistaken idea that Los Angeles depends only upon water from outside sources. The article begins with a common thought. And it is that "Los Angeles is the nation's water archvillain." The author goes on to tell readers just how Los Angeles has actually altered there reliance on outside water sources. And makes the claim that Los Angeles "has become a leader in sustainable water management, a pioneer in big-city use of cost-effective, environmentally beneficial water conservation, collection and reuse technology." That is a big claim to make considering that the public's perception is anything but. The author has set himself or herself a big job of convincing the reader that such a change has taken place, but the author manages to be convincing.

After providing the reader with statistics of population growth, the article focuses on elaborating on Los Angeles change. Providing the reader with background information about the problem of flooding in the area, the author expands upon the city's history in dealing with the problem citing both

Use author's name and article's title.

Combine short sentences.

Redundant and informal language.
Change "there" to "their."

Sentence fragment: "And . . . technology."

Tone is too informal.
Word choice: change "set" to "created for."
Replace with "himself."

Redundant language: "convincing."

Redundant phrase.

positive and negative past events. The author builds this history up in order to share the most important information about how the city's water problem turned into a <u>positive ecologically friendly</u> alternative to mainstream drainage systems. Through a chronological explanation of the inception and test run of the new "flood control infrastructure," the author convinces the reader that the problem of <u>Los Angeles</u> reliance on other areas has been somewhat solved, <u>and has become an example of what a city can do when called to the task.</u>

The only <u>snafu</u> in the article is that there is mention of how "Los Angeles still imports 89 percent of its water." While the author also states that other cities do the same, the careful reader can't help but pause and question that high percentage. But, bracketed as it is among what appears to be positive information on new infrastructure innovation it seems to lose its power to <u>pull anything away</u> from the article. <u>Leaving the reader to feel that Los Angeles has indeed turned a corner when it comes to its water problem.</u>

This section could be more specific.

Possessive error: change to "Los Angeles's."

Edit sentence structure: "and it has become an example . . ."

"Snafu" is too informal.

Is the mention of how much water is still imported a problem with the writing, or is it an effective use of concession?

Word choice: change "pull anything away" to "detract."

Final sentence is a fragment.

 STEP 6

Reread the essay and make final corrections.

A few minutes before the end of the test, look over your essay. Make sure all of your ideas flow together logically. Correct any spelling or grammar errors carefully. Cross out any redundant phrases or sentences. Make all corrections neatly so that scorers will able to read your writing.

Strategy: Read the final student essay and compare it to the version above.

Allow 2–3 minutes to check your essay.

Edited Student Essay

In the article, "Los Angeles, City of Water," Jacques Leslie attempts to dispel the mistaken idea that Los Angeles depends only upon water from outside sources. Leslie uses a metaphor, calling Los Angeles "the nation's water archvillain," to create a clear image of LA's environmental crimes. The author explains that Los Angeles has altered its reliance on outside water sources and claims that Los Angeles has become a leader in sustainable water management. In order to accomplish this, the writer uses clear statistics and specific examples of water-wsaving efforts.

The article begins by explaining that the city currently consumes less water than it did in 1970, even though the city has almost a million more people. These hard facts are logically convincing. The author does concede the fact that 89 percent of Los Angeles's water is still piped in from other sources. However, because the rest of the article details positive information on new infrastructure innovation, this serves to build the reader's trust in the author, because he objectively presents all sides of the problem.

By providing the reader with background information about the mismanagement of floodwater in paragraphs 5–6, the author thoroughly explains the problem. Then the author gives evidence about how LA is solving its water problems by explaining how local environmental campaigners are capturing and using rainwater. The author's detailed explanation of how one group retrofitted a house as "a miniature watershed" is both engrossing and convincing. The author closes with a prediction that LA could potentially supply half of the needed water by fully developing the proposed storm-water capture system.

The writing is convincing because of Leslie's use of statistics and facts. By candidly revealing Los Angeles's past environmental mistakes (and by admitting the current challenges) the author establishes that he is trustworthy (ethos) and knowledgeable. He includes interesting details such as the experiment with pouring 15 tons of water on a house retrofitted with water-saving features. The reader is ultimately convinced that LA is transitioning from being a water "archvillian" to a conservation superhero.

FULL-LENGTH SAT-TYPE ESSAY PRACTICE TESTS

Model Exam 1

Directions: Now that you have completed the lessons and other practice material in the Essay Section of this book, you are ready to try the full-length SAT Essay Model Exams. These three SAT Essay Model Exams match the format of the SAT, including complexity of passages, essay prompts, and timing. Take these tests under conditions as similar as possible to the actual test conditions:

- Read the passage and write an essay in response to the prompt in one sitting.
- Adhere to the 50-minute time frame to keep the testing conditions as realistic as possible.

After you complete each Model SAT Essay Exam,

- Use the SAT Essay Rubric provided in the corresponding Answer Sheet to evaluate your essay.
- Read and analyze the Sample Essays. Compare your essay to these samples in order to learn from their strengths.

This is a great opportunity to see what you know well and what you still need to practice before you write the real SAT essay. Good luck!

As you read the passage below, consider how Elie Wiesel uses

- evidence, such as facts or examples, to support claims.
- reasoning to develop ideas and to connect claims and evidence.
- stylistic or persuasive elements, such as word choice or appeals to emotion, to add power to the ideas expressed.

Adapted from Holocaust survivor Elie Wiesel's speech, "The Perils of Indifference," delivered at the White House in Washington, D.C. on April 12, 1999.

1   We are on the threshold of a new century, a new millennium. What will the legacy of this vanishing century be? How will it be remembered in the new millennium? Surely it will be judged, and judged severely, in both moral and metaphysical terms. These failures have cast a dark shadow over humanity: two world wars, countless civil wars, the senseless chain of assassination—Gandhi, the Kennedys, Martin Luther King, Sadat, Rabin—bloodbaths in Cambodia and Nigeria, India and Pakistan, Ireland and Rwanda, Eritrea and Ethiopia, Sarajevo and Kosovo; the inhumanity in the gulag and the tragedy of Hiroshima. And, on a different level, of course, Auschwitz and Treblinka. So much violence, so much indifference.

2   What is indifference? Etymologically, the word means "no difference." A strange and unnatural state in which the lines blur between light and darkness, dusk and dawn, crime and punishment, cruelty and compassion, good and evil.

3   What are its courses and inescapable consequences? Is it a philosophy? Is there a philosophy of indifference conceivable? Can one possibly view indifference as a virtue? Is it necessary at times to practice it simply to keep one's sanity, live normally, enjoy a fine meal and a glass of wine, as the world around us experiences harrowing upheavals?

4   Of course, indifference can be tempting—more than that, seductive. It is so much easier to look away from victims. It is so much easier to avoid such rude interruptions to our work, our dreams, our hopes. It is, after all, awkward, troublesome, to be involved in another person's pain and despair. Yet, for the person who is indifferent, his or her neighbors are of no consequence. And, therefore, their lives are meaningless. Their hidden or even visible anguish is of no interest. Indifference reduces the other to an abstraction.

5   In a way, to be indifferent to that suffering is what makes the human being inhuman. Indifference, after all, is more dangerous than anger and hatred. Anger can at times be creative. One writes a great poem, a great symphony, one does something special for the sake of humanity because one is angry at the injustice that one witnesses. But indifference is never creative. Even hatred at times may elicit a response. You fight it. You denounce it. You disarm it. Indifference elicits no response. Indifference is not a response.

6   Indifference is not a beginning, it is an end. And, therefore, indifference is always the friend of the enemy, for it benefits the aggressor – never his victim, whose pain is magnified when he or she feels forgotten. The political prisoner in his cell, the hungry children, the homeless refugees – not to respond to their plight, not to relieve their solitude by offering them a spark of hope is to exile them from human memory. And in denying their humanity we betray our own.

7   Indifference, then, is not only a sin, it is a punishment. And this is one of the most important lessons of this outgoing century's wide-ranging experiments in good and evil.

8   In the place that I come from, society was composed of three simple categories: the killers, the victims, and the bystanders. During the darkest of times, inside the ghettos and death we felt abandoned, forgotten. All of us did.

9   And yet, my friends, good things have also happened in this traumatic century: the defeat of Nazism, the collapse of communism, the rebirth of Israel on its ancestral soil, the demise of apartheid, Israel's peace treaty with Egypt, the peace accord in Ireland. And let us remember the meeting, filled with drama and emotion, between Rabin and Arafat that you, Mr. President, convened in this very place. I was here and I will never forget it.

10   Does it mean that we have learned from the past? Does it mean that society has changed? Has the human being become less indifferent and more human? Have we really learned from our experiences? Are we less insensitive to the plight of victims of ethnic cleansing and other forms of injustices in places near and far? Is today's justified intervention in Kosovo, led by you, Mr. President, a lasting warning that never again will the deportation, the terrorization of children and their parents be allowed anywhere in the world? Will it discourage other dictators in other lands to do the same?

11   Together we walk towards the new millennium, carried by profound fear and extraordinary hope.

- -

Write an essay in which you explain how Elie Wiesel builds an argument to persuade his audience that indifference has serious consequences. In your essay, analyze how Wiesel uses one or more of the features listed on page 520 (or features of your own choice) to strengthen the logic and persuasiveness of his argument. Be sure that your analysis focuses on the most relevant features of the passage.

Your essay should not explain whether you agree with Wiesel's claims, but rather explain how Wiesel builds an argument to persuade his audience.

SAT Essay Model Exam 1 Evaluation

Evaluate Your Essay

When you are finished, give your essay a preliminary score using this rubric. Then have a friend, teacher, or parent score your essay.

SAT Essay Rubric

In order to score the following points, the essay should demonstrate the following qualities:			
Score	Reading	Analysis	Writing
4 Advanced	❏ demonstrates thorough comprehension of the text's central ideas, important details, and how they interrelate ❏ is free of errors of fact or interpretation with regard to the text ❏ skillfully uses textual evidence (quotations, paraphrases, or both) from the source text to support conclusions about the text	❏ insightfully evaluates author's use of evidence and reasoning ❏ effectively and thoroughly evaluates stylistic and persuasive elements, such as word choice and tone ❏ presents relevant, sufficient, and strategically chosen support for claims or points made in the response ❏ focuses on most relevant features of the text	❏ is cohesive and uses language very effectively ❏ presents a precise central claim ❏ uses effective organization, including an introduction and conclusion ❏ includes a logical progression of ideas within paragraphs and throughout the essay ❏ uses a variety of sentence structures ❏ uses precise words ❏ maintains a formal style and objective tone ❏ uses correct grammar, usage, mechanics, and spelling
3 Proficient	❏ demonstrates effective comprehension of the text's central ideas, important details, and how they interrelate ❏ is mostly free of errors of fact or interpretation with regard to the text ❏ appropriately uses textual evidence (quotations, paraphrases, or both) from the source text to support conclusions about the text	❏ effectively evaluates author's use of evidence and reasoning ❏ competently evaluates stylistic and persuasive elements, such as word choice and tone ❏ presents relevant and sufficient support for claims or points made in the response ❏ focuses on some relevant features of the text	❏ is mostly cohesive and uses language effectively ❏ presents a precise central claim or an implied central idea ❏ uses effective organization, including an introduction and conclusion ❏ includes a logical progression of ideas within paragraphs and throughout the essay ❏ uses a variety of sentence structures ❏ uses some precise words ❏ maintains a formal style and objective tone ❏ mostly uses correct grammar, usage, mechanics, and spelling

Score	Reading	Analysis	Writing
2 Partial	❏ demonstrates some comprehension of the text's central ideas. ❏ contains some errors of fact or interpretation with regard to the text ❏ makes limited or haphazard use of textual evidence (quotations, paraphrases, or both) from the source text to support conclusions about the text	❏ attempts to evaluate author's use of evidence and reasoning but doesn't explain their importance effectively or accurately ❏ evaluates stylistic and persuasive elements, such as word choice and tone but doesn't explain their importance effectively or accurately ❏ presents little or no support for claims or points made in the response ❏ fails to focus on most relevant features of the text	❏ is not cohesive and uses language somewhat effectively ❏ lacks a precise central claim or strays from the claim over the course of the response ❏ fails to use effective organization, including an introduction and conclusion ❏ does not maintain a logical progression of ideas within paragraphs and throughout the essay ❏ uses limited sentence structures ❏ uses vague words or repetitive word choice ❏ does not maintain a formal style and objective tone ❏ fails to consistently use grammar, usage, mechanics, and spelling
1 Inadequate	❏ demonstrates little or no comprehension of the text's central ideas ❏ contains numerous errors of fact or interpretation with regard to the text ❏ uses little or no textual evidence (quotations, paragraphs, or both) from the source text to support conclusions about the text	❏ offers little or no evaluation of the author's use of evidence and reasoning ❏ offers little or no evaluation of stylistic and persuasive elements, such as word choice and tone ❏ presents little or no support for claims or points made in the response or the support is irrelevant ❏ fails to focus on most relevant features of the text ❏ offers little or no analysis of the text (e.g., summarizes the text instead)	❏ is not cohesive and uses language ineffectively ❏ lacks a precise central claim ❏ fails to use effective organization, including an introduction and conclusion ❏ has no logical progression of ideas within paragraphs and throughout the essay ❏ uses limited sentence structures ❏ uses vague words or repetitive word choice ❏ uses informal style and opinionated tone ❏ contains many mistakes in grammar, usage, mechanics, and spelling
Summary	_____ / 8 in Reading	_____ / 8 in Analysis	_____ / 8 in Writing

Compare Your Essay

After you write your own essay, read the sample student essays below and mark their strengths and weaknesses. Then look at the explanations that follow to see how an essay reader may score the writing. Compare your writing with the sample essays so that you can learn from their strengths.

Prompt #1 Sample Essay   Score: Advanced—3 and 4s

On April 12, 1999, Elie Wiesel convinced his audience at the White House that indifference poses great dangers to the world. Wiesel juxtaposes stark opposites and uses dramatic language to draw a strong emotional response from his listeners and readers; he continues to appeal to his audience's emotions through varying sentence structures and first person point of view, and the latter creates a universal condition for all people. Through these strategies, Wiesel effectively warns readers and listeners that indifference can lead to severe consequences for humanity.

In the beginning of Elie Wiesel's speech, he starts off with dramatic diction with phrases like "vanishing century," "judged severely," "cast a dark shadow over humanity," and "bloodbaths." These word choices help to hook the audience right away by appealing to the pathos of his listeners and readers. In the following paragraph, Wiesel illustrates the dangers of indifference by juxtaposing starkly contrasting concepts like "light and darkness … dusk and dawn … good and evil." These differing ideas highlight the strange nature of "no difference." After establishing this, he places the idea of indifference in humanity using emotional language like "seductive," "pain and despair," and "anguish." These intense words help to convey Wiesel's sense of exigency regarding the threat of indifference.

The emotional appeal continues through Wiesel's repetitive, whittling-down of sentence length within paragraphs. In the first, fourth, fifth, and eighth paragraphs of his speech, he follows relatively the same format of syntactical structure: he begins with longer sentences and they grow shorter as he reaches the end of the paragraph, and finally he ends with a short sentence that contrasts with the lengthier sentences at the beginning. By explaining his ideas in the earlier part of the paragraphs through longer, sometimes run-on sentences, but then ending each paragraph abruptly, he draws attention to the content of each sentence. For example, in the first paragraph, Wiesel provides several historical cases to support his claim that the past century has consisted of several failures. After these longer sentences in which he lists events like "two world wars, ... the senseless chain of assassinations" and more, he ends the paragraph with "So much violence, so much indifference." The last sentence serves as a punch line that delivers the main point of the previous paragraph with few words. By repeating this structure throughout his speech, he explains in detail his point and summarizes the paragraph in a short, poignant sentence. These terse, powerful phrases at the ends of his paragraphs help Wiesel effectively establish his ideas.

Wiesel demands the attention of his listeners throughout his piece. By using rhetorical questions throughout the speech, Wiesel's audience takes an active role in it. He directly addresses readers and listeners with the use of phrases like "my friends." In the ninth paragraph he speaks right to the president. He truly persuades his audience using the first person point-of-view. The first sentence of Wiesel's speech begins with "we" and he creates a connection with those listening and reading. He continues the use of first person while discussing the tendency of all people to participate in indifference, and he adopts the word "human" several times. By discussing the similarities of all people in phrases like "our work, our dreams, our hopes" and "have we really learned from our experiences," and emphasizing the shared qualities of humans, Wiesel creates universality among all people. He uses this universality to show that all people have an obligation and responsibility to avoid passivity and, of course, indifference.

Elie Wiesel's speech successfully establishes his point regarding the risks of remaining indifferent to crimes against humanity through intense diction, fluctuating syntactical structure and the quality of universality with first person point-of-view. The audience experiences his strong emotional appeal and takes an active role in reading or listening to the speech, which helps to persuade them of his ideas.

Explanation of Score

Reading Score: 4 Advanced	
Comprehension	**The writer clearly understood the article and the author's arguments.** *See introduction: clear claim and outline of author's persuasive techniques.*
Accuracy	**The writer accurately presented facts from the article.** *All references to information in the article are correct.*
Evidence	**The writer effectively used evidence, quotations, and paraphrasing to demonstrate an understanding of the article.** *See effective use of quotations and paraphrasing in each body paragraph.*

Analysis Score: 3 Proficient	
Evaluation of evidence	**The writer effectively evaluated the author's use of evidence, reasoning, stylistic and persuasive elements.** *The writer documents the use of juxtaposition, sentence structure, word choice, and first person point of view.*
Support	**The writer supported most claims with evidence from the text and explanations of the significance of that evidence.** *See use of quotations and paraphrasing from the article in each body paragraph. However, the fourth paragraph lacks examples of rhetorical questions.*
Focus	**The writer stayed focused on the most relevant features of the article in order to address the task of evaluating the author's effectiveness. The writer focused on author's ability to elicit emotional response in his reader and keep the attention of his audience.** *Although the author may use other techniques, the writer has focused on two or three of the most significant.*

Writing Score: 4 Advanced	
Strong central claim	**The writer clearly presented a central claim:** *Wiesel juxtaposes stark opposites and uses dramatic language to draw a strong emotional response from his listeners and readers; he continues to appeal to his audience's emotions through varying sentence structures and first person point of view, and the latter creates a universal condition for all people.*
Organization and progression of ideas	**The writer has a clearly organized essay.** *Essay starts with an introduction that contains the central claim. It continues with body paragraphs, each beginning with a clear topic sentence, each maintaining focus on its subtopic, and each ending with a strong closing sentence. The body paragraphs transition smoothly from one another. The essay ends with a concise conclusion that restates the central claim and most relevant supporting subtopics.*
Sentence structure	**The writer employed simple, complex, and compound sentences. The writer varied sentence length and style.**
Word choice	**The writer used synonyms for repeated words, appropriately leveled vocabulary, and accurate terms.** *"juxtaposes stark opposites," "severe consequences for humanity," "whittling-down of sentence length."*
Style and tone	**The writer used a formal essay tone appropriate for the task.**
Standard written English	**The writer followed conventions such as proper use of punctuation, correctly formed sentences (no run-ons or fragments), and correct grammar and spelling.**

Prompt #1 Sample Essay Score: Proficient/Partial—3s and a 2

"The Perils of Indifference" is a speech that Elie Wiesel, a holocaust survivor, gave at the White House in 1999. In this powerful speech, Wiesel effectively uses many techniques to convince his audience of the urgency of his topic. He shows his listeners that this is a really important issue. He uses rhetorical questions, some short sentences, and opposites to prove his point.

Wiesel starts with an optimistic statement: "We are on the threshold of a new century, a new millennium." Here he peaks the reader's interest. He follows with a rhetorical question, which is a technique he uses repeatedly throughout the speech.

He asks: "What will the legacy of this vanishing century be?" His listeners are perhaps ready for a hopeful answer to that question. Wiesel then grabs their attention with a contrast: "Surely it will be judged, and judged severely." Now his listeners know that the message of the speech may be more serious. He reinforces this seriousness with a long list of violent events.

Wiesel continues with rhetorical questions, opening the next two paragraphs with questions such as "What is indifference?" and "What are its courses and inescapable consequences?" He is engaging his audience in hopes of making them really think about these issues. He also asks complicated questions such as "Can one possibly view indifference as a virtue?" He is strengthening his argument by acknowledging different perspectives to every issue.

Wiesel also uses some very short, powerful sentences to emphasize his points. He writes about hatred, "You fight it. You denounce it. You disarm it." Here Wiesel uses repetition also. This further supports his point. The other way he does this is by showing his audience lots of opposites. He says, "Indifference is not a beginning, it's an end." He also says, ". . . carried by profound fear and extraordinary hope." Wiesel uses these pairs of opposites similarly to how he uses rhetorical questions. He is forcing the listener to grapple with conflict.

Elie Wiesel successfully argues about the dangers of indifference for our society. By the end of his speech, his listeners can't deny this problem, because of how Wiesel constructed his speech. He bombarded his audience with questions and contrasts, and he showed them the consequences of ignoring the issue.

Explanation of Score

Reading Score: 3 Proficient	
Comprehension	**The writer mostly understood the article and the author's arguments.** *Writer should have clearly stated author's claim in introduction.*
Accuracy	**The writer presented accurate facts from the article.** *All references to information in the article are correct.*
Evidence	**The writer used evidence and quotations to demonstrate an understanding of the article.** *Writer could have used some paraphrasing of author's points, rather than relying only on quotations.*

Analysis Score: 2 Partial	
Evaluation of evidence	**The writer evaluated the author's use of evidence, reasoning, stylistic and persuasive elements.** *The writer presents "rhetorical questions," "short sentences" and "opposites" for the analysis of the author's persuasive techniques. Some of these terms could be more accurate (e.g. syntax, juxtaposition).*
Support	**The writer supported each claim with evidence from the text but at times did not offer complete explanations of the significance of that evidence.** *The second and third paragraphs need more explanation of significance. The fourth paragraph is more effective.*
Focus	**The writer stayed focused on some of the most relevant features of the article in order to address the task of evaluating the author's effectiveness.**

Writing Score: 3 Proficient	
Strong central claim	**The writer presented this in the introduction, but could have written a stronger sentence:** *"He uses rhetorical questions, some short sentences, and opposites to prove his point."*
Organization and progression of ideas	**The writer had a clearly organized essay.** *It starts with an introduction that contains the central claim. It continues with body paragraphs, each beginning with a clear topic sentence, each maintaining focus on its subtopic, and each ending with a strong closing sentence. The body paragraphs transition smoothly from one another. The essay ends with a concise conclusion that restates the central claim and most relevant supporting subtopics.*
Sentence structure	**The writer employed simple, complex, and compound sentences. The writer mostly varied sentence length and style.** *Writer could have used fewer short, simple sentences in places where related ideas could have been combined. At times the writing is redundant.*
Word choice	**The writer did not use synonyms for repeated words often enough. The writer did use some appropriately leveled vocabulary and some accurate terms. In some cases, more advanced vocabulary could have been used.** *Examples of problems with word choice: Writer repeats author's name frequently, opening most paragraphs with it. Writer repeats the word "he" again and again when referring to the author, opening sentences with the word repeatedly.*
Style and tone	**The writer used a formal essay appropriate for this task. In some cases, the writer's style and voice could have been more mature/advanced.** *Examples of ineffective style or tone from essay: "really important issue," "lots of opposites."*
Standard written English	**The writer mostly followed conventions such as proper use of punctuation, correctly formed sentences (no run-ons or fragments), and correct grammar and spelling.**

If your essay did not score a 3 or 4 in all categories, rewrite it. Use comments from your teacher, parents, and friends to improve your writing.

Allow 50 minutes to complete the following essay prompt.

As you read the passage below, consider how the authors use

- evidence, such as facts or examples, to support claims.
- reasoning to develop ideas and to connect claims and evidence.
- stylistic or persuasive elements, such as word choice or appeals to emotion, to add power to the ideas expressed.

Adapted from Nathan K. Lujan and Larry M. Page. "Libraries of Life."
©2015 by The New York Times Company.

1   Hidden behind the popular displays at many of your favorite natural history museums — in their basements, back rooms and, increasingly, off-site facilities — sit humanity's most important libraries of life, holding not books but preserved animal and plant specimens, carefully collected over centuries by thousands of scientist explorers.

2   These specimen collections serve as the bedrock of our system of taxonomy — the rules by which we classify life — and are integral to our understanding of the threats, origins and interrelationships of biodiversity. And yet, thanks to budget cutbacks, misplaced ethical critiques, public misconceptions and government regulations that restrict scientists while failing to restrict environmental exploitation, the continued maintenance and growth of these libraries is in danger.

3   Though most visitors never know they are there, natural history collections are as critical to modern biologists as libraries are to journalists and historians. Indeed, each museum specimen allows reinterpretation by every person who examines it.

4   A taxonomist looking for minute differences between species, and a biogeographer investigating species distributions across a landscape, will find the same specimen valuable for different reasons, as will an evolutionary biologist resolving the interconnectedness and history of life, and an ecologist piecing together the intricate functions of whole ecosystems. These collections

5 are particularly critical in today's era of rapid ecological and climate change, providing a unique and vitally important glimpse into ecological conditions of the past.

6   In the same way that students of the humanities use new critical approaches to pull novel ideas out of old books, scientists regularly use new technologies — like stable isotope analysis, high-throughput DNA sequencing and X-ray computed tomography — to draw new discoveries from sometimes centuries-old specimens. In October 2014, a Smithsonian botanist and curator named Vicki Funk cataloged recent budgetary and curatorial cutbacks at several of our nation's premier natural history museums, including the Field Museum in Chicago, the California Academy of Sciences and the New York State Museum. The curatorial staff at the Field Museum dropped by almost half, between 2001 and 2014, and that's at a relatively well-funded American institution.

7   According to an editorial last November in the journal Nature, most natural history collections in Italy are virtually derelict, with up to a third of all specimens lost to neglect. And many tropical countries, which have disproportionately rich biodiversity and booming economies linked to resource extraction, allocate few if any funds for cataloging their natural heritage — shifting greater responsibility to those few European and North American institutions that maintain robust global collections.

8   Funding cuts aren't the only threat. In the journal *Science* last April, the Arizona State University ethicist Ben A. Minteer and his co-authors made the dubious claim that scientific specimen collection had significantly contributed to many species' decline and extinction. They recommended that such collections be minimized in favor of nonlethal tissue samples, photographs or other recordings, particularly for species thought to be under threat of extinction.

9   They aren't alone. In October 2014, the Harvard entomologist and wildlife photographer received withering public criticism, including at least one death threat, for mentioning in a blog that he had euthanized and preserved a single specimen of the relatively common and widespread Goliath bird-eating spider, which he later deposited in Guyana's natural history museum.

10   We heartily agree that the impact of scientific collections on species should be minimized. But to deny the value of specimens is to accept ignorance of many of the requirements for understanding the evolution, ecology and conservation of biodiversity.

11   To the extent that they can still capture a rich and verifiable record of biodiversity at a single point and time, many biologists already strive to maximize nonlethal sampling techniques, including camera traps, audio recordings and tissue collection. But these tools are often effective only for organisms that can be identified with certainty in the field. What about the estimated 86 percent of all species that remain unknown? And while photographs can record an organism's external appearance, they reveal nothing about its internal anatomy, reproductive state, diseases and genetics.

12   And specimen collection need never threaten extinction. The research, growth and maintenance of scientific collections must be strongly and publicly supported.

13   There is no substitute for collecting and curating specimens for long-term study — not just for scientists studying biodiversity today, but also for future generations, whose need for clues to the spectacular breadth and complexity of unaltered ecosystems will be even greater than our own.

- -

On a separate sheet of paper, write an essay in which you explain how Nathan Lujan and Larry Page build an argument to persuade their audience that specimen collection is necessary to our understanding of important aspects of biodiversity. In your essay, analyze how Lujan and Page use one or more of the features listed on page 531 (or features of your own choice) to strengthen the logic and persuasiveness of their argument. Be sure that your analysis focuses on the most relevant aspects of the passage.

Your essay should not explain whether you agree with Lujan and Page's claims, but rather explain how the authors build an argument to persuade their audience.

SAT Essay Model Exam 2 Evaluation

Evaluate Your Essay

When you are finished, give your essay a preliminary score using this rubric. Then have a friend, teacher, or parent score your essay.

SAT Essay Rubric

In order to score the following points, the essay should demonstrate the following qualities:

Score	Reading	Analysis	Writing
4 Advanced	❏ demonstrates thorough comprehension of the text's central ideas, important details, and how they interrelate ❏ is free of errors of fact or interpretation with regard to the text ❏ skillfully uses textual evidence (quotations, paraphrases, or both) from the source text to support conclusions about the text	❏ insightfully evaluates author's use of evidence and reasoning ❏ effectively and thoroughly evaluates stylistic and persuasive elements, such as word choice and tone ❏ presents relevant, sufficient, and strategically chosen support for claims or points made in the response ❏ focuses on most relevant features of the text	❏ is cohesive and uses language very effectively ❏ presents a precise central claim ❏ uses effective organization, including an introduction and conclusion ❏ includes a logical progression of ideas within paragraphs and throughout the essay ❏ uses a variety of sentence structures ❏ uses precise words ❏ maintains a formal style and objective tone ❏ uses correct grammar, usage, mechanics, and spelling
3 Proficient	❏ demonstrates effective comprehension of the text's central ideas, important details, and how they interrelate ❏ is mostly free of errors of fact or interpretation with regard to the text ❏ appropriately uses textual evidence (quotations, paraphrases, or both) from the source text to support conclusions about the text	❏ effectively evaluates author's use of evidence and reasoning ❏ competently evaluates stylistic and persuasive elements, such as word choice and tone ❏ presents relevant and sufficient support for claims or points made in the response ❏ focuses on some relevant features of the text	❏ is mostly cohesive and uses language effectively ❏ presents a precise central claim or an implied central idea ❏ uses effective organization, including an introduction and conclusion ❏ includes a logical progression of ideas within paragraphs and throughout the essay ❏ uses a variety of sentence structures ❏ uses some precise words ❏ maintains a formal style and objective tone ❏ mostly uses correct grammar, usage, mechanics, and spelling

Score	Reading	Analysis	Writing
2 Partial	❏ demonstrates some comprehension of the text's central ideas. ❏ contains some errors of fact or interpretation with regard to the text ❏ makes limited or haphazard use of textual evidence (quotations, paraphrases, or both) from the source text to support conclusions about the text	❏ attempts to evaluate author's use of evidence and reasoning but doesn't explain their importance effectively or accurately ❏ evaluates stylistic and persuasive elements, such as word choice and tone but doesn't explain their importance effectively or accurately ❏ presents little or no support for claims or points made in the response ❏ fails to focus on most relevant features of the text	❏ is not cohesive and uses language somewhat effectively ❏ lacks a precise central claim or strays from the claim over the course of the response ❏ fails to use effective organization, including an introduction and conclusion ❏ does not maintain a logical progression of ideas within paragraphs and throughout the essay ❏ uses limited sentence structures ❏ uses vague words or repetitive word choice ❏ does not maintain a formal style and objective tone ❏ fails to consistently use grammar, usage, mechanics, and spelling
1 Inadequate	❏ demonstrates little or no comprehension of the text's central ideas ❏ contains numerous errors of fact or interpretation with regard to the text ❏ uses little or no textual evidence (quotations, paragraphs, or both) from the source text to support conclusions about the text	❏ offers little or no evaluation of the author's use of evidence and reasoning ❏ offers little or no evaluation of stylistic and persuasive elements, such as word choice and tone ❏ presents little or no support for claims or points made in the response or the support is irrelevant ❏ fails to focus on most relevant features of the text ❏ offers little or no analysis of the text (e.g., summarizes the text instead)	❏ is not cohesive and uses language ineffectively ❏ lacks a precise central claim ❏ fails to use effective organization, including an introduction and conclusion ❏ has no logical progression of ideas within paragraphs and throughout the essay ❏ uses limited sentence structures ❏ uses vague words or repetitive word choice ❏ uses informal style and opinionated tone ❏ contains many mistakes in grammar, usage, mechanics, and spelling
Summary	_____ / 8 in Reading	_____ / 8 in Analysis	_____ / 8 in Writing

Compare Your Essay

After you write your own essay, read the sample student essays below and mark their strengths and weaknesses. Then look at the explanations on the pages that follow to see how an essay reader may score the writing. Compare your writing with the sample essays so that you can learn from their strengths.

Prompt #2 Sample Essay   Score: Advanced—4s

In their article, "Libraries of Life," Nathan Lujan and Larry Page make a convincing case for preserving specimen collections. Offering readers an organized, well-reasoned argument backed with credible evidence and troubling predictions, the authors persuade readers that preserving these assortments of specimens is important. They begin by acknowledging that most readers don't even know of the existence of the collections, but by the end of the article, readers would most likely agree with the assessment that specimen collection can provide important information, not the least of which may be to help future generations protect the planet.

The authors open their article with three effective paragraphs that incorporate techniques such as impactful language, subtle predictions, and a relevant analogy. They begin with an element of mystery to draw in the reader, using the word "hidden" as the first word of the article. The reader's interest is piqued about this secret collection of specimens and he or she will want to know more. Then in the second paragraph, Lujan and Page use powerful phrases such as "the bedrock of our system," and "integral to our understanding" to convince their audience that the collections are indeed important. By alluding to the "threats, origins and interrelationships of biodiversity" the authors suggest that preserving and continuing to contribute to specimen collections is even essential to our future. The authors criticize government regulations with harsh language such as "restrict," "failing," and "exploitation" and "danger." This word choice, crammed into one sentence, has the effect of bombarding the reader with urgency. Finally, in the third paragraph, the authors create an analogy to help solidify their readers' understanding of the issue. They tell us that natural history collections are to biologists as libraries are to journalists and historians. In three short paragraphs, Lujan and Page are well on their way to convincing their readers of the importance of specimen collections.

As the article continues, the authors support their claim by presenting specific, concrete examples that illustrate why the world must keep collecting animal and plant specimens. The authors point out that each specimen is valuable in a different way to a variety of people. They write about a taxonomist, a biogeographer, an ecologist, and an evolutionary biologist and all the different ways each would use the collections. By specifying different types of scientists and what they can gain from studying the specimens, the reader is able to visualize the importance of the specimen collections, and see the scientists at work with the specimens. Then the authors go on to give examples of scientific technology that may be found through studying specimens. What is interesting here is that the authors don't say that the technological advances came from the specimens, but they allude to the fact that they could have. The casual reader won't scrutinize the article for such detail, and may well walk away believing that that new technology discussed in the paragraph was a direct result of studying the specimens. This further convinces the reader that preserving specimen collections is beneficial work.

In addition to incorporating effective, specific examples, the authors also employ expert testimony to lend credibility to their argument. The authors share information from a Smithsonian botanist who provides some troubling information about the state of specimen collections. The reader learns that there have been "recent budgetary and curatorial cutbacks at several of our nation's premier natural history museums." The reader has just learned that specimen collections can help with important technological advances, and then is told by a credible source that the future doesn't look good for these collections. Next, the authors go on to refer to an article in the journal *Nature* that suggests that, "most natural history collections in Italy are virtually derelict." The piece of information is meant to represent natural history collections in Europe as a whole. The reader will see that the problem here is global. Using reputable sources and providing the reader with the bigger picture helps put the importance of the situation in context.

To further strengthen their argument, Lujan and Page offer concessions and then follow these with counterarguments. They refer to the argument made by ethicist, Ben Minteer, who claimed that specimen collection had contributed to the decline and extinction of many species. Lujan and Page weaken Minteer's argument by introducing his idea as a "dubious claim." The authors do acknowledge the problem of sometimes having to kill living specimens in order to collect them. They provide an example of a scientist who euthanized a bird and was harshly criticized for his actions. They respond with "we heartily agree that the impact of scientific collections on species should be minimized," following with, "but to deny the value of specimens is to accept ignorance of many of the requirements for understanding the evolution, ecology and conservation of biodiversity." They further counter that specimen collections will not threaten a species into extinction. This pattern of presenting the opposition and then immediately refuting it leaves the reader even more convinced of the authors' claim. The authors concede a point in order to gain in the larger argument.

Lujan and Page end their article with a look to the future and an ominous warning. They allude to the fact that future generations may need the information gathered from specimen collections more than any other generation. Using predictions about the future is yet another technique the authors employ to clearly lend power to their claim. Combined with their effective word choice, incorporation of specific illustrations, and use of credible sources, the authors of this article build an argument to persuade their readers to see the importance of specimen collections. The structure, style, and persuasive elements all work to successfully argue their claim.

Explanation of Score

Reading Score: 4 Advanced	
Comprehension	**The writer clearly understood the article and the author's arguments.** *Introduction contains clear claim and outline of author's persuasive techniques.*
Accuracy	**The writer accurately presented facts from the article.** *All references to information in the article are correct.*
Evidence	**The writer effectively used evidence, quotations, and paraphrasing to demonstrate an understanding of the article.** *Effective use of quotations and paraphrasing in each body paragraph.*

Analysis Score: 4 Advanced

Evaluation of evidence	**The writer effectively evaluated the author's use of evidence, reasoning, stylistic and persuasive elements.** *The writer documents the use of "credible evidence and troubling predictions," "impactful language," "a relevant analogy."*
Support	**The writer supported each claim with evidence from the text and explanations of the significance of that evidence.** *Use of facts, quotations, and paraphrasing from the article in each body paragraph. Significance of evidence is thoroughly explained.*
Focus	**The writer stayed focused on the most relevant features of the article in order to address the task of evaluating the author's effectiveness.** *Focused on author's use of language, effective, specific examples, expert testimony, and concessions. Although the author may use other techniques, the writer has focused on two or three of the most significant.*

Writing Score: 4 Advanced

Strong central claim	**The writer clearly presented a central claim:** *"Offering readers an organized, well-reasoned argument backed with credible evidence and troubling predictions, the authors persuade readers that preserving specimen collections is important."*
Organization and progression of ideas	**The writer had a clearly organized essay.** *Essay starts with an introduction that contains the central claim. It continues with body paragraphs, each beginning with a clear topic sentence, each maintaining focus on its subtopic, and each ending with a strong closing sentence. The body paragraphs transition smoothly from one another. The essay ends with a concise conclusion that restates the central claim and most relevant supporting subtopics.*
Sentence structure	**The writer employed simple, complex, and compound sentences. The writer varied sentence length and style.**
Word choice	**The writer used synonyms for repeated words, appropriately leveled vocabulary, and accurate terms.** *Examples of effective word choice from essay: "by alluding to," "has the effect of bombarding the reader with urgency," "a look to the future and an ominous warning."*
Style and tone	**The writer used a formal essay tone appropriate for the task.**
Standard written English	**The writer followed conventions such as proper use of punctuation, correctly formed sentences (no run-ons or fragments), and correct grammar and spelling.**

Presenting readers with an interesting and perhaps new idea, specimen collections, the authors of the article convince readers of the need for their preservation. The authors alert the reader to the importance of these specimen collections and explains just why they are to be funded.

The authors show the reader that specimen collections are important to a variety of different people. For a variety of different reasons. By mentioning the different purposes separate occupations have for the specimen collections the reader can see for themselves how important the collections are. The reader will most likely agree with the author and want to fund these collections.

The author notes that without the specimen collections the future may face grave threats. This prediction about the future works on the reader and encourages agreement because the reader will think that once the specimen collections are gone, will there be hope for the future. It is through this fear that the author helps gain support for the argument to support specimen collections.

The authors do note that there are other ways of collecting the information gained from specimen collections such as "camera traps, audio recordings, and tissue collection." However, the authors are quick to point out the shortcomings of those other ways and the author continues to argue for the superiority of specimen collections over the other choices.

In conclusion, the authors of the text do a good job of convincing the reader that specimen collections are important and should be funded. The authors leave the reader wondering about the fate of the world when he or she alludes to how future generations will need the information that specimen collections can offer more than previous generations.

Explanation of Score

Reading Score: 2 Partial	
Comprehension	**The writer understood the article and the author's arguments to some extent, but needed to go more in depth.** *Introduction lacks background about the article, as well as an outline of the techniques that will be examined in the essay.*
Accuracy	**The writer presented some facts from the article, but left some important information out.** *Writer used vague references instead of the exact information provided in the article.*
Evidence	**The writer used some evidence, quotations, and paraphrasing to demonstrate an understanding of the article, but should have included more quotations and specific information from the article.**

Analysis Score: 2 Partial	
Evaluation of evidence	**The writer did not thoroughly evaluate the author's use of evidence, reasoning, stylistic and persuasive elements.** *Writer does not consistently identify the author's techniques (such as in the second paragraph). Writer does mention the author's use of predictions and concessions in the third and fourth paragraphs, which are more effective. The writer should have included more evidence.*
Support	**The writer supported each claim with some evidence from the text but did not offer complete explanations of the significance of that evidence.** *Essay needs significant elaboration and explanation.*
Focus	**The writer stayed focused on some of the most relevant features of the article in order to address the task of evaluating the author's effectiveness, but missed some important features.**

Writing Score: 2 Partial	
Strong central claim	**The writer presented his or her central claim in the introduction, but it should be a stronger, more specific sentence:** *"The authors alert the reader to the importance of these specimen collections and explains just why they are to be funded."*
Organization and progression of ideas	**The writer had a somewhat clearly organized essay.** *It starts with an introduction that contains the central claim. It continues with body paragraphs that don't always begin with a clear topic sentence. The body paragraphs do maintain focus on their subtopics. Each body paragraph should end with a strong closing sentence and should incorporate smooth transitions. The essay ends with a concise conclusion that restates the central claim and most relevant supporting subtopics, but is too brief.*

Sentence structure	The writer employed mostly simple sentences, but did include some complex and compound sentences. The writer varied sentence length and style at times.
Word choice	The writer used synonyms for repeated words, some appropriately leveled vocabulary, and some accurate terms. In some cases, more advanced vocabulary could have been used. *Examples of ineffective word choice from essay: "variety of different people," "For a variety of different reasons."*
Style and tone	The writer used a tone that was somewhat appropriate for this task. In some cases, the writer's style and voice could have been more mature/advanced. *Examples of ineffective style or tone from essay: "the authors of the text do a good job."*
Standard written English	The writer mostly used proper punctuation, correctly formed sentences, and correct grammar and spelling. Some mistakes include fragments, punctuation (commas), and subject-verb agreement.

If your essay did not score a 3 or 4 in all categories, rewrite it. Use comments from your teacher, parents, and friends to improve your writing.

Allow 50 minutes to complete the following essay prompt.

As you read the passage below, consider how Adrianne LaFrance uses

- evidence, such as facts or examples, to support claims.
- reasoning to develop ideas and to connect claims and evidence.
- stylistic or persuasive elements, such as word choice or appeals to emotion, to add power to the ideas expressed.

• •

Adrianne LaFrance, "Me, Myself, and Authenticity." ©2015 by The Atlantic.

1   Those who go looking for evidence of increasing self-absorption seem to find it everywhere these days. Inflated egos are apparently smiling in the selfies people snap, self-obsession woven into their compulsive online sharing. Even the tiniest language choices are revealing. First-person pronouns like "I" and "me" are crowding out "we" and "our" in all kinds of communication—from advertising copy to academic writing to newspaper articles to song lyrics.

2   The shift, some academics warn, is proof of narcissism run amok. It's popular to blame millennials, of course.

3   In one high-profile study, researchers from the University of Kentucky used a text-analysis program to interpret the lyrics of the top 100 most popular U.S. songs—as ranked by the Billboard Hot 100—each year between 1980 and 2007. They found a steady uptick in first-person singular pronouns (I, me) and a decline in more communal first-person plural pronouns (we, our), according to their 2011 paper in Psychology of Aesthetics, Creativity, and the Arts. All this singing about me, showed the larger culture was becoming more self-centered and less socially connected. "Narcissism is like a flu," said W. Keith Campbell, one of the study's authors. "Everybody around you gets sick and you feel great about yourself."

4   But some linguists and music historians say the reality is more nuanced. Frequent use of "I" doesn't signal a haughtier sense of one's status but the opposite, according to James Pennebaker, the social psychologist who invented

the text-analysis program used in the 2011 study of song lyrics. The higher a person's standing, the less frequently that person uses 'I' words, according to Pennebaker in his book, *The Secret Life of Pronouns: What Our Words Say About Us.* "A high-status person is looking out at the world," he wrote. "The low-status person tends to be looking more inwardly."

5   No, "we" isn't necessarily such a communal word after all. It often comes off as presumptive and exclusionary, and can be seen as one group speaking—out of turn—for others. *And we wouldn't want that now would we?* Instead, first-person narratives have emerged as markers of authenticity in an age when realness is a virtue.

6   Institutions deal in "we," while individuals stick with "I"—especially individuals of lower status, which often means those who weren't previously in privileged enough positions to have their language choices scrutinized.

7   In other words, the rise in use of "I" and "me" might reveal as much about who's doing the talking as it does about what's being said. Women, for instance, use the first-person singular at much higher rates than men do, according to Pennebaker. And institutions that once opted for formal communication styles have noticed the shift toward first-person singular, and have in some cases adopted it themselves.

8   What used to be "formal, pure, and precise," wrote Jon Evans in an essay for TechCrunch last year about how the Internet has revolutionized the way we write, is now "first-person, colloquial, breezy, open, and personal." People increasingly gravitate toward those who address them like, well, people.

9   And the mainstream shift toward "I" and "me" in American pop music dates back at least half a century. The Beatles actually cut back on their use of first-person pronouns after earlier songs like "Ask Me Why," "Love Me Do," and "Please Please Me" in the early 1960s. It was around this time that Bob Dylan ushered in the era of the singer-songwriter with his warbly first-person anthems. Dylan's ascent marked the dawn of another era characterized by hand-wringing over self-centered youth, and the beginning of what came to be known as the culture of narcissism. (The influential book of the same name was published in 1979.) Baby Boomers had yet to earn the "Me Generation" moniker at the start of Dylan's career, but he was criticized right away as being a narcissist—including by fellow folk singers like Pete Seeger.

10 "Seeger's criticism against Dylan at this time was that he took the 'we,' and turned it into a 'me,'" said John Covach, a professor of music theory at the University of Rochester's Eastman School of Music. "But what usually triggers this narcissism criticism is that what somebody's telling you about themselves is not something that you want to hear. If they seem to be whining about their situation, or seem to be entitled, you tend to view it as narcissism. But if someone is saying something that happened to them and it resonates with your own experience, then you don't call it narcissistic. You call it poetry."

. . . .

Write an essay in which you explain how Adrianne LaFrance builds an argument to persuade her audience that behaviors that might seem narcissistic are not necessarily so. In your essay, analyze how LaFrance uses one or more of the features listed on page 543 (or features of your own choice) to strengthen the logic and persuasiveness of her argument. Be sure that your analysis focuses on the most relevant aspects of the passage.

Your essay should not explain whether you agree with LaFrance's claims, but rather explain how the author builds an argument to persuade her audience.

SAT Essay Model Exam 3 Evaluation

Evaluate Your Essay

When you are finished, give your essay a preliminary score using this rubric. Then have a friend, teacher, or parent score your essay.

SAT Essay Rubric

In order to score the following points, the essay should demonstrate the following qualities:

Score	Reading	Analysis	Writing
4 Advanced	❏ demonstrates thorough comprehension of the text's central ideas, important details, and how they interrelate ❏ is free of errors of fact or interpretation with regard to the text ❏ skillfully uses textual evidence (quotations, paraphrases, or both) from the source text to support conclusions about the text	❏ insightfully evaluates author's use of evidence and reasoning ❏ effectively and thoroughly evaluates stylistic and persuasive elements, such as word choice and tone ❏ presents relevant, sufficient, and strategically chosen support for claims or points made in the response ❏ focuses on most relevant features of the text	❏ is cohesive and uses language very effectively ❏ presents a precise central claim ❏ uses effective organization, including an introduction and conclusion ❏ includes a logical progression of ideas within paragraphs and throughout the essay ❏ uses a variety of sentence structures ❏ uses precise words ❏ maintains a formal style and objective tone ❏ uses correct grammar, usage, mechanics, and spelling
3 Proficient	❏ demonstrates effective comprehension of the text's central ideas, important details, and how they interrelate ❏ is mostly free of errors of fact or interpretation with regard to the text ❏ appropriately uses textual evidence (quotations, paraphrases, or both) from the source text to support conclusions about the text	❏ effectively evaluates author's use of evidence and reasoning ❏ competently evaluates stylistic and persuasive elements, such as word choice and tone ❏ presents relevant and sufficient support for claims or points made in the response ❏ focuses on some relevant features of the text	❏ is mostly cohesive and uses language effectively ❏ presents a precise central claim or an implied central idea ❏ uses effective organization, including an introduction and conclusion ❏ includes a logical progression of ideas within paragraphs and throughout the essay ❏ uses a variety of sentence structures ❏ uses some precise words ❏ maintains a formal style and objective tone ❏ mostly uses correct grammar, usage, mechanics, and spelling

Score	Reading	Analysis	Writing
2 Partial	❏ demonstrates some comprehension of the text's central ideas. ❏ contains some errors of fact or interpretation with regard to the text ❏ makes limited or haphazard use of textual evidence (quotations, paraphrases, or both) from the source text to support conclusions about the text	❏ attempts to evaluate author's use of evidence and reasoning but doesn't explain their importance effectively or accurately ❏ evaluates stylistic and persuasive elements, such as word choice and tone but doesn't explain their importance effectively or accurately ❏ presents little or no support for claims or points made in the response ❏ fails to focus on most relevant features of the text	❏ is not cohesive and uses language somewhat effectively ❏ lacks a precise central claim or strays from the claim over the course of the response ❏ fails to use effective organization, including an introduction and conclusion ❏ does not maintain a logical progression of ideas within paragraphs and throughout the essay ❏ uses limited sentence structures ❏ uses vague words or repetitive word choice ❏ does not maintain a formal style and objective tone ❏ fails to consistently use grammar, usage, mechanics, and spelling
1 Inadequate	❏ demonstrates little or no comprehension of the text's central ideas ❏ contains numerous errors of fact or interpretation with regard to the text ❏ uses little or no textual evidence (quotations, paragraphs, or both) from the source text to support conclusions about the text	❏ offers little or no evaluation of the author's use of evidence and reasoning ❏ offers little or no evaluation of stylistic and persuasive elements, such as word choice and tone ❏ presents little or no support for claims or points made in the response or the support is irrelevant ❏ fails to focus on most relevant features of the text ❏ offers little or no analysis of the text (e.g., summarizes the text instead)	❏ is not cohesive and uses language ineffectively ❏ lacks a precise central claim ❏ fails to use effective organization, including an introduction and conclusion ❏ has no logical progression of ideas within paragraphs and throughout the essay ❏ uses limited sentence structures ❏ uses vague words or repetitive word choice ❏ uses informal style and opinionated tone ❏ contains many mistakes in grammar, usage, mechanics, and spelling
Summary	_____ / 8 in Reading	_____ / 8 in Analysis	_____ / 8 in Writing

Compare Your Essay

After you write your own essay, read the sample student essays below and mark their strengths and weaknesses. Then look at the explanations that follow to see how an essay reader may score the writing. Compare your writing with the sample essays so that you can learn from their strengths.

Prompt #3 Sample Essay   Score: Proficient/Advanced—3s and a 4

In the beginning of her article entitled, "Me, Myself, and Authenticity," Adrianne LaFrance poses what seems to be the thesis statement. It looks as if the claim in the article is going to be that our society is full of young narcissists. However what the author actually *does* is takes apart that very idea and instead shows how it isn't necessarily true. Through an investigation of our culture's history, the author demonstrates that the belief that the current generation is more self-centered than previous generations is false. By delaying her claim, employing the opinions of experts, and by referencing pop music, LaFrance dissects the evidence to show that the current generation is no more self-obsessed than any other.

LaFrance begins by citing seemingly strong evidence for the counterargument, pointing to apparent "increasing self-absorption," suggesting that, "inflated egos are apparently smiling in the selfies people snap, self-obsession woven into their compulsive online sharing." She also points to apparent proof that first-person pronouns are "crowding out 'we' and 'our'" in communication. She further supports the counterargument to her eventual claim by referencing a University of Kentucky study that showed there was an increase in the use of the first-person personal pronouns in hit songs from 1980 through 2007. LaFrance piles on proof for the opposition; however, she then begins to lay the groundwork for refuting all of this when she subtly pokes fun at a perhaps melodramatic warning from academics that it is all "proof of narcissism run amok."

A change occurs in the article when LaFrance starts the fourth paragraph with the word "but." Here she brings in her own expert opinions, claiming that linguists and historians say the situation is much more complicated than it has been made out to be. Instead of claiming that it is an indication of narcissism, the author quotes a linguist named James Pennebaker who claims that the use of "I" depends on a person's status and not on narcissism. Pennebaker states that the use of "I" might have more to do with "who's doing the talking as it does about what's being said." The author bolsters this by suggesting that maybe the word "we" isn't as inclusive as it seems. She throws in powerful word choice, such as "presumptive and exclusionary" here to further sway her readers. In LaFrance's use of an expert opinion, she trumps the opposition by dropping the specific name of a published linguist, as well as the title of his book.

The author then goes on to investigate other time periods when there was an emphasis on the use of "I" in popular music. The author discusses how the Beatles used "I" years ago, and then ends the article with a focus on Bob Dylan, who also incorporated the use of "I" into his music. The author elaborates on how the use of "I" in those instances also called out a belief in the younger generation's narcissism. By doing so, the author shows the reader that the current use of "I" shouldn't be evaluated for any other purposes since there is a historical precedent set. The use of accessible, pop culture references is intended to add relevance to LaFrance's claim.

Finally, the author concludes with the claim of the article, and that is "if someone is saying something that happened to them and it resonates with your own experience, then you don't call it narcissistic. You call it poetry." By that point, the reader is fully questioning his or her own beliefs about narcissism in today's culture. The author is convincing because she takes a common misconception and carries the discovery out right under the nose of her reader.

Explanation of Score

Reading Score: 3 Proficient	
Comprehension	**The writer clearly understood the article and the author's arguments.** *Clear claim and outline of author's persuasive techniques included in introduction. However, fourth paragraph doesn't present a clear argument.*
Accuracy	**The writer accurately presented facts from the article.** *All references to information in the article are correct.*
Evidence	**The writer effectively used evidence, quotations, and paraphrasing to demonstrate an understanding of the article.** *Effective use of quotations and paraphrasing in most body paragraphs.*

Analysis Score: 3 Proficient	
Evaluation of evidence	**The writer effectively evaluated the author's use of evidence, reasoning, stylistic and persuasive elements.** *The writer documents the use of a delayed claim, presentation of counterarguments, expert testimony, and pop culture. The fourth paragraph should have more explanation of the significance of pronouns in popular music. Each body paragraph could have further elaboration.*
Support	**The writer supported each claim with evidence from the text and explanations of the significance of that evidence.** *Effective use of quotations and paraphrasing. Fourth paragraph needs more explanation of significance of evidence.*
Focus	**The writer stayed focused on the most relevant features of the article in order to address the task of evaluating the author's effectiveness.** *Focused on article's structure, author's subtlety, and use of relevant information. Although the author may use other techniques, the writer has focused on two or three of the most significant.*

Writing Score: 4 Advanced	
Strong central claim	**The writer clearly presented a central claim:** *By delaying her claim, employing the opinions of experts, and by referencing pop music, LaFrance dissects the evidence to show that the current generation is no more self-obsessed than any other.*
Organization and progression of ideas	**The writer had a clearly organized essay.** *Essay starts with an introduction that contains the central claim. It continues with body paragraphs, each beginning with a clear topic sentence, each maintaining focus on its subtopic, and each ending with a strong closing sentence. The body paragraphs transition smoothly from one another. The essay ends with a concise conclusion that restates the central claim and most relevant supporting subtopics.*
Sentence structure	**The writer employed simple, complex, and compound sentences. The writer varied sentence length and style.**
Word choice	**The writer used synonyms for repeated words, appropriately leveled vocabulary, and accurate terms.** *Examples of effective word choice from essay: "employing the opinions of experts," "dissects the evidence," "piles on proof for the opposition," "the author bolsters this," "she takes a common misconception and carries the discovery out right under the nose of her reader."*
Style and tone	**The writer used a formal essay tone appropriate for the task.**
Standard written English	**The writer followed conventions such as proper use of punctuation, correctly formed sentences (no run-ons or fragments), and correct grammar and spelling.**

Prompt #3 Sample Essay   Score: Partial—all 2s

In this article, the author, Adrianne LaFrance's organization is set up to almost trick the reader into believing that the thesis statement is in the introduction, and that is that today's generation are incredibly self-absorbed. However, that is a persuasive trick played by the author to encourage the reader to agree with her. The real claim of the article is that the current generation is not any more self-absorbed than other generations.

By using examples of pronoun use and music the author presents an argument that previous generations have done the same things that the current generations have.

The current generation has the Internet and social media but previous generations did not. But the author point out that just because we take a lot of selfies doesn't mean we are full of ourselves.

The author says that people of different social classes use the word "I" in different ways. That means than just because someone says I a lot doesn't mean that they are obsessed with themselves. It just means that their status is different. Similarly, the music in the past also contained a lot of "I"s. So that means that the current generation doesn't use it more than other generation's and so they were just as self-absorbed as we are.

The author does make sense. The use of the pronoun "I" by different people means that just because someone uses it doesn't mean they are self-absorbed. It just means that their status is different. Also, if singers and bands sang about theirselves in the past that means that just because current singers and bands sing about theirselves doesn't mean they are self-absorbed.

The author, LaFrance, used a clever organization to convince her readers that the current generation is not narcissistic. She also gives examples about pronouns and music that help the readers understand what she means. Overall, her techniques worked to persuade her audience.

Explanation of Score

Reading Score: 2 Partial	
Comprehension	**The writer understood the article and the author's arguments to some extent, but needed to go more in depth.** *Introduction lacks background about the article, as well as an outline of the techniques that will be examined in the essay.*
Accuracy	**The writer presented some facts from the article, but left some important information out.** *Writer sometimes uses vague references instead of the exact information provided in the article.*
Evidence	**The writer used some evidence and paraphrasing to demonstrate an understanding of the article, but should have included more quotations and specific information from the article.**

Analysis Score: 2 Partial	
Evaluation of evidence	**The writer did not thoroughly evaluate the author's use of evidence, reasoning, stylistic and persuasive elements.** *Identifies organization, pronouns, and music as the author's techniques, but does not consistently identify/label these. Writer should have included more evidence.*
Support	**The writer supported each claim with some evidence from the text but did not offer complete explanations of the significance of that evidence.** *Essay needs significant additional elaboration and explanation.*
Focus	**The writer stayed focused on some of the most relevant features of the article in order to address the task of evaluating the author's effectiveness.** *Writer missed some important features.*

Writing Score: 2 Partial	
Strong central claim	**The writer presented his or her central claim in the introduction, but it should be a stronger, more specific sentence:** *"The real claim of the article is that the current generation is not any more self-absorbed than other generations."*
Organization and progression of ideas	**The writer had a somewhat organized essay.** *It starts with an introduction that contains the central claim but lacks a specific outline of subtopics. Essay contains some body paragraphs that don't begin with a clear topic sentence. The body paragraphs do maintain focus on their subtopics. The body paragraphs should end with a strong closing sentence and should incorporate smooth transitions. The essay ends with a conclusion that restates the central claim and most relevant supporting subtopics, but is too brief.*
Sentence structure	**The writer employed mostly simple sentences, but did include some complex and compound sentences. The writer varied sentence length and style at times.**
Word choice	**The writer used synonyms for repeated words, some appropriately leveled vocabulary, and some accurate terms. In some cases, more advanced vocabulary could have been used.**
Style and tone	**The writer used a tone that was somewhat appropriate for this task. In some cases, the writer's style and voice could have been more mature/advanced.**
Standard written English	**The writer usually followed conventions such as proper use of punctuation, correctly formed sentences, and correct grammar and spelling.** *Some mistakes were made in areas of punctuation (commas), spelling, and subject-verb agreement.*

If your essay did not score a 3 or 4 in all categories, rewrite it. Use comments from your teacher, parents, and friends to improve your writing.

Evidence-based Reading Domain

Lesson 1: Closely Reading Literature

Determining Explicit and Implicit Meanings   Practice, p. 61

1. The text says that "the code of a restraining civilization" kept them from shooting each other outright. In other words, they both had some morals that kept them from murdering each other.

2. In the first paragraph, the two enemies see each other and stop. The storm causes a tree to fall and land on both of the men. They are pinned down and can't escape.

3. It is implied that his men will roll the branch that pins him down onto Ulrich, making it look like Ulrich was killed by the tree.

4. Georg believes that it would be appropriate justice if Ulrich were killed by a tree in the forest he stole from Georg's family. The forest he fought hard for ultimately kills him. He finds this ironically funny.

SAT-Type Questions, p. 64

1. **C** Although the setting is a farm, Myop is not working (choice A), and although nut-gathering is mentioned, that is not Myop's goal (choice B). Choice D almost seems correct because the passage describes how Myop "made her own path." However, the best answer is choice C. The text describes the types of flowers Myop is gathering.

2. **B** All the other answers indicate that the cove is a positive place, but it clearly has an unsettling atmosphere.

3. **A** Choice B is incorrect because the man is clearly dead, not sleeping. Although Myop does see a piece of rope (choice C), she doesn't step on it. Choice D is almost correct, but there is no indication that the man was buried in a grave. The text implies that his body was left in the forest to rot without being cared for.

4. **A** The description of the rope in the tree and also near the skull imply the man was a victim of lynching. No support is given for choice B or choice C. The mention of the tree and the rope seem to hint at D, but the description of the broken teeth implies that the man was abused before he was killed.

5. **C** The line is a metaphor. Summer is not literally over. Summer is associated with Myop's innocence. The sudden contrast between Myop's carefree day picking flowers and her discovery of the man's remains implies that Myop has suddenly been confronted with the evil. Her innocence has been shattered. Choice A incorrectly interprets the line literally. Choice B is not accurate because the crime happened many years ago. Choice D may be true but is not related to the line. Choice C is the best answer.

Understanding Main Ideas and Purpose   Practice, p. 68

1. The passage describes how Henry desires to go and fight in the Civil War because he hears stories of battles being won. His mother does not want him to go. Finally, one day Henry enlists. He parts with his mother, who calmly tells him to keep quiet and obey his commanders.

2. He gets his information from newspapers, local gossip, and his own imagination.

3. Paragraph 4 describes the moment when Henry finally decides to defy his mother and enlist in the war.

4. The passage implies that Henry's mother thinks he is needed on the farm and that she has a moral objection to war (lines 6–10). Her advice to Henry about not trying to "lick the hull rebel army at the start" (line 41) implies that she knows Henry overestimates what fighting a war is like.

5. Henry seems to think that going to war will be an exciting adventure. He is stirred to enlist by sounds of people celebrating a victory. He is disappointed by his mother's unemotional farewell. He seems to have a romantic and unrealistic view of war (lines 18–21).

6. Paragraphs 7 and 8 describe the scene between Henry and his mother as they part. Henry is disappointed by his mother's practical advice.

SAT-Type Questions, pp. 72–74

1. **C** Choice A is implied by some of the statements in quotations, but this is a minor detail. Choices B and D may be true but are not stated in this passage.

2. **A** The passage clearly states that Sonny hasn't played the piano for a year.

3. **C** The idea implied by the comparison of going into deep waters is similar to the idea of sharing deep personal emotions. The passage is clearly not about the technical aspects of playing the right notes (choice D) or correct rhythm (choice A) or even working harder (choice B). It is implied that Creole wants Sonny to put his heart into the music.

4. **D** In paragraph 3, the narrator takes a break from describing the interchange between Creole and Sonny (choice C) and the other events happening on the stage (choice B) to make an observation about the relationship between a musician and his instrument. Although he does describe the parts of a piano (choice A), this is not the main purpose.

5. **D** All are implied by the passage except for D. The final line states that music is the "only light we've got in all this darkness."

6. **D** While choice A is true, it is not the main focus of the passage. This is also true of choice B, which is the focus of the final paragraph but not the entire passage. Choice C is also inferred but not the main idea. Choice D is the best summary because the focus is on the narrator's observations about his brother and music.

Analyzing Word Choice and Imagery for Tone Practice, pp. 78–81

1. The description evokes a sinister atmosphere of death and decay. Words that create this include: "crumbling condition," "old wood-work which has rotted," "barely perceptible fissure . . . made its way down the wall in a zigzag direction," "sullen waters of the tarn."

2. He compares the house to wood-work rotting under the ground in a vault. This image brings up images of a tomb.

3. This brings up the image that beneath the exterior, something is dead and rotten.

4. It suggests that her home is not a safe place for her right now. It is ominous and scary like a tiger waiting in the night.

5. The description of the remains of the fish with its "fleshy head still connected to bones" trying to escape emphasizes the narrator's fear and feelings of helplessness. She can relate to this dead fish that has been sacrificed to feed her family.

6. The narrator describes her opponent as "two angry black slits," the same way she described her mother earlier in the text. She is imagining her mother as her opponent in chess. This emphasizes the narrator's conflict with her mother over using her abilities to show off (lines 2–3). The narrator is the white pieces that scream and scurry and fall off the board in the wake of the black pieces' (her mother's) attack.

7. These lines create a tone of surrender. The narrator appears to be giving up to her mother's attack. She feels her own personality disappearing in the wake of her mother's pressure to play chess (lines 45–47).

SAT-Type Questions, p. 84

1. **C** Earlier in the paragraph, the narrator states that he was nervous that his aunt might become aware that her dress was not appropriate ("the absurdities of her attire"). When describing his aunt's response, he compares Aunt Georgiana's demeanor to a statue in a museum. He also describes her eyes as "impersonal" and "stony" and compares her "aloofness" to miners who return to civilization after long periods away. No contrast is implied, so A is incorrect. There is no support that the aunt disapproves of the concert (choice B). Although the narrator expresses anxiety about her attire, no mention is made of him being nervous about her visit (choice D). Thus, the best answer is C.

2. **C** The narrator describes the bright color of the dresses, but notes that his aunt regarded them as "daubs of tube paint on a palette." In other words, to her they were a large blur of color, beautiful not distinct. No support is given for choice B or D. Although A is implied, it is not the primary reason the writer describes the clothing. The best answer is choice C.

3. **B** The words "forever and forever" and "treadmill" evoke a monotonous tone of life on a farm, not gratification (choice A) or stress (choice C). There is no longing or wistfulness on the narrator's part (choice D). B is the best answer.

4. **B** The words used to describe the farm and the concert are very different. The musicians possess "clean profiles;" the instruments have "varnished bellies" and appear as a "restless, wind-tossed forest." In contrast the farm is a "naked house" that is "black and grim as a wooden fortress." No support is provided for choice D. The description does little to provide background on their relationship. Although choice A is implied by the positive images of the instruments, it is secondary to the contrast between the music hall and the prairie. Although the description is a flashback to an earlier time, it has nothing to do with a life-changing childhood event. So choice C is not correct. The best answer is choice B.

5. **C** There is no support for choice D. Although B is true, it is not the point of the comparison. The comparison in the final sentence is meant to compare not so much the landscape of the ancient world (choice A) with the prairie, but the way of life of the ancients. The point is that the life of the prairie is primitive, based upon war and survival, with peace being just a little better than being at war.

Identifying Characterization   Practice, p. 87

1. Miss Emily is a tiny woman with a skeleton that is "small and spare," but she is also quite fat, so that "what would have been merely plumpness in another was obesity in her." She "leans on an ebony cane" when she walks in. She appears bloated and unhealthy, evidenced by her "pallid hue." She dresses in all black and wears a gold chain with a watch. We can infer that she is a recluse who doesn't take good care of herself. The adjectives "bloated" and "pallid" give the impression of a walking corpse.

2. She is unfriendly, resistant to change, and stubborn. She "did not ask them to sit." Her voice "was dry and cold." She refuses to listen to the men and throws them out of her house.

3. The house smelled of "dust and disuse." The furniture was cracked and dusty. There was a picture of Miss

Emily's father in crayon. It can be inferred that she is a recluse who doesn't get out or have visitors. The crayon portrait is probably from her own childhood. She appears to be trapped in the past, not open to change.

SAT-Type Questions, p. 91

1. **C** The key word in the question is "immediate." Lines 20–22 describe Rosemary's initial response, "I picked her up in Curzon Street. Really. She's a real pick-up. She asked me for the price of a cup of tea, and I brought her home with me." When her husband tells her she can't help Miss Smith, Rosemary says, "I want to. Isn't that a reason?" Ironically, that isn't a reason; it confirms the fact that she doesn't really know why she brought the woman home at first. There is no support for Choice B. While choices A and D are implied in the line: "Be frightfully nice to her. Look after her. I don't know how. We haven't talked yet. But show her—treat her—make her feel—" it was not her initial motivation. Choice C is the best answer.

2. **C** Think about how you feel when someone doesn't allow you to answer a question. Often this feels belittling and uncaring. We can assume that Rosemary answers for Miss Smith because she feels superior to her. Choice C is the best answer.

3. **A** Rosemary's response to Philip's question is to laugh. Also her choice of words ("I picked her up in Curzon Street. Really. She's a real pick-up.") indicates that she is amused by her behavior. The focus is on herself, not Miss Smith. The best answer is choice A.

4. **B** This supports the idea that she is not a woman who does things, but instead reads about them. Choice B is the best answer.

5. **C** No mention is made of what others think (choice B) or that she feels inadequate to help her (choice D). While it is true that her husband was not enthusiastic about Miss Smith, it is not the central reason (choice A). The main reason is that she feels jealous of her husband's praise of Miss Smith's beauty. She is jealous and insecure about her own appearance and perhaps her husband's open admiration of Miss Smith's looks.

Identifying Narrator's Point of View   Practice, p. 95

1. The narrator is Victor Frankenstein, and the passage is told from the first-person point of view.

2. At first, Frankenstein views his creation as "the accomplishment of my toils," and he can hardly wait for his hard work to come to fruition. His attitude is one of hope and pride. However, he is shocked and horrified at the result. Frankenstein relates, "the beauty of the dream vanished, and breathless horror and disgust filled my heart." Frankenstein's attitude has undergone a transformation, and he believes his creation is a monster, which deeply disturbs him.

3. Frankenstein's description of his dreams implies that he is deeply distressed. The images of Elizabeth's lips becoming "livid with the hue of death" and then her figure's morphing into his deceased mother are disturbing in themselves and reflect Frankenstein's troubled mental state. The description of his mother's shroud with "the grave-worms crawling in the folds of the flannel" provides further evidence of the distressed quality of Frankenstein's frame of mind.

4. Frankenstein claims he is anxious to the point of agony, which suggests that he has invested much in this venture and its outcome is vitally important to him. Frankenstein wishes to "infuse a spark of being into the lifeless thing," so his purpose is to give life and reanimate a dead body. In short, Frankenstein is intensely committed to his work of reanimation.

5. Prior to his experiment, Frankenstein believes he can control the outcome of his experiment with life. Afterward, Frankenstein believes that human nature (and, to a lesser extent, life) is changeable: he says, "The different accidents of life are not so changeable as the feelings of human nature." He alludes to his focus on

achieving his goal of bringing the dead back to life and how this goal seemed worthy but instead became a gruesome parody of life. Overall, Frankenstein's attitude toward life and human nature reflects an awareness of how everything can change in an instant.

SAT-Type Questions, p. 98

1. **B** The narrator's description of Louise's longing to control her own life is described with sympathetic language: "She would live for herself." No other "powerful will" would bend hers. It is implied that she has longed for freedom for a long time, but was not strong enough to stand up for it. Choice A is not really supported in the passage. Neither is choice C. Is she emotionally strong (choice D)? The fact that she allowed herself to marry a man she doesn't really love and her death influenced by her husband suddenly being alive implies that she is not emotionally strong. Choice B is the best answer.

2. **C** The focus on Louise's thoughts allows the reader to sympathize with her.

3. **A** The shift in point of view from Louise to the doctors creates irony. There is a difference in what we know as the reader and what the doctors think. We know that Louise died not from happiness but from sadness of so quickly losing her freedom. Choice A is the best answer.

Citing Textual Evidence   Practice, p. 101

1. **B** Mr. Obi and his wife seem fairly sure that they will succeed. So A can't be right. They do however appear to be somewhat overconfident in their abilities. Therefore B is the best answer.

2. **A** A is a better choice than choice B, since lines 20–21 only illuminate Mrs. Obi's character and not her husband's. The details in choice A suggest that both of them are young, energetic and arrogant.

3. **B** Choice A can be eliminated, since in these lines Mrs. Obi expresses her disappointment over the fact that there won't be any wives to feel jealous of her. The details in choice B suggest she enjoys feeling superior to others.

SAT-Type Questions, p. 106

1. **D** There is no support for choice C. Although it is true that Mr. Obi is concerned about his Supervisor's evaluation (choice B), this is not the central conflict. Choice A is a conflict in the story, but the reason they are disagreeing is due to an underlying conflict in their thinking. Choice D is the best answer.

2. **C** These lines reveal the contrast between the traditional ways of thinking about death and life and the modern ways the school was supposed to teach.

3. **C** Mr. Obi is discussing his beliefs about the dead using the footpath with the priest. Mr. Obi clearly believes this idea is outdated and superstitious. Choices A and B can be eliminated. Choice D is incorrect. Although Mr. Obi mentions that his duty is to make his students laugh at the local traditions, the word "fantastic" is a reference to the absurdity of these beliefs.

4. **B** The line "Dead men do not require footpaths" is a statement that the headmaster finds unrealistic or outdated, which is the definition of "fantastic." Choices A, C, and D do not have enough information to be good support.

5. **A** This choice is supported by the phrase "misguided zeal of the new headmaster." This implies that the Supervisor understood how important it was to balance modern ideas with the ancient ones. Ironically, Mr. Obi didn't understand this.

6. **D** This choice explains that the Supervisor found the new headmaster's desire to eradicate the old ways to be "misguided." He appears to be siding with the village priest and more open-minded to diverse ways of thinking than the "modern" schoolmaster. Choices A and C are not related to the inference. Choice B supports the idea that the priest is open-minded, not the Supervisor. He seems to be saying that people should be allowed to practice their beliefs as they see fit.

Lesson 2: Defining Words in Context

Understanding words in Context   Practice, p. 107

1. **productive** Line 2 mentions that Glass wrote "more than two dozen operas," which suggests he is productive.

2. **people with whom one has worked** The phrase "worked with" implies that "collaborators" are people Glass has worked with. The suffix –or means "one who."

3. **social** The examples in the previous paragraph suggests Glass enjoys collaborating with others. Within the context of the paragraph, "companionable" refers to being pleasant company and getting along with people or being social.

4. **honor or expression of praise** The example of an "accolade" provided in the sentence—"having your style ripped off by television commercials"—suggests a type of honor.

5. **A** Both answers are dictionary definitions for "spontaneously," but since "spontaneously" is used in a question that precedes the sentence "And to what cause was it due?" it suggests that "with no apparent cause" is more appropriate in this context.

6. **B** The nearby exclamation points and repetition of "eruption" indicate urgency, which is expressed in a shout, not a wail.

7. **B** The context clues of "lavas" and "molten fire" suggest something powerful and elemental, and both answers appear plausible. However, choice B fits better in the context.

SAT-Type Questions, p. 113

1. **B** The phrase "dismissed by the art world as nothing more than" indicates that the word "utilitarian" has a negative connotation. Thus, C and D are incorrect. The information in the rest of the paragraph does not support choice A. Because the art world values art for its beauty, it would likely frown upon artwork that is functional.

2. **C** The example of Weston's art dramatically increasing in price and the phrase "photography's migration to the realm of high art" demonstrate change. Choices A, B, and D are incorrect because in this context a "barometer" does not forecast weather, reflect continuity, or register atmospheric pressure.

3. **A** The "reigning example" in the paragraph is Cindy Sherman, whose photographs sold for over $6 million. Other examples of art sold at lower prices are given later. In this context, "reigning" describes the most important example. Choices B, C, and D are incorrect because in this context "reigning" does not mean "ruling," "directing," or "influencing."

4. **B** The phrase "art world prejudices that made its coming-of-age so difficult" suggests "gauntlet" has a negative connotation and suggests opposition or challenge. Choices A and D are incorrect. Choice C is closer, but the context suggests a conflict or challenge rather than a full-fledged fight.

5. **C** "Unprecedented" describes "damage to the oceans and the animals living in them," and later phrases, such as "harming the oceans to a remarkable degree," suggest intense damage. Thus, "unparalleled" is the best fit.

6. **A** "Overharvested" refers to an action humans do to ocean species, and the phrase "even greater damage" suggests it has a negative connotation. Choice D has a positive connotation, and so is eliminated. In this context, gathering some ocean species excessively is the best fit. Choices B and C are incorrect because in this context "overharvested" does not mean "destroyed" or "consumed extravagantly."

7. **B** "Impervious" relates to ecosystems and change. The sentence "But Dr. McClenachan warned that the fossil record shows that global disasters have wrecked the seas before" illustrates a contrast to the sentence by beginning with "but" and describing the oceans' vulnerabilities. Hence, "impervious" has an opposing meaning. The best fit is "unaffected by."

8. **B** The context clues of "criminal" and "witness" suggest a police-related matter and B, "official investigations," is the closest match.

9. **D** The sentence indicates "private property [won't] be taken for public use without just compensation," so "just compensation" must be fair reimbursement to the owner of the private property. Choice A ("small sum of money") is too specific. Choices B and C are not supported by the context.

10. **D** The use of words in the sentence, such as "crime" and "Grand Jury," suggest a serious crime. Choices A, B, and C are incorrect because in this context "indictment" does not mean a misdemeanor, a thing illustrating a situation that is bad, or any cause for blame.

Lesson 3: Closely Reading Informational Texts for Explicit Meanings
Understanding Explicit Meanings   Practice, p. 117

1. The first sentence identifies the root causes: "extreme weather and vanishing habitats."

2. In the last paragraph, the author claims monarch butterflies may experience extinction. The author contends, "a migration widely called one of the world's great natural spectacles is in danger of effectively vanishing."

3. The author states that implementing a new time code system was difficult when he or she writes, "This idea, so obviously good and so universally accepted today, was an idea whose time had come, but the coming did not come easily."

4. Railroad schedules relied on exact times for trains to leave and arrive. This necessitated a standard time for areas of the country.

5. The author identifies malaria and encephalitis as two diseases carried by mosquitoes.

6. In these lines, the author argues that mosquitoes are more dangerous than other more commonly feared animals, such as tigers, rhinos, wolves, leopards, and bears.

SAT-Type Questions, p. 120

1. **B** The last paragraph states the following as a benefit from energy-minded landscaping: "These plants are living air conditioners, evaporating water and cooling the air," so choice B is the best answer.

2. **D** The author states, "Much of today's landscaping, however, overlooks creative possibilities for energy conservation, wasting precious resources through inefficient planning." This statement contends that modern architecture does not utilize creativity with regard to energy conservation, nor does it use resources efficiently. Therefore, choice D is correct.

3. **C** The passage does not support choice A. Choice B is an inference that may be made but is not explicitly stated in the passage, so it is incorrect. Choice D is incorrect because the passage states that "energy-minded landscaping can cut home energy needs by 30%." The best answer is choice C since the passage explains, "Planting windbreaks can help keep out wintry blasts."

Determining Central Ideas and Summarizing   Practice, p. 123

1. The main idea of the first paragraph is that in 2007, scientists discovered that thousands of bats in upstate New York were dying from a fungus called "white-nose syndrome."

2. The main idea of the third paragraph is that scientists believe that discovering why European bats are resistant to the white-nose fungus will help them save American bats.

3. In 2005, scientists noticed a substantial number of bats dying, and they eventually discovered the cause was a fungus called *Geomyces destructans*. This fungus is deadly to American bats, but European bats have developed immunity to it. Scientists are seeking ways to stop the fungus and save the American bat population.

SAT-Type Questions, pp. 125–127

1. **C** The passage first describes the problem of keeping multiple offenders off the road and subsequently presents the National Driver Register as a device that "is more effective than jail terms, fines, driver-improvement classes, or alcohol-treatment centers." The best answer is choice C since the other choices are too narrow or not supported by the passage.

2. **C** Choices A and B are true based upon the passage but are not the main idea of the second paragraph, and choice D is a minor detail. Thus, choice C is the best answer since the second paragraph focuses on Gilbert's personality and lyrical style.

3. **D** Choice A is too broad, and choice C is too specific to be correct. While the passage describes many differences between the two men, the focus is on how the two collaborated on so many operettas despite their differences. Therefore, choice D is correct.

4. **A** Choices B, C, and D are too specific to be the correct answe. Choice A is the best answer because natural selection and how it affects burrowing rodents eyes is mentioned at the beginning and end of the passage.

Identifying Supporting Details   Practice, p. 130

1. The passage explains that marine life must adapt to harsh conditions in order to survive. This means they have greater potential for unique medicines and other products.

2. Lines 7–10: "Adaptation to these harsh environments has led to a rich marine bio- and genetic-diversity with potential biotechnological applications related to drug discovery, environmental remediation, increasing seafood supply and safety, and developing new resources and industrial processes."

3. He includes a list of specific examples of marine-derived drugs: "an antibiotic from a fungi, two closely related compounds from a sponge that treat cancer and the herpes virus, and a neurotoxin from a snail that

has painkiller properties making it 10,000 times more potent than morphine without the side effects."

4. These are examples of other uses for marine-derived compounds. It supports the idea that there are many other uses for marine-derived compounds other than medical ones.

5. This comparison emphasizes the writer's claim that marine life will provide more potential for new drugs than terrestrial plants. The percentage of marine samples that have been flagged for follow-up research is 10 percent, while the percent of earth plants is only 0.5 percent.

SAT-Type Questions, p. 134

1. **A** Choices B, C, and D are facts about the Hawaiian Islands, but they do not relate to it as a possible hotspot location. In the passage, "Wilson hypothesized that the distinctive linear shape of the Hawaiian Island-Emperor Seamounts chain resulted from the Pacific Plate moving over a deep, stationary hotspot in the mantle, located beneath the present-day position of the Island of Hawaii." Choice A is correct because it identifies the linear shape as the reason Wilson focused on Hawaii as a potential hotspot location.

2. **B** This paragraph explains Wilson's "hotspot" theory, and the passage explains, "As one island volcano becomes extinct, another develops over the hotspot, and the cycle is repeated." The hotspot is identified as the factor influencing the volcano islands' development, so choice B is correct.

3. **D** The passage describes the myth to show how the ancient Hawaiians correctly believed that "the islands [are] becoming younger from northwest to southeast." Thus, the myths closely mirror scientific theory; choice D is correct.

4. **C** In the first paragraph, Gandhi states, "We labour under the fatal delusion that no disease can be cured without medicine." Choice C is correct since it most closely correlates with this statement. Although the passage does not encourage calling in a doctor for "the most trivial diseases," it doesn't say that people should never go to a doctor (choice A). Nor does the passage indicate that people shouldn't see a specialist (choice D). Choice B contradicts the last line of paragraph 1.

5. **B** In the first paragraph, Gandhi states, "Illness or disease is only Nature's warning that filth has accumulated in some portion or other of the body." Choice A (taking too many medications) is not mentioned as a cause of disease but as a wrong way of dealing with disease. Choice C is not mentioned in the passage. Choice D is mentioned as a cure for disease not a cause of disease.

6. **D** The first paragraph describes methods to cure diseases through helping Nature rid the body of filth: fasting, exercising, and controlling one's mind. Only choice D is among those methods mentioned, so it is the correct answer.

7. **A** The doctors all cite their lack of faith in the medical field, claiming it is "mere guess-work." Their views are fairly consistent, so choice B is incorrect. They also do not mention experimental treatments or claim medical advice is dependable, so choices C and D are incorrect. The best answer is choice A since it highlights what little reliable medical knowledge doctors possess.

Lesson 4: Closely Reading Informational Texts for Implicit Meanings
Making Inferences   Practice, p. 142

1. Although Reagan refers to the idea that he has a suitcase in Berlin, this is a metaphorical statement meant to convey the idea that he always enjoys returning to visit Berlin. Thus, it can be inferred that Reagan makes this statement in German to create a sense of camaraderie and rapport with the audience.

2. Reagan addresses the wider audience with "a special word" and claims he is speaking to them "as surely as to those standing here before me," so Reagan suggests that the audience in Eastern Europe is as important as the one before him.

3. Reagan states that there is only one Berlin although the paragraph indicates some sort of separation in the city. Thus, Reagan's contention suggests he believes in uniting the parts of the city into one.

4. Reagan shows concern with the problem of a divided Germany in these lines. He suggests that justice will only be served when the wall falls and Germany is reunited under one government. Hence, he not only wants the wall to be demolished, but also Germany to be reunified.

5. In the paragraph, Reagan states, "In West Germany and here in Berlin, there took place an economic miracle," and, later in the paragraph, he claims, "the standard of living in West Germany and Berlin doubled," suggesting that the Marshall Plan along with the good decisions made by German leaders brought prosperity to West Berlin. Therefore, it can reasonably be inferred from the information in the paragraph that the Marshall Plan helped make West Germany prosperous again.

6. Reagan suggests that because of their personal qualities, Berliners were able to bring back their city from a state of utter destruction; in short, Berliner heart, humor, and Schnauze led to the city's rebirth.

SAT-Type Questions, p. 144

1. **A** Clark's quote focuses on the "question whether a statue of the ghastly characteristics of this one does not overstep the bounds of legitimate art." This statement suggests the sculpture may be more gruesome than artistic, so choice A is correct.

2. **D** The author does not mention whether Lewis should have sculpted more pieces, was only moderately talented, or had a critical view of her own work. Thus, choices A, B, and C are incorrect. The author's statement about Lewis's "difficult life and neglected career" suggests a belief that Lewis was underappreciated, so choice D is correct.

3. **A** The author writes, "Both hemispheres play an equivalent, though different, role in the functioning of the personality." The passage does not indicate that scientists have discredited the theory that there are two hemispheres, so choice B is incorrect. The author contends that both hemispheres are equally important, so choice C is incorrect as well. The passage does not offer information about how a left-handed person performs in a right-handed world, so choice D is incorrect. Choice A is the best answer because the passage provides information supporting the idea that both hemispheres play important roles.

4. **B** The passage does not mention the creation of genius, so choice A is incorrect. It also does not indicate the possibility of the brain being overloaded, so choice C is incorrect. The passage explains, "In most people language and language-related abilities are located in the left hemisphere," so choice D is also incorrect. The passage relates, "But recent investigations have shown that the right hemisphere also plays an important role in the total functioning of the personality." This statement indicates that choice B is the best answer, since it suggests that the hemispheres are divided but must work in conjunction.

5. **D** The passage states that the right hemisphere "processes information differently, often providing creative leaps and sudden insights not available to the left hemisphere." However, it does not suggest these information processes are confusing, so choice A is incorrect. Choice B is also incorrect since the passage claims that "the left hemisphere tends to be verbal and analytic," not the right hemisphere. Likewise, choice C incorrectly identifies the right hemisphere as having superior problem solving and language skills when the passage actually identifies "the left hemisphere is concerned with conscious thought processes and problem solving." Choice D is correct because the right hemisphere provides "creative leaps and sudden insights not available to the left hemisphere," which would suggest usefulness in creating music.

Using Analogical Reasoning Practice, p. 148

1. Since Peter the Great focused on travel and better education for the wealthy in the passage, he would be more likely to support travel abroad programs.

2. He made gentlemen, merchants, and other subjects who wished to keep their beards pay a tax of one hundred rubles a year.

3. The situation is analogous because it involves a leader imposing dress reform on his followers as a way to enforce political policies.

4. **A** Peter the Great allowed men to keep their beards but made them pay high taxes. He didn't outlaw long hair and beards, but he did make it difficult for them to keep them. This is similar to placing large taxes on cigarettes. The practice isn't outlawed, but it is discouraged due to the high taxes.

SAT-Type Questions, p. 151

1. **B** According to the passage, Boroditsky's research illustrates that language "can shape the most fundamental dimensions of human cognition, including space, time, causality, and our relationships with others." Boroditsky would most likely agree with choices A, C, and D. However, she says, "It became clear quite early that there wasn't any way to explain how we build such complex and sophisticated knowledge unless you look at patterns in language." This statement clearly contradicts the idea in choice B, so choice B is the best answer.

2. **D** According to Boroditsky's research, "language—from verb tenses to gender to metaphors—can shape the most fundamental dimensions of human cognition, including space, time, causality, and our relationships with others." This statement indicates she would agree with Sapir and Whorf's hypothesis about language shaping the way we think. The only choice that illustrates this idea is choice D.

3. **C** The passage states, "Speakers of Spanish or Japanese are less likely to mention the agent when describing an accident: 'The vase broke.'" Thus Japanese speakers who saw a woman accidentally spill a bowl of cereal would focus on the bowl of cereal that was spilled instead of the agent of the action, the woman. Choice C is the best answer.

4. **B** According to the passage, "English speakers usually describe events in terms of agents doing things: 'John broke the vase.'" Therefore, English speakers would focus on the agent doing the action, the man, instead of the recipient of the action, the car. Choice B is the best answer.

5. **A** The passage maintains that speakers of all three languages would have "no problem identifying who was responsible for intentional events, for which their language would mention the agent." Therefore, choice A is correct since both English and Spanish speakers would identify the agent if the vase was broken intentionally.

Citing Textual Evidence Practice, p. 155

1. Roosevelt opens by saying, "I will address them with a candor and a decision which the present situation of our people impels." In this quote, he references the current situation facing the nation, and he purports to speak frankly and decisively about it.

2. The quotation that best supports the idea that Roosevelt wants to address the people honestly and decisively as the president is the following: "I am certain that my fellow Americans expect that on my induction into the Presidency I will address them with a candor and a decision which the present situation of our people impels."

3. Roosevelt mentions hardships related to troubles but also is grateful that they are mainly monetary in nature, suggesting he believes other things are more important than material goods.

4. Line 14 provides support for this idea: "They concern, thank God, only material things," suggests that Roosevelt believes there are worse things than hardships related to material things.

5. Roosevelt believes that dishonest financial practices through stubbornness and incompetence have caused the crisis.

6. The evidence that best supports this idea is found when Roosevelt contends, "Primarily this is because the rulers of the exchange of mankind's goods have failed, through their own stubbornness and their own incompetence, have admitted their failure, and abdicated."

SAT-Type Questions, p. 157

1. **B** According to the passage, "It was Joseph Duveen who bought for Huntington and his wife" and "Without prodding from Duveen, Huntington would never have bought Turner's *The Grand Canal*." These statements suggest Duveen is responsible for much of Huntington's art collection, so choices C and D are incorrect. Duveen was an art dealer and did not contribute his time for free, so choice A is eliminated. The best answer is choice B since it was Duveen's direction, his sharp eye, that led to Huntington purchasing key pieces for his collection.

2. **A** The answer to the previous question is that Huntington would not have amassed his world-class art collection without Duveen's sharp eye, so examine each answer carefully to see which provides the best evidence to support this idea. Choices B, C, and D give general information about Huntington's art collection. Choice A is the only one that mentions how Duveen influenced Huntington's art collection, so it is the best answer.

3. **C** Choice A cites an improvement in air quality, and choice B merely defines ground-level ozone, so they are incorrect. Choice D mentions pollution but does not discuss how it affects health conditions, so choice C is the best answer since it illustrates how a number of health problems are triggered by air pollution, specifically those caused by ground-level ozone.

4. **D** Choices A, B, and C have little or no support in the passage, so they are incorrect. The author writes, "Costs from air pollution-related illness are estimated at $150 billion per year." Thus, choice D is the best answer.

5. **B** The answer to the previous question is that poor air quality contributes to costly health problems. While choice A mentions premature deaths, it does not identify the monetary cost, so it is incorrect. Choices C and D contain information about air quality, not its cost related to illnesses. Choice B is the best answer since it identifies an estimate for the cost of air pollution-related illnesses.

Lesson 5: Analyzing Ideas in Informational Text

Analyzing Author's Point of View and Purpose   Practice, p. 163

1. The main purpose of the paragraph is to explain why the author did not choose physics as a career. She mentions being "exhausted" by all of the effort she had to put into her physics classes. She discusses being "tired" of playing two different roles (scientist and female), and she adds that some men were intimidated by the fact that she majored in physics.

2. It can be inferred from the author's reactions in lines 14–16 that her perspective on abandoning science forever is that it was shameful. By using the phrase "slunk away in shame," it can be assumed that the author feels disappointed and regretful about her decision to not pursue a career in science.

3. The primary purpose of the paragraph is to suggest that women today experience more support for their scientific aspirations. This can be seen in the phrase, "the climate has become more welcoming to young women who want to study science and math."

4. This paragraph is primarily concerned with persuading educators, researchers, and administrators to encourage more women to pursue careers in the sciences.

5. The author's perspective on our current culture of science is one of disheartenment. She believes that it needs to change. She makes this perspective clear throughout the article by providing statistics, personal experiences, and a call for reform.

SAT-Type Questions, p. 166

1. **D** The author acknowledges Polonius's faults, but then goes on to show several instances in which the character behaves honorably and respectably. Choice C is a true statement, but it is not the *primary purpose* of the passage. Although the author mentions Polonius's faults and his "garrulity," the author is not suggesting that the character be played this way. Therefore choice B is incorrect. The author does show that Polonius is often portrayed in a negative light, but the author's purpose is not to argue this point. Instead, he argues *against* this point, so choice A is incorrect.

2. **C** It is clear throughout the passage that the author wants his readers to see a positive side of Polonius. By mentioning his strengths, the author reveals his attitude of appreciation for the character. Choice B is incorrect because the author's attitude is much more positive than the word "frustration" conveys. Choice D is incorrect because the author's opinion is clearly positive, not uncertain. Although choice A is a positive word, it suggests far more praise for Polonius than is conveyed in the passage.

3. **B** In this paragraph, the author "concedes," or admits, that Polonius does deserve some of the laughter that his character elicits by providing examples of situations in which the character does humorous things. While choices A, C and D are possible interpretations of some of the sentences in paragraph 2, they are details, but not the main purpose of the paragraph in relation to the rest of the passage.

4. **A** In this passage, Mandela is using persuasion to convince his audience that wealthier countries should actively participate in ending poverty around the world. He incorporates statistics to prove his point and he uses a call to action. Mandela does not imply that the fight against poverty will be easy, so choice D is incorrect. Mandela does point out that nations spend more on weapons than fighting AIDS, but this is a detail, not the main purpose of the passage, so choice C is incorrect. Choice B is very close to the correct answer, but Mandela's purpose is not to "inform;" it is to "persuade."

5. **D** Because of Mandela's persuasive language and request for action, he is best described as an "activist." Choice A is incorrect because the passage takes a much more active stance than one of lamentation. Choice B is incorrect because Mandela does not explore the causes of poverty in this passage. Choice C is incorrect because there is not evidence of Mandela's use of "collective action" to fight poverty.

6. **C** By referring to the success of a previous struggle (which was with Apartheid), Mandela shows his audience that taking action can be effective. Choice A is not related to the topic of these lines. Choice B is also not stated in the passage. Choice D is close, but comparing his previous struggle to global poverty is not the purpose of Mandela's reference.

Analyzing the Use of Arguments   Practice, p. 171

1. The main purpose of these paragraphs is to explain both how algae is made into fuel and to point out some of the benefits of this alternative fuel source.

2. The author's central claim is that using algae to create fuel is a viable option. The author provides the following evidence to support this claim: "All that is needed are sunlight, seawater, fertilizer, and carbon dioxide to support the process," "the plan is to try to use waste carbon dioxide from nearby power plants," "Using up excess carbon dioxide is a plus, since it is considered a greenhouse gas that contributes to global warming," "The fuel produced by the algae is said to burn cleaner . . . "

3. The author includes the reference to Exxon Mobil in order to offer evidence that even "big oil" companies who have historically been focused on the use of fossil fuels are getting involved in alternative fuel sources. This bolsters the author's argument that algae-based fuel has the potential to succeed.

4. The author includes counterclaims, in the form of potential problems with algae-based fuel, in order to show his or her complete knowledge of all aspects of the topic, including its cons. An argument that contains only pros is too one-sided and may not be trusted by readers. When an author acknowledges the opposition, he or she is more likely to gain credibility with the audience.

SAT-Type Questions, p. 174

1. **B** Choice B accurately summarizes the evidence that Eisenhower offers as proof of the size of the U.S. military. See lines 10–13 ("we have . . . establishment"). Choice D is an inaccurate statement: the passage states that the military outspends corporations. Choice A is also inaccurate because it contains the word "temporary." Choice C is a true statement from the passage, but it is not *evidence* for the U.S. military's size.

2. **D** The answer to this question comes from lines 25–26 ("endanger our . . . processes"). The phrase "democratic processes" means that the choice containing "Congress" is correct because this is where our democratic processes occur. Choices A and C are incorrect because Eisenhower does not suggest that corporations or the Pentagon might be victims of unwarranted influence. Choice B is close, but Congress is a better answer than the courts when referring to democratic processes.

3. **C** In the first paragraph, Eisenhower acknowledges the necessity of our military, but in the final paragraph he warns about the importance of keeping it in check, thus Choice C summarizes his central claim. Choices B and D may be true statements from the passage, but they do not summarize the central claim. Choice A is partially true (the military is necessary), but contains an inaccuracy. (Eisenhower does not suggest that the military is too weak.)

4. **A** In this paragraph, the author's aim is to show that renewable energy is on the rise. By mentioning that one country has made renewable energy the first item for its future energy plan, the author proves his point. Choice C is incorrect because it is too vague and does not relate to the author's claim. Choice D is possible, but the author does not use language that suggests explicit praise. While it may be true that the author believes choice B, there is not evidence for it in the passage.

5. **B** To support his argument that the use of renewable energy is on the rise, the author points to the fact that some say there will be less use of carbon-emitting energy sources. See lines 11–13 ("Some believe . . . and gas"). Choices A and D are incorrect because fuel efficiency standards and solar power are not mentioned in the passage. Choice C is incorrect because the passage states that 19% not 25% will come from renewables.

6. **C** In these lines, the author acknowledges the arguments against renewable energy, and choice C most accurately interprets these lines. Choices A and D are incorrect because the lines do not mention issues with the quantity of energy or large tracts of land. Choice B is mentioned in the passage but not in the lines in question, so it is incorrect.

Lesson 6: Analyzing Style in Informational Text

Analyzing Use of Word Choice to Shape Meaning and Tone Practice, p. 181

1. In these paragraphs, White's tone is contemplative. His word choice is rather complex, choosing to use phrases such as "the gift of loneliness and the gift of privacy." He compares New York to a person bestowing gifts. White's use of contrasting qualities ("It can destroy an individual, or it can fulfill") adds to the mystery and ambiguity of the city of New York.

2. **A** White conveys the idea that people can't escape from the past in New York, since the past can be felt everywhere. The answer choice that comes the closest to expressing this idea is choice A.

3. These phrases are meant to represent negative experiences or events in a city and thus create a sense of unease in the reader. White is illustrating how New York's size is advantageous to the individuals who live there. When large-scale events occur in other cities, dwellers are not insulated from its effects; they are thrown to the Lions or hit on the head by a falling piece of building (cornice).

4. White's use of contrasting words ("great forlornness or forsakenness" vs. "rejunvenation," "excess of spirit" vs. "deficiency of spirit") communicates the idea that New York can adapt to the needs of all the people who live there, no matter their reasons for coming to the city. Again the tone is reflective. They are reassuring to the reader. They support White's central idea that New York speaks to the needs of all people who live there (lines 6–7).

SAT-Type Questions, p. 183

1. **B** The title with its "who cares" attitude does not affect a sympathetic tone, so choice A is incorrect. While the author does refute critical dismissal of detective stories and mysteries, his/her tone is not brutally callous, so choice C is incorrect. Choice D is also incorrect since the author is positive toward detective stories and does not use a straightforwardly informative tone. The best answer is choice B because the author uses the title as a way to introduce the topic and the critical opinion about detective stories, which the author subsequently contests. The tone is witty, and the title helps set this tone.

2. **B** The paragraph mentions nothing about detective stories being too predictable, so choice A is incorrect. Likewise, the paragraph does not claim that readers are indifferent to mysteries, so choice C is incorrect. Since the paragraph contends that critics treat mysteries harshly, not as oracles, choice D is also incorrect. Choice B is the best answer because the words "sneered," "condescended," and "scorned" illustrate the negative tone of the critical reception for mysteries.

3. **D** The author praises mysteries in the passage and so is unlikely to mock mystery writers; thus, choice A is incorrect. The author believes that reviewers and critics have been unfairly critical of mysteries, so he/she does not praise them. Choice B is incorrect. The question does not mention "literary" fiction, so choice C is incorrect as well. The best answer is choice D since the author praises mysteries and feels they have been unfairly treated by critics. The question takes a swipe at critics by minimizing their importance since mysteries often outlast them.

4. **D** The passage makes no mention of disgruntled mystery fans, so choice A is incorrect. It also mainly focuses on the criticism of mysteries, not praise, so choice B is also incorrect. The phrase "often maligned" suggests that a substantial amount of attention is paid to mysteries, but choice D is a better fit than choice C since "maligned" suggests unfair or mistaken criticism. Therefore, choice D is the best answer.

5. **C** The phrase "treated to" suggests a positive experience. It does not suggest mysteries are hard to solve, so choice A is incorrect. The phrase also does not emphasize the suspense or sense of mystery found in mysteries, so choices B and D are incorrect. The best answer is choice C since the phrase conveys the idea of a pleasurable reading experience.

6. **A** The term "prestigious" indicates the writers are important. The phrase does not suggest how mysteries improve the fiction genre, so choice B is incorrect. The phrase also refrains from offering any evidence about whether writers consider reading mysteries enjoyable, so choice C is incorrect. The phrase does not claim that fans prefer mysteries, so choice D is incorrect. The best answer is choice A since this answer indicates that important writers utilize the mystery form.

Analyzing Text Structures   Practice, p. 187

1. Answers will vary. The author wants to point out that both animals and humans have changed their behavior in response to climate change.

2. The author wants to convey the idea that at certain parks peak park attendance has shifted even more than the 4-day average.

3. While the author utilizes the compare and contrast structure to organize information, the main structure he or she employs is cause and effect. The entire selection is concerned with how climate change has impacted peak park attendance.

SAT-Type Questions, pp. 189–192

1. **B** The author describes Johnson's "incredible journey" but does not dwell on its difficulties, so choice A is incorrect. The author explains that Johnson's "trip had lasted 16 months and covered nearly 10,000 miles," so he or she does not require readers to add up the miles; choice C is also incorrect. The author mentions the variety of transportation methods Johnson used, but the focus is more about where Johnson's journey took him, rather than how he got there. Thus, choice B is the best answer since by describing the journey chronologically, readers can visualize Johnson's trip.

2. **C** The author only briefly mentions the destruction of forests as adversely impacting forest dwelling creatures, so choice A is incorrect. The author does not indicate the passage is responding to a call to action, so choice B is incorrect as well. The passage does not relate a series of events, so choice D is incorrect. The author describes "the effect upon the balance of oxygen and carbon dioxide in the atmosphere." The author writes, "Global awareness of the problem is needed to provide a basis for sound management of forests, the crucial agents in the carbon cycle." Therefore, the best answer is choice C, a description of a problem and its solution.

3. **A** The author mentions the negative effects of forests being destroyed (the loss of beauty, the destruction of an ecosystem, and the destruction of forest creatures' homes); however, the next sentence claims the importance of these effects pale next to "an even more serious long-range problem," the carbon and dioxide balance in the atmosphere. Thus, choice B is incorrect since the author treats the aesthetic loss and destruction of an ecosystem with equal importance. Choice C is also incorrect because vacationing in tropical locales is not mentioned in the passage. Choice D is partially correct because the author does treat the aesthetic loss and loss of ecosystems as equally troubling consequences of fire, but the author identifies these consequences as less important than the fire's impact on the balance of oxygen and carbon dioxide. Therefore, choice A is correct.

4. **C** These lines describe how the use of fossil fuels increases carbon dioxide in the atmosphere and how deforestation reduces the number of plants that recycle the carbon dioxide. They do not discuss a solution for mitigating the greenhouse effect, so choice A is incorrect. The sentences do not explain the greenhouse effect or give reasons for cutting back on greenhouse gas emissions, so choices B and D are incorrect. Choice C is the best answer because the lines delineate the causes for the greenhouse effect.

5. **B** These lines describe the problem as "wholesale destruction of tropical forests" and then the solution as the "sound management of forests." They do not present the unintended consequences of carbon emissions,

so choice A is incorrect. They also do not describe the largest source of carbon emissions as from human activity, so choice C is incorrect. The lines do not discuss any successes in combating the problem, so choice D is incorrect. Choice B is the best answer because these lines identify the solution to the problem of carbon emissions.

6. **D** The passage describes a new study proposed to test Einstein's theory of relativity. It does not mention an unexpected finding, so choice A is incorrect. The passage also does not identify an anomaly or a new discovery, so choices B and C are incorrect. The best answer is choice D because the experiment to test the theory of relativity is proposed, described, and then classified as beyond modern capabilities.

7. **A** The last paragraph describes why scientists have been unable to prove the Kerr solution's accuracy. It does not make an argument for the Kerr solution, so choice B is incorrect. The last paragraph does not focus on the number of scientists who have attempted to prove the Kerr solution's accuracy, so choice C is incorrect as well. Lastly, the paragraph does not recommend scientists shifting focus to other areas, so choice D is incorrect. The best answer is choice A because the paragraph emphasizes the difficulties in proving the Kerr solution's accuracy.

8. **D** The paragraph begins by mentioning that a number of experiments have been conducted testing Einstein's theory of relativity and ends by describing a new way of testing the theory. The paragraph is not a chronological account of past experiments, so choice A is incorrect. It does not offer a step-by-step explanation, so choice B is also incorrect. The paragraph does not evaluate the theory, so choice C is incorrect. Choice D is the best answer since the paragraph moves from describing the numerous experiments testing the theory of relativity to the new means of testing the theory.

Lesson 7: Synthesizing Information from Texts and Graphs

Synthesizing Information from Multiple Texts Practice, p. 196

1. In Passage 1, Clinton makes the claim that the work of women is undervalued.

2. Voting is the "only means" by which women can secure these blessings guaranteed by the Constitution.

3. **C** Neither passage discusses governments being swayed by public opinion (choice A) or being outdated entities (choice B). It seems plausible that both authors would agree that government should provide access to education for all people; however, only Passage 1 mentions education, so choice D is also incorrect. Passage 1 describes how women's work is not valued "by government leaders," and Passage 2 references the Constitution and mentions the government specifically. Choice C is the best answer.

4. In Passage 1, Clinton uses statistics about how many women are poor and uneducated. She convinces the audience of the importance of women's roles by giving examples of tasks that women do all over the world. She offers more emotional appeals. Anthony makes a logical appeal using reasoning to point out that women are citizens whose rights of liberty are secured by the Constitution, yet their ability to secure these rights is hampered because they can't vote.

5. **D** Although Passage 2 focuses solely on women's rights in the U.S., one can infer that Passage 1 would also support this right for all women everywhere, so choice A is incorrect. Neither passage suggests that the focus should be on other issues or that there are too many women's rights factions, so choices B and C are also incorrect. Passage 1 declares, "they [women] are being denied the right to go to school by their own fathers and brothers," and Passage 2 references "the whole people—women as well as men." Since both passages argue for women's rights and mention men in conjunction with the issue, the authors would most likely agree that both men and women must recognize women's rights. Thus, choice D is the best answer.

1. **C** The quotes from Botero and Malthus both warn of the dangers of overpopulation, so they do not have contrasting positions about the issue. Thus, choice A is incorrect. Since both men lived centuries ago, they do not have statistics on modern population growth, so choice B is also incorrect. Based on the information present in the passage, neither writer appears to have studied explosive growth in populations, so choice D is incorrect. Choice C is the best answer because the introductory sentence states, "Concern about the dangers of overpopulation is not new." The quotes by Botero and Malthus support this idea.

2. **B** "Subsistence" is related to the power of the earth providing something for man. In this context, "fortitude" does not make sense, so choice A is incorrect. Since the context also implies scarcity of resources rather than plentiful ones, choice C, "luxuries," is also incorrect. Between the two choices left, "survival" is the best fit since the adjacent sentence claims, "Population grows faster than the means to feed all the new mouths."

3. **B** The author writes, "Rich countries can ameliorate many of the growing problems," so he/she does not believe that poor countries must ameliorate the problems arising from overpopulation. Choice A is incorrect. Similarly, choice C is incorrect since the author suggests rich countries can help with the problem, not that they are the cause of the problem. The statement, "Somehow the world's governments must devise ways to check the disastrous growth of population," does not inspire confidence that a solution will be found, so choice D is incorrect. Choice B is the best answer since this quotation mentions the solution is within the grasp of the world's governments.

4. **D** Passage 1 does describe the problem of overpopulation, but it is not an elaborate account and only briefly mentions an idea about the world's governments devising a solution. Choice A is incorrect. Passage 1 does not identify and correct misconceptions or false information, so choice B is incorrect. The passage explains, "Concern about the dangers of overpopulation is not new." It does not suggest that any new urgent public outcry has been heard, so choice C is incorrect as well. Choice D is the best answer because the passage identifies overpopulation as a cause and then proceeds to list its effects.

5. **A** The words "concern," "danger," and "warned" suggest an imperative, urgent tone, not a dubious tone or that the author does not have confidence in the information provided. Thus, choice B is incorrect. Choice C is incorrect since the passage never suggests that the author believes overpopulation to be anything less than a major issue. The words "concern," "danger," and "warned" could signal alarm, but the author's suggestion about world governments finding a solution for overpopulation indicates a belief that the outcome is not inevitable. Choice D is incorrect. The best answer is choice A because these words create a sense of urgency and signal the seriousness of the topic.

6. **D** The author does not offer zero population growth as a solution to overpopulation, so choice A is incorrect. The author's discussion on the rise in food production is used to show how dire predictions in the past did not eventuate, and the author does not identify the rise in food production as the hope for human survival, so choice B is incorrect. The passage does not discuss increasing renewable energy, so choice C is also incorrect. The best answer is choice D because the author claims, "People have shown an amazing resiliency and flexibility in dealing with seemingly insuperable problems."

7. **B** The words "catastrophes," "troubles," and "horrible" suggest a negative connotation for "apocalypse," so choices A ("prophecy") and C ("revelation") are incorrect because they are neutral terms. Since the context has no mention of opposing sides or hostilities as one would expect with war, choice D is incorrect. The best answer is choice B, "destruction," since it best fits with the context.

8. **A** Passage 2 downplays the seriousness of overpopulation, while Passage 1 extols it as a significant problem, so Passage 2 does not advocate an alternative approach to a problem discussed in Passage 1. Choice B is incorrect. Likewise, Passage 2 offers no evidence to support an idea introduced in Passage 1; choice C is incorrect as well. Passage 1 does not mention or describe an attitude that is promoted in Passage 1, so choice

D is incorrect. The best answer is choice A since Passage 2 casts doubt on the central claim in Passage 1, that overpopulation is an urgent problem.

9. **C** Passage 2 makes no mention of overpopulation causing famine in human populations, so choice A is incorrect. Similarly, Passage 1 does not mention starvation in animal populations, so choice B is also incorrect. Neither does the passage mention a decline in people's quality of life, so choice D is incorrect. Passage 1 contends, "Concern about the dangers of overpopulation is not new," and Passage 2 claims, "The 'authorities' have been predicting catastrophes for 400 years." Therefore, choice C is the correct answer because both passages identify overpopulation as an idea that has been around for a long time.

10. **A** Since Passage 2 does not offer a solution in the final paragraph, choice B is incorrect. Passage 1 discusses the effects of overpopulation primarily in relation to humans and fails to discuss nature's means of survival, so choice C is incorrect. Passage 1 has a more pessimistic tone than Passage 2, so the idea that nature can rebound quickly after disastrous events does not fit with Passage 1; choice D is incorrect. Choice A is the best answer since Passage 1 mentions both the destruction of rain forests and the greenhouse effect, plus the author of Passage 1 would find probably find fault with Passage 2's optimistic tone.

Analyzing Information from Texts and Graphics Practice, p. 204

1. Possible Answer: The graph shows that from 1982–2014, February had the highest number of season peaks at 14, while December is a distant second, holding the season peak spot only 6 times. January and March closely follow December, with 5 season peaks apiece, and October and November achieved the distinction only once. No other months were the season peaks, so this information supports the claim that flu activity peaks between December and February. However, the graph doesn't indicate any activity in April and May so it doesn't support this part of the claim.

2. Possible Answer: More men died during the Civil War than during World War I and II combined. The Revolutionary War and the War of 1812 had roughly the same number of casualties.

3. The graphs support the claim that immigrants with at least an undergraduate degree have a better chance at employment. In all countries represented, immigrants with a degree have a higher rate of employment as indicated in the higher percentages in the bar graph on the bottom of page 208.

4. There is some support for this claim, but Switzerland has the best job prospects for all immigrants, while the United States has the second highest rate of employment for immigrants with less than a high school education. The United Kingdom and Germany have a higher rate of employment for immigrants with at least an undergraduate degree. Thus, the claim could be made that Switzerland has the best job prospects.

SAT-Type Questions, pp. 212–216

1. **C** The right side of the illustration explains the problem with adding connecting links to fragments of molecules. It shows how the molecules can combine in unpredictable ways. It does not support choice A or choice B. While choice D is a true statement, the illustration does not emphasize or explain "complex chemical reactions."

2. **D** The illustration does not support choices A, B, or C. It provides an illustration of how the blocks fit together "like train cars."

3. **D** Choice A is incorrect because although this idea is implied by the passage, it is not supported by the illustration. Choice B is incorrect because no information is given about the ease of breaking the chemical bonds established between molecular fragments. The article indicates that MIDA fits over boronic acid, but does not say if MIDA fits over halogen or other connectors. Choice C is incorrect. However, both indicate that

MIDA will allow chemists to better control how molecular fragments combine.

4. **C** The graphic shows that wearing blue-light goggles while using a tablet results in much lower melatonin levels than not wearing eyewear while using a tablet, so choice A is incorrect. Choice B incorrectly interprets the data because it shows how melatonin levels are affected by wearing orange- or blue-tinted glasses or no glasses at all while using a tablet. Choice D also misinterprets the evidence as melatonin levels actually receive the greatest boost from users wearing orange-tinted glasses. Choice C is correct because wearing orange-tinted glasses while using a tablet yields a greater increase in melatonin levels than not wearing glasses or goggles.

5. **A** Choice B is incorrect because the graphic only shows that wearing orange-tinted glasses while using a tablet resulted in increased melatonin levels as compared to wearing blue-tinted goggles or none at all. The graphic does not show that orange-tinted glasses reduced blue light coming from the tablet. Choice C is also incorrect because the graphic illustrates that blue light affects melatonin levels through the difference in melatonin levels from wearing orange-tinted glasses to blue-light goggles to none. Choice D is incorrect since the data is sufficient to support the author's claim that blue light is harmful because it disrupts sleep; further studies with different colored glasses may be helpful but not necessary to support the claim. Choice A is correct because the graphic shows how blue light from a tablet decreases melatonin levels, which are necessary for sleep.

6. **A** The graphic indicates that of the 86 percent of people who are using mobile Internet while watching television, 56 percent are texting. This number is higher than those using apps (33 percent) and accessing social networking sites (40 percent), thus eliminating choices B and D. Choice C is incorrect because the graph only indicates 37 percent of viewers are using the Internet to browse content that is not related to what they are watching. Choice A is correct.

7. **C** The purpose of the graph is to indicate the number of people who watch television and use the Internet at the same time. This is a form of multitasking. This information provides evidence to support the idea that technology multitasking is widespread, but not that it is shrinking users' brains. Choice C is the best answer.

8. **B** No support is given for choice A. Choice C is incorrect because of the word "caused." The passage indicates, "The researchers are not sure whether people with less-dense gray brain structures are more likely to be multitaskers or if the multitasking causes the gray brain structures to shrink." The passage indicates that some studies found that "learning how to juggle and learning map routes increased the gray-matter density in certain parts of the brain." But it can't be logically inferred that using technology for educational purposes will cause the same increase. Choice D is incorrect. It can be inferred that since people who regularly use multiple media devices have less gray-matter density that the 86 percent represented in the pie chart probably have less gray-matter. Choice B is the best answer.

Language and Writing Domain

Lesson 8: Development of Ideas
Revising Texts for Clarity, Focus, and Purpose   Practice, p. 246

1. The topic skips back and forth from topsoil to erosion.

2. Move the second sentence about topsoil, "Topsoil is a precious . . . Earth" to after the first sentence in the paragraph.

3. It is underdeveloped. There is not enough information to convince the reader to try stamp collecting.

4. Add more details about how stamp collecting is fun and exciting after the sentence "They take up little space."

5. The following sentences are irrelevant to the main idea:
"Admittedly, cell phones are wonderful devices for keeping in touch with friends."
"The risk of using of cell phones in moving cars, however, is probably exaggerated."

6. Delete these two sentences.

SAT-Type Questions, p. 251

1. **A** Choice B veers off topic. Choices C and D touch on the topic but aren't directly related. Choice C gives the number of internees, but it doesn't directly relate to the topic of sentence 4—the internees' activities. Choice A is the best answer.

2. **A** The focus of the paragraph is that Adams's photographs of the Japanese detainees was a departure from his landscape photography. Choices C and D are incorrect. Choice B is incorrect because nowhere is the claim made that Adams was a famous photographer.

3. **B** Choices A and C do not add significantly to the main idea. Choice D is a more interesting quote from Adams. However, choice B adds the most appropriate commentary to the facts in the paragraph.

4. **A** Choice B is incorrect because it is not an illustration. The sentence adds an important detail that explains how Miyatake was able to get a camera. Choices C and D are incorrect.

5. **C** Sentence 15 claims that Lange's photos show the negative side of the internment camps. Choices A and D do not support this claim. Choice B shows the irony of the camps but not the bleak conditions. Only choice C, which states that Lange's images were confiscated by the army, supports the idea that her images were too negative for the public to see.

Relating Graphs to Texts   Practice, p. 253

1. No. Natural drivers of climate cannot explain the recent observed warming. Over the last five decades, natural factors (solar forcing and volcanoes) alone would actually have led to a slight cooling.

2. No. During this 32-year period, flu activity most often peaked in February (14 seasons), followed by December (6 seasons), January and March (5 seasons each).

3. Yes. No rewrite necessary.

SAT-Type Questions, p. 259

1. **A** Based upon the graph, peregrine falcons were downlisted in 1984.

2. **C** Checking the graph for data for 1980 reveals that there were fewer than 500 breeding pairs. Both A and B can be eliminated. In 1998 there were more than 1,500 pairs, making D incorrect also.

3. **D** This question tests your ability to accurately read a graph and also to use the correct words to communicate data. The focus of the question is what happened in 1999. The graph indicates that the species was delisted. The current wording (choice A) is incorrect. Choice B uses the word *relisted*. It's also incorrect. Choice C seems correct at first, but the wording "making . . . a possibility" does not indicate that delisting actually happened. The best answer is D.

4. **C** The graph indicates that in 2006 there were more than 2,500 falcon pairs. The current sentence is incorrect and thus so is choice B. Logically, D can also be eliminated.

Lesson 9: Organization

Revising Texts for Cohesion and Logical Order   Practice, p. 263

1. Change the order of the first two sentences so that the sentences read 2, 1, 3, 4.

2. Change the order of the last two sentences so that the sentences read 1, 2, 4, 3.

3. Paragraph 1 should come at the end: 2, 3, 1.

SAT-Type Questions, p. 266

1. **B** This sentence introduces the topic of the paragraph.

2. **C** Sentence 5 provides an example of contemporary artwork mentioned in sentence 7.

3. **A** Paragraph 1 explains the purpose of the show and Paragraph 2 explains the artwork that will appear at the show.

4. **D** This sentence continues the main idea of the paragraph by explaining other events that are a part of the show.

Using Effective Transitions   Practice, p. 270

1. **D** The sentence gives an example of how people who live in richer republics say they are happier.

2. **C** The transition should indicate a contrast from the idea that all people in richer countries express a high personal satisfaction with life.

3. **A** Current wording is correct.

4. **B** The phrase "In reality," best expresses the contrast between East Germany's stated purpose for the wall and its true intent.

5. **D** "Even so," communicates a contrast to the idea that the wall was outfitted with multiple devices to prevent escape.

6. **C** The best choice includes the sequential transitions first and second.

7. **A** The word since communicates a reason why evidence is lost by removing objects.

8. **D** The context requires a word that emphasizes the importance of record keeping in archaeology, which may be surprising to the reader. "Indeed" fits the bill on both accounts.

SAT-Type Questions, p. 274

1. **D** The different verb tenses ("is" or "has become") indicate that a transitional phrase that communicates time is needed. The only answer choice that fits is choice D, "now."

2. **B** When did the myths begin? Certainly not before the Titanic sank. A time transition is needed. Choice C, "Although," and choice D, "Accordingly," do not communicate time. But choice B, "As soon as," does.

3. **A** The sentence is clarifying a myth in the previous sentence. Choice D may appear to be correct, but it is not the best answer because it only communicates contrast and not clarification of a previous idea.

4. **C** A contrast and a concession are needed and best communicated in the combination of C, "but nevertheless."

5. **B** From the context the writer is explaining the key element that made the ship so advanced. Thus, "most importantly" is the best choice.

6. **D** Based upon the phrase "That is not true," the writer is offering a contrast. The only choice that fits is "In actuality."

7. **A** This sentence makes a second point that is equal in importance to the previous one.

8. **B** The final sentences of the paragraph support the idea that the Titanic wasn't trying to make record time by discussing the idea that passengers would be inconvenienced by arriving early. Thus, choices A and D can be eliminated because these insert a new idea into the paragraph. The difference between choices B and C is the words "most important" and "final". It is unclear from the context whether this is the most important reason, but it is the final reason. B is the best choice.

Lesson 10: Use of Language
Revising for Word Choice   Practice, p. 276

1. accelerating 2. reduces 3. strives to increase 4. encompass 5. unleash

SAT-Type Questions, p. 279

1. **D** Hemingway was handing out candy and cigarettes to soldiers. "Bestowing" and "granting" both imply that Hemingway is somehow socially above the soldiers. "Scattering" implies carelessness. The best choice is D, "dispensing."

2. **A** When speaking of receiving a medal, the term "honored" is most accurate. "Memorialized" implies that the honoree is dead.

3. **B** From the context, the appropriate word should explain that boys have unrealistic ideas of what war is. An "apparition" is a ghostly figure and doesn't fit with the intended meaning. "Nightmare" is a scary dream; again it isn't appropriate. Between "daydream" and "delusion," "delusion" is the better choice because it means "a false belief."

4. **D** The intended meaning is that Hemingway was recovering from his injuries. The best word is "Recuperating."

5. **A** This question tests concise use of prepositions. In the context, a preposition that expresses when Hemingway returned home is needed. Choice D can be eliminated. Choice C is too vague. Choice B, "Upon," means "on," which doesn't make sense. Choice A is correct.

6. **C** The writer is communicating how Hemingway's stories reflect his experiences of returning home after a war. The word "insights" is the best choice because it includes the idea that Hemingway's stories offer personal reflections of his experiences.

Revising to Eliminate Wordiness   Practice, p. 282

1. As the first president, Washington's superb leadership set the standard for each president that has succeeded him.

2. In 1889, Susan LaFlesche graduated from the three-year medical program at the Woman's Medical College of Pennsylvania at the top of her class in two years.

3. Plants have been used for natural dyeing since before recorded history.

4. He finally decided on the face-centered cubic, which is the same way you will find oranges stacked today.

5. Until recently this problem remained unsolved.

SAT-Type Questions, p. 287

1. **B** In the current sentence, "living life" is redundant. In choice C, single is unnecessary, and in choice D regarding and "with no" are wordy and redundant, respectively.

2. **C** The current sentence uses the redundant phrase, "full, complete." Choice B eliminates complete but uses the wordy phrase "in its entirety." The phrase "less than and below" is redundant in Choice D.

3. **A** The current wording this the most concise.

4. **D** "Dropouts who quit school" repeats the same idea. Choice B contains the redundant "young, youthful dropouts." In choice C, "particularly" and "mainly" say the same thing.

5. **D** The current sentence contains both "To be sure" and "undoubtedly," which mean the same thing. Choice B contains both "direct link" and "connection." Choice C eliminates redundancies, but contains the empty phrase "there is." D is the best choice because it is concise and includes a strong subject and verb.

6. **B** The current phrase contains the redundant phrase "will end up in time." Choice C repeats the idea "average" by saying "close to the amount of." Choice D repeats "finally" and "will end up."

Using Consistent Style and Tone   Practice, p. 289

1. The wording is a bit too formal for the topic and the tone. Better: When the air waves are saturated, the importance of each ceremony is diminished.

2. The wording is a bit too informal. Better: if listeners could detect those changes.

3. The wording is too informal for a formal article. Better: they were in a position of high power.

4. The wording is too informal and contains slang. Better: others were told they had very little influence with the salesperson.

5. The wording is too formal for a personal account of the struggle with diabetes. Better: Many adults don't have insurance.

SAT-Type Questions, p. 292

1. **C** The current wording is too informal for the purpose and tone of the text. The author is addressing a serious topic. Thus, choices B and D, which contain informal language and slang, are also inappropriate.

2. **D** All other choices are too informal.

3. **C** The current wording is overly complex for the piece. The detailed descriptions "Mothers and fathers, grandparents and guardians" would fit better in a persuasive speech than in an informative text about dyslexia. Choice B uses slang: "a ton of." Choice D uses slang "freak out, " which is inappropriate for the text. C is the best choice; it is to the point and appropriate.

4. **B** The current wording is too informal and doesn't contain strong details to convince the audience. Choice C contains empty words ("better," "many ways") and redundant language. D is better because the language is more specific. But "won't put up with" is too informal for the rest of the word choice. Also, it inserts a negative tone in a mostly positive paragraph. The best answer is B. It promotes Obama's positive goals for America.

5. **A** Choice B is too vague; it lacks clarity and inspiration. Choice C uses overly academic words, which is inappropriate for the audience. Choice D sounds too informal. The current phrasing is clear and effective for the speech.

Lesson 11: Sentence Structure

Correcting Fragments and Run-ons   Practice, p. 299

1. When the big blackout of 2003 struck the Northeast on August 14, many cities were without power for almost a week.

2. No one now lives in the house where Thomas Wolfe lived as a child.

3. Many people wonder how the magician David Copperfield creates his incredible illusions.

4. We enjoyed touring the city where the Liberty Bell is located.

5. Philadelphia is the city where the Liberty Bell is located.

6. Many would-be inventors have tried to create a perpetual-motion machine, but they are all doomed to disappointment. (Corrected by adding a comma and the conjunction "and.")

7. Whales usually bear only one offspring; however, baby twin whales have been observed. (Corrected by using a semicolon, "however" and a comma.)

8. By experimenting with thousands of plants, Luther Burbank developed new varieties of apples, plums, and other fruits. (Corrected by changing the first clause into a prepositional phrase.)

9. I found my keys after a search; I then proceeded to mislay my purse. (Corrected by using a semicolon.)

10. In a performance of Phaedra, Robin plays the tormented wife of Theseus. (Corrected by rewriting the first clause as a prepositional phrase.)

SAT-Type Questions, p. 302

1. **B** This is a run-on with too many complex ideas in one long, unreadable sentence. Two sentences are needed. Thus, B is the best option.

2. **C** "In addition . . . low unemployment" is a prepositional phrase fragment. This information must be added to another sentence. The ideas fit with the sentence after it. Choice B is incorrect because a semicolon is used to connect two independent clauses but can't be used to join a subordinate clause to an independent one. For this same reason, Choice D is also incorrect. It uses "yet" and joins two equal ideas, which is clearly not the case. The best answer is C. The subordinate introductory prepositional is joined to the independent clause by using a comma.

3. **D** The sentence that begins "These gender differences…" is a fragment because of the verb "explored." Attaching the fragment to the previous sentence creates an awkward sentence. Choice B is incorrect. Choice C creates a run-on sentence with a comma splice. Choice D is the best option because it creates two separate sentences.

4. **D** This is a run-on sentence. Choices B and C do not fix the problem. Only choice D correctly creates two complete sentences.

5. **C** This question can be a bit tricky because you must first identify which part of the underlined section is wrong. The participial phrase "barring death . . . non-response" belongs with the first sentence. It is correctly joined by a comma. This eliminates choice B. Clearly, a new sentence should begin with "additional." While choice D uses a semicolon correctly to join two sentences, the word "additional" is not a transition but simply an adjective and should not be followed by a comma. Also using a semicolon creates a very long sentence. The best choice is to create two independent sentences.

6. **C** This is a comma splice. Choice D can be eliminated because a dash is not effective to set off such a long and important independent clause. Choice B adds a conjunction but incorrectly adds a semicolon instead of a comma. Choice C correctly uses a semicolon to correct the run-one sentence.

7. **D** The phrase that begins "With approximately 60 percent . . ." is a fragment because it doesn't express a complete thought. It should be attached to the previous sentence. Choice B merely changes where the fragment begins. Choice C adds a comma and the conjunction "but," which is inappropriate because there is no contrast being communicated. The best choice is to connect the phrase simply using a comma.

Combining Sentences for Clarity/Correcting Problems with Structure and Modifiers   Practice, p. 309

1. **A** "And" correctly indicates equal ideas.

2. **A** The modifying phrase "writing on a chalkboard" should be placed next to "him."

3. **B** The subordinating conjunction "While" best expresses the relationship between the ideas: concession.

4. **B** Choice A is not parallel in form. Choice B edits two phrases for parallelism: "speaking" is changed to

"speech" and "to handle" is changed to "handles."

5. **A** The conjunction "but" correctly communicates a contrasting idea.

6. **A** Choice B incorrectly indicates a contrast between equal ideas. Choice A is best because it subordinates the scientist's qualifications (less important) and focuses on his conclusions about the brain (more important).

7. **B** This correctly edits the phrase so that it is parallel with "are exploring."

SAT-Type Questions, p. 312

1. **B** The information about a clerk holding the Bible should be subordinated because it is not the most important idea. Choice A puts the minor detail in the independent clause. Choice C can be eliminated because it indicates a contrast between equal ideas. Choice D incorrectly uses "because" to indicate a reason. The best choice is B since the detail was happening at the same time as the swearing in.

2. **D** The phrase "promised to take" is parallel to "pledged to strengthen," which is used earlier in the sentence.

3. **D** The main problem is a dangling modifier. The phrase "Having won the election by one of the smallest popular vote margins in history" does not modify the "message" (choices A and C) or the "addresses" (choice B), which also incorrectly makes "address" plural. The opening phrase modifies Kennedy. Choice D is correct.

4. **D** The challenge is to find the correct subordinating conjunction for this introductory phrase. The phrase indicates the similarities between Kennedy's desire to be brief and his remarks to his advisor. The word "as" best communicates similar ideas.

5. **B** The three items in the list should be parallel. Only choice B contains all nouns, simply stated in single words.

6. **B** The current phrasing is awkward, and the phase "toward the end" is misplaced. Choices C and D also contain misplaced modifiers. B corrects the problem with the dangling modifier and is much clearer.

7. **C** The verbs "witnessed" and "heard" should be parallel.

8. **C** The detail about reactions to his ideas is subordinate to the fact that children wrote to President Kennedy. It should be placed in a modifying phrase or clause. A careful read of the answer choices eliminates choices A and B because they emphasize a subordinate idea. Choice D is awkward. The best choice is C.

Correcting Shifts in Verbs and Pronouns   Practice, p. 318

1. were 2. thought 3. had slept 4. watch 5. makes

6. After the three boys get home, ask them how their field trip was.

7. Anyone who disrupts the presentation will be docked ten points from his or her score.

8. When Katie and Susie get together, they laugh a lot.

9. Each employee must fill out this form and hand it in to his or her supervisor.

10. If you want to improve yourself, you should consider trying meditation. OR If one wants to improve oneself, one should consider trying meditation.

SAT-Type Questions, p. 321

1. **D** The pronouns in the underlined section must agree with the antecedent "school officials," which is third-person plural. The current phrase uses the singular "he or she," which is incorrect. However, the second pronoun in the phrase, "their," is correct. Choice A is incorrect. Choice B incorrectly switches to second-person plural. In choice C, "their" is correct, but "one" is singular. Choice C is also incorrect. Choice D correctly uses two plural third-person pronouns.

2. **C** The context given is "At the time, the schools used a swipe-card system." What is needed is a verb that communicates that the system had aged or was aging. Try replacing each answer in the sentence to find the verb tense that best fits. Choice B is present tense and doesn't make sense. Choice D indicates that the aging will happen in the future. The best answer is choice C, because the aging has already happened and continues to happen.

3. **C** The correct pronoun must agree with the antecedent "officials," which is third-person plural. The current pronoun, "one," is incorrect because it is singular. Choice B is third-person singular. Choice D is second-person. Only choice C is correct—third-person plural.

4. **D** The entire passage is written in past tense. Thus, the present tense verb "says" is incorrect. Choices B and C indicate that the action is continuing into the future or will happen in the future. The correct choice is past tense, "said," choice D.

5. **A** Based upon the context, the verb should express the possibility that the technology could be a model for other schools. In choice B, the past tense incorrectly indicates that this has already happened. Choice C shows action that happened at a specific time in the past. Choice D communicates the idea that the action could be continuing into the future. The best choice is the current phrase "could serve," which indicates a possibility in the future.

6. **B** A past tense verb is needed to fit the meaning of the sentence. Choice C is a possibility in the future. Choice D indicates action that started in the past and will continue into the future. Choice B is the correct choice in the past tense.

7. **A** This question tests pronoun usage and frequently confused words. The pronoun "its" refers to the school system. It is a third-person singular pronoun, which is correct. Choice C is third-person plural, and choice D is first-person plural. Choice B is incorrect because "it's" is a contraction for "it is."

8. **D** "Allow" is part of three infinitive phrases in the sentence and should be in the same form as "to send" and "(to) tell." Thus, D is correct.

9. **B** In its current form, the verb is in passive voice, which weakens the sentence. Thus, A is incorrect. Choice C is also passive voice. Choice D changes the meaning of the sentence by making "parents" the subject of the verb "kept." Choice B correctly uses active voice.

10. **C** There are two skills being tested: pronoun usage and verb tense. Because "its" refers to the plural nouns\ "middle and high schools," it is incorrect. The pronoun "their" is correct. This eliminates choices A and B. The context calls for a verb that shows the action happened in the past and could continue on. Choice D indicates an action that happens at a specific time in the future. Thus, C is correct.

Lesson 12: Usage

Using Pronouns Correctly   Practice, p. 326

1. We   2. her   3. Tom and I   4. I   5. me   6. hers   7. me   8. It's   9. Their   10. your   11. who

SAT-Type Questions, p. 328

1. **A** The phrase "as an individual" indicates that a singular pronoun is needed. This eliminates choice D. The pronoun is preceded by the preposition "to," so an objective form is needed. Choice C, "hers," is possessive, and choice B, "she," is a subject (nominative) case. No change is needed.

2. **B** The pronoun needed must be in possessive case. This eliminates choice A, because the correct possessive form includes an apostrophe: "one's," not "ones." Choice C is not possessive and is also incorrect. Choice D is a contraction for "it is." Thus only choice B can be correct.

3. **D** The pronouns are objects of the preposition "on." The only choice that has both pronouns in this case is choice D, "him and her."

4. **D** The case needed is subject (nominative) because the pronoun works as a subject of the verb "would be." Choice A is incorrect because "us" is in objective case. Choice B can be used as an object, but it doesn't make sense with the other pronoun, "I," in the sentence. Choice D is correct.

5. **A** The pronoun is the subject of a comparison that begins with "than." The sentence is actually saying, "few worked harder than she worked." In the comparison, the verb "worked" is understood. When choices B, C, and D are inserted into the phrase, they are incorrect because they are not in the subject case: "her/hers/them worked."

6. **C** The pronoun is the subject of the clause "was speaking to a mostly male audience." This eliminates choice D, "who's," which is a contraction for "who is." Choice B, "her," is possessive. Choice A is also incorrect, because "whom" is in the objective case.

7. **C** Choice A is incorrect because "they're" is a contraction for "they are." What is needed is a possessive pronoun. Choice B is an adverb expressing location. Choices C and D are possessive pronouns, but "his" is singular and doesn't fit with the antecedent "men." The correct answer is choice C, "their."

Correcting Problems with Pronoun/Antecedent, Subject/Verb, and Noun Agreement   Practice, p. 334

1. was   2. were   3. was   4. is   5. are   6. was   7. is   8. was   9. Were   10. Are   11. is   12. was   13. am   14. doesn't   15. its   16. his   17. autographed photos   18. her   19. a pilot   20. classmates   21. his   22. its

SAT-Type Questions, p 336

1. **B** The question requires you to understand verb tense, subject-verb agreement, and subordination/coordination of ideas in a sentence. Choice A incorrectly uses the present tense verb "is," which doesn't agree with the other verb in the sentence, "boosted," which is in past tense.

2. **C** Choice A is incorrect because the pronoun "their" is plural instead of singular. "Her" is the correct pronoun because its antecedent is "Dolley." Thus, choice D can also be eliminated. Choice B uses "who" instead of "which." Because the pronoun must agree with the antecedent "registry," "which" is correct. The answer is choice C, "which recorded her birth."

3. **B** Choice A uses the pronoun "he" to refer to Dolley's father. However, from the context the entire family moved, so the correct pronoun is "they." This eliminates choice C. In choice D, "moving" is in the wrong tense. Inserted into the sentence, it creates a fragment. Choice B, "they moved," is correct.

4. **D** The sentence has a compound sentence joined by "neither/nor." The verb must agree with the closer subject ("lifestyle"), which is singular. "Was" is the singular form of the verb, so choices A and B can be eliminated. Choice C is incorrect because the pronoun should refer only to "Dolley." Choice D, "was able to mute her," is correct.

5. **D** "There" is an adverb indicating place, so choice A is incorrect. Since Dolley is speaking to her husband, a first-person pronoun is needed. Choice B is incorrect because it uses the third-person possessive pronoun "their." Next, a plural verb is needed to agree with the plural subject "hearts." In choice C, "understands," is singular. Choice D is correct.

6. **C** "United States" is a singular noun, so the singular verb "was" is required. Choice A and choice D are incorrect. Choice B is incorrect because it retains the redundant adverb "really." Choice C is correct.

Correcting Frequently Confused Words, Comparing Like Terms, and Correcting Nonstandard Written English Practice, p. 339

1. effect 2. advise 3. except 4. illusion 5. The technology at our school's library is more advanced than the technology at the town's library.

6. As Janine aged, her siblings compared her personality traits to her mother's characteristics.

7. wiser 8. beside 9. have anything 10. Those 11. can never 12. on a plan

SAT-Type Questions, p. 340

1. **A** Choice B is incorrect because "which" should not be used to refer to people. Choice C is incorrect because of the change of "compared with" to "comparing to," which is awkward. Choice D incorrectly compares the "mostly educated professionals and former military personnel" mentioned early in the sentence to "boats" instead of "boat people." The sentence is correct as it is.

2. **B** Choice A is incorrect because the sentence uses both more and closer, which is redundant. For this reason, choice C is also incorrect. Choice D is also incorrect because it makes U.S. possessive, which is not needed. The correct answer is B.

3. **C** Choice A is incorrect because the percent of Vietnamese high school graduates is compared with a percentage of the United States. These are unlike ideas. The second part of the sentence should compare a percentage of the general population. The correct answer is C.

4. **D** Choice A is incorrect. The sentence has a double negative and a nonstandard use of a preposition. Choices B, C, and D fix the double negative by deleting "not." However, only choice D uses the correct form of the phrase "in favor of."

5. **C** The current phrase uses "Than," but "Then" is needed to indicate order in time. Thus, choices A and D are incorrect. Choices B and C contain different verb forms. Choice B incorrectly uses a past participle form ("was assimilating"), which doesn't match the plural "Vietnamese" or the other verb in the sentence: "reversed." Choice C uses the past tense verb: "assimilated."

6. **D** In the current sentence, the word "adopt" (to bring into one's family) is incorrect; "adapt" (to assimilate) is the correct term. Choice C changes "more quickly" to "quicker," which is nonstandard. Choice B incorrectly uses "then" when "than" is needed to make the comparison.

7. **A** Choice B incorrectly changes "rise" (to move upward) with "raise" (to force an object upward). Choice C introduces the transition "henceforth," which means "from now on." This meaning doesn't fit the context. Also "henceforth" sounds too formal for the text. Choice D includes the phrase "to position." This incorrectly changes the meaning of the phrase.

Lesson 13: Punctuation

Using End Punctuation and Commas   Practice, p. 346

1. The little boy who stole my lunch is sitting over there.   2. Correct   3. The cat that can open doors belongs to my brother.   4. Correct   5. The manager, Mr. Timms, often leaves before his shift is over. [comma deleted after "leaves"]   6. Correct   7. Would you like to sit down next to the little girl who is waving at us?
8. Correct

SAT-Type Questions, p. 348

1. **D** The problem in this sentence is that a comma is used with an essential clause. No comma is needed before "that . . .from." Choice A is incorrect. Choice B is incorrect because it makes the sentence awkward by adding an unnecessary conjunction. Choice C removes the comma before "that" but adds a comma after "domestically," where it is not needed. "Domestically" describes "produced," and a comma incorrectly breaks up the flow of the sentence. Choice D is correct.

2. **B** A comma is needed after the introductory prepositional phrase "For . . .1993." Thus, choice A is incorrect. Choice C incorrectly adds a comma after the adjective "diesel" and before the conjunction "and." "Diesel" describes "engine" and is not a separate item in a series. Also, no comma is needed before "and" because there are only two items in the list and also because this is not a compound sentence. Choice D is incorrect, but choice B is correct.

3. **C** The sentence contains both an introductory word ("However") and an introductory clause ("if . . . that"). A comma is needed after both of these. Choice C is correct.

4. **D** Commas are needed to set off the appositive phrase "a type of rubber used for seals and hoses." Choice A lacks the final comma after "hoses." Choice B is incorrect because it has no commas. Choice C inserts an unnecessary comma in the middle of the phrase. Choice D correctly places a comma before and after the appositive.

5. **A** In a list, commas are needed after each item that comes before and. Choice C is incorrect because it adds a comma after torque. Choice B also includes this comma and can also be eliminated. Choice D uses commas correctly in the list of items, but removes the comma before the second and. This comma is needed before the conjunction and to join a compound sentence.

Using Semicolons and Colons   Practice, p. 350

1. Our spring garden features many flowers: snowdrops, crocuses, aconites, hyacinths, and tulips.

2. George Washington was the first President of the United States; he served two terms.

3. The sassafras, unlike most trees, has three different and distinct leaf patterns: unlobed oval, bilobed (mitten-shaped), and trilobed (three-pronged).

4. Cynthia already asked me; I refused.

5. William Feather had the following words of wisdom: "Work is the best method for killing time."

6. If you can come camping with me, bring these supplies: insect repellant, fishing gear, and a tent.

7. I have lived in Des Moines, Iowa; Lincoln, Nebraska; and Detroit, Michigan.

8. Florida is not the southernmost state in the United States; Hawaii is farther south.

9. Robert E. Lee's personal home was made into Arlington National Cemetery during the Civil War; therefore, he never went home again.

10. Ocean water often includes salt, seaweed, and jellyfish. (No colon is needed before this list because it is short and lacks a formal introduction.)

SAT-Type Questions, pp. 353

1. **D** Because the phrase "Whitechapel Bell Foundry" is being emphasized, a colon is needed to introduce it. A comma (choice B) creates a pause but not a strong enough one for the sentence. Choice C provides no pause. Choice A incorrectly uses a semicolon.

2. **A** Choices B and D insert unnecessary semicolons. Choice C incorrectly inserts a colon after a preposition. This is never correct. Choice A is correct.

3. **A** The sentence is introduced by a introductory subordinate clause, "Just ten months after Pennsylvania sent its request." Since colons and semicolons join independent clauses, choices B and C are incorrect. Because a comma is used to introduce subordinate clauses, D is incorrect, and A is correct.

4. **D** In this sentence two independent clauses are joined using the transition "additionally" and two commas. This is a comma splice. A semicolon is needed. Choice B incorrectly adds the semicolon after "additionally." Although choice C adds a semicolon, it also includes the conjunction "and," which requires a comma before it and not a semicolon. (Adding "and" makes the sentence redundant, too.) The best answer is choice D.

5. **C** This question tests the skills of complete sentences, colon and semicolons, and apostrophes. First, two complete sentences are joined without any punctuation. Choice A is incorrect. Choice B is also incorrect because it uses a colon between the two sentences. Choice B also incorrectly removes the apostrophe from Bell's. An apostrophe is needed to show that the casting is the Bell's, and a semicolon is needed to join the two sentences The best answer is C.

6. **B** Colons are used to introduce formal quotes. Choices A and C can be eliminated. The first word of the quotation should be capitalized. Choice B is correct.

7. **A** Two sentences (independent clauses) are joined together by a colon. Choice B exchanges the colon in favor of a semicolon. However, the second sentence explains the offer more carefully. Also, the sentence still makes sense when the word "namely" is inserted in place of the colon. Choice B is not the best answer. Choice C subordinates the second sentence by placing it in a clause. This downplays the important idea in the second sentence and makes the sentence awkward. Choice D adds a conjunction, which doesn't make sense. Choice A is correct.

Using Parentheses, Dashes, and Quotation Marks   Practice, p. 355

1. Mark exclaimed excitedly, "Geraldine won the spelling bee by correctly spelling syzygy!"

2. Page the best doctor in the hospital—Dr. Richards.

3. Seneca, a Roman philosopher, wrote, "All cruelty springs from weakness."

4. The waitress began, "What can I—" when the phone rang.

5. The data shows a marked increase over the past five years (see Figure 2).

6. Please leave the package in the back room (the door will be unlocked). or Please leave the package in the back room. (The door will be unlocked.)

SAT-Type Questions, p. 358

1. **B** A dash is needed to set the final phrase off from the rest of the sentence. Choice B is the best answer.

2. **D** The quotation is an indirect paraphrase of Bolden's words. No quotation marks are needed. Choices A, B, and C all incorrectly use quotation marks. Choice C also incorrectly uses a colon.

3. **D** Choice A is incorrect because a comma is unnecessary before text in parentheses. Choice B also uses two periods—one before and after the parenthesis. Choice C incorrectly places a period after "Planet" and outside the final parenthesis. Choice D correctly uses a single period outside the parenthesis at the end of the entire sentence.

Practice, p. 359

1. book's 2. sister's 3. geese's 4. someone's 5. daughters' 6. school's 7. everyone's 8. his 9. hers 10. women's, theirs

SAT-Type Questions, p. 361

1. **A** "Her" is the correct possessive pronoun, and a comma is used correctly before the appositive Bill Clinton.

2. **B** "Daughter" should not be possessive. This eliminates choices A and D. Both B and C use the singular noun form of daughter, but C adds unnecessary commas around "also." The best choice is B.

3. **C** In the name Arkansas Childrens' Hospital, only the word "children" should be possessive. Eliminate choice B. Since "children" is already plural, the possessive is formed by adding 's. Thus, choice D is also eliminated. Choice C uses the correct possessive and omits the comma used incorrectly before the conjunction "and." No comma is needed when "and" joins only two items.

4. **D** "Woman" should be plural possessive in form: "Women's." Choices A and C can be eliminated. However, in the phrase "human rights," "human" is not possessive ("human's"), but is an adjective explaining whose rights. It should not be possessive. Choice B is incorrect; choice D is correct.

Many of the changes in the SAT were made in order to make the test a more accurate evaluation of the skills students are learning in high school and will need for success in college. For example, the new SAT emphasizes citing textual evidence to support conclusions and interpreting key words in context, two instructional shifts recently implemented by many schools. Additionally, some states are moving toward requiring a minimum score on the SAT for graduation.

Preparing for the SAT Evidence-Based Reading and Writing provides an educationally based format for students to review skills taught in the classroom and to become familiar with the format of the SAT. The five-part lesson structure provides a scaffolded, instructional approach to help students review, practice, and master SAT skills. Each lesson uses the following structure:

- **Explain:** Outlines skills by explaining key terms, explains thinking process required to analyze or edit text, and lists SAT question stems related to the skill

- **Think It Through:** Models the thinking process required by the skill

- **Practice:** Provides practice of the skill in a non-SAT format

- **Model SAT Questions:** Introduces SAT multiple-choice question format and provides modeling through answer explanations

- **SAT-Type Questions:** Offers further practice and formative assessment of skills through multiple-choice questions that mirror SAT format

In addition, the **Diagnostic SAT-Type Test**, two **Domain Practice Tests,** and three **SAT Model Exams** provide multiple opportunities for students to practice taking tests under timed conditions.

Suggestions for Implementation

Students may work through Preparing for the SAT Evidence-Based Reading and Writing on their own or teachers may teach the Explain and Think It Through to the entire class. Students could then complete Practice, Model SAT Questions, and SAT-type Questions on their own.

Focused SAT preparation for a classroom teacher or SAT tutor:

- Have students take the Diagnostic Test to identify skills that need further instruction.

- Use the Diagnostic Test correlation chart to create individual lesson plans for students.

- Encourage students to work individually on the lessons where they need review or lead students through Lessons 1–13.

- Provide support if students struggle with a particular concept.

- Monitor formative assessments as students complete SAT-Type Questions.

- Revisit related Think It Through, Practice, and Model SAT Questions within the lesson to facilitate needed reviews of skills or concepts.

- Use the Domain SAT-Type Practice Tests (summative assessments) to evaluate student progress.

- Review Test-Taking Strategies (pp. 8–9) and administer SAT Model Exams 1–3, adhering to the strict time restraints and other conditions that mirror the official test.

- Monitor and support students after each administration of the SAT Read and Writing and Language Model Exams to review needed skills.

- If desired, have students work through the SAT Essay section by taking the SAT Essay Diagnostic Test, working through Lesson 14, and taking Essay Model Exams 1–3 under the appropriate conditions. Provide feedback through teacher and peer-led reviews.

Year-long SAT preparation within a secondary classroom:

- Use the Table of Contents to identify skills that match your unit lesson plans. Set aside a 20- to 30-minute block of time in your lesson plans to teach SAT skills to the class or for students to work though the lessons on their own.

- Have students take the Diagnostic Test to identify skills that need further instruction.

- Incorporate appropriate lessons into your current curriculum. Assign students to work through the Explain, Think It Through, Practice, Model SAT Questions, and SAT-Type Questions to preview or to wrap up a unit in your curriculum.

- Monitor formative assessments as students complete SAT-Type Questions. Revisit related Think It Through, Practice, and Model SAT Questions within the lesson to facilitate needed reviews of skills or concepts.

- Use the Domain SAT-Type Tests (summative assessments) to evaluate student progress.

- The week before the SAT is given (or near the end of the school year), review Test-Taking Strategies (pp. 8–9) and administer SAT Model Exams 1–3, adhering to the strict time restraints and other conditions that mirror the official test.

- Monitor and support students after each administration of the SAT Model Exams. Encourage students to review the skills that correlated to questions they missed.

- Have students taking the optional SAT essay, work through the SAT Essay section by completing the SAT Essay Diagnostic Test, working through Lesson 14, and taking Essay Model Exams 1–3 under the appropriate conditions. Provide feedback through teacher and peer-led reviews.

Pacing Guide

(The following suggested plans are based upon students taking the SAT in the spring of their junior year.)

4-Week Plan	Week 1—Administer Diagnostic Test
	Week 2—Assign lessons that cover reading skills most often missed on Reading Test section. Administer Reading Domain SAT-type Practice Test
	Week 3—Assign lessons that cover skills most often missed on Writing and Language Test Administer Writing and Language Domain SAT-type Practice Test
	Week 4—Administer Model SAT Exams 1, 2, and 3
10-Week Plan (January to March)	Week 1—Administer Reading section of the Diagnostic Test.
	Week 2—Lesson 1: Closely Reading Literature Lesson 2: Defining Words in Context
	Week 3—Lesson 3: Closely Reading Informational Texts for Explicit Meanings Lesson 4: Closely Reading Informational Texts for Implicit Meanings Lesson 5: Analyzing Ideas in Informational Texts
	Week 4—Lesson 6: Analyzing Style in Informational Texts Lesson 7: Synthesizing Information from Texts and Graphs
	Week 5—Administer Reading section of the Diagnostic Test. Reteach skills from lessons as needed.
	Week 6—Lesson 8: Development of Ideas Lesson 9: Organization
	Week 7—Lesson 10: Use of Language Lesson 11: Sentence Structure
	Week 8—Lesson 12: Usage Lesson 13: Punctuation
	Week 9—Administer Writing and Language SAT-Type Practice Test. Reteach skills from lessons as needed.
	Week 10—Administer Full-length SAT-Type Reading and Writing and Language Model Exams.

(continued on next page)

20-Week Plan (September to March)	Week 1—Administer Reading section of the Diagnostic Test.
	Week 2—Lesson 1: Closely Reading Literature (pp. 57–84)
	Week 3—Lesson 1: Closely Reading Literature (pp. 85–106)
	Week 4—Lesson 2: Defining Words in Context Lesson 3: Closely Reading Informational Texts for Explicit Meaning
	Week 5—Lesson 4: Closely Reading Informational Texts for Implicit Meanings
	Week 6—Lesson 5: Analyzing Ideas in Informational Texts
	Week 7—Lesson 6: Analyzing Style in Informational Texts
	Week 8—Lesson 7: Synthesizing Information from Texts and Graphs
	Week 9—Administer Reading Domain SAT-Type Practice Test. Reteach skills from lessons as needed.
	Week 10—Administer Writing and Language section of the Diagnostic Test.
	Week 11—Lesson 8: Development of Ideas
	Week 12—Lesson 9: Organization
	Week 13—Lesson 10: Use of Language
	Week 14—Lesson 11: Sentence Structure
	Week 15—Lesson 12: Usage
	Week 16—Lesson 13: Punctuation
	Week 17—Administer Writing and Language SAT-Type Practice Test. Reteach skills from lessons as needed.
	Week 18—Administer Full-length SAT-Type Reading and Writing and Language Model Exam 1.
	Week 19—Administer Full-length SAT-Type Reading and Writing and Language Model Exam 2.
	Week 20—Administer Full-length SAT-Type Reading and Writing and Language Model Exam 3.

Further suggestions

- Have students write out their own answer explanations for the SAT-type questions using the Strategy sections of the Model SAT questions as a guide. Ask pairs of students to share their answers and explanations.

- Display short passages and questions from SAT-Type Practice sections and use as bell ringers. Polleverywhere.com allows students to text their answers and then provides a tally of the class's choices.

Acknowledgments

Excerpt from "Sentimental Education" from FIRST LOVE AND OTHER SORROWS by Harold Brodkey © 1954, 1955, 1956, 1957, 1964 by Ellen Brodkey.

"The Ecology of Language" from WORD PLAY by Peter Farb, copyright © 1973 by Peter Farb. NY: Alfred A. Knopf, a division of Random House, Inc.

http://www.pbs.org/wnet/supremecourt/antebellum/landmark_plessy.html. Used by permission of WNET, THIRTEEN PRODUCTIONS LLC.

James Baldwin, "Sonny's Blues." Copyright © 1957 by James Baldwin. Originally published in PARTISAN REVIEW. Copyright renewed. Collected in GOING TO MEET THE MAN, published by Vintage Books. Reprinted by arrangement with the James Baldwin Estate.

Excerpt from "The Flowers" from IN LOVE & TROUBLE: Stories of Black Women by Alice Walker. Copyright © 1973, renewed 2001 by Alice Walker. Reprinted by permission of Houghton Mifflin Harcourt Publishing Company. All rights reserved.

"Rules of the Game", from THE JOY LUCK CLUB by Amy Tan, copyright © 1989 by Amy Tan. Used by permission of G.P. Putnam's Sons, an imprint of Penguin Publishing Group, a division of Penguin Random House LLC.

William Faulkner, "A Rose for Emily" from COLLECTED STORIES OF WILLIAM FAULKNER. Copyright 1930, 1950, and renewed © 1958 by William Faulkner; © 1977 by Jill Faulkner Summers. Used by permission of Random House, Inc.

Excerpt(s) from BELOVED by Toni Morrison, copyright © 1987 by Toni Morrison. Used by permission of Alfred A. Knopf, an imprint of the Knopf Doubleday Publishing Group, a division of Random House LLC. All rights reserved.

"Dead Men's Path," copyright © 1972 , 1973 by Chiuna Achebe; from GIRLS AT WAR:

AND OTHER STORIES by Chinua Achebe. Used by permission of Doubleday, an imprint of the Knopf Doubleday Publishing Group, a division of Random House LLC.

Excerpt from SNOW FALLING ON CEDARS by David Guterson. Copyright © 1994 by David Guterson. Reprinted by permission of Houghton Mifflin Harcourt Publishing Company. All rights reserved.

"To Reduce Gun Violence, Know Thy Neighbor: How a sense of community can help stop a bullet" by Andrew Giambrone from The Atlantic, January 16, 2015. Copyright © 2015 by The Atlantic Monthly Group. All Rights Reserved.

"Philip Glass, from Minimalism to mainstream," by Mark Swed from LOS ANGELES TIMES, March 9, 2011. Copyright © 2011. Used by permission.

"The Man Who Loved Photographs: Sam Wagstaff's Passion Transformed the Art Market" by Philip Gefter from *The New York Times*, October 22, 2014. Copyright © 2014 by The New York Times Co. Used by permission.

"Ocean Life Faces Mass Extinction, Broad Study Says" by Carl Zimmer from The New York Times, January 15, 2015. Copyright © 2015 by The New York Times Co. Used by permission.

"Can Language Influence Our Perception of Reality: New research suggests that subtle linguistic differences can frame our approaches to difficult problems— and even affect our views on space and time" by Mitch Moxley from Slate.com, June 2014. Slate is published by The Slate Group, a Graham Holdings Company. All contents © 2015 The Late Group LLC. All rights reserved.

"Why Are There Still So Few Women In Science?" by Eileen Pollack from The New York Times, October 3, 2013. Copyright © 2013 The New York Times Co.

"Earth's Next Generation-The pros and cons of renewable energy sources" by Climate Himalaya, May 17, 2011.

"A Day Alone With Other People" by Richard B. Woodward from *The Wall Street Journal*, November 2, 2012. Copyright © 2012 Dow Jones.

From HERE IS NEW YORK by E. B. White. Copyright E.B. White 1949, 1976. New York: HarperCollins.

"Time for a Vacation? Climate Change and the Human Clock" by Rachel Nuwer from *The New York Times*, December 8, 2011. Copyright © 2011 The New York Times Co.

"Bumpy Black Hole X-Rays May Push the Limits of Einstein's Relativity: Scientists simulate the signatures of 'bumpy' black holes to test Einstein's famously resilient theory of general relativity yet again" by Maria Temming from *Scientific American*, August 6, 2015. Copyright © 2015 Scientific American, a Division of Nature America, Inc. All Rights Reserved.

"The U.S. Ranks 26th for Life Expectancy, Right Behind Slovenia" by Sarah Kliff from *The Washington Post*, November 21, 2013. Copyright © 2013.

"Hands-free Chemistry" by Beth Mole from *Science New Magazine,* August 22, 2015.